REAL WORLD
DIGITAL
AUDIO

PETER KIRN

PEACHPIT PRESS
BERKELEY, CALIFORNIA

REAL WORLD DIGITAL AUDIO
Peter Kirn

Peachpit Press
1249 Eighth Street
Berkeley, CA 94710
510/524-2178
800/283-9444
510/524-2221 (fax)

Find us on the World Wide Web at: www.peachpit.com
To report errors, please send a note to errata@peachpit.com
Peachpit Press is a division of Pearson Education

Project Editor: Cary Norsworthy
Production Editor: Simmy Cover
Developmental and Technical Editor: Jim Aikin
Copyeditor: Anne-Marie Walker
Proofreaders: Leona Benten, Emily K. Wolman
Compositor: Happenstance Type-O-Rama
Indexer: Julie Bess
Cover design: Aren Howell
Cover illustrator: William Duke
Cover art direction: Charlene Charles-Will
Interior design: Mimi Heft

ISBN 0-321-30460-8

9 8 7 6 5 4 3 2 1

Printed and bound in the United States of America

TABLE OF CONTENTS

ACKNOWLEDGMENTS

One name is on the front cover, but this book has resulted from the efforts of an extraordinary team. Thanks to everyone at Peachpit Press, including Cary Norsworthy for her tireless leadership, Anne-Marie Walker, Simmy Cover, David Leishman, Eric Geoffrey, and our talented production team. Thanks to Jim Aikin, whose insight and unparalleled experience have guided the whole book, and Tova Friedman for lighting up pages with her illustrations.

Thanks to those who were generous with their knowledge, including electronic music pioneer Curtis Roads at the University of California, Ben Chadabe at the Electronic Music Foundation, Jon Appleton at Dartmouth College, percussionist Paul Wertico, film editor Pawel Wdowczak, Frank Verderosa at Nutmeg Audio Post, hardware researcher Lyndsay Williams of Microsoft Research Cambridge, musicologist Alan Richtmyer, and musicians Tim Place, Robert Henke, and Tim Exile.

Many people in the music industry have contributed products to test as well as technical expertise and ideas, particularly Steve Thomas and Jesse Jost at Cakewalk, Tobias Thon at Native Instruments, Dave Hill at Ableton, Christine Wilhelmy at Apple, Mike Lohman at Shure, Reinel Adejar at Digidesign, LaShundra Hicks at Akai/Alesis/Numark, Marsha Vdovin on behalf of Cycling '74 and Propellerhead, Jim Cooper at MOTU, Leslie Buttonow at Korg, Tara Callahan at Roland, Shane Swisher for Yamaha, Starr Ackerman and Jeni Karlieva at IK Multimedia, and many others, including those at Sennheiser, Novation, M-Audio, Mackie, Denecke, MakeMusic!, Sibelius, FXpansion, Behringer, Edirol, Brian Moore Guitar, Ms. Pinky, Auralex Acoustics, Fervent Software, Executive Software, and TrackTeam Audio.

On a personal note, thanks to my electronic music teacher John Yannelli at Sarah Lawrence College, whose commitment to helping people understand these topics has been a model for me, to Christopher Breen at Macworld for setting me on this path, to my family for endless support of epic projects, and to my partner Jennifer for being a brilliant reader and inspiring me with patience.

INTRODUCTION

Making Music with Technology

Digital audio was once the exclusive domain of those with deep pockets or access to a university or multimillion-dollar recording studio. Times have changed. Today, digital recording and music production are within reach of anyone who can afford a modest computer. And traditional recording is just the beginning: computers are tools for composition, sound creation, and performance, and a means of connecting music and sound to visuals and other media. Sophisticated studios are still valuable places, and professional expertise is irreplaceable. But the amateur in a home studio can produce professional-sounding results too. The production studio doesn't even have to be at "home." People really do make music in coach-class airplane seats and improvise with laptops onstage.

Digital audio tools have become, in essence, a new musical instrument in their own right—or perhaps more accurately, an ensemble of instruments. But while the technology has brought the ability to make amazing music within easy reach, getting the best out of the technology is not guaranteed to be easy. Like learning how to play any musical instrument, learning how to use digital audio technology requires assimilating a lot of knowledge and skills.

The new forms of computer-based music making put new demands on musicians. It's no longer enough to master a single instrument (be it a grand piano or an electric guitar) and leave the rest of the recording process up to other experts. Musicians today need to know how to get the numerous elements of digital audio technology to work together smoothly. Today, you need to be an instrumentalist, composer, conductor, recording engineer, producer, and computer specialist all at once.

This book brings together the information you'll need to master the new skills involved in digital audio production. Although there is a nearly infinite range of musical styles, tastes, and musicians, there are basic needs that all of us have and basic information that we all need at our fingertips.

We need to understand how sound itself works, so we can manipulate audio effectively once it's in the computer. We want to be able to create new sounds and shape existing ones. We need to be able to record performances on acoustic and electric instruments, voice, and the many real-world sounds around us, and we want that recording to resemble the way we hear those sounds before they reach the microphone. We want to share our music, whether through printed scores, CDs, DVDs, online distribution, as soundtracks for video and motion pictures, or in live performance. To make this happen, we need to get past the learning curve of gear, figure out which equipment and software to buy, learn how to plug it in, decide which cable to put where, and learn how to keep everything working.

The first step is often just to pierce the fog of unfamiliar terminology.

"But what does an 'expander' do?"

A student had looked up the name of an audio effect in the manual for a software product he was trying to learn. There would certainly have been room for a full explanation in the manual, since it was a phone book-sized tome. Instead, the author had provided a circular answer that would make sense only to someone who already knew the answer. It said something like "the Brand X digital expansion module provides high-quality expansion of an audio input."

So what does "expansion" mean?

If you've gotten this far, you probably already know *why* you want to learn more about digital audio. Now that this book is in your hands, it's simply a matter of getting started. All of us have been in the same spot as the student I quoted above: all of us are beginners at something, even if we're expert at something else. What we need is a place to start.

WHAT'S IN THIS BOOK

This book is a comprehensive reference for creating music with digital audio technology, centering on the computer. It's a practical guide to the diverse skills you'll need to produce a wide variety of music and sound. You can use it as you would a reference book, particularly if you're a more advanced user, but it's also designed so that if you read it in order you'll develop a solid foundation that you'll be able to build on more easily.

The first four chapters cover the underlying fundamentals of sound plus choosing and configuring gear:

- **Chapter 1** explains how sound works, how we hear, and how sound is translated into digital form. Understanding these fundamentals will help demystify many of the terms and concepts used in audio tools, and will help you get the results you want.

- **Chapter 2** surveys the landscape of available hardware and software gear, explains what each tool does, and shows how to choose the studio setup that's right for you.

- **Chapter 3** focuses on how to configure and optimize your computer and equipment for the best audio performance.

- **Chapter 4** explains how to connect your hardware, from the many potentially confusing cable types and labels to various patching setups.

The next five chapters cover various production techniques. Depending on your interest, you may want to read some or all of them:

- **Chapter 5** is an overview of how software tools can produce a finished song, focusing on two entry-level tutorials, one for the Mac and one for Windows. It explains the use of loops in song production, particularly for backing tracks and live groove-based performances.

- **Chapter 6** explains various microphone types and how they're used to capture sound, including where they're positioned when recording many of the commonly used musical instruments.

- **Chapter 7** explores the different kinds of audio processing and effects. You'll learn what effects are and how to best use them in production.

- **Chapter 8** is an introduction to MIDI and explains how it can be used to capture performances and control software.

- **Chapter 9** covers how to create and edit original sounds on digital instruments, making your computer or hardware synthesizer into an expressive musical instrument.

The final four chapters bring together the earlier topics, showing you how to produce a finished result, whether it's a recorded track for CD or other distribution, a notated score, a video, or a concert performance:

- **Chapter 10** looks at how the raw materials of an audio project can be shaped into a finished recorded track, how to store that track in different file formats, and how to distribute your finished content on CDs, DVDs, and online.

- **Chapter 11** covers how to create, edit, and share a notated score.

- **Chapter 12** explains how to work with video and motion, including how to match sound to image and how to manage and edit time information and digital video formats.

- **Chapter 13** explores the techniques needed to make a computer a performance instrument, whether it's for simple backing tracks or for more elaborate interactive setups that include synchronized visuals.

WHO THIS BOOK IS FOR

This book is written primarily for musicians. The scope of what that word means has expanded: the word "musician" rightfully applies to recording engineers and producers, to composers and arrangers, and to DJs and electronic performers. If you're using computers and other technology to produce music or any other type of sound, this book is written for you.

Topics like acoustics, MIDI, audio processing, synthesis, mixing, mastering, notation, video scoring, and electronic performance have each been the subject of numerous individual books. But the reality is that a wide group of people need to use many or all of these techniques in combination. Products like Apple Logic Pro, Digidesign Pro Tools, Cakewalk SONAR, and others provide resources for handling all of these tasks in a single package. So clearly, there's some overlap in these techniques and among the people who use them.

Because each topic could fill a whole book, it would not have been practical for us to cover every detail. Instead, this book provides an overview in each area, starting with the basics. In these pages you'll find the terminology and concepts that software and hardware manuals may frustratingly assume you already know, as well as some practical advice on how to apply specific production techniques to your music. If you're new to the field, this will be more than enough to get you started doing hands-on work with your tools of choice. If you've been working with the technology for a while, *Real World Digital Audio* will help ease the learning curve as you add more advanced tools to your studio and delve into more specialized books on the subject. You'll find references to some of the seminal works scattered throughout the text.

The "industrial strength techniques" tagline of the *Real World* series challenged us to cover power-user techniques, but we're especially interested in the needs of beginners. The person who has years of recording experience might know absolutely nothing about sound design for synthesizers. So although this book is densely packed, we've made every effort to explain each topic in detail rather than assume what you know.

Real World Digital Audio focuses primarily on the computer, not as the exclusive device for accomplishing every task, but as a hub that you'll sometimes use with other equipment. For an increasing majority of musicians and engineers alike, that's the reality of modern audio production. This doesn't mean some of the techniques discussed in this book can't be applied if you're working with the hardware counterparts of some of the software tools mentioned. New audio hardware often resembles or even incorporates computer software. Ultimately, even as specifics change, many of the underlying concepts remain. But where appropriate, our illustrations do focus on computers and software.

HOW TO USE THIS BOOK

If you're not picking up at page one and reading straight through to the end, you'll find that this book is designed with features to help navigate the breadth of topics covered.

Essentials

You'll find an Essentials box at the beginning of each chapter that introduces the key terms and concepts in that chapter. If you find some of the topics overwhelming, check out the "Where to Start" note at the bottom of the Essentials box for a sense of what "step one" is.

DVD and Hands-on Examples

Hands-on tutorials and tips in each chapter guide you and suggest when to put some of the concepts to practical use with the software demos and content included on the bundled DVD. For an overview of what's on the DVD, see the Appendix.

Of course, if you have your own tool of choice, you'll still find instructions and examples that apply to you. You'll also find additional cross-platform content on the DVD, including royalty-free audio loops and samples that you can use with other applications.

On the Web

Because digital audio continues to evolve daily, you can check www.real-worlddigitalaudio.com for updates to the book, links to current information and news, and other online resources and extras. The Web site also includes a series of *Pro Files*, which are interviews with leading musicians and technologists about digital audio.

Use in a Classroom

 Trial software and saving files: With the exception of Sound-School and the open-source program Audacity, the demo applications on the disc are incapable of saving work, though they can be used for learning purposes.

Although this book isn't an academic book (and there are fine books that are), it is designed to be suitable for an introductory electronic music, computer music, or audio production class, particularly at the high school or undergraduate level. It is biased away from open-ended software like Csound, Reaktor, Max/MSP, and Pure Data, which are often emphasized in academic courses. But the sections on MIDI, synthesis, audio processing, and performance are all relevant to curricula that use those programs.

The modular nature of the chapters means that individual chapters can accompany units on those topics, particularly in the case of recording and audio processing, MIDI and synthesis, notation, or mixing and mastering.

Key symbols

Throughout this book you'll find numerous boxes and margin notes containing extra information. Each item is flagged with a handy symbol that indicates what type of information the item contains. Here are the symbols, and an explanation of what they mean:

The Clarify icon is used when the item provides an in-depth discussion of a concept that is explained briefly in the main text.

The Define icon is used when the item gives a basic definition of an important term or concept.

The DVD icon is used when the item points you to files or tutorial examples on the DVD that accompanies this book.

The Hands-on icon is used when the item provides a procedure that you can try on your computer.

The Tip icon is used when the item gives a suggestion that will save you time or make your workflow more efficient.

The Web icon is used when the item lists or describes on-line resources.

CHAPTER 1

Understanding Digital Sound

Your most important musical tools are your ears, which have the ability to detect the tiny changes in air pressure that we call sound. Digital audio technology converts these changes in air pressure into electrical and numerical form and vice versa. To understand how your digital audio equipment works, it's helpful to know what sound is and how it's perceived and measured.

 Essentials

Understanding Digital Sound

To fully grasp the nature of sound, you'll learn:

- How sound travels through air as vibrations
- How sound can be measured, and what it looks like in software
- How we hear pitch, loudness, and timbre
- How analog and digital circuitry capture and play back sound
- What determines the quality of digital audio, and how it's stored

Essential Terms

- Compression and rarefaction
- Amplitude and frequency

- Doppler effect
- Sine wave
- Fundamental, overtones, partials, harmonics, harmonic/inharmonic
- Phase cancellation
- Key tone, octave equivalency, interval, dissonance, beats
- Essential units: Hertz (Hz)/cycles per second (cps); decibel (dB); semitones and cents
- Transducer; analog and digital; A/D, D/A converters; sampling; sampling rate; bit depth
- Aliasing; Nyquist frequency; noise floor; signal-to-noise ratio
- Compression: lossy, lossless; interleaved/split files

HOW SOUND WORKS

We're so used to being surrounded by sound that we take it for granted, but what is sound, exactly? In terms of the physical event, sound is a series of vibrations that travel through some medium. Unless you're planning on playing your next show underwater in a swimming pool, it's safe to say that the medium is probably air. For practical purposes then, we can describe sound as alternate areas of slightly more compressed and slightly less compressed air that move outward from a source.

When you hit a drum head, for instance, the skin of the drum vibrates, moving rapidly up and down (**Figure 1.1**). Materials like drum heads and strings can vibrate because they're elastic; you can create sound by plucking a rubber band for the same reason. With each outward movement of the drum head, air molecules around the outer surface of the drum become more densely packed, increasing the air pressure slightly. This increased air pressure is called *compression*. With each inward movement, the molecules spread out again, dropping the air pressure, which is called *rarefaction*. The sound of a drum dies away quickly, but even so, the drum head moves up and down a number of times before it comes to rest, creating a series of compressions and rarefactions. The typical waveform graphs you'll see in digital audio software and physics textbooks alike simply show us how these compressions and rarefactions alternate over time. The result looks like the wavy line shown in Figure 1.1.

These changes in pressure don't just occur immediately around the source, or you wouldn't hear anything. The alternations in pressure move outward from the drum (or whatever happens to be vibrating) through the air: they *propagate* outward. These outward-moving variations in air pressure are called *sound waves*. The waves of vibrations are transmitted much like ripples in a pond, although it's important to realize that unlike water waves, waves of sound don't move up and down. Instead, they're *longitudinal waves*: these waves involve forward-and-back vibrations of air in a line between the listener and the sound source (**Figure 1.2**). Once the drum stops vibrating, the waves dissipate, the air pressure becomes stable, and the sound stops.

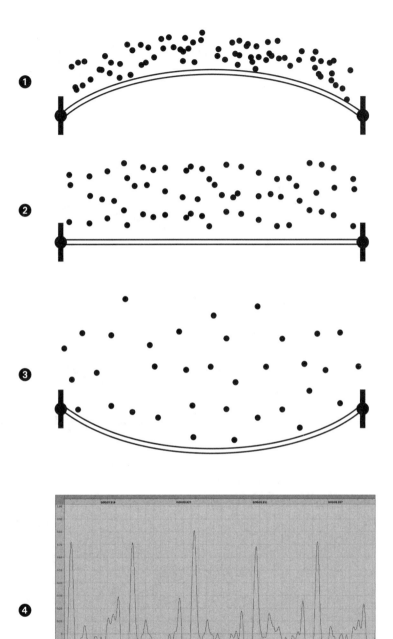

Figure 1.1 As a sound source vibrates, it causes rapid fluctuations in air pressure around it. As a vibrating body like a drum head expands outward (1), it packs adjacent air particles together (*compression*). As it rebounds to a neutral position (2), air pressure returns to normal. As it moves inward (3), air pressure decreases (*rarefaction*). As this process repeats, waves of sound spread outward through the air from the source. In digital audio software, we can observe a graph that represents these air pressure fluctuations over time (4).

It's the wave that moves outward from the source, not the air in the wave. The air vibrates, but when you hear a note from a cello, you're not hearing air that's traveled from the cello to you, any more than when a wave hits the beach in Australia its carrying water from Hawaii. The energy of the vibration is what actually travels, not the water.

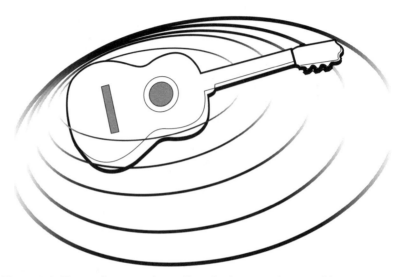

Figure 1.2 Waves of compression and rarefaction spread outward from a source through the air, a phenomenon called *wave propagation*.

Without some material to vibrate, you can't have sound. The answer to the old riddle, "If a tree falls in a forest and there's no one there to hear it, does it make a sound?" is, in fact, yes. The sound of the tree falling radiates outward through the surrounding air as the air molecules around the tree vibrate. The only way the tree wouldn't make a sound would be if there were no air or other material to carry the vibrations.

The science of how sound travels in the air and in physical spaces is called *acoustics*; it's the study of what physically happens to sound waves under different conditions in the real world. (When there is someone around to hear a sound, an additional set of issues comes into play; the study of *psychoacoustics* deals with the perception of sound.)

Acoustics is a branch of physics, but acoustical engineers work with environments that are very familiar to musicians, like concert halls and recording studios. Acousticians need to understand what will happen to sound from an orchestra when it bounces off walls, for instance, or how raucous a restaurant in a soon-to-be-constructed building will sound when it's full of diners. You might not be planning a career in acoustical engineering, but a basic understand of how sound works will help you decide where to place your mic while recording vocals, how to configure a digital reverb effect so your track sounds realistic, and how to perform countless other tasks.

Dimensions of a Sound Wave

To work with digital audio tools, we need to be able to describe sound in ways less vague than simply "areas of air compression" or "vibrations." As we talk about digital audio, we'll be using two key measurements of sound: *amplitude* and *frequency*.

Amplitude

The change in air pressure of each compression or rarefaction is a sound wave's *amplitude*. When we measure or describe amplitude, we're describing the amount by which the air pressure changes from the normal background air pressure, whether positive or negative. Amplitude is a very real phenomenon: if you've ever been at a concert with a loud, booming bass and felt vibrations in your chest, what you felt were the literal, large-amplitude vibrations of the sound, which made your body vibrate.

Using digital audio tools, we can map these up-and-down changes in pressure over time; we'll get a wavy line more or less like the one shown in Figure 1.1. The distance the wavy line moves above or below the straight line in the center is the change in pressure, the amplitude (**Figure 1.3**). Each upward thrust is called a *peak* or *crest*, and each downward dip is called a *trough* because the graph looks like a wave of water in the ocean. The spot where the wave is in a neutral position, representing no change from the background air pressure, is called a *zero crossing*. The overall shape of crests and troughs over time is called a *waveform*. With very few exceptions, every digital audio device you'll ever use generates, processes, or otherwise handles waveforms. (One important exception is MIDI, which is introduced at the end of this chapter and discussed more fully in Chapter 8.)

Figure 1.3 Mapping the change in air pressure over time results in a graph that's shaped like a wave. Each compression, an increase in air pressure, is represented by a crest (1). As air pressure returns to the normal level, it crosses the center line (2), a zero crossing. Each rarefaction, a decrease in air pressure, is represented by a trough (3).

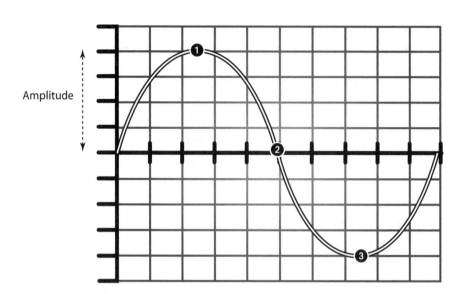

Frequency

 Frequency vs. pitch: Frequency is not quite the same as musical pitch, but we can treat them as roughly interchangeable terms. Pitch is usually expressed in musical terms, using note names like C and D. Frequency is usually expressed in Hz.

Standard measurement of frequency: Hertz (Hz), or cycles per second; the number of complete periods (one upward crest and one downward trough) that occur each second.

As a series of air pressure waves reaches your ear, you perceive continuous sound, not individual fluctuations in air pressure. Your ear and brain can count in a remarkably accurate way how many wave crests and troughs occur in a given span of time.

When the peaks and troughs are closer together, so that more of them hit your eardrum in quick succession, we say the sound is higher in *pitch;* when the peaks and troughs are farther apart, so that fewer of them reach your eardrum in the same span of time, we say the sound is lower in pitch (**Figure 1.4**).

The scientific term for how many peaks (or troughs) of a sound pass a given point within a given time is *frequency*. Frequency is usually described in *cycles per second*. A *cycle* consists of one upward crest and one downward trough. The unit for measuring the number of cycles per second (cps) is the Hertz (Hz). A measurement of frequency in Hertz tells us how many crest/trough pairs occur in the waveform during a time interval of one second.

Another useful way to talk about sound waves is in terms of their *wavelength*, the distance between adjacent crests (or between adjacent troughs). Wavelength is inversely proportional to frequency—that is, sound waves with long wavelengths have low frequencies, while sound waves with short wavelengths have high frequencies. It's easy to see why: if the distance between adjacent wave crests is greater, fewer of them will arrive at your ear in a given amount of time. Figure 1.4 represents this relationship visually.

Period

Figure 1.4 We hear changes in frequency based on how rapidly the air pressure oscillates. The more crests and troughs of a sound wave reach your ear in a span of time (the greater the frequency, or shorter the wavelength), the higher the pitch.

 How fast is sound? In dry, room-temperature air, sound travels about 1,125 feet (343 meters) every second—only marginally faster than a typical commercial airliner's cruising speed. That means that in a large space you can hear the delay of a sound bouncing off a wall. This delay time is used in digital audio to create realistic models of acoustic space.

 The Doppler Effect

When a sound source is in motion and the person hearing the sound is at rest (or vice versa), the perceived pitch changes. That's the reason a train's horn sounds as if it's changing in pitch as it passes you: the waves are pushed closer together (for a higher frequency) as the train moves toward you and spread farther apart (for a lower frequency) as the train moves away. This phenomenon is called the *Doppler effect*. Digital audio software can replicate this effect, a trick used by sound designers for film and TV. (The effect is also used, amazingly enough, by astrophysicists to determine how quickly nearby stars are moving in relation to us. The observed wavelengths of the stars' light depend on their motion.)

Sine Waves and the Geometry of Sound

Real-world waveforms aren't perfect, regular up and down oscillations, nor do they have just one frequency: sound almost always has energy at multiple frequencies simultaneously. This fact is central in the construction of digital audio devices such as equalizers and filters (Chapter 7). However, audio engineers have found it extremely useful to have a basic waveform that can be used as a sort of benchmark or building block to describe more complex waveforms. This basic waveform, the *sine wave*, oscillates repeatedly at a single frequency, and has no sound energy at any other frequency.

Meet the sine wave

The sine wave is a basic, *periodic* wave (one that repeats at regular intervals). It sweeps up and down in a motion that's a bit like the shape of the humps and dips of a roller coaster (**Figure 1.5**). Sounds that we'd describe as "pure," like a flute playing without vibrato, a person whistling, or a tuning fork, all approximate the sine wave. It's even the ideal wave shape for the electricity in your home's power outlets.

Figure 1.5 Computers are capable of producing an approximation of a pure sine wave, as represented here in the waveform display in Apple Soundtrack Pro (top). Shown in a graph of frequency content over time (bottom), this sine wave is a single horizontal band; unlike other sounds, the sine wave carries energy at only a single frequency. The haze around the horizontal band is not due to the presence of other frequencies in the sine wave; it's caused by the limitations of the analysis process.

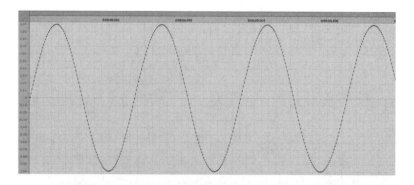

The sine wave is the wave shape you'll most often see illustrated, as in Figures 1.3 and 1.5, but it's not just useful in sound and physics textbooks: any real-world sound can be analyzed mathematically as a combination of sine waves, a property that underlies many digital audio techniques. As a result, you can begin to understand how the complex, irregular world of real sound can be understood as a combination of single frequencies.

Overtones

Most of us would intuitively assume the sound of a single musical note has one pitch, and thus one frequency. In fact, when you pluck the string on a guitar, it produces a single pitch, but the string vibrates not just at one frequency but at multiple frequencies simultaneously (**Figure 1.6**). The enormous variety of sounds in the real world (and in digital audio applications) is due to the complex blending of these various frequencies.

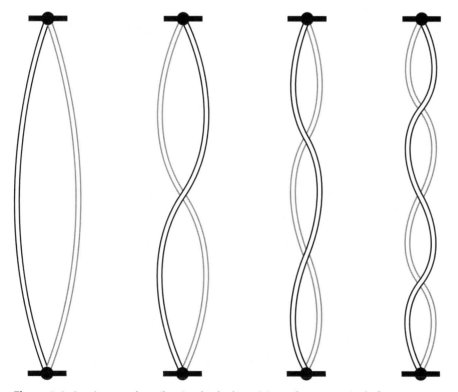

Figure 1.6 A string or other vibrating body doesn't just vibrate at a single frequency and wavelength; it vibrates at multiple frequencies at once. This string is vibrating not only at the full length of the string, but also in halves, thirds, fourths, and so on.

For instance, a string like the one shown in Figure 1.6 not only vibrates at its full length, but at the halves of its length, the thirds of its length, and so on, all at the same time. As the wavelengths decrease by whole-number fractions (½, ⅓, ¼, ⅕ . . .) the frequencies inversely increase by whole-number multiples (2x, 3x, 4x, 5x . . .), so the frequencies that result from the vibrations represented in Figure 1.6 will be successively higher as the wavelengths get shorter.

The lowest of these frequencies (usually the one we think of as the "note" of the sound) is called the *fundamental* frequency, and the frequencies above the fundamental are called *overtones* (the tones "over" the fundamental) or *partials* (since they make up part of the whole sound).

The overtones shown in Figure 1.6 have a special property: each frequency is a whole-number multiple of the fundamental frequency. Any whole-number multiple of the fundamental frequency is called a *harmonic*. This series of frequencies (twice the fundamental frequency, three times the fundamental, four times the fundamental . . .) is called the *harmonic series* or *overtone series*. The sounds of many tuned musical instruments, like the piano and violin, contain major portions of energy concentrated at or very near the harmonics.

Because the frequencies of the harmonic series are whole-number multiples of the fundamental, a sound composed solely of energy at these frequencies will remain perfectly periodic; the resulting waveform will repeat without changing at the frequency of the fundamental.

Not all overtones are harmonics, however. In between the harmonics, real-world sounds often have overtones that aren't as closely related to the fundamental. These overtones are called *inharmonic* overtones or, more often, simply *partials*. (Note that that doesn't mean all partials are inharmonic. All harmonics are partials, but not all partials are harmonics.) Because inharmonic partials aren't related to the frequency of the fundamental, the wave resulting from a fundamental frequency and inharmonic frequencies above it will be irregular over time; it won't have a single, repeating period. Instruments like a wire-stringed guitar, for instance, contain many inharmonic overtones; instruments with complex timbres like cymbals contain even more. (**Figure 1.7** shows comparisons of different sounds.) You'll see these irregularities when you look at the waveform of the sound in a digital audio program.

We don't usually hear the different overtones independently; they combine to form a more complex waveform. However, using a mathematical technique called a *Fourier transform*, it's possible to analyze any complex waveform as being made of a number of simple components, all of which are sine waves. This process underlies many techniques in digital processing, like the spectrum views shown in Figure 1.7, and many digital effects. (See "Fast Fourier Transform: Behind the Scenes of Spectral Processing" in Chapter 7 for one specific example; many other digital processes rely on Fourier transforms as well.)

 You say first overtone, I say second harmonic: Because most sounds contain a series of partials at higher and lower frequencies, we can give a number to each progressively higher partial. But the way we count them can be a little confusing. The first overtone is the first partial above the fundamental. The fundamental, which is a partial, is itself a harmonic (because its frequency is a whole-number multiple of itself, the whole number in this case being 1), so the fundamental counts as the first harmonic. Thus, the first overtone (an octave above the fundamental) is the second harmonic. The second overtone is the third harmonic, and so on.

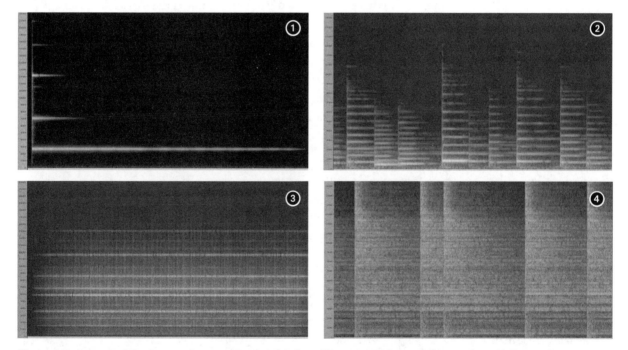

Figure 1.7 Any sound that's not a sine wave has partials, but different sounds vary in harmonic and inharmonic content, as shown here in sound samples viewed by their frequency spectrum. In these diagrams, frequency is displayed on the y-axis, time is displayed on the x-axis, and the amplitude of the partial is shown by the brightness of the area. The pure-sounding small bell (1) is strongest at the fundamental, with almost no inharmonic content and a few clear harmonics. A melody played on a Bösendorfer grand piano has richer harmonic content (2); the ladder-like effect shows the harmonics above each note of the melody. An alarm bell (3) mixes harmonic content (the brighter lines) and inharmonic content (the gray areas in between). A pattern played on a ride cymbal is almost all unpitched noise (4). The bright, leading edges are the initial crash of the stick hitting, but even as the sound decays it retains a mixture of inharmonic content evidenced by the gray areas.

Phase

So far, we've looked at the amplitude of a waveform (the increase or decrease in air pressure) and the frequency (the number of complete up and down oscillations in a given amount of time). These are useful dimensions, but neither of them tells us exactly *when* the oscillation of a wave is up (higher air pressure) or down (lower air pressure). To completely describe a waveform, we need a third dimension: the *phase* of a waveform is the position of the wave within its complete up-and-down cycle (period). At first glance, the whole business of waveform phase may seem too scientific for musicians to worry about, but it has very practical implications, as you'll see in later chapters. Knowing about phase becomes important when you're setting up multiple microphones to record an acoustic instrument, for example.

Phase is described in trigonometric terms as degrees of arc relative to a circle. Why have we switched from waves to circles? Because the sine wave is essentially a perfect circle unfolded geometrically into a wave. The sine function comes from trigonometry, the branch of mathematics that deals primarily with right triangles and circles. Aside from being used to calculate the dimensions of angles and sides in triangles, the sine function is used to determine the position of any point on a circle. That makes it convenient for our purposes in sound, because it lets us accurately refer to specific points along a sine wave as it oscillates up and down.

One period of a sine wave is equivalent to one complete rotation of a circle, so you can talk about any point along the sine wave simply by referring to a quantity in degrees from 0 to 360 (**Figure 1.8**). The beginning of the period starts at 0°, proceeds to the top of the crest at 90°, back to zero amplitude at 180°, to the bottom of the trough at 270°, and back to zero amplitude at 360°. That position along the period of the sine wave is the waveform's phase.

Figure 1.8 You can easily label a period of a sine wave in relation to a circle from 0 to 360 degrees. Any point can be calculated in degrees, but the easiest to spot are 0°, 90°, 180°, 270°, and 360°. The 360° point is the same as the 0° point, because it's the start of a new period.

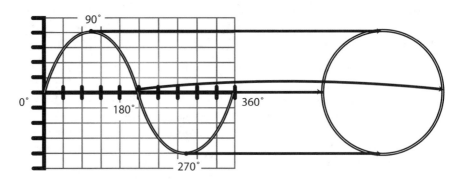

Our ears can't ordinarily detect the phase of sound waves, but phase is just as important as frequency and amplitude for another reason. A waveform's phase determines what happens when it's combined with a similar wave, an event called *wave interference*.

When waves collide

Real-world sound, as noted earlier, rarely consists of a single sine wave emanating from a single sound source: most sound sources produce energy at multiple frequencies. In addition, different sound sources often combine, and it's the more complex, composite waveform that reaches your ear. Just as dropping several pebbles into a pond creates complex, overlapping waves on the surface of the water, the combination of different overtones and different sounds changes the resulting wave shape.

When waves pass through one another or are superimposed, they *interfere*. (This is also sometimes called the *superposition* of waves.) Interference can be *constructive* interference, in which the addition of the two waveforms results in a new wave of greater amplitude, or *destructive* interference, in which the resulting amplitude is less than that of either wave by itself.

If a peak of one waveform combines with the peak of another waveform, or a trough with another trough, the amplitude of the two waveforms will be added, making the composite sound louder. However, if a peak combines with a trough, the amplitude of the waves will be reduced, making them sound softer. If the peak and the trough are of equal amplitude, they'll cancel each other out, resulting in a zero amplitude—that is, in silence (**Figure 1.9**).

Whether you're making a recording using multiple microphones or adding waveforms by *mixing* them in a digital audio program, you need to understand this basic fact: when two waves are added, the amplitude of the resulting wave depends on the phase relationships of the two original waves.In other words, it's the phase of two sine waves that determines whether those waves interfere constructively or destructively. Two sine waves of equal amplitude and frequency that are *in phase*, meaning crests and troughs are aligned with one another, will combine to form a sound that's twice as loud. When the same two sine waves are *180 degrees out of phase*, meaning crests are aligned with troughs, the result will be silence. (The cancellation of out-of-phase waveforms is called, oddly enough, *phase cancellation*.) If the phase of two sine waves with equivalent amplitude and frequency is neither perfectly in phase nor perfectly out of phase, there will still be cancellation, but only partial cancellation: two waveforms that are 90 degrees out of phase will be weakened, but not silenced.

The same principles apply to real-world sounds composed of various partials, but for each individual partial. Wave interference between real-world sounds will only result in complete phase cancellation if all of their partials have exactly the same amplitude and frequency, and if all those partials are 180 degrees out of phase. For that reason, it's extremely unlikely that you'll experience complete phase cancellation in the real world. More often, only some partials will be strengthened or weakened, so that the resulting mix of two sounds will be a little thinner or quieter at some frequencies and a little louder at others because of constructive or destructive interference.

Figure 1.9 When sine waves of equal amplitude interfere and are in phase, they combine, doubling in amplitude (top). If they are 180° opposite in phase, they cancel each other out (bottom), resulting in a zero amplitude.

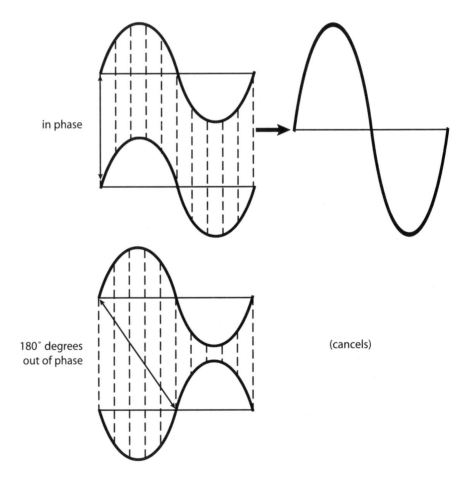

in phase

180° degrees
out of phase

(cancels)

Phase cancellation can become a problem in digital audio work, however, making sounds softer or thinner in color than desired. On a P.A. system in a live performance situation, for instance, speakers situated too close to a live sound source (like drums) can cancel out some of the natural sound from the instrument by overlapping that natural sound with out-of-phase amplified sound. You can use this effect to your advantage: by adjusting the placement of the speakers, you can employ constructive interference from in-phase sounds as reinforcement, making the mix of natural and amplified sound stronger.

A similar problem can occur when recordings are made using multiple microphones. This is particularly an issue with stereo recording or recordings of instruments like acoustic guitar and piano, when the goal is to mix the same source sound into multiple mics. The sound can arrive later at one microphone than the other, meaning you'll have two out-of-phase versions of a similar signal. When the signals from the two mics are blended, you won't hear silence, but you may hear a thinner or quieter sound than you expected. Usually, you can diagnose such problems by comparing the sound of a single mic to the mix of all of the mics, and then adjust microphone placement until you hear the mix you want.

Phase cancellation isn't always a bad thing. The muffler on your car is composed of a series of metal tubes and a resonator chamber that are designed to maximize destructive interference between waves in order to reduce the noise of exhaust from the engine. Active cancellation circuitry in noise-reducing headphones intentionally produces out-of-phase waves to deaden the sound of unwanted external noise; a microphone picks up the external noise and the headphones play back the sound out of phase.

In fact, you can use phase cancellation creatively by intentionally detuning two oscillators from one another in a synthesizer; see Chapter 9 and the discussion of detuning in the section "Intervals and tuning," later in this chapter.

SOUND AND PERCEPTION

Sound isn't just a phenomenon in physics: what happens inside your ear and brain is equally important. *Psychoacoustics* is the study of the subjective perception of sound, sound as we experience it on a daily basis as vibrations reach our ear and are relayed to the brain. Ultimately, of course, it's the human listener we care about in digital audio and music, so it's vital to understand how frequency and amplitude translate into perceived pitch, loudness, and timbre.

 Why phase cancellation matters: Unwanted phase cancellation can deaden certain sounds. You'll need to be mindful of the effects of phase cancellation whenever working with sound, but especially when recording or performing with multiple mics (see Chapter 6) or mixing (see Chapter 10). Wave interference and phase can also be used creatively in synthesis (see Chapter 9).

How We Hear Musical Pitch

If you have any musical training, you probably think about pitch in terms of musical note names, not Hertz. Although the way we hear pitch is based in part on the physical reality of sound, it's also learned through musical experience. We train our ears to hear sound in relation to tuned musical pitches. So what's going on when we hear an audio frequency and perceive it as a certain musical pitch?

Audible range

To be heard by human ears at all, sound needs to be in the audible frequency range. You could feel a 1 Hz oscillation if the amplitude were great enough, but you couldn't hear it. (It's still sound; it's just sound below the range of what you can hear.)

Sound is only audible if it lies between about 20 Hz and about 22,000 Hz. Frequencies below that range are called *infrasonic* or *subsonic*; above are called *ultrasonic*. Subsonic frequencies are sometimes used in audio to modulate other sounds. If a sound contains both partials within the audible frequency range and ultrasonic partials, we'll hear only the partials within the audible range.

At around 20 oscillations each second, or 20 Hz, most healthy adults can begin to hear a sound. The bottom note of the piano (A0) is just below 28 Hz. The A above middle C (A4), 440 Hz, is the note to which most orchestras and other ensembles tune. (This is the first note you hear before an orchestra begins tuning, as played by the oboe.) The top note of a piano is less than 4,200 Hz, but you can hear much higher, up to about 22,000 Hz for a healthy young adult.

Key tone

It's fairly easy to understand how our ears can discern pitch from a single sine wave: the number of compressions and rarefactions in a span of time translate directly to frequency. But your ears can also perceive a dominant pitch in more complex sounds that are rich in partials, sounds that contain energy at many different frequencies. When you hear an instrument play a note and hear the note G, you're not just hearing sound with the frequency that corresponds to G. Your ear detects the sound of one partial as the most significant, the *key tone*. Usually, as with a piano or violin, it's the lowest partial or fundamental, although in rare cases (as with more clangorous sounds like a church bell) the key tone may be one of the overtones. Regardless, your ear identifies that pitch as the important one while hearing the other partials as contributing to the color of the sound. Without this capability, we wouldn't be able to hear a melody.

High, low, and octaves

If you can hum a tune (even badly), you can perceive "high" and "low" frequencies as they relate to one another. That is, you can probably pick out basic contours and recognize one melody from another by identifying which pitches sound higher or lower in relation to one another—at least near the center of the frequency spectrum, where musical pitches occur.

On a basic level, this perception of high and low corresponds to frequency: faster frequencies sound higher in pitch, and slower frequencies sound lower in pitch. The way we hear the ratio of one pitch to another, however, is more complex. We hear sound in musical space along a geometric curve rather than a straight line: that is, if we hear two different frequencies (a musical interval) and compare them to one another mentally, the same difference in frequency in Hz will sound like a bigger change in relative pitch if the frequencies are lower than if the frequencies are higher.

Let's take the simplest interval to calculate, that of the octave, as shown in **Figure 1.10**. If you take any frequency number and double it, you'll get the frequency of a pitch an octave higher. For instance, starting with the frequency 220 Hz, the A just below middle C, doubling the frequency to 440 Hz results in the A an octave higher. Likewise, to get the note A an octave lower, you would halve the frequency to 110 Hz. Each time the frequency doubles, the pitch rises by an octave.

It's not just your ears that make this possible, it's the reality of physical sound. If you cut the wavelength of a string in half, by halving the length of a vibrating string, you'll get a frequency that's twice as high. Keep halving the length of string, and the frequency will continue to multiply by two, the frequency being inversely proportionate to the wavelength. (Or, in the opposite direction, keep doubling the length of string to halve the frequency.) The same thing happens in a software-based synthesizer if we adjust the Transpose parameter to increase or decrease the pitch by an octave: the frequency of the sound being produced by the synthesizer is doubled or halved.

Figure 1.10 Octaves look visually equidistant on a piano keyboard, and most musicians would tell you they sound equidistant (and even sound like the "same note," only higher or lower). But the underlying frequency (shown in Hz) doubles each time, indicating that the way we hear is geometric, not linear.

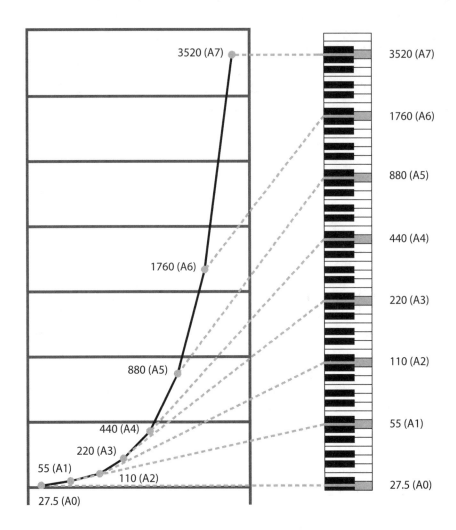

The important related psychoacoustical phenomenon is that we perceive frequencies an octave apart as being very closely related. Musicians would describe the relationship of 440 Hz to 220 Hz as being "the same note, an octave higher." Furthermore, we hear not only the octave itself but the divisions of the octave as being equivalent. The interval between an A and a B sounds the same in the higher octave as in the lower octave, even though the difference between A and B in Hz is twice as great in the higher octave. This way of perceiving pitch space is called *octave equivalency*. It's the reason Western musicians label pitches using the same note names in each octave (A, B, C, D, and so forth) regardless of how high or low they are. (Other forms of octave equivalency are found in many musical cultures around the world, as well.)

As you can see in Figure 1.10, the underlying numbers produce an exponential curve. The distance in Hz to the high A (a distance of 220 Hz) is twice as large as the distance to the low A (a distance of 110 Hz), and so on up and down the curve. But almost all musicians would say the distances sound the same.

This is obviously important when you're working with the many digital audio software parameters that are labeled in Hz. Transposing a lower pitch up by 100 Hz will sound like a bigger change than transposing a higher pitch by the same amount.

Intervals and tuning

Any two pitches can be related to one another by a ratio called an *interval*, the octave being the simplest. The ratio of an octave is 2:1. We hear two notes as being "in tune" or "out of tune" with each other based first and foremost on these ratios. It's the ratio of the frequencies, not the raw distance in Hz, which is most significant to our ears.

The musical pitches we know, such as the notes of a major scale, are specific, learned frequencies. We've heard them so many times that we've learned the relative intervals formed by certain tunings. If you have perfect pitch, you've even memorized the tunings, but even if you can only sing "Happy Birthday," you've unknowingly memorized a series of intervals. But how did these intervals, the ones that sound good and "in tune," arise in the first place?

First, there are acoustic phenomena that can make two notes sound in tune or out of tune. Close intervals with ratios that can't be described using small whole numbers produce an acoustic phenomenon called *dissonance* or *beats*.

Literally, beats are the result of constructive and destructive interference produced by differences in phase between two tones. We perceive these repeated changes in amplitude as a shifting in the sound, which might be very subtle, or a more pronounced, "twangy," rhythmic pattern. (For a dramatic example, think of the out-of-tune old piano in a movie saloon in a Western. We perceive that the piano is out of tune because a piano has three strings for each note, which are supposed to be tuned to the same frequency. When the strings drift out of tune with one another, they produce beats when sounded together.) With pure sine waves of equal amplitude, the frequency of the beating that results when two tones are sounded

 Sounds bad: Acoustical dissonance, which produces the phenomenon called beats, is loosely related to musical dissonance, but the latter is more complex and difficult to quantify because it's related to how intervals are used in various musical styles. The latter topic is not discussed in this book.

together is the difference between the frequencies of the two tones. Tones at 440 Hz and 442 Hz, for instance, would produce a *difference tone* of 2 Hz, which would sound like a regular beating in amplitude twice every second.

Dissonant intervals aren't necessarily bad; on the contrary, they're often used for specific artistic effects. Two slightly detuned sound sources at the unison can be used to create special timbres, as we'll see in the discussion of sound synthesis in Chapter 9. But acoustic dissonance does contribute to our sense of what is and is not in tune.

Because of beating, it's very easy to tell when two pitches don't match at the unison, so the simplest method of tuning—whether you're matching a pitch with your voice or tuning two instruments to the same note—is to tune to unisons. It's also particularly easy to hear the 2:1 ratio of the octave when it is tuned to remove beats, or other simple intervals like the perfect fifth (a ratio of 3:2). Combining these intervals into a tuning system for an entire instrument, however, is far more complex.

Theoretically, it might be ideal to tune to the interval ratios found in the lower harmonics of the harmonic series—the ratios of 3:2 (the perfect fifth), 4:3 (the perfect fourth), 5:4 (the major third), 6:5 (the minor third), and so on. The frequencies of the harmonic series correspond closely to musical intervals with which we're familiar (**Figure 1.11**). The octave, fifth (and by inversion, the fourth), and major and minor thirds are all found in the first six harmonics. In fact, you can tune to simple whole-number ratios for a tuning system that closely matches this series and thus sounds very "tuned"; this system (which is actually a whole family of tuning systems) is called *just intonation*.

(Harmonic number)

Figure 1.11 The harmonic series consists of the fundamental and the series of harmonic overtones representing whole-number multiples of the fundamental (1x, 2x, 3x, 4x, 5x . . .). The series is based on a fundamental pitch, such as A2 (the A an octave and a third below middle C), which is shown here. The series corresponds loosely to the musical notes shown, but not exactly, because of compromises in the tuning system used by most musicians.

The problem with tuning exclusively to whole-number ratios is that it yields intervals of differing sizes. That creates problems for keyboard instruments in particular, because it makes it difficult to use chord progressions that modulate to different keys. In order to get the same set of intervals in the new key, you'd have to retune the instrument. Starting in the 18th century, as music that moved from one key center to another became more common, Western musicians began using various methods for compromising the ratios of pitches so that all pitches and intervals would sound more or less equally in tune in a variety of keys.

The system used most commonly today, *12-Tone Equal Temperament*, makes all adjacent notes on the keyboard sound perfectly equidistant. If you were to play up the white and black notes on a tuned keyboard, each adjacent step should sound the same as every other adjacent step, because the ratio of adjacent pitches to one another is constant. (As usual, we hear geometric ratios as equivalent, not linear differences in Hz.) Unfortunately, this ratio is not based on whole numbers; it's based on the 12th root of 2, which is an irrational number. Strange as it may seem, the ratio is not rational.

As a result, the musical pitches shown in Figure 1.11 only approximate the frequencies in the harmonic series. All of the intervals except the octave are slightly compromised. If you listen closely to a major or minor third in particular, you'll hear beating between the two tones, because the equal-tempered thirds are not the same as the ratios in the harmonic series. But since the tuning system is part of the music most of us hear from birth onward, we take it for granted and don't perceive any out-of-tuneness in its intervals. (Thanks to digital audio technology, it's far easier than ever before to experiment with other tuning systems.)

Musical pitch and digital audio

Certain tasks in digital audio are likely to require that you use musical units rather than audio units. For instance, if you want to transpose a recorded passage to a new key, you'll probably want to do that using terms you're familiar with, like "up a whole-step" or "from D to E" rather than as a ratio or, worse, a unit in Hz. When pitch is described in digital audio applications, the *semitone* is the most commonly used interval; it's what musicians call a chromatic scale degree or the distance between adjacent notes in an octave on a piano (including both white and black keys). When additional precision is needed, we can divide each semitone into one hundred *cents*.

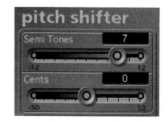

Converting between note names and Hz: You'll find a handy online converter at www.phys.unsw.edu. au/~jw/notes.html.

If an application displays a parameter in Hz and not in pitch, you may have to convert manually when you need to think in terms of pitch. Fortunately, there are a variety of lookup tables and calculators online. Some applications, like Cycling '74 Max/MSP (www.cycling74.com), even include automatic conversion between the two units. All of these assume the most common tuning system, 12-Tone Equal Temperament. In some situations, it's enough if you remember that doubling the frequency raises the pitch by an octave. For instance, a frequency of 1,500 Hz is an octave above a frequency of 750 Hz.

How We Hear Loudness

As with musical pitch, calculating relative loudness is complex because of the details of how we hear.

The terms "amplitude" and "loudness" are often used interchangeably, but although they're related, they're not the same thing. Amplitude is a relative measure both of the physical properties of sound (the relative displacement of air pressure) and of the relative strength of audio signals (both digital and analog). Loudness, on the other hand, is a subjective terms that's dependent on perception. It's what seems loud to you based on the physical capabilities of your ear and the way your brain processes sound.

The human ear is capable of detecting an extraordinary range of amplitudes, which in sound is measured as *sound pressure level*. If we measured these numbers directly, we'd have to work with some decidedly inconvenient numbers: the power range of the human ear is a ratio of approximately ten trillion to one. Unless you like numbers with lots and lots of zeros, you'll probably want a more convenient scale with which to label a volume fader.

Decibel scale

The basic mathematical method of turning this huge range of numbers into a more manageable range is to use a *logarithmic* rather than a *linear* scale. Without getting too far into the underlying mathematics, this means that instead of marking off increments in a numbering system like 1, 2, 3, 4, 5, 6 . . ., you use those simple numbers to represent bigger numbers (the sound pressure level ratios with increasing numbers of zeros on the end).

The original unit for measurements of this type was called the *bel*, after Alexander Graham Bell. Even that number proved to be a little too large for use with sound, so engineers simply eliminated one last zero, giving us the *decibel (dB)*, which is equal to 1/10 of a bel.

You're probably already familiar with another logarithmically derived scale, the Richter scale, which is used to measure the intensity of earthquakes. Like the Richter scale, decibels are a generic measure of ratio. Since we're measuring ratios and not a simple quantity (as with inches or kilograms), the key questions are ratio of what unit, and relative to what? Without a point of reference, the scale doesn't mean anything.

The relative point from which the decibel scale is measured is an arbitrary point that's called 0 dB. When we say that a sound measures 0 dB, we're not necessarily talking about zero amplitude.

Different uses, different scales

Two basic forms of decibels are used in audio, those used to measure acoustic phenomena relative to human hearing and those that measure signal strength in electrical systems. Comparing sound pressure to signal strength is like comparing apples to oranges, even though both are routinely measured in decibels. We all understand the joke in the movie *This Is Spinal Tap* when the character Nigel ignorantly points to a guitar amplifier that "goes to eleven" instead of ten. In the end, units related to loudness are literally all relative.

The dB (SPL) scale measures sound pressure level relative to human hearing. It sets zero as the lowest sound pressure level at which most people can hear a sound. (Again, this is relative, so if you have especially sensitive ears, you may be able to hear sounds that would be measured as slightly below 0 dB.) For electrical signal strength, a variety of units measure either power (including units like the dBm; "m" is short for milliwatt) or relative voltage level (units like dBu and dBV). The good news is you probably won't need to know the difference between dBm and dBu. These letters are tacked on the end of these units in contexts like technical specifications of audio equipment so that engineers know what the reference level of that equipment is.

Loudness and digital audio

In audio software, decibels are usually a relative measure of the strength of an audio signal. For instance, in a mixer view in an application like Digidesign Pro Tools or Cakewalk SONAR, 0 dB would be not the smallest sound you could hear, but an arbitrary measure of level within the application. The signal of a given waveform might be a smaller value (a relatively weaker signal, measured as a negative dB value) or a slightly higher value (a relatively stronger signal). In some applications, 0 dB is the highest possible peak the application can handle, and everything else is measured as lower than 0 dB.

Decibel ratios only loosely correlate to the way we perceive significant volume changes. An increase of 3 dB doubles the relative sound pressure or power level of a sound; a decrease of 3 dB halves it, but the perceived change in loudness is fairly subtle. A change of one or two dB is often undetectable. To get a change that sounds twice as loud, it's often necessary to increase the volume level by 20 or 30 dB.

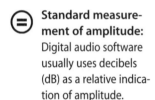

Standard measurement of amplitude: Digital audio software usually uses decibels (dB) as a relative indication of amplitude.

Not all frequencies are created equal, either. Our ears are most sensitive to sounds toward the center of the pitch spectrum, closer to the frequency range of speech, and less sensitive to sounds at lower and higher frequencies. That's the reason the "loudness" setting on many home stereos and consumer audio devices will boost the bass and treble, leaving the middle spectrum untouched. By boosting the bass and treble, a loudness curve has the opposite bias of your hearing, which is more sensitive to the middle frequencies. It boosts the frequencies you have the most difficulty hearing at low listening volumes. The resulting effect sounds fuller and more present, even though the volume for the whole sound has not been boosted by as much as you think it has. (Incidentally, a loudness contour will therefore have very little effect at high listening volumes, because your ears are less biased to the center when sounds have greater amplitude.) The equalization section of Chapter 7 details some of the other ways in which amplitude changes to different frequencies impact perceived sound.

What does matter is the volume change you perceive when you make a change in decibel level. So should you pull out your scientific calculator and start punching up logarithms? Of course not; the decibel was invented to save you that trouble. Instead, you'll most likely develop an intuitive sense of how a certain change adjusts the sound in certain frequency ranges. Sound engineers routinely talk about "boosting the mids [middle frequencies] by a couple of dB," for instance.

Protecting Your Hearing

Healthy young people can hear frequencies from about 20 Hz to 22,000 Hz. As you grow older, some high-frequency hearing is lost. The sound-sensing apparatus of your ear—tiny hypersensitive hairs that line the inner ear—is extremely susceptible to damage. To protect your hearing, avoid prolonged exposure to high-volume sound, take breaks when wearing headphones, and be careful how you set listening volumes. The best way to set volume with headphones is to start very low, turn up to a comfortable listening level, and then leave the level there. Your ears can become desensitized to a level that's causing damage.

High-volume listening puts you at risk for hearing loss and the painful, irreversible hearing syndrome tinnitus. (Having your ears ring or feel fatigued is generally a sign of an extremely dangerous sound level.) For these reasons, you'll often see music-loving audio engineers wearing earplugs at rock concerts. High volume levels aren't just dangerous, they're less accurate: they introduce distortion, making them less than ideal for monitoring.

For more on preventing hearing loss, try the following online resources:

U.S. Center for Disease Control on Hearing & Health (www.cdc.gov/ncbddd/dd/ddhi.htm)

American Tinnitus Association (www.ata.org)

For workplace safety, it becomes vital to measure the exact ambient noise level in dB (SPL); thus you can find lots of detailed information on the dB (SPL) unit of measurement and different volume levels at the United States Department of Labor's **Occupational Safety & Health Administration** (www.osha.gov).

How we hear timbre

As discussed earlier, most sounds contain energy at multiple frequencies, but our ears fuse these together and experience them as a single sound. It's the combination of these component energies that we hear as *timbre*, the color or character of a sound. (That's pronounced *tam-burr*, not "timber.")

The timbre of a sound depends entirely on the frequencies of the partials in the sound and the amount of energy at each frequency (the amplitude of each partial). Different partials will typically last for different lengths of time, as well, so part of what we hear as timbre is the way this frequency content changes over time. The energy of these different partials over time is what allows us to tell the difference between the sound of a tuba and the sound of an electric guitar. This overall picture of the content of the sound is commonly called the *spectrum* of the sound, the distribution of energy across the range of audible frequencies. As you add energy to the overtones of a sound, the resulting waveshape (as you'd see it on an oscilloscope or in a software program) changes. A simple sine wave, as you've seen, has steady, repeated increases and decreases in air pressure resulting in a single frequency with no overtones. As you add harmonics above this pure tone, the resulting waveshape becomes more complex, as shown in **Figure 1.12.** As inharmonic overtones are added, the periodicity of the wave will disappear, and the sense of a defined, clearly audible pitch will begin to be reduced. The more inharmonic content is present, the less well defined the pitch of the sound will be.

In contrast to pitched tones, *noise* lacks perceptible periodicity entirely, as shown in Figure 1.12. Sounds like electrical static and wind are mostly noise in their sound content. On a frequency spectrum, they would have no noticeable harmonics and a fairly even distribution of energy at all frequencies. Theoretical "white noise" has equal energy at all frequencies: it's "white" in the same sense that white light contains energy at all visible wavelengths.

These qualities of timbre become all the more significant when you begin designing your own sounds and virtual instruments. For an extended discussion with hands-on examples, see Chapter 9.

Figure 1.12 When a waveform view in software is zoomed in close enough to allow details to be viewed, you can see the individual periods (cycles) of the wave. A pure sine wave (1) has a simple, repeating period. With added harmonics (2), the periodicity remains, but the shape of the wave becomes more complex. You'll still hear this sound as pitched, but the perceived timbre will be richer. With noisy sounds, like the synthetically generated white noise shown (3), there's no repeated period at all. With no discernible period, you'll no longer hear the sound as pitched; the result will sound like wind or static.

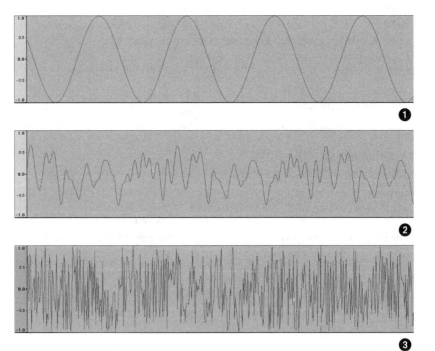

What Sound Looks Like in Software

Now that you've learned the basics of the physics of sound, how will you deal with sound in digital audio software? So far, we've dealt with three basic elements:

- **Time:** Without time, you can't have pitch (since frequency is just repeated oscillations over time) or music (which also exists in time).

- **Amplitude/relative air pressure deviation:** Amplitude is essential to determining the strength of sound materials and to perceived loudness.

- **Frequency content and partials:** We hear the strengths of different partials in the sound over time as its timbre.

Much of the time, digital audio software displays the first two elements onscreen. **Figure 1.13** shows a typical waveform view in audio software, which shows a representation of signal strength or air pressure on the y-axis and time on the x-axis.

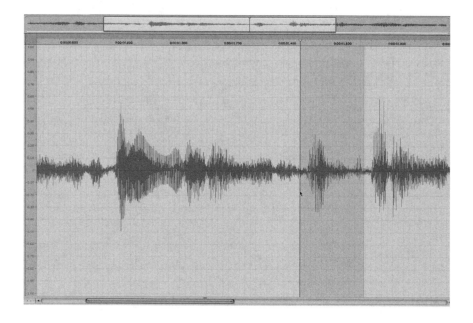

Figure 1.13 A typical wave editor view of a waveform, shown here in Apple Soundtrack Pro. When the display is zoomed out to the time level you'd most often use for editing, you won't be able to see individual wave periods, but you will be able to see overall changes in amplitude.

The height of the waveform on the y-axis of the graph should be roughly analogous to the changes in air pressure of the actual sound, as a result of the digital recording process described in the section "Sound in Digital Form" later in this chapter. Any deviation above or below the center line represents amplitude, as you saw earlier. The display shows the strength of

On the DVD: Basic waveform editors are useful "Swiss Army knife"-style tools for working with digital audio. Audacity, included on the DVD, is a free, open-source, audio-editing package available for Windows, Linux, and Mac OS X.

the recorded digital signal, although the labels on the y-axis are often fairly obscure, labeled simply as –1.0 to zero to 1, or –100% to 100%, rather than something specific like decibels. If they are labeled in decibels, you may see something like 0 dB for the maximum, and a negative value like –96.3 dB, representing the dynamic range of the digital audio software. Some programs provide y-axis labels in exact sample values, such as –32,628 to 32,627, although since this type of data is a little hard to grasp, it's much less common.

When the display is zoomed further out to give you an overview of a longer segment of sound, you won't see the individual oscillations of the waveform, but you will see the overall amplitude profile over time. You'll be able to see where words in a sung or spoken recording begin and end, where drum hits or bass notes happen, and so on. **Figure 1.14** shows a typical screenshot from Sony ACID Pro (http://mediasoftware.sonypictures.com) with an overview of a song arrangement.

Figure 1.14 Waveform overviews as they appear in a song arrangement in Sony ACID Pro. Here, you can see the elements of your song as they relate to one another (beats, notes, and other elements as they appear in the amplitude of the waveforms).

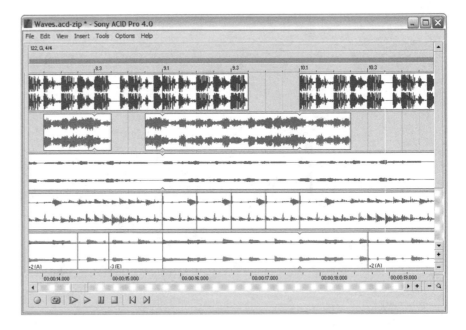

Showing air pressure and time in a basic waveform view isn't the only way to represent sound onscreen. Many programs allow you to view the frequency spectrum of the sound, which is more useful for seeing the timbral qualities of the sound you're editing and fine-tuning parameters of effects and edits in Hz, as shown in **Figure 1.15**.

Hands-on: Visualizing Sound

Using Audacity, you can open and view audio files in Windows WAV format and compressed Ogg Vorbis and MP3 file formats. Try opening some files in these formats and looking at the waveform view. To increase the vertical size of the waveform display, drag on the bottom edge of the waveform view. To zoom in and out horizontally, click the magnifying glass tools represented by the plus and minus signs on the toolbar, or use the commands in the View menu. If you zoom in far enough, you'll see the individual samples in the audio file. They look like squares overlaid on the waveform.

Many applications and plug-ins can also display harmonic content over time in place of the usual amplitude-versus-time view. This can be useful for better understanding the content of sound and can act as a tool in editing and filtering. In Audacity, you can switch the view of your sound from an amplitude graph, which Audacity simply calls its waveform view, to a "spectrum" view that displays frequency information on the y-axis and amplitude as darkness or lightness. To change the view, click the down arrow next to the waveform name and select Spectrum, as shown in Figure 1.15.

Some applications take this concept further. Tools like U&I Software MetaSynth (www.uisoftware.com) enable you to synthesize and edit sound with tools usually found in graphics software, painting with sound in a spectral view. Adobe Audition lets you paint over its waveform view to filter the sound.

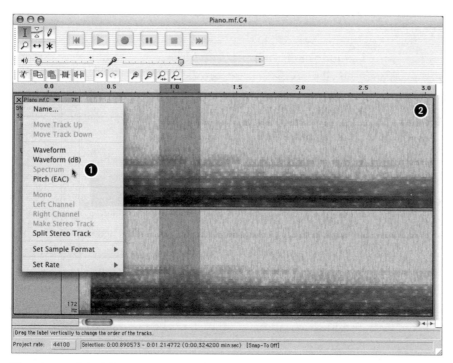

Figure 1.15 Select the Spectrum view from the drop-down menu next to a waveform (1), and Audacity displays a frequency-versus-time graph in which amplitude is displayed as shades of gray (2). The spectrum of a real-world sound contains a range of pitched components that contribute to the color of the sound. You can use this view in Audacity to edit and filter a sound.

SOUND IN DIGITAL FORM

So far we've been talking about sound as it exists in the real world, but most important to us is learning how to manipulate that sound digitally. To translate sound to digital form, or to translate digital information back into sound, we need the assistance of *transducers*. A transducer is a device that translates one kind of energy into another.

Transducers

A device is a transducer if it converts any kind of energy into another form. A thermometer is a simple transducer. It transforms heat into a visual display such as a moving needle. An audio transducer transforms sound waves in the air into some other form, such as an electrical signal. Your ears are themselves audio transducers, transforming sound into nerve impulses that can be sent to the brain.

Early audio transducer technology, like Edison's 1877 tinfoil phonograph, converted sound energy into mechanical energy. These devices directly translated the vibrations in air into grooves in a foil-wrapped cylinder. Inserting a stylus into the groove on the cylinder and attaching the stylus to a megaphone-type horn reversed the direction of the transducer, translating the grooves back into sound.

Today's most common audio transducers—microphones, headphones, and speakers—convert sound into electrical energy or vice versa. Instead of working with sound vibrations to cut grooves directly in a storage medium as Edison's device did, vibrations are translated into electrical signals by intermediate devices such as moving magnetic coils. (See Chapter 6 for details on exactly how microphones do this.) Once in electrical form, the signals can be used for direct electrical processing in sound hardware, they can be stored magnetically (via magnetized metal particles on audio tape), and, via specialized circuits, they can be converted into numerical data that can be transmitted digitally to computers and other digital devices. In the opposite direction, electrical signals can be converted mechanically into acoustical vibrations; for example, an amplified electrical voltage will drive the cone of a loudspeaker in and out, producing sound.

Analog and Digital Audio

Once sound has been transformed into an electrical signal by a microphone, various devices can transmit and store a representation of the sound in either analog or digital form. Even though the title of this book is *Real World Digital Audio*, not *Real World Analog Audio*, you'll use both digital and analog devices in your digital studio, especially since microphones, headphones, and speakers all require conversion of digital audio to analog electrical signals.

Analog and digital equipment both work with transducers that convert sound to voltage and vice versa. Analog circuitry transmits this voltage as a continuous signal that directly represents sound. As with the grooves on a record, any small variation is directly equivalent to the fluctuations in air pressure that constitute sound. Digital circuitry starts with an analog voltage stage, but converts this signal into a numeric form that represents a series of snapshots of the original continuous voltage level. The digital signals are still transmitted as voltages, but minor changes in voltage don't matter, because the signal is encoded and interpreted as a series of zeros and ones (binary numbers). Let's look at each of these in turn to better understand what that means.

How analog audio works

Something is an analog of something else if the two are comparable in some way. The term *analog* in relation to audio refers to a continuously varying electrical signal that represents the original variations in pressure of a sound. In reality, the signal is an approximate, not perfect, representation of the original source because of the limitations of real-world transducers—in this case, microphones—but the variations in voltage (the analog signal) will look approximately like the original variations in air pressure (the sound) (**Figure 1.16**).

Analog audio signals are employed by a variety of devices, such as:

- Microphones and speakers (including those with digital converters; fundamentally, a mic or speaker is still an analog device)

- Standard audio connections, including headphone jacks, the RCA phono plugs on a stereo, and ¼" TRS connectors

- Analog musical instruments, such as analog synthesizers and electric guitars, and their amps

- Analog audio processors, including spring reverbs and analog effect units

- Analog recording equipment, including turntables and cassette and reel-to-reel tape decks

Air pressure   Voltage level

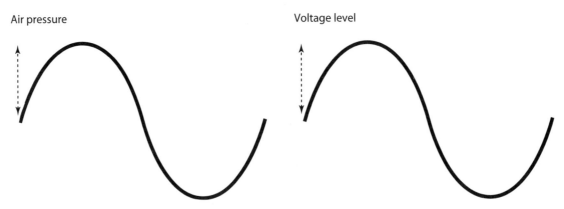

Figure 1.16 An analog electrical signal represents the continuous variation of air pressure in real-world sound (left) as a continuous variation in voltage level (right).

How digital audio works

Since analog electrical audio signals are neatly comparable to the original sound, why would you ever need anything else? The answer is, analog audio has its downsides. First, because it represents sound using a continuously fluctuating voltage level, any variation in that level—like small amounts of electrical interference—will be heard when the electrical signal is passed through another transducer (in this case a loudspeaker) and once more becomes sound. In other words, analog signals are susceptible to noise and loss of quality when being transmitted and copied. Second, you're limited in the ways you can process analog signals. You can't take advantage of the many capabilities of the microprocessors in your computer and other hardware. Since computers are essentially very sophisticated arithmetic machines, you can't use computers to work with sound unless you can convert analog audio signals into numbers. The solution to all of these issues is to use a stream of numbers to represent the analog signal instead of using the analog signal directly.

Any audio system that uses numbers to store, process, and transmit data is called *digital*. The word digital refers to digits, or fingers, because the simplest way to convert observed phenomena to number values is to count on your fingers. To convert the continuous range of analog voltage into numeric form, digital equipment uses a device called an *analog-to-digital (A/D) converter*.

To create discrete numerical values, the converter measures the voltage level at regular time intervals, a process called *sampling* (**Figure 1.17**). You can see a representation of digital samples up close in audio software that has sample-level zooming, as shown in **Figure 1.18**.

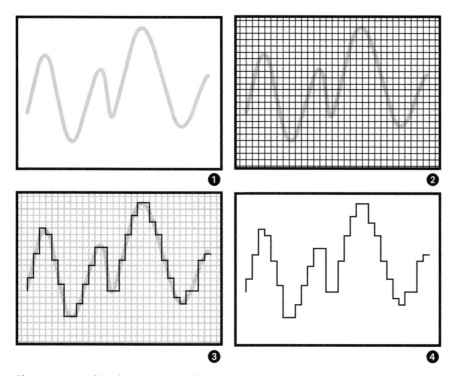

Figure 1.17 A digital converter translates a continuous analog voltage into discrete, numerical values. The input for the converter is an analog electrical signal, which has a continuously variable level analogous to the variations in air pressure in the original sound (1). The converter is capable of translating this data into a "grid" of possible, discrete numbers: on the x-axis, time, a certain number of snapshots per second, and on the y-axis, signal strength, a certain number of numerical values for each of those snapshots (2). The digital converter must round off the continuous levels of the analog signal to these numerical values (3). This results in a digital signal that models the original analog signal as a series of numbers (4).

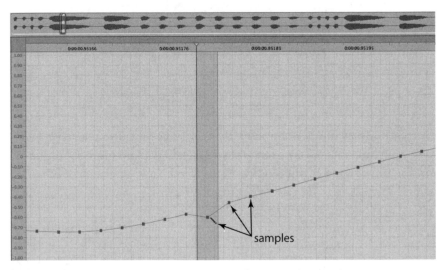

Figure 1.18 If you zoom all the way in with a software application that supports sample-accurate display, you can see the individual samples in the waveform. The lines connecting each sample (each square shown) are added to make the display easier for human eyes to understand; the data itself is just the series of discrete values. (Applications like Apple Soundtrack Pro let you edit individual samples as well as view them.)

 Why you need both digital and analog:
You can't convert directly between sound and digital information. Transducers like microphones, headphones, and speakers ultimately need to convert sound waves to and from continuous analog voltages. Likewise, many audio processes can only operate on digital signals, and computers can only directly process digital sound.

The *A/D converter* converts the incoming signal into digital form, after which it can be processed or stored in the computer. But we also need a way to get that digital data back into the form of an analog voltage. Otherwise, we won't be able to drive headphones and speakers to convert it back into real-world sound. A digital-to-analog (D/A) converter (sometimes called a DAC) does just the opposite of what the A/D does. The D/A converts digital data back into continuous analog voltage.

Devices can be considered digital devices if they contain A/D and/or D/A capability or if they work with digital audio directly. These devices include:

- Computer audio interfaces and stand-alone converters

- Digital effects, such as digital reverb units, multi-effects processors, guitar amp simulators, and many others

- Digital mixers and playback and recording devices, including portable digital recorders like MiniDisc and DAT

- Digital instruments, including nearly all MIDI-based synthesizers, new guitars with onboard digital capabilities, and other devices that are designed to interface with a computer

- Digital connections, including the digital-audio connection that runs from a consumer DVD player to a surround sound receiver

- Computers

Quality in the Digital Domain

Uneducated consumers often think the word "digital" means something is high-quality. In fact, to say something is "digital" says no more about the quality of the sound it will produce than to say that it is "electrical," as you've no doubt already discovered from experiencing poor-quality digital cable and mobile phone reception. Digital media solves some problems. For example, no noise will be introduced after recording, as in analog recorders. But digital recording introduces new problems. Most significant of these is the issue of data loss: since analog-to-digital conversion samples the signal as discrete levels, it removes some of the information present in the original signal. Whether or not that lost data is noticeable is a function of how detailed the sample is.

Two elements work together to define the sampling process: how often the converter takes a sample (the *sampling rate*) and how accurately it can represent that sample as a number (the *bit depth*). It's important in any digital capture device, including any audio device, to record enough information to provide an accurate record of the source signal. The sample rate you choose determines how much frequency range you can record, and the bit depth determines how accurately you can record changes in the level of the analog signal being sampled, which impacts dynamic range and thus the amount of residual noise in the signal.

Sampling rate and frequency range

The sampling rate is how often the A/D converter measures the signal level; the samples are roughly analogous to a series of snapshots. If the converter takes ten samples of the signal each second, it has a sampling rate of 10 Hz.

The frequency range of an A/D converter is determined by sample rate, but probably not in the way you'd assume. The highest frequency you can capture is only half the sample rate. A sample rate of 10 Hz can capture a maximum frequency of 5 Hz, not 10 Hz. The reason is that, without twice as many samples of a source as there are up and down oscillations, you lose some of the oscillations.

Aliasing occurs when the highest frequency being sampled is higher than the highest frequency that can accurately be captured by the A/D converter. Aliasing adds unwanted distortion to the audio signal by artificially lowering the frequency of high partials. Aliasing can occur in a digital audio system as a result of a poorly designed A/D converter, but you're far more likely to hear it when synthesizing high notes using a software-based digital synthesizer. If the synthesizer doesn't use anti-aliasing technology, high notes are likely to turn into random clusters of tone that have no relation to the key you're playing.

To avoid aliasing, you need the sampling rate to be at least twice as great as the highest frequency you want to capture. Why twice as high? When a sound has a high frequency, the peaks and troughs in its waveform will be close together. If the sampling rate isn't fast enough to capture every peak and every trough, the digitized version of the sound will have a different waveform than the original (**Figure 1.19**). If the frequency of what you're sampling or synthesizing is greater than half the sample rate, the original frequency will be lost. When you listen to the tone that was recorded or synthesized, you'll hear a different frequency, as shown in Figure 1.19. This new frequency, introduced by the sampling process, is often called a *foldover* frequency or an alias, because the higher frequency, beyond the range of the converter, is folded over into a lower frequency that lies within the range of the converter.

Original analog signal source

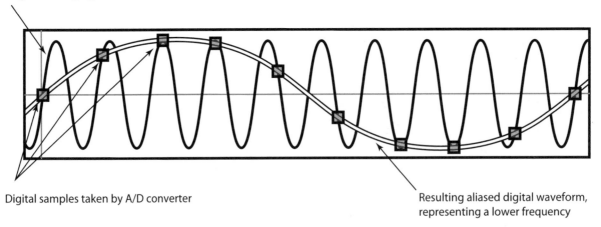

Digital samples taken by A/D converter

Resulting aliased digital waveform, representing a lower frequency

Figure 1.19 Aliasing occurs when an analog-to-digital converter is unable to capture enough data to represent a high frequency. If the digital samples are not taken often enough to capture each up and down oscillation of the source, the digital representation of the wave will be inaccurate: it will contain a lower frequency. The sampling process "folds" the higher frequency into a lower one, so it's called a foldover frequency, or an *alias* of the higher frequency.

Researchers at Bell Labs were familiar with this problem as early as the 1920s and recorded the principle as the Nyquist-Shannon Sampling Theorem. The theorem is simple: to properly sample frequency value x, you need a sample rate of at least twice x. (The maximum frequency that can be sampled without aliasing at a certain sample rate is thus called the Nyquist frequency.) So why do we need the sampling rate to be twice as fast as the highest frequency to be recorded? Because each period of a regular waveform includes both an up and a down oscillation. If the A/D converter takes fewer than two samples per period, it can't capture the full oscillation. In order to capture each "up" and each "down" state, you need to take at least two samples each period. Thus the sampling rate has to be twice the highest frequency to be recorded (**Figure 1.20**).

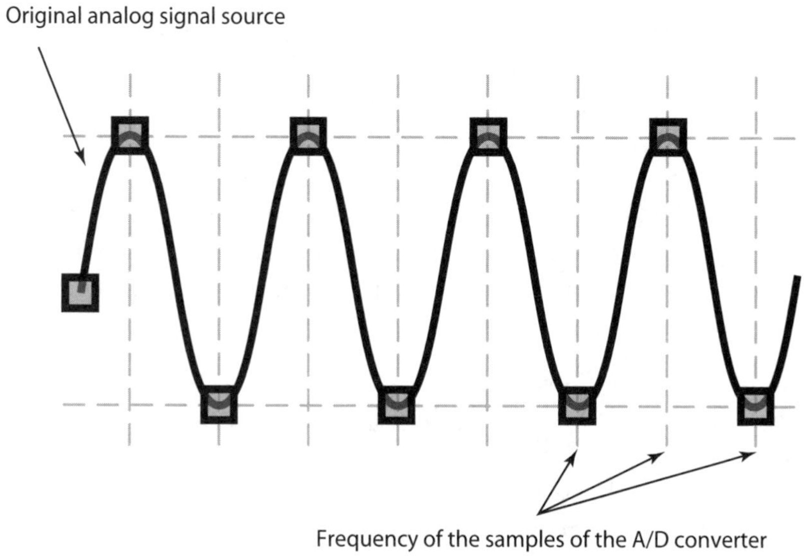

Original analog signal source

Frequency of the samples of the A/D converter

Figure 1.20 To capture the full oscillation of a frequency, you need at least two digital samples for each period of the sampled waveform. With two samples, the A/D will be able to capture both the up and down state of the waveform.

According to the Nyquist-Shannon theorem, to sample frequencies up to the upper range of human hearing (about 22,000 Hz), you'll need a sample rate of about 44,000 Hz, which is, not coincidentally, very close to the standard sample rate for commercial audio CDs, 44,100 Hz.

That obviously enables you to sample frequencies at the top of the range of your hearing, but what happens when the frequencies in the signal reaching the A/D converter exceed the maximum frequency limit of 22 kHz? Left untouched, they would fold over into the audible spectrum as distortion, so A/D converters incorporate an *anti-aliasing filter* that removes these high partials before the audio is converted to digital form.

Bit depth and signal-to-noise

The sampling rate tells us how an A/D converter works in time, and thus how it captures frequency information—the x-axis of the waveform diagrams. The *bit depth* determines the amount of detail that can be recorded about the incoming level of the signal—the y-axis of the diagrams.

With each sample, the A/D converter must measure the incoming signal level and assign it one of a discrete set of numbers. For instance, if the converter can record a whole number between one and eight (that is, rounding off each value it records to 1, 2, 3, 4, 5, 6, 7, or 8), then its bit depth is 3 bits. (A binary bit has two values, either off or on, so it's three bits because $2^3 = 8$: you need three on or off positions in order to count from one to eight). The converter is limited to these discrete values. It can't record that the signal is between two and three; it must round off to one or the other. Needless to say, 3 bits are not nearly enough; 8-bit and 12-bit converters were used in many early digital audio devices, and today 16-bit and 24-bit converters are the most common. With each bit added, the number of possible sound pressure levels that can be stored doubles—16-bit audio has over 65,000 possible levels of resolution; 24-bit has over 16 million. You've probably experienced what happens when you reduce bit depth by talking on a mobile phone: the sound becomes noisier, harsher, and less clear.

The direct impact of the bit depth on the captured signal is on dynamic range: the greater the bit depth, the greater the range of dynamics or amplitude levels you can capture before (at the lowest amplitude level) the signal is submerged in the background noise. Dynamic range is obviously important, given the level of dynamic range our ears can perceive. But its real significance is that, when the number of possible dynamic levels is limited by the use of a converter with a lesser bit depth, the measurement of the analog signal becomes inaccurate. This inaccuracy is perceived by our ears as noise. We hear the errors created by the rounding off of the numbers, called *quantization errors*, as noise.

If we increase the dynamic range of the digital audio system by using a greater bit depth, we effectively reduce the amount of background noise in the system: the difference between the loudest signal that the system can handle and the residual noise is greater. This ratio of distinguishable signal information to background noise is called the *signal-to-noise ratio*. The greater the bit depth, the greater the dynamic range, and the higher the signal-to-noise ratio (sometimes abbreviated "s/n") of the system.

Commonly used sampling frequencies and bit depths

Digital audio resolution is measured in terms of sampling frequency (related to sound frequency range and measured in kHz) and bit depth (related to amplitude and measured in bits). These values are roughly equivalent to image resolution and color depth in digital graphics. Any numbers are theoretically possible for these values, and you can mix and match sampling frequency and bit depth, but the settings you'll encounter most often are

- **16-bit, 44.1 kHz:** The standard for Red Book CD Audio—the commercial audio CD format. Also used for consumer CD-Rs and the most common default for computer audio software.

- **16-bit, 48 kHz:** The standard for digital video (DV), commercial DVD videos, and most digital-broadcast video.

- **24-bit, 96 kHz:** The emerging higher-resolution format increasingly supported by computer audio software and hardware, although not yet a widely adopted standard in the consumer marketplace for listening to music.

A good minimum standard for many types of recording is 16-bit/44.1 kHz, because it's the output quality of commercial audio CDs, and its sampling frequency can record up to the top range of human hearing. (Generally, you'd use 48 kHz sound to match the output sample rate for standard video, not to get a 2 kHz increase in Nyquist frequency—something you're highly unlikely to notice as an improvement in audio quality.)

It may seem counterintuitive that you'd ever want to work with audio capable of manipulating frequencies above the highest frequency you can hear. There are three reasons why you might want sampling rates up to 96 kHz or greater, however. The first reason, although it's hotly debated, is that unheard frequencies above 22 kHz may have an impact on sound in the audible spectrum, making audio output at 96 kHz sound better or more accurate than 44.1 kHz. That's generally a matter of opinion: some claim they can hear this, others can't. The second reason is more concrete: some digital audio algorithms, particularly those associated with number-intensive processes like time stretching and pitch shifting, can achieve better results when they start out with more data.

The third reason is equally important: although it's debatable whether high frequencies directly influence the audible spectrum in a significant way, phase distortion introduced by the anti-aliasing filter is much less likely to occur in an audible frequency range when the sampling rate is higher. The absence of this distortion can result in a subtle but noticeable change in perceived clarity. This doesn't mean you should immediately start recording everything at 96 kHz, especially since that will be costly in hard disk space and processing power. But it does mean there is some difference between the sampling frequencies, and that there's a reason why professional studios pay good money for equipment that can operate at higher sampling frequencies.

Regardless, you know you can get decent results working with a minimum of 16-bit, 44.1 kHz audio. If you do, factors like mic choice and placement, signal level, and other recording quality issues are far more likely to impact the audio quality of your recordings than using a higher sample frequency or greater bit depth.

Digital File Formats

Chapter 10 covers how best to export audio for sharing and distribution. But since you're likely to be manipulating audio file formats long before then, here's a basic overview of the file formats for digital audio you'll encounter most often.

The most critical distinction in audio formats is between compressed audio and uncompressed audio. Compressed audio reduces the amount of data stored in order to save space on hard drives and other recording media, and to speed transmission times over the Internet. To do this, it removes information that is less critical to your ear for hearing the source material. If the compression algorithm has no impact whatever on the sound—if the original sound can be reconstructed perfectly from the compressed file—the compression is said to be *lossless*.

 Untangling Confusing Terms

Bit depth is sometimes also known as word rate, or bit resolution; all the terms mean the same thing.

Resolution is sometimes used in place of bit depth or sampling rate, but confusingly so. Technically these terms would be either bit resolution or sampling resolution, since resolution is a generic term for accuracy.

Bit rate is the combination of the sampling rate and bit depth; it represents the total amount of data per second (bits per second, bit/s, or bps). For instance, CD-quality audio, with 16-bit bit depth and 44.1 kHz sampling rate, is measured as 1,411.2 kbit/s. Bit rate should not be confused with bit depth; it's usually referred to in regards to audio and video compression.

The Analog vs. Digital Debate

Ever since digital technology was introduced to the masses with the advent of consumer CD players, audio lovers have debated the relative merits of digital and analog technology.

Certainly, analog technology has its advantages. Because of the unique characteristics of certain analog components, sought-after analog equipment can color the sound in desirable ways, the quality many describe as "warmth." This is especially true in analog synthesizers, which produce sound entirely from the voltage generated by analog circuits. Although the basic sound of these instruments can be replicated using digital technology, much of their character and personality comes from their analog design. Like an acoustic instrument, no two are the same. In the area of recording, well-maintained, high-end analog equipment can achieve a theoretical frequency range that's greater than that of the standard commercial audio CD format.

Using analog signals exclusively has disadvantages, however. Analog signals are more susceptible to noise and interference than digital, and analog copies are susceptible to generational quality loss, which is not usually a problem with digital audio. (Generational loss is what happens when you make a copy of a copy of a copy, and the quality deteriorates as noise is added.) Digital is not completely immune to storage and transmission issues of its own, but if you make regular backups of computer audio files, for instance, you can maintain a pristine copy of your work with no loss of fidelity whatsoever.

Digital also has some unquestionable advantages: countless audio processes and techniques are possible only using digital technology, and many other techniques are easier or more flexible when digital audio is employed. That's not to disregard the feel and sound of analog techniques. There's no reason why you can't bring "vintage" analog gear into your studio and use it alongside your computer rig.

Most people use some combination of digital and analog equipment, choosing the right tool for the right job. And ultimately, all digital audio has to be transformed back into analog signals to be reproduced as audible sound.

Unfortunately, most audio compression formats are *lossy*, meaning that when they remove data to save space, they also reduce the quality of the recording: information critical to the sound is lost. This may be in the form of sound in certain frequency ranges that is weakened or cut completely, or in the form of *artifacts*—noise and other unwanted sounds that are added to the sound in the process of compression. Once you've lost sound information due to lossy compression, there's no way to restore that data, so you'll nearly always want to maintain an uncompressed version of any important recording. Also, many audio applications are not compatible with compressed formats.

Tip: When in doubt, save a file as WAV on the PC and AIFF on the Mac. It's the safest bet for compatibility with the vast majority of programs. If given a choice, choose "uncompressed WAV" and "interleaved AIFF."

Formats like commercial audio CDs and WAV and AIFF file formats are generally lossless, uncompressed audio formats. Formats like MP3 and MP4, Real Audio, Windows Media, and Apple AAC files purchased from online music stores like MSN Music, Napster, and the iTunes Music Store are all lossy.

The other element to consider when choosing an audio file format is whether the file is mono or stereo, and how the stereo data is stored. For stereo files, some programs offer a choice of *interleaved* files, which store left and right audio tracks in a single file, or *split* files, which divide the file into one file for the left channel and one for the right. MOTU's Digital Performer (www.motu.com) on the Mac, for example, requires separate left and right files, but most programs prefer the more common interleaved files. Surround files introduce still more issues, and file storage is evolving. For more on surround mixing and sharing, see Chapter 10.

MIDI

Although recorded digital audio can be manipulated in many ways, the data contained in the digital audio depicts only the sound(s) of the instrument(s) being played. The recording contains no information about which notes were played or what physical gestures the musicians made to perform them. In the centuries before digital technology entered the picture, it was useful to record musical sound and to transcribe musical performances as written scores. In a similar way, digital technology gives us a way of recording and transmitting musicians' performance gestures in digital form.

MIDI (the *Musical Instrument Digital Interface*) is a digital protocol with which we can describe musical events and physical gestures, and record and transmit them in a standardized format between devices and computers. Chapter 8 is dedicated exclusively to MIDI, but here's a quick overview.

MIDI data acts as a control language, enabling hardware and software to send and receive musical performance information in real time. The MIDI specification involves three separate elements:

- **A file format:** If you've worked with "MIDI files," you've been using the common file format specified for storing MIDI information. You don't have to have a MIDI file to use MIDI—you can also use it as a live control protocol or even store MIDI data in a nonstandard file format—but the standard file format is a convenient way to store and exchange MIDI data.

- **A protocol specification:** MIDI is a standard way of describing music in a digital form that can be understood by hardware and software. Musicians already have a language for music: one musician can say "middle C" or "B♭ minor " or "eighth-note," and other musicians will know what that means. Likewise, a standardized protocol allows different devices to speak the same language when talking about musical events.

- **A standardized interface:** MIDI requires a physical interface and cabling between hardware units for controlling other devices in real time. This interface is often a USB or FireWire connection, although special-purpose MIDI connectors are still common, as shown in **Figure 1.21**.

Figure 1.21 A standard 5-pin MIDI cable can carry data about notes and other events between a variety of equipment. Your MIDI device may use USB or FireWire to carry the same data. (Photo courtesy Hosa Technology, Inc., www.hosatech.com)

MIDI and digital audio are often used side by side in computer software, and both can be used to produce music that we can listen to, so newcomers aren't always clear on the profound differences between them. It's important to understand that they're entirely different technologies. MIDI data is much more compact and far easier to edit, but MIDI only produces sound when it's sent to a synthesizer (either hardware or software) or some other type of electronic instrument. The instrument produces the actual sound: MIDI only gives the instrument instructions about what notes to play and so on. MIDI is roughly analogous to a printed score: it makes no sound until it's played by a musician. You need a MIDI instrument to render the "score" of MIDI as sound, just as you need a musician to render a written score as audible music.

Some of the basic, common kinds of data MIDI transmits include the following:

- **Note messages** tell the receiving instrument which notes to play (**Figure 1.22**). Note messages also contain information about *key velocity*, which indicates how hard the musician struck the key on the keyboard.

- **Controller data** represents physical movements, like turning a knob, sliding a fader, moving a wheel, or depressing a pedal.

- **System messages** include events like start and stop messages for synchronizing equipment, and device-specific information—for example, information that tells a particular Yamaha model how to configure itself.

MIDI can be used for controlling software and instruments expressively in real time. MIDI can also be used for controlling lighting and video, and for controlling the playback of many types of audio software (not just synthesizers). It's even used in unusual applications like collecting data from sensors and controlling robotic mechanisms.

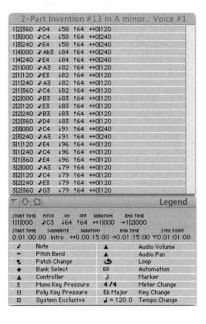

Figure 1.22 At the lowest level, MIDI is simply a list of performance control events. This event list view in MOTU Digital Performer is accompanied by a legend. The numbers are, from left to right, bar/beat location, pitch, how hard the note was played, how lightly it was released (not used here, hence all those 64's), and duration. For more information on MIDI and how to edit it, see Chapter 8.

Putting It Together

Now that you have a basic grounding in how sound and digital audio work, you're ready to tackle more advanced concepts. You'll find a knowledge of acoustics particularly helpful when dealing with recording in Chapter 6, effects processing in Chapter 7, synthesis in Chapter 9, and mixing in Chapter 10. In the meantime, now that you have a basic handle on the terminology, the next step is to get your digital studio working, the subject of the next three chapters.

 Theory overload?
If all of this textbook-style material has left you itching for some hands-on experience, take an excursion to Chapter 5 for quick tutorials in loop-based song production, or try some of the hands-on exercises later in the book.

 Further Reading on Digital Audio and MIDI

The Computer Music Tutorial (MIT Press, 1996) is the single most comprehensive reference on digital audio theory. It looks like a phone book, but the first chapter, John Strawn's overview of digital audio concepts, is a perfect companion to this chapter and should be very approachable now that you've gotten your feet wet. The chapter focuses on the fundamentals of audio signals and how they're represented digitally. Later chapters cover the math and physics behind concepts covered in this book, which you'll find useful if you get deeper into advanced interactive computer music software.

For more than you ever wanted to know about digital audio file formats, see the absurdly comprehensive file format list, complete with links to full specs, at The Sonic Spot (www.sonicspot.com/guide/fileformatlist.html).

Countless free tutorials are available on the Web covering many of the topics discussed in this chapter. One of the best resources is the free, open-source encyclopedia, the Wikipedia (www.wikipedia.org). The contributing community has plenty of information on digital-audio terminology, especially because some of the same concepts used in digital signal processing are used in nonmusic applications, too. Try search terms like "digital audio," "analog," "harmonic series," "anti-aliasing," "digital to analog converter," and "MIDI." You'll find in-depth articles and links to other Web resources.

CHAPTER 2

Choosing Your Tools

Finding a digital studio setup that fits the way you work is as personal as choosing a musical instrument. You need to identify your needs, figure out which tools meet those needs, make sure they're compatible with one another, and think about your budget. In this chapter we'll survey the available tools in the order in which audio makes its way from live sound to digital form—from recording and playback to the computer—so you'll be ready to shop for exactly what you need or desire.

 Essentials

Choosing Your Tools

You'll need some or all of the following equipment for digital audio, depending on your needs:

- Microphones and cabling for recording, studio monitors and headphones for playback

- Computer audio interface to get high-quality audio to and from your computer (essential), mixer (optional but useful)

- Controller inputs for easy access to software parameters

- Capable computer, which can be either a general-purpose machine or specialized

audio hardware (key specs: fast CPU, fast/large hard drive(s), RAM, generous I/O)

- Software/hardware specific to your production needs, for recording, songwriting, editing and arrangement, mastering, playing instruments, DJing, video scoring, and producing printed notation

Essential Terms

- DSP
- AD/DA conversion
- Digital audio workstation (DAW)/sequencer
- Hosts and plug-ins

Where to Start:

If you're overwhelmed by choices and costs, consider getting up and running quickly with an entry-level audio interface bundled with some basic software.

INPUTS AND OUTPUTS

A studio setup won't get far without the ability to get sound in and out of the electronic and digital domains and connected to the computer. Additional hardware gives physical control for the virtual parameters of software. We'll start building our studio by assembling the gear we need for inputs and outputs. The ultimate goal is a complete creative workspace, as shown in **Figure 2.1**.

Figure 2.1 A fully equipped, computer-based studio in action. M-Audio (www.m-audio.com) set up this studio, so it features its products. Notice that even this digital audio manufacturer still uses some vintage keyboards. (Photo courtesy M-Audio)

❶ Transducers (microphones, monitors, headphones) are essential for getting sound in and out of the electronic domain.

❷ A separate control room isolates the recording area from the sound of the computers.

❸ Keyboards shown here include keyboards with sound production abilities and instruments designed for controlling soft synths, such as this USB-powered M-Audio Radium.

❹ Control surfaces with banks of knobs and sliders, like the Evolution US-33e shown here, provide remote access to software parameters (see p. 55).

❺ An audio interface, like the M-Audio FireWire models shown here, gets audio in and out of the computer (see p. 50).

❻ External hardware like these vinyl turntables and cross-fader are great for those times when software just doesn't feel and sound the same as analog equipment.

❼ Make sure you have a computer capable of running audio software (see p. 60), and an application for recording and hosting software instruments and effects (see p. 71). Shown here are Apple PowerBooks running Ableton Live.

Recording and Playback: Transducers

As explained in Chapter 1, electronic music systems of any kind, analog or digital, must use transducers to convert sound to and from vibrations in the air. For example, to play back sound, you'll need studio headphones and/or speakers, and you'll need microphones for recording.

Make sure your playback equipment is "pro." Pro devices are very different from consumer models, even those in the same price range. Consumer audio equipment is often intentionally "sweetened," emphasizing certain frequency ranges, because that's what consumers are accustomed to hearing. That's a disadvantage when you're trying to adjust your audio mix for a wide range of equipment, so pro "studio" models are designed to be truest to the original sound.

Prices on all these products range from a few dollars to tens of thousands of dollars, but that doesn't mean you won't find inexpensive workhorses in pro studios. See **Table 2.1** for help identifying pro-level equipment that won't break the bank.

 Gear vendor examples:

Shure
(www.shure.com)

M-Audio
(www.m-audio.com)

Edirol
(www.edirol.com)

Tapco
(www.tapco.com)

Event Electronics
(www.eventelectronics.com)

Mackie
(www.mackie.com)

Sony
(www.sony.com/professional)

Sennheiser
(www.sennheiser.com)

AKG
(www.akg.com)

Table 2.1 Recording and Playback Gear: Where to Start

Transducer	What You Need to Know	Starting Price Range	Basic Examples
	If you're recording directly in stereo, you'll need a matched pair of microphones or an integrated stereo mic. Match microphones to intended use: an inexpensive, rugged vocal microphone might be better for adding live vocals in a club than a pricey studio condenser.	$100 buys a standard pro dynamic microphone; condensers have dropped to under $200 but higher-quality models cost more.	Shure SM57 (pictured) and Beta 58A, and related models are good general-purpose percussion and vocal microphones. M-Audio makes entry-level dynamic and condenser microphones ideal for computer audio use.
	Passive monitors are unpowered and require a separate amplifier. Active monitors are powered, self-contained units. Check prices carefully: monitors are often listed per unit instead of per pair, a bit like a one-way airplane ticket.	Decent active entry-level monitors start at around $200 a pair; for serious studio work, consider the $400–500+ "mid-range" models.	Beginning users can opt for speakers from M-Audio and Edirol. Mid-range options include: Tapco S3 Event Electronics TR-8 Mackie HR824 (pictured)
	Some studio headphones are available in alternate DJ models. They're more rugged and allow easier one-eared listening.	Many "starter" headphones around the $100 price point are also standards in the studio.	Sony MDR-7506 Sennheiser HD-280 (pictured) AKG K-240S

Computer Audio Interface

The line-in and headphone jacks on your computer are fine for occasional recording and listening, but dedicated audio/MIDI interfaces like the one shown in **Figure 2.2** offer higher audio fidelity and more connection options. They might also feature extras like bundled software.

Figure 2.2 A hardware audio interface, such as this Edirol FA-101 Firewire interface, shown here in front and rear views, will be the primary connection between your computer's audio software and the outside world. (Photo courtesy Edirol)

Why not just use the audio I/O built into your computer? First, these interfaces usually lack the number and size of connections you need, and rarely accommodate the lower signal level generated by guitars, microphones, and turntables. Some computers lack sound inputs altogether. Second, built-in interfaces tend to be too noisy for recording, especially if they're not properly insulated against interference and computer noise. In addition, their dynamic and frequency ranges often aren't as good as those of dedicated audio interfaces.

Interfaces for every budget and need are readily available, so your primary job is to navigate three essential elements on the specifications sheet: inputs and outputs (I/O), digital-to-analog (D/A) and analog-to-digital (A/D) conversion quality, and the means by which the device communicates with your computer (*bus*).

> **(?) Audio Interface Checklist**
>
> Identify your needs and keep these elements in mind when you're buying an audio interface:
>
> **Inputs**
> - ❏ Enough inputs for instruments, inputs and preamps for microphones
> - ❏ MIDI connection for MIDI devices (if needed)
>
> **Outputs**
> - ❏ Standard stereo pair
> - ❏ Multiple outputs for surround sound
> - ❏ Extra output for cueing (DJs only)
> - ❏ Extra output for alternate mixes for other musicians
>
> **Adequate resolution**
> - ❏ 16-bit, 44 kHz sample rate for everyday use
> - ❏ 24-bit bit depth and 48 kHz, 96 kHz, or 192 kHz sample rates for high-quality capture (see Chapter 1, "Understanding Digital Sound")
>
> **Right bus for your computer**
> - ❏ Laptops: CardBus, USB 1.1/2.0, or FireWire
> - ❏ Desktops: USB 1.1/2.0, FireWire, or PCI
>
> **OS compatibility**
> - ❏ Drivers available for your OS of choice
>
> **Extras**
> - ❏ Software bundles and hybrid devices (keyboards with integrated audio/MIDI interfaces or audio interfaces combined with control surfaces) can add value.

Ins and outs of I/O

Since one of the primary reasons for buying an interface is to add additional inputs and outputs, you'll want to first think about what equipment you have and how many inputs you'll need to record simultaneously. For instance, if you're a vocalist playing an external keyboard, you'll need one input for the vocal mic and two for the external keyboard, for a total of three inputs. If you need surround or other multichannel outputs, you'll also need multiple simultaneous outputs beyond the standard two-channel stereo. See **Table 2.2** for some of the most common setups.

Aside from analog audio I/O, other connections are necessary for hooking up specific MIDI and digital equipment:

- **MIDI:** If you have equipment with standard MIDI connections, you'll need either an audio interface with a MIDI connection or a self-contained MIDI interface.

- **Digital Audio I/O:** For a higher-quality audio signal and synchronization, digital audio equipment often includes digital as well as analog connections.

Chapter 3 explains different connection types and how to manage them.

Table 2.2 Typical Analog Audio Configurations

Number of Analog Connections	Examples
Two in, two out	Digidesign Mbox; Mackie Spike
Four in, four out	M-Audio 410; Lexicon Omega (www.lexicon.com)
Eight in, eight out	MOTU Traveler (www.motu.com); Edirol FA-101

Extras: All these interfaces also include digital I/O, and the 4x4 and 8x8 devices add MIDI.

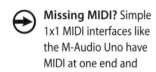

Missing MIDI? Simple 1x1 MIDI interfaces like the M-Audio Uno have MIDI at one end and USB at the other.

D/A-A/D conversion

Specifications for bit depth and sampling rate are significant to audio quality, as explained in Chapter 1, although 16-bit 44.1 kHz is sufficient for most users. The quality of the digital audio circuitry itself plays a considerable role as well, so you might want to check the reviews of an interface you're considering in pro audio publications like *EQ* and *Sound on Sound*. Some pros even purchase pricey stand-alone D/A converters, although those with home studios are more likely to use the converters built into their interface.

Myth dispelled: Many users assume FireWire is "better" than USB 1.1, but that's not exactly right. With well-written drivers, USB 1.1 can perform quite well in recording and playback. FireWire simply has greater bandwidth than USB 1.1, allowing more channels.

Connecting to your computer

Different interfaces connect to the computer via various connection types, or *buses*, such as FireWire and USB (**Table 2.3**). Based on available bandwidth, buses can offer multichannel audio with nearly real-time performance. (Faster buses allow more channels.)

Table 2.3 Buses for Audio

Name/Alternate Names	Used for	Examples
Laptop		
CardBus/PCMCIA	Extremely compact laptop audio interfaces	Echo Audio Indigo (see **Figure 2.3**) (www.echoaudio.com)
Desktop		
PCI/PCI-X (high-speed variant)	Inexpensive desktop interfaces and high-end, high-bandwidth multichannel systems; especially popular on PC platform	Digidesign Pro Tools|HD platform (high end) E-mu interfaces (budget) (www.emu.com)
Both Laptop and Desktop		
FireWire 400/FireWire 800 (high-speed variant) Also called IEEE-1394	High-bandwidth multi-channel audio; appears on some external audio gear	Metric Halo interfaces (www.mhlabs.com)
USB 1.1 (Most common variant of USB)	Lower-bandwidth multichannel audio; connections to control surfaces and some MIDI gear	Lexicon Omega
USB 2.0 (High-speed variant of USB)	High-bandwidth multi-channel audio	Edirol UA-1000

Figure 2.3 Echo Audio's Indigo cards fit into the CardBus slot on many Mac and PC laptops. (Photo courtesy Echo Audio)

Bundled software

Digidesign has always sold its hardware and software as a single bundled package, from its entry-level Mbox to its high-end Pro Tools|HD. But other vendors also typically sweeten their audio interface packages by including free software. These are often limited editions rather than full-blown versions of the software you'd buy separately, but they can be a good starting point. Bundled software includes packages like Pro Tools LE (available via Digidesign only), the full versions of entry-level audio workstations like Mackie Tracktion and Steinberg Cubase LE, and limited editions of programs like Propellerhead Reason and Ableton Live.

Controller Input Devices

 Interface/software bundle vendor examples:

Digidesign
(www.digidesign.com)

M-Audio
(www.m-audio.com)

Lexicon
(www.lexicon.com)

Steinberg
(www.steinberg.com)

Mackie
(www.mackie.com)

You can make music on a computer using just a mouse and QWERTY keyboard. Applications like Ableton Live and Apple Logic even let you type on your keyboard to play instruments. But for more tactile feedback, controller input devices let you assign onscreen settings to physical knobs, faders, buttons, and piano-style keyboards (**Table 2.4**).

Table 2.4 Options for Hands-on Control

Cost	Task	What you'll need	Examples
$100 – $150			
	Shuttle through a mix with ready access to keyboard shortcuts	Custom keyboard or shuttle controller	Logickeyboard (www.logickeyboard.com) Contour Designs ShuttlePro (pictured) (www.contourdesigns.com)
$150 and up			
	Manipulate software parameters	Basic control surface with knobs and/or faders	M-Audio Evolution UC-33e fader box or DJ-oriented X-Session (pictured) FaderFox for Ableton Live and Mackie Tracktion (www.faderfox.de)
	Play a software instrument while adjusting sound parameters	Keyboard with knobs, faders, or other controls, either with a USB or MIDI interface	Alesis Photon x22 (www.alesis.com) Novation X-Station including built-in synth and audio interface (pictured) (www.novationmusic.com)
$800 and up			
	Control your mix with motorized response to automation	Motorized control surface	JL Cooper controller line (www.jlcooper.com) Mackie Control Universal (pictured)

Hybrid Devices

With all the devices available, you could wind up with a lot of different pieces of equipment. So to reduce complexity and cost, manufacturers increasingly are combining functions into integrated devices (**Table 2.5**).

Table 2.5 Hybrid Hardware Examples

Function	Examples	Best for
Audio interface + keyboard + control surface	Alesis Photon X-25, M-Audio Ozonic, Edirol xx	Musicians playing soft synths on the go
Audio interface + motorized control surface	Yamaha 01X, Tascam FW-1884 (**Figure 2.4**), Digidesign 002	Integrated home studios and mobile recording
Audio interface + mixer	Mackie Onyx, Alesis MultiMix USB	Project/home studios that need to route and mix lots of external gear

Figure 2.4 The Tascam FW-1884 combines a motorized control surface with a multichannel audio interface to turn your computer into a fully powered recording workstation in one device. (Photo courtesy Tascam)

CHOOSING THE RIGHT COMPUTER

Choosing an OS

Few technology issues inspire more passion than the choice of an operating system. Fortunately, both Windows and the Macintosh OS are excellent choices. Each OS has made major strides in recent years in terms of available software, hardware compatibility, reliability, and ease of use. Nor should Linux be ignored as an option. While less pro-level music software is available for Linux than for the Big Two, Linux can be installed on a PC or Mac alongside the primary OS, and Linux software is mostly free.

Mac vs. Windows

Cross-platform development on Mac and Windows, once an expensive and difficult endeavor, has become commonplace in recent years. Many developers now share the same code on both platforms, enabling them to release applications for both platforms simultaneously with almost complete feature parity (**Figure 2.5**). Each OS has its own array of exclusive applications as well, but each lineup is strong enough that choosing the better of the two is an entirely personal decision (**Table 2.6**).

Figure 2.5 Switching between Mac and Windows versions of cross-platform software like Ableton Live is nearly seamless.

Table 2.6 Applications and Platforms (Partial List)

Only on Mac	Apple GarageBand, Apple Logic Audio, MOTU Digital Performer, U&I MetaSynth, BIAS Peak and Deck
Only on PC	Cakewalk product line (SONAR, Project5), FL Studio ("Fruity Loops"), Sony ACID and Sound Forge, Adobe Audition, Tascam GigaStudio
Cross-platform	Digidesign Pro Tools, Steinberg product line (Cubase, Nuendo), Native Instruments product line (Traktor, Reaktor, Kontakt), Ableton Live, Propellerhead Reason, MakeMusic Finale, Sibelius, Cycling '74 Max/MSP and Jitter, Plogue Bidule, IK Multimedia product line (AmpliTube, SampleTank)

The Mac platform has the advantage of including Apple's free entry-level software GarageBand. In addition, it has two Mac-only front ends to Digidesign hardware (Logic and Digital Performer) that offer an alternative to using Pro Tools, as well as unusually easy MIDI and audio configuration.

The PC generally offers slightly better audio performance-for-money value and more hardware choices. In comparison, both platforms are capable, affordable, and have more applications than anyone could ever exhaust.

 Is Your OS Up-to-Date?

Both Windows and Mac OS went through generational differences involving OS releases that used the letter or Roman numeral "X." Make sure you can run at least the following versions. Earlier versions can cause incompatibility problems with some audio software.

Mac: Mac OS X 10.2.8 or later (10.2 overhauled audio and MIDI support)

Windows: Windows XP SP1 or later (any XP version will work; SP1 improved USB support)

Linux: 2.6 kernel or later (2.6 kernel integrated audio driver support)

Although you are typically better off with a new OS version, be careful not to upgrade too soon. New releases often require updates from music software companies that can lag behind an OS release by weeks or even months.

 Foreign exchange program: If you need to exchange files between PC and Mac, nearly all cross-platform apps share a single file format that works on both platforms.

Linux

Until recently, Windows and Mac were the only options for running audio, but Linux developers and advocates have been hard at work to make it a viable alternative. The Linux operating system has a small but dedicated band of converts for audio use, including many developers and conservatory electronic music programs. Here's the good news about Linux:

- **Free software:** Linux applications are generally free and are open source products under the GNU General Public License (GPL), meaning they can be used at no cost (donations are often suggested). In many cases, if you're a developer, you can use the source code. A growing number of powerful, unique audio and music applications are available on Linux for free.

- **An OS built just for digital audio:** Special *distributions* or *"distros"* of Linux are available that have been preconfigured for music production. Just install or boot from the OS and everything is set up for you, including a selection of free digital audio applications, notation software, effects, instruments, and tools.

- **Linux alongside Mac and Windows:** You don't have to give up your current OS. Most Linux installations let you choose between Linux and your existing OS on your Mac or PC on startup.

- **Linux without Linux:** Mac OS X users can run an increasing number of Linux applications without Linux, thanks to OS X-native ports and OS X's ability to run windowing environments like Apple's X11. Other applications can run on Windows, too, thanks to cross-platform development tools.

The bad news about Linux is:

- **Only geeks need apply:** Linux isn't for the faint-of-heart, since it lacks the software choices and driver support of Windows and Mac, and can be tricky to configure, although preconfigured operating systems can help.

- **Limited software selection:** Mac and Windows still have a dramatically larger selection of software and capabilities for audio, at least at the moment.

- **Competing drive formats:** Moving files to your existing Mac or PC drive can be difficult.

 Resources for Linux

AGNULA project (www.agnula.org): Extensive audio links and tutorials from this audio-specific development project.

ALSA (www.alsa-project.org): Provides drivers for audio and MIDI hardware included in many music distros; check for compatibility.

Rosegarden (www.rosegardenmusic.com), **Ardour** (www.ardour.org): Full-featured digital audio workstation packages built specifically for Linux; Rosegarden includes notation and MIDI functionality, to boot (**Figure 2.6**).

Audacity (http://audacity.sourceforge.net): Must-have multichannel audio editor.

MetaDecks (www.metadecks.org): Developer of Linux software Metadecks, an audio editor with DJ-style interactive scrubbing, and live audio software AUBE.

terminatorX (http://terminatorx.cx): Real-time DJ application with vinyl-style scratching and sequencing.

Jack (http://jackit.sourceforge.net): A "low-latency audio server," virtual-connection software you can use to connect multiple applications to each other or interfaces on Linux as well as Mac OS X.

Fervent Software Studio-to-Go (www.ferventsoftware.com): Makes a mail-order, bootable CD-ROM for Intel PCs to run a full-featured Linux music studio, complete with Rosegarden preconfigured and support for Windows VSTs. (You can install to a hard drive, too, if you like.)

Linux software is nearly free or most often "pay what you can." If you're broke, it's free, but if you can donate some spare change, you will help the initiative continue to evolve.

However, if you're on a tight budget, if you're a programmer, or if the idea of a self-contained OS and applications just for music is appealing, Linux is worth a look—even if only to run alongside your existing OS. And even if you don't use Linux directly, odds are you'll be using hardware powered by it or open source or commercial software developed on it in the near future.

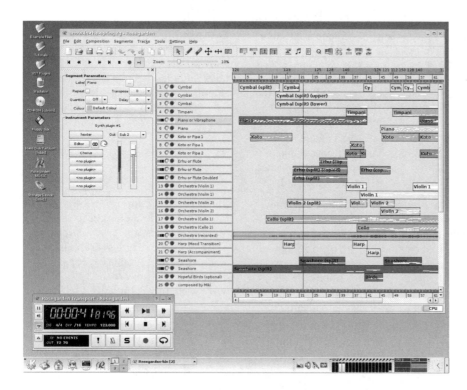

Figure 2.6 Rosegarden is a free, open-source audio application you can run on your Mac or PC hardware under a Linux operating system. (Screenshot courtesy Fervent Software, Ltd.)

Configuring Your Computer

Whether you're buying a new computer or using an existing system, specifications are important (**Table 2.7**). If you're just doing MIDI or music notation, older machines are likely to be sufficient, but live digital audio is system-intensive. In these situations, your computer has to perform mathematics on data that changes 44,100 times per second or more, outputting the results with minimal delay. Digital videographers and 3D graphic artists can afford some rendering time, but musicians often can't.

Table 2.7 Essential Specifications

Factors to Consider	Minimum/Optimal	Importance	Research/Budget
CPU speed	800 MHz processor for a single basic application/1–3 GHz processor	The primary CPU performs tasks like effects processing and sound generation in many programs.	**Research:** Check software requirements to see how processor-intensive the software you want to use is. **Cost:** Functional bare-bones computers start at about $500.
Hard drive capacity	60 GB free for recording/ As much as you can afford (250 GB +), dedicated drive	Recorded audio eats hard drive space fast: a CD's worth of audio is about 600–700 MB, and that only includes the finished, mixed songs. Once you start recording layers of audio tracks, you'll have multiple recordings for each minute of sound.	**Research:** Calculate how much space you need at www.glyphtech.com/site/ sales_drivecalc.html. **Cost:** Large, fast internal hard drives start at around $100; external drives suitable for audio have dropped below $200.
Hard drive speed	7200 rpm for simultaneous multitrack recording/Audio or A/V-optimized drive	4200 and 5400 rpm drives, like the internal drives that usually ship with laptops, choke when recording multitrack audio, causing dropouts, or they cease to record.	**Research:** Check drive specs carefully. Examples include audio-specific drives from Glyph Technologies (www.glyph.com, pictured—photo courtesy Glyph Technologies) or the portable high-speed ComboGB drive from Wiebe Tech (www.wiebetech.com).
RAM	512 MB/1 GB +	If you're using a software sampler, the amount of RAM is vital: these applications usually load samples directly into RAM, so you'll need more RAM for bigger samples.	**Research:** Memory prices fluctuate as often as week-to-week based on supply and demand, so it's best to comparison shop—computer manufacturers usually inflate RAM prices. Check tracking sites like DealRam (www.dealram.com) for the best deals. **Cost:** You can usually significantly upgrade RAM for under $100, so buy as much as you can afford.
Buses	At least USB 1.1 and one high-speed bus (FireWire, CardBus, or PCI)/USB 2.0, FireWire 400/800, PCI (desktops), other fast connections	You'll need connections for your audio interface, hard drives, keyboards, control surfaces, and other audio gear.	**Research:** Apple systems ship standard with these connections; PC users should max out their systems.

Table 2.7 Essential Specifications *(continued)*

Factors to Consider	Minimum/Optimal	Importance	Research/Budget
Screen real estate	One 1280x1040 display/ Larger screens, second monitor	Audio software interfaces take up lots of space; multiple monitors prevent you from having to switch between windows.	
Quiet operation		The quieter the system, the less you'll have to deal with noise added to recordings.	**Research:** Consider a system designed to run quiet or, for complete control, use an extender and place the system in a different room from your recording booth, or use a noise isolation cabinet such as those made by AcoustiLock (www.acoustilock.com).

Going Non-native: Hardware DSP Systems

Ever-faster processors have led to more and more *native* or *host-based* software that relies on your CPU to function. But there are still benefits to using specialized hardware to power virtual instruments, effects, and other audio tasks.

Even with faster chips and multiple processors, your built-in CPU provides only a finite amount of processing power, and audio applications have to compete with each other and with operating system tasks for attention. This can cause *latency*, a delay between when you play a note or record a sound and when the software responds. If the CPU can't keep up, you may run out of processing power altogether, making audio skip and pop.

Digital signal processing (DSP) chips are designed especially for off-loading tasks from your CPU. They're available in add-on hardware that connects to your computer via PCI or FireWire in the form of either an audio interface or a dedicated peripheral like the PowerCore Compact in **Figure 2.7**.

Effects and instruments must be specifically coded for DSP platforms, so you'll need a specific DSP hardware product and plug-ins designed for it. Available platforms include TC Electronic's popular PowerCore platform, which can connect to a laptop via a FireWire version, or Digidesign's PCI-based TDM hardware, which is integrated into products like Pro Tools|HD.

Figure 2.7 TC Electronic's Power Core Compact (www.tcelectronic.com) attaches to your desktop machine or laptop via FireWire, and provides extra processing power for high-quality, low-latency effects and instruments at home, in the studio, or on the road. It's available for less than $1,000.

Although basic cards with DSP can be purchased for about $100, the price of pro systems range from $1000 to tens of thousands of dollars. You can live without dedicated DSP processing power, but it can make your audio creation experience more efficient and reliable. See Chapter 6 for more on processing audio.

Where to buy

Turnkey systems:
Korg SoundTree
(www.soundtree.com)

Sweetwater Audio
(www.sweetwater.com)

Tekserve
(www.tekserve.com)

Custom systems:
Alienware
(www.alienware.com)

Carillon
(www.carillondirect.com)

MusicXPC
(www.musicxpc.com)

**Audio-only hardware
and hybrids:**
Muse Research
(www.museresearch.com)

Open Labs
(www.openlabs.com)

PlugZilla
(www.plugzilla.com)

Preconfigured and music-specific machines

Digital audio works well with off-the-shelf systems, but you can buy preconfigured music-specific products that range from simple bundles to custom audio-specific hardware:

- **Bundles:** Packages that combine computers, interfaces, and software range from around $1,500 to high-end five-figure options.

- **Turnkey systems:** Bundles that have all software and hardware installed and "optimized." You can turn them on without having to configure any settings. Many education vendors also sell turnkey configurations for school labs. Package prices vary; typical well-equipped configurations run from about $2,000–$3,500.

- **Custom systems:** Custom pro audio PC systems add optimized custom PC hardware to turnkey systems. Many include rack-mountable, low noise cases for use with other racks of audio gear, like the Carillon AC-1 (**Figure 2.8**). Some even have special audio controls, like knobs and transport controls, integrated with the case. They often add a comparatively small price premium: Carillon's systems, for instance, start at about $1,000 without a monitor. (Since Apple no longer licenses clones, Macs aren't included in this category, although some users have built compact Macs like the Mac Mini into custom cases.)

- **Audio-only hardware and hybrids:** You may not even need a traditional computer to run computer digital audio, thanks to new computer-powered gear designed just for audio (**Figure 2.9**). The Muse Research Receptor and the PlugZilla, for example, are both Linux-based audio boxes designed to wed the flexibility of software synthesis and effects with the ruggedness and stability of traditional hardware. They'll run Windows plug-ins and even provide dongle copy protection support via USB. The Neko is a full-featured keyboard with an integrated Windows PC for virtual instrument support. The Neko and PlugZilla aren't for those on a tight budget; they each cost over $3,000 and up. But the Receptor is competitive with current PCs at just over $1,000, and you can expect more of these devices in the future.

Figure 2.8 By appearance alone, you can see some advantages of custom audio computers like this Carillon AC-1. It's rack-mountable, rugged, and comes with special pro audio controls built in. Bundled "turnkey" software is ready to use right out of the box.

Figure 2.9 Computer, or audio hardware? New hybrid devices are both, like the Muse Research Receptor rack-mounted effects and instruments box and the Open Labs Neko keyboard. The devices run Linux and Windows, respectively. (Photos courtesy Muse Research, Open Labs)

MUSIC AND SOUND PRODUCTION TOOLS

Software Capabilities

With literally thousands of features in many modern music programs, how do you decide which software will help you be more creative and productive? There are no easy answers. Since current software offerings tend to blur the boundaries by including features from various categories, you may indeed be able to find one program that will do everything you need. In such a case, you can choose a tool based less on what it does than on how its user interface looks and feels to you. This is largely a subjective matter, however, so instead of getting sidetracked into the "knobs vs. sliders" debate, let's look at the basic capabilities found (in one form or another) in many commercially available music programs.

Specialized multitrack recording/editing applications include:
BIAS Deck (Mac)
Adobe Audition (Windows)
(See the next section, "Sequencing")

Find out how to do it:
Chapters 5, 10

Multitrack recording/editing

Multitracking is the recording and editing of multiple simultaneous audio signals. Before digital audio software, you needed multitrack analog tape decks and eventually digital decks for multitracking. Now, multitrack features are found not only in "studio" software as you'd expect, but many other creative music and sound applications as well (**Figure 2.10**).

Figure 2.10 Traditional mixer view in Adobe Audition.

Specialized sequencing applications include:
Digidesign Pro Tools
Steinberg Cubase SX
Mackie Tracktion
Ableton Live
Apple Logic (Mac)
Cakewalk SONAR (PC)
Rosegarden (Linux/Mac)

Find out how to do it:
Chapters 5, 8, 10

Sequencing

Sequencing is the construction of songs from MIDI, audio, and mix automation data. It's separated here from multitracking because it involves more than just audio.

The term is somewhat misleading because of its history: it's a throwback to vintage analog equipment, which constructed simple patterns out of sequences of voltages. (Does this sound like a tough way to make music? It was!) Sequencing later came to mean, in more general terms, arranging sounds and musical information into songs or mixes, first for MIDI alone and eventually for both MIDI and audio.

A *sequencer* now means any program with MIDI and audio recording, editing, and arranging functions (**Figure 2.11**), including programs like Cubase, Logic, SONAR, and Digital Performer. These programs are often called *digital audio workstations*, but products in that category include many functions besides sequencing, including those found in the next few sections.

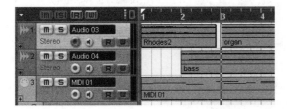

Figure 2.11 Typical sequencing interface with MIDI and audio, here in Cubase SX.

Waveform editing

Waveform editing, also called *sample editing*, involves detailed modifications to individual sound files. This can include the ability to edit sound at the level of the individual sample, as well as using other general tools for audio manipulation and batch processing. A waveform editor is to a multitrack editor as a text editor is to a page layout program. Most audio programs provide some kind of waveform editing, whereas others are dedicated entirely to the task (**Figure 2.12**).

Specialized waveform-editing applications include:
Audacity
Sony Sound Forge (Windows)
Adobe Audition (Windows)
BIAS Peak (Mac)

Find out how to do it:
Chapter 10

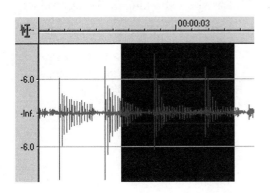

Figure 2.12 Waveform editing in Sony Sonic Foundry.

Specialized pattern-based editing applications include:
FL Studio (Windows)
Cakewalk Kinetic (Windows)
Propellerhead Reason

Find out how to do it:
Chapters 5, 8

Pattern-based editing

Pattern-based editing, sometimes called *beat-based editing*, mimics the limitations of primitive drum machines and constructs musical patterns for drums and instruments out of regular metrical patterns (**Figure 2.13**). This approach naturally appeals to people producing dance music, but because it's simple, easy, and quick, it's useful for sketching quick drum patterns or basslines for other musical genres as well. Since pattern-based features were common on early synthesizers and drum machines, many software instruments include some kind of pattern-based editing. It's also found throughout certain specialized workstation apps.

Figure 2.13 A drum machine-style pattern editor in FL Studio.

Specialized looping applications include:
Ableton Live
Sony Music ACID (Windows)
Apple GarageBand, Soundtrack, Logic (Mac)

Find out how to do it:
Chapters 5, 10

Looping

Pattern-based editing uses loops of musical material, usually in the form of MIDI. *Looping* refers to tools that loop audio. These applications can modify the tempo and sometimes beat positions of audio samples without changing pitch. Programs like GarageBand and ACID can take advantage of special loop libraries containing hundreds of sampled grooves and instrumental materials. Again, they're indispensable for dance music, but can be used in any musical genre to sketch ideas, create backing tracks, or produce entire songs (**Figure 2.14**).

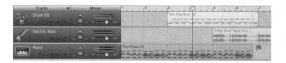

Figure 2.14 Quick song construction with loops in GarageBand.

Synthesis (instruments)

You can produce an entire mix without ever recording a note. *Synthesis* is the creation of sound entirely in the digital domain. Synthesis techniques range from emulations of vintage equipment, like Arturia's painstaking re-creation of the original Moog Modular, to cutting-edge sound creation techniques only possible on the computer, like Apple's Sculpture in Logic Pro.

All software instruments involve some kind of synthesis, but sometimes the term *virtual instrument* is used to specifically refer to emulations of real-world, nonelectronic instruments (**Figure 2.15**).

Figure 2.15 Native Instruments' B4 virtual instrument, an emulation of the Hammond organ.

Specialized synth applications include:
Native Instruments Reaktor, Absynth (synthesis), B4, FM7 (virtual instrument) Arturia Storm (synthesis) and vintage synth products Tascam GigaStudio (sample playback) IK Multimedia Sample Tank, Studiophonik (sample playback)

Find out how to do it:
Chapter 9

Signal processing (effects)

A digital *effect* is anything that takes an audio signal and changes it in some way, for example, reverbs, acoustic space simulators, delays, mastering, EQ, compression, sound-munchers, weird spacey sound warpers, and whatever else you can imagine. *Signal processing* is simply the use of effects. As the name implies, it's the processing of a signal.

Figure 2.16 Signal processing in MOTU's MasterWorks EQ, included with Digital Performer.

Specialized signal-processing applications include:
TC Electronics Native Bundle Waves Renaissance Maxx Bundle Sony Oxford Collection

Find out how to do it:
Chapter 7

**Specialized guitar-
processing applications
include:**
Native Instruments Guitar Rig
IK Multimedia AmpliTube

Find out how to do it:
Chapter 13

Guitar processing

Although it's technically just another form of digital effect, guitar processing deserves special mention. With the aid of software-modeled amplifiers, effects, and speaker cabinet simulation, software guitar processing can do what would otherwise require a lot of external equipment.

Figure 2.17 GuitarRig simulates a rack of guitar amplifiers and effects.

**Specialized mastering
applications include:**
Apple WaveBurner (Mac;
included with Logic Pro)
Steinberg WaveLab (PC)
iZotope Ozone (Mac/PC plug-in)
IK Multimedia T-racks (Mac/PC
plug-in)

Find out how to do it:
Chapter 10

Mastering

Mastering is a general category of tasks related to preparing music and sound for distribution. It includes effects intended to smooth, sweeten, and balance the sound's dynamic and frequency range, and the process of exporting for broadcast, CD distribution, or Web sharing for a single song or a group of songs (as in an album).

Figure 2.18 You can prepare audio via effects and author a CD in Apple's WaveBurner mastering tool.

DJing

DJs have special requirements, like the ability to manage large libraries of music, cue music by prelistening to it before the crowd in a club hears it, adjust tempo and pitch, and cross-fade between audio signals. Because these same features can be useful to non-DJs as well, general-use applications like Ableton Live have become more appealing to DJs and non-DJs alike.

Specialized DJing applications include:
Native Instruments Traktor
Ableton Live
MegaSeg (Mac)

Find out how to do it:
Chapter 13

Figure 2.19 Use your mouse to cue, scratch, and cross-fade with the free Tactile 12000 (www.tactile12000.com).

Notation

Music *notation* or *scorewriting* is the production of printed scores readable by musicians. Music notation usually interfaces with MIDI data, since it's a convenient standard for storing musical information. Although notation features in programs like Logic and Cubase are useful for quick song scores, composers and arrangers require various specific additional features depending on the complexity of their music and the technical requirements of musicians and publishers.

Specialized notation applications include:
Sibelius
MakeMusic Finale

Find out how to do it:
Chapter 11

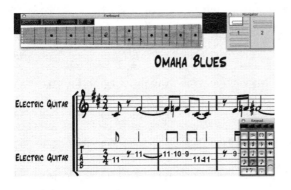

Figure 2.20 Preparing guitar notation in Sibelius' G7.

Specialized modular and interactive applications include:
Native Instruments Reaktor
Cycling '74 Max/MSP
Pure Data

Find out how to do it:
Chapter 13

Modular and interactive control

Early synthesizers produced sound by connecting individual components, or *modules*, with patch cords. The approach was time-consuming but infinitely flexible because each module had just one task, and following the path of a signal was as easy as following the associated cable. Modern digital audio software adapts this method to allow the creation of custom sound and MIDI processing configurations, and *interactive control* that lets software respond to and control everything from MIDI to audio to live video signals.

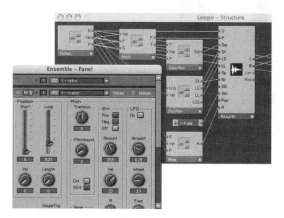

Figure 2.21 Behind Reaktor's interactive instruments is a modifiable, modular structure so you can create any sound, effect, or interactive instrument you can imagine.

Specialized tools

Some applications have specific functions for certain markets. These functions aren't included in general-purpose audio workstations yet, but if they're critical to the work you do, you'll want to check them out:

• **Music learning** utilities help students and musicians study music theory, musicianship, and composition.

• **Music accompaniment** applications create automatic backing tracks to help musicians practice.

• **VJ/Video** software creates interactive, real-time imagery, and is growing in popularity in clubs, art galleries, and onstage.

Building a Software Studio

One of the advantages of software audio production is that it affords nearly infinite flexibility. Since no two users are the same, no two software setups have to be the same. There are two primary approaches: buy an integrated workstation that does everything you need or assemble just the tools, instruments, and effects you need a la carte. Thanks to plug-in technology and other means of integrating software, there's a broad middle ground as well.

Integrated workstations

A *Digital Audio Workstation* (DAW) combines a variety of features and work methods into a single application. A DAW is defined by the ability to start, develop, and finish music and sound production within a single application. It can include some or all of the features mentioned earlier:

- **Audio features:** Audio recording, waveform editing, mastering features, and file conversion/export

- **Sequencing features:** Editing of MIDI and audio via traditional mixing interfaces, pattern-based editing, looping, or some combination of all three

- **Effects and instruments:** A complement of included effects and instruments and/or support for third-party plug-ins

- **Additional extras:** Many include guitar processing, notation, video/scoring features, or even basic modular and interactive functions for combining components

A number of applications fit into this general definition of a DAW:

- **Digidesign Pro Tools** refers to both hardware and software, but the Pro Tools application itself is a definitive DAW. It's in a league of its own for its dominance in pro studios, although competitors have made some inroads in recent years. The primary difference between Pro Tools and other software is that Pro Tools requires Digidesign hardware in order to operate.

- **"Big Four" DAWs:** Steinberg Cubase (now with pro sibling Nuendo), Cakewalk SONAR, MOTU Digital Performer, and Apple Logic (**Figure 2.22**) all began as MIDI sequencers nearly 20 years ago. As Pro Tools added MIDI capabilities, these four DAWs added audio, and upgrade-for-upgrade each app has tried to top the other with sprawling feature lists.

- **The New-Wave DAWs:** The all-in-one approach of Pro Tools and the Big Four can sometimes overwhelm creative music production, so a new generation of applications has focused on simplified interfaces and streamlined workflows. Not everyone would consider Tracktion, ACID, Live, Reason, FL Studio, or even GarageBand a DAW, but that hasn't stopped devoted users from adopting them for studio production and performance. Many users combine these tools with more traditional DAWs to take advantage of the strengths of each.

Figure 2.22 Apple's Logic Pro is a good example of a single software workstation that does almost everything. It combines features like (1) traditional mixing via a channel strip interface, (2) detailed editing of MIDI and audio data, (3) included instruments and effects like the Sculpture physical-modeling synth, and (4) a notation view for editing and printing scores.

Naturally, it can be difficult to distinguish the differences between applications with deep, overlapping feature sets. The choice is entirely personal: If you visit the studio of any top musician or producer, you'll likely find a wide variety of these applications in use.

What Does Pro Tools Mean?

"Pro Tools" can mean a wide variety of capabilities, since it refers to hardware and software tools ranging from the entry-level Pro Tools LE and Mbox to systems costing tens of thousands of dollars. Unlike most of its competitors, the Pro Tools product line is sold only as an integrated hardware-software system, with proprietary plug-in formats not supported by other software/hardware (with one exception, listed below). If you're considering using Pro Tools, keep these details in mind:

- When you buy Pro Tools hardware, whether you're buying an entry-level LE system or a high-end HD system like the one shown in **Figure 2.23**, you get Pro Tools software.

- You can't buy Pro Tools software separately; if you want Pro Tools software, you have to buy Pro Tools hardware.

- You can't run Pro Tools software without Pro Tools hardware plugged in. The Pro Tools application requires the hardware in order to run (an important consideration for laptop musicians). Pro Tools|HD users often purchase a portable Mbox so they can work with mixes on the go.

"Closed" vs. "Open"

Pro Tools is considered a "closed system" not only because it requires proprietary hardware, but because its TDM and RTAS plug-in formats are proprietary or closed rather than open. They work only with Digidesign systems, and the creation of new plug-ins is restricted to Digidesign-licensed developers. Users disagree passionately about whether the proprietary Digidesign approach or the open approach is better, but each has its own advantages.

Open plug-in formats like VST, Audio Units, DirectX, and LADSPA allow more consumer choice. You can use them on a variety of hardware and software (not just one proprietary system), and because anyone can write a plug-in, many more are available—many of them cheap or free.

On the other hand, although Digidesign RTAS/TDM plug-ins are fewer in number, they tend to be more consistent in quality overall because Digidesign exerts quality control over developer access to the format. High-end TDM plug-ins also take advantage of DSP hardware instead of taxing your CPU (see the sidebar "Going Non-native: Hardware DSP Systems," p. 61). The success of Pro Tools in studios is largely due to this arrangement. Invest in Pro Tools hardware, and you have an integrated system for reliably running a wide range of low-latency, high-quality effects.

Using Pro Tools Hardware and Plug-ins with Other Applications

If you're a Mac user, you don't have to use the Pro Tools application to take advantage of your high-end Pro Tools|HD hardware and plug-ins. You can use Digidesign hardware and effects within Apple Logic and MOTU Digital Performer if you have Digidesign hardware.

Digidesign's Pro Tools LE hardware, including the Mbox and 002, will work with other applications, just like any other audio interface.

 Music learning:
Sibelius Educational Suite (www.sibelius.com)

ECS Media (www.ecsmedia.com)

Music accompaniment:
MakeMusic SmartMusic (www.smartmusic.com)

PG Music Band-in-a-Box (www.pgmusic.com)

Soundtrek Jammer (www.soundtrek.com)

VJ/Video software:
Isadora (Mac, PC) (www.troikatronix.com)

motion dive.tokyo (www.digitalstage.net)

Vidvox VDMX and GRID (www.vidvox.net)

Cycling '74 Jitter (www.cycling74.com)

Figure 2.23 A complete, professional Pro Tools studio configuration might include racks of Digidesign Pro Tools|HD hardware (far left), a full configuration of modular motorized control surfaces (center), plus Pro Tools software, running here on the Mac. Full systems of this sort can cost as much as tens of thousands of dollars. Pro Tools systems start at under $400, though the low-end systems only include a subset of the capabilities here.

To learn more: See Chapter 4 for more on configuring your system and Chapter 7 for how to use these plug-ins in your mix.

Combine software for a custom studio

Developers have devised ways of combining applications, allowing you to build a studio from a combination of software. Audio software fits into one of three categories:

- **Host:** A single application, usually your DAW, that provides access to your interface, mixing, and arrangement capabilities, and *hosts* additional plug-in effects and instruments as well as *client* applications (**Figure 2.24**).

- **Plug-in:** A piece of software that runs only inside a host environment.

- **Stand-alone:** A separate application that runs on its own. To use a stand-alone app with a host, you'll need a technology like ReWire to route audio and MIDI data between them. Or if the software doesn't support ReWire, system-level technologies like Jack will work with all applications.

Using a combination of software from these three categories, there are an almost infinite number of possible software setups thanks to common open formats (**Table 2.8**). As long as you have a host of some kind, whether it's a simple freeware/shareware host or a full-fledged workstation, you can add a la carte instruments, effects, and other tools at will. Even without running a host, you can run a stand-alone application whenever you need it.

The only caveat is that plug-ins must be written to take advantage of a host environment via one of a number of standards: open formats used by multiple applications (VST, DX, AU, and LADSPA); proprietary formats for specific compatibility with a product, like Digidesign's RTAS and TDM; or other host- or hardware-specific formats. Since not all applications support all formats, you may need to use wrapper programs from companies like FXpansion (www.fxpansion.com) to extend compatibility.

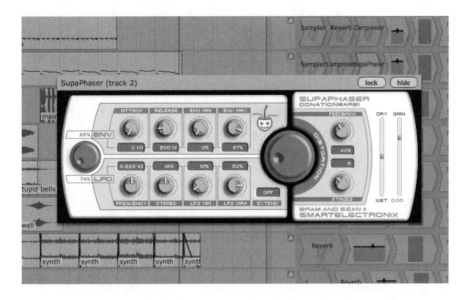

Figure 2.24 Starting with a host like Mackie's Tracktion shown here, you can add capabilities via commercial, shareware, and freeware plug-ins, such as this donationware phaser effect from www.smartelectronix.com.

Table 2.8 Plug-ins and Audio/MIDI Routing Platforms

Platform	Plug-in Support	MIDI and Audio Between Supported Applications	Audio Between Any Applications
Windows	VST, DX	ReWire	N/A
Mac OS X	VST, AU	ReWire, Core Audio's Inter Application Communications (IAC)	Jack OS X
Linux	VST, LADSPA	None currently available	Jack
Digidesign systems (Mac/Win)	RTAS, TDM	ReWire	N/A

Adding Hardware to Your Studio

Many novice users build their initial studio using software to save space and money. That doesn't mean, however, that hardware isn't worth a look for many of the same tasks software performs. Hardware has a number of potential advantages:

- Tactile, physical control (particularly indispensable with musical instruments)

- Reliability and durability

- Zero-latency responsiveness and instant-on gratification

- Distinctive sounds not possible with software

In short, hardware is fun to use, and there's no reason it can't be integrated into a computer studio. You can generally control external digital hardware via MIDI and synchronization controls or the more advanced of tools like Apple Logic's Environments. You don't need computer control of every-thing—often simple audio routing will work well—but see the sidebar "Hardware-Software Connections Checklist" for some good questions to ask.

Products to consider include:

- **Instruments:** Whether you're a guitarist, keyboardist, drummer, or looking for something different altogether, there's an instrument for you.

- **Effects devices:** Process vocals and instruments before they reach the computer, or route audio out from your mix (especially easy with a dig-ital mixer).

- **Guitar amps:** You can mic guitar amps directly instead of using soft-ware amplification.

- **Multitrack workstations:** Portable models are perfect for road recording without lugging your computer, whereas other models can act as a replacement for computer DAWs.

- **Groove boxes and toys:** Create beats for dance music using straight-forward hardware controls, optionally coupled with a computer (**Figure 2.25**).

Figure 2.25 You could perform the same functions as this Korg ElecTribe exclusively in software, but some users like the feel of physical hardware and the sense of creativity hardware interfaces give them.

 Hardware-Software Connections Checklist

For complete integration with your studio, look for any of the following specs on a hardware device.

Essential for control:

❏ MIDI inputs and MIDI-controllable parameters

❏ MIDI outputs and assignable MIDI controllers to send MIDI data

❏ (For beat sync) Receives synchronization via either MIDI or digital audio connection

Nice to have:

❏ Digital audio connections

❏ Direct computer connections: USB, FireWire, or FireWire-based mLAN

❏ Software editing

 Major hardware manufacturers include:

Korg, general equipment (www.korg.com)

Roland, general equipment (www.roland.com)

Yamaha, general equipment (www.yamaha.com)

Alesis, general equipment (www.alesis.com)

Tascam, recording (www.tascam.com)

Samson, recording (www.samsontech.com)

Stanton, turntables and DJ accessories (www.stantondj.com)

Gibson, guitars and general equipment (www.gibson.com)

Fender, guitars and general equipment (www.fender.com)

Resources: Where to Buy

Retail sales outlets include:

Guitar Center
(www.guitarcenter.com)

Sam Ash
(www.samashmusic.com for retail store, www.samash.com for online sales)

Fully-staffed online resellers who provide sales advice include:

Sweetwater
(www.sweetwater.com)

Full Compass
(www.fullcompass.com)

Kelly Music & Computers
(http://kellysmusicand-computers.com)

GOING SHOPPING

Now that you understand the mind-boggling quantity of products available for digital audio, it's time to shop for them. Here are some tips to make your shopping trip successful.

- **Plan your budget in advance:** Plenty of inexpensive options are available to you, so don't be afraid to budget before you shop.

- **Try before you buy:** Download software demos, get hands-on experience at your local music store, and check out training sessions and get practical experience with hardware and software at music technology conferences and music store events.

- **Demand personal attention:** Many retail (or even online) stores have knowledgeable, working musicians on staff. They should also know which products to avoid because they'll see returns from unsatisfied customers. Make sure you can ask questions and get intelligent answers. If you can't, go elsewhere.

- **Check return policies on hardware:** It's happened to the best of us: a product we thought was going to sound fabulous turned out to be extremely poor quality. Unfortunately, software usually can't be returned because of piracy concerns.

- **Check maintenance policies:** Before you agree to a retailer's "extended service plan," find out what the manufacturer's warranty is. Retailers are required by U.S. law to tell you. Then, make sure you read the fine print of any extended options.

- **Save the receipts, and add insurance:** You'll need receipts for rebates and returns, tax purposes, and insurance. Audio equipment can be a significant tax deduction if it's related to your profession. Even if it's a hobby, you can record hobby expenses on your income tax in the United States. Additionally, since warranties and extended service plans don't cover theft or damage, you can often cover your gear under your existing home insurance (if the gear is at home) and/or personal property insurance (when you're on the road). Bring receipts to your insurance company and find out what it will cover.

- **Get ready to download:** Aside from online shareware and freeware, commercial software is sometimes cheaper without the box. And even if you buy boxed software or hardware, check online for updates—the CD is rarely the latest release.

In the next chapter, we'll unpack all your new gear, boot the software, and learn how to connect and successfully configure your setup.

 ## Choosing the Right Software

With so many choices, which music software should you buy? This is not a question with an easy answer. Plus, as manufacturers add new features, the picture changes slightly every month, so any of the specific points below may be out of date by the time you read this. For up-to-date features lists, you'll need to check manufacturers' websites. Here are some things to keep in mind as you shop, and a few caveats that are valid in mid-2005:

1. It's all good. Even the most limited of today's music production tools are stunningly powerful compared to anything that existed ten years ago, and the sound quality of all of them is extremely high. You just about can't go wrong.

2. If you plan both to record external audio tracks (vocals, for example) and use software synthesizers, a general-purpose DAW from the Big Four list (Cubase, Digital Performer, Logic, SONAR) should probably be your first stop. While many of the newer loop-oriented "synth studio" programs will record and play audio tracks, the most popular of them (Reason) won't do so.

3. The traditional DAWs all have entry-level versions that cost less. In the synth studio realm, only FL Studio has low-cost versions and upgrades.

4. If you want to use sampled beats onstage, Live is probably the way to go. While ACID Pro is still popular among Windows users, it's strictly a studio tool. Project5 has added some Live-like performance features in version 2.0.

5. Even the traditional DAWs now ship with a selection of included synths and effects, but the included instruments are not likely to be as good as third-party plug-ins. If possible, budget for one or two high-quality plug-in instruments, and make sure your main workstation program will host plug-ins. (Again, Reason won't.)

6. Pro Tools is well named. Most versions require expensive Digidesign hardware, and compatible plug-ins also tend to be high-priced.

7. Ask about the included sound library. Some programs (Live, ACID, Reason, FL Studio) come with fairly extensive libraries of samples and other content to get you started. While most DAWs will time-stretch loops much the way ACID and Live do, they may not ship with as much, or any, content.

8. If you're planning to collaborate with other musicians, you'll open the door to endless headaches unless you're all using the same software. Find out what your bandmates or potential collaborators are using before you whip out the credit card.

9. Need to print out parts for live musicians? Get a traditional DAW. Softsynth studios and loop programs don't have notation editing or score printout.

Choosing the Right Software *(continued)*

10. If you want to use external MIDI synths, most programs (other than Reason) will accommodate you, but the MIDI editing capabilities of ACID are inferior. For advanced MIDI use, a traditional DAW is a better choice, because these programs all started out as MIDI sequencers, and have editing tools the newer programs lack.

11. While a scoring program such as Finale or Sibelius will do basic MIDI sequencing, they're not recommended for advanced sequencing tasks. If you want to use synthesizers to create recordings, get a real sequencer.

12. If you're using a Mac, you have fewer choices: Live but not ACID or Project5, Reason but not Project5 or FL Studio.

13. Try not to be stampeded by one or two sexy "pro" features. High-end programs have 5.1 surround mixing, for instance — but will you really need it? Ditto for ultra-high sampling rates: Even 96kHz is not really needed for most projects.

14. Don't neglect the "other guys." Programs like Mackie Tracktion (a DAW), Arturia Storm (a synth studio), Bitshift Phatmatik Pro, Cakewalk Kinetic, and Native Instruments Traktor DJ Studio (all sampled beat players) are worth checking out.

15. Many programs have downloadable demo versions. Others have downloadable manuals, which will give you a much better idea what the program is all about than just reading the marketing copy on the website.

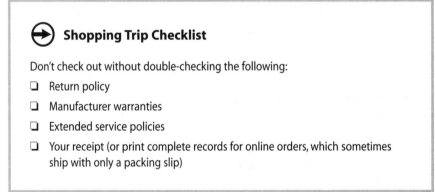

➔ Shopping Trip Checklist

Don't check out without double-checking the following:

❑ Return policy

❑ Manufacturer warranties

❑ Extended service policies

❑ Your receipt (or print complete records for online orders, which sometimes ship with only a packing slip)

CHAPTER 3

Setting Up Your Equipment

Whether your audio environment is a home studio, recording studio, DJ booth, or bedroom, you can set it up to produce a clean sound and to function as an efficient workspace, as long as you can decipher a bit of technical jargon. Manufacturers and audio pros tend to assume you have the knowledge and experience they have, even when you don't, but getting a grasp of the basics isn't difficult.

 Essentials

Setting Up Your Equipment

Getting up and running with your gear means thinking through every aspect of your workspace:

- Make your studio comfortable and easy to use

- Use speaker placement and acoustic treatments to make the sound of your recordings and playback as true to the original as possible

- Properly hook up equipment, being mindful of physical connectors and signal level and type, both digital and analog

- Reduce noise interference and preserve signal integrity

- Manage digital audio protocols to maintain compatibility with your equipment

Essential Terms

- Sound isolation/sound treatment

- Coaxial versus optical

- Connector types: $\frac{1}{4}$", XLR, $\frac{1}{8}$" minijack, RCA/phono, TOSLINK, BNC, 4mm

- Tip/ring/sleeve

- Preamplifier

- Impedance

- Grounded, ground loop

- Balanced/unbalanced

- Digital formats: S/PDIF, ADAT Optical, AES/EBU, AES3, TDIF

Where to Start

Mixers and interfaces generally come with helpful connection diagrams. Once you're hooked up, plug in a microphone or instrument and follow signal flow from the source through to your computer, checking to make sure sound is reaching each component.

SETTING UP YOUR WORKSPACE

Ergonomics

 Everything within reach: Arrange your workspace for efficiency; for instance, a pegboard fitted with hooks is perfect for keeping cables de-tangled, visible, and available.

Set up your space so that your computer, keyboards, control surfaces, and other often-used devices are within arm's reach. Avoid placing a mouse or trackball where you have to stretch to reach it, and keep the computer screen near eye height so you don't have to hunch over to see it. Even your work chair requires some thought: pro studios have comfortable chairs with wheels so engineers can shift location easily and work long periods without fatigue. Repetitive strain injuries are a danger with computer music work, so take regular stretch breaks. Many online workplace health resources can help ensure that your setup won't result in injury. Regular exercises like those at MyDailyYoga.com (www.mydailyyoga.com/yoga/rsi.html) can help you stay loose during extended work sessions.

Sound Isolation and Sound Treatment

Major recording studios aren't valuable just because they have a lot of cool audio toys: their major edge is that professional engineers designed and built them to sound good, making adjustments to the physical space to prevent any sound contamination. *Sound isolation* is the separation of the audio you want to record from outside influences. Specifically, *sound treatments* are materials that are added to a space to improve acoustic perception, including the use of consumer products like acoustic foam. This includes several related techniques:

- *Soundproofing* reduces sound leakage through walls, windows, and doors in your work environment. Soundproofing generally adds mass at these weak points to reduce the amount of sound that can get in and out. If you can't afford to rebuild walls, keep in mind that the goal of all soundproofing is never perfect sound isolation. You can at least consider the weakest points of your studio, like windows and doors.

- *Absorption and diffusion* treatments help avoid the slap and echo and unevenness that can be caused by walls or irregularities in a room (**Figure 3.1**).

- *Bass traps* are designed specifically to control bass frequencies in locations like corners.

Figure 3.1 This room's acoustic properties have been improved by the use of professional sound treatments, including the flat foam Auralex SonoFlat panels on the walls, which are designed to absorb mid- to high-frequencies. (Photo courtesy Auralex Acoustics)

Of course, even the addition of carpeting to the floor can make a big impact on the sound, replacing the hollow, characteristic sound of a room with the warmer, more appealing sound you'd expect from a professional recording studio. A few hundred dollars' investment could be a wise choice for recording work; cheap microphones in a well-treated space often sound better than expensive microphones in an untreated space. See the sidebar "Sound Treatment Resources" for some suggestions on where to start.

 Recording booth on the cheap: Do you need to record vocals in a hurry and can't install sound treatment products or build a booth? Remember, your main enemy is reflections from walls and corners. Set up a couple of wardrobe frames, and hang blankets on them on three sides. Have your vocalist enter from the back and record inside the "booth" for isolation. Similar tricks can work in a hotel room. Just don't start hanging cardboard egg cartons around your apartment—pros agree they're not effective.

Sound Treatment Resources

Information about sound treatment alone could fill a book (and has), but you can find some great resources online:

Auralex (www.auralex.com) is the largest manufacturer of sound-treatment products, and its Web site is a treasure. It's the most comprehensive resource online, with tutorials, room calculators, and links to lots of information.

Primacoustic (www.primacoustic.com) carries a full range of acoustic-treatment products, including studio-in-a-box solutions (starting at about $500), which contain everything you need to treat a room and are ideal for a home or project studio.

Studiotips (www.studiotips.com) is an ideal first stop before you build a studio. It offers in-depth information on acoustics, soundproofing, and wiring, plus a file area, various calculators, an active forum, and more.

Several sites aimed at improving home theater and music listening environments are just as useful to digital-audio hobbyists and pros. Art Ludwig (www.silcom.com/~aludwig), an engineer and audiophile, has an extensive guide to acoustics theory, including some practical information on do-it-yourself sound treatments. AudioRevolution (www.audiorevolution.com/equip/cheaptreatments/index.html) has a DIY guide for sound treatments for under $100.

Sound on Sound magazine (www.soundonsound.com/sos/jul00/articles/faqacoustic.htm) has newbie-friendly, frequently asked questions on sound treatment. For a printed reference, Paul White's *Basic Home Studio Design* (Sanctuary Press, 2000) is indispensable. It's a simple guide aimed at home and project studios, and it doesn't assume an extensive grounding in acoustics or a big budget.

Speaker Placement

Like real estate, speaker placement has three rules: location, location, location. Speakers are affected by proximity to other objects, like walls or your desk, and proximity to your ears. To get the best sound, follow these principles:

- **Keep your setup symmetrical:** Place each monitor at an equal distance from other objects to maintain even sound throughout the room. Move furniture if you have to.

- **Don't put speakers in a corner or against a wall:** Walls artificially enhance bass; put a little bit of space between your speakers and the walls.

- **Mind your ears:** Generally, speakers should be approximately at ear level, and far enough apart from each other and your ears that you achieve correct stereo separation (**Figure 3.2**). Surround sound requires additional adjustment to create the proper surround field.

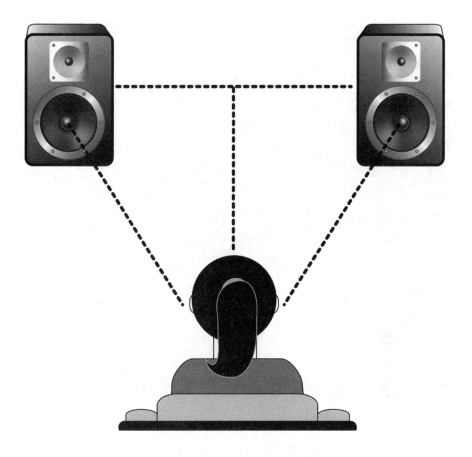

Figure 3.2 The general rule for determining stereo speaker placement is to imagine an equilateral triangle between the listener and the two speakers, so the distance between the speakers is about the same as the distance from the speakers to the listener.

- **Consider a stand:** Placing a speaker directly on a shelf or desk creates two problems: frequencies are transmitted through the surface and reflect off it, impacting the sound, and the height of the speaker may be incorrect. A speaker stand can resolve both these issues.

- **Experiment:** No rules can completely describe the many minute details of your personal audio space. Try moving speakers and other objects to different locations, and see how changes impact the sound.

Better sound from monitors: One of the cheapest, easiest ways to improve sound in your studio is to add acoustic foam beneath your monitors. These isolate your monitors, so that sound doesn't travel into your desk, shelf, or stand. Auralex's (www.auralex.com) MoPADs, or Monitor Isolation Pads, cost about $30 a pair and can be configured to tilt your monitors up or down if needed (**Figure 3.3**). Even if you're using a stand, isolation pads can be a worthwhile investment.

Figure 3.3 Auralex MoPAD monitor isolation pads. (Photo courtesy Auralex Acoustics)

CONNECTING PHYSICAL HARDWARE

If you don't have experience connecting audio equipment, your first glimpse at a professional's collection of cables can be daunting. Audio cables come in a variety of shapes and sizes. Fortunately, these connectors, despite their physical differences, do the same thing: they carry signals between equipment. Here are some specific factors to pay attention to:

- **Physical connector types:** Jacks and plugs are differently shaped connections on your equipment. Generally speaking, a plug (the "male" side of the connection) has protruding pins and is found at the end of a cable, while the jack (the "female" side) is found on a panel and has one or more recesses into which the plug's protrusions fit. You'll want to match up the physical connectors so you're not literally trying to fit a square peg into a round hole. You won't need to buy all new cables, though. If a connection doesn't fit, you may be able to buy an adapter. Adapters won't convert one *type* of signal to another, however.

- **Coaxial versus optical cabling:** Most cables are *coaxial* or "coax," meaning they're shielded wire cables that carry voltage on the center ("hot") lead, around which is wrapped a braided shield that connects to ground. The voltage on the hot lead can be an analog or encoded digital signal; in some cases, analog and digital cables are interchangeable, even though the signals aren't. Optical cables transmit digital data as light, not electrical voltage, and are exclusively digital.

- **Digital versus analog:** What kind of data are you sending? Analog signals can be understood by any analog input or output, though noise and other problems can be caused by level mismatches. Digital signals require that the receiving device speak the correct digital language. If a device isn't set up for that signal, it won't work.

- **Voltage level (analog):** If the signal is transmitted as analog voltage, what's the *level* of the signal? Different equipment uses different levels.

- **Stereo versus mono, multichannel:** How many channels of audio are you transmitting? If you try to transmit stereo signal over a mono cable, you'll lose a channel because you'll be missing the electrical connection for that channel.

Once you learn the basics of these connector types, you'll no more try to plug your S/PDIF digital input into your analog aux than you would your toaster into your phone jack.

 Digital signal advantages: Audio transmitted digitally doesn't suffer fidelity degradation or added noise the way analog audio does. Multiple channels can be transmitted compactly, as in ADAT Optical, which transmits eight uncompressed audio channels over a single fiber-optic cable.

Connector Types

A variety of different plug types for connecting audio equipment has evolved over the years; your studio probably already has several types. **Table 3.1** indicates the major connectors you're likely to encounter.

Why are there so many formats with so many odd names? The connectors' origins are usually historical. The ¼″ jacks are called "phone" jacks because they were invented for use on telephone switchboards. Phono plugs were first used on phonograph connections in home stereos; but your home studio might now include CD, DVD, and game systems with the same connection, often still referred to as "phono" plugs. Many of the names are associated with individual manufacturers, such as RCA and Toshiba's TOSLINK, even though these connectors have become industry standards.

Certain connectors are associated with certain applications. The ¼″ and XLR connectors are seen more often on pro equipment (**Figure 3.4**). A

Figure 3.4 You can plug both ¼″ and XLR male plugs into a Neutrik "combo" jack (www.neutrik.com). These jacks are commonly found as a space-saving (and cable-saving) solution on equipment that needs to accept both instrument/line and microphone inputs, as shown here on the M-Audio 410.

simple reason is that an XLR connection, for instance, is less likely to come loose than the ⅛″ connection found on an iPod headphone jack. RCA and ⅛″ connectors are more common on consumer or portable equipment.

The one format that's a bit different is the TOSLINK digital connector. TOSLINK connections appear on consumer DVD players and game systems as well as pro multichannel digital equipment. Usually, the port into which the TOSLINK plug is connected has a removable plastic widget to protect it. Instead of voltage, these connectors carry encoded digital audio signal as light; an LED emitter flashes at the transmitting ends and is conveyed by fiber optics to a receiver.

Table 3.1 Jacks and Cables at a Glance

Type	Name/AKA	What It's For	Digital or Analog
	¼″ (Guitar cables, phone plugs, jack plug, patch cord)	Guitars, instruments, head-phones, general-purpose equipment connections (line inputs)	Analog
	XLR (Mic connec-tors, cannon/canon plugs, symmetrical connectors)	Microphones, AES/EBU pro digital connections, general-purpose pro audio/video use (variants with different pin numbers for single-jack stereo, etc.)	Both
	⅛″ (Minijack)	Portable equipment, consumer equipment and headphones, computer audio	Both
	RCA (Phono plug)	Consumer equipment (particularly home stereo), DVD and CD digital and analog connections, S/PDIF digital connections, consumer digital surround, computer audio	Both
	TOSLINK (FO5 (as in Fiber Optic 5mm), "optical")	S/PDIF digital connections, digital surround	Digital
	BNC (Bayonet Neill-Concelman)	Pro connections (more common in video than audio), cable TV connections	Both

Myths dispelled: TOSLINK is a physical connector, not a format or protocol. Digital protocols like AES/EBU and S/PDIF can be transmitted on TOSLINK or on other connector types.

Don't confuse "phone" and "phono" plugs: RCA plugs are phono plugs (as in phonograph); ¼″ plugs are phone plugs (as in telephones).

Table 3.1 Jacks and Cables at a Glance *(continued)*

Type	Name/AKA	What It's For	Digital or Analog
	4mm (Banana plugs)	Speaker connections, vintage gear; rarer	Analog
	Speaker terminals	Bare-wire connections for speakers, secured with a screw or spring-loaded attachment (shown)	Analog
	MIDI	Synthesizer and control surface connections	Digital
	USB	Computer peripheral connections	Digital
	FireWire (IEEE 1394)	Multichannel computer audio connections, Yamaha mLAN and other studio equipment	Digital

MIDI and USB cable photos courtesy Hosa Technology, Inc.

🔑 Tip, Ring, Sleeve: What Those Stripes Mean

Have you ever noticed that some ¹/₄″ and ¹/₈″ plugs have an extra stripe of darker material on the shaft? This non-conductive material isolates different electrical connections, all of which are carried on the same plug. If there are two non-conductive stripes, two signals can reach a correctly wired jack at the same time. The connections on the plug are called tip, ring, and sleeve (TRS) depending on their location on the plug. Even if you're not soldering your own cables, it's important to know this: a stereo cable with a TRS plug can carry either a stereo signal, a mono balanced signal, or a mono unbalanced signal (see the explanation of balanced and unbalanced connections later in the chapter). Here are the most common configurations:

TS (Tip/Sleeve, one stripe) is used for mono connections like guitar cables.

TRS (Tip/Ring/Sleeve, two stripes) in a stereo configuration carries both left and right channels on one plug; sometimes called *stereo plugs* (**Figure 3.5**). TRS can also be used for mono-only balanced connections.

With a mixer, a TRS cable can be used to route effects as an insert cable (see p. 104).

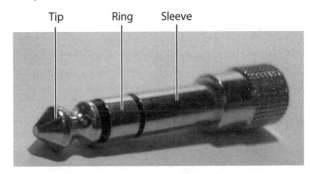

Figure 3.5 ¹/₄″ TRS cable.

Video

Video connections use many of the same connectors as analog and digital audio. Pro video applications generally use XLR or BNC cables, whereas consumer video equipment often uses RCA phono plugs. Phono plug connections can be either *composite* or *component* video. Composite video carries the video signal on one cable, whereas component video provides the complete signal on three separate cables, one for each of three color channels. Specialized video connectors include S-Video (also called Y/C) connections, which are transmitted on 4-pin mini-DIN connectors to provide greater color depth than composite video. There are also unique connectors for new high-definition digital video formats like HDI and DVI.

Mixing connecter types

A cable is simply a pipe. Despite the physical differences between connectors, you can route analog signal through any coaxial cable. There's nothing to stop you from connecting an XLR microphone to a minijack; you can purchase special adapters or cables that connect from XLR to mini.

 Resources for Cables

In a fix, Radio Shack (www.radioshack.com) has locations everywhere and a decent cable selection. For more variety and pro-quality options, turn to your local music shop or these resources:

Leading cable manufacturers:
www.monstercable.com
www.hosatech.com/hosa/index.html

Online cable retailers:
www.gigcables.com/index.html
www.impactacoustics.com
www.bettercables.com

Don't overlook your local stores. Brooklyn, New York has a shop that's dedicated exclusively to cabling; Mikey's HookUp has been featured on VH1 (www.mikeyshookup.com). Specialized retailers like Griffin Technology (www.griffintechnology.com) carry cables aimed at computer users.

Armed with some standard parts and a soldering iron, you can even build your own cables. A number of online sites offer step-by-step tutorials, such as the tutorial at MediaCollege (www.mediacollege.com/audio/connection).

Connectors and "gender"

While evoking somewhat unfortunate and politically incorrect imagery, cable connectors are universally labeled by gender. Most cable types are available in both *male* and *female* versions, like the XLR connectors shown in **Figure 3.6**. The male connectors, like the end of your headphone cable, have some sort of protrusion, whereas the female connectors, like the headphone jack on the iPod, have a recession into which the male connector fits.

Usually, the male connector is used for a cable and the female connector is used for a port, but not always. You'll need a female-to-male connector if you want to extend a cable length, for instance, and microphones often have male connectors on the microphone and female connectors on the cable.

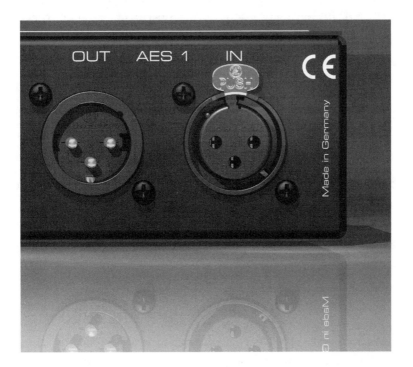

Figure 3.6 Male (left) and female (right) digital XLR connectors, as seen on an RME ADI-4 DD digital format converter. (Photo courtesy RME, www.rme-audio.com)

Mono, Stereo, and Multichannel Connections

In addition to choosing a connector type, you must figure out how many channels of audio you need to transmit.

Mono signals involve only one channel. Therefore, using an analog connection, you'll need only one electrical connection to carry audio signal.

If you're transmitting a *stereo* analog signal, you'll need electrical connections for two channels: left and right. This can be done either with two mono cables or with a stereo cable. A stereo cable can carry a mono signal, but a mono cable can only transmit half of a stereo signal. Note, however, that a single-connector cable can carry a stereo digital signal.

You can also transmit surround audio and other multichannel formats either via multiple mono and stereo connectors or through specialized digital formats that transmit multiple channels using one cable.

Voltage Levels

As discussed in Chapter 1, "Understanding Digital Sound," analog signal translates sound amplitude into an analogous voltage level. If the voltage level of this incoming signal is too weak, a signal will sound faint. If it's too strong, it will sound distorted. *Preamplifiers*, whether they are external devices or part of your interface (for example, a dedicated jack), increase the voltage level. External preamps are often connected between devices like microphones, guitars, and turntables to a mixer or interface input. Integrated preamplifiers are either in the form of jacks or switchable preamplifiers. By setting a button or switch to "pro" or "consumer," "line" or "mic," you're activating or deactivating preamplifier circuitry to adjust the voltage of the incoming signal. Whichever level you choose, the signal for your devices must be set at the same level.

Line level and consumer vs. pro: "Line level" can refer to either consumer or professional level. Consumer equipment transmits audio signal at –10 dBV ("consumer line level" or sometimes "instrument level"), whereas professional equipment uses a hotter signal of +4 dBu ("professional line level"). Many interfaces and mixers have a switch between these two levels so you can match the signal levels of your devices.

Microphone level: Microphone level uses a much lower signal level, ranging from about –40 dB to –60 dB; this signal level must be amplified to –10 dB or +4 dB when being connected to other gear. Many interfaces and mixers have a simple mic/line switch that activates an internal preamplifier. With the switch in the mic position, the preamp is on; when it's switched to the line position, the preamp is off. Therefore, if you're using a separate mic amp in the signal chain prior to the input, you should choose line-level input on your interface to turn off the built-in preamp.

Guitar level: Guitar level, like microphone level, must also be amplified, though it has a larger signal range of –60 db to 0 db. Inputs may also have a switch for this input, as in **Figure 3.7**.

Non-optical digital connections use voltage too, but you don't have to worry about the signal level unless you're building your own digital audio circuitry!

Figure 3.7 Typical inputs, shown here on an M-Audio Fast Track USB interface. The input level button switches between guitar-level and line-level signal. (Photo courtesy M-Audio)

① Left and right phono plugs
② ¼″ TRS line/instrument balanced mono input
③ XLR balanced mono microphone input

Impedance

Impedance, which is measured in Ohms, is the resistance of direct current to alternating current. Even if you don't care to understand how it works, you'll need to make sure the impedance of an audio signal you want to use is appropriate for the input into which you're plugging it. According to author Craig Anderton in *Home Recording for Musicians* (Amsco), "For minimum signal loss in an audio system, in most cases an input impedance should be approximately ten times greater than the output impedance feeding it."

Using the correct impedance is especially relevant when you're connecting an output of an electric guitar. If the input isn't correct, the full frequency range of the instrument will be compromised, making for a dull sound. The solution is to use an input specifically designed for the guitar. Some computer audio interfaces are designed for this purpose, as are some mixer inputs. Most often, a guitarist will plug into a guitar *direct box*, which amplifies the signal and solves the impedance problem.

Noise and Hum

You've probably had the experience of plugging equipment in, turning it on, and hearing a loud hum. Even digital audio relies on analog voltages, which means your computer music setup involves lots of electricity. If that electricity isn't properly *grounded*, meaning the audio wiring is properly isolated from the power wiring, electrical interference will be added to your mix in the form of noise and hum.

 How Ground Loops Happen

Electricity makes digital music possible, but it can be the enemy. The setup pictured in **Figure 3.8** is quite likely to produce a ground loop. Most buildings have just one ground, probably a connection in the basement or crawlspace that connects the wiring to the earth. Each wall outlet should provide a connection to that ground. This isn't likely to be a problem until you plug one piece of gear (like your computer) into one outlet, then plug another piece of gear (like powered speakers) into a different outlet. At this point, there's likely to be more resistance in one of the ground connections than in the other, which will cause a current to flow through the ground loop. When you plug the audio cables between the speakers and the computer's audio interface, you create a full loop, and your audio rig may suffer from unwanted hum.

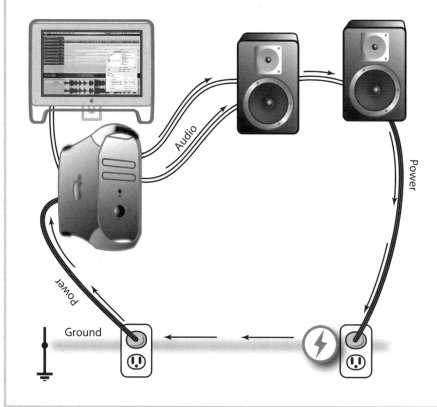

Figure 3.8 This is one way to create a ground loop. Any setup with multiple routes to ground will have the same result.

Audio systems require a neutral *ground* as a reference point, a zero voltage level. Without that reference, your equipment can't separate the sound of the music from electrical noise. In an audio cable, the reference is provided by the ground wire. The ground isn't necessarily connected to the earth as in a true ground, but does connect to some conducting material within the transmitting and/or receiving device that serves as a ground reference. Unfortunately, the moment you connect two or more electrical devices to one another, you create the possibility of a *ground loop.* That is, the combined circuit has two (if not more) paths to ground, one of which may have more resistance than another. This can cause a current to flow through the ground loop. This current, in turn, will cause the audio wiring to act as a radio antenna, picking up a hum at 60 Hz. This "60 cycle hum" reflects the 60 Hz frequency of the AC power grid in North America.

Ground loops are the most common source of hum problems. Each device in your setup should have a direct path to ground through its three-connector power plug. If all of the power plugs are connected to the same wall outlet through a junction box, ground loops are less likely, but are still possible.

In simple terms, the easiest way to eliminate ground loops is to make sure interconnected sound equipment is plugged into a single wall outlet or a power line from that connection. If you still hear a hum, there are two solutions. If you're handy with a soldering iron, you can create cables in which the ground connection is severed at one end (but not both ends, as the shield in the cable provides protection against radio signals). Another alternative is to use a three-to-two power plug adapter on one of the devices in the signal path. It's important not to use such adapters on all equipment, however, as a "floating ground" can be hazardous to your health. For other ideas on reducing noise and hum, see the sidebar "Wired for [No] Sound."

Balanced and Unbalanced Connections

The use of *balanced* connections is a means of reducing noise interference, especially when cables have to run long distances. Balanced connections require a ground wire plus two additional electrical connections. This configuration is sometimes called *symmetrical* because, in addition to the ground, there is a wire carrying the signal and a wire carrying an inverted copy of the signal. The "hot," positive signal is "balanced" around the ground by the "cold," inverted signal. When a balanced connection is made, the receiving device (such as a mixer or computer audio interface) inverts the cold signal a second time and adds it to the hot signal. At this point, any noise that has been added while the signal was traveling through the cable will cancel out, because the second inversion of the cold signal will reverse the polarity of the noise on that cable. Positive noise plus negative noise equals no noise.

Most consumer devices are unbalanced, carrying only the signal and a ground, as on stereo minijacks and RCA plugs. Because they're used in fairly simple setups with little wiring, manufacturers can save money by not worrying about creating balanced connections. But when wiring covers longer distances, connections become more prone to noise, so pros prefer balanced connectors like XLR and TRS. **Table 3.2** provides examples of balanced and unbalanced connections and which signals they carry.

Table 3.2 Balanced/Unbalanced at a Glance

Balanced

Mono TRS $^1/_4$″, $^1/_8$″	signal, inverted signal, ground
XLR Analog, Digital	3 pins: signal, inverted signal, ground

Unbalanced

Mono TS $^1/_4$″, $^1/_8$″	signal, ground
Stereo TRS $^1/_4$″, $^1/_8$″	left signal, right signal, ground
RCA Analog, Digital	left, right or in, out

Digital Connections

Several *protocols* are available for transmitting digital audio. Each of these formats is a specification for transmitting information, and each is different and essentially incompatible. For instance, you can't directly plug an ADAT Optical output into a S/PDIF input. You'll need to know which protocols devices are using to ensure compatibility. Unfortunately, it's not as simple as looking at a jack or cable, because it's possible to transmit different formats over the same physical connector.

If you're using consumer and semi-pro equipment, the primary digital formats are S/PDIF and ADAT Optical. Most computer audio interfaces use at least one or the other; some use both. S/PDIF is used for stereo digital audio and compressed multichannel audio such as DTS and Dolby Digital Surround, whereas ADAT Optical is used for 8-channel uncompressed digital audio. Since these formats appear on everything from consumer DVD players to keyboards to digital mixers and recorders, typical users will be able to connect all their digital equipment using these two formats.

Manufacturers do sometimes get lazy about labeling inputs and outputs, but it's usually possible to guess which connections are which. S/PDIF, for instance, is so ubiquitous that a connector using it may simply be labeled "optical" or "digital."

Pros tend to use a slightly different mix of digital formats than consumers and semi-pros. Digidesign Pro Tools|HD and other higher-end equipment use AES/EBU. Also known as AES3, it's transmitted over balanced XLR cables, which perform better over longer distances and have more rugged connectors, making them better suited to demanding applications. Although AES3 is supposed to be the industry standard, Alesis's ADAT Optical and Tascam's TDIF format are also popular for multichannel communication (**Table 3.3**, page 99).

 Wired for [No] Sound

Are you getting hum and other noise in your system? Isolate the problem by unplugging all components. Next, starting with the amplifier, replug each component one by one to see if you can locate the source. Then try these strategies for avoiding hum and noise in your systems:

- **Use balanced cables whenever possible:** If you are using unbalanced connections, try to keep them short (ideally six feet or less).

- **Use a single power source for audio equipment:** Plug audio equipment into a single power source, such as a power strip connected to one wall outlet, thus ensuring a single path to ground.

- **Don't coil wires:** Audio amateurs often coil microphone cables around the stand. Bad idea: you've just created a very effective magnetic field, producing additional hum! Keep wires straight; instead of coiling, bind them with gaffer's tape or cable ties.

- **Use trunks for organization:** If you have a lot of cables, bundle them together using cable coils and other wrapping systems, taking care not to cross cables. Bundle similar cables together into snakes.

- **Keep power and audio cables separate:** Power cords generate interference that can be picked up, even by shielded audio cables. Keep them away from each other if possible, and if not, cross the cables at a 90 degree angle.

- **Don't wrap power and audio cables together:** Bind them separately.

- **Invest in shielding:** Shielded audio cords and speaker wire have a stronger immunity to interference. Some power strips even include RFI/EMI filtering for additional protection, and many speakers intended for computer use include special shielding.

- **Isolate sources of interference:** CRT computer monitors, cell phones, power blocks, and many other devices produce interference. Some are so loud that they're easy enough to locate by ear. When in doubt, put some distance between them and your audio setup and speakers.

Got the format mismatch blues? If you have lots of digital equipment and want to easily select them or convert between different formats, consider a digital patch bay or format converter. M-Audio's CO3, for instance, features multiple ins and outs, converts between all formats, and performs other utilities like input switching and jitter correction, a means of solving connection issues between digital components.

Even though you need to know which format is which, you don't need to worry about choosing one or another: you'll use whatever format your equipment supports.

When you have two pieces of digital gear, your best bet is to make a digital connection. Use analog connections when you want to take advantage of analog equipment and processing or the flexibility of analog insert points.

When digital audio connections are used, one device needs to be the *word clock master* for purposes of synchronization. (Word clock is the high-frequency signal that aligns the bits and bytes of the digital audio signal.) If you're using only two digital audio devices, such as the S/PDIF input on your computer audio interface and a synthesizer that has a S/PDIF output, the receiving device will most likely configure itself automatically to synchronize its own digital audio to the incoming signal. But when three or more digital audio devices are connected, as in a setup that includes a digital mixer, you'll need to consult the owner's manuals for information on setting up word clock sync. Pro studios use specialized hardware to provide a high-quality digital audio synchronization source to which all of the devices can be synchronized. If you hear occasional clicks and pops in a system that includes two or more digital audio devices, consider the possibility that they're not all synchronized to the same word clock.

 What Do You Mean by "Pro"?

The divide between AES/EBU and S/PDIF, like many cabling formats, is "pro" versus "consumer." Both formats are used by pros, so why is AES/EBU, which uses XLR connectors, more "pro"—more likely to be used in critical studio and live performance applications?

- **Durability:** Consumers tend to favor cabling that's cheap, but cheaper cabling can be more fragile. A band performing in front of tens of thousands of fans seven nights a week will probably want more rugged cabling, whatever the expense.

- **Solid connections:** Consumer cabling tends to favor connections like phono plugs and minijacks, which come loose too easily for professional applications with hundreds of wires. BNC and XLR are bigger, but they're also less likely to loosen.

- **Low noise, long length:** At home, you may never need a cable more than six feet long, but pro applications may route audio over 100 feet. Even digital signal degrades over distances that long, which is why pros will opt for AES/EBU over S/PDIF when rigging the band at a stadium.

Of course, you don't have to be a pro to consider each of these factors. Even if you're using so-called consumer cables like minijack and RCA, you may want to invest in better cables. Inexpensive cables often break easily and have poor shielding, so consider pro-quality cables for better reliability and sound.

Table 3.3 Digital Audio Protocols at a Glance

Type	Acronym for	Also known as	Uses	Connectors
S/PDIF (pronounced "SPID-iff," "spuh-DIFF," or "ess pee diff")	Sony/Phillips Digital Interconnect Format	SPDIF (without a slash), unbalanced digital, "optical," "digital coax," or even simply "digital," IEC958 "Digital audio interface"	Consumer home audio equipment, portable audio recorders, computer audio interfaces, and various consumer, semi-pro, and pro audio equipment	RCA, TOSLINK, BNC
ADAT Optical	Alesis Digital Audio Tape	Lightpipe, simply "ADAT"	Alesis multichannel equipment and other multichannel devices, many computer audio interfaces, standard on the Apple Power Mac G5	TOSLINK
AES/EBU	Audio Engineering Society / European Broadcast Union	AES3, balanced digital	Pro equipment	XLR (AES3), BNC (AES3id, not as common)
TDIF (pronounced "tiddiff" or "teediff")	Tascam Digital Interface Format	"DA-88" (after the multichannel recording device that popularized the format)	Tascam multichannel equipment and compatible	Specialized 25-pin connector

Get the Hook-up: Real-world Examples

Now that you're more familiar with the many different formats and connection types possible, you'll find that all those jacks on a pro mixer or audio interface start to make a lot more sense.

The easiest way to figure out how to plug in equipment is to look closely at the gear. Devices tend to follow certain conventions of structure, layout, and available inputs and outputs.

Figure 3.9 and **Figure 3.10** illustrate typical configurations that you might confront when using real-world gear. The MOTU Traveler FireWire interface and Mackie Onyx mixer each have layouts of connections that are common on competitive products. Part of what makes them appealing to pros is that they have an arrangement of connections that's predictable and useful in a wide array of situations. By looking in detail at these

Bring a map: Well-documented gear should come with example routing layouts, which are well worth taking the time to read. Most manufacturers let you download manuals, so make sure gear includes friendly documentation before you make your purchase.

Figure 3.9 The back panel of the MOTU Traveler FireWire audio interface covers the full range of connectors you'll likely use in digital audio. The interface's eight analog inputs and outputs are laid out on the right, with digital I/O on the left; the two can be used simultaneously. (Photo courtesy Mark of the Unicorn)

configurations, you'll have an idea of how to connect the cables and connections in your own studio, even if you're hooking up equipment you haven't yet used.

Computer audio interface

Computer interfaces are the connection between guitars, keyboards, turntables, microphones, digital recording decks and other devices and the digital realm of the computer, whether they're recording one input or a complex multichannel setup. Below is a detailed explanation of the numbered items in Figure 3.9.

❶ 1–4 Neutrik combo inputs and preamps (analog)
❷ 5–8 TRS inputs (analog)
❸ 1–8 TRS outputs (analog)
❹ S/PDIF unbalanced input and output (digital)
❺ Clock synchronization connections (digital)
❻ FireWire 400 connector (digital)
❼ AES/EBU balanced input and output (digital)

Analog connectors:

You'll use inputs 1–8 for up to eight simultaneous analog inputs, which could be any combination of instruments, equipment, and microphones.

1. Inputs 1–4 are analog instruments with preamps for instruments or mics. MOTU has opted for handy Neutrik "combo" connectors. They double as both balanced XLR and ¼″ TRS connectors, so you don't have to worry about having the wrong cable.

2. Inputs 5–8 are simple balanced TRS jacks. If you want to plug microphones into these jacks, you'll need a preamp.

3. Lines 1–8 out are balanced TRS outputs. Many users will simply plug a stereo pair into their amp or powered speakers. Lines 1–2 are appropriate for this as their label "main" suggests. Lines 3–8 are for outputting to surround speaker setups or other multiple-speaker applications, to add analog effects to individual tracks via external hardware, or to output to an analog mixer.

 If You Can't Hear Anything . . .

From newbies to pro engineers with decades of experience, this situation happens to everyone: everything's plugged in, everything's turned on, and there's the sound of . . . silence. Don't panic. Just try to resolve the issue step by step:

1. **Follow the signal flow:** If audio routing had one commandment, this would be it. Starting with your sound source, trace the signal through each connection, from source to destination.

2. **Don't rely on your ears alone:** On each device that has visual meters, confirm that signal is being received.

3. **Check gain, mute switches, and solo buttons:** A disturbing number of popular mixers have gain knobs labeled with black indicators on black backgrounds and mute and solo buttons that look the same whether they're turned on or off.

4. **Swap cables:** A good way to test a connection is to swap a connection that isn't working with one that is. Cables fail regularly, and this is an easy way to tell if that's your problem.

Digital connectors:

You'll use the digital connectors for tasks like bringing in audio for your projects from digital recorders, or bouncing out to a CD, or even sharing audio with a second computer. Synchronization data will allow seamless connections with that equipment, essential for sync-dependent work like video.

4. Unbalanced S/PDIF RCA connectors are for "consumer" digital connections. Note that there's only one input jack and one output jack. Unlike analog RCA plugs, digital connections can carry more than one channel on the same jack.

5. Use these connectors to exchange synchronization data with other equipment.

6. The FireWire connector plugs into the computer and can even provide power if the computer supports bus power.

7. Balanced AES/EBU XLR connectors are for "pro" digital connections. More equipment has RCA S/PDIF connectors, so for many, the XLR jacks will go unused.

Not shown in Figure 3.9 are the MIDI in and out ports, which are located on the side of the interface.

Hardware mixer

Mixers provide sophisticated routing options for inputs and outputs, providing recording and effects options for analog and digital equipment that's external to the computer.

Figure 3.10a The layout of the Mackie Onyx 1220 is modeled on the influential Mackie 1202-series analog mixers. It's typical in design of many compact mixers. What you'll see immediately, of course, is a lot of inputs and outputs and knobs. You don't need to use all of them every time you mix. The advantage of traditional mixers is that they offer lots of routing flexibility for those times when you do need it, and they put everything up front, making settings and I/O visible and accessible. (Photo courtesy Loud Technologies, Inc.)

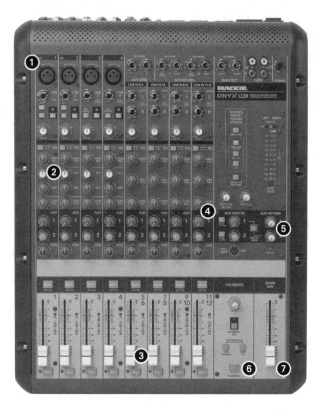

1. Inputs with preamps
2. Built-in EQ knobs
3. Faders, stereo pair
4. Aux send knob
5. Aux return knob
6. Talkback button
7. Main outputs (L/R)

1. Like the Traveler, the Onyx has four inputs with mic preamps. Note that the ¼″ jacks for inputs 1 and 2 are unbalanced only. They're guitar inputs, designed for the impedance of a guitar. These inputs can stand in for a direct box, but you should use a direct box if the guitar is a long distance from the mixer because the inputs are unbalanced.

2. Commonly found on mixers but almost never on a computer interface, each channel has independent EQ controls for adjusting the audio's frequency content, plus "aux" (as in auxiliary) send knobs for routing part or all of the signal to other equipment. Even if you're using computer effects, a built-in EQ on the mixer often comes in handy, and you might even prefer the sound.

3. Even if you're mixing in the computer, physical faders may still be useful in monitoring situations. Here's an example: assign your computer's output to this stereo pair (5/6), and you have an instant master fader for your computer mix. Plug a microphone into channel 1 for vocals, your guitar into channel 2, and your keyboardist's output into stereo pair 7/8. Now you can route each of these into tracks in your software for recording, and also easily control the live signal. Just be careful not to route channels 5/6 back into the computer during recording, as this may create a disastrous feedback loop.

4. The *aux send* is an output intended for sending an independent mix; the aux knob sets the level of this output. Applications can include sending a mix to stage monitors or to an effect processor.

5. An *aux return* is an input used to 'return' signal sent to an effect processor via the aux send. For instance, you might route an aux send to the input of a digital delay, then 'return' its signal by connecting the delay's output to the aux return input.

 Mixer or Interface?

Computers, interfaces, and mixers have blurred in function over the last few years. For example,

- **A computer can be a mixer:** Combining a computer and audio interface means any computer can function as a mixer.

- **An interface can be a mixer:** The MOTU Traveler doesn't even need a computer. In stand-alone mode it's a self-contained digital mixer.

- **A mixer can double as an interface:** The Mackie Onyx, although it will look instantly familiar to users of Mackie's traditional analog mixers, can double as a computer interface with the addition of an optional FireWire card.

Although these devices share some basic functions, each device has its own form and structure. The Traveler has a fraction of the routing flexibility of the Onyx, and any changes to a mix must be made on its small LCD front panel with limited physical controls. The Onyx, on the other hand, is more expensive and less portable than the Traveler. As long as the laws of physical space remain, and audio pros' habits lead them to desire certain device designs, these three equipment categories are likely to remain intact in some form.

6. *Talkback* is used to allow communication between a control room and a performer in the recording studio, or in a live environment, between a console in the audience and someone onstage.

7. Since these main outputs are on the top of the mixer, they're a natural candidate for hooking up to a recorder for a quick stereo recording of a mix.

Figure 3.10b The back panel on the mixer houses I/O you won't need to access as often, like the connection to your speakers. (Photo courtesy Loud Technologies, Inc.)

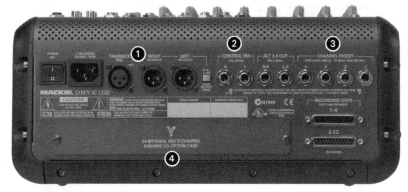

❶ Main outputs
❷ Control room outputs
❸ Channel inserts
❹ FireWire connection for computer

 How equipment differs: The fundamental channel/bus structure of nearly all mixers is the same, but different components of this structure are combined in different ways. More channels let you add more inputs. More buses let you group signal into configurations of 4, 8, or more tracks instead of the simple left/right two-bus mixer shown in Figure 3.10a. Additional buses are essential for surround sound and outputting to multitrack recordings.

1. Main L/R outputs are the connections you'll use for your powered monitors. (For unpowered monitors, you'll plug into your amp first.)

2. *Control room* outputs are intended for powering a second set of monitors for the isolated room with the mixer in a recording studio, or the monitors by the board in a live performance situation. If you have only one room and one set of monitors, you won't need these outputs; you'll use the main outputs.

3. *Channel inserts* give you an additional way of working with effects. Instead of returning a modified signal like an aux return, they "insert" changes to the entire audio signal before it reaches the fader. This is useful for devices like compressors and other devices you want to apply to the whole signal.

4. Here's where the Onyx becomes a true digital extension of your computer. With an optional FireWire card, all of the tracks on the mixer are digitally connected to your computer for recording and editing.

CHAPTER 4

Preparing Your Computer for Audio

You tune guitars and pianos, so why not tune your computer? Using a computer as a musical instrument and audio-production studio places demands on it that are different from other day-to-day applications. It's essential to know how to configure your computer for audio and MIDI support, and the optimizations you can make to improve audio performance. With your physical studio in place, let's prep your computer for optimum audio productivity.

 Essentials

Preparing Your Computer for Audio

To complete and optimize your computer setup:

- Install and configure drivers for your OS and specific application

- Install any plug-ins (effects, instruments) for your platform

- Deal with copy protection schemes effectively

- Optimize and back up storage

- Trim and optimize your OS for maximum performance

Essential Terms

- Driver formats: DAE, Core Audio, WDM, ASIO, MME, ALSA

- Plug-in formats: VST, AU, LADSPA, DX, TDM, HTDM, RTAS

- Latency, buffer size, recording offset

- Copy protection

- Defragmentation

Where to Start

Check your hardware documentation first to install drivers, then follow the driver-configuration instructions for each application. Look over any optimization tips, particularly disk and OS optimization, to make sure your machine is reaching maximum performance. (You may want to skip some of the advanced tips if you're not comfortable adjusting core system settings.) Most important, decide on your backup plan now, before you lose data.

CONNECTING YOUR VIRTUAL STUDIO

Installing and Configuring Audio Hardware

Audio hardware interfaces use specialized *drivers*, software that enables them to communicate with your operating system and applications. Regardless of which operating system or hardware you use, installation and configuration of your audio interface involves three basic steps:

1. Install driver(s) for your audio interface. You'll typically do this from the CD that shipped with your interface or, if one is available, an updated copy downloaded from the manufacturer's Web site. Instructions are OS-specific and occasionally devices don't need drivers installed; see "Audio Drivers and the OS."

2. Configure your choice of hardware (shown at left: the driver for the Lexicon Omega, www.lexiconpro.com) in your audio application. If you use multiple applications, you'll likely set up each individually. For applications that don't have audio driver settings, set up global audio defaults in the OS's configuration.

3. If needed, configure the audio driver for performance settings, such as buffer size and maximum number of audio tracks.

Audio Drivers and the OS

Each OS has its own driver format:

*   **Mac OS X:** Core Audio (http://developer.apple.com/audio)

*   **Windows:** Microsoft's WDM/DirectSound (www.microsoft.com/ windows/directx/default.aspx), Steinberg's ASIO

*   **Linux:** ALSA (www.alsa-project.org)

You'll need to install a driver or drivers for the appropriate system before you begin working. Exceptions include built-in audio hardware on your computer, which typically doesn't require you to install separate drivers, and particularly on the Mac, many USB audio/MIDI devices that are "class-compliant" or work automatically with the OS's built-in USB drivers.

On both Mac and Windows, Digidesign's Pro Tools hardware (www. digidesign.com) uses its own audio system called *DAE* (Digidesign Audio

Engine) to provide support for Digidesign hardware and its onboard DSP chips. Pro Tools software runs exclusively on DAE; Apple Logic (www.apple.com/logicpro) and MOTU Digital Performer (www.motu.com) can be switched to the DAE system for use with Digidesign hardware. DAE acts as both an audio driver for Digidesign hardware and an environment for running Digidesign's TDM and RTAS plug-in formats. (See "Installing Plug-in Effects and Instruments" on p. 113.)

Mac OS X: Core Audio

Whether you're listening to a simple beep in the Finder, a song in iTunes, or an eight-channel surround sound mix in Logic or Steinberg Cubase (www.steinberg.de), you're listening to OS X's built-in audio system, *Core Audio*. All application audio is routed through this low-latency audio system, so once you've installed your audio hardware, you can use it with any OS X application.

Core Audio also adds special functionality that could make your Windows-using friends jealous, particularly, the ability to assign several applications to different channels on a single piece of hardware, the ability to switch audio inputs and outputs at the OS level on the fly, and utilities that route and record audio from any OS X applications.

If you're not a programmer, all you really need to do is install a driver for your audio interface. Once you've done that, you can sit back, relax, and make music. Core Audio will enable OS-wide audio features automatically.

Configuring audio on Mac OS X

Configure your applications: Applications that let you select audio inputs and outputs should automatically recognize any hardware that's plugged in and has drivers installed. You can even plug in and use multiple devices simultaneously; just set each application to the audio device you want it to use (**Figure 4.1**).

 Pre-OS X Macs: Do you have a "vintage" Mac running Mac OS 9 or earlier? Unfortunately, most new hardware and software doesn't officially support pre-OS X systems. Your best bet for audio hardware may be to find a compatible OS 9 ASIO driver. (See an explanation of ASIO in the following section. Originally, ASIO was a cross-platform format for Windows and Mac before Core Audio supplanted it on Mac OS X.)

 Geeky details: For info on the nuts and bolts that make Core Audio work, see Apple's extensive documentation and links: www.apple.com/macosx/features/audio; http://developer.apple.com/documentation/MusicAudio/MusicAudio.html

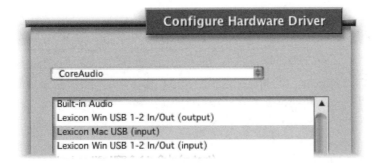

Figure 4.1 Set the application you're using to the desired audio device, as shown here in Digital Performer.

Configure OS-level defaults: If an application doesn't provide hardware configuration options, it will simply use the default input and output specified in the Sound Preference Panel in System Preferences (**Figure 4.2**). (Applications that do provide input and output controls generally override these settings.)

Set default output settings for system events (like the default system beep).

Set input and output settings for applications that lack individual configuration.

Figure 4.2 Sound preference panel.

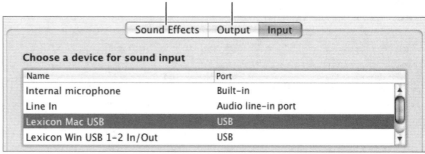

No drivers needed: Many *class-compliant* audio and MIDI devices, including some interfaces and keyboards, don't require drivers at all; generic driver support is built-in. Plug in your device, boot your computer, and you're done.

For additional control over Core Audio settings, use Apple's Audio MIDI Setup, which is included in your Utilities folder. From there you can make global settings to your audio drivers. You can also create, save, and switch between global MIDI configurations so other OS X applications will recognize your external MIDI setup or setups. For more information, see the discussion of MIDI configuration and recording in Chapter 8.

Windows: WDM and ASIO

Windows lacks some of the niceties of Mac OS X for audio, but that doesn't mean you can't get high-performance audio on Windows, too. You'll choose from two reigning driver models:

- **WDM (Windows Driver Model):** Microsoft's standard format for drivers, designed for Windows 98 SE and later. Audio drivers tap into the Windows DirectSound library.

- **ASIO (Audio Stream Input Output):** Originally developed by Steinberg, this driver model is used by many applications and hardware manufacturers.

Occasionally, you'll see an *MME* (Multi-Media Extensions) driver, the "legacy" Windows driver format that has been replaced by WDM. MME doesn't perform as well as WDM and ASIO, however, so you'll want to opt for WDM or ASIO drivers if they're available.

Table 4.1 Windows Users: Choosing a Driver Format

Problem	Solution
You don't know which driver to use for your interface	Try WDM first, then ASIO
You don't know which driver to use for Steinberg's Cubase or Nuendo	Use ASIO
You have legacy audio hardware that doesn't have new WDM or ASIO drivers	Use MME, but only if you have to (it increases latency)

 Geeky details: WDM audio drivers and MME drivers are sometimes called DirectX drivers because they access DirectSound, Windows' standard sound library, which is a subset of the DirectX library. This is a developer library for Windows apps, roughly akin to Apple's Core Audio and Core Video, that provides support for everything from 3D graphics in games to sound playback and recording.

Configuring audio on Windows

Application settings: Your first stop for configuring audio in Windows is within the application. Keep in mind that since Windows uses WDM, MME, and ASIO drivers, and not all programs support all three formats, you may have different audio options in different programs (**Figure 4.3**).

 Windows installation tip: If you see a warning that says your hardware "failed Windows logo testing," don't panic: it simply means Microsoft hasn't tested a device in its compatibility labs. Microsoft generally doesn't test audio hardware drivers, so this message appears regularly; click "Continue Anyway."

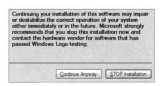

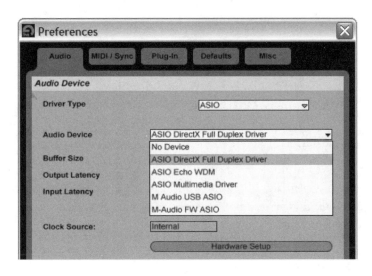

Figure 4.3 Select audio input/output driver settings for each application. You may have a choice of multiple drivers in programs that support multiple formats, as shown here in Ableton Live.

Configure OS-level defaults: Like the Mac, Windows XP has global settings for default audio and MIDI devices; they're found in Sound and Audio Device Properties (**Figure 4.4**). Keep in mind that many audio applications will override these settings, but they are a good way to check what drivers are installed on the system for connected devices.

Figure 4.4 Choose Start > Control Panel > Sound and Audio Devices > Audio for default audio and MIDI playback devices. This setting is used mainly by applications like Windows Media Player and iTunes because they lack separate settings.

If you're using WDM drivers, you'll have the option of using multiple devices simultaneously or routing multiple applications' outputs to a single device.

To allow multiple applications access to the ASIO driver, open settings for the driver in any ASIO application and select the "Release ASIO Driver in Background" check box.

Troubleshooting Windows Drivers

Updating or reinstalling a driver can often resolve problems with audio devices that don't appear properly. To update your drivers:

1. Open Device Manager (Right-click My Computer, then choose Properties > Hardware > Device Manager).

2. Find your device, and confirm that it's enabled (see **Figure 4.5**).

3. If it's enabled and still isn't working, right-click it and choose Update Driver. If that doesn't work, right-click and choose Uninstall, then reinstall the driver and reboot.

Figure 4.5 The contextual menu for a Windows device lets you disable, enable, and update drivers.

Linux: ALSA

Like Mac OS X, Linux focuses on OS-level support for multichannel audio handling. Originally, this was part of an OS layer called OSS (Open Sound System), now developed commercially by 4Front Technologies (www.opensound.com). The preferred means of supporting audio drivers under Linux, however, is ALSA (Advanced Linux Sound Architecture). ALSA is included in many Linux distributions and doesn't require separate driver installation, so your audio card may be compatible with Linux without any additional effort.

Configuring Your Interface

 Is your hardware supported? Since most manufacturers don't write Linux drivers for their audio cards—leaving that task to the Linux community—check www.alsa-project.org to see if your card is supported. Newer chipsets often aren't. Laptop users should also check out www.linux-on-laptops.com for installation tips.

Latency

No matter how efficient your audio driver and operating system are, it takes time to route data through your computer. The delay introduced by the computer and interface is called *latency*. Windows XP, Mac OS X, and Linux have *low-latency* drivers that keep this delay short. They're low-latency, though, not zero latency.

Eliminating latency is important for keeping timing accurate, especially when overdubbing. To achieve zero latency, many audio interfaces feature "zero-latency monitoring" or *direct monitoring*: headphone jacks on the interface monitor the incoming sound instead of the outgoing sound. Another solution is to connect headphones to a mixer plugged into your audio interface. See Chapter 6, "Recording Instruments and Sound."

Performance settings

Audio applications typically have driver controls, such as *buffer size* and *offset,* that impact latency. The buffer size impacts audio data transferred between software and the audio interface, and is set on an application-by-application basis. Some programs (but not all) also have an additional offset value that can be used to compensate for a constant audible delay by sending mix data early. Offset can thus be used for manual *latency compensation* for an audio interface; some systems can calculate this compensation automatically (**Figure 4.6**).

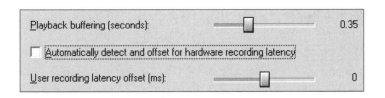

Figure 4.6 Buffer size and offset settings in Sony Music Acid (www.sonymediasoftware. com/products/acidfamily.asp). Note that the box in the center lets the program set offset automatically.

In many cases, the defaults work just fine. Some applications, including Cakewalk SONAR (www.cakewalk.com) and Apple Logic, even include wizards to help you make the proper settings. However, there are instances where you may need to make an adjustment to these settings:

- **If latency is too great:** The buffer size may need to be decreased. Be careful; if the buffer is too small, audio will skip.

- **If audio output is skipping or stuttering, or you hear clicks and pops:** The buffer size may need to be increased. If the buffer is too small, the software is unable to keep a steady stream of audio traveling to the interface.

- **If you can hear a regular, constant delay:** Try setting the offset (output or input latency) to compensate.

Many interfaces also include specialized applications to access features that can't be accessed on the interface's breakout hardware. Using these applications, you can test your interface, set hardware options, and in some cases use custom routing options and other special features specific to your equipment.

Installing Plug-in Effects and Instruments

As discussed in Chapter 2, plug-ins and technologies like ReWire (www. propellerheads.se/technologies/rewire) and Jack (http://jackit.sourceforge.net) can be used to extend the capabilities of your audio software. Plug-ins require special installation, which we'll look at according to format.

Standard native plug-in formats

Standard, native formats run on the CPU and are supported by a wide variety of hosts on each platform, as shown in **Table 4.2**. The capabilities of each are similar, so whichever format you use will be dependent on the host application you use.

Each software program supports different formats. If you have a plug-in that's incompatible with your program, you can use an inexpensive *wrapper* application that lets plug-ins work with hosts that otherwise wouldn't support them. Apple Logic and MOTU Digital Performer on the Mac, for instance, don't support VST, but you can add support via a wrapper from Audio Ease or FXpansion.

Other vendors support all the major formats: on Mac, Ableton Live (**Figure 4.7**) supports VST and AU; on Windows, Ableton Live, Image-Line FL Studio (www.flstudio.com), and Cakewalk SONAR all support both VST and DirectX.

Table 4.2 Open standard plug-in formats

Abbreviation/Full Name	OS	Developed by
VST (Virtual Studio Technology, VSTi for instruments)	Windows/Mac	Steinberg
DX (DirectX, DirectSound, DX, DXi for instruments)	Windows	Microsoft
AU (Audio Units, components)	Mac	Apple
LADSPA	Linux* (Linux Audio Developer's Simple Plug-in API)	Open Source (www.ladspa.org)

*Linux LADSPA plug-ins are also supported by some Mac OS X applications and utilities ported from Linux, including Jack OS X (www.jackosx.com).

 Resources for wrappers:
FXpansion (Mac, PC, Digidesign): www.fxpansion.com
Audio Ease (Digital Performer): www.audioease.com
Cakewalk (PC): www.cakewalk.com

Digidesign plug-in formats

Digidesign's DAE system uses proprietary plug-in formats, as discussed in Chapter 2 (see "What does Pro Tools mean?", p. 73). Digidesign's formats are either hardware DSP-based, running on the DSP chips in the Digidesign hardware, or "host-based," native plug-ins that run on your CPU via DAE, as shown in **Table 4.3**. You can use many or all of these plug-ins using DAE hosts like Apple Logic and MOTU Digital Performer.

Figure 4.7 Ableton Live supports multiple plug-in formats for instruments and effects.

Table 4.3 Pro Tools Plug-ins

Name	Host or Hardware-based?	Used for
RTAS (Real-Time Audio Suite)	Host	Basic real-time effects and instruments
TDM (Time-Division Multiplexing)	Hardware	High-end effects and instruments on Pro Tools TDM and HD systems (**Figure 4.8**)
HTDM (Host TDM)	Host	Effects with higher latency than TDM but more flexibility than RTAS

 Geeky details—your cell phone and Pro Tools, distant cousins: Time-Division Multiplexing itself isn't a proprietary technology, it's a standard means of processing digital signals developed in the telecommunications industry and used in many digital mobile phones. (Phone systems have to process digital audio, too.) The Pro Tools TDM platform and other digital audio hardware that uses DSP chips makes use of similar technologies, adapted for pro sound and music applications.

Figure 4.8 Hardware DSP-accelerated plug-ins look like software plug-ins but, via the Pro Tools TDM system, run on Digidesign hardware instead of your CPU. Shown here is Freeze, a plug-in in GRM Tools that lets you manipulate fragments of audio input as loops (www.grmtools.org).

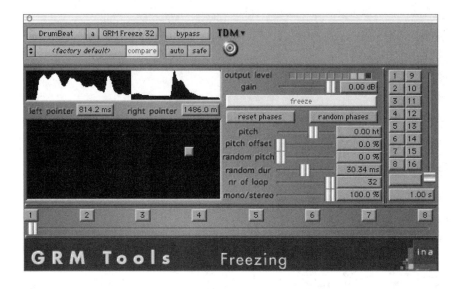

Where the Plug-ins Go

Some plug-in installers automatically determine correct folders for installation. Others, including many free plug-ins you download from the Web, assume you know where to install them. Either way, you'll need to know where to find those plug-ins after they're installed.

Mac OS X

Mac OS X uses a shared folder for plug-ins. Nearly all your Mac apps should automatically look at this folder. You can find this folder in the Library folder located in the root folder of your drive: [*your boot volume*] > Library > Audio > Plug-Ins (**Figure 4.9**).

You can often identify a plug-in type by its file extension: .component files are Apple Audio Units and .vst files are VSTs. Most other files have a .bundle extension.

Figure 4.9 With Mac OS X, Apple consolidated all the different plug-in formats in one location so they're easier for you—and your applications—to find.

Some plug-ins are proprietary to specific systems, like those included with Apple Logic and Ableton Live. These are sometimes hidden or located in a separate location. However, shared plug-ins are the ones you usually have to manage.

Windows

Windows doesn't have a consolidated plug-in folder. Instead, plug-ins can be installed to different locations on your drive.

DirectX plug-ins can go wherever you like. When they're installed, they register with Windows, and any application with DirectX will find them automatically. This means you can put them in a location that is convenient for you. Since DirectX requires DirectMedia, you might need to download an update from Microsoft if you haven't updated your system recently.

VST plug-ins may need to be installed separately for each application (**Figure 4.10**). On Windows, VSTs are DLL (dynamic link library) files. To install them, drag a copy of the DLL into the VST folder of each application you want to have access, for example, C:\Program Files\[*application name*]\VSTPlugins

Some applications allow you to share the Steinberg VST directory (C:\ Program Files\Steinberg\Vstplugins) or use a VST folder of your choosing. Check your application's documentation for details.

Tip: Here's an easy way to turn plug-ins on and off, for troubleshooting or convenience. Duplicate each plug-in folder in the Plug-Ins folder, then label the duplicate "Disabled" (e.g., VST Disabled). Drag any plug-ins you want to turn off into this folder. Incorrectly written plug-ins can cause crashes, although some major applications like Logic and DP now include validators to check for troublesome plug-ins.

Name	In Folder	Type	Date Modified
VSTPlugins	C:\Program Files\AudioMulch 0.9b16	File Folder	6/11/2004 8:34 PM
Vstplugins	C:\Program Files\Steinberg	File Folder	7/18/2004 3:47 PM
VSTPlugins	C:\Program Files\SynthEdit	File Folder	6/12/2004 2:19 AM
Vstplugins	C:\Program Files\Ableton\Live 3.0	File Folder	6/12/2004 1:45 PM
vstplugins	C:\Program Files\Adobe\Audition 1.5	File Folder	8/26/2004 3:40 PM
Vstplugins	C:\Program Files\Steinberg\Cubase SX 2	File Folder	9/27/2004 9:32 PM
Vstplugins	C:\Program Files\Steinberg\Cubase SX 3	File Folder	9/27/2004 11:35 PM

Figure 4.10 Windows VST plug-ins must be installed in each application folder.

 Plug-in Installation at a Glance

Where can you find the plug-ins you've installed?

- **Mac OS X:** Library > Plug-Ins (shared)
- **App-specific Windows VST:** Vstplugins folder in each application folder
- **Shared Windows VST:** Steinberg > Vstplugins
- **DirectX:** Can be located anywhere on your drive
- **Digidesign:** DAE Plug-Ins folder

MAINTAINING YOUR VIRTUAL STUDIO

Copy Protection and Dongles

Audio developers are very concerned about piracy issues. They point out that piracy is rampant in the music software market. Even some free software has been cracked to remove serial number protection, and a sample audio file created by Microsoft for its Windows Media Player showed the use of pirated software in its file header. Although some large manufacturers are doing big business, an audio-software developer may only be breaking even or creating software as a labor of love. Whether they're overreacting to the situation is a matter of debate, but many developers have decided they need additional help to protect their software.

Copy protection methods

Unfortunately, many of the mechanisms used by music developers to protect their software from piracy mean extra effort for legitimate users. The degree of software protection spans a wide range:

- **Unprotected:** Some software is entirely unprotected—you can do with it what you want—including a variety of free and open-source software. If you want to remain legal but still keep programs free, it's possible to assemble very compelling all-free software studios, an option frequently used by academic institutions.

- **Serial number authorization:** Software from developers like Cakewalk is authorized by serial number only. Enter a code from the CD or manual, and the application is authorized for life. To authorize a second machine (like a laptop), all you have to do is install the program again and enter the code.

- **Hardware copy protection:** Increasingly, software developers are opting for USB-based hardware keys, commonly called "dongles." Just as a car won't run until you insert the key, software won't run without the dongle.

- **Online authorization (Challenge and Response):** Instead of physical hardware, online authorization software or "challenge and response" software requires you to connect via the Internet or manually enter a code to authorize a software installation on a computer (**Figure 4.11**).

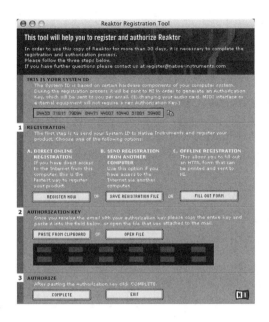

Figure 4.11 Challenge-and-response copy protection combines a serial number with a code sent over the Internet to authorize the machine, as shown here in Native Instruments Reaktor (www.native-instruments.com).

Coping with copy protection

There's no question which of these methods, other than completely unprotected software, is most convenient for users: serial number authorization is the riskiest for developers but easiest for the rest of us.

Hardware copy protection may initially seem like the least appealing solution for users. There's no one format for dongles; aside from the somewhat popular iLok system (www.ilok.com), each new dongle product requires another hardware key (**Figure 4.12**). Even worse, although developers will usually replace a malfunctioning key, if you break or lose a key, many will charge you 50%–100% of the purchase price of the original product. (Some will be more reasonable if you send in the broken remains of a dongle; check individual vendors' policies before you buy.)

Figure 4.12 These dongles from Apple and iLok act like software keys. One downside is you may need to purchase a hub to use multiple dongles.

Dongles do have some advantages over online authorization, however. If a company ceases its business operation, the lack of an online authorization can leave its product disabled. Even if the company is completely reliable, you may not be able to automatically reauthorize a product without an online connection, which you might not have access to in that grungy basement club in the middle of a gig. Depending on the scheme, it's usually easier to move a software license from one computer to another via a dongle. With Cubase, for instance, you can switch between a Windows laptop and a Mac desktop just by moving the USB dongle.

Since a software studio of any size is likely to use a combination of these copy-protection methods, it's best to have some strategies for dealing with all of them:

• Store serial numbers in two centralized places: one on the hard drive in a text file, so you can quickly access it if you need to on the road, and one in a physical form just in case the drive fails.

• Keep hardware keys on a key chain with removable key rings so you always have them handy. Some users also stock a key chain with a USB flash drive for emergency storage.

• Test online-authorized software before gigs.

Whether your software is copy protected online or via a hardware dongle, it will shut down without proper authorization (**Figure 4.13**).

Figure 4.13 This is the alert message that users see when trying to run Apple Logic Pro without the USB key.

 Fighting piracy: Software developers, via the International Music Software Trade Association (www.imsta.org), have banded together to form www.be-cool.org, a campaign site that encourages users to use software legally. Studios and musicians can list themselves as "piracy-free zones" or chat on a forum. With any luck, users who embrace legal software—whether purchasing commercial software or using legal, open-source software—will help discourage odious copy-protection schemes.

Maintaining Storage

Digital audio lives on storage. As you work, your computer pulls enormous amounts of audio data directly from your hard drive. That means you need to be conscious of how you set up and maintain your storage. To ensure maximum performance of your audio projects, try the following strategies:

- **Keep available space on your startup disk:** The operating system and many audio applications rely on temporary files stored on your startup disk. If you have too little room, performance may suffer. Keep at least a couple of gigabytes free (10% of your drive is a good rule). Check available space by right-clicking a drive in Windows and choosing Properties, or by selecting Utilities > Activity Monitor > Disk Usage on Mac OS X.

- **Consider a separate partition:** Separate partitions on the same volume as the startup drive aren't as safe as a separate drive, but they can still be useful. Although they're still vulnerable to physical failure, separate audio partitions are less likely to be impacted by a directory structure problem on the startup volume. Use a disk-formatting tool to set up new partitions, or use Windows utilities like Symantec Partition Magic to partition a drive without having to reinstall drive data (www.symantec.com).

- **Use a separate disk for recording:** The internal startup disk will work fine for playing back audio, but ideally, you'll want to record audio on a separate, dedicated drive—meaning a separate physical drive, not just a separate partition. You can bend this rule a bit with simple, stereo recording—laptop musicians often sample directly onto their slow, internal startup disk during performance—but for serious multi-channel work, a second drive is a must.

- **Perform regular checkups:** Just as you should routinely see a doctor, you should routinely check up on your drive to keep it running its best and prevent or identify system problems before they happen. The OS automatically verifies the startup disk regularly, but to check additional volumes and fix problems the built-in verifier missed, use a third-party disk utility or built-in utilities. On Mac OS X, run Utilities > Disk Utility and verify/repair disk permissions and/or verify/repair disk. (To repair a problem with the startup drive other than permissions, boot from another drive or the OS X install CD.) On Windows XP, you can verify a disk by running chkdsk (Start > Run, then type chkdsk.exe).

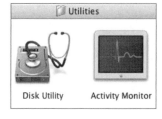

Defragmentation utilities:

Mac OS X:
Tech Tool Pro
from Micromat
(www.micromat.com)

Windows:
Built-in utility: Start >
Programs > Accessories >
System Tools > Disk
Defragmenter

Diskeeper
(www.executivesoft-
ware.com), **Figure 4.14**

Tip: Defragmenting a
disk sometimes wipes
out software copy-
protection authorizations.
Make sure you have your
serial numbers and origi-
nal program discs handy
before you proceed.

- **Defragment your disks:** See the sidebar "Defragmentation: Still Essential for Audio."

- **Back up your data:** See the sidebar "Backup: The Most Important Maintenance Step."

- **Make it a routine:** Using Mac OS X 10.4 and later, you can schedule simple and complex tasks using the Automator. With earlier versions of OS X, you can use the UNIX command-line utility cron or the $8.99 utility Macoroni (www.atomicbird.com), or even hack iCal to do the work for you (http://hacks.oreilly.com/pub/h/1712). Using Windows XP you can schedule tasks by selecting Start > Control Panel > Scheduled Tasks.

 Defragmentation: Still Essential for Audio

Defragmentation takes data and free space that is scattered in different locations on your drive and moves them to contiguous blocks, improving performance. Without it, audio recordings can wind up with skips and pops or other performance problems. Modern operating systems are smarter about how they maintain hard drives, so you may have heard that defragmentation is a thing of the past. Unfortunately, that's not the case yet. Because audio recording is especially performance-intensive, audio developers still recommend that users regularly "defrag" or "optimize" their data disk. For best performance, defrag both your startup disk and your project drive.

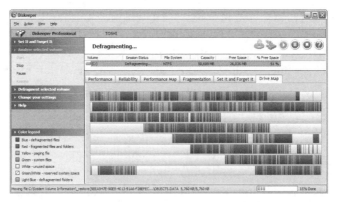

Figure 4.14 Diskeeper will take these noncontiguous blocks of data and make them more accessible for better performance. Diskeeper is a worthwhile upgrade from the built-in defrag utility in Windows, offering "set it and forget it" options so you can defrag without interrupting your work.

Backup: The Most Important Maintenance Step

There's an old adage in the computer world: there are those who have lost data and now have a backup plan, and those who will lose data soon. Hard drives fail frequently, either through data errors or mechanical malfunction. Also, although Windows XP now includes system restore points, on both Windows and Mac it's sometimes necessary to revert to backed-up files to recover from other system problems.

Now that hard drives are dirt-cheap, the easiest backup strategy is simply to buy drives in twos and mirror data. That way, you won't lose your audio files, and you won't have to reinstall applications or reconfigure operating system settings in the event of a failure. If you have 250 gigabytes of data to back up, buy a 250 GB backup drive. Because you'll only be using them for backup, you won't need top-of-the-line models, and some vendors like Iomega bundle backup software with the drive, saving you even more money.

Ideally, you should create a bootable disk, which is perfect for emergencies (or for swapping when a drive fails ten minutes before a gig!). For additional protection, archive important projects to recordable DVD.

Backup Utilities

Windows XP comes with a backup utility, found in Accessories > System Tools, but it's only installed by default on Windows XP Pro. Windows XP Home users need to manually install Backup from their original install CD (not a restore CD), by launching [cd drive]:\VALUEADD\MSFT\NTBACKUP.msi

Apple's .Mac includes a free backup utility. It's not very useful for full backups, but can be helpful for archiving audio-project files to your online iDisk, a CD/DVD, or external drives, and is even preconfigured to back up iTunes music. Download the latest version at www.mac.com if you're a .Mac member.

Your best option is to synchronize an entire volume, creating a bootable second volume in the process so you can swap the two. Backup software like Symantec's Ghost (www.symantec.com) on the PC and Prosoft's Data Backup (www.prosoft.com) on the Mac will automatically copy changed files to an external drive.

Optimizing for Audio Performance

Close other applications and processes: Windows XP's Task Manager (press Ctrl-Alt-Del) and Mac OS X's Activity Monitor (in the Utilities folder) each let you monitor memory and processor usage (**Figure 4.15**). With these utilities you can see if any tasks are bogging down your system. Be sure to quit unused applications and processes before doing any serious audio work. You can also tell if you need to install more physical memory by examining page ins/page outs data in these utilities. If you're short on memory, the system pages data to the disk more often, causing a major hit in performance.

Figure 4.15 Mac OS X's
Activity Monitor.

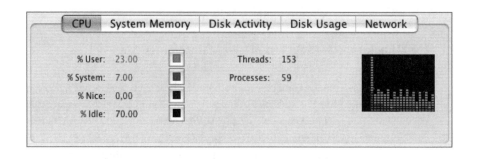

Disable unused fonts: Fonts can consume memory and, in the event of corruption, can cause system instability. (If you're unsure about whether or not to disable certain fonts, only uninstall the fonts you've added; other fonts may be critical to the system.)

Keep two user accounts: Both Windows XP and Mac OS X let you maintain separate user accounts with different system settings. Many users maintain a separate audio-optimized account, installing all their fun free-ware and shareware goodies on a day-to-day account while keeping the audio account as trim and clean as possible. (Installers usually have a choice to "install for all users" or "install for current user.") Of course, this might be overkill if you keep your primary account lean.

Reinstall the operating system: Although it should be a last resort, a sluggish system is often cured by reinstalling Windows XP or Mac OS X. If you're installing a major OS upgrade, it might be the perfect opportunity to reinstall the OS. Both operating systems give you options for clean installs and to archive existing drivers and settings. You may be surprised by the performance boost you get in overall responsiveness and stability and audio performance.

Keep your software up to date: Sometimes software troubles are not caused by user actions: developers are routinely fixing problems with their software. For general computer software updates, check out www.versiontracker.com (Windows/Mac), www.macupdate.com (Mac only), and www.freshmeat.com (Linux), and visit sites like www.kvraudio.com for the latest music-specific version updates. Mac OS X and Windows XP also both feature self-updating utilities, although you should be cautious when using newly released updates. Sometimes the latest and greatest .1 update to an OS also contains new audio incompatibilities.

Never Blow a Gig: Tips for Live Digital Audio

Onstage or even in the studio, these settings will ensure that you're set for silent running and solid performance:

Turn off energy saving features: Power management features can cause performance problems and other anomalies. On the Mac, these settings are located in System Preferences > Energy Saver (**Figure 4.16**); on Windows they're in Control Panel > Power Options:

- Turn off automatic sleep settings. Sometimes a computer will fail to recognize an audio device when it wakes up.
- Turn off automatic hard drive shut down/sleep. Spinning down disks adds wear and tear to the disk, and can cause audio playback delays.

Disable system sounds: There's nothing worse than hearing a resounding system beep live onstage.

- On Mac OS X, open System Preferences > Sound > Sound Effects. Reroute system sound to internal speakers, and uncheck user interface sound effects and "play feedback when volume keys are pressed."
- On Windows, choose Control Panel > Sounds and Audio Devices > Sounds. Select "No Sounds" as your sound scheme to disable all Windows sounds. From Control Panel > Accessibility Options > Sound, turn on SoundSentry. Now, instead of an annoying beep, Windows will unobtrusively flash the active caption bar. You'll still catch the error, but you won't disturb your audience.
- To be twice as safe and prevent other applications' unwanted noises, set "default audio output" on either platform to your internal soundcard. (See pp.107–110.)

Make your audio drive bootable, just in case: On both Windows and Mac OS X, you can create a bootable portable drive using your installer CD or a specialized utility. Having a second drive that can boot into Windows or OS X could save the day if your primary drive fails.

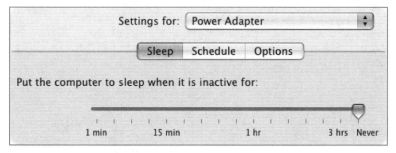

Figure 4.16 OS X's Energy Saver preference panel.

Mac power tips

Create a slimmer OS X: Diablotin is a useful, free utility for turning various system components off and on for troubleshooting or slimming down your system (http://s.sudre.free.fr/Software/Diablotin.html).

Lose languages: Consider installing only one language for support, or remove unused languages with the free utility Monolingual (http://monolingual.sourceforge.net).

Guard against viruses: Mac OS X generally doesn't suffer the virus problems Windows does, but it's smart to take precautions to keep it that way. Virex is available free with Apple's .Mac Internet service, which includes lots of other features and discounts that are generally worth the $100/year fee (www.mac.com).

Maintain your system: Cocktail ($14.95) is a must-have utility for maintaining your system. It runs a number of essential UNIX-based maintenance scripts that OS X sometimes fails to run automatically, especially if you turn off your computer instead of leaving it running all the time. Launch Cocktail (**Figure 4.17**) and click the Pilot tab; you can then run the scripts manually or schedule them to run regularly (www.macosxcocktail.com).

Improve disk performance: Disable journaling on all audio drives. It's not necessary and can cause a minor hit in audio performance. Run Utilities > Disk Utility, click a drive, and select File > Disable Journaling.

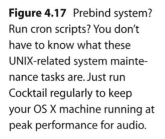

Figure 4.17 Prebind system? Run cron scripts? You don't have to know what these UNIX-related system maintenance tasks are. Just run Cocktail regularly to keep your OS X machine running at peak performance for audio.

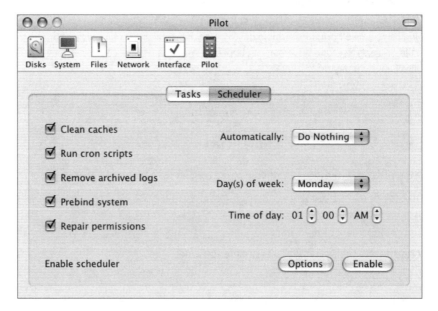

Save disk space: Identify space-wasting files using Omni Group's Omni-DiskSweeper, which lists the directories and files that use the most space on your drive. It's excellent for finding useless files on your hard drive and slimming down audio projects. The software is free, or you can pay $15 to enable a "Delete" button (www.omnigroup.com).

Windows power tips

Adjust System Performance Options: Choose Control Panel > System > Advanced > Performance > Settings. You'll find useful settings in this box under Visual Effects and Advanced:

- **Visual Effects:** Choose "Adjust for best performance" or "Let Windows choose what's best for my computer," or turn off individual items as you like. These options remove some GUI eye candy, but saves CPU cycles. Many settings are available in this tab. If you just want to turn off shadows and effects, select Control Panel > Display > Appearance > Effects (**Figure 4.18**) and uncheck the appropriate settings.

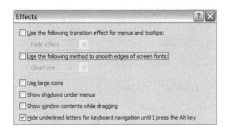

Figure 4.18 Windows XP's Visual Effects settings.

- **Advanced:** If you're using ASIO hardware drivers and want to reduce latency, choose "Background services" instead of "Programs under Processor scheduling." This isn't necessary for WDM drivers.

Clean out your Registry: The Windows Registry is a large database of system information that can also be a source of difficult to identify stability problems. At worst, corrupted entries in the Registry can cause unexpected software behaviors and slow performance, or even prevent your machine from booting. Messing around with the registry yourself can be dangerous, but utilities like Rose City's $21 Registry First Aid will do the work for you (www.rosecitysoftware.com/Reg1Aid). Using such a utility should become part of your Windows maintenance routine—it's like flossing for your computer.

Clear hard drive space with Disk Cleanup: Windows includes a utility for freeing up disk space. Choose Start > Programs > Accessories > System

Tools > Disk Cleanup. Ignore the More Options tab, and don't compress unused files, but use the other check boxes to free up much-needed space.

Turn off unneeded system services: This technique is potentially dangerous, so you should first research what you're doing so you don't disable a service the OS needs, and as always, backup. You can disable background services so they don't take up memory and CPU cycles, resulting in a big boost in audio performance and stability. Select Start > Programs > Administrative Tools > Services.

Protect your computer from the Internet: Spyware, viruses, and other Internet security issues can plague any computer. But they're especially devastating for audio because foreign applications can consume memory and processing power, causing instability. Here are some essential steps to protect your computer:

- **Take advantage of Security Center:** Windows XP SP2 and later include a central location for checking on your security settings; select Control Panel > Security Center. If you don't have SP2 or later, consider upgrading. If you do, launch Security Center and make sure that you have an active firewall, automatic updates, and virus protection when you access the Internet. If you haven't purchased a separate firewall, you can use the firewall built into XP; it's sufficient for basic use.

- **Upgrade to better Internet security if you can:** You'll need an additional tool for virus protection, and you may prefer a more full-featured firewall than XP provides. The Zone Labs Zone Alarm firewall (www.zonealarm.com) and Grisoft AVG anti-virus software (www.grisoft.com) are each available in free versions.

- **Protect your computer from spyware:** After all the optimization you've done, the last thing you want on your PC is *spyware* or *malware*, which are dangerous and system-taxing hidden utilities that install themselves without your permission when you're browsing or using downloaded software. Several good utilities are available for finding and destroying spyware. Spybot Search & Destroy is an excellent choice and it's free (www.spybot.info).

- **Turn off all utilities for performance and recording:** You should have all these utilities on for Web browsing and day-to-day use. But if you're going onstage or entering a major recording session and you won't be online, disable these utilities to save memory and processing power, and to avoid distracting dialog boxes.

CHAPTER 5

Quick Songs with Patterns and Loops

New software makes mixing musical elements more like playing with blocks: combine pre-built elements, like musical patterns and recorded sound loops, and within minutes you can produce a piece of music that sounds like a professionally recorded song. You can use this as-is or as a sketch for creating original material.

 Essentials

Quick Songs with Patterns and Loops

We'll apply the building-blocks production approach, using audio loops and patterns, to two scenarios:

Create a Backing Track with Apple GarageBand

- Build a linear song arrangement
- Mix and export music to a CD or iPod

Build a Custom Groovebox with Cakewalk Kinetic

- Edit and assemble individual grooves
- Apply basic effects
- Play an interactive song structure from a keyboard

Essential Terms

- Loops
- Patterns

Where to Start

You can use loops and patterns with many applications, so if you've already got a sequencer, fire it up and try working with the free loops included on the DVD. In this chapter we'll work with applications that import and play loops. Tutorial files are located on the DVD so you can hear the finished project.

Mac: Apple GarageBand (www.apple.com/garageband) is available preinstalled on recent Mac models and is included in Apple's iLife application (www.apple.com/ilife); Apple Soundtrack (part of Final Cut Pro) and Logic Express/Pro have similar features.

Windows: Cakewalk Kinetic (http://cakewalk.com/Products/Kinetic/) is available in a fully functional demo version included on this book's DVD.

PATTERNS AND LOOPS

You can quickly and easily sketch musical ideas in software like Kinetic and GarageBand thanks to their fluid use of pre-built, repeating musical components. You can then store, edit, and develop your sketches.

- *Patterns* are chunks of MIDI data, and are played by a virtual instrument. Since patterns are stored as notes and rhythms, not as audio recordings, it's easy to change individual notes or radically change their sound by assigning them to a different instrument.

- *Loops* are short audio recordings, often one, two, or four measures in length, that can be repeated seamlessly. You can adjust their tempo and pitch independently (though with some degradation in audio quality), but it's difficult to edit individual notes since you must digitally modify the original recording.

- *REX files* combine some of the features of audio and MIDI. Each file contains a number of separate samples (usually single notes) that are played by a MIDI file. REX files require special playback software.

On the DVD: Expand your loop library with an exclusive free collection of loops from SmartLoops (www.smartloops.com), which includes Apple Loops for use with GarageBand and ACID loops for use with both GarageBand and Kinetic (along with many other programs). Also on the DVD you'll find tips for making the most of loops musically.

We'll look at two applications that represent simplified, "sketchpad" versions of professional workflows: Apple's GarageBand on the Mac and Cakewalk's Kinetic on Windows. Both applications are serious tools, even if they lack some of the bells and whistles of their higher-end counterparts. GarageBand uses a timeline approach, which is similar to full-blown studio Digital Audio Workstations (DAWs) like Logic, whereas Kinetic's "virtual hardware" approach reflects how DJs and remix artists work. Both programs can be integrated with pro apps if you decide you need features like score printing, surround sound, and editing features that these applications lack.

Is It a Pattern, or Is It a Loop?

Since editable MIDI patterns and audio loops function differently, the software must provide a way of distinguishing which is which. In GarageBand, audio is blue and MIDI is green, both in tracks and in loops. As in other applications, you'll also see that the two contain different kinds of data: audio is represented as a waveform, whereas MIDI is represented as note data (**Figure 5.1**). In Kinetic, everything is a pattern unless it's specifically labeled as an audio loop.

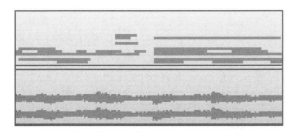

Figure 5.1 MIDI note data as graphical bars (top) and audio data as a waveform (bottom) in GarageBand.

Pitch/Tempo Independence

In the days of analog tape, the only way to adjust pitch was to raise or lower the speed at which the tape moved. Any change in speed generated a change in pitch. With digital data, it's possible to manipulate pitch and tempo independently. You can adjust MIDI data to any tempo or pitch imaginable, and thanks to digital audio processing techniques, the pitch and tempo of audio can also be modified independently, though when the changes are large you'll probably hear changes in the character of the sound.

Specialized loop formats ease the audio pitch/time-shifting process by adding meta-information to the file, in one of several standard file formats (see the sidebar "Standard Loop Formats"). By storing original tempo information and markers to locate where beats begin (**Figure 5.2**), these formats make adjustments more musically accurate and aurally satisfying. Instead of time-stretching the entire file at once, the audio software can stretch or manipulate beats individually. You can modify the tempo or pitch of the audio without this information, but it generally requires more manual labor for the best results.

Tempo	Key	Beats
140	E	16
120	C	16
130	C#	8
128	G	16
100	F	16
95	G	32
126	C	4

 Don't stretch too far: Changing the pitch or tempo of an audio loop by too great an amount can result in unpleasant audio effects. If you don't want those sounds, don't stretch the loop as far, or use a different loop. These effects aren't necessarily bad: in fact, some musicians have intentionally used the unusual sounds that result.

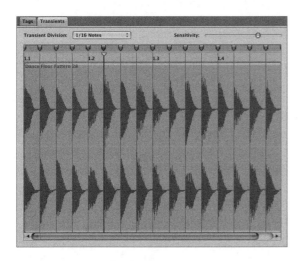

Figure 5.2 Loop formats store the location of each beat for more accurate manipulation. Your software reads this information and adjusts automatically, like the beats stored in this Apple Loop.

Standard Loop Formats

Applications like Sony Acid and Apple GarageBand helped popularize looping. But now many applications—including all the major DAWs (see Chapter 2, "Choosing Your Tools")—have integrated the technique. Some applications, such as Ableton Live, work fluidly with raw audio files in standard formats like WAV and AIFF. But specialized formats can help make looping more seamless—provided your loops are prepped ahead of time, either by you or by a sample designer.

These specialized audio formats include *metadata* that stores information like key, original tempo, and the positions of beats (**Figure 5.3**). Formats include:

Apple Loops: Audio in Apple Loops is stored in standard AIFF files, so the raw audio can be used by any application that can read AIFF, including PC software. Some Mac apps (like MOTU Digital Performer) can read beat locations from Apple Loops, and Apple's GarageBand and Logic can search through keywords, key, and tempo using the Loop Browser. You can create and edit Apple Loops using the free Apple Loops Utility included with Logic Pro or available for download at http://developer.apple.com/sdk/#AppleLoops.

ACID: Originally developed for the PC app Sony ACID, ACIDized files are now widely used on both the Mac and the PC. ACIDized files contain tempo, beat, and key information, but not keywords. Just as Apple Loops are AIFFs with additional information, ACID files use the standard WAV format, so even if your software doesn't natively support the ACID information, it can use the loop as a plain WAV.

REX: These audio files are created using ReCycle by Propellerhead. They are widely used on the Mac and the PC because of the flexibility of REX file slices, although the format doesn't contain keywords or key information.

GarageBand is designed to work primarily with Apple Loops but it also supports the popular ACID format.

Kinetic's audio loops use the ACID format.

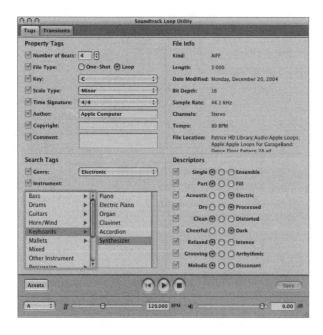

Figure 5.3 Loop files store not only audio but meta information as well. An Apple Loop, shown here being edited in the Soundtrack Loop Utility (now called Apple Loop Utility), includes information like keywords, instrument type and genre, tempo, and key.

Musical Uses

Drum machines that emulated the patterns of rock drummers were among the first commercial pattern-based hardware. Hip-hop and so-called dance music seized on the unique, mechanical sounds they provided.

People often refer to loop-based music or pattern-based editing as though they're new forms of music—often associating them solely with dance music and electronica—but the underlying concept isn't new at all. Musical traditions of all cultures use repetition and pattern.

By carefully stitching patterns and loops together and using variation, you can create pieces that sound more organic and musical—or, if you prefer, more mechanical and odd. Either way, there are endless musical possibilities.

We'll look at two ways people most commonly use loops and patterns. The first is to create a backing track for rehearsing, songwriting, or performing, letting the loops fill in for parts you can't play. The second is to build repetitive grooves for interactive dance music. Although we'll use GarageBand for the former and Kinetic for the latter, each is capable of both activities.

 Quick start: Pros like Us3 producer Geoff Wilkinson use loops and samples to help develop ideas and get an initial groove, then replace them with recorded music.

CREATE A BACKING TRACK (GARAGEBAND)

When you need accompaniment for practicing, backing tracks to fill in missing players for performances, or a way of quickly turning musical ideas into sketches, loop libraries like the one found in GarageBand are invaluable. GarageBand ships with a vast collection of ready-made musical materials, including selections from many different musical genres. You can make music in GarageBand without ever using these loops, but they can easily complement other recorded parts or stand on their own. Using sounds included with GarageBand, we'll create a country/folk rock arrangement, then record audio parts, and mix to create a completed song.

On the DVD: You'll find a completed GarageBand project created via the steps here. If you're on Windows or don't own GarageBand, MP3 files are also included so you can hear the results.

Since GarageBand matches the tempo of loops automatically, it's possible to combine loops even if they had a different original tempo. GarageBand doesn't match the rhythmic feel of materials, so you may have to audition a few clips to find one that sounds right.

GarageBand at a Glance

GarageBand is at its core a full DAW without a complex user interface (**Figure 5.4**). It combines basic multitrack recording, editing of audio and MIDI, a complement of effects and instruments borrowed from Apple Logic, and a loop browser and loop library.

Figure 5.4 Basic Garage-Band 2.0 interface.

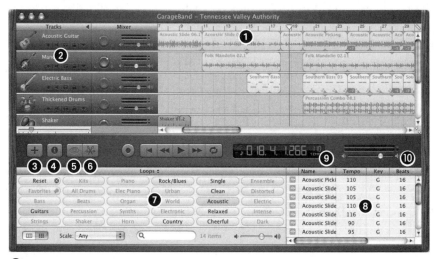

❶ Multiple tracks combine audio and MIDI, including linear material, loops, and patterns
❷ Record-enable, mute, solo, lock tracks, and hide/show automation of volume and pan
❸ Add instrument
❹ Edit instrument settings
❺ Open loop browser
❻ Edit track/region
❼ Select loop category
❽ Audition loops
❾ Master transport and tempo
❿ Master volume

 Want more loops? You can find loops and instruments to suit any taste, from classical-sounding and jazz to rock and electronica, from Apple, third-party companies, and even free online. Before using a loop in a commercially released song, it's important to read the fine print, as some loops are sold with licensing restrictions.
Apple Jam Packs (www.apple.com/garageband/jampacks)
Big Fish Audio (www.bigfishaudio.com)
East West (www.soundsonline.com)
iCompositions: tools guide, third-party products, and free loops (www.icompositions.com/tools)
SmartLoops (www.smartloops.com)

Basic GarageBand Workflow

Here are the basic steps you'll work through to create a song in GarageBand:

1. **Start a song:** Select key and tempo.

2. **Pick out loops:** Browse in the loop browser for the loops you want, then drag them into your song for use as backing tracks, temporary "comp" tracks, or even a whole song.

3. **Arrange your song (or backing tracks):** Drag loops to move them to different starting points or drag their end points to extend them so that they repeat for more bars.

4. **Record yourself:** Add your own performances from your MIDI keyboard, microphones, or guitar input.

5. **Edit:** Edit MIDI loops or parts of your performance.

6. **Add effects and mix:** If desired, adjust the effects on tracks, and change the panning and volume.

7. **Wrap it:** Export to iTunes or CD.

 ACID-compatible: ACIDized WAV files commonly found on the Web (and included on this book's DVD) can be used with GarageBand. The only disadvantage is you can't browse and search them with the Loop Browser; otherwise, they'll work just like Apple Loops.

Optional Hardware

You can complete this GarageBand walkthrough with just a computer (see **Figure 5.5**), but additional hardware offers other options:

- An audio interface will enable additional inputs. With GarageBand 2 or later you can record multiple inputs simultaneously (depending on how capable your computer is).

- A MIDI device like a keyboard or MIDI guitar will let you play in parts.

- An iPod or other playback device will let you take your backing track with you.

Figure 5.5 If you don't have a MIDI keyboard handy, you can enter notes with your mouse by selecting Window > Keyboard. Better yet, in GarageBand 2 or later, select Window > Musical Typing to use your computer's QWERTY keyboard to input notes.

Tutorial 1: Start a Song and Choose Loops

We'll begin this walkthrough by using loops as they're found in the Loop Browser, and then walk through the steps to add them to the process.

To select loops, click the appropriate categories in the Loop Browser. For example, click Reset in the upper-left corner of the loop categories to ensure all categories are deselected, then click Bass > Rock/Blues > Edgy Rock Bass 01.

To make sure we're placing the loop in the right place, we'll refer to measure (bar) numbers (using the abbreviations "m" and "mm" for measure numbers). You can find bars and beats on the ruler at the top of GarageBand: the numbers are bar numbers, and each tick is a beat.

Loop ingredients:

Guitars > Rock/Blues > Acoustic Vamp 01

GarageBand tools:

Loop Browser
Automatic Loop Placement
Cycle

1. **Choose the tempo, time signature, and key:** Start GarageBand and either respond to the prompt when the program starts or select File > Create a New Project. For this tune, choose 110 bpm (beats per minute) 4/4 time, in G Minor. (If you're using GarageBand 1.x, you can't specify major or minor.)

2. **Clear the piano:** We don't need a piano track right now, so let's delete it: select it and press Command-Delete. GarageBand Tracks can use processor cycles even when they're inactive, so deleting them reduces the load on your CPU.

3. **Browse loops:** The Loop Browser at the bottom of GarageBand's window lists the available loop categories by instrument and genre. If it's hidden, click the blue eye-shaped icon to display it. Clicking on

categories or searching lets you choose loops; you can click on any loop to *audition* it before you add it to your arrangement. The Reset button clears selected categories.

Tip: Not all the loop categories are shown. To view even more options, mouse over a blank part of the toolbar (your cursor should change to a hand) and drag up to expand the window.

4. **Find a "starter loop" you like:** You want your backup band to provide you with some musical inspiration, so find a loop that immediately makes you want to play. Typically, you'll choose the instrument you want first and genre/style second to narrow your choices. For this tune, click Guitars > Rock/Blues > Acoustic Vamp 1 to set the mood.

5. **Add the loop to your song:** Once you've found the loop you want, drag it to the empty space below the time ruler at the top, making sure your position (indicated by a vertical line) matches up with the "1" on the ruler for the beginning of the song (m. 1). GarageBand automatically configures a track to play your guitar loop. A loop that's been added to a song is called a *region*.

6. **Try out the mix:** You could simply click Play at this point, but to loop the playback, click the *Cycle* button first. GarageBand automatically sets cycle points for the first four measures, indicated by a yellow bar on the top timeline. This makes it convenient to jam with your instrument or vocals as the loops play, or audition new loops you're considering adding. Click Cycle again when you're done to return to nonlooped playback.

Tip: In cycle playback, you can adjust how much of your song is looped by dragging the yellow bar. Drag the center to move it around or the edges to change the loop start and end points.

Tutorial 2: Create a Basic Arrangement

One loop repeating indefinitely is a long way from a full song. By dragging additional loops from the Loop Browser to new tracks, we'll create new parts and add some musical structure to our song. This will mimic the entrances of live musicians.

Loop ingredients:

Shaker > Shaker 01, Shaker 02

Slide Guitar > Acoustic Slide 06, 01, 02

Slide Guitar > Acoustic Picking 21

Guitars > Country > Folk Mandolin 02

Kits > Country > Southern Beat 02

Bass > Country > Southern Bass 02, 03

Kits > Rock Blues > Ensemble > Percussion Combo 08

GarageBand tools:

Loop placement and stretching

1. **Extend the loop:** If you position your mouse over the upper-right edge of the Acoustic Vamp 1 region, your cursor changes from an arrow to a loop. Drag to the right, and you can seamlessly repeat the audio. Too many repetitions can become boring, so repeat it just once, ending it at m. 9. (You can see where a loop repeats by observing where its edges curve, as at m. 5.)

2. **Add another instrument:** Staggering the addition of new sounds helps shape the song, so before we bring in our drummer, let's get the groove going with just a shaker: try Shaker 01. Drag it into the empty area below the guitar track to create a new track, lining up the shaker entrance two bars after the guitar at m. 3.

3. **Mix it up:** Since real musicians (we hope) don't play exactly the same part ad infinitum, we'll add some variation: Drag to repeat Shaker 01 once more (ending at m. 7), then add a bit more intensity to the end of the guitar phrase by adding Shaker 02 (mm. 7–9), then add Shaker 01 once more (mm. 9–11). The acoustic guitar can switch patterns, too.

Place Acoustic Slide 06 at m. 9 next to the previous loop. We'll leave two bars of silence in the shaker part; a drummer also playing shaker would need time to pick up her sticks.

4. **Get the song rolling:** Adding multiple instruments gives us the sense of an ensemble and makes this piece start to sound like music. Create new tracks by adding and extending drums and mandolin parts. Add another Acoustic Slide region to the existing acoustic guitar track. Since we can shape the music as much by what we leave out as what we put in, create a bass track but have the bass enter four bars later than the other parts. Then add more musical variety by giving the acoustic guitar a solo: add a different Acoustic Slide at m. 20, dropping out the other parts.

Get the song rolling:

mm. 13–20: Southern Beat 02, Folk Mandolin 02, Acoustic Slide 01

mm. 17–20: Southern Bass 02

mm. 20–24: Acoustic Slide 02

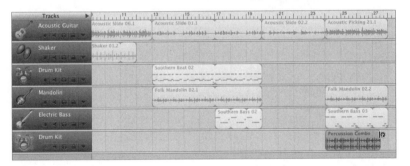

5. **Thicker ensemble:** After the guitar break, we'll thicken things up a bit with more instrumental layers in measures 24–28. For a fuller percussion pattern, we'll add a new percussion track to the bottom (*Percussion Combo 08* needs its own track because it's an audio region, not MIDI, like the Drum Kit track). We'll also have the guitarist switch to picking and bring back mandolin and bass (switching to Southern Bass 03 for variety). Now click the leftmost transport button (single left-pointing arrow) to return the track to the beginning, then click Play to hear the results. (The arrangement will end a bit abruptly, but it's a start!)

Thicker ensemble— all in mm. 24–28:

Percussion Combo 08
Acoustic Picking 21
Folk Mandolin 02
Southern Bass 03

Tutorial 3: Develop a Song Structure

To further mimic the way real musicians play, we'll make the repetitions tighter and less mechanical, and add chord changes so the song doesn't get stuck in one harmony for its duration.

Loop ingredients:

Strings > Ensemble > Orchestra Strings 02

GarageBand tools:

Region duplication

Region transposition

1. **Tighten it up:** By removing unneeded repetition, we can make this song a little more exciting. First, remove two bars each of the first acoustic vamp and shaker regions: drag the right edge of the acoustic vamp so that it ends at m. 7 (instead of m. 9) and the right edge of Shaker 01 so it ends at m. 5 (instead of m. 7). Second, move the rest of the song arrangement left by dragging across the other regions to select them and dragging them until they line up again with the acoustic guitar and shaker regions. (There shouldn't be any gap between them.)

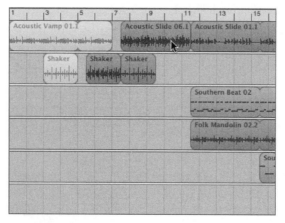

2. **Halve the Acoustic Slide:** Because *Acoustic Slide 02* has an internal repetition in it, we don't really need it to last the full four bars. To divide it in half, drag its right edge: mouse to the center of its edge so that your cursor changes to a straight line with a right arrow (instead of the loop), then drag left so that it ends at m. 20. Once again move the remaining regions: move the remaining four loops left from m. 22 to m. 20 to fill the gap. It's a lot of work, but it's worth it. Listen to how much tighter the arrangement sounds.

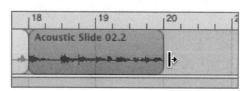

We'll create individual duplicates of the guitar and bass (1) so we can change their pitch and leave the mandolin and percussion (2) loop as is. We'll create a four-bar pattern (3), two two-bar patterns (4), and two one-bar patterns (5) by Option-dragging them into place.

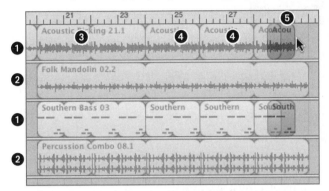

3. **Duplicate and divide regions to add chord changes:** By dividing separate regions, we can create a song structure. Duplicate the bass and acoustic picking regions: Shift-click to select both regions, then hold down the Option key and drag them to m. 24. Shorten the copied regions so they're only two bars in length, extending them from m. 24 to 26 (you'll need to use the center edge of the acoustic picking region, just as in step 2). Then Option-drag the new two-bar regions to mm. 26–28 and 28–30 to duplicate and move them two more times. Shorten the regions at mm. 28–30 so they're only one bar in length, and Option-drag one last time so you have one-bar regions at m. 28 and 29. Finally, extend the last folk mandolin and percussion combo regions so they extend from m. 20 to m. 30. (We won't transpose either of these regions.)

4. **Transpose regions:** Now that we've divided the regions, we can transpose them. Select the second and final guitar and bass regions (mm. 24–26 and m. 29); hold down the Shift key and click each region to select them simultaneously. Click the track editor button (the one that looks like a pair of scissors cutting a waveform), and slide the Region Pitch fader (under Track, on the left) to transpose the regions' pitch to –7. (For those with some musical background, the fader works in semitones or half steps, so –7 is equivalent to the musical interval of a perfect fifth downward.) Select the guitar and bass in m. 28 and transpose them to –5. (We'll leave the other parts alone: the mandolin sounds fine where it is, and you obviously wouldn't transpose the

Why so many steps?
GarageBand's loops tend to get stuck in one key. By dividing regions, we can create a harmonic structure (chord changes) by applying pitch changes to the loops. We'll have chord changes that last 4 bars, then 2 bars + 2 bars, then 1 bar + 1 bar.

Transpose regions:

mm. 20–24: Not transposed

mm. 24–26: –7

mm. 26–28: Not transposed

mm. 28–29: –5

mm. 29–30: –7

drums.) Listen to the song: it should sound like a standard blues/rock chord progression. When you're done, switch back to the Loop Browser by clicking the "eye" icon again.

Finish the song:

mm. 32–48: Percussion Combo 08

mm. 32–52: Southern Bass 03

mm. 36–44: Folk Mandolin 02

mm. 35–36: Acoustic Slide 02

mm. 36–52: Acoustic Slide 01

mm. 32–52: Orchestra Strings 02

5. **Finish the song:** To give this short excerpt a sense of wholeness, we'll add one more *Acoustic Slide 02* before bringing back the percussion combo and bass (mandolin and more slide guitar). Sparing no "expense," add one final ingredient: *Orchestra Strings 02*—an element your real band probably can't afford. (If you are wondering why there are so many repeats, sit tight: we're going to fade out the end, so we'll need some extra repetitions.)

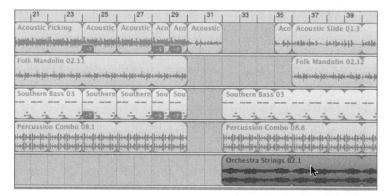

Tutorial 4: Mix and Record

With the basic elements in place, it's time for some fit and finish. Adjusting the panning, volume and fades, and effects of the mix will help get the exact sound you want. At this point you can also record your own vocals or acoustic instrument, adding them to the computer-generated tracks.

1. **Adjust pan and volume:** At this point, all the tracks are *panned* center and mixed at exactly the same volume, so it's hard to differentiate parts. To adjust settings for an entire track, open the Mixer panel by clicking the triangle next to Tracks (if it's not open already). Adjust the pan knob and volume until they sound right to you. To begin with, adjust the volume fader for the strings so that they don't overwhelm the other parts; adjust its volume fader slightly to the left.

2. **Sweeten the sound:** GarageBand offers various built-in effects for modifying your sound. Select the second of the two Drum Kit tracks (the one with the audio drums) and click the Track Info button (the one with the letter "i" on it). Click "Drums" in the left column and a number of presets appear in the right column; try selecting different settings and auditioning the sound. (These effects work in real time as your project plays, so simply click Play and try different settings.) If you want to fine-tune the preset or see how it was created, click Details. You can save your own presets as Instruments. For now, let's leave the drums with no effects. To change the master effects through which all the tracks are routed, select Master Track. Try the setting Rock/Pop > Live Gig.

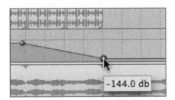

3. **Fade out the end: S**o the song doesn't end abruptly, we'll fade out the tracks. You could fade out the whole mix by adjusting the Master Track (Tracks > Show Master Track), but for more subtlety we'll adjust them

Effect ingredients:

Master Track > Rock/Pop > Folk Rock

GarageBand tools:

Volume and pan for tracks, volume/pan automation

Effects presets

Master track

Real instrument, software instrument

Recording

Editing

individually. To bring up pan/volume automation for a track, click the triangle below the track name. Click once on the blue or green filled-in area in the Track Volume lane where you want the fade to begin. Then click where you want the fade to end, and drag the ball down so the volume is lowered. Repeat this process for each track. GarageBand automatically adjusts the volume gradually between these two points for a smooth fade. Continue to fine-tune these adjustments until your fades sound just right. Try letting the drums just drop out, creating gradual fades of several bars for the remaining parts.

4. **Add your voice or instrument:** Now that the "backing" part of our backing track is done, the rest of the music is up to you. (If you just want to play live over the GarageBand track without recording yourself, you can skip the remaining steps and continue to the next section.) Set up your recording by clicking the New Track button. If you're recording your voice or instrument through an audio interface, select Real Instrument and the setting you want. Choose the instrument preset and appropriate input, and turn on monitoring to check the input through GarageBand. If you're recording via a MIDI keyboard or other controller and want to use your computer to generate the sound, select Software Instrument. (If you're using a guitar, you can plug in directly and take advantage of GarageBand's built-in amp simulations, or mike your guitar's amp.)

5. **Record and edit:** In GarageBand 1.x, simply select the track on which you want to record. In GarageBand 2 and later, you can *arm* one or more tracks (enable it for recording) by clicking the Record button under the name of the track(s). In all versions, once you're ready, click Record or press the R key to begin. When you're done, you can edit your recorded track (or any of the tracks in the song) by selecting the Edit Track button. If the track is a green MIDI track, you can directly edit notes, either via a graphical view or, in GarageBand 2 and later, in traditional music notation.

Share Your Work: iTunes

Once your mix is done, you're ready to save and share your work. File > Export to iTunes will automatically mixdown or bounce your audio to a single stereo mix and include it in an iTunes playlist. Some strategic use of GarageBand and iTunes, however, can make this feature even more useful:

• **Choose a playlist name:** From the GarageBand menu, select Preferences > Export (**Figure 5.6**). By changing the playlist from the default, you can manage projects more effectively in iTunes.

• **Make iTunes your personal musical assistant:** Create a playlist of songs-in-progress you're working on, for instance, or store rehearsal sets, performance sets, or albums, by setting different playlist names. Using iPod preferences, you can selectively load these on your iPod, too.

• **Export to a CD:** By right-clicking on a playlist title in iTunes, you can burn a CD.

• **Compress to AAC in iTunes:** By default, GarageBand saves to the uncompressed AIFF file format, so even the short tune we just created is a whopping 20.5 MB—too big for e-mail or the Web. Right-click on the song in iTunes, and you can convert your song to the high-quality compressed AAC format, the format used by the iTunes Music Store. Drag that file out of iTunes to the desktop or a folder for emailing or uploading. (Unlike music store songs, it's not copy-protected.)

Figure 5.6 By customizing GarageBand's export settings (left), you can create a custom playlist, so your next rehearsal session will have all your current backing tracks. From iTunes, you can listen to your tracks, burn a CD, or drop songs on your iPod (right).

Getting More Advanced with GarageBand

GarageBand may be considered a "beginner" application, but it's advanced enough to be used by pros like John Mayer, punk rocker and BBC Radio 6 host Tom Robinson, and Barenaked Ladies' Ed Robertson, who uses it for backup tracks during performance and for sketching. Here are a few of the more advanced features you can utilize once you outgrow the basics of fiddling with loops:

- **Use notation and editing:** Record your instrument or MIDI device in your own tracks and edit them, adjusting pitch, timing, and MIDI events where needed. Using GarageBand 2 and later, you can even view your work as a score. (See Chapter 8 for more on using MIDI; GarageBand has some powerful MIDI editing features.)

- **Make your own loops:** Just because you're working with loops doesn't mean you can't use original material. With GarageBand 2 and later, you can save any region as a loop: drag it to the Loop Browser or select it and choose Edit > Add to Loop Browser. You can even categorize it for later use (**Figure 5.7**). Since Apple Loops can be used with any digital audio program (even the Loop Browser in Logic), you can easily move short segments of audio to other projects.

Figure 5.7 When you create a new loop, GarageBand lets you add category information.

Learn more: Writer/producer/musician Francis Preve has written a book devoted to advanced GarageBand use. Check out *Power Tools for GarageBand: Creating Music with Audio Recording, MIDI Sequencing, and Loops* (Backbeat Books, 2004).

- **Work with Logic and other software:** Since the audio quality of programs like GarageBand is basically the same CD-quality digital audio you'll get from other applications, there's no reason you can't sketch in GarageBand and then move to another program for additional editing options. Logic will open GarageBand projects. You can also export audio tracks or loops to other programs, but you'll need to recreate your song arrangement from scratch, as other programs can't load GarageBand song files.

MAKE A GROOVE BOX (KINETIC)

DJing by just shuffling records can be a little boring, but triggering grooves interactively and playing over them, well that's more fun. Software like Kinetic makes this easy: you can manipulate, mix, and even create grooves from drums, beats, bass, and instrumental sounds. Kinetic is packed with audio and MIDI loops, just like GarageBand. But unlike GarageBand, instead of painting loops in one at a time, you can trigger groups of them all at once, locking them to beats so that the dance floor doesn't miss a beat.

Kinetic at a Glance

Kinetic's interface is inspired by physical hardware (**Figure 5.8**). Its central interface element is a 16-part mixer with traditional channel strips and

On the DVD: Follow along with these steps using a 30-day demo of Kinetic; the project you save can be used with the purchased version. In addition to a finished version of the project, you'll find an exclusive sample project from Cakewalk. (Mac users, if you want to hear the results, MP3 files are provided, as well.)

ACID support: Kinetic supports the popular ACIDized loop format used by many PC programs, so you can choose from a wide variety of loop libraries.

faders, plus a 4x4 grid for triggering grooves. The top of the screen is dedicated to mixing, the middle to editing parts, and the bottom to arranging songs (although if you're DJing, you're likely to ignore the bottom and trigger grooves live, using the arrangement feature to record your set).

Figure 5.8 An overview of Kinetic's interface.

➊ Section for mixing grooves
➋ Section for editing parts
➌ Section for arranging songs (or recording a set)
➍ Groove picker for triggering grooves
➎ Mixer for setting volume and pan for parts of grooves
➏ Select a pattern or audio loop, grouped by genre
➐ Select an instrument to play the pattern
➑ Play/record arrangements
➒ Draw in arrangements

Kinetic is a groove box, loop library, and software synth (with virtual instruments from Cakewalk and Roland) all in one. Since it integrates all these elements, you can use it to build a groove, starting from the smallest element and working up to the song:

1. **Patterns and Audio Loops:** Patterns and loops are the basic musical elements of your song. Just like GarageBand, Kinetic can handle both MIDI data and audio, although all of the audio loops shipped with Kinetic are drums (other drum patterns and all of the other instrument parts are MIDI).

2. **Patches:** Patches include the settings for instruments that will play your patterns, plus (via the Audio FX Bin) effects for both patterns and audio loops.

3. **Parts:** Once you've selected an audio loop, or a pattern and a patch, you can assign it to one of the 16 available parts—that is, the slots on the mixer—to create a groove from multiple parts (patches).

4. **Grooves:** Those 16 parts (complete with mixing, panning, and effects) can be combined into a single groove selected by the Groove Picker. A groove might include just one simple part or a combination of drums, bass, leads, and pads—up to 16 parts at once. Up to 64 grooves can be used in a song.

Sixteen parts may not seem like much, but typically you'll only layer 4–5 parts at a time. Multiply 16 parts times 16 grooves in the Groove Picker, then multiply those times four (the A, B, C, and D selectors), then add the ability to play synths over top of the mix, and you have enough music to carry you through the night.

🔑 Basic Kinetic Workflow

Here's a typical way to work with Kinetic to create your own project:

1. Create a new project, either using a blank file or a template.
2. Press Play to start the grooves.
3. Edit grooves by browsing and selecting pre-built patterns and patches, or record or draw in your own patterns, edit them, and add effects.
4. Create grooves by combining up to 16 parts into a groove.
5. Choose different grooves by selecting banks A–D and buttons 1–16 to trigger grooves, or paint them into the Song Arranger.

Optional Hardware

You can complete this walkthrough with just a computer (and Kinetic is unusually well-suited to jamming on an airplane with your laptop and headphones), but using additional hardware does have advantages:

- A keyboard allows you to play virtual instruments over the top of your grooves.

- A control surface (or keyboard with knobs and/or faders) makes it easy to trigger grooves and effects without laboring over your laptop and mouse.

Tutorial 1: Patches, Patterns, and Grooves

We're going to begin our Kinetic walkthrough with the ingredients at left. By adding musical elements to the Groove Picker, we'll gradually assemble a basic arrangement with bass, drums, and keyboards—our first "groove."

Groove ingredients:

Patch 1: Bass > 101 Bass 3
Pattern 1: Bass > US Hard House > USHardHse2_bs
Patch 2: Drums > Kits > Hip-Hop 1
Pattern 2: Drums > Hip-Hop > HipHopEast1_drm
Patch 3: Pianos > El Piano > Cuttin' Analog
Pattern 3: Leads > Trance > Trance2_lead

Kinetic tools:

Groove Picker
MIDI Patterns and Sounds
Choosing Pattern & Patch
Part mixer (volume and pan)

1. **Create a project:** Choose File > Project to start your set. You can use a set that's already configured by choosing File > Project From Template File, but we'll start ours from scratch.

2. **Start playback:** To audition beats in Kinetic's browser, Play must be activated first. (You may have noticed the Play button pulsing to entice you to click it!) Select a tempo (and, if you like, a swing setting) from the top of the screen, then click the Play button in the Groove Picker keypad. Try 126 bpm. Note that you can use the Spacebar to play and stop. If channel 1 isn't selected in the mixer, select it by clicking in an empty part of that channel.

3. **Pick a patch, then a pattern (Groove 1, Part 1):** Kinetic assumes you're creating a traditional dance music track with bass, drums, leads, and pads. Building up the groove one element at a time can be more interesting and musically useful, so we'll start with bass. You won't hear anything until you choose an instrument, so select your Patch first.

Then, find a pattern you like, browsing by genre. (You may want to adjust the Patch so it works well with the pattern.) Let's try 101 Bass 3 (patch) playing USHardHse2_bs (pattern).

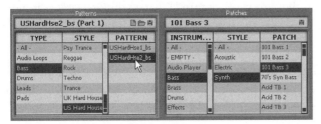

4. **Add a drum part (Groove 2, Part 2):** We want more than just bass, so right-click on groove A1 and choose Copy Groove 1 To: > Next Preset [A2]; the bass pattern appears in both A1 and A2. Now we can add another part. Click part 2 in the mixer to highlight it, and again pick a patch and pattern. In honor of Cakewalk's Boston roots, we'll add some East Coast hip-hop drums with Drums > Kits > Hip-Hop 1 playing Drums > Hip-Hop > HipHopEast1_drm.

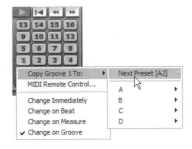

5. **Add some keyboard (Groove 3, Part 3):** As before, right-click on Groove 2 and choose Copy Groove 2 To: > Next Preset [A3]; the bass and drum patterns will now be heard in grooves A2 and A3. Click part 3 in the mixer to highlight it, and again pick a patch and pattern. This time, try Pianos > El Piano > Cuttin' Analog playing the pattern Leads > Trance > Trance2_lead.

Ignore these directions: Part of the fun of MIDI is the ability to quickly hear a pattern on a different instrument—sometimes with radical results. Try playing patterns on the wrong instruments. Even experimenting with drums on keyboards and the reverse can produce interesting results. These alternative selections aren't just useful in Kinetic: sometimes trying this technique on your own MIDI recordings can free up your creativity.

6. **Switch between grooves (Groove 1, 2, 3):** Here's the fun part: you can now bring the drums and lead part in and out, locked to tempo and phrase, by clicking on Groove Picker buttons 1, 2, and 3. Set "Change on Measure" in the Groove Picker to "Change on Groove" so it will automatically change at the end of a groove (two bars here) instead of just at the end of the bar.

7. **Mind the mix:** Try adjusting the mix of your three parts: adjust the volume faders if you're not happy with their blend, and adjust the pan pots off center (make one part a little to the left, one to the right) to give this mix more space.

Tutorial 2: Build Up a Set of Grooves

To build up the Kinetic song, we'll add the patterns and patches at left. After each addition, right-click on the pattern button in the Groove Picker and copy the groove to the next preset. This will allow you to switch back and forth, cueing different elements in and out of the mix with a single mouse-click.

Groove ingredients:

Patch 4: Pianos > Keyboards > Vintage Clavi

Pattern 4: Pads > Jazz > Jazz2_pad

Pattern 5: Audio Loops > Tribal > 129 TRIBAL LOOP 1

Patch 6: Synth Pads > Analog > --..---..- (think Morse Code)

Pattern 6: Drums > Dream Trance > DreamTnc1_drm

Kinetic tools:

Audio FX

Included effects

Audio Loops

Muting

1. **Add effects (Groove 3, Part 3):** The keyboard part (which should be in mixer channel 3, if you've been following the list of parts given above) is working fairly well, but it's a little dull. After selecting this mixer channel, click Part Editor > Edit Patch to add effects. Right-click under Audio FX, then choose Effects > Project5 > Modfilter. You'll see four of Modfilter's most commonly adjusted settings on the right (for more settings, double-click the Modfilter to see its full interface). Above those four knobs, click the drop-down list to choose a preset like Little Engine or Sweep, Med.

Now add a second effect to the chain by selecting Effects > Project5 > Tempo Delay. If necessary, drag the Tempo Delay to the right, so it will process the output of the Modfilter. Try the Pinging Double-Time preset, but set Sync to 50% to tighten it up, and increase the Time Right setting to add more stereo delay. Now you have a tempo-synced delay effect for a richer groove.

2. **Add Clav (Groove 4, Part 4):** The tune is sounding a little mechanical, so let's add some funk. Copy A3 to A4, then add Jazz2_pad on the Clavi to part 4. It already sounds like a Hohner Clavinet, but it'll cut through the mix better if it's routed through a swirling phaser effect as is popular with real Clavs (see Chapter 7 for more on phasers). Select Part Editor > Edit Patch > Audio FX and choose Effects > Project 5 > Classic Phaser, then choose the Phatty Quad preset. Slightly increase the Sync setting to your preference. (Notice that although we have two sounds that are technically keyboards, they're different enough in pitch range to sound good together.) Again, copy your groove (from A4 to A5).

3. **Add an Audio Loop (Groove 5, Part 5):** So far, we've been using MIDI parts only. Try Audio Loop Tribal Loop 1 on part 5. You don't need to select a patch; Kinetic automatically selects the Groove Player (although, just as with a MIDI patch, you can add effects by clicking Edit Patch). This overlaps with our original Hip-Hop drums, so mute them by clicking the M button just below its name on part 2. Muting, pan, and volume are all specific to grooves, so muting the drums on groove 5 won't mute them on grooves 1–4.

4. **Create more grooves:** From here on, you can copy your grooves to wherever you like. Remember to copy the groove each time so you can make changes in the Groove Picker one step at a time. To quickly round out this particular tune, we'll switch the Clav in part 4 to a new pattern (Trance1_pad) on groove 6, add another part on groove 7 (Part 6,

DreamTnc1_drm), and gradually mute parts to thin out the texture and round out the song. Then remove the part 5 drums in groove 8, the part 1 bass in groove 9, the part 4 Clav in groove 10, and the Trance1 beeps in groove 11.

Tutorial 3: Ready for the Dance Floor

With the grooves in place, you're set to turn your home studio (or club, if you want) into a dance inferno. The key to producing this result is real-time, tempo-locked triggering of the grooves we've just assembled.

Kinetic tools:

MIDI Remote Control

Para-Q

Song Arranger, Export

MIDI Controller (optional)

1. **Change grooves:** Try out your custom groove box by clicking on different buttons in the Groove Picker. Thanks to the Change on Groove setting, everything will sync up nicely. Move sequentially through grooves to build up or remove parts of the mix, or try jumping through the structure out of order for changes with more contrast. If you have a keyboard, add an instrument on another part and jam over the top.

2. **Thin out the mix:** Try switching back to groove 1 with just the bass for four bars (perhaps between grooves 5 and 6)—the sudden sparseness makes for some dynamic contrast. Notice that we've covered ourselves by assigning the Tempo Delay effect to the analog keyboard patch. This traditional DJ trick ensures that when other parts drop out, delay spills over the silence rather than the sound stopping abruptly.

3. **Control grooves:** If you have a MIDI device—a keyboard or any other controller—you can use that instead of a mouse to control the grooves. Just right-click on the button or knob in the Kinetic interface you want to assign. For example, right-click one of the grooves, select MIDI Remote Control, and click Learn. Press the button or key you want to use to switch to that groove, then click Stop Learning. (Alternatively, enter the information manually with Control Source, although Learn is generally

easier.) Repeat this procedure for the other grooves, and you can "play" your grooves using your keyboard or other device.

4. **Control a filter sweep:** A must-have physical control is a DJ-style filter sweep: it's no fun with a mouse, but it's perfect for a fader, mod wheel, or (best of all) a knob. (See Chapter 7 for more on equalization and filtering, but you'll probably recognize the sound.) Select part 5 (the Groove Player) and select Edit Patch. Right-click Audio FX and add a 2-band parametric equalizer: Effects > Project 5 > Para-Q. Increase Gain 1 to 100%, then assign a MIDI knob or slider to Frequency 1 (right-click, select MIDI Remote Control, and follow the Learn procedure in step 3). Now, using your knob or slider, gradually sweep through the filter with this groove playing.

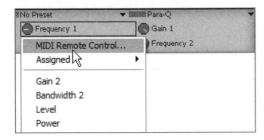

5. **Play, record, share:** Using the Song Arranger, it's possible to paint grooves into the arrangement with the mouse, but instead (especially if your live MIDI controller performance is hot) click the Record button in the Arranger or hit the R key before triggering the grooves. Click

Stop when your set is done, and your whole set is recorded. Click Export Song to save it as a WAV file and burn it to disc or convert it with iTunes, Windows Media Player, or another program. (The MP3 converter in Kinetic costs extra, but you can convert your songs to MP3 or OGG for free in Audacity.)

Getting More Advanced with Kinetic

Kinetic may be an entry-level app, but as a groove station it integrates perfectly with other parts of a software studio. Here are some of the more advanced features Kinetic offers:

- **Make your own patterns:** With a MIDI keyboard (or simply by painting in notes or drum hits), you can create your own beats and melodic materials for the patches. You can even paint or record right over the top of the patterns we used in the preceding sections, because the pattern loops as it plays. Just select a pattern and click Edit Pattern.

- **Paint over the groove:** Using the Auto (automation) tool (**Figure 5.9**) in both the Part Editor and Sound Arranger, you can paint over your patterns and grooves to automatically adjust volume, pan, MIDI controllers (see Chapter 8), and even effect and instrument settings.

- **Save as Template:** By choosing Save as Template, you can build a custom groove toolkit for yourself for easy modification, so you don't have to repeat some of the steps we performed in this walkthrough.

- **Export audio loops, work with Project5:** Aside from exporting a song as audio, you can also export a single groove (complete with effects) for use in a program like Ableton Live (also included on the DVD). In addition, you can save files as Project5 files for use with Kinetic's "pro" sibling. Project5 is a more extensive program that is also based on hardware-style synth patches and pattern editing. Using Project5, you can expand the possibilities of what you can do with Kinetic alone.

- **ReWire Kinetic to other programs**: Since Kinetic is essentially a collection of virtual hardware plus some pattern editors, you can use ReWire to incorporate Kinetic into other programs you're using, like SONAR, Live, and Cubase. ReWire will automatically route audio from Kinetic into any of those programs, syncing to its tempo, a perfect setup for live performance with Ableton Live or studio sessions with other programs.

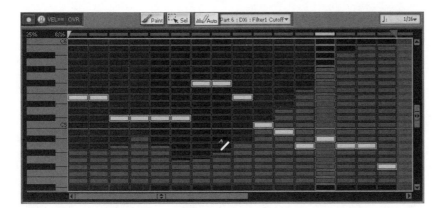

Figure 5.9 Record, paint, and edit your own patterns, then paint automation and MIDI data over the top of them using the Pattern Editor.

CHAPTER 6

Recording Instruments and Sound

If you understand how microphones work, you can use them to capture only the sounds you want, reject the sounds you don't want, and record your source as you want your listener to hear it. We'll first look at the ways in which microphone designs differ, and then see how they're typically employed in specific recording situations. Once you've chosen and set up your mic or mics, you can then try recording to disk using your own application or one of those provided on this book's companion DVD.

 Essentials

Recording Instruments and Sound

By learning about various kinds of mics and how they work, you'll have the tools you need for the recordings you want to make:

- How mic characteristics impact what kinds of sound they capture best
- Mic patterns and how they affect sound coming from different directions
- General strategies for miking close, at a distance, and for stereo
- Specific strategies for individual instruments
- Hands-on recording: monitoring, setting levels, and using Audacity and Ableton Live (included on DVD)

Essential Terms

- Diaphragm/capsule
- Mic characteristics: frequency/amplitude response; directionality
- Transient
- Polar response/mic pattern: omni, cardioid, supercardioid, bidirectional
- Mic constructions: dynamic; ribbon; condenser; boundary
- Phantom power
- Headroom
- Distortion/clipping
- Overdubbing

Where to Start

Make sure you have access to a good condenser and dynamic mic (see p. 164 for some examples), plus extras like a pop filter and stand. Then, try some of the hands-on tutorials at the end of this chapter.

MICROPHONE CHARACTERISTICS

Many different kinds of microphones are available, but fundamentally, they all work on the same principle: sound waves move a plate or membrane (*diaphragm*) inside the mic, and this movement is translated into electrical voltage. The exact details of how this is implemented impact the way recordings sound.

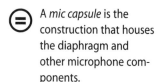 A *mic capsule* is the construction that houses the diaphragm and other microphone components.

While trying to figure out whether a given mic is the right choice for a particular recording chore, we need to look at several qualities:

- **Amplitude response:** Sensitivity to sounds of different loudness

- **Directionality:** Sensitivity to sounds coming from different angles

- **Frequency response:** Sensitivity to different parts of the frequency spectrum as well as specific low-frequency characteristics (**Figure 6.1**)

Figure 6.1 Frequency response curves vary by mic. A smooth response (top; a Shure KSM-32) responds relatively consistently across the frequency spectrum. (The dotted line shows the proximity effect: bass frequencies are boosted when the source is 15 centimeters from the mic as opposed to 60.) A less consistent curve (bottom; a Shure SM-58) might reduce low frequencies and accentuate mid frequencies. Smooth is not necessarily better: the response on the bottom can be perceived as a "warmer" sound and is intended for use with vocals. (Images courtesy Shure, Inc.)

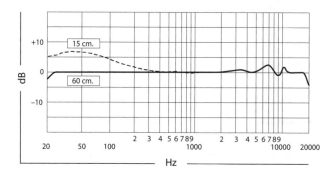

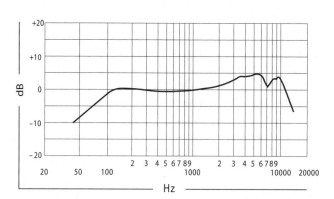

Different methods of microphone construction have certain shared properties. If you use the wrong mic for the job, you could fail to capture the sound you want, or even damage your mic. For instance, diaphragms respond uniquely when sound waves cause them to move, particularly with short, intense sounds (transients, as shown in **Figure 6.2**). Heavier diaphragms respond slowly to this abrupt change, thus distorting the sound of the transient, whereas lighter ones respond more quickly and are more likely to be damaged by sounds that are too powerful. You would thus match diaphragm size—and other physical properties of mics—to the qualities of the sound source you're recording. Put simply, use a fragile mic right against your guitar amp or kick drum, and you could break the mic! Other mic characteristics don't threaten the health of your mic, but can threaten the quality of your recordings, based on the position, frequency range, and amplitude range of your sound.

 A *transient* is any sudden change in signal. In audio recording this term is used to refer to the abrupt peak caused by sounds like a gunshot, drum hit, or the attack of a brass stab.

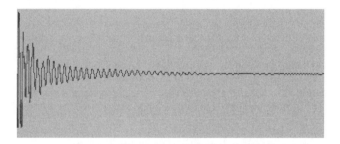

Figure 6.2 An example of a transient signal: a 2-second bass drum sample has a sharp transient at the beginning.

We'll observe frequency and amplitude response by different microphone types, but directionality can be easily described in terms of general *patterns*.

Mic Patterns

Microphones tend to be most sensitive to sounds that arrive directly perpendicular to the mic capsule, or *on-axis* (**Figure 6.3**). You've probably noticed TV reporters pointing their microphones at an interview subject in order to exploit this fact. Different microphones vary in how sensitive they are to off-axis sounds. A mic's relative sensitivity to sounds from different angles is called its *polar response* or, more commonly, a mic *pattern*.

On-axis

Figure 6.3 Directional microphones are most sensitive on-axis or near it, relative to the facing of their diaphragms. (Shure SM-58 image courtesy Shure, Inc.)

 Resources: Microphone Manufacturers

AEA
(vintage reproductions)
(www.ribbonmics.com)

AKG Acoustics
(www.akgacoustics.com)

Audio Technica
(www.audiotechnica.com)

Blue
(www.bluemic.com)

Crown
(www.crownaudio.com)

Electro-Voice
(www.electrovoice.com)

Neumann
(www.neumann.com)

Røde
(www.rodemic.com)

Royer
(www.royerlabs.com)

Sennheiser
(www.sennheiser.com)

Shure
(www.shure.com)

Studio Projects
(www.studioprojectsusa.com)

Directionality

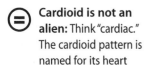

Cardioid is not an alien: Think "cardiac." The cardioid pattern is named for its heart shape.

A directional mic picks up sounds best from the front, whereas an *omnidirectional* mic picks up sounds fairly evenly in a 360-degree radius. Different mic patterns are directional to varying degrees (**Table 6.1**). Keep in mind that microphone response patterns differ at different frequencies. Even if you're using an omni mic, you may find sound coming from behind the microphone to be more hollow than sounds from the front.

Table 6.1 Basic Mic Patterns

Polar Response	Name, Width	Description and Applications
	Omnidirectional (widest)	Omni mics pick up sound nearly equally from all directions, so they're useful for picking up larger fields of sound or ambient sound, or in situations where direction from the source is uncertain. They're the most forgiving in terms of placement.
	Cardioid (narrower)	Cardioid microphones are the most commonly used, basic directional mics, because they respond well to sounds in front of them while rejecting potentially unwanted ambient sounds behind. This makes them especially useful for live applications, since they're less likely to pick up audience noise.
	Supercardioid/ Hypercardioid (narrowest)	Supercardioid microphones have a narrower pattern and are used to prevent bleed in crowded situations or other recordings that need to reject ambient sounds. Care must be taken in placement, however, because their narrowness is more unforgiving. Since, unlike cardioids, they are sensitive to the rear, you'll also need to keep monitors and other sources out of this area. Sometimes the terms super and hyper are used interchangeably.
	"Shotgun" (narrower supercardioid)	Supercardioid patterns are available in varying degrees: the narrowest versions of this pattern are "shotgun/long gun" or simply "gun," which reject more off-axis sounds in both front and rear.
	Bidirectional (sides are dead)	Bidirectional or "Figure of Eight" microphones pick up sounds from the front and rear while rejecting sound on the sides. "Front" means the front of the capsule, not the mic head. Because the capsule is mounted sideways, these microphones pick up sound from the sides.

Images courtesy Sennheiser Electronic Corporation. From top: Sennheiser MD 21-U dynamic, MD 421-II dynamic, MKH-50 condenser, MKH-70 condenser, MKH-30 condenser.

Proximity effect and cardioids

Cardioid microphones exhibit another unique behavior: their bass response becomes more pronounced as a sound source nears a microphone. This phenomenon is known as the *proximity effect*. You can try it with a cardioid mic by monitoring yourself as you get closer to the mic capsule while speaking. In some cases, as in miking instruments, this can be undesirable, but for spoken or sung vocals it's not uncommon to use it to intentionally add bass to the sound.

 Tip: Do you want a deeper "radio" voice? Try moving closer to your cardioid mic (you'll want to use a pop filter for the best results). You're now making intentional use of the proximity effect.

Choosing a mic pattern

You'll choose microphone patterns depending on the recording application. Journalists might work with omni microphones because they won't lose a critical interview if the subject speaks off-axis. Or they might use a highly directional mic if they need to reduce ambient noise. General music applications typically involve cardioid microphones, which screen out unwanted ambient sound while remaining flexible about positioning to the front. Extremely dense ensemble recordings may require multiple, discretely placed supercardioid or hypercardioid mics to prevent bleed.

Some microphones have a specific, fixed pattern and either are labeled as such or can be identified using manufacturer specifications. Others have a switchable capsule so you can adapt the mic to a specific recording situation (**Figure 6.4**).

 Patterns aren't perfect: Mic patterns are only ideal models of mic performance. Real cardioid mics don't completely eliminate sound from the rear (though they do reduce it), and reflections from nearby surfaces will further color your recording.

Figure 6.4 By using a mic with switchable patterns, you can change patterns without swapping mics. Neumann's U 47 first popularized this feature. Shown here are the knobs on its current stereo USM-69 mic. (Photo courtesy Georg Neumann GmbH)

Mic Type and Construction

Microphone *types* or *models* are families of microphones that share a means of construction and accompanying acoustic characteristics. The two most common types are dynamic and condenser mics, although ribbon mics are popular for recording as well. Traditionally, dynamic mics have been more affordable, but today many high-quality condenser mics compete even in the sub-$200 range; ribbon mics almost always command a higher price.

Because different mic designs produce various trade-offs, there's no perfect mic: even beginners should consider assembling a small "mic cabinet" of models for maximum flexibility and creative options. Typically, this would include at least a matched pair for stereo recording and a combination of condenser and dynamic mics. Even two or three good mics will provide additional choices for recording.

Needless to say, this isn't just "buying advice." Once you have several microphones to choose from, you'll regularly select certain microphones for different applications, so knowledge of mic types is critical to creating the recording you want.

 Tip: Starter mic ideas
A great recording can begin with relatively inexpensive mics; two matched dynamic mics and a condenser mic would be a good starting point. Here are some typical examples, although there are many options:
Dynamic: Shure SM57 / 58 / Beta 58 ($80–150 street), Blue The Ball or USB-compatible Blue Snowball ($100–150)—Ideal for drums, vocals, onstage
Condenser: Røde NT-1A ($200, shown), Studio Projects C1 ($200)—Ideal for vocals, instruments

Dynamic

Dynamic mics use a moving magnetic coil to produce voltage (**Figure 6.5**), so they're sometimes called *moving-coil* mics. They operate on the principle that any coil moving perpendicular to a magnetic field will create current, a process called *electromagnetic induction*. The fact that they require a physical coil to be moved is their primary advantage and disadvantage: dynamics are unusually resistant to air pressure and are the most rugged mics, but they're not as good at picking up high frequencies.

If you want a mic that can take some physical abuse or record loud sources, make sure you use a dynamic mic. You'll find it's invaluable for many other recording applications, too, which is why you won't find a pro studio in the world without an SM57 on hand.

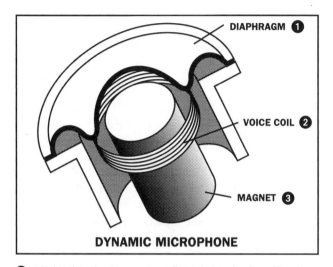

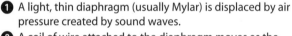

DYNAMIC MICROPHONE

Figure 6.5
Inside the dynamic capsule. (Illustration courtesy Shure, Inc.)

 Dynamic examples: Shure SM57/58, Sennheiser MD421 mk II (shown at the bottom of p. 164, courtesy Sennheiser Electronic Corporation)

Needs power? No

Pros: Rugged, wide amplitude range, often more affordable

Cons: Not as good at capturing high frequencies, tend to "bias" low-end, produce a weaker signal

Best for: General-purpose recording, loud recordings like drums and guitar amps, onstage applications

❶ A light, thin diaphragm (usually Mylar) is displaced by air pressure created by sound waves.
❷ A coil of wire attached to the diaphragm moves as the diaphragm moves.
❸ As the coil of wire moves it disrupts a fixed magnetic field, generating current, which is fed out of the mic as output signal.

 Genre-bending mics: You can't rely on rigid categories to understand microphones, because engineers are always breaking the rules. Case in point: Blue makes popular, powered dynamic mics like the USB-connected Snowball (pictured, courtesy Blue Microphones), an exception to the "rule" that dynamics don't need to be powered (see sidebar "Phantom Power", p. 167). By powering the mic, engineers are able to mix desirable qualities of condensers and dynamics, and make a mic that can be used in a wider variety of recording situations.

Condenser

Instead of using air pressure to create voltage by induction, condensers are already charged and use pressure to measure a change in charge in their circuitry. Two charged metal plates, one acting as a diaphragm and the other fixed, react to sound waves (**Figure 6.6**).

Condenser mics have a relatively smooth frequency response and are ideal for capturing softer instruments and high-frequency sounds, perfect for applications like recording acoustic guitar. Because they're more sensitive, however, they're not as suited to close miking or high-amplitude situations like kick drums. They also require power, either in the form of an internal battery or from an external source (see sidebar "Phantom Power").

Condensers are categorized by diaphragm size; you can immediately recognize them by the size of the microphone head. Narrow, *small-diaphragm* mics are usually less expensive and can be used onstage as handhelds, or to record instruments. Broader, *large-diaphragm* condensers are bigger and often more expensive, but offer higher recording quality.

Condenser examples: Shure KSM/27 (shown, courtesy Shure Inc.), AKG C1000S

Needs power? Yes

Pros: Smoothest overall frequency response

Cons: Less rugged; not suitable for close miking of loud sources

Best for: General studio recording, acoustic guitars, instruments and vocals where ruggedness is less critical

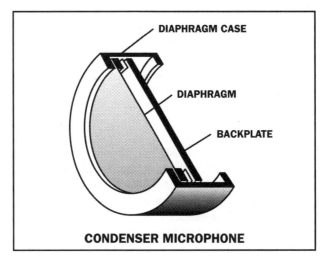

CONDENSER MICROPHONE

Figure 6.6 In a condenser mic, two charged plates form a capacitor. One of the plates, a light, thin metallic membrane called a diaphragm, moves in relation to the thicker, fixed metal backplate as air pressure from the sound pushes and pulls it. As the distance between the plates changes, current flows to or from the capacitor, forming the output signal. An internal amplifier (either transistors or tubes) makes this signal usable by increasing its strength. (Illustration courtesy Shure, Inc.)

Variations on construction have allowed the production of very inexpensive mics, although they sacrifice some recording quality. If you have a portable cassette recorder, it probably uses an *electret* mic. Electret condensers' diaphragms are internally charged, making electrets extremely cheap to manufacture, but they have thicker diaphragms and thus sacrifice high-end response. *Back-electret condensers* use the same principle, but by using a thinner membrane material, they behave more like the expensive models. Condensers for under $100, for instance, use this approach.

You say tomato, I say to-MAH-to: Condenser mics are sometimes called capacitor mics because the electrical terms capacitor and condenser are used interchangeably depending on the country you're in. If you're in the United States, you probably call the mic a condenser, even though you call the circuitry a capacitor, whereas if you're in the United Kingdom, you'll probably call both the mic and circuit "capacitor."

 Phantom Power

Phantom Power is a means of providing electricity to a condenser microphone without using additional cabling. Using one of the connections in a balanced cable, it provides a 11-52V DC power supply (often labeled simply '48V') to charge the condenser plates. Condensers can use a battery instead of phantom power (**Figure 6.7**), but phantom power is generally preferred.

Phantom power can be supplied by a number of sources:

- The balanced connection on a mixer
- The balanced connection on a computer audio interface
- Dedicated phantom power supply

On a mixer or computer audio interface that supports phantom power, there's usually a phantom power on/off switch.

Dynamic mics don't use phantom power, but if you do happen to apply phantom power to a balanced dynamic mic, it will function just as though phantom power were off.

Warning: You should only plug a microphone or other device into a phantom-powered jack if you're certain the device is compatible with phantom power. Check your documentation if you're unsure. Nearly all common microphones with balanced XLR jacks will work, as will many direct boxes, but some older mics or mics with unbalanced or high-impedance outputs could be damaged, and you should never plug in an unbalanced device into a mic input without first turning off phantom power.

Figure 6.7 Condenser mics and other mics that need power can draw it from a battery, as in the Sennheiser K-6 power system shown here, or from phantom power supplied by a mixer or interface through the XLR cable. (Photo courtesy Sennheiser Electronic Corporation)

Ribbon

Ribbon microphones are closely related to dynamic mics; sometimes they're even called "ribbon dynamics." Like dynamics, they generate signal by disrupting a magnetic field, but they use an extremely thin ribbon instead of a diaphragm and coil (**Figure 6.8**).

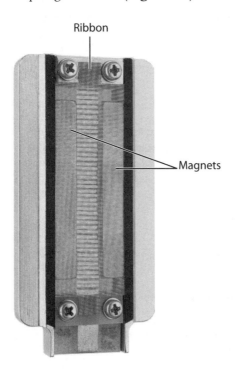

Ribbon

Magnets

Figure 6.8 Inside a ribbon mic. A single corrugated ribbon stands in for the diaphragm/coil combination in a dynamic mic. The ribbon is suspended between magnets. As it moves with air pressure from sound it disrupts the magnetic field and generates voltage, just as with a dynamic mic. (Photograph of R-121 transducer courtesy Royer Labs)

Ribbon examples: Royer R-121 (shown, courtesy Royer Labs), Beyerdynamic M130/160

Needs power? No

Pros: Consistent frequency response, subjectively warm sound

Cons: Expensive, sensitive to wind and air (although some modern designs are more rugged)

Best for: "Smooth" or historical sound, strings and other instrumental recordings, warm vocal recordings

The ribbon microphone was extremely popular in years past, thanks to classic mics like the RCA 44 and 77 (**Figure 6.9**) and Shure Model 55. If you've seen a black-and-white photo from the '30s, '40s, or '50s featuring a big, classy-looking mic (possibly with the NBC or CBS letters on the side), it was probably a ribbon mic. That doesn't mean ribbon mics are just museum pieces; their unique characteristics remain popular. Many of the historical designs have been revived in improved replica form: AEA, for instance, makes modern versions of the RCA mic, even aping the logo. New designs from AEA and mics in more compact form factors from manufacturers like Royer Labs are more rugged and compact than traditional ribbon mics.

Figure 6.9 Left: A ribbon classic: the original RCA Type 77-DX. (Photo courtesy Stanley O. Coutant; microphone from his private collection, www.coutant.org) Right: AEA's R84 mic has the looks and figure-8 polar response of an RCA mic, but has been updated with a more rugged design and improved sound. (Photo courtesy Audio Engineering Associates)

RECORDING APPLICATIONS

Mic Placement Strategies

There's more than one way to select and place microphones. After having reviewed the science of microphones, bear in mind that recording is an art. The placement of your microphones determines what your listener will hear. There are some established conventions that achieve certain results. We'll look first at the basic underlying techniques, then move on to some specific examples.

Distant and close

Any recorded sound comprises both *direct* and *indirect* or *reflected* sound. Direct sound travels straight from the source to the microphone and is the "cleanest" sound because it is unchanged from its source. Indirect sound reflects off surfaces in the room or recording environment before reaching the microphone; it is colored in the process and arrives with a small delay.

 Just do it: Sometimes the best way to learn about mic placement is simply to try it. Set up a microphone near a source and begin monitoring the results. Be sure to experiment with distance and angle.

By using different mic placements, you can affect the mix of direct and indirect sound. The most basic forms of microphone placement are *close* and *distant* (or *ambient*):

• **Close miking** is the use of microphones near the source, as in a vocalist singing directly into a microphone or the placement of a mic directly next to a guitar amp or kick drum. Close miking picks up mostly the direct sound.

• **Distant (ambient) miking** is the use of greater space between a mic and source, such as a *boundary* mic onstage or a stereo mic in the audience of an orchestral performance, and tends to pick up more reflected sound.

The blend of direct and reflected sound you want to record depends on the result you're trying to achieve. If you want an intimate guitar recording, one that might sound as though your ear were up against the body of the instrument, you'll want as little reflected sound as possible. On the other hand, if you're recording a choir performance in a cathedral, you'll want to capture some reflected sound since this is a desirable quality of the space.

Either way, excessive reflected sound can cause problems. *Phase cancellation* occurs when certain partials arrive 180 degrees out-of-phase with respect to the direct sound. Phase cancellation causes some frequencies to disappear, thus creating a hollow sound. One way to compensate for this problem is to use boundary mics for distant miking (see the sidebar "Boundary Condenser (PZM)"). Too much reflected sound can also make a recording sound muddy. Solutions include employing more direct miking or setting up acoustic barriers to prevent reflected sound from reaching the mic.

To obtain the desired mix, many recordists use some combination of close mics and distant mics. Even with only two microphones, this combination will give you options when blending the two signals.

Boundary Condenser (PZM)

Examples: Crown PZM-30D, AKG C 542 BL, Neumann GFM 132 (**Figure 6.10**)

Needs Power? Yes

What they are: Condenser mics with omni patterns, specially designed in a flat housing to make use of an internal boundary plate and/or flat mounting surface

Why use them? Allows surface mounting, compensates for problems with distance recording, avoids sound coloration near surfaces, unobtrusive appearance

Best for: Distance recording (as on a stage), recording surfaces (as on a piano lid)

Boundary microphones, often called PZM (Pressure Zone Microphones) after the trademark of their original creator Crown, are specialized condenser microphones designed to be mounted to a solid surface like a floor, wall, or piano lid. By utilizing the surface, they can compensate for reflected sound that would otherwise interfere with the quality of a distant-miked recording. (With traditional mics, reflected sounds and direct sounds arrive at different times, canceling out some sound. With boundary mics, reflected and direct sound is in phase.)

Some boundary mics include bass filters, which eliminate rumble sounds. All have an omni pattern, but of course half of the omni pattern is lost on the boundary side of the mic.

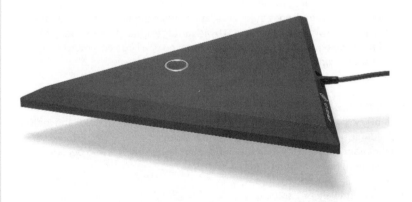

Figure 6.10 The flat design of boundary mics like Neumann's GFM 132 opens up placement locations that aren't possible with other mics. (Photo courtesy Georg Neumann GmBH)

Table 6.2 Stereo Mic Placement Options

Placement	Technique	Pros and Cons
	**Stereo microphones:** You can purchase a single stereo microphone that contains two diaphragms (one for each side), with separate left and right connections. Shown here is a cutaway of the Neumann USM 69 stereo condenser, showing the positioning of its two transducers. (Photo courtesy Georg Neumann GmbH)	**Advantage:** Added convenience of using only one mic. **Disadvantage:** Limited control over the stereo image.
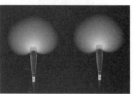	**Spaced (A/B):** When two microphones are mounted some distance apart, natural delay will create a stereo image. You'll want to use similar or (ideally) matched cardioid or omni microphones. There are a variety of approaches to A/B miking, ranging from using angled mics inches apart to using mics several feet apart and parallel.	**Advantage:** Good wide-range stereo field. **Disadvantage:** Mixing to mono is problematic as phase cancellation can result. Too large a space can be unconvincing in some cases.
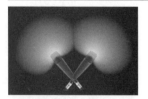	**X/Y pair:** Mounting two similar or matched cardioid or bidirectional microphones at 90–110° angles allows an overlapping stereo field with no phase problems. (Bidirectional mics will include sound captured from the rear, as well, blending it with the front.)	**Advantage:** Reliable sound with no phase cancellation. Bidirectional X/Y pair adds ambience. **Disadvantage:** Creates a less convincing stereo image of a large ensemble.
	**Middle/Side (M/S):** This system combines a cardioid or omni mic with a bidirectional mic. The cardioid mic picks up sound directly forward, and the bidirectional mic fills in the sides. This system requires an M/S decoder to separate the middle and side to right and left, either via hardware or a software plug-in (**Figure 6.11**).	**Advantage:** No phase cancellation and full control over mix of direct (mid) and indirect sound (side). **Disadvantage:** Requires M/S decoder.

Figure 6.11 An M/S decoder takes two mono mic inputs set up as middle and side, and converts them into left and right. The MOTU M/S decoder is included with Digital Performer and is labeled with cardioid and bidirectional patterns (1), so you can tell which signal is which and avoid any confusion. You can control the mix of the two signals with the stereo knob at the center (2).

With a stereo microphone, or an A/B or X/Y pair, mixing stereo signals is easy: one mono channel is left (so you'll pan it all the way to the left when mixing), and one is right (so you'll pan it right). With M/S miking, you'll mix directly in the decoder or, after decoding, use the left and right channels as you normally would.

Putting it together

For a full recording of an ensemble, you'll use a combination of mic strategies:

- **Overall pickup:** A mono microphone (or stereo pair) that picks up the general sound of the space and source—both direct sound and ambience.

- **Ambient mic:** A mic designed just to pick up the recording environment more than the source, such as the ambience of the room or audience noise (surround-sound live recordings, for instance, will often mic the audience for the rear channel).

- **Instrument mics:** Mics that are intended to focus on direct sound, for either miking each individual instrument or using additional *accent* mics to add a little bit of focus to the overall pickup.

You'll then match your mic pattern and characteristics to the instrument (or other source) and sound you want to capture.

 When in doubt, go stereo: When miking ensembles, you'll at least want a basic stereo configuration (X/Y, A/B, M/S, or spaced). This is especially common when recording classical music ensembles. Then, gradually add accent mics or "spot mics" and other individual mics to get the mix you want.

Live Sound vs. Studio

Microphones behave the same onstage as they do in the studio. But in live applications you'll have different needs. You'll need a system that's more rugged and one that avoids feedback, since you can't monitor strictly through headphones while performing. (You could, but your audience wouldn't hear you!)

When you go onstage, adapt your mic strategies:

- **Use mics that stand up to abuse:** Select mics that can take physical abuse and can be used as handhelds by vocalists. Consider dynamic mics since you'll be able to position them closer to the source, keeping your mix loud and avoiding feedback.

- **Reduce the number of mics:** By using fewer mics, you reduce the potential for feedback.

- **Take advantage of dead spots:** Select directional mics, and make sure onstage monitors and audience noise line up with the mic's dead spots to keep your mix accurate and to help reduce feedback.

Miking Common Instruments

 Hold the EQ: It's better to get the tonal quality you want with your choice and placement of your microphone than to try to change the tone later in the signal path using equalization. You can always add EQ during the mixing process, at which point you'll have more creative choices if your original recording sounds good. See Chapter 7 for more on equalization and other effects.

An infinite number of potential sound sources and ways to mike them are available, but the best way to begin is to consider the following factors:

- **What sound does your source produce?** Determine your source's amplitude and frequency characteristics.

- **How (and where) does it produce that sound?** Mic placement should exploit where particular sounds are best heard on the instrument or source.

- **What sound do you want?** Do you want to capture the full frequency and amplitude range of the instrument, or will some rejection of low- or high-frequency sound "warm" the recording or eliminate unwanted sound components?

With these issues in mind, we'll look at conventional means of miking the instruments you're likely to record most often.

Vocals

Vocals are fairly straightforward to record because there's only one sound source and you already know where it is: the vocalist's mouth. In this situation, you'll face just a few challenges:

- Make sure your vocalist (and you) use good mic technique: hold the mic steady if it's handheld, or even better, use a stand. Don't touch the grille of the mic head.

- Generally, keep the mic 3–4″ from the vocalist's mouth (**Figure 6.12**). You might want to move it a few inches farther away depending on the vocalist's singing style or if you desire more indirect sound. Move the mic slightly closer if you want to intentionally utilize proximity effect to thicken or deepen the sound.

Recording vocals:

Number of mics: 1

Best pattern: Cardioid (omni distant miking for large ensembles)

Best placement: Close miking (a few inches to just over a foot)

Tips: A dynamic mic is best for rugged applications; condenser/ribbon mics are best for the spoken word. Use a pop filter if you can.

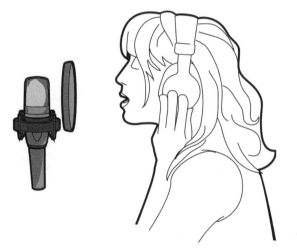

Figure 6.12 Keep your mic close to your vocalist's mouth; consider a pop filter to control plosives and sibilance.

- You'll need to deal with *plosives* and *sibilance*, the blasts of air produced by normal speech, and excessive sibilance, which consists of high-frequency *s*, *sh*, *f*, and other similar consonants. A pop filter, also known as a pop shield (**Figure 6.13**), is cheap and will help overcome plosives, while for sibilance—the hissing sound produced by consonants like the letter "s"—you may want to have the vocalist point their mouth slightly to the side of the mic.

If you have more than one singer, either give each singer a mic or, if that's not possible, choose a mic with a wider pickup pattern. Onstage, omni isn't ideal, but a wide cardioid pattern will still be effective.

Cheap pop filters: The material in commercial pop filters is similar to ordinary nylon panty hose, so intrepid DIY types have built their own, using an embroidery hoop as a frame. Christopher Stark has instructions online at www.kaiaudio.com/projects/xplosive.html. Other solutions include placing socks over the microphone head.

Figure 6.13 An inexpensive pop filter will combat the effect of plosives in vocal recording, and bursts of air in any instrumental recording. Sennheiser MZP 40 shown. (Photo courtesy Sennheiser Electronic Corporation)

Piano

Recording piano:

Number of mics:
2 or more

Best pattern: Omni

Best placement: Close-miking soundboard or stereo pair pointed at the lid

Tips: Thanks to the lid of a grand piano, it's possible to use a boundary mic. Regardless, you'll want to keep the piano lid open (half- or full-stick).

The key to recording acoustic pianos is to pick up both high and low strings while deemphasizing the distracting sounds of action and pedals.

Condenser mics are preferred; one of the mics could be a boundary mic taped to a grand piano's lid. Of all the instruments, the piano's full-frequency range is especially well suited to a high-end condenser, particularly for solo music.

Because the piano's rich sound is a result of internal reverberation and sympathetic resonance of stings, you don't want to place your mics too close to the strings. Leave at least 6 inches so your recording balances sound from individual strings with the sound of the soundboard. Ideally, you'll want two mics, so as to cover both the bass and treble strings (if you have an upright piano, simply open the top).

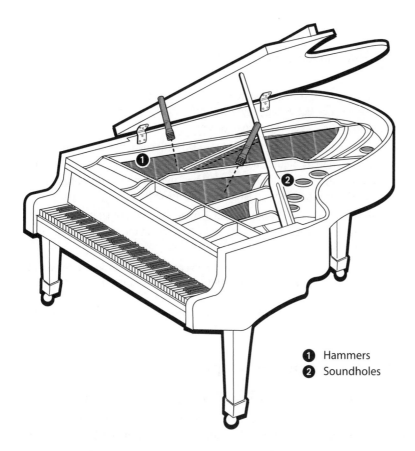

Figure 6.14 A typical close-miking setup for a piano for two mics. Many others are possible, such as placing a mic closer to the soundholes, using boundaries on the piano's lid, or even having distant miking pointed at the piano's lid.

❶ Hammers
❷ Soundholes

The sound of a piano varies at different parts of the instrument: hammers have a more percussive sound, whereas the soundboard tends to be richer and fuller. To get the sound you want, you can change the positions of your two microphones, or use even more mics (especially if you're working with a longer concert grand). If you only have one mic, don't fret: choose an omni pattern and position for the sound you want. The sound is richest over the strings, most percussive at the hammers, and thinner at the sound holes, and you can emphasize treble or bass by relative position over the corresponding strings.

 Grand tour of the grand: A grand piano gives you more physical space to explore than any other instrument. So try experimenting with different parts of the inside of the soundboard and various distances from the instrument to get the sound you want.

Vintage Keyboards and Organs

Electronic keyboards usually feature line-level outs or even digital outs and computer connections, but vintage keyboards don't. Here are some tips if you're lucky enough to have a classic keyboard or organ:

- Keyboards like the Rhodes can be recorded either directly or through an amp, often using a technique similar to what you'd use with a guitar. If you are running directly from the keyboard without an amp, consider a tube pre-amp to "warm" the sound or to add fatter distortion/overdrive.

- Electronic organs that use rotary Leslie cabinets require separate miking for the cabinet: position a mic at the top and another at the bottom to capture both rotors.

- Pipe organs, like choirs, are all about ambient sound, so consider a stereo mic setup pointed at the pipes from a distance of ten feet or more.

Electric guitar and bass (amps)

 Recording amps:

Number of mics: 1–2

Best pattern: Cardioid

Best placement: Close miking the amp or a combination of close miking and ambient miking

Tips: The "American" (versus "British") sound tends to employ condenser mics over dynamic mics, but be sure to give your condenser some distance so it isn't damaged!

You can hook up an electric guitar directly into your direct box ("DI" box) or interface, but if you have an amp you love and want to capture the way it colors your sound, you'll need to mic the amp (**Figure 6.15**). The traditional way of doing this is to point a dynamic mic at the screen of the amp, even positioning it close enough to touch the surface of the amp. (Don't try this with your expensive condenser mic!) The result is a very thick, aggressive sound. You'll typically get the best results with the amp turned up and the mic at an angle to the amp, pointed indirectly at the cone.

If this setup doesn't give you exactly the sound you want, you may want to add a second mic (more often a condenser), either for distant miking or pointed at the back of an open-backed amp cabinet. This second mic can be used to add some subtle additional sound or to make it clear that your garage band is playing in a real garage!

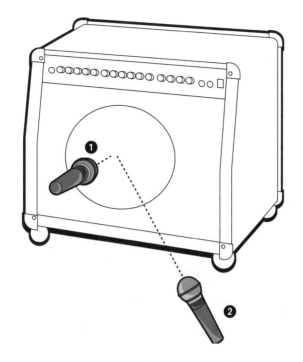

Figure 6.15 Various possible miking locations for an amp: (1) consider a dynamic mic right up against the screen pointed on-axis at the speaker cone; (2) a condenser or dynamic off-axis a little further away; (3) distant miking for more ambient sound; or a mic pointed at the back of an open-cabinet amp.

The other option is to make the amp entirely virtual, either by using a hardware amp simulator from a vendor like Line 6 (www.line6.com) or using a software solution, like IK Multimedia AmpliTube, Native Instruments Guitar Rig, or Guitar Amp Pro in Apple Logic Pro (**Figure 6.16**). These software packages emulate the miking techniques described in this section, so even if you're going virtual, it's helpful to have knowledge of guitar miking.

Bass tips: Bass is often recorded directly for a cleaner sound, but you can mic a bass amp just like a guitar amp. Large-diaphragm condensers are especially useful for picking up bass sounds. IK Multimedia also makes software models of Ampeg bass amps (www.amplitube.com).

Figure 6.16 Software and hardware amp simulators let you switch mics, placement, amps, and effects all within the software, as shown here in Apple's Logic Pro.

Acoustic guitar

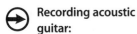

Recording acoustic guitar:

Number of mics: 1–2

Best pattern: Cardioid

Best placement: Close-miking amp or a combination of close miking and ambient miking

Rules are meant to be broken: Condensers are usually favored for acoustic guitars, but if you want edgier guitar to emphasize finger-plucking or rhythmic playing, substitute a dynamic mic.

Acoustic guitar has a full frequency range, making it an ideal test for a high-quality, large-diaphragm condenser. Steel-strung guitars are generally close miked from the soundhole (slightly off-axis), whereas the more delicate sound of a classical nylon guitar is better served by miking the bridge.

Because of the range of sounds from the fretboard, bridge, and soundhole, acoustics are well suited to a two-mic setup as well. Possibilities include:

• X/Y pair (see p. 172) centered on the soundhole

• One mic on the fretboard, one on the bridge

• One mic on or closer to the soundhole, one on the bridge

With two mics, you can experiment with different setups for the exact balance desired in stereo.

Figure 6.17 Possible mic placements for guitar on the (1) bridge; (2) soundhole; and (3) fretboard—any of the three can be combined to taste.

Drum kit

Miking drums is perhaps the most idiosyncratic of recording techniques, but a basic setup involves individual mics for kick, snare, and hi-hat, with overhead condensers for toms and cymbals. If you want a grungy "garage" sound, you could mic the whole kit via one distance mic, but for more clarity, consider bringing out some individual elements of the kit.

There are some conventions for how to best mic individual drums. Using Paul Wertico's studio setup (**Figure 6.18**) as an example, we'll look at these one at a time. Paul is a Shure artist, but even if you're using another brand, the same basic principles apply.

 Recording drums:

Number of mics: From two to many; varies (average around 5–6)

Best pattern: Cardioid/ supercardioid

Best placement: Distant miking is possible, although close miking is more popular with multiple mics

Tips: Substitute supercardioid instead of cardioid if you want a tighter, cleaner sound with less spillage. Boundary mics work well on bass and snare, and even good budget models are often effective.

Figure 6.18 Seven-time Grammy Award-winning percussionist Paul Wertico has his home kit set up in his studio just the way he likes it. (Photo courtesy Paul Wertico)

❶ Overheads
❷ Hi-hat
❸ Toms
❹ Snare
❺ Bass ("kick")
❻ Distance mic

1. **Overheads:** Overhead condensers (cardioid) in a spaced pair or X/Y pair will pick up a balance of cymbals and the overall sound of the kit. Paul uses two Shure KSM32 condensers.

2. **Hi-hat:** A condenser mic (cardioid) can be pointed at the hat slightly off-axis. (Some like to double up miking the hi-hat and snare via a mic placed between them—a bidirectional pattern can work well.) Paul uses one Shure SM81 condenser.

3. **Toms:** For individual miking, dynamic mics (cardioid) can be used above the head, either for each tom or in pairs. Alternatively, use overhead condensers (cardioid) to pick up the toms with the cymbals. Paul uses three Shure A98SPM miniature condensers.

4. **Snare:** A dynamic mic (cardioid/supercardioid) can be angled at the inside top rim, close to the surface of the snare (1″), pointed away from parts of the kit that could leak. Paul uses one Shure SM57 dynamic.

 It's the drums: Drum miking is as much about drums as microphones—if not more so. Drum damping and tuning will radically affect the sound of the kit and with it your recording, so if you're not getting the sound you want, adjust the drums.

5. **Bass ("kick"):** A dynamic mic (cardioid/supercardioid) or specialized condenser can be pointed at the head (adjust distance to your preference). Large-diaphragm mics like the Shure Beta 52A often work well, although a smaller diaphragm inside the kick is also effective. Consider using a pillow or blanket inside the drum; the damping effect will keep your kick sounding sharp instead of muddy. You can even lay a dynamic mic directly on the pillow or blanket. Paul uses either one Beta 52A (specialized kick dynamic) or one Shure SM91 (specialized kick condenser).

6. **Distance mic:** For additional ambient sound, a condenser mic (cardioid) can be used at a distance of a few feet from the kit, although the above setup should cover the sound of the kit itself. Paul uses two KSM32s (not pictured), which he also uses as "floaters" for additional percussion and general-purpose recording tasks.

 Tuned Percussion

Other percussion instruments require specific techniques, similar to those used with a kit.

- **Pitched mallet instruments** like vibes, marimba, and xylophone are usually miked in spaced stereo pairs with condensers positioned above the bars.
- **Hand percussion instruments** like congos, bongos, djembe, and other instruments played with the hands can be recorded with dynamic mics, typically close miking smaller instruments and leaving a foot or more for deeper, larger instruments.

If you are short on microphones, make sure you have at least one overhead mic (ideally about a foot from the top of the drummer's head), and then focus on bringing out other focused sounds, like the bass and snare. (If you're sampling individual parts, of course, you can just record one drum at a time.)

Brass instrument family

Most brass instruments can be miked individually, pointing a mic at the bell (the opening of the instrument). To better tolerate the blast of wind these instruments produce, the instrument should be placed off-axis (or the player should play off-axis from the mic), particularly at close distance.

- Trumpet and trombone are often close miked (**Figure 6.19**). Consider a windscreen to further protect the mic from wind blasts.

- Tuba and French horn are usually miked from a few feet away. With the horn, it's customary to focus on capturing more reflected sound, placing the instrument near a reflective wall.

- For ensemble recordings, use a combination of relatively close mics (high enough off the ground and far enough back to capture the whole section) and ambient mics.

Recording brass:

Best mics: "Instrument dynamic mics" and ribbon mics are preferred for brass.

Tips: Pros use diffusion walls behind brass ensembles to get a diffused sound of the whole group, with a stereo pair as the pickup.

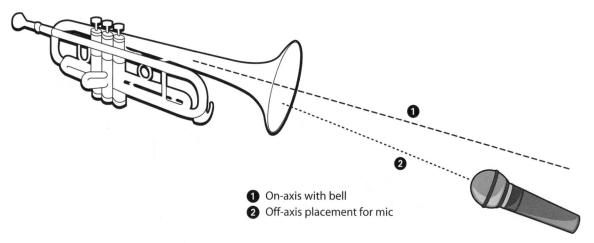

❶ On-axis with bell
❷ Off-axis placement for mic

Figure 6.19 A typical brass mic placement involves close miking the instrument slightly off-axis from the bell, as shown here on a trumpet.

Woodwinds

Recording woodwinds:

Best mics: Large-diaphragm condenser, mini-condenser, specialized pickups

Tip: Focus on lower fingerholes in placement.

Back off: Distance is essential to getting good woodwind recordings. Get too close and you'll have too much reed/mouthpiece sound; a few inches (or even feet) of distance can help balance out the sound.

In contrast to brass instruments, woodwinds radiate sound from the length of the instrument; different sounds can be captured in various positions. Most woodwinds are close miked at a distance of a few inches to a foot. The best positions for recording each instrument are generally:

- **Clarinet:** Lower fingerholes (**Figure 6.20**)

- **Saxophone:** Middle of the instrument, angled slightly toward the bell, to pick up sound from both locations. (Adjust the position to your preference—aim at the bell, use a pickup on the bell for the brightest tone, or point slightly away from the bell for a fuller tone; see Figure 6.20.) Ribbon mics are popular for sax recordings as well, with the addition of tube mics for warmer recordings of genres like Latin and jazz.

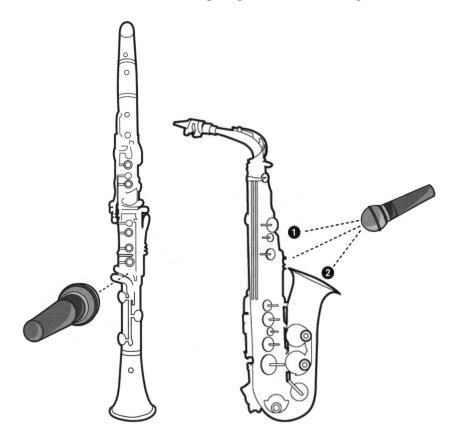

Figure 6.20 Unlike brass instruments, most woodwinds are miked at the fingerholes, as shown on the clarinet (left). On the saxophone (right), you can choose to emphasize the sound from the (1) fingerholes or the (2) bell by how you aim the mic.

- **Flute:** Roughly in the middle of the instrument: closer or further away from the mouthpiece for more or less breathiness.

- **Bassoon:** Lower fingerholes, often lower than the other instruments, or even recorded slightly to the side of the mic.

Strings

String instruments radiate sound from the f-holes—the curved holes on the face of the instrument. To pick up the sound resonating in the instrument blended with the sound of the bow, position a cardioid microphone on-axis with the instrument. The mic can be positioned anywhere from a few inches from the instrument (which will create a sharper, more cutting sound) to 2´–3´. Because of the wide frequency range of a resonating string instrument, this is another case that calls for a high-quality condenser mic, especially for solo recording.

 Recording strings:

Best mics: Large-diaphragm condenser, mini-condenser, specialized pickups

Tip: Focus on f-holes for placement.

Figure 6.21 Typical mic placement for a cello. Since other instruments of the string family share a similar shape, mic placement is basically the same.

Engineer with a baton: If you're recording large ensembles, you may rely on a conductor or group leader even more than your mics: they're essential to providing the balance you need for the recording.

 Don't throw away that cheap mic: Inexpensive portable electret condenser stereo mics, like those manufactured by Sony to complement MiniDisc recorders or those built into a recorder like the Edirol R-1, can get surprisingly good sound—and they fit in your jacket pocket.

 Harmonicas

Harmonicas deserve special mention because a jazz, rock, and blues recording tradition is associated with them. Close miked, standard dynamic mics work well with harmonicas, but harmonica players may use a specialized mic like the Shure 520DX dynamic "Green Bullet" so they can cup their hands around the entire mic for wah effects (**Figure 6.22**).

Figure 6.22 The round shape of Shure's Green Bullet makes it ideal for harmonica players. (Photo courtesy Brett Sherman)

General-purpose sampling

What about other types of recordings, such as "found sound" on-site recordings, special effects, and Foley sound-effect recordings for video? Large-diaphragm condensers or stereo condensers (the latter are especially useful for on-location work) are useful for general-purpose sampling because of their broad, flat frequency response. In general, think about the source. You may find similarities to the instrumental categories mentioned earlier.

DIGITAL RECORDING

With your microphones in place, you're ready to begin recording to disk. Double-check the input and output settings in your software first. On Mac OS X, look for preferences under the application menu (the menu with the name of the program, like Audacity or Live), and on Windows select File > Preferences. You can then proceed to record.

Setting Levels

With an input enabled, you'll need to make sure you have the right input level. If the signal is too weak, the recording will be too quiet, and amplifying it to an audible level will add noise. If the signal is too strong or "hot," it can cause distortion. By setting your input gain so that the level saturates your dynamic range without distorting, you'll get the cleanest possible recording. This means you need to watch your meters while you're recording and make appropriate adjustments as needed (**Figure 6.23**).

 For more information, see:

Chapters 3–4: Connect and configure your equipment

Chapter 7: Add signal processing to sweeten your sound or add compression and effects

Chapter 10: Mix sources together and edit and arrange your sound

Chapter 13: Record on the fly during a performance

Figure 6.23 Watch your meters (left) to set the right level. If you need to, adjust input gain in your hardware or software, as shown here in Audacity (right).

Headroom

Every device has a dynamic range (the amplitudes it can accommodate from minimum to maximum). On analog equipment, there's an additional range above the maximum recommended level (labeled on a meter as 0 dB), up to the level at which signal significantly distorts or *clips*. This range is often colored red on equipment meters. If you've ever gone "into the red," you've exploited the additional range, which is called *dynamic headroom* (**Figure 6.24**).

On analog equipment, you'll want your meters to read approximately 0 dB as often as they can, with an occasional excursion slightly "into the red." Meters on analog equipment can show a little bit of clipping when the signal isn't actually significantly distorting. Digital equipment works differently: because amplitude is stored as a number and not as a continuous voltage, its

 Get the right levels:

Analog: 0 dB, or a little more or less

Digital: Approaching but never crossing 0 dB

maximum is really its maximum. Generally speaking, digital equipment doesn't have any dynamic headroom; therefore, you'll have to set your inputs so that your levels get near the 0 dB threshold without crossing it.

Figure 6.24 Analog signal (left) has additional headroom beyond 0 dB, but anything above 0 dB on a digital meter (right) will result in digital clipping.

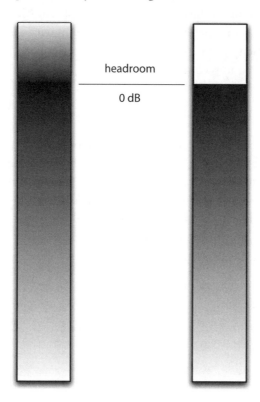

headroom

0 dB

Distortion

"But wait," you may be saying, "I love distortion!" Odds are, you like analog distortion, a "fuzzy," warm sound generated by analog equipment pushed just past its headroom. From distortion pedals to "overdriving" recorded tracks, musicians have long made use of slight *overdrive* (pushing a device just past its amplitude maximum) to get a desired effect.

Digital devices distort differently: instead of rounding off the top of a waveform as it passes beyond the amplitude maximum, they slice off the tops of the sound waves, creating a straight line (**Figure 6.25**). This result is called *digital clipping*, and it's almost never desirable. In fact, if you want to achieve analog-style distortion, you'll need software that can emulate the result. (See Chapter 7 for more on this effect.) Unless you want the specific and unpleasant sound of digital clipping, make sure your digital meter never crosses the upper threshold. The signal input level can't generally be turned down once the signal has entered the computer; if it's too hot, you need to turn it down at the source or adjust the input trims on your audio interface.

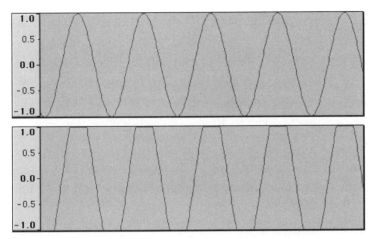

Figure 6.25 A saturated digital signal makes maximum use of the full amplitude range of the recording (top). But go beyond the maximum, and digital clipping will occur (bottom), as shown here with a sine wave.

Monitoring

Monitoring, listening to the sound that's being recorded, is key to a successful recording. If you're recording on top of existing tracks, you'll need to hear both those tracks and the live sound in order to play with tight timing. You can monitor the live sound through the computer as you're recording, but latency introduced as a signal routed into and out of the computer can make timing difficult. Some interfaces offer direct monitoring features that route zero-latency audio directly from the interface's input to headphones plugged into the interface. Lexicon's Omega, for instance, even lets you adjust the mix of what's coming directly from your mic or instrument and what's coming from your computer (**Figure 6.26**). Other interfaces have options available in their software driver control panels.

If you don't have an interface with this feature, you can also set up zero-latency monitoring using a mixer. Plug your headphones and the sound source you want to record into this device, route the output from your computer to the mixer, and then record the new track by routing its signal from the mixer to your interface using an aux send. (If you record the mixer's main output, your new track will have the previously recorded tracks embedded into it.)

Figure 6.26 The monitor mix knob on the Lexicon Omega computer audio interface lets you listen exclusively to the sound you're recording (direct), exclusively to the audio from your computer (playback), or to an adjustable mix of the two.

Audio applications can also give you the option of turning monitoring on or off: Ableton Live's "Monitor" can be set to monitor inputs only when the track is armed (Auto), or it can be manually enabled or disabled.

Recording Methods

Whether you're using a simple cassette multitrack recorder or a sophisticated pro digital studio, there are several different approaches to recording:

- **Simple recording:** Basic recording involves recording one mono or stereo signal at a time: click/press Record, then click/press Stop.

- **Overdubbing:** Overdubbing is the addition of tracks, one or more at a time, on top of existing material, which remains unchanged. You can overdub with any software that supports multitrack playback, including Audacity and any DAW.

- **Simultaneous multitracking:** As opposed to sequential overdubbing, multitracking is the recording of two or more discrete inputs (one drum track and one guitar track, for example) at the same time. On a computer, this is accomplished with a multichannel audio interface and multitrack recording software or DAW.

- **Punch recording:** Punch recording involves beginning to record at a point other than the beginning of the song, "punching in" (starting recording), and then "punching out" (stopping recording), often replacing other material in the same track. For instance, if you have a perfect take but don't like one bar, set the punch in and out points to that bar and record only over it.

- **Looped recording:** Even if your music doesn't involve loops, looping can make recording easier. For instance, if you need a "perfect" take of a four-bar phrase, loop that four-bar phrase using an application that supports multiple takes, and keep recording takes over the loop.

- **Sampling:** Sample-based software takes the idea of looped recordings one step further: using a sample recorder or an application like Ableton Live, you can record and play back takes on the fly, even in a performance.

🖐 Hands-on: Roll It!

Now you're ready to record in your application of choice. The basic workflow in any application goes something like this:

1. Set your input device(s) for the program.

2. In a multitrack application, set the audio input for the track you want to use.

3. *Arm* the track: record-enable it so it's ready to record. (Some software automatically monitors any record-enabled track; if yours sets monitoring manually, set up monitoring on the track, too.)

4. Set the playback position to the beginning of your project, or set the in and out points for punch recording.

5. Click Record!

Let's take a look at some hands-on examples using Audacity and Ableton Live, as included on the DVD.

Audacity

Once your inputs are set up, recording in Audacity is as simple as clicking the Record button on the transport. Each new recording take will add an additional track (**Figure 6.27**). You can use this to store multiple takes, saving the one you like, or to create a mix of multiple recordings. Use the Solo and Mute buttons to choose which tracks to hear.

 On the DVD: Audacity multitrack recorder (free, Mac/Windows), Ableton Live audio workstation (save-disabled demo, Mac/Windows)

Similar environments: You'll find basic waveform-level recording in applications like BIAS Peak and Deck (Mac), Sony Sound Forge (Windows), and Adobe Audition (Windows).

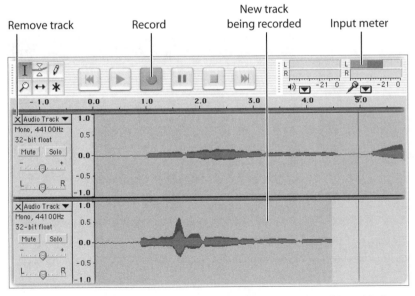

Figure 6.27 Overdubbing mono tracks in Audacity. New tracks will be added on the bottom with each new take.

Ableton Live

Ableton Live (www.ableton.com) is more typical of the multitrack recording interface in a DAW. Since Live displays level in inputs before you select them, it's easy to tell whether the input on your interface is live. Live's first tutorial will familiarize you further with the application and recording.

Live can record audio (and MIDI) in one of two ways (**Figure 6.28**). You can record whole tracks in linear fashion, just as you might in another DAW, by using the *Arrangement View*. Unique to Live is a second option: you can record individual audio/MIDI samples into clips, which you can manipulate and play back in real time for faster studio work or even a live performance. Either is a valid way to work, and you can move clips back and forth between the two views, so you don't have to choose one or the other permanently.

Either way, once you're ready to record in one of these two views (**Figure 6.29**):

1.   Make sure your inputs and outputs are visible in *Session View* (View > In/Out).

2.   Select an input for an individual track, making sure the input's meters are active. (If not, double-check your connections and hardware and software settings.)

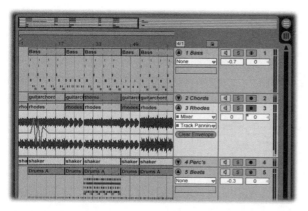 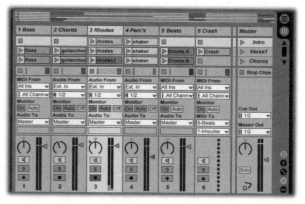

Figure 6.28 Ableton Live is structured to let you work through a linear song structure or a collection of clips to be triggered individually or in groups. Record audio into an overview of your song in Arrangement View (left), or record into a clip slot in Session View (right).

3. Arm the track in the view you want to use:

   Arrangement View: For linear recording into your arrangement, arm the track in Arrangement View.

   Session View: If you want to record a clip into a clip slot for later use (either looped or as a triggered file), arm the track in Session View.

4. Record into your arrangement or clip slot:

   Arrangement View: Click Record in Live's transport controls. When you're done, click Stop.

   Session View: Click the Record button of the slot into which you want to record. When you're done, click the Clip Stop button.

 Similar environments: DAWs like Pro Tools, Cubase, Logic, and DP also feature mixer and arrangement views and mixer-style record-enable buttons, although the clip approach to on-the-fly sampling is specific to Live.

Figure 6.29 To record in Live, first set up your inputs and arm (record-enable) your track (left); then either click the record button on a clip slot in Session View (top) or click the Record Transport button at the top of the screen in Arrangement View.

CHAPTER 7

Processing and Effects

If you're new to recording music, you might be surprised by the extent to which even a natural-sounding vocal on the radio depends on the arsenal of software and hardware devices known as *effects*. Whether you're trying to fix problems, "sweeten" recorded tracks, or send your listeners on a sonic roller-coaster ride, you'll need to master digital audio *signal processors*. This type of processing is usually handled by plug-in programs called effects.

Essentials

Processing and Effects

In this chapter we'll discuss:

- What signal processors are
- How to apply non-realtime signal processors and route real-time signal processors
- Equalization and frequency: filter types and uses
- Dynamics processors and amplitude
- Time-related effects: delays and reverbs
- Specialized processors: distortion, modulation, and utility

Essential Terms

- Signal processor, filter, effect
- Non-destructive and destructive editing

- Routing: channel strip; insert/send/return/bus; side-chaining
- Equalization (EQ): highpass, lowpass, band-pass filters, parametric/graphic EQ
- Filter parameters: cutoff frequency, center frequency, bandwidth, Q/resonance, stop-band, passband
- Dynamics: compressor/expander/limiter/gate/de-esser
- Time: delay, echo, reverb
- Convolution, impulse, impulse response (IR), Fast Fourier Transform (FFT), fuzz/overdrive/distortion
- Modulation: tremolo, vibrato, chorus, flanger, phaser, ring modulation, low frequency oscillator (LFO)

Where to Start

Using your own audio software or one of the DAW/host demos included on the DVD, try out some effects, especially parametric EQ, dynamics processors, and delay/reverb. See p. 210 for some ideas.

BASICS OF SIGNAL PROCESSORS

What Is a Signal Processor?

On the DVD: The included demo copy of Ableton Live will enable you to try the hands-on effects routing and audio processing examples in this chapter.

Natural sound filters are everywhere. Your mouth and tongue modify the sound of your vocal cords to produce recognizable vowels. A concert hall alters and enhances the raw sounds coming from the instruments in a symphony orchestra. Even the racket coming from your neighbor's stereo, if you live in an apartment, sounds very different after it has passed through the wall. Digital signal processing (DSP) lets you emulate those natural effects, along with others that originated in classic analog synthesizers, as well as creating newly imagined digital sonorities.

Processors and effects versus filters: In common usage, the term "effect" is often used instead of "signal processor" to refer to any process that takes a signal (input) and changes it in some way (output). The term "filter" can be theoretically defined in exactly the same way, as any process with an input and output. However, for the purposes of this book (and in common usage), "filter" refers to a device that boosts or reduces certain frequencies in a signal (see "Equalization," p. 212).

Anything that takes a sound input, modifies it, and returns a sound output is considered a *signal processor*. Many types of signal processors are available, and all of them impact one or more of the following basic elements of sound:

- **Frequency:** The pitch and harmonic spectrum of a sound. Examples of effects that work in the frequency domain are equalizers and low-pass filters.

- **Dynamics:** The changes in amplitude (loudness) of a sound, from soft to loud. Examples of effects that work in the amplitude domain include compressors, limiters, expanders, and gates.

- **Time:** When a sound begins in relation to the rest of the music, and how often (and in what manner) it's repeated. Examples of effects that work in the time domain include reverb and delay lines.

Digital Signal Processing

Many processors we commonly use today are based on the designs of earlier analog equipment. The way they work, and even the labels for knobs and faders, come from a tradition of audio gear. That's a good thing: with the software plug-ins included in your audio software, you can use the same techniques heard in your favorite recordings of the past few decades. Thanks to Digital Signal Processing (DSP), musicians today have more control over traditional effects, and can also create new kinds of sounds that weren't possible before.

 Ten Signal Processing Ideas

Before we get into the nitty-gritty details of how signal processors work, here are some common tasks for which you might use them and locations for descriptions of each:

- **Reverse** a track for a special effect (p. 203)
- Use an **equalizer** to bring out the high frequencies of recorded cymbals (p. 212)
- Use a **DJ-style filter** to sweep through a groove (p. 222)
- Run an electric guitar through a **wah effect** (p. 236) and **amp simulator** (p. 248)
- Use a **compressor** to add punch to a drum loop or vocals (p. 228)
- Add a classic **phaser** effect to an electric piano (p. 253)
- Give your track a sense of space by using a **reverb** (p. 242) on an effects **send** (p. 206)
- Make your track sound "retro" or digital-gritty using **digital distortion** (p. 247)
- Create a far-out spectral effect using an **FFT-based processor** (p. 246)
- **Tune** your guitar (p. 263)

Most DSP is performed in real time using specialized processors or your computer's CPU. Other effects cannot be performed in real time. Instead, they require you to process audio first, modifying the actual audio file, before you can hear the results of the effect.

Destructive vs. Nondestructive Editing

Non-realtime effects are usually applied as *destructive edits*; that is, they modify the actual waveform itself, so that your audio file now irrevocably incorporates the added effect. That doesn't necessarily mean you can't change your mind later: many audio editors have multiple levels of undo, while others will make copies of the file each time you make a change, either by default or as an option. Real-time effects are by nature non-destructive: the audio file is unchanged; effects are simply added to the audio signal, not the waveform, during playback.

Destructive edits have some advantages. You can apply an effect or other edit to an audio file, then move the audio file to another application that doesn't have the effect, yet still hear it with the effect. Destructive edits don't require processing power after the edit is performed, since the effect isn't operating in real time. (Some newer waveform editors use non-destructive edits that can be saved destructively in the finished file; see **Figure 7.1**.)

Figure 7.1 Apple's Soundtrack Pro is an example of a waveform editor that applies effects and edits entirely in real time, non-destructively. By storing each effect as an "action layer," you can use Soundtrack to adjust effects, reorder effects processing, and make other changes as you go.

Destructive audio file edits can also be useful when batch-processing audio (**Figure 7.2**). For instance, if you wanted to perform noise removal and filtering on a whole batch of sound recorded for a video, you might set up basic settings for all the audio, batch-process them in an audio editor like Apple Soundtrack Pro or Adobe Audition, and then bring them into your DAW for later editing.

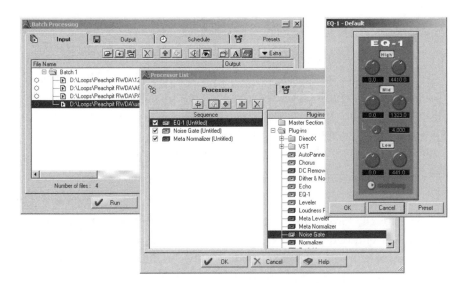

Figure 7.2 A waveform editor with batch processing capabilities can apply a string of effects destructively to a large group of files, an essential timesaver when you have a lot of audio to clean up, process, and convert. Steinberg's WaveLab editor is employed here for preprocessing a group of files.

(≡) Delay Compensation

Some effects appear to be functioning in real time, but introduce a slight delay between their input and output. This includes plug-ins with "look-ahead" features that fill a memory buffer with audio prior to processing, and hardware DSP systems like the Universal Audio UAD-1, TC Electronic PowerCore, and Digidesign hardware. If you're using a DAW with *automatic delay compensation* (sometimes called *plug-in latency compensation*), your software will automatically compensate for the slight delay introduced by feeding audio slightly early to plug-ins that require it. The compensation feature works invisibly in hosts that support it, requiring no interaction on your part. Delay compensation works only with recorded audio, not live inputs; because recorded tracks are stored on the hard disk, it's possible to feed the audio to the effect early.

Digidesign's DAE audio drivers include built-in delay compensation for use with TDM plug-ins. With other hosts and hardware DSP you'll have to check your DAW's specifications, though recent versions of Logic Pro, Digital Performer, SONAR, and Cubase all support this feature. If you're working with a DAW or plug-in that doesn't support automatic delay compensation, you may need to shift a track slightly in time when using such an effect in order to keep the effect's output in sync with other tracks. On the other hand, if you don't use plug-ins that require it, you may never need to worry about delay compensation.

Using Non-realtime Effects

You'll usually find effects that are applied to a sound file in non-realtime in waveform editors, either in the audio editor included in your DAW or in an independent waveform editor like Audacity (on the DVD). Usually, you'll simply select either all of an audio waveform or the part of the waveform to which you want to apply the effect, then use a menu command and wait as your software applies the effect permanently to your audio file.

Fades

A fade gradually lowers the loudness (amplitude) of either the beginning (fade-in) or end (fade-out) of a sound to zero, using a straight line or curved shape. *Cross-fades* gradually fade out the amplitude of one sound file while fading in the amplitude of another, so that the resulting mix shifts from one sound to another. (For a comparison, see **Figure 7.3**.)

Can it be done in real time? While you can use automation to create fades by adjusting the volume level of a track's fader (see Chapter 10 for information on automation), fades can usefully be applied as destructive edits. In addition to automated fades using track faders, most DAWs have the ability to apply non-destructive fades and cross-fades to audio via a fade tool or by automatically cross-fading sounds that are dragged on top of one another. The advantage of non-destructive fades is that they're easier to adjust after the fact, though you may prefer to use destructive fades for fine-tuned effects and batch processing.

Speed, Tempo, and Pitch

Changing the speed impacts audio just as it would on a tape player or record player, modifying both pitch and tempo simultaneously. (In other words, if you speed up audio, you'll get the classic higher-pitched "chipmunk" effect; slow it down and you'll get a slower but lower-pitched "Darth Vader" sound.)

Thanks to digital processing, you can also modify pitch independent of tempo or vice-versa. Unfortunately, this process tends to introduce unpleasant sound artifacts, especially when you make more drastic changes (double-digit metronome marking tempo changes or pitch changes greater than a couple of semitones). Different sound material will behave differently, some plug-ins and settings will help compensate, and audio recorded at a higher sample rate can perform more accurately, but you'll still want to use this process judiciously.

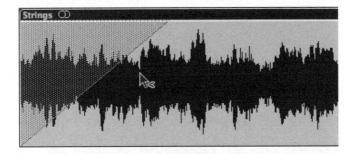

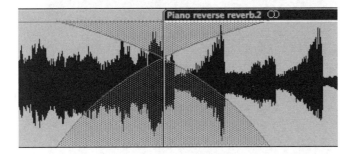

Figure 7.3 Three fades: a destructive fade-in, as applied in a waveform editor (top); a non-destructive real-time fade-in, as applied with the fade tool in a DAW (middle); and a cross-fade between two sound files (bottom).

Can it be done in real time? Speed, tempo, and pitch shifters are all available in real-time versions, though they often make compromises in audio quality in order to be more processor-efficient.

Normalization

Normalizing amplifies an entire sound file or a segment of a sound file so that the loudest sound's peak is increased to the highest amplitude range available, or some other specified amplitude level. Normalization analyzes audio for the highest signal peak (the loudest sound in the audio), then amplifies the entire file so that peak is at 100% signal level (–0 dB) or some other level you determine.

While mixing, of course, one can simply turn up the fader of a channel for the same result (a louder sound), so normalization might seem unnecessary. It's useful, though, for matching different sound levels to be used in the same track prior to mixing, at least as a rough approximation. Usually some additional adjustment is necessary while mixing. Some sound engineers also normalize files in preparation for outputting to a CD or other medium, but this should be considered only a quick-and-dirty way of mastering and should be applied to the entire set of tracks, not individual tracks. (Applying normalization to individual tracks prior to mastering can actually interfere with the mastering process because it's a fairly inaccurate way of balancing the overall perceived loudness of audio; subjective adjustment with your ears is often preferable.) For more control over the dynamics of a sound, you'll need dynamics processors like compression and limiting; see p. 228.

Can it be done in real time? Normalization doesn't work in real time, since it requires an analysis of an entire audio file (see **Figure 7.4**).

Figure 7.4 Normalization increases the overall volume of a sound file so the loudest peak is amplified to a specified amplitude level (here –3 dB; sometimes 0 dB).

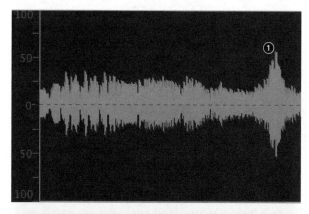

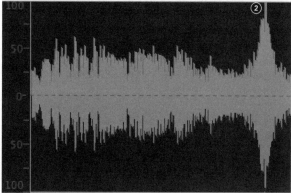

❶ Highest peak before normalizing.
❷ Highest peak after normalizing; amplified to –3 dB.

Reverse

This effect reverses an entire section of audio so that it plays backward, from the end to the beginning. Because we're used to hearing the way real-world sounds decay, the "sucking" effect of reversed audio decays can sound very strange (in a good way, if you like the sound). For instance, a picked guitar note, when reversed, will begin quiet (the end of the decay), gradually get louder, and then end with the attack of the pick. Reverse can be used as a special effect, or more subtly in small doses to add punch to the entrance of a note.

Can it be done in real time? Reversing is impossible in real time with live audio input (though pre-recorded audio can obviously be played backward in real time). However, some plug-ins provide near real-time operation for short segments of audio by using a memory buffer to store live input for reversing. For instance, ndc Plugs' Tempo Sync Reverser (Windows/Mac VST plug-in) reverses a specified time segment of your live audio input, triggered by MIDI. Real-time reversing of buffer-recorded audio is especially useful in conjunction with a delay, as with Expert Sleepers' free Mac-only Meringue plug-in (http://www.collective.co.uk/expertsleepers/meringue.html).

Signal Routing with Real-Time Processors

Processors, by definition, can't function without an input, so you must first hook up the signal processor to a sound source. You'll likely use processors during one or more of the following stages:

- **Before and during recording:** Sometimes effects are added directly to the sound source. For instance, you may be recording a guitar whose sound is being modified by stompbox effects pedals, or a hardware synth that has built-in effects that enhance its sound programs.

 Non-realtime Processing in Audacity

Try basic processing for free using Audacity; select the part of a waveform you want to process and explore the options on the Effects menu. To fade the sound from zero at the beginning of the file up to the sound's full amplitude at the cursor position, click your cursor in the waveform where you want the fade to end, select Edit > Select… > Start to Cursor, and Effect > Fade In. To fade from a point of the sound down to zero at the end, click where you want the fade-out to begin, select Edit > Select… > Cursor to End, and Effect > Fade Out. For other effects that you would normally apply to the whole file, select Edit > Select All to modify the entire file at once, and try options like Effect > Change Pitch, Change Speed, and Change Tempo, Effect > Normalize, and Effect > Reverse.

- **After recording:** When a track is recorded "dry" (without effects), effects can be used on playback to modify the sound.

- **On the final mix:** Once the multitrack recording process is complete, *mastering* effects can be used (either by inserting them on your DAW's master output bus or by using specialized mastering software on the stereo mix after it has been created) to modify the sound of the entire mix. (See Chapter 10.)

The easiest way to work with signal processors, and the place you're likely to use them most often, is at the channel level. You'll access these processors via a user interface object called a *channel strip*.

What's a channel?

A channel is any path of audio from input (which could be either a live input or an input from a file previously recorded to the hard drive) to output. On a mixer, for instance, each fader is associated with a separate channel, and allows you to control the amount of signal that passes from the input to the mixer's master fader. An eight-channel mixer is one with eight input/output paths for signal, a little like an eight-lane automobile highway. Those eight outputs can be combined at the master fader so you can hear and mix them as one stereo mix; hence the term mixer.

For the purposes of applying real-time effects, we'll be working with channels, because by definition signal is routed into and out of an effect via a channel. Having channels is essential to organizing which effects will be applied to which signals: for instance, the signal on one channel might be a vocal, on another it might be a guitar solo. (Channels should not be confused with tracks: a track is a location in software or another storage medium into which signals can be recorded and on which sound files can be positioned for playback. For more on tracks, see Chapter 10.)

Channel strip

Traditional hardware mixers make it easy to evaluate and adjust settings for each channel of your mix, because they align faders and knobs visually in vertical columns. In one way or another, nearly all software that works with multiple audio channels has adopted this basic model, which is called a *channel strip* (**Figure 7.5**). At its heart is the simplest of all signal processors, the level fader, which does nothing other than change the level (gain) of the signal fed through it.

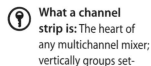

What a channel strip is: The heart of any multichannel mixer; vertically groups settings and processing for a channel

How to use it: Set up inputs and outputs, then add effects (via inserts/sends)

When you'll use it: Any time you want to set up an input/output or software instrument for use, for setting individual channel level and pan, and for adding effects

Gain is the level (or strength) of a signal. In computer software or audio equipment, gain is the technically correct term for adjusting signal strength, not "volume," since the signal doesn't become actual sound until it reaches speakers or headphones.

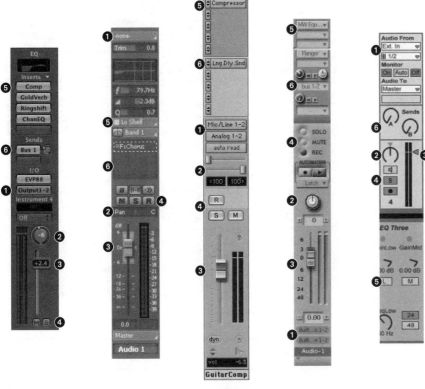

Figure 7.5 Channel strips group signal processors, routing, and level adjustments (as shown from left to right in Apple Logic Pro, Cakewalk SONAR, Digidesign Pro Tools, MOTU Digital Performer, and Ableton Live).

1 Input and output signal routings
2 Pan
3 Level
4 Solo/mute/record buttons
5 Effects inserts
6 Effects sends

Channel strips also show effects routing via two ways of adding signal processors: *inserts* (for modifying sound on a channel) and *sends* (which can be used to route sound from multiple channels to a single effect).

Inserts

An insert is so named because it is "inserted" into the signal path. The entire audio signal passing through the channel strip is routed into the insert, is modified in some way, and is then passed on to the channel's fader and output bus. In other words, you use an insert to modify sound before it reaches the fader (**Figure 7.6**). With multiple inserted effects, a signal can be fed through multiple processors in sequence.

Inserts are most useful with processors that need to be applied to a specific channel in order to shape that channel's whole sound, such as filters, chorusing, and delay.

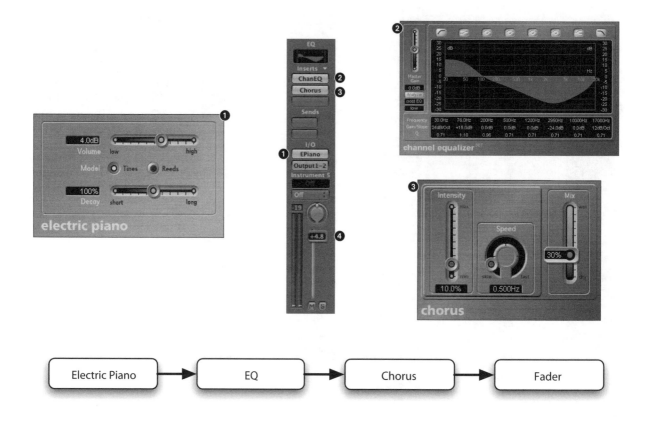

Figure 7.6 Signal starts at the electric piano source (1), is routed through two inserts (2, 3), and then arrives at the fader (4), as shown in Apple Logic Pro.

Sends/returns and buses

Wet/dry balance: Some effects let you choose how much of the *dry* (original source) sound you use versus the amount of *wet* (modified) sound you use; the wet/dry blend is routed to the effect's output.

Inserts process an entire signal at once, which is comparable to holding a colored filter up to the lens of a camera. If you want to process only a portion of a signal, so that you hear the original source on its own mixer fader while a processed sound is heard on a separate fader, you'll need to use a send for the effect rather than an insert. A send, short for "auxiliary send," routes the signal to an additional output, called a return. (This scheme is often commonly called busing, and the send/return configuration a bus.) Both your original channel and the return are routed to the final mix, effectively allowing your signal to be in two places at once: the signal is present on the original channel, with any inserted effects you've added there, and is also routed, at a specified level (the send level) to a return channel (also

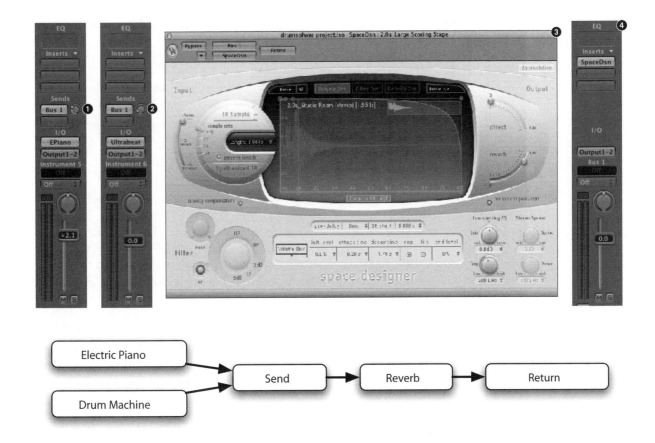

Figure 7.7 Sends allow you to route multiple channels to the same effect(s) (on an effects bus), controlling the level of each signal being sent to the bus. Here, signals from a keyboard and drum machine are both fed to send bus 1, but the sends on the two channels are set to different levels (1, 2). A reverb is inserted on the send bus (3), and the output of the send bus is returned to the main output bus (4).

called an auxiliary channel), where you can apply other effects. Since more than one channel can be fed to a send/return, the return channel can mix as many channels as you'd like, with the balance of each set by the send level on each channel feeding it (**Figure 7.7**).

Using the return channel, you can process a signal from multiple channels through a single effect. One reason to do this is to give the impression that the sounds in the various channels coexist in a signal acoustic "space." You might, for instance, want to make several instruments in a band sound as if they're playing in the same room. By routing portions of their sound to a send/return with a reverb on it, you could add the sound of the reflections of a virtual room to all the instruments simultaneously. Here's how to route a send/return:

1. Send signal from one channel or multiple channels to the send bus; a send level knob or the equivalent will let you determine how much signal you want to process from each of the individual channels. You may be able to choose a *pre* or *post* send to determine whether your signal is processed before or after the channel's fader and panpot. If you want the amount of signal going to the send to drop when the channel fader goes down, a post-fader send is what you need. But if you want to be able to lower the fader without affecting the send level, use a pre-fader send.

2. Add one or more signal processors to the send *bus*, which is where the actual processing occurs. Unlike an insert effect, effects on a send bus are usually set to 100% wet, because the dry sound is being heard through the individual channel(s).

3. After processing, the output of the signal processor feeds a *return* that (you guessed it!) returns signal to the main mix. You then have separate level controls for the dry signal (the source fader or faders) and the wet signal (the return fader), so you can adjust the mix however you like.

What's the difference between applying a single effect via a send to multiple channels and simply adding that effect as an insert on each channel? Each time you add an insert effect, you're creating a separate *instance* of that effect. For example, if you apply a reverb plug-in called "Reverb-o-rama" as an insert to channel 1, and then add Reverb-o-rama inserts to channels 2 and 3, you have three instances or copies of that plug-in. (This is hence also called "instantiating" the reverb, because you're creating an instance of it.) Each reverb has individual parameters, and you'll use roughly three times the number of CPU cycles as with only one Reverb-o-rama. That's fine if you've got CPU power to spare and want completely different settings for each channel. More often, though, both for convenience and to conserve CPU cycles, you'll route channels 1 through 3 to a send, add Reverb-o-rama to that send bus, and then adjust the balance of wet reverberation to dry signal by adjusting the level fader on the return for that bus. (See **Figure 7.8** for a diagram of this imagined scenario.)

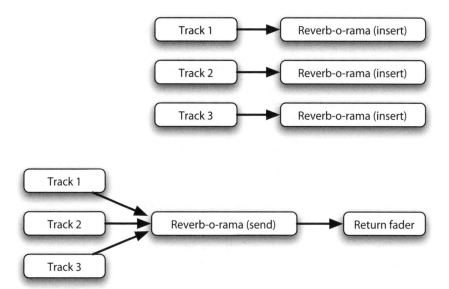

Figure 7.8 Applying the same plug-in effect to multiple inserts creates multiple instances of that plug-in, as shown here with our imaginary "Reverb-o-rama" plug-in (top). Each will have separate controls, and will require additional CPU cycles. By applying a reverb to a send (bottom), you can apply reverb to all the tracks with just one instance of the same plug-in (though you'll lose individual control over plug-in parameters for those tracks).

Choosing between inserts and sends: If you're applying individual effects to individual channels, you'll probably use an insert. The main reason you'd want to use sends is the ability to apply a single effect to multiple channels at once, for creating a single acoustic "space" in which those channels are mixed together for processing (as with a reverb), or simply to save the extra CPU cycles required to add more effects to more channels. You can also use sends to adjust the wet/dry balance on effects that lack a wet/dry setting (not all software plug-ins have such a setting). For this application, you'd use the source channel as the "dry" signal and the send for the effect, adjusting the balance of the wet signal via the return's volume fader.

Side-chaining

Side-chaining lets you route audio directly into an effect from a second audio source, such as another channel, bus, effect, or instrument. Side-chaining plug-ins offers additional capabilities, such as the use of inputs from other channels as modulators to generate rhythmic effects. Here are some possibilities, employing effects described later in the chapter:

- **Create a selective delay:** Side-chain the input of a gate to a drum pattern, then send the output of the gate to a delay, so only the heaviest hits on the drum pattern are delayed.

- **Shape a track rhythmically:** Side-chain a drum track (or other rhythmic source) to a noise gate on another track, such as a continuous pad you want to "break up," giving it the same rhythm as the drums, or a bass part or other instrument you want to tighten. The source will feed the gate, so that you hear the second track only when the amplitude of the first track crosses a threshold (as it does with each loud drum hit, for instance).

- **Make music "duck" under spoken word:** A technique commonly used in broadcast radio and similar applications is to automatically reduce the volume of music as an announcer speaks. This is called "ducking." To produce this effect, place a compressor on the music track, and side-chain the voice-over to a compressor, leaving the compressor's output gain at 0 dB (or turning off the "make-up gain" feature). This will quiet the music each time the announcer speaks.

Sometimes side-chain routings are labeled as such, while at other times you'll simply have an option for an external input, or a modulation labeled "via" that side-chains internal modules of the plug-in. Not all DAW software or effects allow side-chaining.

✋ Hands-on: Add Effects in Ableton Live

Insert Effects:

1. **Pick an effect:** For built-in Ableton effects and instruments, select the Live Device Browser (1). For non-Ableton VST/AU/DX plug-ins, choose the Plug-In Device Browser (2). Here, we've selected the built-in Chorus effect, which you might want to add to a keyboard or guitar part.

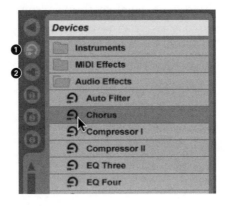

2. **Add the effect:** Select the track you want, and drag your chosen effect to the Track View. (If you don't see a window that shows "Drop Audio Effects Here," just double-click the track title.) You can route effects in sequence by adding more effects; they're routed left to right.

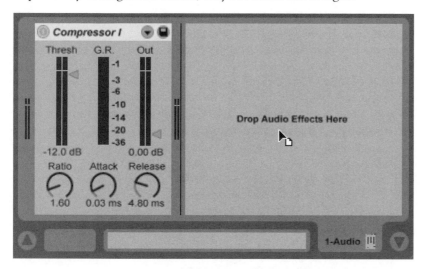

3. **Turn it on/off:** Turn effects on and off using the "power button" in the upper-left corner of each effect.

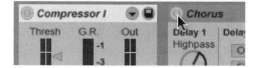

Send Effects:

1. **Set your send:** Make sure your sends/returns are visible (View > Sends and View > Returns). Pick an audio track, and adjust the send knob to determine how much of your signal to send.

Use third-party plug-ins: To make sure Live finds your third-party AU, VST, and DX plug-ins, double-check your preferences. Use Preferences > Plug-In > Active Sources to turn on/off different formats and set a default VST folder. (On the Mac choose Live > Preferences and on Windows choose Edit > Preferences.)

2. Add the effect: Drag your effect from the Device Browser (or drag it with settings intact from another track), and drop it on a Return track. (Here we've selected Live's built-in Reverb, a likely candidate for use as a send effect.)

3. **Choose pre/post:** By default, Live's sends occur post-fader, so the level and panning of the send signal will be determined by the volume and pan settings of the channel fader(s). If you'd rather set volume and pan solely with your return, choose Pre. Either way, you can adjust volume and pan on your return track just as you would with any other Live track.

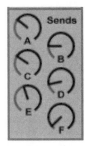

4. **Add more returns:** If the default two sends/returns aren't enough for you, use Insert > Insert Return Track to add as many as you'd like—just remember not to overload your computer's processor!

EQUALIZATION

If you've used treble and bass controls on a car stereo, "Hi," "Mid," and "Low" knobs on a mixer, or home stereo settings like "Loudness" or "Bass Boost," you've already used *equalization*. Despite the name, equalization (EQ) doesn't boost the loudness of the low frequencies so that they're at the same level as the high frequencies or vice-versa: it adjusts the relative volume or gain of various frequency ranges within a signal. (The more generic term "filter" is sometimes used in place of the term "equalization.")

We hear a sound's timbre based on its harmonic content—the relative amplitudes of the overtones (partials) of a given sound (see Chapter 1, p. 9)—so adjusting the loudness of whatever overtones happen to be present within a frequency range will impact the perceived timbre of the sound. You already have a harmonic filter in your mouth: when you form different vowel shapes during speech, the shape of your mouth filters out certain frequency ranges. (There are digital and analog filters that mimic this very effect.) Likewise, by filtering certain frequencies, equalizers can be used to solve recording problems, adjust the timbral balance of recordings, and even achieve special effects.

You can conceptualize the effect of equalizers on a graph of frequency versus amplitude, as in **Figure 7.9**. The frequency axis of the graph (the x-axis), represents the different components of the spectrum of the input sound, its partials. The amplitude axis (y-axis) represents the amplitude change of those partials when passed through the filter. With the equalizer's response shown as a curve on this graph, any rise above the 0 dB point represents a boosting of overtones, while any dip below represents reduction in amplitude. (Note, however, that if the sound being EQed has no overtones present in the frequency range you're adjusting, the EQ will make no difference.)

Equalizers are grouped by different characteristic shapes on this frequency graph. By mastering these different shapes, you'll be able to manipulate different parts of the frequency spectrum.

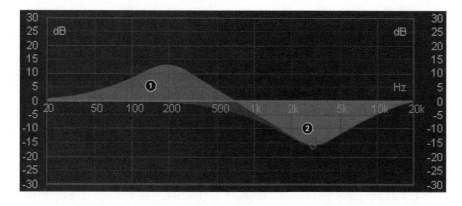

Figure 7.9 Filter response of equalizers is typically represented as an X/Y graph.

❶ A peak rising above 0 dB represents an increase in amplitude of that part of the frequency spectrum.
❷ A dip falling below 0 dB represents a decrease in amplitude.

EQ Shapes

High- and lowpass EQ

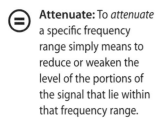

What high- and low-pass EQs do: Allow the sound energy at some frequencies to pass unchanged while others are weakened, above or below a specified frequency

How to use them: Set a cutoff frequency, above which (in the case of a lowpass filter) or below which (in the case of a highpass filter) sound energy (partials) will be weakened

When to use them: When you want to remove a large chunk of audio content at the high or low end, such as eliminating low-end rumble (via a highpass filter)

Attenuate: To *attenuate* a specific frequency range simply means to reduce or weaken the level of the portions of the signal that lie within that frequency range.

Highpass and *lowpass EQs* are the simplest form of filters. A highpass filter can also be referred to as a "low-cut" filter, while a lowpass filter can be referred to as a "high-cut" filter. Both of these filters "pass" partials in part of the frequency range unaltered while reducing or cutting the rest.

Filter is not a yes-or-no process. Filters don't operate by totally blocking off the partials in certain frequency ranges; rather, they weaken the sound energy of partials by different amounts depending on the frequency of the partial. Each filter has a *cutoff frequency,* which is usually a user-editable parameter. In the case of a lowpass filter, the further above the cutoff frequency a partial is, the more it will be attenuated (weakened). Partials close to the cutoff frequency will not be attenuated by very much, so they'll still be audible, but partials several octaves above the cutoff frequency will be attenuated by a great deal, and probably won't be heard at all. In the case of a highpass filter, the same thing happens in reverse: Partials below the cutoff frequency are attenuated, and the further they are below the cutoff, the more they're attenuated.

If we diagram the amount by which partials at various frequencies are weakened, we'll see a sloped pattern. The further above (or below) a specified cutoff frequency, as we've just noted, the more the partials are reduced in amplitude by the filter. Some filters have steeper slopes than others. The slope of a filter's response pattern is measured in dB per octave.

Common filter slopes include 6, 12, 18, and 24 dB per octave. If the filter slope is 12 dB per octave, for instance, a partial one octave above the cutoff frequency will be attenuated by 12 dB; a partial two octaves above the cutoff will be attenuated by 24 dB; and so on. Thus a 6 dB per octave slope is more gradual or gentle compared to a 24 dB/octave slope, and will allow partials that fall further past the cutoff frequency to remain more audible. The slope of a filter is also known as the *rolloff,* because the filter "rolls off" sound energy past the cutoff frequency. Some filters let you choose a slope from among several options, whereas others have a fixed slope.

The cutoff frequency is usually defined as the frequency at which the filter reduces the input signal by 3 dB (**Figure 7.10**). The portion of the frequency spectrum that lies beyond the cutoff frequency (that is, above the cutoff in the case of a lowpass filter or below the cutoff in the case of a highpass filter) is called the *stopband,* because partials in that region will be stopped. The portion of the frequency spectrum on the other side of the cutoff frequency is called the *passband*, because partials in that region will pass through the filter unaltered.

Partials that are at or near the cutoff frequency may be boosted if the filter is *resonant*. Thus, increasing the "resonance" setting of a filter with adjustable resonance will emphasize the cutoff frequency and frequencies near it.

High- and lowpass filters are best for dramatic changes to large ranges of frequency content, or for cutting narrow ranges all the way at the top or bottom of the spectrum (like low-end rumble or extremely high-pitched hiss). They're not as good at removing broad-spectrum noise, the kind most often found in noisy recordings, because they'll tend to remove a lot of the frequency content you want to keep; specific noise reduction tools are better-suited to that purpose. (See p. 261.) They're also not as good at fine-tuned adjustments to narrower ranges or for fixed amounts of reduction. For more nuanced tasks, you'll need two other kinds of EQ: shelving and peaking.

 Specific filter types: A *rumble filter* is simply a highpass filter (i.e., a filter that reduces low-end frequencies) with a low cutoff frequency for getting rid of extremely low "rumblings" that can creep into a recording.

A *bandpass filter* is a filter that reduces both lows and highs while leaving unaffected a range of frequencies in between (the passband). You can create a bandpass filter by combining a highpass filter and a lowpass filter in series. Set the cutoff frequency of the highpass filter to the lowest frequency of the desired passband, and the cutoff of the lowpass filter to the highest frequency of the desired passband.

A *resonant filter* is any filter that emphasizes frequencies on or around the cutoff frequency (Figure 7.10).

Shelving EQ

High- and lowpass filters attenuate all frequencies beyond the cutoff; you can sometimes choose different slopes or even boost frequencies around the cutoff slightly with resonance, but you can't specify a fixed amount of

 Don't get confused: "Highpass" = cuts low "Lowpass" = cuts high

 What a shelving EQ does: Boosts or cuts frequencies above or below a certain frequency

How to use it: Set the cutoff frequency (if one is provided; some shelving EQs have a fixed cutoff frequency) and an amount (gain) by which to boost or cut

When to use it: To boost or cut a range of frequencies by a variable amount, such as slightly reducing a sound's high end

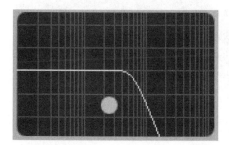

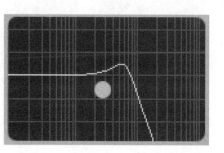

Figure 7.10 The slope is the "rolloff" pattern of a filter beyond its cutoff frequency (left). In the case of a resonant filter, in addition to the frequencies that are attenuated, frequencies around the cutoff are boosted (right).

attenuation, and you can't boost large frequency ranges. Shelving EQs, in contrast, allow a broad range of frequencies to be boosted or cut by a fixed amount. They also have a slope, but rather than continuing to slope past the cutoff, the shelving filter's curve levels off again (**Figure 7.11**).

Shelving filters are typically used for subtle reductions of a frequency range— for instance, reducing some of the high-frequency content of a sound that's too shrill.

Peaking filter

What a peaking filter does: Boosts or cuts frequencies around a certain frequency: a "bell-curve" filter

How to use it: Set a center frequency, choose (if your filter allows it) a value to determine how broad or narrow the filter is (Q), and set the cut or boost amount

When to use it: For precise control over a specific range of frequencies, such as "warming up" a sound by boosting the mid-frequency range

High- and lowpass filters represent the "brute force" approach to filtering, adjusting all of the sound energy beyond a cutoff frequency. *Peaking filters* let you choose both ends of the frequency range that will be affected, allowing you to manipulate a narrower range of frequencies.

The response curve of a peaking filter is shaped like a bell curve. Here are some additional parameters to give you full control over the shape of that curve:

- **Center frequency:** The frequency around which you want to increase or decrease signal.

- **Gain (slope):** "Height" of the curve; the amount by which signal is increased or decreased (in dB) at the center frequency.

- **Bandwidth:** "Width" of the curve; range of frequencies being manipulated, measured as the distance between the –3 dB points on either side of the center frequency.

- **Q** (as in Quality, sometimes called Resonance or Emphasis): "Selectivity" of the curve; describes the narrowness or broadness of the overall filter settings. Q and bandwidth are sometimes used interchangeably, but "Q" is more likely the label you'll see on your software or gear.

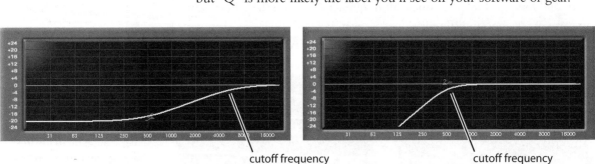

cutoff frequency   cutoff frequency

Figure 7.11 A shelving filter (left) eventually levels off once it reaches a maximum level of cut or boost, as opposed to a high-pass filter (right), which continues to cut frequency content along a steady slope. (Shown: ParaEQ in MOTU Digital Performer)

Peaking filters are useful for adjusting the strength or weakness of specific ranges of partials. For instance, if a sound is muddy because its low- or mid-frequency range is too intense, you might reduce the sound in that range by focusing a peaking filter on a frequency around the center of the "muddiness," turning down the gain, and adjusting the Q to reduce the range of the filter. But keep in mind, as discussed in Chapter 6, you don't want to fall into the trap of using EQ to fix problems in an initial recording. Try to resolve issues with mic choice and placement first, leaving EQ for fine-tuning and creative control.

 Notch filter: A *notch filter* can be thought of as a peaking filter with a very high Q, for focusing on and cutting a tiny range of frequencies (hence, a notch).

 Resonance versus Q: Resonance and Q are the same thing. *Resonance* is usually used in place of the term Q for analog filtering, since it has specific connotations in regard to Moog synthesizers and filters, and other classic analog instruments and effects. A higher resonance is a higher Q.

What Q Means

The term "Q" is useful because it presents a simple, easy-to-read number that describes how selective your filter curve is. The higher the Q number, the more fine-tuned your adjustment will be. A filter with a low Q impacts a broad range of frequencies around the center frequency—better for subtle adjustment of a larger frequency range—whereas a peaking filter with a high Q impacts a very narrow range of frequencies, better for "razor blade" adjustments to the spectrum. (See **Figure 7.12** for a comparison.) For instance, if you want to give your sound some additional presence in the midrange around 800 Hz, you can set your center frequency to 800 Hz and Q to 1.5.

The Q number is calculated by dividing the center frequency by the bandwidth. For example, if a filter's curve is centered at 400 Hz, with cutoff frequencies (–3 dB) at 500 Hz and 300 Hz, Q would be calculated by dividing 400 by 500 minus 300, which is 400/200 = 2.

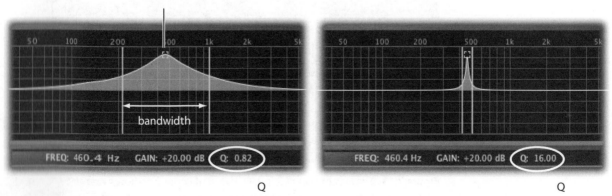

Figure 7.12 Set the Q low (left) to cover a wider range around the center frequency, or set the Q high (right) for a narrow range. (Shown: MasterWorks EQ in MOTU Digital Performer)

EQ Filter Tools

What an EQ does: Combines several filters into a single tool so you can increase or reduce the relative strengths of different frequency ranges all at once

How to use it: Switch on as many bands as you need, and set the frequency, gain, and Q for each band

When to use it: For general-purpose adjustment to the frequency content of a sound, such as adjusting the timbre of recordings or removing unwanted hum, hiss, and other low-level sonic artifacts

The actual EQ you'll find in a DAW or equivalent will most likely include three (or more) filters in a single plug-in. This is true of equalizers with names like "parametric EQ," "multiband EQ," "3-band EQ," "graphic EQ," and "DJ EQ." (If you're using a modular system like Reaktor or Max/MSP, or the filters built into a synth, you may see individual filters instead; you can then combine them using modular routing into a variety of combinations.)

Multiband parametric EQ

Sometimes you need to use more than one filter on a given sound. You might want to get rid of some rumble, slightly reduce the midrange, and enhance the treble sparkle of a drum recording all at the same time. If so, you'll need multiple filters in one. Enter the multiband *parametric EQ* (**Figure 7.13**).

Figure 7.13 The Masterworks EQ in MOTU Digital Performer shows off the advantages of implementing EQ in software. You can drag each band's center frequency and gain freely, and preview your sound file as you work. Most of the time, subtler adjustments to the overall curve are what you want.

Peaking filters are useful for adjusting the strength or weakness of specific ranges of partials. For instance, if a sound is muddy because its low- or mid-frequency range is too intense, you might reduce the sound in that range by focusing a peaking filter on a frequency around the center of the "muddiness," turning down the gain, and adjusting the Q to reduce the range of the filter. But keep in mind, as discussed in Chapter 6, you don't want to fall into the trap of using EQ to fix problems in an initial recording. Try to resolve issues with mic choice and placement first, leaving EQ for fine-tuning and creative control.

 Notch filter: A *notch filter* can be thought of as a peaking filter with a very high Q, for focusing on and cutting a tiny range of frequencies (hence, a notch).

Resonance versus Q: Resonance and Q are the same thing. *Resonance* is usually used in place of the term Q for analog filtering, since it has specific connotations in regard to Moog synthesizers and filters, and other classic analog instruments and effects. A higher resonance is a higher Q.

 What Q Means

The term "Q" is useful because it presents a simple, easy-to-read number that describes how selective your filter curve is. The higher the Q number, the more fine-tuned your adjustment will be. A filter with a low Q impacts a broad range of frequencies around the center frequency—better for subtle adjustment of a larger frequency range—whereas a peaking filter with a high Q impacts a very narrow range of frequencies, better for "razor blade" adjustments to the spectrum. (See **Figure 7.12** for a comparison.) For instance, if you want to give your sound some additional presence in the midrange around 800 Hz, you can set your center frequency to 800 Hz and Q to 1.5.

The Q number is calculated by dividing the center frequency by the bandwidth. For example, if a filter's curve is centered at 400 Hz, with cutoff frequencies (–3 dB) at 500 Hz and 300 Hz, Q would be calculated by dividing 400 by 500 minus 300, which is 400/200 = 2.

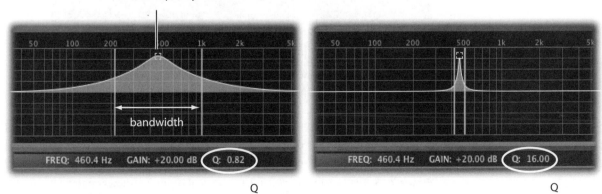

center frequency

bandwidth

FREQ: 460.4 Hz   GAIN: +20.00 dB   Q: 0.82

FREQ: 460.4 Hz   GAIN: +20.00 dB   Q: 16.00

Q

Q

Figure 7.12 Set the Q low (left) to cover a wider range around the center frequency, or set the Q high (right) for a narrow range. (Shown: MasterWorks EQ in MOTU Digital Performer)

EQ Filter Tools

The actual EQ you'll find in a DAW or equivalent will most likely include three (or more) filters in a single plug-in. This is true of equalizers with names like "parametric EQ," "multiband EQ," "3-band EQ," "graphic EQ," and "DJ EQ." (If you're using a modular system like Reaktor or Max/MSP, or the filters built into a synth, you may see individual filters instead; you can then combine them using modular routing into a variety of combinations.)

Multiband parametric EQ

Sometimes you need to use more than one filter on a given sound. You might want to get rid of some rumble, slightly reduce the midrange, and enhance the treble sparkle of a drum recording all at the same time. If so, you'll need multiple filters in one. Enter the multiband *parametric EQ* (**Figure 7.13**).

Figure 7.13 The Masterworks EQ in MOTU Digital Performer shows off the advantages of implementing EQ in software. You can drag each band's center frequency and gain freely, and preview your sound file as you work. Most of the time, subtler adjustments to the overall curve are what you want.

What an EQ does: Combines several filters into a single tool so you can increase or reduce the relative strengths of different frequency ranges all at once

How to use it: Switch on as many bands as you need, and set the frequency, gain, and Q for each band

When to use it: For general-purpose adjustment to the frequency content of a sound, such as adjusting the timbre of recordings or removing unwanted hum, hiss, and other low-level sonic artifacts

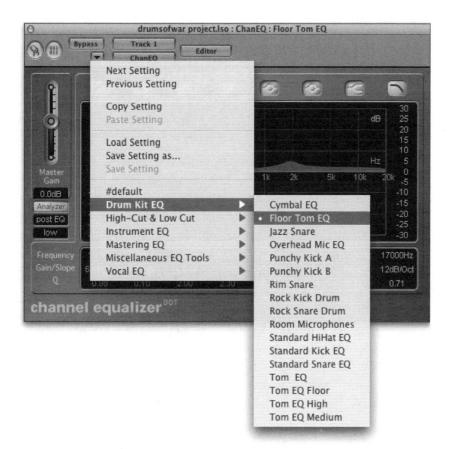

Figure 7.15 For a sense of common creative and utility applications of EQ, surf the extensive presets in EQ plug-ins like the one included with Logic Pro.

Graphic EQ

Graphic equalizers are composed of a series of fixed bandpass filters for creating an overall frequency curve. They provide gain controls for various frequency bands but not control over bandwidth (**Figure 7.16**). Because their Q and center frequencies aren't adjustable, they don't offer as much control as parametric EQs, but some users prefer to work with fixed bands rather than the movable bands of a parametric EQ. Graphic equalizers in software model the function of classic, professional graphic EQs, and sometimes their desirable imperfections ("warmth").

What a graphic EQ does: A series of filters arranged at fixed frequency intervals cuts or boosts the frequency content of sound

How to use it: Isolate individual octaves or create overall curves; the only controllable parameter is gain

When to use it: For a traditional sound of a "classic" hardware graphic EQ

Figure 7.16 Anwidasoft's GEQ31V Windows/Mac VST plug-in (www.anwida.com) looks, works, and sounds like a traditional analog hardware graphic EQ. It's intended to add some of the warmth and distinctive sound of its predecessors.

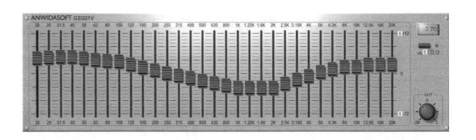

 What a DJ-style EQ does: A simplified 2-band or 3-band shelving EQ attenuates large blocks of frequency content at once

How to use it: Adjust the gain of high, mid, and low bands (or just high/low)

When to use it: For radical timbral changes to your sound via controls familiar to users of DJ hardware

 Sweep it: As shown in the Chapter 5 tutorial on p. 155, you can use an EQ to sweep through different timbres. The same trick works in any application that has an EQ.

"DJ-style" EQ

DJs have added to the musical language of EQ by using simple EQs to achieve timbral effects. Because the controls are reduced to low, mid, and high filters, for instance, DJ-style EQs can produce drastic results quickly, without the need to adjust parameters like Q. Drum loops, because they contain broad-spectrum, noisy signal, are perfect for radical filter changes: assign the EQ to a knob, then turn the knob gradually. You'll hear the drum loop go from muffled to brassy. This effect has become so common that it's spread to many forms of music that use electronic beats. Some EQs of this type are designed to color the signal as an analog filter would, even when the controls are set to zero, as in Ableton Live's EQ Three (**Figure 7.17**).

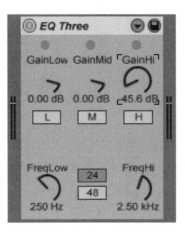

Figure 7.17 Ableton Live's EQ Four is a traditional parametric EQ, but DJs, remix artists, and electronica lovers may be happier with the simple DJ-style EQ Three shown here.

Step filter (and other musical effects)

Since filter cutoff and resonance (Q) have a distinctive effect on the timbre of sound, they can be used for rich musical effects by modulating their settings over time. Electronic music often uses modulated filters; for example, distinctive rhythm-synced step filters, adopted from analog equipment, are popular in electronica and dance music. To achieve this effect, you can use mix automation in your sequencer (or take advantage of features like Ableton Live's clip envelopes) or a specialized effect like the one shown in **Figure 7.18**. By synchronizing changes to the beat or sweeping through filter changes over time, you can make filtering an active part of your music.

 What a step filter does: A pattern sequencer drives filter cutoff and resonance settings for rhythmic and melodic filtering effects

How to use it: Draw in "step" patterns for filter and/or resonance, and sync the filter with your music's tempo

When to use it: For analog-style, grooving filters

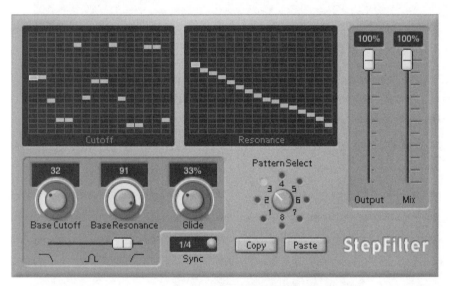

Figure 7.18 With Cubase SX's StepFilter, you can draw various patterns to control filter cutoff and resonance in time with your music. Try disparate patterns for a more rhythmic/melodic effect or continuous curves for a gradual sweeping effect.

Painting with Filters

Most digital filters emulate analog controls with knobs, a fixed number of bands, and rounded analog-style filter shapes. However, software is capable of providing almost any imaginable interface and filter method. Applications like U&I Software's MetaSynth (Mac-only, **Figure 7.19**) allow you to use painting tools to visually edit a spectrum. Not only can this be more intuitive, since you can easily see the impact your filtering has on the spectrum of the sound, but it allows fine control not possible with other methods.

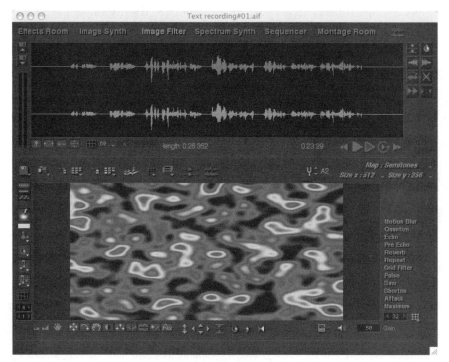

Figure 7.19 MetaSynth (www.uisoftware.com) features envelopes and filters that can be manipulated using visual tools, normally associated with graphics applications, for audio shaping not possible with knobs.

✋ Hands-on: EQ in Ableton Live

If your recorded sound doesn't sound quite "right"—perhaps the sound is a bit flat and lifeless in the treble, and too much bass has made it muddy—a parametric EQ can help you make adjustments. By creating different EQ curves, you can bring out some frequencies while de-emphasizing others. To begin, drag the EQ Four from the Device Browser (see p. 210) to the audio or instrument track you want to process. It will appear as shown in **Figure 7.20**.

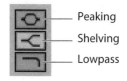

— Peaking
— Shelving
— Lowpass

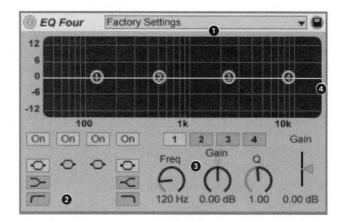

Figure 7.20 Live's EQ Four is a typical four-band parametric EQ flexible enough for any basic filtering task. You'll find (1) a menu of presets; (2) controls to turn bands on and off and set them to a filter shape; (3) knobs to adjust individual parameters for each band; and (4) a graphical display of your overall EQ curve on which you can directly drag each band.

1. **Create a highpass filter:** Select band one (1, near right) since it's the lowest band, and change it to a highpass filter by clicking the highpass icon (2). Now your EQ will cut out low frequencies (such as rumble).

2. **Create a lowpass filter:** Select band four and change it to a lowpass filter (the icon is the mirror image of the highpass icon). You'll notice this cuts high frequencies but boosts signal at the cutoff, so adjust the Q setting (far right) to 0.74 for a more typical lowpass. Now your EQ will cut out high frequencies. (If you leave your highpass filter activated, you've just created a bandpass filter.)

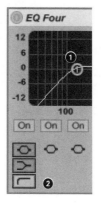

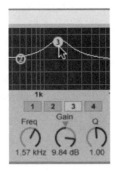

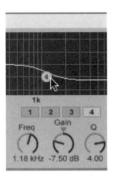

3. **Create a peaking filter:** Bands two and three are fixed as peaking filters. You can adjust them by clicking the band number and then adjusting frequency and gain knobs, but try just dragging the number around the graph. (It's a bit more fun!) Adjust the Q knob all the way to 12 for a very narrow filter, then widen it by reducing the Q. Now you can accentuate or reduce any frequency range you like.

4. **Create a shelving filter:** Clear your settings by selecting the Factory Defaults from the presets menu (use the down arrow in the upper-right corner of the EQ Four). Select band four and choose the shelving filter mode (1). Set its gain to –7 or –8 dB, set its frequency below 3 kHz, and adjust the Q to 4. (There's nothing special about these settings, they just make it easy to see what a shelving filter does.) Try dragging the fourth band's control (the circle with the number four) around in the display for a better sense of how the shelf shape works. Increase the gain to a positive dB to boost signal.

5. **Put it all together:** Now that you know the basic shapes, you can draw whatever overall EQ curve you want. Since Live can loop audio easily, your best bet is to start a loop, add an EQ to the track, and make EQ adjustments by ear until you like what you hear. (Click the power button in the upper-left corner to compare your modified sound to the original.) For instance, set band 1 to a steep high-cut filter at a low frequency to eliminate rumble, band 2 to a medium Q and small gain decrease to reduce some midrange, band 3 to a lower Q and small gain increase to brighten the high mids, and band 4 as a shelving filter with a fairly high cutoff to reduce some of the brassiest high-pitched sound. See **Figure 7.21** to see how frequency ranges respond to adjustments.

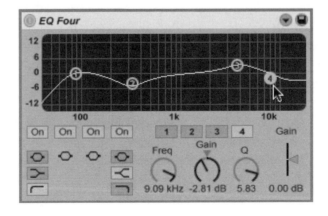

6. **Try some presets:** As in any effect in any program, checking the presets is a great way to learn. In EQ Four, check out:

    *   **Phat Low:** Gives some extra punch to your bass

    *   **Curved:** Adds nice presence to the sound; try guitar and drums for starters

    *   **Notch 4:** Features four notch filters (remember, notch filters are just peaking filters with high Q settings); move them around to select specific frequencies to remove or boost for extreme filtering.

    The Vocal presets are modeled after the way your mouth shapes sound when you form vowels. If you ever wondered what your favorite drum loop would sound like played inside your mouth, here's your chance!

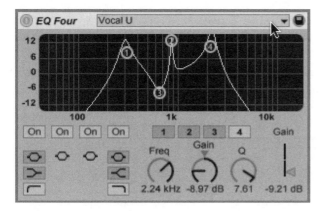

In other software: You'll find that most parametric EQs work similarly to Live's EQ Four. (Many also use icons for parametric, shelving, and peaking filters.)

Figure 7.21 To create an EQ curve with the sound you want, you'll need to listen to your sound in different ranges of the spectrum. Here are some approximate ideas of how much to boost or cut, and in what ranges. Different instruments will vary, so once you have a sense of the basic ranges, your ear will be your best tool.

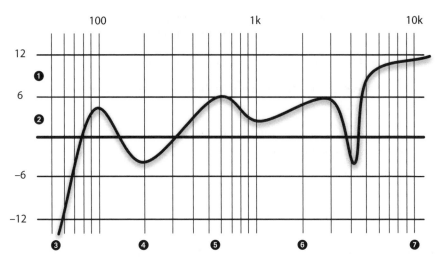

❶ 6–12 dB: Drastic adjustment

❷ 0–6 dB: Typical adjustment

❸ 50–100 Hz: (Bass range) Increase for bass "boom"; decrease to help clarity

❹ 200 Hz: (Low musical range) Increase to add fullness; decrease to reduce muddiness

❺ 400–880 Hz: (Vocal range) Increase for clarity; decrease to enhance presence

❻ 1.5kHz–7kHz: (Overtones) Increase for punch and presence; decrease if sound is thin

❼ 10+ kHz: (Overtones) Increase for brightness; decrease to reduce hiss/ess

DYNAMICS PROCESSORS

Dynamics processors modify the amplitude range of sound, from quieting noises you want to deemphasize to "squeezing" the overall range so tracks can sound louder to adjusting certain loudness levels of sounds. You could keep one hand on the fader at all times and manually adjust dynamics, but dynamics processors are capable of performing efficient, automatic edits that produce effects your fingers can't.

Compressor

Compressors take the overall dynamic range and compress it to a smaller range by reducing the amplitude of a signal when it rises above a certain thresh-old. Counterintuitively, you'll typically apply compression to make your track sound louder. After bringing the loudest peaks of a sound down within a more manageable range using a compressor, you can safely turn up the entire track's volume, which will bring out sounds that otherwise might be too soft to hear easily. The behavior of a compressor is controlled by a number of parameters:

- **Threshold (dB):** The threshold is the amplitude level beyond which the compressor begins to reduce the level of the signal: when signal amplitude exceeds this value, the compressor becomes active.

- **Ratio (input:output):** Ratio determines the amount of gain reduction that will be applied when the input passes the threshold; it's a ratio of the input gain to the output gain. If the ratio is set to 3:1, a 3 dB increase in input gain beyond the threshold results in just a 1 dB increase in the output. Some compressors also include a *knee* setting, which adjusts the curvature of the point where reduction begins; not surprisingly, this point looks like a "knee" (**Figure 7.22**).

- **Attack/release (ms):** In order to reduce the output level as the input level rises past the threshold, compressors act like an automated volume fader. Attack and release timings determine how quickly or slowly the compressor makes its gain adjustments. Attack is the amount of time during which the reduction begins to take effect, and release (sometimes called decay) is the amount of time during which the compression goes away, returning the output level of the signal to the same level as the input level. Imagine you are watching a mixer: whenever a signal crosses the meter beyond a certain number of decibels (the threshold), you reach for the fader and pull it down more or less quickly (the attack); when the signal crosses back below the threshold, you return the fader to its original level (release). Typically, you'll want to strike a balance between settings that are too short (creating an audible pumping sound, though that can be useful for a special musical effect, as mentioned in the following tip) and settings that are too long (which can sound artificial).

- **Output gain (dB):** Output gain (more descriptively called "make-up gain") simply adds volume to the sound after it's been processed by the compressor. Compression makes the overall sound softer, since it's reducing the gain of the signal whenever the signal rises past the threshold. By adding output gain, you can restore the overall average amplitude of the sound, amplifying softer sounds in the process.

What a compressor does: Reduces overall dynamic range by making louder sounds quieter

How to use it: Set a threshold above which the signal will be reduced, an amount of reduction, and the timing characteristics (attack and release times), then set the output gain to make the overall sound louder

When to use it: By "smoothing out" the dynamic range of a track, you can use compression to make sound "denser" and louder by increasing output gain. Compression is often applied to instruments like drums, guitar, and vocals.

Milliseconds (ms): Short periods of time are usually indicated in audio software using the term milliseconds (abbreviated ms). A millisecond is 1/1000 of a second; there are 1000 ms in a single second. You'll often see envelope attack and release times and the delay time in delay effects indicated in ms.

Figure 7.22 Apple Logic Pro's Compressor has a built-in visualization of the output:input gain curve. The input gain is graphed on the x axis and the output gain on the y axis.

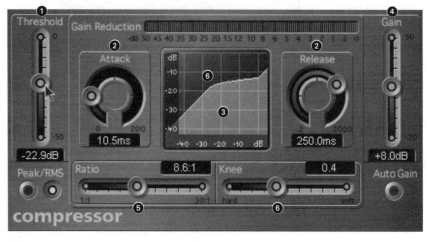

❶ Threshold level

❷ Attack and release settings

❸ Curve shows the proportion of output gain (y axis) to input gain (x axis).

❹ Output gain

❺ Ratio sets the slope of the curve.

❻ Knee rounds off the area around the threshold.

The best way to learn about compression, as with other processors, is to try it out. A small amount of compression can smooth out wide dynamic ranges and make your signal sound more intense or more even, but too much can make it sound flat and lifeless. Just compressing a signal as far as you can isn't always a good idea: changes in dynamics are part of what makes music exciting.

Compression can be applied both at the track level and in mastering (see information about mastering with compression in Chapter 10).

Limiter

Dynamics processors that limit signal to a certain amplitude threshold are called *limiters* (**Figure 7.23**). Limiters are basically compressors with a large input:output ratio in which signal above the threshold is always reduced to nearly the same level (a flat slope). Because of the different uses of a limiter, you'll have a slightly different choice of settings:

- **Threshold:** Maximum amplitude above which a signal can't rise.

- **Release:** Functions like the release setting on a compressor except that in this case to reduce pumping, you'll do the opposite of what you'd do with a compressor. Since the output ratio is flat beyond the threshold, you want as short a release time as possible.

What a limiter does: Prevents the signal from rising past a certain amplitude level

How to use it: Set a threshold amplitude and release time (you won't use an output gain as you would on a compressor)

When to use it: To prevent system overload by setting a fixed maximum output level, particularly in broadcast media applications. You can also use it creatively for extreme-ratio compression. If you want a compressor with more "squashing" power, a limiter is your best bet.

- **Look-ahead:** A look-ahead feature predicts what the peak of audio will be by storing a short segment of the signal in a buffer, analyzing the contents of the buffer before applying limiting for best results.

- **Input/output gain:** Like the compressor, limiters often include input and output gain settings.

Limiters are integral to analog-to-digital converters in hardware (like digital recorders and computer audio interfaces). Limiters integrated with the A/D circuitry moderate the incoming signal and protect digital circuitry by limiting signal to a safe level. Hard-limiters will create digital distortion if signal exceeds their maximum threshold; some audio hardware employs soft-limiters designed to deliberately produce harmonics for a "pleasant" distorted sound. (See "Distortion," p. 247.)

 Pump it up: Normally, you'll want to adjust attack and release settings for smooth gain transitions, but by setting both very low (less than 10 ms), you can create a pumping, rhythmic effect, which works well on drums.

Figure 7.23 Bomb Factory's hardware-style BF76 Peak Limiter, bundled with Digidesign Pro Tools, shows an analog meter to demonstrate when signals peak "in the red"; the limiter adjusts gain beyond that threshold. The BF76 is an emulation of the Universal Audio 1176 "peak limiter," in turn a descendent of vacuum tube limiters like the Universal Audio 175 and 176.

Expander

Expanders are generally the inverse of compressors (as you might expect), but have two different variants: downward and upward.

A *downward expander* decreases the gain when the input signal falls *below* a threshold to provide the impression of a larger dynamic range. In compressors louder signals become less loud, whereas in an expander quiet signals become even more quiet. The same parameters otherwise apply, with a reversed input:output gain relationship from the compressor.

What an expander does: Increases the dynamic range of a sound by decreasing volume when the signal level falls *below* an amplitude threshold or increasing volume *above* (the opposite of a compressor)

How to use it: Set threshold, ratio, attack, release, output gain—just as on a compressor, only with a reversed effect

When to use it: For artistic purposes to create additional contrast between loud and soft sounds on drums or vocals, or to reduce the level of background noise during a live recording

An *upward expander* also increases apparent dynamic range, but it does so by *increasing* the level of a signal (rather than decreasing signal, as on a compressor) when the input level is *above* the threshold, as shown in **Figure 7.24**.

The easiest way to differentiate compressor/limiters and expanders is to think about what they do to overall dynamic range, as shown in **Figure 7.25**. Expanders are useful for expanding the "crispness" or "punchiness" of sounds with dynamic contrasts, like drums, by emphasizing louder sounds and deemphasizing quieter ones.

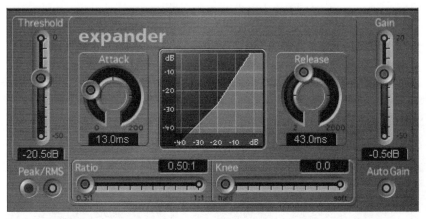

Figure 7.24 Logic Pro's expander is an upward expander. As you can see from the input:output ratio, it's the inverse of a compressor.

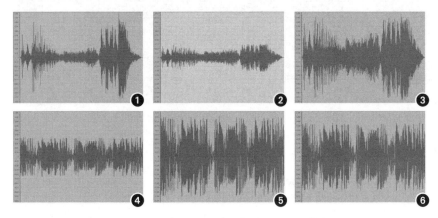

Figure 7.25 Top: A compressor takes a signal with a large overall dynamic range (1), reduces the gain of louder signals for a smaller overall dynamic range (2), and then (3) boosts the smaller signal range with gain. The impression is of a louder sound overall. Bottom: An upward expander takes a signal with a small overall dynamic range (4) and increases the gain of louder signals (5) before finally reducing gain (6), resulting in a greater overall dynamic range. (A downward expander has the same basic effect as an upward expander, but reduces soft sounds instead of increasing loud sounds.)

Noise Gate

Whereas limiters, expanders, and compressors all adjust signal amplitude smoothly, a *gate* makes a sharp attenuation in sound, reducing or completely cutting the signal when the signal drops below a threshold (**Figure 7.26**). Similar to an upside-down limiter, a gate silences sounds that drop below a certain amplitude level. The main parameters you'll be editing in a noise gate are:

- **Threshold:** Usually, gates cut portions of the signal that drop below the threshold, although some gates will allow you to "flip" the threshold, reducing or cutting louder signal instead of softer signal, which can create unusual rhythmic effects.

- **Reduction:** The reduction amount is the amount of attenuation performed by the gate when triggered.

- **Look-ahead:** Gates, like limiters, benefit from the look-ahead function in order to be able to react smoothly when the signal hits the threshold.

- **Attack/hold/release:** Like other dynamics processors, a gate is configurable with attack and decay settings, but it adds an additional setting: *hold*. The hold setting determines how long it remains open (or, in reverse mode, how long it remains closed).

- **External input (optional):** Gates can be triggered externally. Triggers can include manual input (that is, pressing a key or clicking a button), MIDI input, or a side-chained audio input from another channel, again opening up creative rhythmic possibilities.

- **Frequency range:** Some gates are frequency specific, combining a gate with a frequency filter.

What a gate does: Reduces a signal when the signal falls below (or, more rarely, above) a threshold with an immediate, rather than gradual, adjustment

How to use it: Set a threshold and the amount by which you want the signal reduced—including completely cutting the signal, if you prefer

When to use it: To suppress noise during low-amplitude lulls in sound (like a cough during a break). You can also employ gates creatively for rhythmic dynamic effects.

Gates and drums: By adding a gate with a high threshold to a drum track, you can create punchier, more rhythmic drums. A short attack with longer hold and release times will isolate the attacks of the drums and eliminate some of their decay. More extreme settings can create odd rhythmic effects.

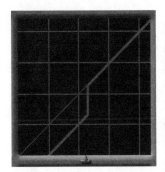 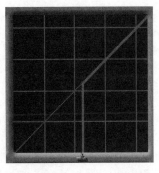

Figure 7.26 A gate can either reduce signal below the threshold (left) or cut it completely (right). (Shown: MasterWorks Gate in MOTU Digital Performer)

Gating other elements: A gate doesn't have to be a dynamics processor. A gate can be any processor triggered by specific amplitudes, like Logic Pro's bizarre Spectral Gate, which lets you work with gated frequency components individually for off-the-wall, alien-sounding filtering.

The most common application of a gate is as a noise gate: set the amplitude to the level below which you want sounds to be suppressed, regions where nothing louder than that level is occurring will be reduced or cut. For rhythmic effects, use the gate to reduce or eliminate sounds below a higher threshold, for instance isolating the transients of a drum loop or other percussive track.

Combining Dynamics

As you may have noticed, compressors, limiters, expanders, and gates are all closely related in function. Many hardware and software processors combine some or all of these functions into a single general-purpose dynamics processor (as in **Figure 7.27**). This consolidation can simply add convenience, by providing a single interface for multiple effects, or can enable you to use multiple dynamics processors in tandem. To help you remember which of these processors does what, **Table 7.1** offers a basic comparison.

Figure 7.27 Instead of using different plug-ins for each function, Cubase SX's Dynamics plug-in combines a compressor/expander, gate, and limiter.

Dynamics processors can also be combined with frequency-specific filters for hybrid processors like multiband compressors, which allow different compression settings for different frequency ranges (**Figure 7.28**). A *de-esser*, for instance, is a specialized processor for removing high-frequency "ess" sounds generated by vocals and some instruments, and is really at its heart a bandpass- or highpass-specific compressor.

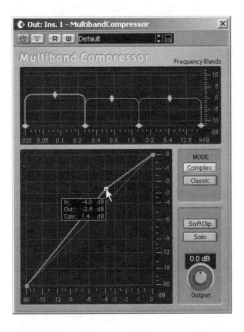

Figure 7.28 Multi-band compressors like the one included with Cubase SX allow different settings for different frequency ranges, for finer control of dynamics.

Table 7.1 Dynamics Processors at a Glance

Type	Graph (input vs. output)	Part of the Signal Affected	Increased/ Decreased
Compressor		Above threshold	Decreased; ramp
Limiter		Above threshold	Decreased; flat
Expander (upward)		Above threshold	Increased; ramp
Expander (downward)		Below threshold	Decreased; ramp
Noise gate		Below threshold (sometimes switchable)	Decreased or cut; flat

Fixing loudness— other solutions: If you're using dynamics processors to adjust the relative mix of your tracks, remember that amplitude isn't the only element in determining how you hear the mix. Different tracks will vie for your ear's attention if their frequency range is similar, so you can sometimes make more "room" for other tracks by subtly adjusting EQ. Your first step should be even simpler: make sure all your tracks aren't panned center. By using left/right (or surround) panning, you can help your ears separate different parts of the mix.

Envelope followers— other applications: Envelope shapers and followers are found throughout synthesis and filtering, because they were often incorporated in vintage modular synths. For more on the general uses of envelopes, see Chapter 9.

Table 7.2 When to Use Dynamics Processors

Desired Result	What to Do
Make overall dynamics more present, louder sounding	Use a compressor or limiter to reduce dynamic range, then increase overall gain
Keep amplitudes from getting too loud	Use a limiter to set a maximum threshold
Create a "pumping," punchy track on sounds like drums and bass	Try a compressor with a short attack time
Reduce noise and other unwanted sounds between musical events	Use a noise gate or downward expander to reduce quieter noise (also consider noise reduction software; see p. 261)
Make a punchier track with a wider dynamic range; increase accented transients	Use an expander or gate to accentuate louder sounds

Envelope Follower

Envelope followers translate changes in volume of an input into a control signal to be routed either to another process within the same effect or to a separate device or plug-in. In other words, an envelope shaper provides a way of controlling an effect, "following" the amplitude shape of an input signal. Envelope followers are the basis of a number of plug-ins, and can also be used to control parameters in plug-ins like filters: you might route an envelope follower to filter cutoff, for instance, so the filter cutoff follows the amplitude of the input (such as in an "auto-wah" effect). Unless you're using a modular sound environment, an envelope follower usually won't be a discrete plug-in; it'll be integrated into a plug-in you're using, often labeled simply "envelope" or "attack/release."

Envelope Shaper

Dynamics processors use basic *envelopes*—the attack and release times—to smooth out the effects of the processor. Envelope shapers are designed to explicitly shape the envelope of the *input sound* (**Figure 7.29**). When a transient crosses a defined threshold, the shaper adjusts the transient's gain according to the attack/release shape you define. (An envelope shaper is basically an envelope follower fed into a gain control; the net effect is a processor that re-shapes the amplitude envelope of an input.)

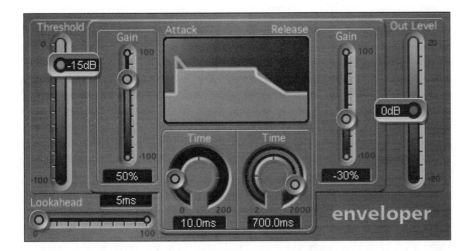

Figure 7.29 Envelope shapers like the Enveloper in Logic Pro allow you to change the envelope of an audio input directly.

Any transient has a basic envelope shape or *attack and release phase*. Simply put, the attack is the beginning of the transient as its level increases, and the release is the end as its level decreases. By changing the slope of each, you can change the envelope, and thus alter the punchiness of the sound. Typical settings include:

- **Attack** (timing and gain)

- **Release** (timing and gain)

- **Threshold**

- **Look-ahead**

- **Gain**

Of these settings, the most critical are the attack and release times and gain. Using the envelope shaper, you might:

- **Increase attack gain:** By boosting the gain of an attack, you can make a drum hit punchier.

- **Decrease/cut attack gain:** Attenuating the attack gain makes the transient fade in more slowly, giving the attack a more rounded sound.

- **Increase/decrease release gain:** Since the tail end of your input signal contains the decay of the sound and reverb content, you can emphasize or deemphasize the reverb/decay by increasing or decreasing the release gain, respectively.

What an envelope shaper does: Shapes transient signals gradually with an adjustable envelope (attack and release times)

How to use it: Set gain cut or boost for attack and release

When to use it: To smooth out timing problems, create rhythmic envelope shapes, tighten drum tracks, create punchier attacks, emphasize or deemphasize reverberation, or for other tasks

With the envelope shaper's threshold set low, boost or attenuation will impact the entire signal; this has the most pronounced effect, and one that's not possible with other dynamics processors, so it's the most typical setting. (Some envelope shapers even lack a threshold control for this reason.) By increasing a threshold, however, you can create a more specific result.

Attack and release timings are even more significant when using an envelope shaper than with other dynamics processors, because they directly shape the new amplitude envelope you create. When the times are set very high, the effect is gradual, whereas an extremely low setting will create a "glitchy" stuttering effect. Most of the time you'll want to set times in the 250 ms range, but as with the other parameters, you're limited only by your creative desires.

✋ Hands-on: Dynamics in Ableton Live

Two dynamics processors you might use often are a compressor and a gate. By adding a compressor, we'll be able to squeeze the dynamic range of a track, making it sound tighter and louder, as you might do on instruments like guitar and vocals. If you have drum tracks with long decays, they may still sound muddy, so we'll bring out the attacks of the drums by using a gate. We'll also look at how a noise gate can be used to reduce unwanted sounds in pauses in the music.

Compressor

1. **Add a compressor:** Compressor I is a very simple compressor with all the controls you'll most often need. Drag it from the Device Browser onto an audio or instrument track. (Live's Compressor II adds look-ahead and filtering, so you can work with specific frequency ranges.)

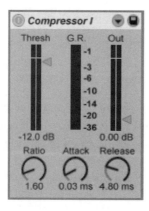

2. **Set the threshold:** Watching the incoming level meter, adjust the Thresh control so that it's just below the highest peaks in the signal. As the compressor activates, the "G.R." (gain reduction) meter in the center should be red.

3. **Set the ratio and timing:** Increase the ratio until you hear the compression you want, then adjust attack and release until the compression timing sounds right. Try a short attack (0.02 ms) and long release (60 ms) for a pumping effect, then try decreasing the release for more subtle compression.

4. **Adjust the output gain:** The signal should sound softer now, so to make up for the loss in overall amplitude, increase the output gain. Watch the meters and find a gain amount that pushes the meters into the orange part of the meter but not the red.

Gate

1. **Add a gate:** Live's Gate is similar to the Compressor: you'll find a meter with a threshold and timing controls. The reduction amount (1) determines how much the gate cuts a signal that falls below the threshold (or above, in flip mode). The indicator (2) should be green when a signal is passing through the gate.

2. **Set up a noise gate:** To use the gate as a noise gate—reducing or eliminating sound during pauses in the music—set the threshold (Thresh) just above the signal level of the noise, as shown in the image at bottom left. Leave the gate to its other defaults, because the Factory Settings preset in Live work well for a basic noise gate.

3. **Gate drums:** To bring out the attacks of a drum part, set the threshold higher (far right) and increase the cut to "-inf." Keep the attack short (0.2 ms) so you maintain the sharp leading edge of the drum sound, but adjust the hold and release times to about 10 ms or more each.

In other software: Most DAWs have some kind of dynamics processor if not a separate compressor and gate. Be sure to watch input level and output meters to check the level in whatever program you use.

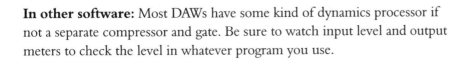

Time-Related Effects

Delay/Echo

What delay does: Repeats the signal at specified time(s)

How to use it: Set a time interval, repeat and filtering options (if available), and mix (dry/wet)

When to use it: Use shorter time intervals to create doubling effects, and larger intervals for rhythmic effects. Use tempo-synced delays to create rhythmic patterns that synchronize with the tempo of your music.

A basic *delay* or *echo* effect repeats an input signal at a specified time interval. The most basic parameters are:

- **Delay time:** The length of the delay, usually in ms but sometimes syncable to the tempo of your project.

- **Dry/wet mix:** Natural reflections are softer than the original sound, so it's common to reduce the amplitude of the delayed signal.

- **Feedback:** A simpler means of presenting multiple delays is with a feedback loop. Instead of just feeding the signal into the delay once, feedback routes the output of the delay (the delayed and possibly filtered sound) back into the input of the delay, in a loop. A feedback level parameter controls the amount of signal routed from the delay output back to the input. Set to its lowest setting, you should hear only one delay. At its highest setting, delays will build on top of one another, and will often ultimately distort.

Delay and echo should not be confused with *reverb*: delays simply repeat the signal, which can simulate basic reflections in an acoustic space but without some of the timbral and spatial controls found in a reverb. (See p. 42.)

Variants on this theme give you different sets of options, all of which may be incorporated in software in different combinations:

- **Stereo delay:** Allows special effects, either by providing separate left and right delay controls, or by automatically feeding delays to left and right channels at different times for a "ping-pong" effect.

- **Multitap delay:** Repeats the delayed signal multiple times (or "taps"), often with individual level, pan, and feedback controls for each repetition.

- **Filtered delay:** Inserts a multiband filter prior to the delay, so that different frequency components are delayed separately.

- **Tape echo:** Produces a wide range of sounds from "spacey" vintage sounds to the distinctive sound of modern dub electronica, which in turn borrows from a Jamaican reggae tradition that used tape echoes. Vintage echoes (**Figure 7.30**) relied on looping the signal through one or more reel-to-reel tape machines for warm, analog delays and unusual special effects. With feedback, the delay can continue to repeat over itself infinitely, even increasing in level until hair-raising distortion is achieved. Software emulations incorporate simulations of analog circuitry to create warm distortion.

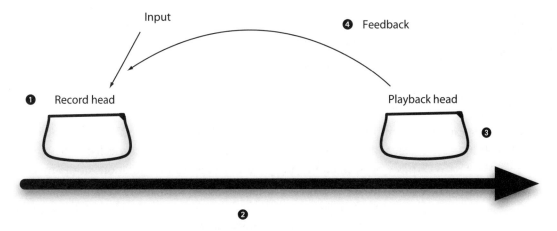

Figure 7.30 Early tape delays took advantage of the distance between the record head and the playback head of the tape recorder. A signal was fed to the record head (1), recording it on the tape. The tape then had to travel (2) the physical distance from the record head to the playback head. By the time the signal reached the playback head (3), the playback output was delayed. If you took that playback output and routed it back to the record head (4), you could create an endless loop of delays that built one atop another. The resulting warm echoes (from a single delay) or far-out effects (from feedback) are still sought after today in digital simulations. Digital delays simply create the delay through number-based algorithms, but if you have a two-head tape recorder, you can re-create the scenario shown. (Just keep in mind, different recorders create different delay lengths if the distance between heads or the speed of the tape varies!)

Reverb

What reverb does:
Simulates the many combined reflections created by acoustical spaces such as concert halls and tile-lined bathrooms

How to use it: Use predetermined settings that mimic real-world spaces, and/or manually adjust reflectivity, room size, and reverb length, balancing the wet reverberation with the dry source

When to use it: To make sound seem as though it is heard in a different space than the one in which it was recorded, for subtle, natural effects, or for more dramatic special effects

Real spaces sound the way they do because of the combination of closely spaced reflections of sound off of different surfaces, such as walls and other objects. When we hear sound, we hear a combination of:

- Direct (*dry*) sound.

- Individual reflections (*early reflections*) from nearby hard surfaces.

- Other reflections so closely spaced and overlapping that our brain can't perceive them as separate. Instead, they combine to form an overall *reverberation*, which is *filtered* by the natural properties of the space.

Imagine the sound you hear in a large cathedral or stadium: there's the direct sound coming from the performer, distinct echoes (early reflections), and a general wash of reverberation, which gradually dies away.

The most direct, though not the easiest, way to create a reverb effect is to play back your source in a space. Some pro engineers still drag speakers and a microphone out to a concrete stairwell to get a reverb "just right."

Since running to a stairwell or a parking garage wasn't always practical, predigital reverbs resorted to other means. *Plate reverbs* mechanically vibrated a piece of steel, employing pickups to record the vibrations in the metal. The plate sound was typical of recordings in the '70s and early '80s, but it required big plates: around 6´x 3´! *Spring reverbs* worked on the same basic principle but used coiled springs, allowing them to be incorporated into instruments and guitar amps; if you have a vintage amp with a reverb, it's most likely a spring reverb. Since both methods create a distinctive sound, they're both commonly emulated in software.

Specialized digital reverbs produce more realistic results with far greater control over timbre.

 When is reverb "in good taste"? Reverb is like ketchup on a burger. Most people like adding a little, but not everyone agrees on how much to use. Both analog and digital recordings can sound a little lifeless if they're completely dry (unless your recording already includes some natural reverb). A very short, low-level reverb can make a track sound warmer and more natural. The key is not to overdo it: add reverb in small amounts to taste. You'll also find you don't have to add reverb to every track in the mix: sometimes just adding a little reverb to one or two tracks provides the illusion of all the tracks being in a real space, especially if it's a subtle effect you want. Add too much reverb, and your sound will be overly muddy. Keep adding, and it'll sound like you used a large ice cave for a studio—a bad idea unless you're specifically going for that effect!

Conventional digital reverb

Most digital reverbs (like Audio Damage's reverb in **Figure 7.31**) use a combination of digital processes to produce the illusion of natural reverberation—multiple delays, equalization, envelope shaping, special filters, and other processes. These blend into the sound of the *reverb tail*, the simulated reflected sound generated by the reverb. Although the underlying algorithm is mostly invisible to the user, a number of useful parameters are commonly found on a typical reverb:

- **Predelay:** The interval before a reverb tail is added to the original signal; in real-world situations the sound of reverberation reaches your ears slightly later than the dry sound. In a large concert hall or gymnasium, where the walls are far from the sound source, the delay between the dry sound and the beginning of the reverberation may be more than 50 ms.

- **Early reflections:** This parameter controls the level of discrete initial reflections—the clearly heard delays at the beginning of the reverb tail, before individual delays combine into a wash of reverberation.

- **Size:** Overall size of the simulated space (sometimes displayed in feet or meters as the length of one side of a cube); typically determines the density of the reflected sound.

- **Time:** The length of the reverb tail.

- **Diffusion/reflectivity:** Simulates the extent to which surfaces diffuse or reflect sound (a stone cathedral will be highly reflective; a crowded club will be highly diffusive).

- **Width:** Describes the stereo quality of the output signal.

- **Dry/wet:** Particularly important in reverb: make your sound too wet, and you'll lose the clarity of your source.

- **High damping:** Determines whether the high-frequency portion of the reverb tail dies out (is damped) more quickly than the low-frequency portion, or perhaps more slowly. Different rates of high damping are characteristic of different reflective surfaces: a hard surface such as tile will produce less high damping than a soft surface such as carpet.

Of these parameters, the most critical are the size, time, and dry/wet settings; nearly all reverbs will provide at least these three. Reverbs also often include filter and sometimes even envelope parameters.

Figure 7.31 Audio Damage's Deverb uses many of the concepts found in a typical digital reverb. The two most essential controls on any reverb are the (1) size controls for how big your virtual room will be and (2) wet/dry mix to balance the reverberation sound with your direct sound. Audio Damage also offers some unusual goodies: (3) dual filters with a "digital rot" knob for a grungier sound, plus (4) MIDI control for rhythmic reverb effects (www.audiodamage.com).

Convolution reverb

 Get on the bus! Reverb processors are notoriously the most processor-intensive of all effects. Some even provide controls for directly reducing CPU load by simplifying calculations at the cost of some reduction in sound quality. You'll usually want to use a reverb on an effect send bus rather than apply several of them independently to each channel. On the other hand, if you're using contrasting reverbs for different channels, then it may be worth the increased processor load to achieve the individualized sound you want.

Conventional digital reverbs can sound very convincing, and we're now accustomed to hearing the effect they generate. Thanks to the proliferation of faster CPUs, a newer technique called *convolution* has also become practical in real time, allowing musicians to use hyperrealistic convolution reverbs and create special effects. Convolution reverbs are not necessarily better than synthetic reverbs—on the contrary, sometimes the "classic" sound of a traditional digital reverb is ideal—but they can create effects synthetic reverbs can't come close to reproducing.

Of course, if you wanted the ultimate realistic recording of the way your mix sounds in Notre Dame Cathedral, for example, you could simply drag some speakers into the center of the church, play back your mix, and record the result. Since the folks who run the church probably won't let you do that, the next best thing is to use a pre-recorded, single sound that represents all frequencies at all amplitudes in a single moment of time, a sound that models the way the space resonates (**Figure 7.32**).

This perfect sound, called an *impulse*, exists only in theory, but in the real world a sound designer can come close to producing it with a starter pistol. The sound of a starter pistol is loud (it saturates the range of possible amplitudes), noisy (it covers nearly all of the audible frequency spectrum), and brief (faster than a speeding bullet). It contains energy at the entire range of frequencies you would likely want to hear in the space. Record the reverberating sound of the starter pistol firing, and you've effectively recorded the entire frequency spectrum as it resonates in your chosen acoustic environment. This recording of the reverb tail of the impulse is called the recording environment's *impulse response* (IR).

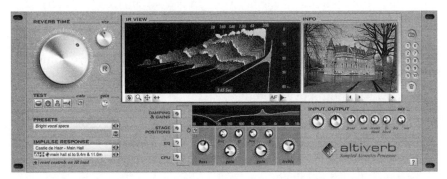

Figure 7.32 You may not be able to record your mix in the Main Hall of the Castle de Haar in Kasteellaan, Netherlands, but with a convolution reverb, it can sound as if you did. AudioEase's AltiVerb (www.audioease.com) was the first commercial computer convolution reverb and includes extras like 3D spectral profiles and (just for fun) photos of the sampled spaces.

Using a digital audio technique that combines the frequency spectra of two sounds over time (a process called convolution), the reverb can combine your input with the impulse response so that the reverb can model what your sound would sound like if it were in Notre Dame Cathedral, a cave, the bathroom in the headquarters of the software developer, or in any location for which you have an impulse file. Here's how it works:

1. A sound designer creates or records the *impulse*, typically by recording the sound of a starter pistol or some other loud, brief transient.

2. The impulse is played live in an acoustic environment, and the result is recorded; the new recording is that environment's distinctive *impulse response* (IR), modeling how it responds to all possible frequencies.

3. The convolution reverb combines your audio source with the impulse response, convolving them into an output signal.

4. The output you hear is an extremely accurate depiction of what it would be like if your source were actually heard in the modeled environment, provided the source and listener were positioned in the same locations as the impulse and microphone.

Free Mac convolution: Convolution of two audio files, complete with a unique time-smearing effect, was first popularized on the Mac with a free program called SoundHack (www. soundhack.com). It's still a favorite among sound designers for the bizarre effects it can create.

Most convolution reverbs include a set of IR sound files (literally, the recording of the impulse in physical spaces) as well as synthetic IRs. Convolution effects also usually include the ability to add your own recorded IRs in case you feel motivated to try recording them. (It's a tricky process, so if you're not up to the challenge, you can take advantage of a variety of impulse files that are available for purchase or free download on the Web.) The convolution process does much of the work, so the typical parameters for the reverb are often simply time (reverb tail length) and dry/wet mix. But many convolution reverbs also add extensive envelope shapers and filtering for finer control over output.

Convolution can be used to create other effects aside from reverb—for example for "morphing" sounds into one another. As seen in real-time digital reverbs, convolution is one of a class of spectral effects that use a digital-processing calculation called the *FFT* (see the sidebar "Fast Fourier Transform").

 Fast Fourier Transform: Behind the Scenes of Spectral Processing

From essential to off-the-wall plug-ins, many real-time effects rely on *FFTs* or *Fast Fourier Transforms*. The FFT is a mathematical process that allows real-time transformations of audio signals. It's essentially a number-crunching shortcut that converts sound between the frequency and time domains. The algorithm can separate sound into component sine waves at multiple frequencies, allowing powerful spectral processing from convolution to other spectral effects and resynthesis. Most likely, if the name or documentation of an effect uses the word "spectral," it's an FFT-based effect.

If you've looked at a software real-time spectrograph of a sound, you've actually seen an FFT at work. Whereas other time- and frequency-based plug-ins, such as analog-style shelving and peaking filters, work with rounded areas of a signal's spectrum, FFT-based spectral processors can manipulate individual frequencies, convolve different sources, and allow wild sonic effects, all in real time. You can work with FFTs directly using modular sound systems like Cycling '74 Max/MSP and Native Instruments Reaktor, and find them in plug-ins like those from Delay Dots (www.delaydots.com), GRM Tools' ST Bundle (www.grmtools.com), and Apple Logic Pro (**Figure 7.33**). FFTs are also at work in spectral analysis graphs, noise reduction tools, pitch correctors, and all sorts of other essential tools.

Incredibly, although FFTs are behind much of the most cutting-edge sound technology today, genius mathematician and scientist Carl Friedrich Gauss had worked out the basic idea as early as 1805. Gauss was too busy discovering properties of magnetism, polygons, astronomy, and differential mathematics to publish his findings, so it took until 1965 for others to reinvent what he had discovered. Not until the last few years did computer processors make calculating FFTs practical in real time. (As recently as the mid-1990s, composers and musicians would leave computers running overnight to get the results they needed!) You can expect to see spectral effects multiply in the coming years as computers continue to get faster.

Figure 7.33 Logic's Spectral Gate uses FFTs to create, in Apple's own parlance, "some pretty wacky filtering effects." Powerful individual frequency control, thanks to the FFT, enables that wackiness.

SPECIALIZED PROCESSORS

Distortion

Distortion is one of those things novice recordists are taught to avoid, but as early electric guitarists discovered, it can be as essential an effect as EQ and compression. Electric guitars actually sound thin and weak without some distortion. One reason why players choose particular amps is to add the timbral qualities of gentle (or not-so-gentle) analog tube distortion. Without it, the sound of the instrument is actually quite dull. You can also use distortion to process anything from vocals to keyboards to drum loops, sparingly or in massive quantities.

There are many flavors of distortion, but a typical distortion effect uses an amplifier to increase the volume of the input sound, bringing it up to or beyond the headroom available either in the actual circuitry or in a software reproduction thereof. Distortion is an *amplitude-dependent effect,* which means that changing the input amplitude alters the harmonic character of the output. Typically, distortion alters the loudest peaks of the waveform and in the process adds harmonic content to the sound. The most common parameters are:

- **Level:** Alternatively referred to as amount, drive, crunch, fuzz, dirtiness, ugliness, or various expletives depending on the creativity of the effect's designer, all of these parameters control one factor: the level of the amplifier and thus the amount of the distortion effect.

- **Tone:** Because distortion adds harmonic content, a simple filter is often added to the output to control the timbre of the effect. Generally, a filtered sound will be warmer and less edgy, whereas an unfiltered sound will be harsher or "dirtier." A few distortion effects also have a filter on the input, allowing you to boost certain overtones and thereby change the character of the distortion.

What distortion does: Produces "bad" sounds that sound "good," either the warm, fuzzy crunch of analog distortion or the glitchy, hard-edged destruction of digital distortion

How to use it: Turn up the effect a little for a subtle effect or a lot for sonic mayhem

When to use it: Essential for producing the customary sounds of guitars and vintage keyboards, but can also be added anywhere some crunch is desired to create a slightly dirtier sound or for more irreverent special effects

Analog devices naturally tend to add warm distortion because of the physical properties of analog circuitry and tubes. But in the absence of these properties in the digital domain, digital effects must simulate analog distortion by emulating their effect on the sound. There's a variety of breeds of distortion, each of which is specific to the way certain circuitry or algorithms respond timbrally.

General distortion effects

The terms *fuzz, overdrive,* and *distortion* are often used interchangeably to describe the distortion effects found on guitar distortion pedals and overdriven analog equipment. Fuzz and overdrive usually refer to transistorized distortion, which produces a harsher sound.

Fuzzy wah: Combine fuzz distortion with a wah filter (see p. 253) for a distinctive dirty, modulated sound that's popular on keyboards, organs, and guitars. (See Figure 7.34 for an example.)

Various analog-style distortions can be accomplished, either with actual analog circuitry or software emulation. (See three examples in **Figure 7.34**.) All are capable of producing warm, pleasant distortion or more grating distortion that is nonetheless organic in character:

- **Overdrive:** If it lacks a more specific label, an overdrive or simply a distortion effect often emulates the distortion generated by transistor circuits. These are the most common distortion effects, and they can sound pretty raunchy.

- **Tube distortion:** Tubes distort in a gentler, warmer fashion than transistors, an effect that software can emulate through a variety of means. Some new hardware even resorts to using actual tubes to get the effect right.

- **Exciters:** Exciters and enhancers are subtle distortion effects that produce artificial harmonics in a high-pitched range, where they add sparkle to dull recordings.

- **Guitar amps:** Guitar amp simulators combine tube or other distortion effects with some means of modeling the effect of the physical amp cabinet on the sound. Some even emulate specific amp-miking setups. Amplitube Uno, for example, included on the DVD, is a simple amp simulator with guitar effects.

- **Turntable (vinyl) distortion:** Turntable distortion involves two elements, harmonic distortion and added noise. Even- and odd-harmonic distortion occurs naturally because of the geometric relationship of needle to groove when the tone arm of a record is set incorrectly. Random noise or "crackle" occurs when the needle runs across dirt and scratches on the record. Software is capable of digitally reproducing both, although many musicians prefer to simply record the latter effect using an actual record, by sampling part of the record that's otherwise silent and mixing it in with digital recordings.

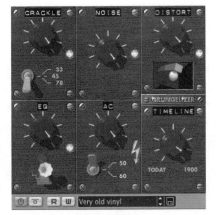

Figure 7.34 Three typical examples of software distortion: from left to right, DaTube is a tube distortion emulator from Cubase SX; the aptly named Grungelizer, also from Cubase SX, simulates vinyl equipment and low-fi analog gear; and the Fuzz-Wah effect from Logic Pro combines a fuzz distortion effect with a wah modulator.

Digital distortion

Digital distortion can be generated by amplifying a signal past the available capacity of the circuit or software (overdrive), or by forcibly truncating the sound to a lower bit rate and/or sampling resolution. Both methods create garish electronic sounds:

- **Overdrive:** As opposed to the fuzzy, rough-edged distortion generated by analog circuitry, overdriving digital circuitry or software chops off the tops of waveforms, creating a flat-topped wave shape that sounds similar to a square wave. The sound is intense, and unlike the product of analog distortion, is often radically unlike the original source. Use this technique with caution: the result is painful and sometimes dangerous to your equipment and hearing, so turn down your monitoring level.

- **Downsampling/bit rate reduction:** Like digital overdrive, bit rate and downsampling effects—often called *bitcrushers* (**Figure 7.35**)—take advantage of an aspect of digital recording you normally try to avoid. By aggressively reducing either the number of bits used to encode the audio or the sampling frequency (or both), data loss and aliasing introduce pitched artifacts and noise. With a modest reduction, your tracks can sound as though they're being played by a used Nintendo game system or early '80s computer. With additional reduction (decreasing the available bandwidth by an exponential factor), you'll hear harsh, "screaming" digital effects.

Figure 7.35 Looking for a way to make your $6,000 digital setup sound like a $20 purchase from eBay? Ableton Live's Redux could be your solution.

- **Distortion without overdrive:** *Waveshaper distortion* is a digital distortion process that doesn't overdrive the signal or introduce clipping. Instead, it reshapes incoming signals, remapping each sample word of the input to a new output sample at the waveform level, adding the harmonic tones that make distortion desirable. Waveshapers typically provide controls over input scaling (the degree to which the effect is added), and tonal controls for different effects like imitating tube distortion.

Modulation

An *oscillator* is any signal source with a continually changing value, whether it's a simple sine wave, repeating on/off switch (square wave), or even an audio sample.

When you take a sound source and transform it in a rhythmic, repetitive way over time, whether by moving a knob or speaker back and forth or even by cupping your hand over your ear, you're *modulating* the source.

The simplest modulation effects apply a regular, repeating transformation, such as you'll hear coming from the Leslie rotary-cabinet speaker often used with Hammond organs: a motor in the cabinet physically rotates the speaker in a circle, which causes the sound to bounce off of nearby walls to create an effect that is at once spatial, spectral (because of phase cancellation between certain overtones when they bounce off of different walls), and pitch-based (because the Doppler effect is introduced by the speaker's motion). Once the rotation speed is fast enough, instead of hearing discrete sweeps, you'll hear a beating or tremolo effect.

Modulation effects work on the same principle. Instead of using mechanical modulation, as in a rotating speaker, they apply a regular change to a specific parameter of the effect, such as a filter cutoff frequency. The most common modulation source is a simple *low-frequency oscillator* (LFO). Quite often the LFO is used to produce a sine wave, which since it represents the shape of a continuous circular motion is perfect for creating sounds like the rotating Leslie. (In fact, you could rightfully consider the motor of the Leslie a mechanical sine-wave oscillator!) Other modulation effects can be achieved with other waveforms or signal sources. A triangle wave, for instance, is commonly used to achieve effects like panning modulation, because it moves evenly between two values. (For more information on different waveshapes and their use in both synthesis and modulation, see Chapter 9.) Using an oscillator to move a setting up and down is basically the same as taking a knob and repeatedly turning it up and down, but with automation.

LFO

Because an LFO (low-frequency oscillator) cycles more slowly than an oscillator intended to directly produce sound, it can be used as a modulation source to produce sweeps whose individual ups and downs are audible. For example, if a sine wave LFO is set to 1 Hz and the sine wave is used to modulate the cutoff frequency of a filter, the cutoff will sweep through its range once every second, producing a 60 bpm wah-wah-wah effect. Using a 1 Hz LFO is equivalent to physically rotating the knob back and forth once every second.

LFOs are employed in numerous types of modulation effects, from simple tremolo and wah filters to elaborate "auto-filters" that resemble synthesizers more than filters; see Chapter 9 for more information on filtering in a synthesis context.

General modulation applications

You can achieve a number of effects with a simple, regularly repeating LFO, so they're typically built into effects with modulation features, or can be applied to any signal you wish in modular environments like Reason, Reaktor, and Max/MSP. Effects based on this form of modulation are popular in vintage keyboards, guitar effects, and organs. They often create interesting effects when applied to other sources as well. The following settings are the most significant (covered in greater detail in their specific synthesis and instrumental applications in Chapter 9):

- **Waveform:** Some LFOs will produce only sine waves, but triangle, square, ramp, and sample-and-hold options are sometimes available. (See the explanation of basic waveform types in Chapter 9.)

- **Rate (speed):** The frequency of the LFO, and thus the frequency of the effect. If you're lucky, your effect will offer a *sync* option that automatically matches the effect rate to the tempo of your music in case you want a beat-locked effect. In this case, you'll likely see a menu of rates that includes real-world note values, such as sixteenth-notes.

- **Depth:** Range of modulation that will be generated by the LFO.

- **Phase:** Also called *stereo width*, the phase setting controls the degree to which the modulation wanders between left and right stereo channels. If degrees are used instead of a percentage, choose 180° to center the effector −180° to shift between channels.

- **Dry/wet:** Mix of the effect.

Because some LFO-based effects are similar to one another and all create different variations of a "swirling sound," they're often confused. Some vintage guitar equipment even labels effects incorrectly! Different effects do result in different sounds, however:

- **Tremolo (amplitude):** The LFO modulates *amplitude*, either in mono or separately for left and right channels; typical of vintage guitar amps and many synths (**Figure 7.36**). If the LFO is inverted in the left or right channel, so that the amplitude of one channel increases while the other is decreasing, the tremolo effect becomes a stereo panner.

Figure 7.36 Regular modulation of amplitude creates tremolo. You can see the regular "swirling" shape of the amplitude here. Logic Pro's Tremolo effect has separate controls for left and right channels so the effect can operate in stereo.

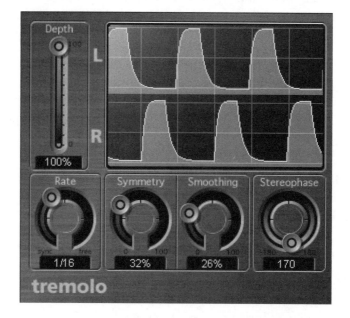

- **Vibrato (frequency):** The LFO modulates *frequency* (pitch). (This terminology will make sense to string players: tremolo is achieved by rapidly repeating a note with the bow, whereas vibrato involves bending the pitch up and down with the finger.) The major characteristic of a Leslie rotary cabinet is vibrato, which is created by the Doppler effect as the speaker twirls.

- **Chorus/flanger (delay):** The LFO modulates the delay time of a short (less than 50 ms or so) delay line. The delayed signal rises and falls in pitch due to the modulation. When the dry signal is combined with the delayed signal, phase cancellation causes the overtones of the sound to beat in a way that sounds rich and pleasing. The shorter the delay time, the higher pitched the phase cancellation will be. Increasing the delay feedback will intensify the effect. Some chorus effects include several independent delay lines, each of which delays the input by a different amount and is modulated by an LFO with a slightly different rate. These *multi-voice* chorus effects can produce a very rich sound. In flanging, the delay time is typically shorter and more feedback is used.

- **Phaser (filter):** Phasers use one or two independent LFOs to create a phased modulation of *filters*. Shifting nonharmonic notches in the spectrum or *comb filtering* creates a distinctive sound that has been wildly popular for use with electric pianos since the '70s.

✋ Hands-on: Modulated Filter in Ableton Live

The brilliance of modulated filters is the ability to create changes over time, and if you like, sync them up to tempo so those changes occur in time with your music. We'll use Ableton Live's Auto Filter for some basic, rhythmic sweeping effects.

1. **Add the Auto Filter:** Find a track with a wide frequency range— drums are a good choice—and drag the Auto Filter from the Device Browser. You'll see a familiar parametric filter (1), but now you can modulate it over time, with the LFO (2) and time sync options (3).

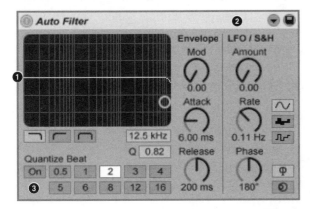

2. **Adjust the filter:** Let's forget about frequency and Q for a second: drag the round ball on the filter up and to the left until you've made a major impact in sound. Drag it in different patterns, and you'll see why a filter like this is a great candidate for assigning to a MIDI controller.

You can choose a peaking or high/low-cut filter; place it where you like and make sure the round ball has a high value vertically (high resonance/Q).

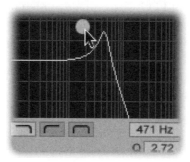

3. **Add LFO modulation:** Now we'll modulate the effect automatically, putting the "auto" in "auto filter." Increase the Amount knob on the LFO, and you should begin to hear a regular change. (If not, increase the Amount, or try moving the filter around.) Adjust the Rate knob to change how quickly or slowly the LFO sweeps through its changes. Remember, 1 Hz is once per second, so an LFO rate of 10 Hz will create ten sweeps each second.

4. **Create different modulation shapes:** Ready to spice up your filter effect? By default, the LFO sweeps gradually through settings (1). By switching to one of the stair-stepped "sample & hold" modes (2), you can use abrupt changes instead. By adjusting the phase control (3), you can create an effect that moves in stereo between your left and right speakers. For more stereo action, spin mode (4) creates different LFO rates for your different speakers. You can also shape the effect itself with the envelope controls: start by increasing the Modulation value (5).

5. **Sync the effect to tempo:** Any effect that's measured in time, including an LFO, has to be manually adjusted to the tempo so that it lines up with beats in the music. Using a tempo-slaved effect, you can have settings automatically shift in time with your music. Click the sync button, then choose a time interval in sixteenth-notes (so 4 is one beat, 2 is half a beat, 16 is a bar of 4/4 time, etc.). As you adjust the global tempo setting of your software, the effect will respond automatically.

Other software: Look for two key parameters that mean you can have fun with a filter using modulation: "LFO" and "sync." If they're available, try sweeping analog-style shifts or beat-synced rhythmic effects.

Ring modulation

Ring modulation (ring mod for short) is an effect in which an audio source is modulated either by an internal oscillator or by another audio input (**Figure 7.37**). The ring modulator outputs the sums and differences of all of the frequency components of the two signals. That may sound a bit oblique to read, so your best bet is to try out a ring modulator—the sound is unmistakable. The sum and difference process creates upward and downward shifting of the frequency spectrum, not simply of the pitch. This has a radical impact on harmonic relationships, so the main appeal of the ring mod is that its output often sounds almost nothing like its input!

In small amounts, ring modulation can create phasing-type effects, whereas greater amounts generate strange metallic, clanging sounds. The alien sounds that result have popularly been used for the robotic sounds of *Star Wars* characters and are associated with the evil Daleks of British sci-fi TV show *Doctor Who*. (British electronic music mavens debate exactly how the latter was created, although the process must certainly have been ring mod-like in the early days. In fact, engineers on a new BBC show are using new Moog ring mod hardware.)

 What ring modulation is: A means of modulating sound that outputs the sum and difference tones of all of the overtones in two signals

How to use it: Feed an audio input and set an amount (using either a second audio signal or an internal oscillator as a modulator)

When to use it: Create rich phase effects, metallic sounds, and evil alien voices shouting, "Resistance is useless!"

Figure 7.37 The Mooger-fooger ring modulator lets you modulate an input with an adjustable LFO. Bob Moog didn't invent ring modulation, but he helped popularize it; retro-style ring modulators that sound like his original hardware are available in new hardware form and in software emulation via Bomb Factory for Digidesign Pro Tools.

 What a vocoder is: A means of analyzing and "resynthesizing" audio by combining two signals: the characteristics of one, broken into frequency components and their relative strengths, are applied to another

How to use it: Feed two audio inputs to the vocoder: one signal (the carrier) to be heard in processed form, and another signal (the modulator) to provide the harmonic spectrum that will be imposed on the other. Alternatively, with a vocoder that generates a synthesis signal via built-in oscillators, combine the built-in carrier signal with an external modulator.

When to use it: To create robotic-sounding vocals, synthesized-sounding timbral effects, and dramatic, far-out filters

Vocoder

Short for VOice enCODER, the vocoder was originally developed for low-bandwidth (and, if need be, secret) transmission of voice messages. The "magic" of the vocoder was based on an understanding of how speech works, separating the production of the raw vocal sound (vocal cords) from the message (the words formed by your mouth). You'll find vocoders today as plug-ins, and in some synth and effects hardware, including some popular keyboards like the Korg MicroKorg and Alesis Ion/Micron.

Here's how it works: human speech can be considered to have two main components: the basic sound of your vocal cords (in terms of the vocoder, the carrier), and the modulating effect of your mouth, which produces vowels like "ooh" and "ah." What we hear as speech is a mix of the basic vocal cord sound and the filtering effect of your mouth. The idea behind the vocoder is to break up speech into those two components and then put them back together again, by applying the analyzed qualities of the formants (modulation) to a basic sound (carrier).

To use a vocoder, you'll need two inputs: one will act as the modulator (the equivalent of the formants of your mouth), and one as the carrier (because it will "carry" the qualities of the modulator as the output signal).

- **Modulation audio source** (a.k.a. "analysis" signal or "formant" source): The modulator is routed into a bank of bandpass filters, which divide the signal into frequency components. Envelope followers then measure the moment-to-moment amplitude level of each frequency component, providing a group of simultaneous control signals that will be applied to the carrier. (If you're using speech, this is the speech source.)

- **Carrier audio source** (a.k.a. "synthesis" source): The carrier is sent through its own set of corresponding bandpass filters. Usually a harmonically rich sound (such as a synthesizer sawtooth wave) is preferred for the carrier. The control signals generated by the modulator's envelope followers are routed to level controls for the outputs of the carrier's bands (sometimes called Voltage-Controlled Amplifiers or VCAs), so that the level of each band in the carrier is controlled by the level of the corresponding band in the modulator.

You don't hear the modulator signal in the final output; instead, you hear the output of the carrier signal after it has been transformed by the modulator signal. (See **Figure 7.38** for a diagram of the routing scheme.) Because vocoding requires two audio inputs, you'll need either a vocoder with a built-in synthesis engine (for providing the carrier), or a side-chained second input. (Since some hosts don't provide side-chaining capabilities, this can lead to some awkward work-arounds; you'll need to check the documentation for your host and vocoder.) The advantage of using a synthesizer as the carrier source is you can easily adjust the frequency of the carrier, or, if the synthesis source allows, even "play" the vocoder with a MIDI input. (See **Figure 7.39** for an example vocoder from FL Studio.)

Figure 7.38
The basic routing scheme for a vocoder. Two inputs are processed into a single output.

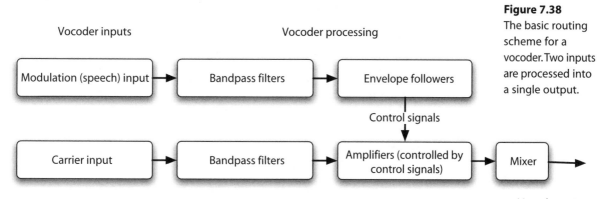

Vocoder inputs   Vocoder processing

Modulation (speech) input → Bandpass filters → Envelope followers

Control signals

Carrier input → Bandpass filters → Amplifiers (controlled by control signals) → Mixer

Vocoder output

Figure 7.39 A classic vocoder effect, as featured in FL Studio, with controls for the synthesis source (1), bandpass filters (2), envelope follower (3), and mix between the carrier and modulator and dry and wet effect (4).

Each step of the process of the vocoder process provides options for controls; which are adjustable depends on your individual vocoder, but possibilities include:

- **Oscillator:** Vocoders with a synthesis section for providing the carrier internally will have controls for generating different kinds of signals. (If you're using an external source, these will be irrelevant, and some vocoders lack internal oscillators.)

- **Filter banks:** Various controls for the filter banks let you adjust the timbre of the vocoder's output, by adjusting the filters for the carrier and modulator. You may be able to switch the number of bands. Increasing the number of bands requires more CPU processing, and the pinpoint accuracy provided by a high number of bands can actually make the "speech" effect less intelligible rather than more. (Some vocoders have fixed filter banks and settings.)

- **Envelope:** Parameters for the envelope follower let you adjust how the carrier responds to the modulation source.

- **LFO:** Some advanced vocoders can even modulate the modulated signal via an LFO or other modulation source, for shifting and sweeping filter effects.

- **Voiced/Unvoiced:** Since human speech is a combination of voiced sounds (tonal sounds and vowels) and unvoiced sounds (noisy sounds, mostly the high-pitched noise found in consonants like "s" and "th"), a vocoder capable of high-quality vocal reproduction will include parameters for triggering different sounds for each in the synthesis engine.

- **Mix Levels:** Level settings allow you to add some unprocessed carrier or modulator signal in the output.

For the classic vocoder speech effect, the modulator is a vocal input, but it doesn't have to be. For instance, you could modulate a string patch with drums, or any other combination of inputs. You will need to use inputs that have similar spectral content for the vocoder to be effective, however. Inputs in the same pitch range work best. If you don't hear the effect you want, you may want to try compressing and/or overdriving the dynamics of a carrier signal whose dynamic level changes too drastically.

 Where you've heard vocoders: The robotic, "singing computer" effect of a classic vocoder has been used in songs like Wendy Carlos's "Timesteps" in Stanley Kubrick's film *A Clockwork Orange* (in which a vocoder sang Beethoven's "Ode to Joy"), by Laurie Anderson ("O Superman!"), Kraftwerk ("We Are the Robots"), Daft Punk, and to more subtle effect with Star Wars' Darth Vader. If you're not a fan of the classic effect, though, vocoders with 16, 20, or more bands and non-vocal use are capable of producing unusual filtering effects that sound nothing like any of these examples.

Pitch Correction

Using real-time FFTs, pitch correctors like Antares' AutoTune (**Figure 7.40**) can remap a monophonic (one-voice) audio signal to a scale or mode for fine-tuning a vocalist or for special effects. Pitch correction plug-ins only correct intonation; they can't turn a lousy singer into a good one. They're best at adding minor pitch corrections to a few notes here or there, which can rescue a take that's nearly perfect except for a few small intonation problems. Plug-ins of this type are generally faster and easier to work with than the laborious process of selecting individual notes and manually adjusting the pitch. That's the reason why pitch correction has started to show up even in consumer-level software like Apple's GarageBand (albeit minus a lot of the power and control of a professional tool like AutoTune).

 What pitch correction is: An effect that automatically makes pitch changes to incoming audio signal, mapping the intonation of instruments or voices to a scale or mode

How to use it: Hook up an audio input, define a scale for tuning (either using a pre-defined scale, like E major, or creating a custom tuning map), and set timing and sensitivity controls

When to use it: Fix minor intonation problems with instruments and vocals, map sounds to exotic tunings, or create special effects with extreme settings—just don't expect any miracles with a horrible singer

Where you haven't heard pitch correction: Contrary to widespread belief, the effect in Cher's "Believe" is not an extreme application of AutoTune: it's a good, old-fashioned vocoder. High responsivity settings in AutoTune will produce a "flipping" sound as pitch translates from one note to another, but not the robotic effect heard in the song. Producer Mark Taylor told *Sound on Sound* magazine in 1999 that the effect was a DigiTalk vocoder. (http://www.soundon-sound.com/sos/feb99/articles/tracks661.htm)

 Black gold: The technology for AutoTune was originally a seismic data analysis process called auto-correlation, used to locate underground oil. The technology turned out to be gold for Antares Technology's founder, an ex-oilman; many people refer to pitch correction simply as "AutoTune."

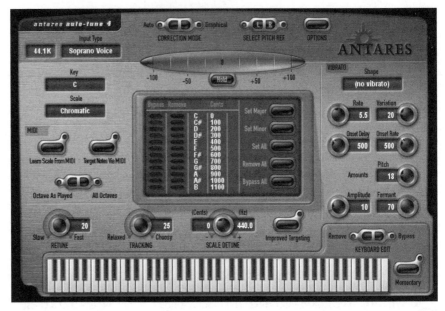

Figure 7.40 Antares' AutoTune (www.antarestech.com) is a ubiquitous plug-in for pitch correction, with many advanced settings for customizing tuning and timing, or, if you prefer, some default automatic settings that work for many music styles.

The more expensive pitch correction plug-ins used by professionals offer all kinds of customization and control, but two basic parameters are the most significant: the tuning table, and the response or timing. The tuning table is the scale or mode to which you wish to tune; it could be C minor, E Phrygian, a drone, an Indian raga, or a custom tuning of your own design, depending on how customizable your pitch correction tool is. The most common application, of course, is simply to choose the key and mode of the song and use pitch correction to automatically correct notes from your singer or instrumentalist to the proper intonation. However, other special effects are possible by "abusing" the settings.

Timing controls determine how quickly the notes will be adjusted to the "correct" pitch. Make the plug-in too responsive by setting the timing too short, and the output sound will "flip" up or down to a note in an artificial way; set timing too long, and you'll be able to hear the pitch corrector changing the pitch. Finding a middle ground is essential to producing natural-sounding results, though again some producers have experimented with intentionally choosing extreme settings for special effects.

Pitch correction has become widespread in commercial studio recordings, which has also made it controversial. It is possible to overuse automatic pitch correction, which has added to complaints about modern pop songs sounding artificial and "over-produced." Great singing often doesn't correspond to the plain-vanilla tuning of a modern piano. Classical singers sometimes make sharped notes slightly higher and flatted notes slightly lower, while rock, jazz, and blues traditions have long involved nuanced bends around pitch. Misused or overused, pitch correction can erase some of the human elements that make vocals enjoyable. It's important to remember that, like all effects—EQ, compression, reverb, and delays included—pitch correction can't make a mediocre singer sound great. (In fact, if you do want to radically change the way a vocal sounds, your best bet is a vocoder.) In smaller doses, though, pitch correction can save recording time and rescue a good but imperfect recording.

Noise Reduction/Restoration

There are a variety of solutions to removing unwanted sound from a recording. You can manually edit out pops and clicks with a sample-accurate waveform editing tool, though that process can be time-consuming. You can reduce noise and hiss with filters, but that can remove too much of the sound you want to keep. You can use noise gates to remove broadband noise, but that does nothing for noise that overlaps with your program sound.

General-purpose restoration plug-ins and noise reduction processors are designed to address these problems in real time, via a combination of specialized techniques and some of the previously-mentioned, generic processors, adapted to the purpose. These tools can help with:

- **Broadband noise:** Specialized noise reduction tools remove sounds like wind, fluorescent lighting hum, hiss, and other noisy sounds. This includes FFT-based reduction, which attempts to identify noise by its spectral content. Some processors sample noise from a location on the recording that contains only that ambient noise; select a portion of the waveform containing only noise and hit a command like 'sample' or 'learn,' and the noise reduction plug-in will attempt to remove that content from the rest of the file.

 What noise reduction/ restoration is: A specialized plug-in for eliminating unwanted sounds from a recording, particularly broadband noise like tape hiss or air conditioner noise. (Many general-purpose restoration plug-ins combine various functions beyond simple noise reduction.)

How to use it: Adjust plug-in settings to strike a balance between removing unwanted noise and maintaining the program material you want heard. With broadband noise reduction, this often involves sampling noise in a spot on the recording where only the noise can be heard. This "noise profile" can then be applied to the rest of the track.

When to use it: While restoration tools usually can't rescue recordings that are so far gone that you hear mostly noise, they are useful for fixing more minor problems like removing hiss, ventilation noise, vinyl pops, and related issues

- **Clicks, pops, and crackles:** Analog pops and crackles created by dusty records or digital clicks and other recording problems are all forms of unwanted transients. They can be removed with specialized real-time digital pop filters. Some are fairly automatic, while others require that you select the region containing the unwanted pops.

- **Hum and rumble:** Hum created by sources like power sources and various sources of low-end rumble are frequency-specific problems. As such, they're best solved by a notch filter or narrow parametric filter. You can use an EQ for this purpose, but some specialized restoration tools also incorporate filtering.

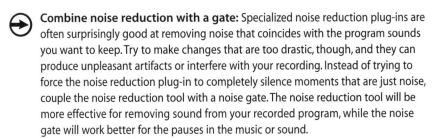 **Combine noise reduction with a gate:** Specialized noise reduction plug-ins are often surprisingly good at removing noise that coincides with the program sounds you want to keep. Try to make changes that are too drastic, though, and they can produce unpleasant artifacts or interfere with your recording. Instead of trying to force the noise reduction plug-in to completely silence moments that are just noise, couple the noise reduction tool with a noise gate. The noise reduction tool will be more effective for removing sound from your recorded program, while the noise gate will work better for the pauses in the music or sound.

Utilities

Some audio software includes tools that can be inserted as effects in order to accomplish common tasks, such as signal analysis and automation of regularly performed work.

- **Testing:** Test tone generators provide a quick way to generate basic signal for checking your equipment, speaker placement, and other tasks; they're usually just simple sine and noise generators.

- **Meters and analyzers:** Just as most studios once kept an oscilloscope on hand to visually evaluate sound, meters provide visual information on sound spectrum, correlation, and other elements of your signal. They're critical for equipment calibration and can be useful in editing and filtering as well.

- **Tuners:** Simple tuning software helps you tune guitars and other instruments (**Figure 7.41**).

- **MIDI triggers:** By sending a MIDI message that's triggered by the amplitude of a signal, you can automate special effects (for example, triggering a filter with a drum pattern) or use "replacement" utilities to automatically convert sampled audio grooves to MIDI information.

- **Pitch-to-MIDI conversion:** Going a step further than amplitude-based MIDI triggers, pitch-to-MIDI converters can be used to generate both pitch and timing information from recording sound. Generally they work only with single-voice instruments (like a trumpet).

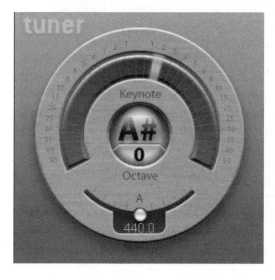

Figure 7.41 Tuner in Logic Pro.

(⊙) **On the DVD: Try Out Signal Processing**

Now that you're armed with the necessary lingo, the best way to learn about signal processing is to do it yourself. To try some of these effects, fire up these tools on the disc:

- Ableton Live's demo includes EQs, dynamics processors, reverb, delays, distortion, and special effects, including most of the categories mentioned in this chapter. You can also use it to try out effects (like those included on the DVD), because it's a Mac/PC-compatible host with multiple-format support that will run most plug-ins, even with Live in demo mode.
- Cakewalk Kinetic's demo includes a range of effects processors from Project5.
- Audacity includes a number of basic non-realtime effects and can host LADSPA and VST effects.
- IK Multimedia Amplitube Uno, included on the DVD, is a standalone amp simulator with built-in guitar effects (**Figure 7.42**).

Try out a selection of free effects processors for Windows and Mac using one of the included hosts or your own.

Figure 7.42 Amplitube Uno, in addition to simulating the coloration of a guitar amplifier, provides two basic guitar effects: distortion and 3-band EQ.

 Plug into plug-ins: Once you become addicted to real-time software signal processing, you're likely to hunger for more plug-ins. Here are a few sites to check out:

KVR Audio (www.kvraudio.com): Offers a massive database of "open standards" plug-ins (VST, AU, DX, LADSPA) with daily updates, including freeware plug-ins for every platform

FXpansion (www.fxpansion.com): Offers "wrappers" to make your DAW software compatible with plug-in formats the DAW doesn't support on its own. (VST, DirectX, AU, etc.)

Digidesign (http://digidesign.com/developers/plugin_info/): Offers a comprehensive guide to plug-ins for Pro Tools and Pro Tools LE with downloadable demos

Real World Digital Audio's companion site (www.realworlddigitalaudio.com): Offers the latest plug-in news and a guide to freeware instruments and effects

CHAPTER 8

MIDI: Notes, Rhythms, and Physical Control

If you're like most musicians, you think about sound as notes and rhythms rather than as frequency and time in seconds. You express music in sound but also in physical gestures like strumming a guitar, playing a keyboard, scratching a turntable, nudging a foot pedal, or tweaking a fader or knob. Using MIDI data, you can store and manipulate these musical gestures digitally, making it easy to record and edit performances and sound mixes.

 Essentials

MIDI—Notes, Rhythms, and Physical Control

To use MIDI, you'll first need to understand how MIDI devices and software communicate, then how to record, edit, and manipulate MIDI data:

- Learn when to use MIDI
- Make MIDI connections and configure your studio
- Understand MIDI's data structure and how different messages can be mapped to musical expression and control
- Record, edit, and manipulate MIDI performances to create a song
- Use MIDI to control your mix and your instrument parameters in real time

Essential Terms

- Controller, receiver, sequencer
- In/out/thru
- RMC pickup, piezo sensors/drum triggers
- Channels, multitimbral
- MIDI data messages: note-on/off, velocity, aftertouch, control change, program change
- Advanced MIDI: Most Significant Byte/Least Significant Byte
- System messages: MIDI clock, MMC, MSC, MTC, SysEx
- Tap tempo, quantization
- Splits, step entry
- General MIDI (GM)

Where to Start

Try using an external keyboard to play a virtual instrument like SampleTank2 FREE, included on the DVD. Check out the data you've recorded using a MIDI monitoring tool, like MIDI-Ox for Windows and MIDI Monitor for Mac, also included on the DVD.

Ins, Outs, and Thrus of MIDI

Sending, Receiving, and Sequencing

As explained in Chapter 1, MIDI (the Musical Instrument Digital Interface) is a simple way of storing sequences of musical events. It's the player piano concept brought into the modern age: By separating the mechanism that produces sound (the piano) from the score (the piano roll), MIDI lets you store, edit, and play back performances.

Obviously, you'll want three things: a way of sending MIDI messages (a *controller*, usually a keyboard), something to receive and respond to the messages (typically a *sound module* or virtual instrument), and some software in which to record and edit your MIDI performance (a *sequencer*) (**Figure 8.1**).

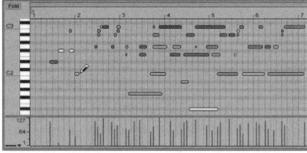

Figure 8.1 Using MIDI usually involves at least two things: a controller, like a keyboard (left), drum pad, or fader box, and something to control, like the built-in sounds on a keyboard, another piece of hardware, or a software virtual instrument (upper right). Add a means of storing the MIDI data, typically a MIDI sequencer (lower right), and you can record and manipulate MIDI performances.

Controllers

The MIDI device that originates the messages is called a *controller*. Any device that can transmit MIDI can be a controller. Some examples include:

- Music keyboard

- Fader box, control surface

- Foot pedals, footswitch boxes

- Digital drum pads

- MIDI-enabled guitar or bass

- Virtual turntable or scratch interface

- Sequencer (software or hardware)

As long as the device has a MIDI out port or a software driver to convert its output to MIDI, it can be a controller. It doesn't even have to be a traditional musical instrument: tools are available for translating the output from QWERTY keyboards, game controllers and joysticks, graphic tablets, electrical sensors, video cameras, and more into MIDI data. Your MIDI controller could be you waving your arms in front of a webcam, playing with a sock puppet with sensors, or anything else that can be made to transmit MIDI data.

Receivers

To produce sound, you can either use the internal sound generation facilities on your controller, if it has any, or give the controller something to control: a *receiver*. Without internal sounds for stand-alone operation or a receiver to produce sounds, your controller is like a conductor without an orchestra: MIDI needs a sound source or other device to respond to the MIDI messages. Common examples of receivers include:

- Software virtual instrument

- Mix and effects settings

- Hardware sound modules and effects

- Video playback and VJ gear

- Lighting (many standard light boards include MIDI inputs)

 MIDI receiving devices: Unconventional possibilities for MIDI receivers include robotics, lasers, and pyrotechnics, but the most common application is a keyboard controller that triggers a virtual instrument.

Many devices, especially hardware keyboards, have the ability to act both as *controllers* (producing MIDI control data) and as *receivers* (producing sound, video, or some other event).

Sequencers

Is it live, or is it sequenced? Sequencers work well for recording and editing, but MIDI is also useful onstage. Because MIDI data is simple and standardized, it's easy to build everything from basic real-time transposers to sophisticated interactive setups. MIDI effects in sequencers or modular MIDI systems like Max/MSP, Jade, Pure Data (Pd), Reaktor, and Logic's Environments let you create custom performance rigs that work as you play.

Of course, the real joy of MIDI isn't just the ability to use one piece of equipment or software to control another: it's the fact that you can record and edit MIDI events. Any device with the ability to record and play back MIDI is considered a *sequencer*. This includes both hardware keyboards with built-in sequencers and the MIDI sequencers integrated within DAWs like Cubase, Pro Tools, and Live.

Sequencing MIDI data lets you record, edit, and arrange compositions. You might use sequencing as a simple writing tool for recording ideas and adjusting and arranging them, or to create instrumental performances so complex that you couldn't play them in real time. Since MIDI stores only event information and not sound, it's possible to make edits with MIDI that are difficult or impossible with audio recordings. For example, you can change a recorded part to another instrument, make quick, fine-tuned pitch adjustments without having to select audio waveforms, draw in unplayable notes and rhythms, or make radical alterations to tempo.

What if you're "all virtual"? You might think that MIDI doesn't concern you, because you make music directly in software and don't have a controller. Well, think again: if you're playing a virtual instrument in a DAW or loop-based "virtual studio," you're using MIDI every time you click with the pencil tool to add a note. If anyone tells you, "MIDI is dead," they're wrong—for now, at least. (See the sidebar "OSC: MIDI's Successor?" on p. 324.)

Connecting Instruments and Devices

USB and FireWire

Connecting a USB or FireWire MIDI device to your computer is basically plug-and-play. Connect the USB or FireWire cable to your computer, as in **Figure 8.2**, and your software should recognize the device automatically. (Some devices require driver installation first.) If you have more devices, just plug them in via USB or FireWire ports as well. If you're out of USB ports, connect a USB hub (making sure your devices have enough power), and you're done.

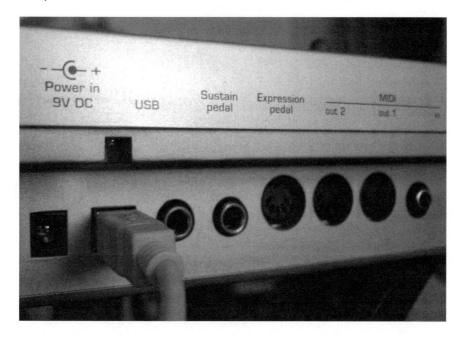

Figure 8.2 If your device has a USB or FireWire port, you can plug it directly into your computer. If you have MIDI ports, too, as on this Novation X-Station, you can use them to connect additional equipment, even if it lacks USB and FireWire computer connections, and then use all your gear and instruments simultaneously.

5-pin MIDI

Now that computers are ubiquitous in music-making and an increasing number of instruments include onboard USB or FireWire ports, you may use MIDI happily for years without ever plugging in a standard 5-pin MIDI cable. However, there's still a lot of equipment that uses 5-pin MIDI ports, and since the port hasn't changed since its introduction over two decades ago, a wide range of new and old gear is available for computer-based music.

Connecting MIDI to a computer does require some additional steps. Since computers lack MIDI ports (unless you have an internal interface with onboard MIDI), you'll need a separate piece of hardware to make the connection. Many audio interfaces have built-in MIDI ports, as do some USB- and FireWire-connected instruments, so you can connect your MIDI equipment to one of these devices, and then connect that USB or FireWire device to your computer. If you lack an audio interface or USB- or FireWire instrument with a MIDI port, you'll need a USB-to-MIDI adapter like the

M-Audio Uno (**Figure 8.3**). The Uno has only one in and one out port; if you have a lot of MIDI gear, a multiport MIDI interface becomes desirable.

Figure 8.3 The M-Audio Uno MIDI interface is so compact you could easily mistake it for a cable. With USB at one end and MIDI at the other, it's an easy way of connecting a MIDI device to your computer.

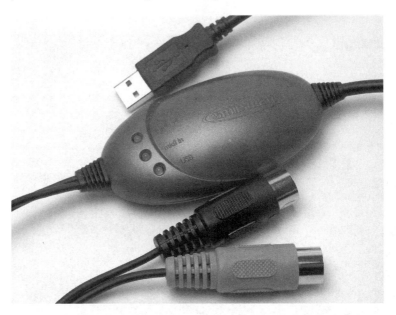

Gear with standard 5-pin MIDI ports also requires a different cabling arrangement than connections like USB. MIDI is unidirectional (data flows in only one direction within a given cable). If you have two devices and you want each to be able to receive information from the other, you'll need two cables.

The three basic MIDI connections are in, out, and thru (**Figure 8.4**):

- **In:** Receives MIDI data from external sources.

- **Out:** Transmits MIDI data originating within the device to external destinations.

- **Thru:** Repeats whatever messages are received at the in port—thus, messages from an external source (like a computer) travel "thru" the device to any connected gear.

Figure 8.4 A full complement of standard 5-pin MIDI ports. Typically, these will be in, out, and thru, from left to right as viewed from the front of the instrument, although many manufacturers arrange ports differently.

Since data flows only one way, you'll connect ins to outs and outs to ins. Thru ports are also connected to ins. If you're just using one device to control another, you'll need only one cable: you'll connect the MIDI *out* of the controlling device to the MIDI *in* of the device being controlled. For example, if you want to control a sound module with a keyboard, you'd connect the out of the keyboard to the in of the sound module. For bidirectional communication, you'll need two cables. For instance, if you want to play the pads on a MIDI drum machine, record your playing with your computer, and then play back that performance using the drum machine's internal sounds, you need data flowing in both directions between the computer and drum machine. One cable will transmit data from the drum machine to the computer, and the other cable will transmit data from the computer to the drum machine.

If you want to connect multiple devices to a single port on your interface, you can use the thru ports. The thru port repeats data received at the in port, so the data can travel "through" the device to another device. By connecting the thru of each device to the in of the next device, you can chain multiple instruments. See **Figure 8.5** for a diagram of how these different cabling setups work in practice.

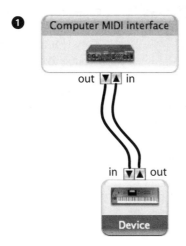

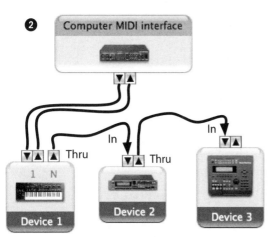

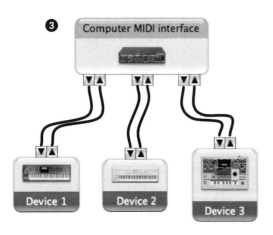

Figure 8.5 Three common MIDI setups:

❶ Basic interconnection: A single device's in and out ports can be connected to a computer MIDI interface via two cables. For instance, you might connect an external keyboard with internal sound capabilities to your computer (via a dedicated MIDI interface or the MIDI port on an audio interface). The keyboard's MIDI out will send the notes you play to the computer for recording by a sequencer. When the sequencer plays those notes back, they are transmitted to the keyboard's MIDI in, allowing you to hear the music that has been recorded.

❷ MIDI chain: Chaining multiple devices allows MIDI data to travel through a single port on the interface to multiple devices. For instance, if you want notes played by the keyboard or computer sequencer to produce sound on a synthesizer sound module and a drum machine, you could connect the thru port of the keyboard to the in port of the sound module (Device 2), and the thru port on the sound module to the in port on the drum machine (Device 3). The disadvantage of this setup is that the chained devices can only receive data through the chain: they can't transmit data generated with onboard keys or controls. For instance, you couldn't record yourself playing the pads on the drum machine with your computer's sequencer.

❸ Multiport MIDI interconnection: If you need multiple MIDI devices to both receive and transmit, you'll need a multiport computer MIDI interface (or multiple MIDI interfaces). Each port includes both in and out connections.

🔑 **No thru traffic?** Just because you have a device with only in and out and no thru port doesn't mean you can't chain devices to it. Some equipment has a merge function that combines the data received on the in port with data generated by the device, so the out port is effectively both an out and a thru port. Check your device's documentation to see if this is the case.

🔑 **What are those other ports for?** Most MIDI keyboards have additional ¼" jacks near the 5-pin MIDI ports for inserting pedals, for punch in/out, sustain, expression, and other functions. Pedals built by one manufacturer may work with keyboards from other manufacturers, but some are not compatible.

Keyboards

The first MIDI devices were keyboards, and keyboards have remained the model for a generic MIDI device. In addition to the obligatory keys, a typical MIDI keyboard usually includes controllers for modulation ("mod") and pitch-bend somewhere on the left side of the instrument (**Figure 8.6**). Often, these controls are in the form of two wheels, one for pitch-bend and one for modulation, though some manufacturers prefer X/Y joysticks, paddles, flat faders, or other controls. Some low-end keyboards lack pitch and mod controls altogether.

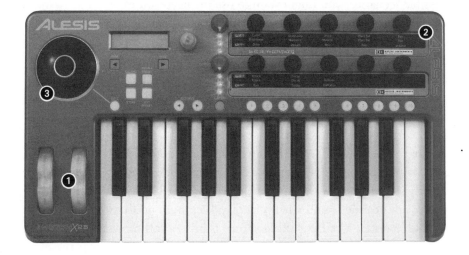

Figure 8.6 This Alesis Photon X25 has various means of transmitting MIDI data aside from the keys: (1) conventional pitch and mod wheels, (2) knobs for controlling sounds in software synths, and even (3) an infrared "AXYS" dome for manipulating sounds by waving your hands in the air. The Photon is aimed at computer users, so it omits internal sound generation. Since it has a USB port, though, you can directly connect it to a computer without a MIDI interface.

Many keyboards have additional faders, knobs, and other controllers capable of sending MIDI. In addition to controlling any internal sounds (if the keyboard has an internal synth), you can use these to control another MIDI hardware instrument or, more likely, the parameters on your software. You might use a bank of faders and knobs, for instance, to control the mix of an arrangement in a sequencer or the timbral controls of a software synth. Some keyboards have more exotic controllers, like a set of pads for triggering samples and drum sounds, or even infrared controllers in front of which you can wave your hands.

In response to the popularity of computers and powerful software-based synthesizers, many keyboards do not produce sound on their own. With such keyboards you'll need to plug in a sound module via MIDI or connect to your computer's software synth to play sounds.

Not hearing anything?
In addition to local-off settings, many keyboards can turn off MIDI receiving for local-only performance. Since you'll want your keyboard to receive MIDI when working with a computer, make sure your keyboard is set to receive MIDI data.

For the many other keyboards that do produce sound, the *local on* and *local off* settings determine whether the MIDI data from the keyboard, pitch wheel, mod wheel, and other controls will be sent to the internal sound generation facility. With the keyboard set to local on, your playing will produce sound on the instrument, as well as being transmitted via the MIDI out port to your computer or other connected devices. With the keyboard set to local off, the sound generator in the instrument will respond to MIDI data received from an external source (like your computer sequencer), and anything you play will be sent to the MIDI out port, but your playing won't produce sound directly. Why would you want to do this? There are two possible scenarios: you might want to use the keyboard to play a software instrument while a sequencer triggers the internal sounds on the keyboard, or you might want to enable a MIDI thru (also, confusingly, called MIDI echo) setting on the computer so that MIDI data is routed through the computer and then back to the synth. If you're using a keyboard that has its own internal synth along with a software sequencer, you'll normally keep the keyboard in local-off mode: if it's set to local-on, the sequencer's MIDI thru will cause each note you play to be heard twice, because each MIDI message will reach the keyboard's internal synth both directly (via local-on) and again after passing through the computer. These doubled notes will usually sound strangely hollow or blurred due to phase cancellation. If you're not hearing sound when you play, keep in mind that you might want to double-check whether your keyboard is in local-off mode.

Guitar and bass

Since electric guitars and bass are by definition analog devices, you'll need to translate your playing into MIDI if you want to control MIDI instruments or input and edit MIDI notes. The connection is one-way: you can use a guitar as a MIDI controller, but MIDI obviously can't play your guitar, so you'll have to use a synthesizer to produce sound with recorded MIDI performances. There are two basic elements to a MIDI hookup for guitars and basses:

- **The pickup**: To capture your playing as analog signal
- **Signal-to-MIDI conversion**: To convert the analog signal captured to digital form, as MIDI pitches and rhythms

Electric guitars and basses ordinarily combine the sounds from all the strings on a single cable as an analog electrical signal. If you're playing single-note lines and carefully muting the other strings, you may be able to use your standard instrument pickups for MIDI. Using a specialized pickup (sometimes called a hexaphonic pickup because it has a separate output for each of the six strings), you can isolate signal from each string for more reliable tracking and the ability to capture multiple notes played at once.

Many pickups use a 13-pin connector called the Roland RMC connector for plugging into guitar tone modules and effects from Roland, Yamaha, and Axon (www.terratec.com). These pickups can be connected to a module like the Roland GI-20 (or similar device), which outputs MIDI via USB for easy connection to a computer (**Figure 8.7**). Plug a 13-pin guitar plug into one end of the GI-20, and then plug your computer into the other end via a USB cable. Now you can do most of what a keyboardist can do with your MIDI instruments and sequencer. (You'll also find that playing idiomatic guitar phrases on these instruments is easier than it is with a keyboard.)

To reduce the number of separate components for digital connections, specialized guitars like the Brian Moore iGuitar (www.iguitar.com) come from the factory with a specialized pickup and RMC connection (**Figure 8.8**). (Brian Moore's iGuitar.USB adds USB out for audio, though it still needs to connect via the RMC connector to a device like the GI-20 for MIDI.)

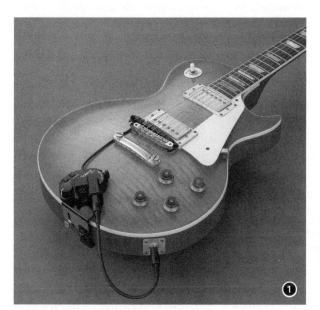

Figure 8.7 A specialized pickup like the (1) Roland GK-3 can isolate the sound of each of your bass or guitar's strings. (Roland's GK-3B is designed for bass.) This pickup connects via a 13-pin RMC connector to a device like the (2) Roland GI-20. The GI-20 converts pitch from the pickup to MIDI, outputting to MIDI connections and USB for your computer. You can then use your guitar or bass to play software instruments. (Photos courtesy Roland Corporation, U.S.)

Figure 8.8 Brian Moore's iGuitar has an integrated six-string pickup and on-board RMC connector, so you can plug it directly into a module like the GI-20 for MIDI control and connection to your computer. (Photo courtesy Brian Moore Guitars, Inc.)

 Do you really need MIDI? If you just want to plug in your instrument and play, adding effects and recording audio, a normal pickup and audio connection are fine. You can then add effects via hardware or software amp simulations with effects, like the AmpliTube Uno software included on the accompanying DVD. You'll need to enable your guitar or bass for MIDI if you want to:

- Play virtual instruments or synths using your instrument as a controller
- Enter specific pitches for notation and songwriting by playing your instrument
- Record and edit individual MIDI notes (for edits that are specific to MIDI, like easier editing of pitch)

Drums and percussion

Percussionists have two basic options for MIDI: you can either capture MIDI events from a traditional acoustic drum kit by adapting it with *piezo sensors* and audio-to-MIDI conversion or use a digital drum system designed specifically for use with MIDI. Both systems convert your drum hits into MIDI events, which enables you to play virtual drum kits in software or hardware instruments, trigger sampled sounds, match the software's tempo to your playing, start and stop videos, or perform other MIDI tasks.

Piezo sensors (or simply "drum triggers") are extremely simple electrical devices that happen to be perfect for use with drums. They're thin pieces of material (*piezopolymer*) that produce an electrical pulse when disturbed by vibrations. If you attach a piezo to a drum head or shell and hit the drum, the piezo produces a brief electrical pulse. Piezo triggers can either be taped directly to the drum head or mounted in specialized trigger attachments like the ddrum triggers in **Figure 8.9**. (The latter arrangement is generally preferable, as it's less fragile and tracks playing more reliably by maintaining consistent pressure with the drum.) The trigger produces an electrical signal, carried via standard audio cables, which can then be converted into digital MIDI data.

To convert the analog electrical signal to MIDI, you'll need a *trigger-to-MIDI* converter. You can purchase newer models like the Roland TMC-6 or scour eBay and other used equipment sources for inexpensive older models.

Figure 8.9 Drum triggers let you treat an acoustic drum kit like a digital kit, for controlling samples or tracking tempo with a computer. These ddrum drum triggers are specially designed for the purpose. A metal casing protects the trigger from accidental hits, while a clamp lets you attach to the side of the drum without adhesives, maintaining the proper pressure. The trigger outputs a signal via a standard audio cable, which can be converted via trigger-to-MIDI hardware for use with MIDI. (Photo courtesy Armadillo Enterprises, Inc. / ddrum Percussion)

Do you really need MIDI? If you're happy just recording the sound of your acoustic kit, you don't need MIDI triggering, but MIDI gives you some capabilities that can turn a skilled drummer into a veritable one-person band:

• **Sound like anything:** Used as a controller for a hardware or software instrument, your drum kit can sound like piano, guitar, or whatever you want.

• **Trigger any sampled sound:** Because drums produce transients, they're perfect for triggering samples. You may want to mix samples with the sound of your live playing.

• **Track tempo:** With a tool like Circular Logic's Mac/Windows InTime Tempo Tracking System, a MIDI-enabled drum setup can produce tempos other equipment can follow. Play your drums live, and a song being played by your software will keep time with you. (Circular Logic has tips and tutorials at www. circular-logic.com.)

As an alternative to piezo sensors, you can use software-based audio-to-MIDI conversion, like the donationware Mac/Windows VST KTDrumTrigger by Koen Tanghe of Smartelectronix, which is included on the DVD. This type of software analyzes close-miked acoustic drums and outputs a MIDI note each time the incoming signal passes a threshold set by the user. A major advantage of software-based conversion is that you can use recorded audio or sampled loops as triggers. In addition to doing some adjustments to make them accurate, you'll also need a host software application that supports receiving MIDI from plug-ins; some major DAWs lack this capability.

Whether you're using piezos or audio-to-MIDI conversion, you may need to experiment with your setup to get the results that you need, by adjusting triggering thresholds and watching for errors.

If you decide to go all-digital rather than banging on real drums, you can use digital drum pads. Digital drum pads either include built-in MIDI ports or use pads with integrated piezo sensors attached to a MIDI converter. Options include hardware for use with:

• **Hands:** Drum pads for use with your hands, like M-Audio's Trigger Finger and Akai's MPD-16, both of which divide pads into a 4x4 grid (as used on Akai's wildly popular MPC-series samplers), or Roland's Handsonic HPD-15, which arranges pads in a circular layout familiar to those who play hand percussion like bongos.

• **Sticks:** Drum pads for use with sticks, like KAT Percussion's DrumKAT and TrapKAT, and drum pads from Yamaha and Roland.

• **Mallets:** Digital mallet instruments, like KAT Percussion's MalletKAT.

• **Feet:** Hardware kits can provide digital triggering via foot pedals that work like an acoustic drum kit's kick and hat pedals; Hart Dynamics, for instance, makes specialized pedals.

• **Whole Enchilada:** Fully digital, complete drum kits with kick, hats, mesh drum triggers, synthesis, and MIDI conversion, like Roland's V-Drum system (**Figure 8.10**) and Yamaha's DTX series.

Figure 8.10 Roland's V-Drum series includes all of the instrument types you'd find in a full acoustic drum kit, from hat to kick to tom, but with mesh pads—all the sound is digital. The V-Drum outputs both MIDI and multiple audio outputs; the audio is generated internally by synthesized or modeled drum sounds. Shown here is the mid-range TD-12K kit. (Photo courtesy Roland Corporation, U.S.)

Resources for MIDI percussion equipment:

Roland: digital drum pads and fully digital kits (www.roland.com)

Yamaha: drum triggers, digital drum pads, and fully digital kits (www.yamaha.com)

ddrum: drum triggers, pads, and kits (www.ddrum.com)

Hart Dynamics: electronic drums, triggers, kick/hat pedals, and kits (www.hartdynamics.com)

KAT Percussion: digital mallet instruments and digital pads (www.alternatemode.com)

DIY and cheap solutions: Because piezo sensors are simple electrical devices, building custom drum pads is a popular project for do-it-yourselfers. A quick Google search for "Drum Trigger DIY" will bring up many alternative ideas. You don't have to build your own triggers just to save money, but piezo sensors run just a few dollars (you can find half a dozen for around $30), and vintage trigger-to-MIDI converters are often as little as $80–100 on eBay (or less at a local garage sale). You may find integrated pads worth the extra money, since they tend to provide more consistent results.

Other instruments

Keyboardists have some advantages over other musicians when it comes to MIDI, but other options are available for other instruments:

- **Pianos:** Some acoustic pianos, like Yamaha's Disklavier line, include built-in MIDI outputs so they can be used as a MIDI controller. The Disklaviers can even respond to MIDI, so they can be triggered by a sequencer. If you don't have access to such an instrument, you can use an add-on device like the Moog Music Piano Bar (www.moogmusic.com) to convert keyboard performances played on any piano to MIDI.

- **Wind instruments:** Wind controllers like Yamaha's WX5 (**Figure 8.11**) are specialized digital instruments intended to provide the flexibility of a MIDI keyboard with the expressivity of a wind instrument. The WX5 can even mimic different fingering layouts like flute and sax. Inexpensive breath controllers provide breath input without any fingering, which is useful even if you're not a wind player. You'll usually need a conversion box, such as a Yamaha keyboard with a breath controller input, to make use of them.

Figure 8.11 Yamaha's WX5 opens up the MIDI world to wind players. It has both recorder and single-reed mouthpieces, plus lip and wind sensors, so experienced wind players will find familiar means of expression, while wind beginners will find a unique new digital instrument for playing electronic instruments. (Photo courtesy Yamaha Corporation of America)

- **Accordion:** Even accordions are going digital: Roland's V-Accordion has onboard MIDI to capture your accordion performance or play other instrument sounds with the accordion keyboard.

- **Pitch-to-MIDI:** Pitch-to-MIDI software or hardware converts incoming audio signal to MIDI data, meaning you can use any instrument you choose (though it typically works only with instruments that play one note at a time—not chords). Examples include Antares Kantos (www.antarestech.com), a Mac/Windows synth plug-in that can be controlled by monophonic input like voice, and Lateral Solutions' Guitar Synth (www.lateralsol.com), a Windows application that converts pitch to MIDI in real time and can be connected to other Windows applications via MIDI-Yoke (included on the DVD). For more control, you may prefer to build your own simple converter in a modular environment like Max/MSP.

Configuring Sequencers and MIDI Software

Once your equipment is connected to your computer via MIDI, you can configure your software to communicate with your hardware. With data flowing in both directions, your software can record and edit performances that originate on your hardware instruments and other MIDI devices, and your hardware can control parameters in software.

Since MIDI instruments treat MIDI data (the data that provides the control) separately from audio data (the sound the instrument makes), you'll need to make sure both MIDI and audio are properly routed in the software.

Programs and channels

If you only ever needed to control one instrument sound with one MIDI input, you wouldn't need to separate MIDI data. However, real music has ensembles. If, for example, you want to play a bass on the bottom half of your keyboard and a piano with the top half, or play back a sequence from software involving a drum kit, horns, and organ, you need a way of separating information (so the horns won't try to play the drum sounds or vice versa). MIDI uses *channels* to route data between multiple sources and destinations. The MIDI specification has 16 channels, numbered 1–16.

Sometimes each device will be assigned its own channel. For instance, if you have two hardware synths and a hardware drum machine, the synths might respond to messages on channels 1 and 2, respectively, while the drum machine might be assigned to channel 3. But often, a single device will be configured as if it were several "virtual" devices. A hardware synth, for example, might play a drum kit on channel 1, an organ on channel 2, and a horn sound on channel 3, all at the same time. A MIDI device that can do this is referred to as *multitimbral*, because it can produce several timbres (sounds) at once. A multitimbral instrument has several *parts* (usually four, eight, or 16), each of which is assigned both a MIDI channel and a sound program. Using a multitimbral instrument is a bit like assembling a virtual ensemble (**Figure 8.12**). For instance, you might arrange a few of your 16 channels into a jazz quartet:

- **Channel 1:**   Acoustic piano

- **Channel 2:**   Upright bass

- **Channel 3:**   Alto sax

- **Channel 10:**   Drum kit

Sound programs: The terms *voice, tone, preset,* and *patch* are all used interchangeably to refer to sound programs. A sound program is a group of settings for parameters, which together determine what sort of sound the instrument will make.

Each of the sound presets for piano, bass, sax, and drums is assigned to a different MIDI channel to create the ensemble. (Many multitimbral instruments default to channel 10 for the drums. It's just a convenient location; you can use whichever channel you like.)

MIDI is technically limited to 16 channels, but it's possible to use 32, 64, or even more channels by assigning 16 channels to each of a number of *ports*. A port is any standard 1–16 channel MIDI connection, usually representing a physical MIDI connection but sometimes referring to a virtual MIDI connection in software. If you want 64 channels, for instance, you'll need four MIDI ports. Most of the instruments that can respond to MIDI data, however, are limited to 16 channels (or fewer), so the only reason to use a multiport configuration is if you're using several MIDI instruments at once, each of which needs to use a number of channels simultaneously.

Figure 8.12 SampleTank2 FREE, included on the DVD, is a multitimbral instrument. Using different channels (1), you can set up a virtual ensemble of various instruments (2).

Configuring a MIDI input

To play into your sequencer using a keyboard or other MIDI controller, you'll need to set up a MIDI track to receive MIDI from the keyboard as you play. Create a MIDI track, then select the MIDI *input* port to receive data from your keyboard or other controller. Many sequencers will receive on all MIDI channels at once by default. If you want to receive on only one channel while ignoring others, select that channel; otherwise, receiving on all channels at once will do the job. If you want to record on multiple tracks at once, with each track recording from a different channel, you'll need to specify the channel on each track and arm those tracks for recording.

Configuring a MIDI output

If you want to use the internal sounds on your external hardware to play back recorded MIDI performances transmitted by your sequencer, you'll need to set an *output* port and channel in the sequencer that corresponds to that device. Now, not only can you record your performances, you can play them back as well (**Figure 8.13**).

 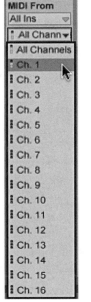

Figure 8.13 To use a hardware MIDI device with a sequencer, first set MIDI input and output on the sequencer's MIDI track (left); then, if needed, choose the channel (center) you want to record. If you want to record the sound from the MIDI device, not just the MIDI data, you'll also want to set up an audio track to record the audio from the device (right).

Software instruments can make MIDI routing easier, although different applications handle these instruments in different ways. Some applications have "virtual instrument" tracks that bundle MIDI and audio data together, handling the two seamlessly. They'll automatically route the MIDI data to your software instrument, and route the audio into your mix. Others require you to set this up manually: you'll set up a MIDI track just as you would with hardware, then set up a separate audio channel in the mixer to handle the audio output from your virtual instrument.

Whether your instrument is a virtual instrument in software or an external hardware synth, you'll want to choose a sound *program* for it. Sequencers often allow you to choose a program for each MIDI track, but some virtual instruments require you to set a patch from their own onscreen interface. Hardware instruments will almost always respond to MIDI program change messages transmitted from your sequencer, although hardware instruments usually also have onboard controls for selecting a patch. (Just remember that you'll probably want to set the patch in software as well so that the next time you load your sequence, you don't wind up with a tuba playing your harp line.) For more details, see the section "Programs and Banks," later in this chapter.

Configuring and recording audio

MIDI track archive: After recording (rendering) external synth tracks as audio tracks in your DAW, mute the MIDI tracks but don't delete them. If you later want to change anything, you'll find it easier to edit MIDI than audio.

If you're using only the MIDI features of your hardware and software, you may not need to route audio signals in or out of the computer at all: with your external synth hooked up to speakers, you'll hear its output when your sequence plays back. However, if you want to add audio effect plug-ins on your computer to the output of your synth, or record the synth's audio output so you can hear the song when your synth isn't hooked up, or output the final mix of your song to a CD, an MP3, or another audio format, you'll need to get the audio from your synth into the sequencer/DAW.

To record audio from an external hardware instrument, you'll need to connect your hardware's audio output to your computer interface, set up an audio track in your sequencer software for recording, choose the appropriate audio input from your hardware, and hit the Record button. Even if you're using a FireWire/USB device, you'll need to route audio to a track. Some of these devices include an audio output that's carried on the same USB or FireWire cable that carries MIDI, saving you the trouble of connecting audio cabling, but you'll still need to manually set up audio recording to capture the sound of the synth.

Even if you're using a virtual instrument, you'll need to record its audio output before transferring your song to a system that lacks that instrument or plug-in. This process differs from one sequencer to another, but the basic process is to automatically render audio from plug-ins if you have such an option, or, if not, to manually route the audio output of the virtual instrument to an audio track, just as you would a hardware synth.

How MIDI Models Performances

MIDI data is simply a series of number values, from 0 to 255, that allow control events to be universally understood by different hardware and software. When you press a key on a keyboard connected to your computer, the keyboard transmits a series of numbers to the computer that represent which key you played and how hard you hit it. (See the sidebar "Behind the Scenes: Anatomy of a MIDI Message" for details.) It's then up to your computer software—an electric piano plug-in, for instance—to decide what (if anything) to do with that numeric data.

It may be hard to believe that simple messages with 256 values can describe musical performances. However, by combining different messages for different events—a specific message type for notes, another for turning a certain kind of knob, and so on—MIDI is versatile enough for a surprisingly wide range of musical uses. Also, because the message structure is so simple, it's easy to understand MIDI messages and manipulate them fluidly. Most MIDI users seldom bother with the numbers. Except in a few specific situations, the numerical data is hidden from you to make your life easier. The essentials are described later in this chapter.

MIDI Specification and Implementation

Interpreting MIDI is a little like interpreting HTML on Web pages: Everything is supposed to work the same way everywhere, but your mileage may vary. Some elements are fixed (notes and pitch-bend usually work in a standard way), whereas others are more flexible. The MIDI Specification itself is published by the MIDI Manufacturers Association. When people say "MIDI," they're usually referring to the MIDI 1.0 Specification. Manufacturers use the technical documentation of this specification to insure that their MIDI hardware and software will work with other MIDI products in an error-free manner.

 Mac OS X and Audio MIDI setup: On Mac OS X, you can test MIDI devices and configure MIDI setups using Apple's Audio MIDI Setup utility, located in the Utilities folder. Click the MIDI Devices tab to create, edit, and switch between saved MIDI configurations. Some MIDI apps will automatically use this setup to recognize which devices are connected to MIDI ports and which channels they use, although others will require you to configure MIDI hardware individually for each application.

(○) Essential MIDI Tool Belt

MIDI data is basic enough that once you're used to MIDI messages, the easiest way to troubleshoot is to watch the MIDI events themselves. In addition to a sequencer event list, which displays recorded MIDI as events labeled in English (with number values where needed), some utilities let you view and modify MIDI messages as they're transmitted. Tools for Windows and Mac can display incoming data in real time and even modify it on its way into your software for tasks as simple as a quick transposition or as complex as MIDI data splitting and conversion. Even beginners will want to have these free/donationware utilities on their hard drive. You'll find all four on the included DVD.

Mac OS X:

Nico Wald's MidiPipe (http://homepage.mac.com/nicowald/SubtleSoft) provides a set of simple real-time tools for modifying MIDI in real time. With this software you can drag filters, splits, modifiers, tuners, players, and more into a "pipe" for custom MIDI setups (**Figure 8.14**).

Snoize's MIDI Monitor (www.snoize.com/MIDIMonitor) is perfect for tracking down strange MIDI problems or testing equipment. It simply displays and filters incoming MIDI messages.

Windows:

MIDI-OX (www.midiox.com) is an all-purpose MIDI utility that performs diagnostics, provides a MIDI message display, does filtering, mapping, scripting, logging, and recording, and can export MIDI data as a MIDI file. Yes, you can leave it running in the background so that brilliant idea you improvised won't be lost forever (**Figure 8.15**). A companion utility called MIDI Yoke lets you route MIDI between Windows apps (fairly easy on the Mac thanks to Core MIDI but not otherwise possible in most Windows software).

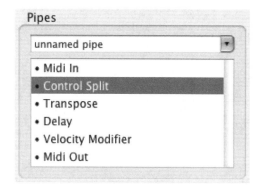

Figure 8.14 MidiPipe lets you assemble custom modifiers into "pipes" of commands for real-time modification to MIDI input. It's easy to drag around the widgets you need for quick MIDI slicing and dicing.

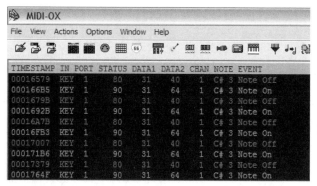

Figure 8.15 MIDI-OX is a general-purpose MIDI utility for Windows that does just about everything you can think of with real-time MIDI data.

Hardware usually comes with a MIDI Implementation Chart (check the back of the manual) that shows how the instrument sends and responds to different MIDI messages. Unfortunately these charts are not easy to read. Software sometimes comes with an implementation chart, but not always. If you can't find information in the manual, you'll have to resort to trial-and-error to troubleshoot MIDI problems.

Notes, Pitch, and Velocity

The MIDI message you'll use most often are, naturally, notes. Note messages include three elements:

- Note-on or note-off on a channel (1–16)

- Note number (0–127), which is often used by a MIDI receiver to determine what pitch to play

- Velocity (1–127), or how hard the note is hit. (For technical reasons, a note-on message with a velocity of 0 is interpreted as a note-off.)

The most common form of velocity is *attack velocity,* the velocity with which the note is hit, though some keyboards also send *release velocity,* indicating how quickly you let go of a note. Release velocity is not often used, since there's no such equivalent on an acoustic piano, but it can add expressivity. Keyboards whose sensors don't detect release velocity always send a release velocity value of 64.

Note-on and note-off

MIDI was developed for use with keyboards, so you'll have an easier time understanding it if you're a keyboardist, or can think like a keyboardist. When you play a keyboard, you press down on a key to make sound, and then release the key to end the sound. Accordingly, MIDI notes are divided into two events (**Figure 8.16**):

1. **Note-on:** Starts a note (press a key, and the sound begins).

2. **Note-off:** Turns off a note (let go of the key, and the sound stops).

Both note-on and note-off are accompanied by a note number value (so the receiving MIDI device knows which note to play) and velocity amount (generated by a sensor that determines how hard you hit the key).

 Note-off versus a "zeroed" note-on: Sending a note-on with velocity 0 is equivalent to sending a note-off, so some devices use this message instead of a true note-off. Usually the distinction is invisible to the user.

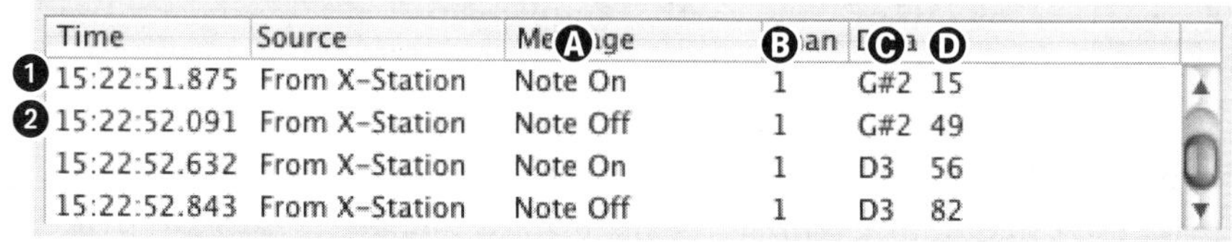

Figure 8.16 Two notes played on a keyboard produce four MIDI messages: each note has a note-on and note-off message (A), accompanied by a channel number (B), note number (C), and velocity (how hard the note was played) (D). (Shown in Subtlesoft MIDI Monitor)

Time	Source	Mege	B an [C 1 D
❶ 15:22:51.875	From X–Station	Note On	1 G#2 15
❷ 15:22:52.091	From X–Station	Note Off	1 G#2 49
15:22:52.632	From X–Station	Note On	1 D3 56
15:22:52.843	From X–Station	Note Off	1 D3 82

❶ A key is pressed, producing a note number and attack velocity value.

❷ A key is released, producing a note number and a release velocity value.

➜ Behind the Scenes: Anatomy of a MIDI Message

Like most forms of digital data, MIDI messages are made up of bytes. As a musician, you'll seldom need to worry about the bytes themselves. But if you know a little about how computers work, you may be curious: How can so many different types of messages be crammed into such tiny packages? And why does the number 128 keep coming up in discussions of MIDI?

First, let's cover the rock-bottom basics. Computers work with *bits* (short for *binary digits*). A bit is a number that has only two possible values: 0 or 1. A byte is a larger unit that contains eight bits. So there are only 256 possible bytes in the world—the numbers from 0000 0000 to 1111 1111. (256 is equal to 2 to the 8th power.)

The MIDI Specification defines two types of bytes: status bytes and data bytes. A status byte always begins with a 1, and a data byte always begins with a 0. Of the 256 available bytes, then, 128 are status bytes and 128 are data bytes. Thus any individual data byte can have a value between 0 and 127.

Each MIDI message consists of a status byte followed (in most cases) by one or two data bytes. The specific meaning of the data bytes depends entirely on which status byte preceded them. So with 128 possible data bytes, MIDI can represent many different things.

Most MIDI messages contain three bytes—a status byte followed by two data bytes. Here's how such a message breaks down:

1. **Status byte:** Describes the kind of message and the channel for which the message is intended. Notes, control changes, and program changes are all different message types, so they use different status bytes. For instance, the status byte might indicate "here's a played note on channel 14." At this point, the note that was struck is still unknown.

2. **First data byte:** The number after the status byte, which can range from 0 to 127, provides more information. If the status byte is a note-on, the first data byte indicates the note number, such as 60 for Middle C.

3. **Second data byte:** The third and last number, which again can range from 0 to 127, either adds more detail to the first data byte or provides some other related piece of information. If the status byte is a note-on, the first data byte provides a note number to specify which key was struck, and the second data byte describes the velocity (speed) with which the key was struck. For instance, the complete three-byte message might specify that Middle C on channel 14 was played with a velocity value of 64, which would be a medium amount of force. Note that a few MIDI messages, notably channel pressure (defined later in this sidebar), don't have a second data byte. They're two-byte messages (one status byte and one data byte).

Inside the actual MIDI messages, all three data bytes are binary numbers (strings of 0's and 1's). Since long strings of binary digits are hard to read, rogrammers usually work with this data using the hexadecimal numeral system, which represents numbers using six letters (A–F) and ten numbers (0–9). For instance, the decimal number 26 becomes 1A in hexadecimal. There's not much reason for you to worry about the hex codes as an end user. (For an excellent explanation of how to read hex codes if you are coding software or DIY MIDI hardware, see http://en.wikipedia.org/wiki/Hexadecimal.)

Here's an example of a MIDI message: press the note E4 and you generate three numbers:

144 52 42

The first number (status byte, 144) indicates note-on, channel 1. The second number (first data byte, 52) is the note number corresponding to E2. The third number (second data byte, 42) is the velocity, how hard the E was hit.

Since all MIDI messages must begin with a status byte, messages can be categorized technically according to the different status bytes:

- Note-on
- Note-off
- Pitch-bend
- Key pressure (sometimes called poly aftertouch or poly pressure)
- Channel pressure (more commonly called aftertouch; the pressure after a note is played)
- Control change (control number and value, for one of 128 possible controllers)
- Program change (for changing an instrument from one sound program to another)

These are all MIDI Channel messages, which means you can use them on up to 16 channels at the same time within one MIDI data stream. The remaining messages, called System messages, control an entire device or an entire music system or perform some other specialized function rather than being used to generate music. They include system-realtime, system-common, and MIDI Time Code, all of which are related to system timing synchronization, and system-exclusive. Most system-exclusive messages are defined by individual manufacturers. (MIDI Machine Code [MMC] is a type of system-exclusive data.)

System-exclusive messages can be much longer than three data bytes. By sending a "start of exclusive" byte, followed by data bytes, followed by an "end of exclusive" byte, the manufacturer of a piece of gear can make system-exclusive messages as long as needed.

Duration and "stuck notes"

MIDI has no way to represent the duration of notes: an instrument simply begins making sound when it receives a note-on message and then ends the sound shortly after it receives a corresponding note-off. This may sound limiting, but it uses a lot less data. Imagine for a moment that you're a MIDI device. If you couldn't just say, "I've pressed G" and then, somewhat later, "I've let go of G" by using note-on and note-off messages, you'd have to say something like, "I've pressed G, and now I'm still pressing G, and now I'm really still pressing G, still pressing G . . ." and so on; you'd need a lot more than just two simple messages.

If an instrument fails to receive a note-off message, it will keep producing sound indefinitely (or until the sound naturally decays, or possibly until the instrument is shut off). This phenomenon is called a *stuck note*. There are a variety of reasons why a MIDI device might fail to send note-off. Playback of a MIDI sequence might be stopped after a note-on has been sent but before the corresponding note-off has been sent. Most sequencers handle this situation automatically. But if the sequencer rudely crashes between the note-on and the note-off, a receiving hardware synth will get a stuck note. Most MIDI hardware and software includes an "all notes off" or *panic* button so you can recover from stuck notes. The panic command turns off all notes on all devices on all channels.

The MIDI hold pedal (also called a sustain or damper pedal) can also be a source of stuck notes, if for some reason a synth has received a hold pedal on message but no hold pedal off message. This can happen, for instance, if the pedal is pressed as it is connected. Try toggling your hold pedal if notes are sticking.

Note number

Don't panic! Memorizing control change (CC) numbers isn't always necessary, but here's a really important one to have handy. To stop stuck notes, send a CC 123 (all notes off) or a CC 120 (all sound off, which also turns off the hold pedal). (See the section "Adding Expressivity.")

MIDI defines 128 note numbers, from 0 to 127; note 60 defaults to Middle C on the keyboard. Note numbers are assigned to half-steps on the keyboard, so B is 59, C♯ is 61, D is 62, and so on, though your software will probably display notes using musical note names instead of numbers. (Middle C is often shown as C3. Octave numbering isn't standardized in MIDI, though, so some equipment refers to Middle C as C4 instead.)

Velocity

MIDI velocity data indicates how hard a key has been struck. A velocity-sensitive device senses the speed with which a key travels downward when you strike it and sends a number from 0–127 as the attack velocity. (Some instruments also respond to the speed with which you release the note—the release velocity.)

The most obvious application of velocity is to make a sound louder when you hit a key harder. But since both the loudness and the timbre often change on real instruments as you strike them with more force, velocity may make other adjustments to the sound as well. A virtual piano plug-in, for instance, might provide samples of a real piano played at different dynamics, and trigger the appropriate recorded sample based on the incoming MIDI velocity for a more realistic sound. The nature and amount of velocity response is determined by the receiving instrument, not by the MIDI message itself.

Velocity does have one major limitation, and it comes back to the fact that MIDI models keyboard performance. On wind and string instruments, you can adjust the loudness of a note while playing it: a string player can adjust the pressure of the bow in the middle of a note, for instance. Not so on a piano: the dynamic level of the note is determined by the beginning of the note; the player can't affect the sound after that. Since MIDI note messages use only attack and release velocity, MIDI instruments tend to behave more like the piano. To add expressivity in the middle of the note, you'll need a separate message. (See "Adding Expressivity," p. 293.)

Hands-on: Try playing a keyboard

We'll use SampleTank2 FREE with Ableton Live, both of which are included on the DVD, so we can set up a software instrument and try playing it. (You can use SampleTank Free with any host you have, not just Ableton Live; see the installation instructions on the DVD for details.) First, let's try setting up a keyboard and playing around a bit to see how MIDI works in practice—and to make sure we're getting sound.

1. **Verify your MIDI settings:** To make sure you can receive and send MIDI in Live, check Preferences > MIDI/Sync > Active Devices. You'll see inputs and outputs listed by port; double-check that each input and output you want to use is lit green by clicking the square next to the port. (Notice that you won't see individual devices connected to those ports. So if you have a Kurzweil keyboard connected to the MIDI, which is connected to an M-Audio interface, you'll select the M-Audio interface to send MIDI to the keyboard, not the keyboard itself.) If you don't have a MIDI device available for input and you want to test your setup, select the Computer Keyboard item to use your QWERTY keyboard.

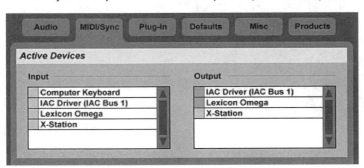

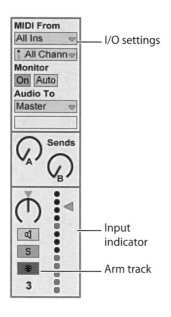

I/O settings

Input indicator

Arm track

2. **Add a MIDI instrument:** MIDI instruments in Live work just like effects inserts: drag them from the Device Browser to a MIDI track to use them. (If you don't have a free MIDI track, create one by selecting Insert > Insert MIDI Track.) You can use one of the built-in instruments in the Live Device Browser, but here let's try SampleTank2 FREE: drag it to your MIDI track. Then enable input by arming session recording on that track: click the arm button (for MIDI, it looks like a 5-pin MIDI port). Try playing your MIDI input or computer keyboard. You should see the MIDI track meters move as you play, and a small indicator in the upper right corner of the screen (MIDI input indicator) should light up.

3. **Edit SampleTank's settings:** Even though you see the MIDI indicators light up, you won't hear any sound because you haven't yet loaded a program or patch. To see SampleTank's full interface, click the Edit Plug-in Panel button on the Device title bar. (It's the icon that looks like a wrench.)

4. **Load a program:** In SampleTank's Browser, you should see all the preloaded SampleTank2 Free patches included on the DVD. (If not, check the DVD installation instructions and troubleshooting advice.) Double-click the 73 EPiano for an electric piano sound reminiscent of a classic, early '70s Rhodes. The program is automatically loaded into the active part/channel (channel 1). For an acoustic piano, try double-clicking HQ Free Piano mk II.

Make Your Playing More Musical

As you play MIDI instruments, try experimenting to make them more expressive (especially if you're using a keyboard or other MIDI instrument).

Velocity: Notice how hitting the keys harder on the 73 EPiano changes the sound, especially in the lower register. It should change from a mellower, rounder sound to a harder-edged, slightly distorted sound as you increase your attack velocity.

Range: On many instruments, the use of different samples in different ranges allows SampleTank to more closely emulate the sound of the original instrument. On the electric piano, the upper register is more bell-like in sound. On the acoustic piano the effect is subtler, but the bass is unmistakably richer in sound, as it should be. Try playing in the different registers to take advantage of their unique timbres.

Hold pedal: If you have a MIDI hold pedal, connect it to your instrument's hold pedal jack. You won't get the same resonant sound that you get on a real acoustic piano, but by using the pedal in a pianistic way, you will be able to more closely mimic the musical sound of a traditional piano technique.

Adding Expressivity

Specifying which note a synth or other electronic instrument should play (with MIDI note number) and how hard to play it (with MIDI velocity) are a start, but to make a MIDI instrument expressive, you'll want some additional control. MIDI provides other kinds of controls, some of which have fixed definitions and produce standard types of musical effects, whereas others can be assigned more flexibly. You can add these effects to your sequencing software by drawing them in with a pencil tool or other editing features, or by using physical hardware during performance. To use these controls as you play, you'll need both a hardware controller capable of sending the appropriate message and an instrument (hardware or software) capable of receiving the message and responding to it. For instance, to control vibrato, you might use an expression pedal attached to a keyboard in conjunction with a software plug-in in which vibrato amount is assigned to the expression pedal. Your MIDI setup for keyboard playing should ideally include at least a pitch wheel and modulation wheel ("mod wheel") at the left end of your MIDI keyboard, and a pedal or two plugged into jacks at the rear of the keyboard. (Non-keyboard MIDI instruments may send similar data using other physical controls.) Even with just these few controls you can make your performances more expressive (**Figure 8.17**).

Although pitch-bend, control change, and aftertouch are often called "continuous controllers," there's really nothing continuous about the MIDI data. Your hardware will generate a series of discrete numbers quickly enough and close enough together that the result will sound continuous to your ear as the receiving instrument gradually changes the pitch or another attribute of the sound.

Figure 8.17 To start adding more expression to your performance than a keyboard alone can provide, explore the uses of the pitch wheel (which sends pitch-bend data) and "mod" wheel (control change 1, modulation), as shown here on the Alesis Fusion. (Photo courtesy Alesis, Inc.)

Pitch-bend

Pitch-bend data allows you to move the pitch of notes smoothly up or down while they're sounding. Pitch-bend is usually controlled by a pitch wheel or some type of stick controller. In the neutral, centered position of the wheel or stick, pitch is unchanged. As you push the wheel or stick (pitch wheels most often move toward and away from the player, whereas pitch sticks move left and right), the pitch changes gradually within a specified range (typically a couple of semitones). This effect is called "bending," by analogy with the way guitarists bend their strings to pull the pitch of the string upward.

Pitch-bend has a full data range of 0–16,383, not 0–127 (see the sidebar "This One Goes to Eleven: Beyond 128"). Since this range offers more precision than is usually needed, however, some software simply refers to the 0–127 "coarse" range for convenience.

Coarse versus fine: A coarse setting is a more significant change of value, whereas the fine setting is a more detailed fraction of the same value. For example, in monetary dollars and cents, the dollar would be the "coarse" amount and the cent would be the "fine" amount. In MIDI, coarse and fine refer to amounts of values like pitch-bend.

Some music software displays pitch-bend data using the values 0–127, with a center value of 64, meaning "no change in pitch." More often you'll see it displayed from –63 to +64, with 0 as the center value. If your software displays the full data range (0–16,383), it will probably show a full downward bend as –8191 and a full upward bend as 8192, again with 0 as the center value (**Figure 8.18**).

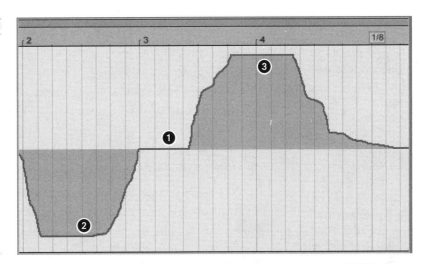

Message	Chan	Data
Pitch Wheel	1	3072
Pitch Wheel	1	2816
Pitch Wheel	1	2560
Pitch Wheel	1	2048
Pitch Wheel	1	1664
Pitch Wheel	1	1408
Pitch Wheel	1	1280
Pitch Wheel	1	1152
Pitch Wheel	1	1024
Pitch Wheel	1	768
Pitch Wheel	1	640
Pitch Wheel	1	512
Pitch Wheel	1	384
Pitch Wheel	1	256
Pitch Wheel	1	0

Figure 8.18 Pitch-bend data is a specialized MIDI message. As you turn the wheel, you generate a series of MIDI values like the data shown on the left. With the wheel centered, the pitch is unchanged (1). Turning the wheel all the way down (2) bends the pitch downward, and turning it up (3) bends the pitch upward.

Aftertouch

Some keyboards are capable of sensing how hard the player presses down on a key after it reaches the bottom of its travel. This pressure during the middle of a note is called *aftertouch* (other terms that mean the same thing are *key pressure* and *channel pressure*). On a keyboard, you generate aftertouch data by pushing down on the note after you've played it. Aftertouch is often used to add vibrato or open a synthesizer's filter for a brighter sound.

There are two types of aftertouch: channel pressure and polyphonic pressure. When a keyboard is equipped to sense and transmit channel pressure, there is only one sensor, which runs horizontally under the keys from one end of the keyboard to the other. When a keyboard is equipped to sense and transmit poly pressure, each key has its own pressure sensor, and transmits pressure data in a format that also includes key number as part of the MIDI message. Poly pressure sensors are more expensive to build, so poly pressure is not found on nearly as many keyboards. To find out whether your software or hardware instrument will respond to poly pressure (or for that matter to channel pressure), you'll have to consult the manual.

With polyphonic aftertouch, you can press down harder with one finger while holding a chord to add vibrato to that one note.

 Which type of aftertouch?

Affects individual notes: Polyphonic aftertouch (also known as key pressure or polyphonic key pressure)

Affects a whole channel: Channel aftertouch (also known as channel pressure or "mono" aftertouch/pressure)

Control change messages

MIDI provides additional controls via *control change (CC)* data. Control change messages are numbered (you guessed it) from 0–127. Some of the controller numbers are assigned to particular tasks. A piano-style hold pedal, for instance, always transmits CC 64, whereas a modulation wheel usually transmits CC 1. CC 7 is used for master volume. Other CC numbers are left open in the MIDI spec; some MIDI devices ignore them, while others use them for different purposes (**Table 8.1**).

Since there are so many controllers available, you'll use some to add color to your musical performances, while others remain available for controlling other elements, like effects settings, synthesis parameters, mixer faders, or anything else you want to assign. With a hundred or more choices per device, you have a lot of flexibility.

Some controllers, like the hold pedal, act simply as on/off switches: Press the pedal and the CC 64 data value goes to 127; lift your foot and the CC 64 value drops back to 0. Other controllers are called *continuous controllers* because they can take advantage of the full range of values between 0 and 127. This is true of faders and knobs (**Figure 8.19**).

Figure 8.19 The modulation wheel is a typical controller, capable of generating a stream of control change messages. As you turn the mod wheel on a Korg MS2000 keyboard (1), you generate a series of numbers from 0 (down) to 127 (up) (2), which will appear in your sequencer as a modulation contour (3). The modulation data can be assigned to a synthesis parameter like vibrato amount. (Photo courtesy Korg USA)

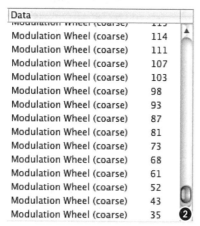

Data	
Modulation Wheel (coarse)	114
Modulation Wheel (coarse)	111
Modulation Wheel (coarse)	107
Modulation Wheel (coarse)	103
Modulation Wheel (coarse)	98
Modulation Wheel (coarse)	93
Modulation Wheel (coarse)	87
Modulation Wheel (coarse)	81
Modulation Wheel (coarse)	73
Modulation Wheel (coarse)	68
Modulation Wheel (coarse)	61
Modulation Wheel (coarse)	52
Modulation Wheel (coarse)	43
Modulation Wheel (coarse)	35

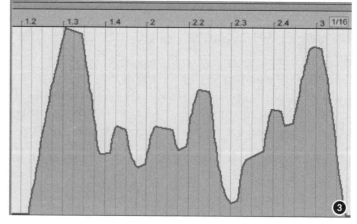

Table 8.1 Important MIDI CC Messages

Name	Control Change (CC) #	Function
Modulation	1	Commonly assigned to the keyboard's mod wheel, but the nature of the sound changes produced by the modulation is not defined. The mod wheel is often used to add vibrato, change the speed of a Leslie rotary speaker simulator in an organ sound, or add a phaser effect to an electric piano (Figure 8.19).
Breath	2	Seldom used with actual breath controllers, which are not common; sometimes transmitted by a joystick or a third wheel in the left-hand controller section of a keyboard. As with modulation, the nature of the sound changes produced by breath controller data is left up to the designers of the synthesizer and its sound programs.
Volume	7	Controls the overall loudness of the musical part assigned to a channel. Unlike velocity, which controls one note at a time and can be mapped to different timbral qualities as well as note loudness, volume data controls the loudness of an entire channel all at once—it's essentially a volume knob for that instrument (in the case of a monotimbral instrument) or for a multitimbral part (in a multitimbral instrument). 0 is silent; 127 is the maximum.
Pan	10	Left/right pan for a channel. A CC 10 message with a value of 0 pans the sound hard left, 64 pans it to the center, and 127 pans it hard right.
Expression	11	Used for dynamic expression within a part by controlling a percentage of the volume setting. (In other words, setting volume with CC 7 is akin to moving a mixer fader, whereas expression data would be used for crescendos and decrescendos on a note or chord while it is being played.)
Hold pedal	64	Also known as the sustain or damper pedal, the hold pedal acts (more or less) the way it does on the piano: hold it down and notes continue to sound even after their keys are released. You'll find the other two piano pedals defined in MIDI, too: the sustenuto pedal is controller 66 and the soft pedal is controller 67. Not all instruments respond to 66 and 67, but most respond to 64.

This One Goes to Eleven: Beyond 128

In some cases, MIDI needs more than 128 data values. Fortunately, there's an easy solution: if you can only use numbers from 0–127, use two numbers. Instead of 128 possibilities, you now have all of the combinations of two numbers from 0–127, for up to 16,384 combinations (128 x 128).

The first byte in a two-byte chunk of data is called the Most Significant Byte (MSB). It's followed by a Least Significant Byte (LSB). The standard computing technology used is a little misleading, because one isn't necessarily more important than the other—it's just a convenient means of remembering which is which.

The standard MIDI pitch-bend message has two data bytes. (Pitch-bend messages use just the status byte—the "here comes a pitch-bend!" byte—followed by two numbers for the amount, instead of just one.) This allows for the full 16,384 data levels, although some devices and software will ignore the finer resolution and just use the information in the MSB, ignoring the LSB entirely.

Control change messages have only one free data byte, because the first byte after the status byte is used to specify which controller is being transmitted. To get two data bytes, you need two control change data messages, one for the MSB (the coarse setting) and one for the LSB (the fine setting). Two data bytes are used for values that need more detail, like tuning. Many instruments don't respond to CC LSB data—but in case you run into one that does, you might like to know that the CC message containing the LSB has a CC number that's higher than the MSB message by 32. For instance, if the MSB is a mod wheel message (CC 1), the LSB will be transmitted as CC 33 (because 1 + 32 = 33).

 For more information on the MIDI specification, see (among a number of sites):
www.midi.org
http://users.chariot.net.au/~gmarts/midi.htm
www.borg.com/~jglatt/tutr/miditutr.htm

A complete version of the MIDI 1.0 Specification is available for sale at www.midi.org.

 Hands-on: Realistic-sounding reeds with mod, pitch-bend, and range

The keyboard instruments in the previous hands-on example ("Try playing a keyboard," p. 291) didn't allow you to use the modulation or pitch wheels, with good reason. When was the last time you heard a piano that could bend pitch? With an instrument like a saxophone, though, your playing will sound unrealistic if it lacks elements like vibrato and pitch-bend; it'll sound too much like it was played with a keyboard instead of the real instrument. (Photos are of the Novation X-Station, which, like many keyboards, combines pitch and mod on a single X/Y joystick. Although the physical hardware is different, the MIDI messages function exactly as on other instruments.)

To try adding some expressivity using MIDI controls, load the Alto Sax patch in SampleTank2 FREE. (Double-click Alto Sax in the Browser.)

- **Modulation:** Play a sustained note—sounds a little lifeless, right? Now, gradually add a little bit of vibrato by moving the modulation wheel on your controller keyboard. Real reed instruments vary the amount of vibrato over time, so use different amounts of modulation for a more authentically organic, expressive sound. You'll find vibrato sounds more musical if you add it to some notes and not others, or add vibrato just to the end of a note. For some inspiration, listen to your favorite sax recordings and also think about how singers use vibrato. (Many sax players claim their instrument is closest to a human voice.)

- **Pitch-bend:** Sax players can easily perform short "scoops" up to a note or down from a note by relaxing their jaw as they play, a technique more common in jazz than in classical playing. To create a scoop up in MIDI, shift the pitch-bend wheel just below center (or to the left of center, depending on the orientation of your pitch-bend hardware), play a note, and then release the pitch wheel. Since it's spring-loaded, it will return to center pitch on its own. For a fast scoop, let go of the pitch wheel as you hit the note. With practice, and some attention paid to recordings by real sax players, you can make this sound realistic. Scoops down use the same technique in reverse: play a note at pitch, then scoop down at the end by moving the pitch wheel just before you release the note. (To make sure the release portion of the note doesn't scoop up again, hold the pitch wheel in place while the note decays to silence.)

• **Range:** An essential way to make a virtual instrument sound realistic is to play it in the same range as the real instrument. The alto sax sounds most natural when played in the range from F below the treble clef to the F two octaves above (F2–F4).

❶ Pitch and mod wheels on SampleTank display
❷ Optimal range

This general advice isn't just for replicating acoustic instruments. If you've created a synthetic instrument or analog sound, think about what makes it musical. In effect, you've invented a new instrument, so it'll sound more musical if it behaves as though it were a physical instrument.

Programs and Banks

When an instrument receives a program change message, it switches to a different sound program, choosing the program from among those stored in its internal memory. (Note that some very good software synthesizers, such as those in Propellerhead Reason, don't respond to program change messages.) Like everything else in MIDI, program change messages are assigned a number between 0 and 127. Program changes can be transmitted directly from the front panel of most keyboards, which is useful in live performance. They can also be stored in a sequencer track to ensure that the instrument being played by that track makes the correct sound each time the sequence is played. Program changes are often inserted at the beginning of every MIDI track in a song for precisely this reason.

Program change messages are just numbers, however, with no particular meaning. Program 12 in one synth might be a flute sound, whereas program 12 in another synth might be a distorted electric guitar. As a result, if you create a track in a MIDI sequencer and add a program change to the track, you're likely to run into problems if you should later decide to send that track to a different MIDI instrument for playback. More than likely, the sound of the new instrument will be incorrect.

The General MIDI (GM) format, found on many hardware synths and a handful of specialized software synths, is a way of dealing with this problem. If an instrument has the GM logo on its panel (or can be switched to a GM mode), then the result of sending it a program change message with a given value becomes predictable. Program 7, for instance, will always be a harpsichord, and program 36 will always be a fretless bass. Although this is genuinely useful, General MIDI is designed more for consumer music applications such as playing prerecorded arrangements of popular tunes on a home keyboard than for serious musicians. With the explosion in the variety of software and hardware available and a wide variety of instrument libraries, you'll find most instruments use their own patch numbering scheme.

Sound programs are organized into *banks,* so that instruments can include more than 128 sounds and so that patches can be organized into useful categories. (You might find an instrument bank and a percussion bank, for instance.)

To change programs, you'll use the program change message and select a patch (program) number from 0 to 127. At the time when MIDI was first developed (the early 1980s), nobody imagined that synthesizers would ever have enough memory to store hundreds of sound programs or that musicians would have a need for so many programs. So the number of possible program change messages is limited. To switch from one bank of sounds to another, the bank select message must be used. Bank select was grafted onto (or spliced into) the control change message area. A CC 0 message gives the coarse (MSB) value for the bank, and a CC 32 message provides the fine (LSB) value. Thus, up to 16,384 banks of 128 sounds each can be chosen via MIDI, which ought to be enough to make anybody happy. Unfortunately, various instruments respond to CC 0 and CC 32 messages in different ways. You may need to experiment and read the synth's manual in order to select the desired program. To get to, let's say, sound bank H, one synth might use a CC 0 value of 7, while another uses a CC 0 value of 0 followed by a CC 32 of 7.

Program numbers:
127 or 128? Confusingly, some manufacturers number MIDI messages 1–128 instead of 0–127.

To change from a patch in the current bank to a patch in another bank, you'll need to send two messages: first send a bank select message, then send a program change. (You have to send the messages in that order, because an instrument waits to change to the new bank until it receives the next program change number. So even if you're changing from bank 1, patch 1 to bank 2, patch 1, on most instruments you'll need to send a bank select followed by a program change.)

System Messages

MIDI also uses system messages. These messages apply to the entire music system that's interconnected using MIDI, not just to individual instruments. The three types of system messages are system-realtime, system-common, and system-exclusive.

The most important system-realtime messages are used for synchronization among devices (sequencers, for example) that engage in real-time recording or playback. In this category are clock messages (sent 24 times for each quarter-note), start, stop, and continue. You can even use MIDI sync data to synchronize sequencers running on two or more computers by connecting them with MIDI cables. (See Chapter 12 for details.)

System-common messages include song select and song position pointer (again, for use with sequencers) and a few other kinds of messages. But the best known and yet most mysterious of MIDI's system messages is system-exclusive, also known as sys-ex or SysEx.

SysEx

System-exclusive messages are designed to address specific hardware devices. These messages are a "back door" through which each manufacturer can create whatever MIDI features a particular instrument may need. The beginning of a SysEx message specifies that the data is intended for a specific model built by a specific manufacturer. All of the other MIDI gear in the system should ignore a SysEx message that's not addressed to them. What SysEx is used for is entirely dependent on the equipment's manufacturer.

One advantage of SysEx messages is that they aren't limited to a specific length, because they simply use a "stop" (also called EOX, or "end-of-exclusive") message to indicate that the message has concluded. Since SysEx can involve a lot of data, it's usually used for initializing a device, downloading an updated operating system from the computer to a piece of hardware, or sending other large chunks of information. Data is "dumped" to a device via a SysEx in a single large chunk, rather than by sending values for individual parameters during a performance as with MIDI data messages like notes and controllers. That said, some manufacturers use SysEx messages instead of data messages for real-time controls, and specialized SysEx data called MIDI Machine Control and Show Control (see sidebar) allow for real-time commands not possible in the channel message area of MIDI.

MIDI Time Code and MIDI clock

Timing information is essential to synchronizing playback systems such as sequencers when they're running on different computers or hardware instruments. When synchronization is used, one device or piece of software is designated the master clock source (**Figure 8.20**), and any other hardware or software should follow the clock signals coming from the master. (In common parlance, the other devices are called slaves.) MIDI provides two methods of synchronization: MIDI clock and MIDI Time Code (MTC).

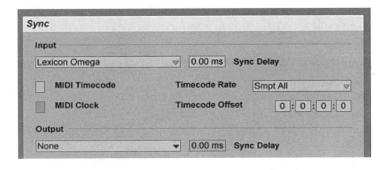

Figure 8.20 MIDI sync settings in Ableton Live let you synchronize the tempo and start/stop times of multiple devices.

MIDI Machine Control/MIDI Show Control

A specialized form of SysEx message, MIDI Machine Control (MMC) is designed for controlling systems for recording and playback remotely, and is used by recording systems like the Tascam DA-88. MMC includes more sophisticated commands than the usual system-realtime start/stop/continue commands. MMC has been expanded into a protocol called MIDI Show Control (MSC) intended for use with other equipment like lighting and special effects. MSC can even be found powering the multimedia elements of rides at Disney World.

MIDI clock is the simpler of the two types. It's sent as a regular, repeating message, 24 times for each quarter-note of the master clock source; thus, it acts like a virtual metronome. Receiving devices count the clock messages being received. After 24 clocks, they should reach the next beat. If the tempo of the master slows down or speeds up, any slaves that are synced using MIDI clock should also slow down or speed up at the same rate. MIDI clock provides *tempo-dependent* synchronization.

When playback starts not at the beginning of the song but somewhere in the middle, the master should also send out a message called song position pointer (SPP), which tells the slave devices where to start playback. The slave will advance its transport to the point indicated by the song position pointer and then wait for a start message to begin playback.

You can use MIDI clock to synchronize applications running on multiple computers. Since sequencers are capable of syncing tempo and song position via MIDI clock, all you have to do is connect the computers via MIDI, choose one program as the master clock source, make sure it's sending sync information to the correct MIDI output, switch the other program into external clock mode, and make sure it's receiving its sync signal from the appropriate MIDI input. You don't have to be using MIDI in any other way for this technique to be useful: tempo-synced audio effects, for example, will automatically synchronize, making this solution perfect for collaboration or performance. (See Chapter 13 for more on real-time performance.)

For clock synchronization that is not tempo-dependent but is based on actual minutes, seconds, and film/video frames, you'll use the MTC. MTC uses standard SMPTE (Society of Motion Picture and Television Engineers) time references, in hours, minutes, seconds, and frames, and it's configurable to different frame rates for different media (film, video, etc.) (See Chapter 12 for more information on working with film and video.) Even if you're not using film or video, MTC can be useful for handling time in nonmusical increments.

RECORDING PERFORMANCES

MIDI is limited in some ways. But recording, editing, and performance are where it really shows off its flexibility. Is your rhythm a little "out"? Hit the quantize button, and your performance will be magically corrected so that it's right on the beat. Do you need to sight-transpose because your singer can't sing in the key you spent so much time learning the song in? Hit a button, and you're in the right key. Wonder what that bass line would sound like arpeggiated? With one command you can pump out tempo-synced musical patterns. Want to try a different orchestration, a different groove, or a different arrangement, or change a few notes? A MIDI performance, once recorded into a sequencer, can be edited in myriad ways that would be difficult or impossible if the same performance were recorded as audio, even to create scenarios like twenty-fingered piano chords or ridiculously fast, intricate runs that would be impossible in the real world.

Recording into any MIDI sequencer allows you to record a performance that's fully editable and reproducible as long as you have the plug-ins and/or hardware with which it was originally produced. Many of these techniques also apply to playing music into notation software; see Chapter 11 for more on notation.

Tempo and Roll

One advantage of MIDI is that you can set a different tempo for recording than the ultimate playback tempo. If a part is difficult, for example, you might record it at half-tempo and then speed it up in playback.

Keeping your performance in tempo is essential to synchronizing parts and being able to quantize rhythms, as described later in this chapter. You'll often want to record with a metronome enabled. (If you don't like the monotony of a metronome, your software will probably let you play along with a drum loop or some other rhythmic material.) To make sure your performance lines up with metronome ticks, you'll want to first set a manageable tempo. If you're playing along with previously recorded audio tracks, however, this technique won't work.

To make sure you start recording on time and in tempo, you'll also probably want to set up a couple of *pre-roll* measures—what musicians call "bars for nothing," or measures prior to the beginning of the song that contain only a count. (These bars give you a "warm-up" time to get ready to play—think "a five, six, seven, eight!")

What if your music isn't that regular, and changes tempo as you play? You have two options: one is to play strictly in time and add tempo changes later, and the other is to play with tempo changes or rubato as you record. If you opt for the latter, you can either turn off the metronome and not worry about synchronizing with bars and beats or, if your program allows it, tap in a tempo (usually using a foot controller) as you play to set the metronome to your playing rather than the other way around. (See the sidebar "Tap Tempo.")

Most DAWs have a track that includes meter changes and tempo shifts. This is often called a *conductor track* (because it's akin to a conductor beating time).

 Tap Tempo

Tap tempo lets you tap in a rhythm in real time during recording or playback. Your MIDI devices will automatically speed up or slow down to match the tempo. You can use tap tempo to match your MIDI tempo to live playing on acoustic instruments, to set up tempos that shift organically, or any time you want to "conduct" your MIDI devices and have them respond. (VJs, you might even use tap tempo to match your visuals to a band; see Chapter 12 for more.)

You can employ tap tempo in two ways:

- Use a hardware device with built-in, preconfigured tap tempo that can send MIDI clock information to other synchronized devices.

- Use software with tap tempo that's assignable to a MIDI controller so you can use a custom controller of your choice (like a hold pedal).

For an example of the second method, Ableton Live has a "tap" control that's assignable to any MIDI controller (**Figure 8.21**). You may want to assign this to a foot pedal so you can tap with your foot while you play. If a pedal isn't available, you could also assign a nonsounding note on your keyboard or even click the tap tempo button with your mouse, though either of these techniques can interfere with your keyboard performance.

Figure 8.21 Tap tempo lets you set tempo in real time by tapping out the beats, so you can conduct your MIDI devices.

Overwrite and Merge

You can overdub with MIDI just as with audio, adding more tracks to your arrangement and using different instruments or MIDI channels to create layers. Since MIDI stores performance events rather than sound, you can also easily add new MIDI data to an existing MIDI performance within a single track. For instance, if you're not a skilled keyboardist, you might record your right-hand part first, then rewind the sequencer to the start of the song and add your left-hand part while listening to the right hand, or overdub a modulation controller over a sequenced track.

In *overwrite* mode, your software will erase the previous recording on a given track and replace it with the new recording, which is useful if you want to replace a lousy take with a better one. If you want to layer more notes into the track, switch to *merge* mode and the newly recorded data will be combined with the old. Just remember, MIDI messages are channel-wide, so if your first take incorporated hold pedaling or pitch-bends, the new take will be affected by those messages as well.

Some DAWs also allow you to do multiple takes without stopping, so you can set a section of a song to loop and try a part several times, then choose among them to decide which you like best.

Splits

You have two hands, so why not take advantage of them? By employing a keyboard *split,* you can use different areas of a keyboard (*zones*) for different sounds. For instance, you could make the bottom of the keyboard an upright acoustic bass and the top an acoustic piano (one of the most common split arrangements).

You can create a split in either the sending or receiving instrument, depending on which supports split creation (not all instruments do). Using a MIDI keyboard, for instance, you could assign one half of the piano to one channel and the other to a different channel, and then arm two tracks for MIDI recording at the same time, assigning one track to each channel. If you create the split in the receiving device, you won't need separate channels; you'll simply set it up to produce a different sound in each half of the keyboard.

Step Entry

Sometimes it's preferable to enter notes individually rather than play them live. *Step entry,* also called step record mode, is a data entry method that involves creating notes one ("step") at a time. Some DAWs have dedicated step entry interfaces that let you choose exact rhythms, pitch, velocity, and other values; many people swear by step entry for precise programming of drum parts and other song elements (**Figure 8.22**). Even if your software doesn't have a dedicated step entry window, you should be able to insert one note at a time using a pencil tool for the same effect. Step entry is similar to the drawing facility in notation software and piano roll editors, and to the data entry used in pattern editors (see the section "Pattern Editing," later in this chapter).

Figure 8.22 Step entry, as shown in MOTU Digital Performer, lets you record notes one at a time instead of playing them in real time.

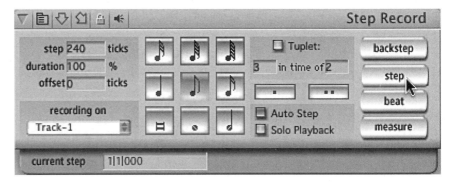

QWERTY and Onscreen Keyboards

What do you do if you don't have a MIDI keyboard handy? For example, you might be composing music on your laptop on a flight to Los Angeles. Some programs will map your computer's QWERTY keyboard to MIDI, so you can easily try out instruments or record a quick bass line. Apple Logic Pro, for instance, displays a keyboard with the Caps Lock key, while Ableton Live will automatically respond to the QWERTY keyboard on any record-armed MIDI track. The QWERTY keys aren't velocity-sensitive, of course, but your software may let you adjust the velocities of the notes you're about to enter using another key combination. If it doesn't, you'll still be able to edit the velocities when you're done entering the notes. Many programs also include onscreen keyboard displays you can click to audition notes. Such keyboards are either built into the display for a virtual instrument (as with synths from IK Multimedia and Native Instruments, for example), or are shown as a mouseable onscreen keyboard in a sequencer, as in GarageBand's Keyboard.

EDITING AND MANIPULATING PERFORMANCES

Since MIDI is just a series of numbers that represent musical events, editing is literally simple arithmetic (in contrast to the heavy-duty number-crunching required for audio). In fact, your sequencer handles all the arithmetic for you. Editing MIDI data is a fairly easy process. You can move notes forward or backward in time, a few at once or track-wide, change pitch individually or transpose entire sections, and rearrange your music with incredible flexibility.

Editing Views and Methods

MIDI sequencers let you look at your recorded music using a few common views: piano rolls (which usually include graphical controller editing), event lists with the actual MIDI data, and pattern editors designed for rhythm-locked edits.

Piano roll and notation

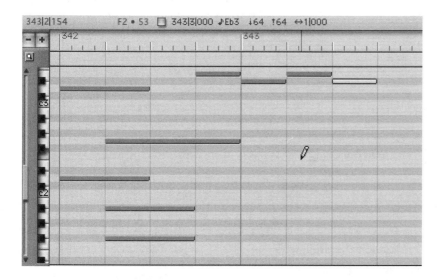

Piano roll views present pitch as the y-axis of a grid, usually with a virtual piano keyboard along the left edge of the window so it's easy to spot which pitch is which. Time is mapped to the x-axis. You can draw notes with a pencil tool, drag them around, copy and paste them, or shorten or lengthen individual notes or whole groups of notes. (Pictured: MOTU Digital Performer)

Graphic controller editing

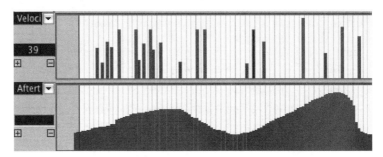

Graphic views offer a powerful way to edit controller data using some of the drawing tools familiar from many graphics programs. Typically, controller data is presented as a graph (also called a strip) along the bottom of the piano roll view. In the strip, you can choose to display pitch-bend, aftertouch, or control change information. You might, for example, draw in a smooth rising ramp for modulation to gradually introduce vibrato on an organ part.

By applying a snap-to-grid option, you can lock your changes to the beat. Thanks to grid options, in fact, there's some overlap in functionality between graphic editors like the MIDI clip editor found in Ableton Live and pattern editors like Reason's Matrix step sequencer. However, a step sequencer *always* places note and controller data on a fixed rhythmic grid. By turning off the grid in a piano-roll or graphic controller editor, you can place events at any point in time. (Pictured: Steinberg Cubase SX)

Event editing

Position				Status	Cha	Num	Val	Length/Info			
------------ Start of List ------------											
2	3	2	150	Note	1	C3	81	.	.	2	100
2	3	2	151	Note	1	C2	81	.	.	2	56
2	3	3	76	Control	1	64	127	EXS24#1			
3	1	1	28	Note	1	C4	56	.	.	3	96
3	1	1	30	Note	1	G3	82	.	.	3	117
3	1	1	31	Note	1	F3	83	.	.	3	138
3	1	1	46	Note	1	G#4	82	.	2	1	209
3	1	1	53	Note	1	C5	81	.	3	1	23
3	1	1	102	Control	1	64	0	EXS24#1			
3	1	3	56	Control	1	64	127	EXS24#1			
3	2	3	233	Note	1	A#2	81	.	.	2	117
3	2	3	235	Note	1	A#1	82	.	.	2	61

Graphic views are friendly, but from time to time you may need to work directly with the MIDI data—especially when you want to precisely adjust a single data value or look at data that's not shown in a graphic view. Event lists display the actual MIDI messages, showing time, message type, and exact value. (Pictured: Apple Logic Pro) The exception is that MIDI notes are displayed with durations, even though note duration is not a MIDI data type: the note-off messages are seldom displayed separately.

Pattern editing

Pattern editors, also called drum editors, always assign musical events to a rhythmic grid. Some emulate hardware drum machines or analog hardware synthesizers for creating intentionally mechanical rhythmic patterns popular in electronica and other forms. Others are designed for creating drum patterns.

To create a drum groove in a pattern editor, you might gradually build up one part at a time. For instance, you could start with a kick drum, then add a hat, snare, tom, and cymbal, until you have a composite pattern you like. By building up this pattern over time (see the Kinetic tutorial in Chapter 5), you can create a song structure; then create variants for breaks and variety.

Bass patterns and rhythmic synth patterns also work well when played by pattern editors. Since some pattern editors let you control other parameters, you can use them for rhythmic timbral changes, filters, and other effects. (Pictured: A pattern-based drum module in Arturia Storm)

Quantization

Quantization is essentially a "snap-to-grid" feature for notes. If your recording isn't quite on the beat, quantization will move the notes to the nearest beat (**Figure 8.23**). There are several basic variants of quantization:

- **Note-on only:** Shifts only the beginning of each note without changing note lengths.

- **Note-on and duration:** Shifts both the beginnings and the ends of notes to the grid.

- **Percentage:** Moves notes part way to the grid, thus tightening up the rhythmic feel without making the part completely rigid.

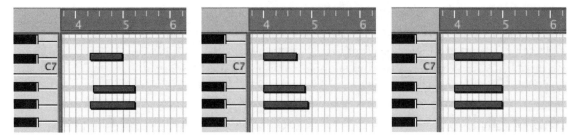

Figure 8.23 Quantization takes notes that are behind or ahead of beat locations (left) and shifts the beginning of each note to the nearest beat (center) based on a grid you specify (common grid values include eighth-notes, sixteenth-notes, eighth-note triplets, and other rhythmic values). If you quantize durations (quantize note-off messages as well as note-ons), the ends of notes will also be aligned with the grid (right).

- **Random:** Adding a small amount of randomization can allegedly "humanize" the quantization, preventing your music from sounding too mechanical. But what it really does is make your tracks sound as if they were performed by a random number generator; better humanization requires a more sophisticated algorithm.

- **Swing/shuffle:** Adds a small delay to the weak beats or offbeats, producing music with a long-short, long-short feeling that's natural in music like jazz, hip-hop, and some rock.

The main setting for quantization is the grid to which you want to quantize. You should choose the smallest value used in the recorded music. If you never play a note value smaller than a sixteenth-note, for instance, you'll usually send the quantization to the sixteenth. If your track includes both duplets and triplets, you'll wipe out the triplets by quantizing to a duplet value. Fortunately, you can select a group of notes and quantize them to a different value; you don't have to quantize the whole MIDI track at once. You can separately quantize duplets and triplets.

Quantization can't read your mind, of course. If a note was played far enough behind the beat that it's closer to the next beat, quantization will shift it to that beat. That means quantization can sound very strange if your original recording is too far off the metronome tick. On the other hand, you can use forced quantization in arrangements, turning melodic lines into chords (set quantization to a whole-note, for instance) and producing other effects.

Quantization can be performed as a MIDI playback effect, using a MIDI plug-in or a sequencer feature called *playback quantization*. With playback quantization you can hear the effects of quantization even though your recorded notes haven't actually been moved around, so you can change your mind about a quantization setting if you like. (Notation software often uses playback quantization.)

In general, quantization isn't just for fixing bad timing. It's also good for creating a rhythmic feel. Think of it as using a rhythmic filter on your music. This analogy is particularly apt when you use different swing settings or groove quantization (see the following section). You can use quantization to make music more mechanical, but it can also make music swing. Both are musically useful effects, so which you choose depends on the result you want. Dance music often uses rigid quantization, for instance, whereas a sequenced jazz, pop, or Latin track might use a looser quantization setting to maintain a live-sounding feel.

Groove quantization

Groove quantization is a specialized form of quantization that allows you to align your performance to a more complex and (hopefully) more musical grid—a grid that sounds like the musical groove played by a master musician. Instead of just setting a regular quarter-note grid, for instance, you could set up a complex, arhythmic grid. Groove quantization can also change velocity values, since a groove isn't just when you play but how you accent different beats. You apply groove quantization just like any other quantization, but the results are often more musical. Your sequencer may come with a selection of grooves, and may also allow you to create your own.

Quantization and audio

Quantization used to be MIDI-specific, but with new technology, the line between MIDI and audio has started to blur. Programs like MOTU Digital Performer and Steinberg Cubase can divide audio into beat "slices" (for instance, separating a recorded drum groove into individual drum hits) and quantize the hits separately, or extract a groove from audio to apply to MIDI or to other audio (with both rhythmic feel and dynamic level for accents).

Groove quantization gets even more interesting when you start extracting grooves from audio and moving grooves from one part to another: it lets you extract a rhythmic "feel" from one source and apply it to another, whether from MIDI to MIDI, MIDI to audio, audio to MIDI, or audio to audio. For example, you might have a jazz drum loop and really love the feel of it: try extracting it as a groove, and then apply it to the Hammond organ recording you played on your keyboard to see how it sounds.

Quantizing controllers: In some (but not all) software, the quantization commands will allow you to move controller data forward or backward along with notes that are sounding during the controller moves. This very desirable feature allows your pitch-bends, for instance, to maintain their timing relationship to the bent notes.

Quantization isn't specific to MIDI: The term describes any process that rounds off continuous values into discrete values. Any time you record analog signal and convert it to digital, you're quantizing the continuous signal into digital values, so quantization is a digital audio term, too.

Hands-on: Recording and editing MIDI clips

Ableton Live treats MIDI clips much like audio clips: you can record into clips, drag them into Session View clip slots or Arrange View tracks, loop them, arrange them in scenes, crossfade them, and do nearly everything else you can do with audio. Whether you're programming a drum track or recording a long piano solo for a new concerto, the easiest way to approach recording and editing Live's MIDI clips is to familiarize yourself with the clip edit interface. For this exercise you can use whatever MIDI instrument you want, from your own hardware to SampleTank to the built-in Live instruments Impulse, Simpler, and Operator.

1. **Record a clip:** With input set for the controller you want to use, record-enable the track on which you want to record (1). If you're using a software instrument, just drag its plug-in to the track and Live will use it automatically. If you're using an external hardware instrument or a ReWire device (like Propellerhead Reason), set the MIDI To setting to the device and channel you want to use (2). When you're ready, click the Record button in a clip slot (3) to record into a Session View clip, or switch to Arrange View to record into your arrangement. If you want to merge MIDI data with an existing Arrangement track or Session clip, make sure Overdub (OVR) is selected at the top of the screen.

2. **Edit a clip:** Double-click a prerecorded MIDI clip in either Session or Arrange View to edit it. (Or, if you prefer to enter notes manually, double-click an empty MIDI clip slot in Session View to create a new, blank clip.) Once in Clip View, you'll have access to various editing capabilities:

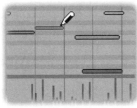

- **Draw Mode:** To toggle Draw Mode on and off (changing your cursor to a pencil so you can draw new notes, controllers, and envelopes), use Ctrl-B (PC) or Cmd-B (Mac). The Draw tool will use the active grid settings.

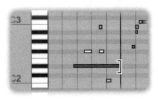

- **Editing:** With Draw Mode off, the cursor changes to an arrow. Drag the center of a note to move it around or drag the leading or trailing edges to adjust the attack or release, shortening or lengthening the note. Drag the note up and down to change the pitch. Hold down Alt (PC) or Cmd (Mac) and drag vertically to change the note's velocity: the note will get darker with a higher velocity, and the Velocity Marker at the bottom of the Clip view (the series of vertical lines) will move up or down.

- **Grid:** Drawing and editing tools will snap to the visible grid (watch the thin vertical lines in the Clip editor). You can change the grid from the Options menu; with the Draw tool (pencil), the grid will make it easy to create rhythmic patterns for parts like drums and basslines. To ignore the grid for finer editing, hold down the Alt key (PC) or Cmd key (Mac) while you drag horizontally (drag first, then hold down the modifier key), or shut off the grid using Ctrl-4 (PC) or Cmd-4 (Mac).

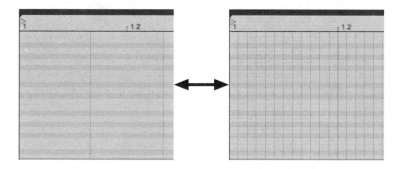

3. **Quantize notes:** Live's quantize feature will use whichever grid is visible:

- **Select:** Choose the notes you want to quantize: select all (Edit > Select all) to modify the whole clip or select just certain notes by dragging a marquee selection area around them (turn off Draw Mode, then drag from a blank area of the clip over the notes you want to select). You can also Shift-click to add notes to the selection individually. (Quick trick: click or Shift-click the keys on the keyboard on the left to select all the notes of that pitch.)

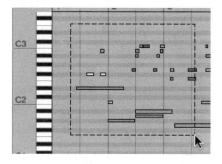

- **Perform quantization:** Make sure the grid shown is the grid you want to use (adjust it using the Options menu if needed), then select Edit > Quantize (Ctrl-U on PC, Cmd-U on Mac). Notice that Live quantizes only note-on events (note start times), not durations.

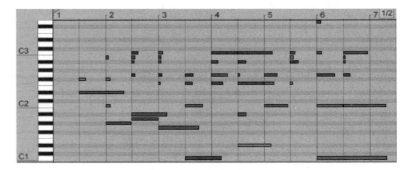

4. **Edit controllers with envelopes:** Using Live's Envelopes editor, you can draw controller data atop your MIDI clip, from pitch-bend to any of MIDI's available control changes (Live automatically ignores messages like bank select, since they aren't useful in this context). Turn on the Envelopes view (1) and select the data type you want (2). Then, for changes synced to the tempo/beat grid, turn on Draw Mode (Ctrl-B or Cmd-B). Draw in changes (3) where you want them to go, and Live will automatically snap to the active grid.

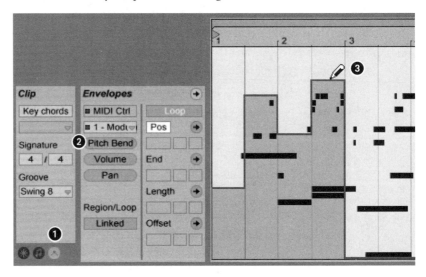

5. **Gradual changes:** For gradual changes of control data instead of beat-synced, sudden changes, turn off Draw Mode and double-click to add or remove breakpoints. Drag the breakpoints up and down, and Live will create smooth transitions between them. (Breakpoints employ the same basic concept as keyframes in digital video and motion graphics.)

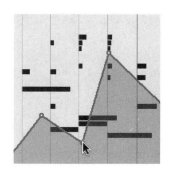

MIDI Effects

Normally we associate the terms "effects" and "plug-ins" with audio, not MIDI, but MIDI is actually much easier than audio for software developers to manipulate in real time. Because MIDI is just a string of numbers that represent your performance, it's easy to add, subtract, or modify incoming note numbers, velocity, and other data. Most MIDI-savvy DAWs include a range of MIDI effects that can be used as "channel inserts" just like audio plug-ins, such as:

Can't get the grid you want? Live bases its Clip grid on the settings for that clip, just as with audio. So if you're not seeing the grid you want or expect, try adjusting the values for time signature (in the Launch Box) and original BPM (in the Notes Box).

• **Split:** Automatically splits pitches into different channels for instruments that lack an internal split feature

• **Echo:** Repeats a note one or more times for an echo effect

• **Quantize/groove quantize:** Quantizes as you play (or adds live quantization to recorded tracks)

• **Arpeggiate:** Automatically produces melodic or harmonic patterns around an input note or chord (**Figure 8.24**)

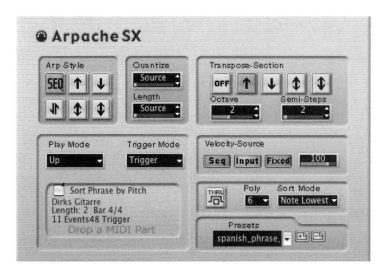

Figure 8.24 Arpeggiators like Cubase SX's powerful Arpache SX can automatically play melodic patterns based on an input note, in time with the music, for various musical effects.

Of course, this is only the beginning: just about any transformation that you can imagine can be wrought on the MIDI data using user-programmable tools like Max/MSP, Pd, and Plogue Bidule. These programs also handle audio, but they can manipulate MIDI with simple arithmetic, and creating your own MIDI widgets is a great way to learn to use this type of software. For more information and ideas, see Chapter 12.

Live MIDI effects

MIDI effects can be added in Ableton Live just like audio effects: open the Live Device Browser (1) and drag the effects you want to a MIDI track (2).

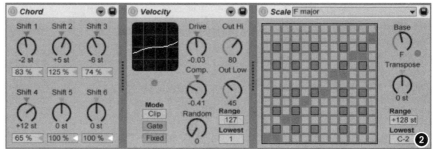

Here's what you can do with Live's effects:

- **Chord** adds up to six pitches (transposing the note you play) to create chords around an incoming pitch.

- **Pitch** is a simple transposition; it's perfect if your guitarist decides she doesn't like G♭ major.

- **Random** randomizes a specified number of pitches.

- **Scale** constrains notes to a certain scale, like pentatonic or F major.

- **Velocity** works like a virtual compressor/gate or randomizer, modifying velocity values.

Check out the presets for some ideas: live MIDI processing can be useful for both melodic and percussive parts. For some wild results, try importing MIDI files—ever wondered what a Bach invention would sound like with some random pitches?

Using Control Surfaces

Another common function of MIDI, aside from recording and playing back musical parts, is to provide a way to control and record mix and synthesis parameters. By assigning a device as a *control surface,* as described in Chapter 2, you can manipulate parameters in software or hardware with physical controls (**Figure 8.25**). You can use control surfaces to control both your mix and instruments.

Figure 8.25 A control surface links the physical to the virtual. When you move a physical controller to generate a MIDI message, you can affect one or more parameters configured to receive that message. For example, a bank of eight sliders might be programmed to send CCs 9 through 16 to control volume levels on a software mixer.

Some control surfaces and MIDI instruments are preconfigured to work with certain software, in which case you can just plug and play. If you need to edit the way these devices and your software work together, you'll have to modify your MIDI control change assignments.

Templates

The easiest way to link a control surface to onscreen controls is to use templates, which save you from having to manually configure your controller and receiver to work with each other. (With only a few exceptions, nearly all MIDI control change assignments differ from one manufacturer to another.) At the very least, you may be able to use a template on either the controller or receiver side to match the two up. But for optimal performance, you may be able to load templates on both sides so your controller is set up to send the MIDI data your software or device needs to receive and the receiving software or device is set up with MIDI assignments for all the necessary parameters. Fortunately, many control surfaces and keyboards intended for use as computer controllers now come with templates, and others can be downloaded online. Some software packages, like Propellerhead Reason, are designed to automatically detect a range of common devices; the application sets up both the software and the hardware for you (**Figure 8.26**).

Figure 8.26 Propellerhead Reason automatically recognizes some common keyboards and control surfaces, and automatically configures its software settings as well as the connected hardware for use with preconfigured layouts.

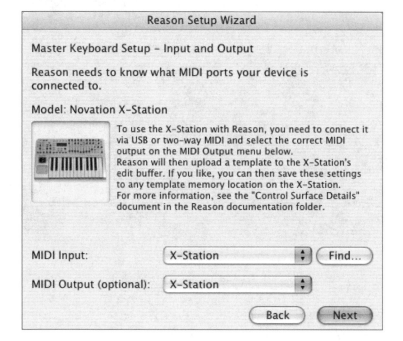

If there isn't an appropriate template available, another option for setting up your software to receive messages from your control surface is to edit MIDI assignments on both devices. But first check your gear's documentation and MIDI implementation chart for details on what data your device sends and receives, and how this data is configured and routed. Usually, you'll be able to control whatever needs to be controlled via basic MIDI messages and control changes, although in some cases you may need to use specialized messages like SysEx.

MIDI Learn

In order to get software to respond as desired to MIDI data, you may be able to make use of a MIDI Learn function. This function, found in most software instruments, allows you to point at a parameter you want to manipulate (like an onscreen fader), then move the physical control you want to associate with it. The software detects the control change messages being sent and remembers the control change number so that it can respond to subsequent messages that have the same CC number. MIDI Learn can be a bit slow to set up if you have lots of parameters to assign, but it's a nearly foolproof setup method. Your instrument may also allow you to save the result as a template so you can reuse it. One "gotcha" when using MIDI Learn is that many synths allow only one onscreen control (usually a knob or slider) to be assigned to any given CC number. If you try to assign a second control to the same CC number, the first control will "forget" its assignment.

 ### Hands-on: Assign a MIDI fader

If you want custom control of your software, the MIDI Learn mode is usually the easiest way to attach your physical controls to controls onscreen. In this example you'll "teach" Ableton Live a controller assignment by turning on the program's MIDI mappings, selecting something to trigger or adjust, and then performing the action you want assigned to that parameter in the software.

1. **Turn on MIDI Map Mode:** Click the MIDI button in the upper-right corner of the screen. The elements that can be assigned will change color, indicating that MIDI Map Mode is on. (The adjacent KEY button works the same way for QWERTY computer keyboard assignments.)

2. **Click something you want to assign.** This can be a loop, a fader, a knob, the crossfader, a filter parameter—whatever you want. Usually, clips are better assigned to single triggers (such as MIDI notes), whereas knobs should be assigned to continuous controllers (like a mod wheel or expression pedal).

3. **Move, twiddle, or play something.** On your MIDI hardware, press a note, or touch/twiddle/adjust a knob, fader, pedal, ribbon, X-Y pad, joystick, infrared sensor, or anything else you have on any MIDI gear that's handy. Live will then assign the note, message, or control change that was sent to the item you clicked.

With MIDI Map Mode on, you can assign as many controls as you want. Then turn off MIDI Map Mode and try it out the controls: your hardware controls should manipulate the onscreen controls.

Applications: Work with mixing and instruments

Thanks to MIDI's open-ended nature, you can use a MIDI control surface in many ways. You might want to control one instrument parameter during performance or run an entire lighting rig with pyrotechnics. That said, here are just a few common applications:

- **Mixer:** Trying to use a mouse to control mix faders and pan knobs is (literally) a drag. Instead, use the faders on your keyboard or dedicated control surface. Not only is working this way easier, but unlike a mouse, a control surface lets you adjust more than one level at a time. If you're using a motorized controller that has two-way communication with your software, the physical faders will automatically snap to the right positions for the current spot in the song.

- **Virtual organ:** Assigning eight faders to organ parameters can give you drawbar-style control of a software organ simulation. Moving the draw-bars while playing is an essential part of technique on a Hammond organ.

- **Synth editor:** For control of envelopes, filters, and other aspects of an instrument's timbre, assign faders, knobs, modulation wheels, X/Y pads, infrared sensors, and whatever else you can get your hands on for real-time sonic shaping.

- **Guitar stompbox:** Assign a switched foot controller to effect parameters and expression pedals to volume or other continuous controls for real-time foot controls. In fact, you don't have to be a guitarist to benefit, since most musicians already have plenty do with their hands while playing (**Figure 8.27**).

- **Drum/sample pad:** If you have drum triggers, digital drums, or a drum pad (a few keyboards even have drum pads built in), try triggering drum sounds or samples with your fingers. Alternatively, if you're using a program like Ableton Live, Max/MSP, or VJ software, in which you can control arrangements in real time, you might use the pads to start clips or scenes.

Figure 8.27 Don't forget your feet! Guitarists have used foot controls for years to turn effects on and off, trigger sounds, start and stop recording, and other applications. Keyboardists, flutists, turntablists, and bagpipe virtuosos can do the same thing, freeing up their hands for playing the instrument.

Using Standard MIDI Files

MIDI is intended as a protocol not only for control, but for file sharing as well. The Standard MIDI File (SMF) format stores recorded MIDI data in a form that can be imported by most MIDI-compatible applications (as well as some hardware). SMFs include notes, controllers, and all other MIDI performance data; system-exclusive data can also be included. The SMF format also allows for the storing of lyrics, which is useful for exporting to notation software and, of course, for karaoke. (Commercially available SMFs of pop songs are used by many karaoke music systems.) What SMFs don't include is the other data contained in a proprietary project file format used by your DAW: there's no audio, no mixing data, and no arrangement information other than what is contained in the MIDI tracks themselves. (For alternatives, see "Interchange Formats" in Chapter 11.)

You can save multi-track MIDI compositions as SMFs, for exporting to a different application. You'll lose any audio data and other application-specific information, but SMFs can be used to take an arrangement created in a sequencer and import the material into a notation package to create a finished score. Under United States Copyright law, you can even register an SMF file to copyright a composition (www.copyright.gov).

.MID files: Usually SMF files are saved with a .MID file extension; sometimes you'll see the .SMF extension, though it's not a standard designation.

In addition to full songs, you can use SMF files to save and re-use short MIDI clips (like drum patterns, basslines, or small phrases), exchanging them among programs with MIDI clip features, including Live, Kinetic/Project 5, GarageBand, and others. In some ways, the SMF format is better suited to these smaller clips than to the storage of an entire music composition, since in these cases you won't need all the extra information stored in a DAW project file.

From time to time you may see references to SMF Type 1 and SMF Type 0. Type 0 SMFs collapse multitrack MIDI recordings into a single track; this track will play multitimbrally when loaded into a sequencer, because the notes retain their original channel information. But the fact that track information is lost can sometimes cause difficulties when trying to determine which musical part is which, especially in music notation software. Type 1 SMF files maintain separate tracks, which is often more convenient for editing. The main reason the single-track format is used at all is for backward compatibility with obscure software and older music hardware.

When exporting MIDI data from your sequencer, you should generally choose Type 1 SMFs; if the software into which you're planning to import the file supports the SMF format at all, it'll almost certainly support Type 1.

 OSC: MIDI's Successor?

MIDI has many advantages: it's simple, it's a standard available on hardware and software built during the past two decades, and it's capable of doing a surprising number of things. But it's not without shortcomings. When you go beyond the realm of pedals, keyboards, and faders, MIDI's rigid way of defining music performance can get awkward fast. Much of the MIDI spec is both too undefined to make devices work together seamlessly and too narrowly defined to customize for what you want. Most important, the data bandwidth of MIDI is painfully narrow: MIDI uses absurdly small, rigid chunks of data. People have talked about replacing MIDI almost since the moment of its inception; even in 1983, for instance, some people complained that MIDI's data transmission rate (about 31,000 bits per second) was too slow. But over the years, no alternatives have caught on.

So, are there any alternatives now? One does look promising, and like electronic music itself, it's getting its start in academia. OpenSound Control (OSC) is being developed at the Center for New Music and Audio Technologies (CNMAT or "senn-mat") at the University of California, Berkeley (www.cnmat.berkeley.edu/OpenSoundControl).

Unlike MIDI, OSC is built for modern networking equipment and protocols, so it's easy to transmit data over networks, wirelessly, or over the Internet. Using concepts like client/server and packet communication, the same basic ideas that power the Internet, it's possible to collaborate with others in real time—something that's difficult in the rigid world of MIDI.

OSC doesn't have prestructured messages the way MIDI does (control change numbers, for instance). Instead, synthesizers and other devices can define their own data structures based on what they need, using something that's a little like a cross between object-oriented programming and Web addresses. Elements defined in OSC actually have addresses, like Web pages.

In fact, OSC's biggest advantage — that it's not anything like MIDI — is probably its biggest obstacle as well, since musicians, developers, and hardware engineers have grown accustomed to the comfortable idiosyncrasies of MIDI. But that hasn't stopped implementations of OSC in popular software like Cycling '74 Max/MSP, Native Instruments Reaktor and Traktor DJ, Macromedia Flash, and the free Mac/Linux/Windows application Pd (www.puredata.org).

If you're a newcomer to synthesis and interaction, you're probably not ready to work with OSC: it requires some knowledge of software development and network protocols. But you may come across devices that use OSC, like a range of new sensor interfaces for creating new instruments, and even fun projects online that adapt graphic tablets and game controllers for music using OSC. One of the more promising devices is the Lemur LCD touchscreen, a *Star Trek*-like gadget that connects via OSC to your computer using a 100-Base-T Ethernet cable for controlling your software (**Figure 8.28**).

MIDI, for its part, appears to be here to stay. But today you can supplement MIDI with other means of communication that are better suited to more complex situations. Looking into the future, maybe something like OSC will ultimately become the new standard.

 OSC is changing quickly. You can track developments at the CNMAT OSC site and at realworlddigitalaudio.com.

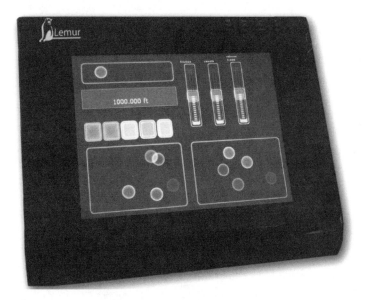

Figure 8.28 The Lemur touchscreen, developed by Jazz Mutant (www.jazzmutant.com) and distributed by Cycling '74 (www.cycling74.com), will give you an idea of what's possible with OSC. The Lemur's single-cable connection, big data bandwidth, and easy setup wouldn't have been possible with MIDI. Looking as if it was lifted from science fiction, the Lemur lets you create custom onscreen parameters and use multiple fingers at once for control—something that's not possible with tablet PCs and traditional touchscreens. The Lemur is just one of many new pieces of cutting-edge hardware and software created by people who are experimenting with OSC. (Photo courtesy Cycling '74)

CHAPTER 9

Synthesis and Software Instruments

Unless you're working exclusively with recorded sound, you'll want to master software instruments. We'll first look at the basic synthesis methods available, both those employing recorded (sampled) sounds and those whose sounds are truly "synthetic." Then we'll delve into what those synthesis methods mean for your music, whether you're just using and editing presets and sound libraries or building your own custom sound patches.

 Essentials

Synthesis and Software Instruments

We'll look at the underlying theory of synthesis and how to apply it:

- How you can create and customize sounds with synthesizers
- Different synthesis methods: how they work, what they sound like, and which are best suited to different musical tasks
- Working with prebuilt sounds (soundware)
- How samples and drum kits are mapped for expressive, realistic playing
- Analog-style waveshapes and what they sound like
- Using envelopes, modulation, and effects for more dynamic sounds

Where to Start

Try your hand at some basic sampling and virtual analog synthesis by following the hands-on examples for SampleTank FREE, Ableton Live, and Native Instruments Reaktor SoundSchool, all on the disc.

Essential Terms

- Synthesizers/synthesis
- Program, patch, and preset; multi; global
- Oscillator, voice, polyphonic/monophonic
- Synthesis types: analog subtractive, modular, frequency modulation, additive, sample playback, physical modeling, granular
- Sample playback: soundware, key zones, velocity cross-switching
- Envelopes; breakpoints
- Modulation

BASIC TYPES OF SYNTHESIS

When we talk about digital synthesis, we're really talking about the ability to make computers and digital hardware into playable musical instruments. Your digital audio workstation software can produce sound, but by most definitions it's not a musical instrument. (Applications like Ableton Live, which can be used onstage as well as for recording, are in a gray area.) A synthesizer is able to respond to MIDI input in real time, turning your performance on a MIDI keyboard or other controller into musical sound. With a synthesizer, the input is MIDI and the output is audio.

Instead of strings, hammers, reeds, pipes, membranes, and metal bars—the means by which acoustic instruments function—synthesizers use the basic sound creation elements of the electrical and digital worlds. These can be used to mimic recognizable acoustic instruments or to create sounds you can get only from electronic instruments.

What Is Synthesis?

The term "synthesizer" was controversial among early instrument builders. They were concerned the moniker would imply that electronic instruments were "artificial" replacements for acoustic instruments rather than unique instruments in their own right. In fact, "synthesis" doesn't mean the creation of something from nothing or the creation of something fake. Synthesis is the process by which simpler elements work together to create a more complex, coherent whole.

A *synthesizer* is any musical instrument, either hardware or software, that creates sound by electronic means in response to input from a player. The input is often in the form of a live performance on a MIDI controller keyboard, but could also be from a sequencer track, a pattern generator, or some other control mechanism. The resulting sound could be highly artificial, or it could be a software-simulated orchestra. (Usually, the use of the term "synthesizer" also implies that the user can edit the sounds being created in significant ways by adjusting the settings of various synthesis parameters. An electronic instrument that plays only preset sounds is not usually considered a synthesizer.)

The method by which the synthesizer produces sound varies from one model to another. A synthesizer may rely on recorded audio samples (as is probably the case with instruments that specialize in electronic piano and simulation of orchestral instruments), or it may produce sound by generating and processing basic waveshapes and digital models.

Synthesizers can be called *synths, soft synths* (software synthesizers), or *virtual instruments* (a term that often refers to synths that mimic either acoustic instruments or specific hardware like an electric piano).

Where You'll Find Synthesizers

Software-based synthesizers are found either as stand-alone applications or as plug-ins. (Many instruments can run in either mode.) As a stand-alone, a soft synth receives MIDI input and sends its audio output directly to your computer's audio interface. In plug-in mode, the synth appears inside your DAW of choice. External MIDI signals are routed into the synth by the DAW, which also sends the synth any MIDI messages that have been recorded into the track to which the synth is assigned. The audio output of the synth passes through the DAW's mixer, where it can be processed in various ways or even captured ("bounced") as a new audio track.

After capturing the output of a plug-in synth as an audio track, you can remove the synth from your DAW project, as the synth itself is no longer needed.

Many DAWs come with a collection of soft synths, and others can be added as third-party plug-ins. Other applications that contain synths (like Propeller-head Reason, www.propellerheads.se), although not plug-ins, can be coupled with your DAW for use as an instrument via ReWire. You can also build your own software instruments using modular programs like Cycling '74 Max/MSP (www.cycling74.com), Native Instruments Reaktor (www.native-instruments.com), and Synthedit (www.synthedit.com).

In this chapter, we'll focus on software for the sake of simplicity, but you'll find that most of the principles discussed apply to hardware as well. The primary difference is the user interface, although as some higher-end keyboards add large-screen LCDs and, conversely, soft synths allow for easier use of hardware controls, even that difference is eroding.

Elements of a Synthesizer Patch

Unlike an acoustic instrument like a piano or kazoo, the way a synthesizer sounds and behaves when you trigger a note isn't fixed. It's the result of a combination of settings on the synth. After adjusting various parameters to create a specific sound, you can store all of the instrument's settings together as a group called a program, preset, or patch.

In Chapter 8, we looked at the concept of a *program* as it's termed by MIDI. The terms *program, preset,* and *patch* are generally interchangeable. All of

Lend a hand: It's best to explore synthesis with some kind of input that allows you to play music on the synthesizer. The most common, of course, is the MIDI keyboard, so in this chapter we'll refer repeatedly to a "keyboard" as an input. As we discussed in Chapter 8, you can use all kinds of other devices as MIDI inputs as well. So if you're playing a MIDI guitar, a MIDI trumpet, or a MIDI accordion, you can substitute those.

these terms refer to some kind of stored instrument settings, a combination of a configuration that creates the sound itself with parameters for how the sound should behave when played (**Figure 9.1**). On a software synth, these settings are stored in files on your hard drive. If the patches are sample based, they'll also include either the audio data or a pointer to an audio file somewhere on the hard drive. With a synth that isn't using sample playback, the patch is simply a record of the settings you've chosen. We'll use the term "preset" to refer to the "factory" patches installed with a soft synth, and more generally refer to these settings as patches.

Figure 9.1 SoundSchool Analog mimics a hardware instrument in that there are fixed memory locations in which you can store patches. SoundSchool calls patches "snapshots," hence the camera icon in the main toolbar (not shown). If you run out of empty slots in the active bank, you can switch to a new bank, so you're not limited to the 128 slots shown here. Just don't forget to choose File > Save All Banks when you're done. Since the synthesizer is running in the computer's RAM, all of your edits will be lost unless they are saved to disk.

Part of the point of using a synthesizer is to take advantage of the ability to change patches or programs so that they meet your musical needs. Creating your own custom programs is often called synthesizer *programming*. (Except in rare cases, synthesizer programming means editing parameters in a patch, not programming in the sense of writing lines of code.)

Making your synth your own

You can approach using synths in several ways. You can use the supplied factory presets simply by loading them from the list and not worrying about what the knobs and buttons do. This is usually the best way to become acquainted with what a synth can do, and if you're using something like a virtual piano, you may not have any desire to go beyond the factory defaults.

Most of the time, though, you'll find yourself wanting to edit the factory patches slightly, if not more radically. A preset might sound just a little too bright, for instance, in which case adjusting the filter will solve the problem. You may also want to go beyond tweaking, adding some effects to an instrument until it sounds quite different from the original.

In other cases, it's easier to work from scratch, building up the sound you want from basic elements rather than starting with a preset loaded with lots of options. In this case, you'll want to forgo the factory presets altogether.

Regardless of your approach, you should save your sounds and their settings so you can use them again later. To accomplish this, soft synths generally include at least some of the following functions for managing individual patches:

- **Load:** Loading a patch replaces any sounds and settings (or those active on the current part, if the synth is multitimbral) with those stored in the patch. You usually won't be able to produce sound until a patch is loaded, although some synths automatically load a default patch for you on launch.

- **Save:** Saving a patch stores all active sounds and settings for the current part, either overwriting an existing patch or saving to a new patch. (Some instruments, including SoundSchool, save to RAM for temporary use rather than to your hard drive, so there may be a separate option for storing your patch permanently.)

- **Create basic/empty patch:** Many synths either include a basic patch with all the bells and whistles turned off or let you create one. This is especially useful for creating sounds from basic ingredients, focusing on individual elements without lots of built-in effects and filters kicking in. (Note that some synths, apparently anxious to show off all their features, include a fancier preset as the default. This is the case with SoundSchool Analog, as used in this chapter. Its "45 - My Default" preset enables many parameters by default, so later in the chapter we'll use more basic presets to begin plain-vanilla sound design.)

- **Duplicate:** Duplicating creates a copy of an existing patch so you can edit it while leaving the original untouched. This is handy if you're frequently editing existing patches. If your synth lacks such a function, you can simply open an existing patch and save it with a different name after editing.

- **Organize:** Many synths let you store patches in folders or banks to keep them organized, as in **Figure 9.2**. It's a big improvement over storing everything in one giant list of patches, in which it can be hard to find the sound you want.

Figure 9.2 Applied Acoustics' Lounge Lizard basically functions as just one instrument, an electric piano. But by organizing factory and custom presets into folders and subfolders, the synth lets you save and recall every slightest tweak to its various parameters without having to hunt through an enormous list of presets.

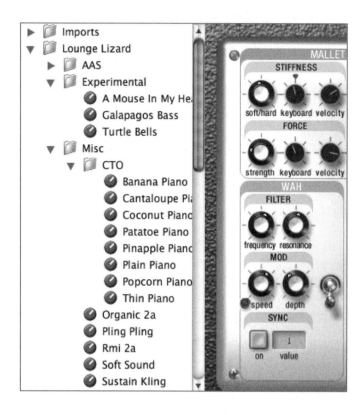

 Why are patches called patches?

In early analog synths, sounds were constructed using combinations of patch cords, which interconnected the various modules of the synthesizer. Since there was no software to save these custom instruments, musicians would have to either remember or write down the locations of the tangle of cables they had set up. Literally, their sound design was a patch: a mess of cords that produced certain sounds and behaviors.

Many of the edits you'll make in a synth are local patch settings, specific to the settings for an individual sound program. On multitimbral instruments, several individual programs can be combined into a larger unit called a *multi* or *combi*—a patch that combines a bass and piano, for instance, or one that layers several sounds at once. The edits made in a multi/combi are usually made in a separate area, and won't affect the data in the individual presets. Most synths also have some kind of *global* settings for storing parameters that affect all patches loaded on the instruments.

Nearly all synths have at least load and save capabilities. Your best strategy as you're experimenting with a synth is to save variants of sounds frequently, storing them in a specific folder so you can go back later and choose your favorite tweaks.

Oscillators

On an acoustic instrument, there is typically one component that is the source of the actual sound. On a piano, guitar, or violin, it's a string. On a clarinet or sax, it's a reed. On a drum, it's the membrane of the drum head.

This source vibrates and produces the sound, which is then modified by the body of the instrument into the sound we hear.

At the core of any electronic instrument are one or more *oscillators* (**Figure 9.3**). In true analog synthesis, the oscillator produces a continuous electrical signal that translates directly into sound (that is, the oscillation of the electrical signal is translated directly by the transducer into vibrations). In digital synthesis, the oscillator produces a digital signal. Analog synths have a limited repertoire of signal shapes, based on the capabilities of electrical circuits, but digital synths can use more complex models of sound and can use recorded audio waveforms (samples) as a signal source. (*Virtual analog* synths are digital synths that replicate the waveshapes and other features of analog synths, as we'll see later in the chapter.) Whether analog or digital, this signal can be combined with signals from other oscillators, processed through filters and amplifiers, or processed through effects.

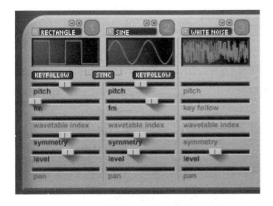

Figure 9.3 Oscillators are the source of the sound in any synth, whether they're generating sound using a previously recorded sample or some other waveform. Here in MOTU's MX4 synth, the three oscillators being mixed are using basic "virtual analog" wave sources, the same waveshapes you'd find on a 30-year-old hardware synth.

Voices and polyphony

A *voice* is usually considered to be a single channel of audio in an instrument; a four-voice synthesizer, for instance, can play four distinct sounds at once. If each note triggers only one sound, a four-voice synthesizer can also play four notes at once.

Instruments capable of playing multiple notes at once are called *polyphonic*. Early synthesizers like the original Minimoog were capable of playing only one note at a time, and thus were called *monophonic* instruments. Although it's impossible to play chords on a monophonic instrument, they are useful for bass and solo lead lines. Many polyphonic instruments today can be set to a monophonic mode to let you play them like the early monophonic instruments popular in jazz and rock; others can reduce the number of available voices to decrease the resource load on your computer system.

So why do we refer to both voices and polyphony, since they seem to have similar meanings? Voices relate to sounds, whereas polyphony relates to notes—the number of keys you're pressing at one time. If each note triggers one voice, the two terms mean the same thing. But if each note triggers more than one voice, the amount of polyphony will be less than the number of voices. For instance, if a synth preset layers four sounds to each note, four voices will be used for each note played, so an eight-voice synth playing that preset will yield only two-note polyphony. Most (although not all) software instruments allow the total number of available voices to be set to a higher or lower value. Reducing the voice count can be useful if your CPU is working too hard.

Pitch and tuning

As mentioned in Chapter 8, MIDI has no conception of pitch; notes are simply numbers that the synth converts into musical pitch. You'll typically find overall settings for how the synth turns MIDI notes into pitches among the other settings for a patch (**Figure 9.4**).

Figure 9.4 Typical pitch parameters, as found in the EXS|24 sampler included with Apple Logic Pro (www.apple.com/logicpro). The Transpose, Tune, and Fine controls determine overall pitch, and the Glide setting lets the synth slide between pitches. Note the legato/mono/poly and voice settings at the top, for determining polyphony and available voices.

The simplest setting is a *transposition* setting, which transposes all pitches up or down in half-step. This can be handy on days when your singer has a cold and can't quite reach the high notes. Sometimes this parameter is labeled "pitch" or "coarse."

For finer tuning, which may be necessary to keep in tune with another instrument, there may be a "fine" adjustment or a "master tuning" setting. The master tuning acts like a digital tuning fork against which the instrument's pitches are determined. (This isn't just for power users, because different countries tend to use different references for tuning. Orchestras in the United States often tune to the pitch A at 440 Hz, for instance, while ensembles in countries like France prefer a slightly higher A at 444 Hz.) The global tuning parameter is typically set to either +/- values in cents or a global setting in Hz. Sometimes there's even a "random" pitch amount, as shown in Figure 9.4, which is designed to introduce fluctuations in pitch. This supposedly mimics the drift on dirty or unreliable vintage analog oscillators. In reality, it tends to sound very unlike that, but it can be useful for special effects.

When the *portamento* or *glide* feature is enabled, the synth can move smoothly between pitches, like a slide trombone, instead of jumping from one discrete pitch to another, like a piano. Glide is equivalent to what's usually called a *glissando* in musical terms. Rocker Keith Emerson helped popularize the sound of a gliding synth, most famously in the Moog synth solos in the Emerson, Lake, and Palmer song "Lucky Man." (To try it yourself, see the sidebar "Hands-on: Glide Through SampleTank FREE.")

Generally, synths tune the relative pitch of notes within the scale according to the system used on modern pianos, which is called 12-tone equal temperament. If you're interested in exploring other tunings, such as historical tunings or foreign tunings, some synths support the use of *tuning tables*. These act as lookup tables that translate MIDI note numbers into other pitches. (Korg's OASYS instruments and several Native Instruments synths support this feature, for instance.) Why would you want to do this if you're not a student of ancient Pythagorean tunings or Indonesian *pathet*? Alternative tunings can add variety to a synth sound by producing unexpected pitches.

Basic Methods of Synthesis

Before you begin working with instruments and designing your own sounds, it's helpful to understand some of the taxonomy of electronic instruments. Different synths are grouped by how they produce sounds and by how they're used. Each method has varied in popularity over time, but thanks to soft synths, all of them are readily available for mixing and matching on a computer.

 Tuning outside the lines: The best solution for tuning tables is to use Scala files, a standard file format that can be loaded by a variety of soft synths and even some hardware. For microtonal control of synths that lack tuning tables and can't import Scala files, there are several free and shareware tools available online for micro-tuning; they usually fake these tunings by sending pitch wheel adjustments.

Scala file information: www.xs4all.nl/~huygensf/scala

Mac (LE version for Windows): Max Magic Microtuner (http://launch.groups.yahoo.com/group/16tone)

Mac-only: Open Tuning (www.open-tuning.com)

Little Miss Scale Oven (www.nonoctave.com/tuning/LilMissScaleOven)

Windows: Algorithmic Arts MicroTone (www.algoart.com/microtone.htm)

Hands-on: Glide Through SampleTank FREE

Keyboardists tend to be unaccustomed to thinking about the pitches between notes, since on a piano it's not possible to bend pitch. Using a glide or portamento feature on a synth, you can add slides between notes to your playing, even if your input device is a keyboard. To hear how it sounds, use IK Multimedia's SampleTank FREE, included on the disc. (You'll need to first load SampleTank into your host of choice.)

SampleTank's glide controls: SampleTank labels its glide function *portamento*, so look for the section of the synth's interface on the right labeled Port (**Figure 9.5**). The Port. Time knob controls how long it takes for the synth to glide from one note to another. You'll need to set the drop-down menu just below this knob to Legato; in Mono and Poly modes portamento is turned off. (Note: this isn't true of all synths; many allow both glide and poly modes to be enabled simultaneously.)

Play an eerie portamento soprano voice: Load the included preset Soprano Ahh by double-clicking it. If you play individual, separated notes, this patch will sound just like a normal sampled female singer. But try connecting the notes: as you press each new note, continue to hold down the previous note. (Once you've pressed down the next note, you can release the previous note. The idea is to make your playing legato—hence the name.) You should hear a subtle "scoop" as the vocal sound glides between the pitches. You can make this more pronounced by increasing the Port. Time to around 500 ms or more. The vocal sound then bends gradually from one note to another.

Slide on a synth pad: Load the included preset L.A. Dreams 2pac. By default, this patch loads in Poly mode, so if you hold down more than one note you'll hear a chord, not a glide. Switch it to Legato mode by selecting the drop-down menu under Port. Time and increasing the Port. Time to about 2 s. As you play each note, hold down the previous note, as in the previous example. You'll hear slow glides between notes and may have a flashback to Vangelis' synth-filled score for the film *Blade Runner*.

Figure 9.5 SampleTank features a portamento feature typical on many synths. Enable Legato mode and set a portamento time, and it will glide between notes.

Analog subtractive synthesis

The first synthesizers were called *analog instruments* because the regular, continuous signal output by their oscillators is an analog to the vibration of real-world sound sources like an instrument's strings, as well as to the pressure variations in the air as sound travels. Part of the reason for their enduring popularity is that their sound is unique. Since there aren't acoustic instruments capable of producing anything resembling a sawtooth wave, early instruments like the Moog have become beloved for their distinctive sounds. Just as the first saxophones sounded unique and ultimately found their way into the orchestra (at least in Europe), analog instruments have become part of the language of music.

When people refer to "analog synthesis," they're generally talking about a specific synthesis method known as *subtractive synthesis*. It's so named because the oscillators produce simple waveforms with rich harmonic content. Filters on the synth shape that harmonic content over time by removing certain harmonics, much as the body of an acoustic instrument colors the sound the instrument makes.

 Analog subtractive synthesis:

Aliases: "Analog"; "modular"

What it's good at:
Distinctive, electronic sounds; expressive playing with full timbral control; retro street cred

What it's not good at:
Sounding like acoustic instruments

Hardware examples:
Moog Minimoog (including the modern Minimoog Voyager); Buchla 100- and 200-Series; Dave Smith Evolver

Software examples:
Reason SubTractor; Arturia's Moog emulations (**Figure 9.6**)

Try it out on the disc:
Native Instruments SoundSchool; Green Oak Crystal

Figure 9.6 Arturia's emulation of the 1960s-era Moog Modular reproduces the way it works down to the tangle of patch cords necessary to connect separate modules, a configuration that gave rise to the term "modular synthesis."

The earliest analog synthesizers, designed by Robert Moog on the East Coast of the United States and Don Buchla on the West Coast, were called *modular* synthesizers, because they were constructed using independent modules that could be bolted into a rack. By interconnecting modules via patch cords in different combinations, it was possible to create different sounds and performance setups for a somewhat custom instrument. This approach survives in software-based modular music production environments like Csound, Max/MSP, and Reaktor. Most analog instruments aren't truly modular, but the division of different parts of the instrument by function—oscillators, envelope generators, filters, low-frequency oscillators (LFOs), and the like—remains, even if the connections between these parts is relatively fixed.

When they first became available, analog instruments were large, heavy, and meticulously assembled by hand, and cost as much as a house. Most "analog" instruments now are really digital instruments that inherit the basic sound design principles and timbral qualities of their analog predecessors. Since digital synths don't generate real analog signals, they're technically *virtual analog* synths; they replicate the signal characteristics of analog circuitry using digital oscillators.

You'll find subtractive principles in a number of guises in today's soft synths:

- **Analog emulation:** Some instruments directly mimic the look, feel, function, and sound of vintage analog gear.

- **Analog-style synthesis:** Because the technique of subtractive synthesis is so popular, many synths re-create this basic working method but with an interface of their own contrivance.

- **Modular design:** Even some instruments that aren't analog-style synths *per se* still inherit elements of their design from the original modular layout. Nearly all synthesizers have remnants of the early modular synths' envelope generators, filters, modulation sources, and other features.

FM and additive synthesis

Subtractive synthesis isn't the only means of combining oscillators and producing sounds from simple components. Two others we'll look at in this chapter take a different approach. Frequency modulation (FM) synthesis uses two or more oscillators to modulate one another, all within the audible frequency range, resulting in complex, bell-like timbres. Additive synthesis sums individual overtones (which may or may not be produced by separate oscillators) to produce new, complex timbres in a manner roughly equivalent to the way drawbar organs work, producing a composite sound from multiple basic components. The Hammond Organ operates on this principle.

Basic FM and additive techniques were possible in analog synthesis, although they were used far less often than subtractive synthesis. FM was less popular with early analog synths because it requires finely tuned oscillators for the best results. The tuning inconsistencies common in early oscillators get in the way of reliable FM sounds. FM and additive have grown in popularity with the advent of digital oscillators and with faster CPUs and DSP chips.

FM synthesis:

What it's good at:
Rich, bell-like timbres and unique sonic effects; broad sonic palette

What it's not good at:
Realistic strings; providing quick results for newcomers to sound design

Hardware examples:
Yamaha DX7 (and DX series)

Software examples:
Native Instruments FM7 (**Figure 9.7**); Oxe FM synth (free Windows-only VSTi; www.oxesoft.com); Logic's EFM1

Try it out on the disc:
Ableton Operator (part of Ableton Live demo); Green Oak Crystal; basic functionality in Native Instruments SoundSchool

Figure 9.7 Native Instruments' FM7, a modern reinterpretation of the Yamaha DX7, uses six oscillators for its frequency modulation. Filtering and distortion in the FM7 allow for thick, morphing tones, and multisegment envelopes allow for rhythmic effects.

Additive synthesis:

Alias: "Fourier synthesis"

What it's good at:
Producing rich, organ-like, complex sounds

What it's not good at:
Much less common than subtractive synthesis; less fruitful in sonic possibilities; processor-intensive in the digital domain

Hardware examples:
Kawai K5 and K5000

Software examples:
Camel Audio Cameleon 5000 (www.camelaudio.com, **Figure 9.8**); White Noise Additive (Windows-only, www.whitenoiseaudio.com/additive)

 Splitting hairs on "samplers": Many instruments marketed as samplers really aren't. Technically, an instrument is a sampler only if it's capable of recording sound from a live audio input. If not, it's a "sample playback synth," not a sampler. Nowadays, you can record audio into your DAW and drop it into the synth or otherwise import audio. For that reason, the term "sampler" is usually used to connote a sample playback synth into which the user can load any new sample as needed.

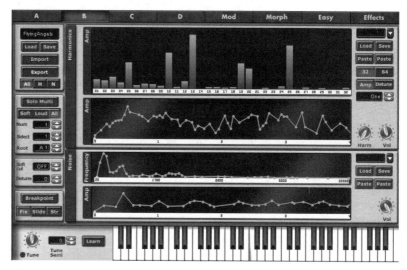

Figure 9.8 One advantage of additive synthesis is that it lends itself to morphing and individual harmonic control, both of which are exploited in Camel Audio's Cameleon 5000. A "morph square" lets you morph between different sounds, and the program lets you control individual harmonics via a graphical interface (shown here) or even by importing an image file.

Even though the techniques of additive synthesis programming are beyond the scope of this book, we will look at some of the basics of FM synthesis in the context of subtractive synthesis, since basic FM is supported in SoundSchool.

Samplers and sample playback

Analog subtractive, additive, and FM synthesis are great for producing distinctive sounds, but you can go only so far with basic waveforms when it comes to mimicking the complexities of real-world sound. Rather than finding electrical or digital substitutes, the obvious way to make an instrument sound as if it incorporates real-world sound is to simply use recorded sound as a signal source. When you play a note, a sample playback instrument reproduces the recording, which can then be routed through envelopes, filters, and effects as with other synthesis methods.

The limitation of using recorded sound is that you sacrifice control over the sound source when you trigger a static recording instead of a mutable waveform. Sound designers have attempted to compensate by adding more recorded waveforms, with additional sounds triggered in different regions of the keyboard and played at different velocities. But that increases the memory requirements of the patch, since it requires additional sounds to be played back from RAM or the hard disk. Also, the effect of playing sample-based instruments can feel less expressive than instruments using other synthesis techniques. Despite the loss of some expressive control, the sound is lifelike, since it uses actual recordings.

Sample-based instruments aren't limited to mimicking acoustic instruments. Sampling can be a way of creatively reworking recordings (as hip-hop musicians have done with vinyl) and of creating new instruments (for instance, creating a drum kit from sampled pots and pans).

You'll find sample playback in all kinds of virtual instruments. Instruments designed to replicate hardware and acoustic instruments are the best-known example, covering territory ranging from guitars to full orchestras. Sample playback is also used on several software percussion instruments like Native Instruments Battery and audio groove boxes like Spectrasonics Stylus RMX (www.spectrasonics.net), among many other examples.

You'll also find many commercially available libraries of sampled sounds, either in audio file format or specially designed for specific sampler formats. These collections of sounds are often called *soundware,* or *sound libraries,* because the focus is on downloading or installing a library of sounds instead of purchasing or downloading a dedicated software instrument.

 Sampling/sample playback:

What it's good at: Reproducing the sound of acoustic instruments; incorporating real-world sounds

What it's not as good at: Can be less expressive to play; high RAM requirements

Hardware examples: Akai S-series samplers; Korg Triton keyboard (sample playback)

Software examples: Native Instruments Kontakt; MOTU MachFive (**Figure 9.9**); Steinberg HALion; TASCAM Giga-Studio; Audio Key Rig (basic sample playback)

Try it out on the disc: SampleTank FREE (sample playback)

Figure 9.9 Samplers and sample playback synths map audio files to the keyboard, triggering those recordings when notes are played, as shown here in MOTU's MachFive sampler.

Other Synthesis Methods

Sound designers in search of new sounds continually develop variations on the synthesis methods discussed in the previous sections, and exploit other techniques as well. If you're familiar with the basics of sample playback and virtual analog synthesis in particular, you'll find some familiar landmarks in most synths, including similar use of filters, effects, and modulations, although other techniques may require learning some new skills.

Granular synthesis

Inspired by particle physics and the thinking of experimental composer Iannis Xenakis, *granular synthesis* conceives of the sound world as composed of tiny sonic grains instead of the repeating waveforms discussed elsewhere in this book. Thanks to research by Curtis Roads and others, and developments in digital technology, it's now possible to produce thousands or millions of the tiny sound grain events and turn the theory into sound.

Great—so what does it sound like? Although it's not terribly useful for producing, say, the sound of a trombone, granular synthesis is capable of some unusual sounds. It can create complex organic waves of tiny sound particles or resynthesize live audio. In fact, granular techniques are behind many of the time-stretching and pitch-shifting algorithms in commercial software applications.

Delving into granular synthesis isn't for the faint of heart, but here are some places to begin:

- **Native Instruments Reaktor:** Reaktor has built-in granular capabilities; with Reaktor 5, load GrainStates SP from the Ensembles > Classics > Sample Transformer directory.

- **Csound (free):** The text-interface, cross-platform modular environment of Csound (www.csounds.com) is appealing for granular synthesis because of the relative simplicity of its grain opcode; see the tutorial on the subject at www.csounds.com/mastering/em_04.html.

- **Max/MSP:** There are various externals for Max for granular synthesis; a good place to start is the cross-platform ~mdegranular (www.michael-edwards.org/software/mdegranular).

- **Further reading:** Curtis Roads's *The Computer Music Tutorial* (MIT Press) has an excellent chapter that explains the underlying concepts behind granular synthesis technology.

Generally speaking, simple granular synthesis involves describing a particle type as a tiny envelope of sound and defining the parameters of the grain "cloud," based on random distribution of grains in sonic space. Other granular synthesis techniques (like those employed by some of the Reaktor ensembles and the ~mdegranular object for Max/MSP) require two audio inputs, meaning you can input your own audio file.

Physical modeling

Unlike granular synthesis, which as a synthesis technique has been largely limited to the avant-garde, physical modeling is gaining popularity in the mainstream. It's not new, but it previously required high-end hardware and had unpredictable results. Recent computer developments have made it more practical.

Physical modeling is a way of replicating the physical properties of instruments via mathematical models. These models describe the properties of a vibrating string, the traveling waves through the instrument, the wooden body resonating, and so on. Physical modeling is sometimes called *component modeling* because conceptually it divides instruments into the various components that produce sound.

Using physical models, it's possible to more accurately represent phenomena that are otherwise difficult to reproduce, like the effect of overblowing a flute or imagining what a glass-stringed violin would sound like resonating in an aluminum tank. Physical models work well for bowed string instruments, wind instruments, and plucked instruments like Clavinets, guitars, and harps, as well as for imagined instruments combining these principles.

Physical modeling is found in a growing number of instruments:

- **Hardware synths** like the Korg OASYS (www.korg.com) and Alesis Fusion (www.fusionsynth.com) keyboards

- **Sculpture** in Apple Logic Pro (Mac)

- **String Theory**, a free VST plug-in (Windows, www.cortidesign.com/ugo)

- **String Studio** from Applied Acoustics (Windows/Mac, www.applied-acoustics.com), as well as their Tassman synth studio

These instruments vary in scope. Sculpture, although capable of producing some traditional sounds, specializes in extensive timbral controls and effects for far-out imaginary sounds. String Theory specializes in reproducing real instruments from Clavinets to guitars and violas; extensive presets and musical labels like "string" and "damper" make it a bit more accessible.

Here are some tips for creating and editing physical modeling patches:

- **Make small adjustments:** Because of the nature of physical modeling, tiny changes to one parameter like string density can have sudden, dramatic impacts, so adjust one parameter at a time in small increments.

- **Work with components:** Adjusting the model for the string or resonating object is nearly always the best place to start, but on its own this model may sound devoid of personality. That's true of all forms of synthesis, but wave sources can sound especially naked with physical modeling. Both Sculpture and String Studio, for instance, have extensive EQ banks for mimicking the way the body of an instrument changes its sound, and distortion for further altering its character.

- **Think about real instruments:** Even if you're creating an underwater glass bassoon played by aliens, consider the properties that make real instruments function when played. Parameters like the mass of the terminating or damping object are pretty abstract, until you think about the way your finger stops the strings on a guitar.

- **Try morphing parameters:** If your physical modeling synth allows it, try changing the nature of the physical material being modeled during the course of a sound by assigning material parameters to an envelope. This allows some distinctive effects not possible with other techniques.

For instance, a typical workflow in Sculpture (**Figure 9.10**) would be to choose a basic material first, adjust the first object for the primary means of exciting the object (like bowing), add a second and third object for additional details (like adding noise to the sound and damping upon release for the KeyOff value), fine-tune the material, and then add effects and modulation.

As with any instrument, successful sound design and performance with physical modeling synths takes practice. In 1994, when reviewing the first commercial physical modeling synth (Yamaha's VL1), Ernie Rideout wrote in *Keyboard* that the instrument was one on which you'd want to practice—both programming and playing.

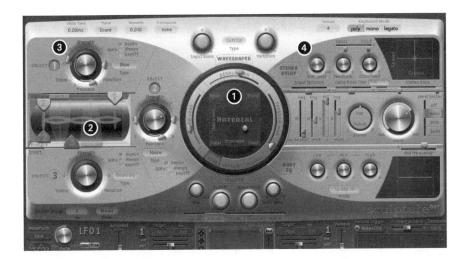

Figure 9.10 Physical modeling synths like Apple's Sculpture provide new control over sounds that mimic acoustic instruments or imagine new ones. Sculpture looks a bit like an alien spacecraft cockpit at first. The best way to approach it, true to its underlying design, is to think of it in terms of its different components. (You'll see many similar editing sections in other synths, like String Studio, although in somewhat simplified form.)

❶ The Material control determines how the vibrating body of the instrument behaves, based on how resistant it is to being blown, struck, or bowed (its stiffness), and how long it resonates once excited (its "inner loss" and "media loss").

❷ This preview of the string in action shows what's happening to the resonating body as notes are played.

❸ Objects numbered 1, 2, and 3 on the Sculpture panel itself are the objects that excite or "play" the virtual instrument. For instance, with object 1 set to Blow, we can create a virtual woodwind of our own design. Other options include settings like Bow, for bowed string instruments, and Pluck. (One advantage of physical modeling is that you can break the rules, blowing and bowing steel at the same time, for instance.)

❹ Many of the other controls, although intimidating at first, are actually traditional effects sections. (Apple simply chose to include every effect they could think of in the main interface!) The various controls at the bottom of the interface are modulation and envelopes.

SAMPLERS AND SAMPLE PLAYBACK

Before we get into the nitty-gritty of creating some textbook virtual analog sounds, let's begin where most musicians start today: with synths that play back recorded sound.

There are three basic levels to working with sampled instruments. You can use prebuilt samples as is, you can edit prebuilt samples to your liking, or you can create your own samples from scratch. We'll look at soundware libraries first. But even if you don't plan to build your own samples, it's important to know the basics of how sample playback instruments work, both to edit them and to play them expressively.

Soundware Libraries

If you are shopping around for soundware libraries to use with a sampler, you should pay attention to both content and format. Soundware content varies from libraries of loops to fully sampled instruments, so you'll need sampled content that matches what you want to do. That could mean simple instrumental samples, prebuilt loops or sliced-up rhythms, individual notes or whole phrases, or any number of other variations.

Beyond having soundware that's musically useful, the most important issue is making sure it comes in a format you can use. If you don't have a sampler capable of importing libraries, you'll probably want a soundware library that comes with its own plug-in. Many libraries, for instance, ship with the cross-platform Native Instruments Kontakt player or Intakt editor (**Figure 9.11**). (Be sure to check whether the plug-in format lets you edit patches. Some play in a simple player, while others provide basic editing capabilities for tweaking the samples.)

Figure 9.11 Soundware libraries used to include just sounds, but in the age of soft synths, many now come with virtual instrument players or even full-fledged sample editors. The Spectrasonics Atmosphere plug-in, for instance, comes with a 3 GB library of sampled waves and also includes various controls for editing patches and layering sounds.

If you do want to import soundware into your own sampler of choice, you'll have to wade through the range of available formats. The basic possibilities are:

- **Raw audio:** Sample libraries in audio CD, WAV, and AIFF are compatible with all samplers, but you'll probably have to map samples to keys by hand. Raw audio gives you the greatest compatibility but also requires the most work (although it is popular among some of the free samples downloadable on the Web).

- **Hardware sampler formats:** Even in the era of software, many sample libraries are still available in Akai, E-mu, and Kurzweil hardware sampler formats. Most major soft samplers support at least one of these formats, either natively or via a conversion utility.

- **Soft sampler formats:** With the rise of software samplers, the unique formats of software samplers have become "standards" of their own. Unfortunately, there isn't one universal format. Tascam GigaStudio (www.tascamgiga.com), EXS|24 (the sampler in Apple Logic), Native Instruments Kontakt, and Steinberg HALion (www.steinberg.de) formats are common, and you'll see even more arcane options. Even the long-discontinued Digidesign SampleCell format appears frequently.

- **Soft studio formats:** Some software-based virtual studios allow the use of multisamples, stored patches, and other user content. The most ubiquitous by far is Propellerhead Reason, which since its inception has supported the ReFill format. You'll find plenty of content on the Web, both free and commercial, that include multisamples for Reason's samplers. TrackTeam Audio (www.trackteamaudio.com) has extended this concept to Ableton Live by designing a special installer for Live content. Their LiveFills include multisamples, as found on the DVD. You'll also find libraries designed for Apple GarageBand that combine sampled instruments with loop libraries. (Since GarageBand is based on Logic's EXS|24 sampler, some of these work with Logic, too.)

Building Presets with Samples

Early mechanical "samplers" responded to notes by playing loops of tape containing recorded sound. Press a key, and the tape played back. Modern digital samplers are more sophisticated, but the same basic concept remains: the sampler has to create the illusion of an instrument when all it's really doing is playing recordings. As a result, sample playback must deal with issues like how to adjust the pitch of samples across a keyboard, when to trigger each sound sample, and how to loop a sample so it can produce sound continuously for as long as a note is held down.

Mapping to keys

Most acoustic instruments sound markedly different in one pitch range than in another. For the ultimate in realism, it's possible to create an individual

Soundware resources:

Several major publishers are devoted to producing and distributing sampled content, including Big Fish Audio (www.bigfishaudio.com), East West Sounds (www.eastwestsamples.com or www.soundsonline.com), Zero-G (www.zero-g.com), PowerFX (www.powerfx.com), and S4/Advanced Media Group (www.samples4.com).

The European-based Web site Samplepoolz (www.samplepoolz.com) is dedicated entirely to covering the latest news and reviews of soundware, and has links to downloads and other resources.

You can find free and for-sale ReFills for Reason at Propellerhead Software and community sites like ReasonStation (www.reasonstation.net)

Analogue Samples (www.analoguesamples.com) has a vast library of samples of old analog gear, with free downloads. If pianos are more your speed than Buchlas and Moogs, opt for piano sampling specialist Post Musical Instruments (www.postpiano.com).

sample for each note on the keyboard, but for most purposes it's neither practical nor necessary: although the result would be very realistic, it would require enormous memory resources. Instead, sample designers have looked for ways to stretch samples across multiple notes.

In the simplest case, a single audio sample can be stretched across an entire keyboard. The easiest way for the instrument designer to adjust the sample to the required pitch is to play the sample faster or slower depending on which note is played. (As noted in previous chapters, the actual process is different from speeding up or slowing down a tape deck or turntable, because it involves digitally interpolating the file, but the audible effect is similar.) This kind of sampler is easy to use and is useful for certain special effects, although it's not practical for building realistic sampled emulations of acoustic instruments.

The alternative to changing the speed of a sample is to change the pitch while maintaining the length of the sample. This way, for instance, a drum groove mapped across the keyboard can change pitch without getting any faster or slower. Different samplers use different algorithms to try to improve the audio quality of this process, but there are still certain realities to stretching sound, as we've seen in previous chapters. Although it's possible to minimize artifacts through the use of certain interpolation algorithms, timbre will change noticeably as the harmonic range of the sample shifts up and down. Also, one sample can't accurately represent the way many instruments differ in timbre across their pitch range. (The thick bass strings of a piano, for instance, are timbrally distinct from the thin strings of its top register.) Usually, the only patches that stretch a single sample across the keyboard are ones for which only one sample is needed, like drum loops.

For instruments, most sample patches use *multisampling:* they sample the sound source at various pitches and then assign each sample to a range of keys, so that a given sample needs to be pitch-shifted up or down by a few half-steps (**Figure 9.12**). Each set of pitches to which a sample is mapped is called a *zone.*

Our ears are extremely sensitive to timbre and pitch shifting, so the trick for a sound library developer is to minimize the boundaries between different sounds; otherwise, the listener will recognize immediately when the sampler switches from one zone to the next.

Figure 9.12 A typical mapping editor, shown here in Native Instruments Kontakt. There's not an individual sample for each note of this piano multisample, but it's close to that: there's a sample for every two or three notes.

The choice of the number of samples used in a given multisample is a matter of economy. Many piano sample libraries, for instance, come with several sizes of the same piano multisample. The "XXL" version of the piano may have a separate sample (or more likely, several different samples) assigned to each key. A "lite" patch might have new samples for only every few keys and is more suitable for use in an ensemble when you're trying to save memory. A "super-sized" patch might pull out all the stops and contain whole gigabytes of sample data. Such a patch is best for use in a solo context when the computer doesn't have to do anything else.

Drum kit mapping

With instrumental patches, you want a close match of samples up and down the keyboard. With drum kits, however, you want just the opposite: you want a distinct sound for each note, because you'll assemble your "kit" by assigning different sounds to different MIDI keys (**Figure 9.13**).

Figure 9.13 Instead of stretching similar samples across the keyboard, drum samplers like FXpansion's Guru focus on assigning individual drum sounds (1) to different notes. You can then use MIDI to trigger those sounds with a keyboard, electronic kit, or MPC-style drum pads (2). Some drum samplers, like Guru, add a pattern sequencer (3) so you can assemble grooves.

At a basic level, mapping a kit involves setting up a range of notes in which a different drum sound (tom, kick, snare, and so on) is assigned to each key. Here's where the General MIDI (GM) specification comes in handy: because the layout of drum sounds on the keyboard is standardized, it's possible to swap to a new kit without having to reedit the sequencer track, and it's easier for your fingers to find where notes are mapped. For that reason, many drum kits map to the GM key locations, even if they're not part of a bank of GM sounds. (For more on General MIDI, see Chapter 8.)

Creating realistic hi-hats introduces another wrinkle. Real hi-hats (a double cymbal that can be played with either a drumstick or a pedal) can be either open or closed. You could simply sample a hi-hat played in those two states, but once the samples were assigned to adjacent MIDI keys, you'd be able to play an open hat and a closed hat at the same time, which is normally impossible. An open hat will continue to sound after it's struck, but once it's closed the sound is damped. Being able to do both at once is the equivalent of being able to close a pair of handheld crash cymbals without the sound stopping. (Hint: it's not possible in the real world.)

By grouping samples together, you can create sampled hi-hats that respond in a more realistic manner. Group the open and closed hat sounds together, so that when a closed hat is played, it mutes or "chokes" the open hat. This feature, found on many sample playback instruments, is sometimes called mute groups, choke groups, or hi-hat groups. On simple prebuilt drum kits, you most likely won't have to do anything special to program a realistic-sounding hi-hat response, because the soundware's designer will have done the work for you. If you're building your own kits, you'll need to set up the group you want and set the polyphony or muting options for that group. Of course, drummers know that even this is a gross simplification of what it's like to play a real hi-hat, which can be played various other ways as well, each producing a unique sound. That's why instruments like Native Instruments Battery have 72 slots for drum sounds in a kit instead of eight. The beauty of mute groups is that they work not only for open and closed states, but for any type of switching you want.

Because of these special considerations, a specialized drum sampler is often a good idea if you're doing lots of detailed drum kit-style work. Advanced samplers like Kontakt, MOTU Machfive, and Steinberg HALion all include the necessary features, but you'll find extra options and a streamlined interface in software like Native Instruments Battery, FXpansion GURU, and the LinPlug RMIV, and in hardware like the Akai MPC-2000.

Of course, a "drum kit" doesn't have to involve drums at all. The notes of the "kit" can be anything you want: sound effects cues for a theater production, sampled vocals for a hip-hop song, different slices of a drum groove for mixing up beats, or any other combination of distinct sounds.

Loop and start points

Drums, percussion, plucked instruments like guitars and harps, and pianos all make a sound that starts with a strong, percussive attack and then dies away gradually to silence. Pluck a guitar string, for instance, and the instrument sounds and decays; there's no way to lengthen the sound other than by plucking the string again. Creating sampled instruments for these kind of instruments is simple: press a key, and you trigger the sound. If you release the key before the sound has had time to decay, the sampler can simply stop the sound.

 Specialized drum sampling features: Drum instruments are unique in that each note represents a truly distinct sound. Specialized drum machines usually offer individualized control over each drum, for independent tuning, filtering, and effects. Many also include pattern sequencers for assembling drum grooves.

 GM drum mappings: For a reference to basic GM drum kit mappings, see www.midi-hits.com/ GM_Drums.html.

String instruments, brass, woodwinds, and any other sounds that can sustain pose a challenge. You'd expect them to continue to sound for as long as the MIDI key is held down, whether it's for just a few seconds or for several minutes. Short of sampling ten minutes of each sound, you need a way of making the sample sustain for as long as the longest note you might play.

The solution is to loop the sample data so that when the recording is played back the sampler will jump from a later point in the sound to an earlier point and then continue. But you won't want the entire sample to loop, because instead of continuous sound, you'd hear the attack and decay of the sample repeating. Instead, samplers let you mark a section of the sample, usually near the center or at the end, and loop it. That way, you'll be able to maintain a distinct attack before the loop, followed by a looping "steady-state sustain" (**Figure 9.14**). Professional sound designers use special tools to cross-fade the end and beginning of the looped region to disguise the loop points. (This is generally tricky, since your ear can easily detect repetition and patterns in the sound caused by looping, much the same way that you can see where patterns in wallpaper occur on a wall.) Typical sample playback controls include the following:

- **Start and end points** let you designate the length of the overall sample, from attack to decay. These controls can be useful even if you're not looping audio, because you can use them to vary loops and grooves, and for special effects.

- **Loop locations** let you specify which portion(s) of the audio will loop when a note is held down. The sampler will play from the start point, into the looped portion, and then begin looping the looped section, so you'll need sound from somewhere in the middle of the sample. (Getting the loop to sound right usually requires delicate adjustments.)

- **Loop method** settings, included on some samplers, let you determine how the loop behaves—whether it loops continuously or just a few times, and in what direction the loop travels. Back-and-forth looping can sound smoother than an ordinary forward loop.

- **Loop cross-fade** controls adjust the blending of the end of the loop with the beginning of the loop to cover the audible seam between the two. This also requires some delicate adjustments, although you might turn it off for certain special effects.

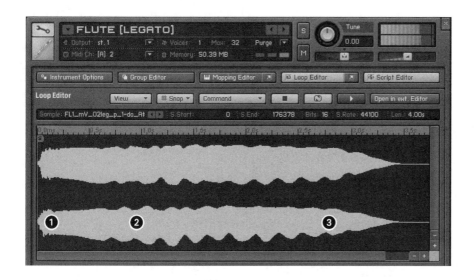

Figure 9.14 A typical sustaining instrumental sound has an attack (1), sustain (2), and final decay (3). By looping the sustained portion in a sampler, you can create a sample that can be played for any length of time. (Shown: Loop Editor in Kontakt)

Velocity and playing techniques

When you play an acoustic instrument with more or less force, it doesn't just get louder or softer in the way that a sound does when you turn the volume knob: it changes in timbre. Typically, playing harder causes more overtones (a brighter sound) as well as an increase in volume. In addition, there's usually more than just one way to play an instrument; you might play a cello pizzicato, plucking instead of bowing the strings. Each time you want to add an additional timbral quality to an instrument, short of what you can accomplish with filters, modulation, and effects, you'll need to add an additional audio file and a means of triggering it via MIDI.

The most common technique is called *velocity cross-switching*. When velocity cross-switching is used, the sampler plays a different sample depending on the velocity of the MIDI note received. For instance, you might sample an instrument playing mezzo-forte (medium loud) and then sample it again on the same note playing fortissimo (very loud) to capture the timbral differences between the two. With each of these samples mapped to a different velocity range, the fortissimo sample will play only when you play your keyboard harder. Programming good-sounding velocity cross-switching is even more of an art than balancing multisamples across the keyboard, because the realism of the instrument's response is highly dependent on how you play.

Velocity cross-switching isn't the only way of switching between samples on the same note, although it is the most common. Some samplers allow you to use other methods, such as moving the mod wheel, tapping a foot pedal, or even assigning unused MIDI keys on the keyboard as switches; see the sidebar, "Orchestral Sample Libraries."

 Orchestral Sample Libraries

A realistic-sounding sampled orchestra is both the most sought-after and the most elusive of sampled instruments. It's sought after, of course, because hiring a real orchestra to play your composition is expensive. But sampling an orchestra is difficult for several reasons: orchestras mix ensemble and solo playing, have a wide variety of instruments, and employ a variety of playing techniques.

Ensembles and solos: In terms of distinguishing between ensembles and solos, there are two schools of thought. One is to sample individual instruments and ensemble playing separately, and trigger them separately. The other, rarer technique is to sample only individual instruments and construct the ensemble sound the way real orchestras do, by constructing a section out of solo instruments. The latter technique is more processor- and memory-intensive, although it allows more flexible ensemble creation, which works better for tasks like producing all-string orchestras and the like. (Garritan Personal Orchestra, www.garritan.com, uses this technique; see **Figure 9.15**.) A hybrid technique used by those who specialize in MIDI realizations of orchestral scores is to blend a sampled ensemble with one or more solo string samples.

Figure 9.15 There are various approaches to creating the illusion of an ensemble in an orchestral library (or a library devoted to any large ensemble, like a chorus). The Garritan Personal Orchestra library, for instance, lets you build up sections from individual players.

Range of instruments: There's no way around the sheer size and complexity of an orchestra. Real orchestras are expensive in terms of union wages, but virtual orchestras are similarly expensive in terms of CPU cycles and RAM. The best-sounding orchestral libraries tend to take gigabytes of hard disk space and RAM. On the upside, installing an orchestral library means you'll have access not only to sampled ensembles, but to solo instruments as well.

Triggering different playing techniques: Velocity-switched samples are a start, but the range of playing techniques in an orchestra means you'll need more control than a MIDI keyboard alone can provide, particularly in the string section. Legato passages sound different from stacatto passages, pizzicato (plucked) strings sound different from arco (bowed) strings, to say nothing of effects like *sul ponticello* playing (bowing near the bridge), brass mutes and effects, and others. To make matters worse for the keyboard-centric world of MIDI, orchestral instruments can easily get louder and softer during a note under the control of the player, something that's impossible on a piano. Orchestral libraries are programmed so they can be played using a number of techniques, including:

- **Use of continuous controllers:** By mapping a MIDI control change message type, such as modulation wheel (CC1) to instrument volume, you can have continuous control of that parameter for more realistic playing.

- **Pedal switching:** Orchestras don't have sustain pedals, so you can use the pedal to switch between samples, such as triggering a legato sample.

- **Key switching:** For additional switches between samples for different playing techniques, some sample libraries assign a nonsounding MIDI note to a switch. For instance, you might hit the bottom note of your keyboard to turn pizzicato on and off.

Integration with notation software: Since one of the most common uses of orchestral libraries is producing demos of orchestral scores, many people want to use orchestral libraries with their notation software. Unfortunately, some of the idiosyncrasies of orchestral sample design can wreak havoc with notation software's automatic playback. You may need to do some extensive tweaking to make your scores play to your satisfaction. For this reason, newer releases of Sibelius (www.sibelius.com) and Finale (www.finalemusic.com) have added more integration with orchestral libraries. For additional advice, the Web sites of sample library developers like Garritan are often a good resource for tutorials, templates, scripts, and tips from users. Getting good orchestral results isn't one of those "skip the manual and try it yourself" endeavors.

Skip the samples entirely: Traditional sampling isn't necessarily your only choice for reproducing the sound of the orchestra. Synful Orchestra (www.synful.com), for instance, uses a combination of samples spliced together from full recorded phrases with additive synthesis technologies to create the illusion of acoustic instruments. Synful calls the technology Reconstructive Phrase Modeling; it's not quite sampling, not quite synthesis, but a further sign that sound designers will continue trying new ways of creating virtual orchestras. As with a sampled orchestra, you'll need to use additional controllers to make up for the difficulty of playing an orchestra with a keyboard. Synful uses the expression (cc 11), mod wheel, and pitch bend controllers.

Virtual orchestral chops: Although we've covered the basic issues of orchestral sample design, we're ignoring the broader issues: making a virtual orchestra sound like a real one is an art, to say nothing of the challenges of orchestration (ask Ravel and Beethoven on the latter). Many users expect to plug-and-play an orchestral sample library and get perfect results, particularly when working with notation software, and that's still fairly unrealistic.

Notation packages geared for integration with orchestral sample libraries will certainly turn out basic mock-ups, but if you need to polish a demo by editing MIDI, you may need to hone your MIDI orchestration skills. Paul Gilreath's book *The Guide to MIDI Orchestration* (Musicworks Atlanta, 2004, www.musicworks-atlanta.com) covers the subject and was co-edited by Jim Aikin, who is also the technical editor of this book. You might even find general orchestration books helpful; refer to authors like Kent Kennan, Samuel Adler, Walter Piston, Nikolay Rimsky-Korsakov, and others.

RAM vs. hard-disk streaming

With each step in developing realistic and expressive sample playback, we've added more samples. That's a fundamental downside of sample playback as a synthesis technique: you need prerecorded sound for nearly everything you want to do. Playing back all the audio files takes additional resources: your CPU will take a hit, but the major drain will be memory capacity for the samples. Assuming you can fit your sample library on your hard drive, you also need to be able to play them back. The preferred method is to load them into RAM, which can be accessed more quickly than a hard drive. Many samplers offer a "stream from disk" option that reads samples from the hard drive to conserve RAM. Even streaming requires a significant amount of available memory (512 MB or more for optimal performance), so the main advantage of streaming is that it allows the samples to be virtually unlimited in length. You'll also want to check to see if your sampler can deactivate unused parts to save memory, or delete samples from an edited preset if you know they won't be required by the current project.

Filters, modulation, and effects

You can add expressivity to sample playback instruments without loading more samples by shaping the sound once it emerges from the oscillator. Here, sample-based synths have a lot in common with virtual analog synths, as you'll see in the next section. The basic possibilities of what you can do with sound beyond the oscillator—adding filters to manipulate the sound spectrum, using envelopes to shape amplitude and other parameters in time, modulating signal with other sources such as LFOs, and adding real-time effects—can all be applied to sampled instruments as well as those that use other synthesis techniques. In fact, line up a virtual analog synth next to a sampled synth (or some other synth type) and in many cases the filter, modulation, and effects stages will be nearly indistinguishable.

You'll want to consider effects as part of your toolbox, too. Samplers' effects can range from the everyday (phasers, distortion and saturation, and EQ) to the exotic (surround panners and convolution). See Chapter 7 for a description of some of these effects.

Hands-on: Basic sampling techniques in Ableton Live

Ableton Live's Simpler (single-sample playback synth) and Impulse (8-slot drum sampler) are about as bare-bones as samplers get. There's plenty they don't do: Simpler can handle only one sample at a time, and Impulse can't group samples into user-defined hi-hat mute groups or even store more than eight sounds at a time. Their overriding character is that they're fairly generic, making them perfect for our purpose—getting some experience with sampling.

You can easily drag clips into Simpler from Live's Session View or the File Browser, so combined with the instant recording features of Session View, you can use it to quickly turn a sample into a sampled instrument. (That's the idea.) Simpler isn't capable of multisampling, but the assumption is that if you're playing live or improvising, you probably don't want to be meticulously setting up sample zones anyway.

1. **Load a sample into Simpler:** Set up Simpler by selecting a blank MIDI track, then double-clicking Devices > Instruments > Simpler. Activate MIDI input by clicking the Arm Session Recording button on that track. Then drag a file—any file will do—from the File Browser or Session View into the box at the top of Simpler marked "Drop Sample Here" (**Figure 9.16**).

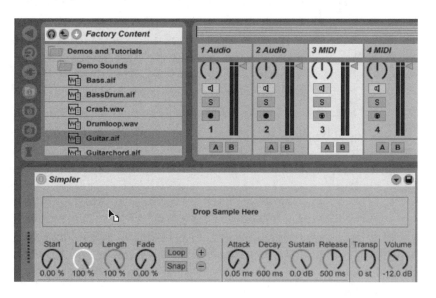

Figure 9.16 Adding a sampler gives you another real-time tool for mixing up sound in studio improvisation and onstage. In Live, you can drag any audio file to Simpler.

2. **Try playing:** If you play up and down your MIDI keyboard (or use the ASDF row on your QWERTY keyboard), Live transposes the clip up and down, and changes the speed accordingly. (Note that some samplers can maintain a single speed and change only the pitch.) We haven't enabled looping yet, so your clip simply plays from the beginning when you hold down a key and stops playing when you let go of the key or when the clip reaches its end, whichever happens first.

3. **Choose which part of the clip plays:** Playing the entire clip may not be what you want: you might want to play just a segment of the clip, like the first few hits of a drum loop, for instance. Simpler lets you control how much of the clip is played and how much is looped. To control how much of the clip is played, adjust the Start knob (to determine where playback begins when you press a key) and the Length knob (to determine how far it will play before it stops or loops). If you're having a hard time seeing the waveform, click the plus and minus buttons to zoom in and out.

4. **Set up looping:** Activate the loop button, and Live will loop the clip; the clip will keep playing repeatedly from the beginning for as long as a key is held down. At this point, Live is simply looping the segment of the sample specified with Start and Length. If you want to loop only a portion of the clip so that Simpler plays from Start when you first press a key but then loops a segment from between the beginning and end of the clip, adjust the Loop knob. It's best to adjust this knob while the clip is playing, so hold down a note and gradually turn the knob. As you increase the Loop setting, you'll see a black line move from right to left, turning the active portion of the clip a brighter shade of green, showing you which part of the clip is getting looped as you hold down the note. In other words, if you set the Loop knob at 50% and hold down a key, Simpler will play from the Start point through the length of the clip, then begin looping from halfway through the clip, repeatedly playing the second half of the clip until you let go of the key (**Figure 9.17**).

5. **Set up a basic cross-fade:** For drum loops, basic looping is fine, but anything with continuous sound will need some cross-fading so the loop point isn't overly audible. If you increase the fade knob, you'll see two lines slant in from the edges of the loop points. These lines represent where the cross-fade occurs.

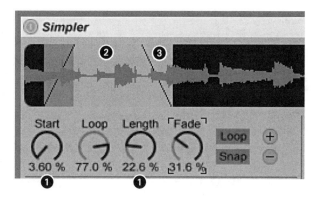

Figure 9.17 With just one sample, it's easy to see how looping works. The highlighted area shows the portion of the wave Simpler is playing, based on the Start and Length parameters (1). The brighter portion (2) shows the section that will loop, as determined by the Loop knob. The diagonal lines (3) show where the loop is cross-faded.

6. **Put it to use:** Now that you've got the basics under your belt, try out Simpler with some different sound sources. Using drum grooves and other rhythmic material, you can use Simpler to slice and dice beats, playing with the Start, Loop, and Length knobs to mix up rhythms. (Try assigning them to MIDI controllers using Live's MIDI Learn capability, and you can mix and mash beats from your keyboard in real time. This is great for onstage beat mangling.) It's best to use Simpler with drum beats, but you can use it for other materials, too: try continuous instrumental samples, single tones for ultra-basic sample design on the fly, or even vocals and spoken word clips.

Hands-on: Set up a drum kit with Live's Impulse

As with Simpler, you can use Impulse to easily trigger clips in performance, building a virtual kit out of any sounds or slices you like. You can even drag them in on the fly in a performance or improvisation.

1. **Load a kit:** With a new MIDI track, load Devices > Instruments > Impulse. From the presets menu, load Studio Montreal for a basic kit.

2. **Edit individual slots:** Like Simpler, Impulse has boxes onto which you can drag clips, but it has eight instead of one. Each of these is a separate drum hit or other sound, triggered by a separate MIDI note. What makes this a drum sampler rather than a standard sampler is that it treats each sound individually rather than transposing them up and down the keyboard. If you click each of the boxes in the Studio Montreal set, you'll see the knobs on the bottom move; each slot has separate settings for its filters, panning, volume, and so on (**Figure 9.18**). You can also time-stretch each clip with the Stretch knob.

Figure 9.18 Impulse is the mirror image of Simpler: it's a drum sampler instead of a general sampler. Instead of one sound mapped across the keyboard, it has eight sounds, each assigned to one MIDI note. Click each of the slots (1), and you have separate editing parameters (2).

More sample playback tutorials: For more on how to use a sample playback synth and to see some of the possibilities this technique affords for sound design and playing, see the SampleTank FREE folder on the disc. You'll find tutorials on bass sounds, guitars, synth pads, and effects.

3. **Try a hi-hat pair:** Impulse lacks the groups found on a more advanced drum sampler, but it does have a position for an open hat in the eighth box. Click Open and you'll see a Link button in the bottom-left corner. If you trigger the open hat (K on your QWERTY keyboard) and then immediately trigger the closed hat (J on your QWERTY keyboard), the closed hat will mute the open hat, as it would on a real hi-hat. With the J and K keys, you can try reproducing the catchy hat riff from Donovan's "Mellow Yellow," if you're so inclined.

SYNTHESIS BUILDING BLOCKS: VIRTUAL ANALOG TECHNIQUES

Early analog instruments were based on what could be easily accomplished with electrical circuitry. Surprisingly, that hasn't made the way they work any less relevant in the digital realm.

First, of course, there's the desirability of analog sounds, which have had a profound impact on the course of music over the past few decades. Analog techniques are essential for reproducing those familiar sounds, but they're important for other sound production tasks as well.

The simple waveforms, filters, and modulators of analog synthesis make excellent basic building blocks for sound production in general. Just as a child's building blocks set tends to incorporate simple, geometric forms like cubes and cylinders, analog synthesis gives us basic geometric sounds (like the sine and square wave) that can be combined into more complex constructions.

As a result, you'll find the same elements, concepts, and interfaces from vintage analog synthesis on sophisticated digital synths. You'll use analog-style envelopes, filters, and modulation on instruments that use sampled audio as wave sources instead of analog-style waveforms like sine, saw, and square waves. Most instruments follow the basic structure shown in **Figure 9.19**.

Figure 9.19 The basic signal routing structure of virtual analog instruments is identical to the vast majority of synths, including digital synths. Even though the analog-style oscillators may be replaced with other signal sources and synthesis techniques, many of the basic modulation, filters, and effects will be similar.

Just reading about synthesis is a fairly fruitless endeavor, since it's the sound result in which we're interested. For that reason, in the discussion on the following pages you'll want to follow along with Native Instruments' Reaktor SoundSchool Analog, included on the DVD. (See the sidebar, "Hands-on: SoundSchool Analog.")

Basic Waveshapes and Timbre

Harmonics in sound and the basic waveshapes were discussed in Chapter 1, but now we'll use these principles in music making.

Analog circuitry easily generates simple waveforms via basic, repeating electrical patterns. The simplest circuits, for instance, simply turn voltage on and off, like a repeating light switch, producing a signal called a *pulse wave* (after the on and off pulses created) or a *square wave* (describing what the signal looks like on an oscilloscope).

The different waveshapes produced can be either listened to or used as modulators (for altering other signals). When a wave comes from an audio oscillator, the different waveshapes have different harmonic content, giving each of them a different sound. Oscillators in a synth can almost always be switched, so that a single oscillator can produce any of several different waveshapes. (On vintage analog oscillators, this switch was typically in the form of a dial for selecting different waveforms. Now that switch is an onscreen setting, often in a pop-up menu.)

 Disclaimer—simulated analog sound: *Virtual analog* synthesizers can reproduce the basic interface, working method, and sound of their analog forebearers. Behind the scenes, though, they use digital algorithms to replicate the function of analog circuitry, so technically they're not analog. Synthesis pioneer Bob Moog claimed that even the virtual analog instruments that bear his official endorsement don't sound as good as his true-analog hardware. You can let your own ears be the judge, but be aware that for the purpose of this section, although the techniques are basically the same as they would be on real analog equipment, the sound is digitally generated.

Hands-on: SoundSchool Analog

Native Instruments' Reaktor SoundSchool Analog is a custom instrument, built in Reaktor, designed to demonstrate analog synthesis for learning purposes. It's not just a learning tool—it's also a fun instrument to play. But its basic layout and functions are perfect for our purposes, because they're relatively generic and similar to many instruments you'll come across. Perhaps the most important feature is the integrated real-time oscilloscope, with which you can see as well as hear the sounds you're producing.

The version of SoundSchool included on the DVD is a stand-alone product, not a plug-in, so once the application is installed following the instructions on the DVD, all you have to do is load the application. The software will configure itself to the audio and MIDI defaults on Mac or Windows, but if you need to change your audio or MIDI settings, select System > Audio + MIDI Settings.

You don't need a MIDI keyboard to use SoundSchool; you can use your QWERTY keyboard to produce notes. The white notes of the piano of each octave are mapped to the rows of your keyboard beginning with the letters 'Q' (upper octave) and 'Z' (lower octave). The intervening black notes are mapped to the rows of keys above each of those rows, so to play chromatically from C to G, you'd play Q 2 W 3 E R 5 T. Give it a try: load SoundSchool and try pressing some QWERTY "notes." Of course, it'll be much easier to play an actual MIDI keyboard or other MIDI controller, but for programming sounds the QWERTY keyboard is fine.

Before we get started, see **Figures 9.20** and **9.21** for a brief overview of SoundSchool's interface. Most important to our first hands-on examples will be the oscillators, labeled in gold in the interface, and the oscilloscope display (labeled "Scope") in the bottom-right corner. Mix, filters, and modulation are labeled in blue in the interface.

Figure 9.20
SoundSchool's interface.

❶ Oscillator controls, which we'll use to look at basic analog waveshapes.

❷ Oscilloscope, which shows an amplitude versus time graph of the sound signal. Play a note, and you'll see a close-up representation of the waveshape of that sound. You can use the time control to adjust how much of the time axis is displayed, although the default is generally fine for these examples. Use the freeze button to hold a waveform image without keeping the note active.

❸ Toolbar (see Figure 9.21).

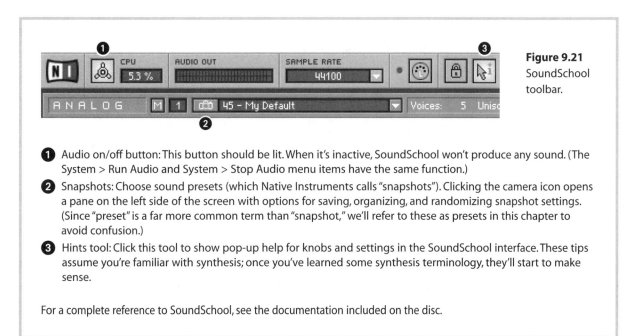

Figure 9.21
SoundSchool toolbar.

❶ Audio on/off button: This button should be lit. When it's inactive, SoundSchool won't produce any sound. (The System > Run Audio and System > Stop Audio menu items have the same function.)

❷ Snapshots: Choose sound presets (which Native Instruments calls "snapshots"). Clicking the camera icon opens a pane on the left side of the screen with options for saving, organizing, and randomizing snapshot settings. (Since "preset" is a far more common term than "snapshot," we'll refer to these as presets in this chapter to avoid confusion.)

❸ Hints tool: Click this tool to show pop-up help for knobs and settings in the SoundSchool interface. These tips assume you're familiar with synthesis; once you've learned some synthesis terminology, they'll start to make sense.

For a complete reference to SoundSchool, see the documentation included on the disc.

As discussed in Chapter 1, real-world instruments all produce sounds containing sound energy at different frequencies. A sound vibration at a particular frequency is called a partial. The words "harmonic" and "overtone" have similar meanings, but the frequency of a harmonic is always a whole-number multiple of the frequency of the *fundamental,* which is the frequency we hear as the base pitch of the note. For example, a fundamental at 100 Hz would have harmonics at 200 Hz, 300 Hz, and so on.

The relative strengths of the various partials contribute to what we hear as *timbre* (tone color). Different waveshapes have different combinations of harmonics, from the sine wave, which contains only a fundamental tone with no overtones, to the sawtooth wave, which contains all the overtones (although higher overtones are progressively weaker). White noise (which is also available as a waveform on many oscillators, although some synths have a separate noise source instead) contains not only all of the harmonically related overtones, but all of the possible partials—in theory, an infinite number. A noise signal contains sound energy at all frequencies. Oscillators of these wave types can be combined with one another, or filtered, so that you hear different harmonic content for additional timbral possibilities. Let's begin by taking a look at (and listening to) the waveshapes most often used in analog synthesis.

Hands-on: Hear and See Basic Waveshapes

You'd rarely use a basic waveshape completely unaltered as an instrumental patch, but it's still helpful to hear what these waves sound like. In SoundSchool, select the preset number that demonstrates each waveform from the preset drop-down menu at the top of the screen. Press a note on your MIDI keyboard, or press a QWERTY key. Try some different pitches, listen to the sound, and watch the oscilloscope. You'll notice some "rough edges" on the oscilloscope on some of the waveforms. These are slightly modified to avoid higher harmonics that would distort on a digital system.

Sine wave

Sine wave

Harmonic content:
No overtones

What it sounds like:
Plain, similar to a flute without vibrato or breath noise; you've heard it in test tones

Why it's useful: Can be used in combination with other sine waves (or other signals) to form more complex tones

Try it: SoundSchool preset 28—Basic Sine

Sine waves (**Figure 9.22**) are the most basic of the basic waveshapes: they're pure tones, free of overtones. As a result, their sound is plain vanilla. Since we're more accustomed to hearing sounds with partials at various frequencies, sine waves sound quite dull on their own. They're often used as test tones for calibrating audio equipment and software. Some acoustic instruments make sounds that resemble a sine wave, like the tone of a glockenspiel, a flute playing without vibrato, and other pure-tone instruments.

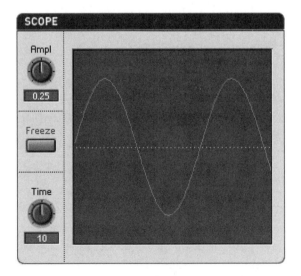

Figure 9.22 The sine wave is a pure tone, and sounds very muted.

Sine Waves: They're Everywhere

A single sine wave doesn't sound like much, but you can model any real-world sound with a combination of sine waves. Think back to dropping pebbles in a pond. Drop a single pebble, and simple, regular waves radiate out across the surface of the water. But if you start to layer waves atop other waves (as you would if you drop multiple pebbles in the water), you can create more complex waves. Each pebble creates a simple waveform, a sine wave. But when those waves overlap, they produce an irregular, tumultuous effect.

The theory behind this effect isn't new. Genius French mathematician and physicist Jean Baptiste Joseph Fourier figured it out in 1800. Fourier suggested that any complex periodic function (in physics and abstract math as well as sound) could be broken down into sine wave components. (Fourier was a busy guy; he not only solved major math and physics problems, but went on battle campaigns with Napoleon, governed lower Egypt, and theorized about the planetary greenhouse effect.)

If you can break down any sound into sine wave components, you can also theoretically produce any sound by combining sine waves. (See "FM and additive synthesis," p. 339.) This is sometimes called Fourier Synthesis after Jean Baptiste's mathematical achievements.

The ability to convert sound back and forth into its sine wave components is behind many of the digital effects we use in music software, too. See the discussion of Fast Fourier Transforms in Chapter 7.

Although they're not as useful alone, used in combination with other waves, sine waves are essential to synthesis. They're the basis, for instance, of both additive synthesis and FM synthesis, both of which utilize sine waves to form more complex sounds.

Triangle wave

Triangle waves (**Figure 9.23**) are similar to sine waves, but do not have a rounded shape. As a result, they add harmonic content (higher overtones) along the lines of a square wave. The harmonics in a triangle wave are much weaker than those in a square wave, however.

Triangle wave

Harmonic content:
Odd harmonics; higher harmonics are very weak

What it sounds like:
Muted, like the sine wave, but with slightly more color

Why it's useful: Used for basses and leads; combined with other waves

Try it: SoundSchool preset 29—Basic Tri

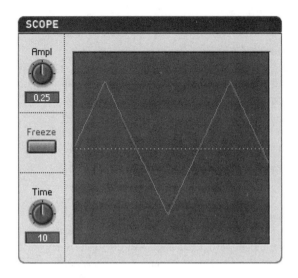

Figure 9.23 The triangle wave has a mellow sound with a few weak harmonics.

Sawtooth wave

Sawtooth waves (**Figure 9.24**) don't just look like the teeth on a saw. Because of the rich set of harmonics, they sound buzzy and "saw-like" as well. They're rich enough in sound that many people use them as is for bass sounds. They're also the classic basis for subtractive synthesis, so-named because filters are used to remove some of the harmonic content from a sound. Sawtooth waves are often compared to the sound of a trumpet: just listen to a high-pitched sawtooth wave and add a lot of imagination.

Sawtooth wave

Harmonic content: All harmonics; higher harmonics are progressively weaker

What it sounds like:
Rich, fat, and buzzy; the classic analog synth bass sound

Why it's useful: Rich and strident on their own, saw waves can be filtered to produce subtler timbres with less harmonic content

Try it: SoundSchool preset 27—Basic saw

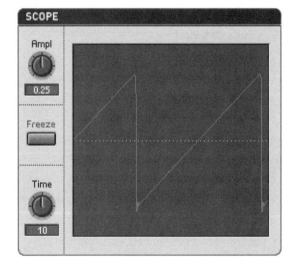

Figure 9.24 Sawtooth wave (note the slight rough edge at the corners; a mathematically perfect waveform will have precise corners, but that isn't always desirable).

Hands-on: Saws, Sines, and Symmetry

SoundSchool doesn't have dedicated oscillator switches for the triangle and sawtooth waves. They're combined in a single oscillator setting. Instead of switching between triangle and sawtooth, you'll adjust the Symmetry control (labeled "Symm"). As its name implies, this parameter impacts the shape of the waveform. The resulting sound changes, too: more asymmetrical waveshapes have additional harmonic content.

From a sine wave to a sine-saw hybrid: Let's give symmetry a try. Start with a sine wave; load preset 28. Switch from Oscillator 2 to Oscillator 1 by turning Mix > Osc 2 down to 0 and Mix > Osc 1 up to 1. Both oscillators are producing sine waves, but to perform this experiment you'll need the symmetry parameter on Oscillator 1. Symmetry is set to 0 for a pure sine wave. While holding down a note, gradually increase the symmetry value by dragging up on the Symm knob, as shown in **Figure 9.25**. (Native Instruments' label is a bit misleading: a higher value actually results in more asymmetry, not more symmetry.)

Figure 9.25 Adjusting the symmetry of the oscillator in Tri/Saw mode gradually morphs it from a triangle wave into a sawtooth wave.

Watch what happens to the Scope view, and listen to the sound. As the sine wave gets more asymmetrical, it becomes richer in harmonics, sounding and looking more like a sawtooth wave than a sine wave. (Try a little comparison: turn the Symm knob all the way to 1.0, and listen to the sine wave. Then select the sawtooth preset, number 27, and play the same note. They're not exactly identical, but they're very similar.)

Triangle and sawtooth from the same wave: Now you'll see why there's just one Oscillator 1 setting called "Tri/Saw." Load preset 29 for a triangle wave. Again, the Symm knob is set to 0 by default. Hold down a note and increase the value of the Symm knob, and you'll gradually morph from the triangle wave to the sawtooth wave.

Musical uses: Being able to adjust waveform symmetry has two main uses in synthesis. First, you can create subtle timbral variations to basic waveforms, as you heard. Second, since many synths allow real-time control over the symmetry parameter, you can sweep between waveshapes as you play. (You can do this in SoundSchool by assigning a MIDI controller to the knob.)

Square wave

Square wave

Harmonic content: Odd harmonics; higher harmonics are relatively strong (as with a sawtooth wave) rather than falling off rapidly in energy (as with a triangle wave)

What it sounds like: Rich but rounded, hollow; very similar to the sound of a clarinet playing without vibrato

Why it's useful: Used for basses and leads; combined with other waves

Try it: SoundSchool preset 26—Basic Square

Like a sawtooth wave, the square wave's upper harmonics (see **Figure 9.26**) are relatively strong. Unlike the sawtooth wave, however, the square wave has only odd-numbered harmonics, giving it a full, rich, but slightly hollow sound. It lacks the buzz of the sawtooth's even-numbered harmonics. In its middle range, you'll find a square wave sounds reminiscent of a clarinet played without vibrato.

Preset 26 in SoundSchool is the most common, basic square wave. True to its name, the dimensions of the wave are square: the signal spends as much time in the "up" position as in the "down" position. If we call the "up" position a pulse, the width of each pulse is equal to the width between pulses. SoundSchool, like many analog synths, lets you adjust the width of the pulse. Hold down a note and try increasing the value of the Symm knob. The width of the pulse will gradually get narrower, and you'll hear a thinner sound. (With a narrow pulse width, the sound is similar to the Hohner Clavinet, the electric keyboard popularized by Stevie Wonder.) As you narrow the pulse, the energy of the fundamental decreases, and the wave acquires more energy in the high harmonics. A narrow pulse has all of the harmonics, not just odd harmonics as with a square wave.

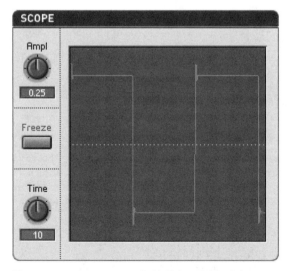 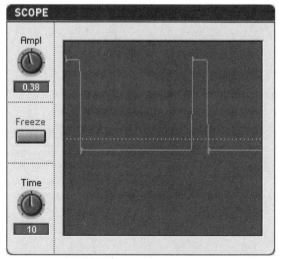

Figure 9.26 Square wave (left); if the width of the wave narrows (right), the wave is called a pulse wave and has different timbral qualities (it contains all harmonics, but less energy at the fundamental).

SoundSchool calls the parameter for the width of the pulse "symmetry," but most synths refer to it as pulse width or *duty cycle*. Some allow continuous adjustment, whereas others require you to choose from preconfigured widths. Later in this chapter, you'll use this parameter in modulation, which is naturally called *pulse width modulation*.

Envelopes

At its core, a keyboard is nothing more than a row of buttons—velocity-sensitive buttons, to be sure, but essentially the performer is limited to switching notes on and off. A simple electronic sound, like the beep on your microwave oven, fits into that basic design: it turns on, you hear sound; it turns off, the sound stops. But the sounds of instruments we love have always been more complex.

An acoustic piano, for instance, also has a keyboard that acts like a series of buttons: press one, and a lever strikes a string. Release the key, and a damper ends the sound. The keyboard of a 9-foot Steinway concert grand is still an on/off device: the sound is anything but. There's the sharp, striking attack as you hit a note, shifting harmonic content after the note is struck; the gradual, dying sound as that sound fades away; and with the release of the note, the tapered damping as a felt damper deadens the vibration of the string.

In short, acoustic instruments produce sounds that change over time. Synthesis needs a way of shaping sounds that's more sophisticated than a binary on/off system. From early analog synthesis to the latest software synths, electronic instruments have used *envelopes* to model changes over time.

What's an envelope?

An *envelope* (see **Figure 9.27**) is a representation of how a parameter of a sound, such as loudness, changes over time. In synthesis, envelopes are created by *envelope generators,* which are dedicated modules in the synth that output control signals. The control signals are routed to whatever is being controlled. The envelope generator makes no sound; it simply controls something else. Imagine you're conducting a cellist with your hand, raising your hand to coax more volume from the player and lowering it when you want the player to back off. Your hand is the equivalent of the control signal from the envelope generator: it produces an envelope (the shape of the volume you want over time), which the player translates into the volume of the sound (the actual amplitude).

Narrow pulse waves versus square waves: All square waves are pulse waves, but not all pulse waves are square waves. As the width of a square wave narrows (so it's no longer square), it is called a pulse wave. Narrow pulse waves have different harmonic content than square waves.

Harmonic content: All harmonics (instead of only odd)

Fundamental: Less energy than a square wave

High harmonics: More energy than a square wave

The most common use of an envelope generator is to control amplitude, but many synths give you other options as well. Unless you're using modular software, you'll usually choose a prerouted destination for the envelope generator to control, then adjust the shape of the envelope. SoundSchool Analog has a typical envelope generator configuration: one for amplitude and one for the filter. The filter envelope can also be routed to pitch, symmetry, or the amplitude of either or both of the oscillators. Each of these routings can be used for different effects.

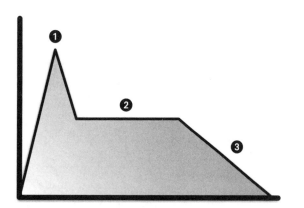
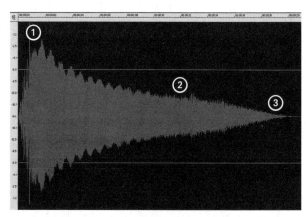

Figure 9.27 What we refer to as a synthesizer envelope is simply a change in the level of a control signal over time. This is usually charted as an X/Y graph with time as the x-axis and control level as the y-axis. If the envelope shown were used to control amplitude, the synth's sound would quickly get louder and then somewhat softer—the attack portion of the note (1), then sustain at a fixed level (2), then fall back to silence (3), as shown here both in an envelope (left) and the waveform it approximates (right).

Envelope shapes

Theoretically, an envelope can be any shape you want, but many synths, inspired by early analog designs, use a standard four-parameter envelope design. For this design, you can thank Columbia-Princeton Electronic Music Center head Vladimir Ussachevsky, who suggested to Bob Moog that a four-parameter system would be the best way to generate note shapes similar to those made by real instruments, from violins to drums. Many musicians have agreed, and the system has remained popular.

On the original Moog Modular, the four settings were labeled T1, T2, T3, and sustain. Today they are called attack, decay, sustain, and release, or ADSR. You'll see those four knobs on the SoundSchool Analog, with a graph of the resulting envelope below them. The Moog labels are helpful in that three of the settings (T1, T2, and T3, or attack, decay, and release) control the amount of time that passes between one envelope level and another when you press or release a key, whereas the sustain parameter controls the level at which the envelope stays for as long as you hold down the key. **Figure 9.28** shows what happens when you press a key and the synth's envelope generator responds.

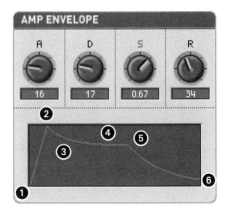

Figure 9.28 This image shows what happens when you press a key down on your synth in relation to your synth's envelope generator controls.

❶ You press a key.
❷ The level rises from zero to the maximum level over a span of time (the attack time).
❸ The level falls (or "decays") to the sustain level over a span of time (the decay time).
❹ The level stays at the sustain level for as long as you hold down the key.
❺ You release the key.
❻ The level falls back to zero over a span of time (the release time).

Each of the points along the envelope is called a *breakpoint*. Some digital synths allow you to design more complex envelopes by adding breakpoints wherever you like. You can use a multisegment envelope to create sophisticated rhythms. For everyday playing, though, ADSR envelopes are versatile enough to cover many of the sound designs you'll need.

Hands-on: ADSR and amplitude

Let's try working with these different knobs and see how they impact sound. Load SoundSchool preset 26—Basic Square. Notice that the Amp Envelope is simply a big blue rectangle: this is an on/off envelope. The attack is 0 (instantaneous) and the sustain is 1 (full level). The decay knob happens to be set to 57, but that's irrelevant, because the decay setting affects the sound only when the sustain level is lowered. Try pressing and releasing a key. The sound turns on, then turns off; its amplitude goes from zero to maximum almost instantly and returns to zero almost instantly. Looking at the sustain

Tip: To keep your square waves from overlapping one another, set Voices (at the top of the screen) to 1, converting Sound-School into a mono-phonic synth. Otherwise, notes sounding at the same time will interfere with one another on the Scope.

Mario, anyone? If this walkthrough gives you flashbacks to video games, it's because Nin-tendo's original console and Game Boy used basic square waves and noise oscillators. If you like the effect, try reduc-ing the sample rate and using an LFO for vibrato (see the discussion of LFOs later in the chapter).

knob, you can see why: the sustain amplitude is at its maximum level, 1. Press a key and, while you're holding it down, adjust the sustain knob. The amplitude of the waveform changes, just as it would with a conventional volume knob.

Set the sustain knob to about .3 and the decay knob to about 50, and you'll create a basic decay/sustain envelope. As you play notes now, each note will decay from its full amplitude to the sustain amplitude and continue sound-ing until you release the key. You can see this happening by watching the Scope: the amplitude of the note (the height of the square wave) decreases from the time you press down the key until the sustain level is reached as you hold down the key.

The notes still begin and end abruptly because the attack and release knobs are set to 0. (The A, D, and R knobs in SoundSchool display time in ms; as you'll see if you turn on tips and mouse over the knob: 0=1 ms, 20=10 ms, 40=100 ms, and so on. The value 0 isn't actually 0, but 1 ms is close enough to zero to sound instantaneous to our ears.)

If you increase the attack knob to 30, the beginnings of the notes will sound less sharp and more "rounded" as the sound gradually increases to maxi-mum amplitude with each note you strike. For a gradual attack, try a value of 50 or more. That sounds a little strange with this plain square wave, so return the knob to a more realistic setting of 20. At that level, the note still has a fairly sharp attack, but there's an audible beginning to the sound.

Just as the attack knob determines how quickly the sound rises to maximum amplitude after you hit a key, the release knob determines how long it takes for the sound to return to zero after you let go of the key. (This is potentially confusing terminology because musicians commonly call this property the "decay" of a pitch, but in synthesis terms, release happens after you let go of a key.) Try increasing the knob to 40 or more, and you'll hear the note con-tinue to sound after you release the key. Decrease it to 25 for a subtler effect.

You've just created a typical envelope for pitched instruments that sustain pitch, like woodwinds. But what about sounds like percussion, which have fast, brief attacks? They can be modeled with ADSR envelopes, but the envelopes will have a different shape.

Open preset 30—Basic Noise. Initially, pressing a key sounds like turning on static on your TV. To make this sound more like a snare drum, you'll need to mimic what happens when you hit a snare: there's a brief initial attack, then the sound quickly delays. Decrease the sustain value to 0 (to mimic the drum's damping effect) and the decay to 40 to create a steep envelope. (For slightly more realistic attack and release, try values of A=8 and R=40.) The sound is primitive, but reminiscent of a snare hit, and is a result of manipulating simple noise with a basic amplitude envelope. (If it sounds familiar, this effect was used in early video games for drums; you'll create richer-sounding percussion later when using filters.)

To see how envelopes are used in practice, you can browse through some of the presets included with SoundSchool; see **Table 9.1**.

Table 9.1 Common Amplitude Envelope Types

Although their timbre is unmistakably analog and electronic, these sounds are reminiscent of common instruments because of their envelopes. (These are classic envelope shapes for these kinds of instruments, so expect to see similar envelopes on other synths.)

 35—Basic Sub Bass has a sharp attack, which you'd expect of a plucked electric bass.

 72—Gittar also has a sharp attack, but decays quickly like an acoustic guitar or harp.

 56—Sreng sounds vaguely like a bowed cello, due to a gentler attack. Adjust it to make it slightly more realistic: increase the attack to 40 and nudge the release to 45.

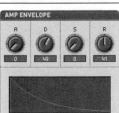 75—Tomm mimics the sound of a drum by eliminating the sustain entirely and decaying quickly. Try small adjustments to the D knob on the Amp Envelope to make this tom more muted (shorter decay) or more resonant (longer decay).

Beyond ADSR: Other Envelope Schemes

The four-parameter attack-decay-sustain-release envelope is the most common, and it's especially ubiquitous on virtual analog equipment. But that doesn't mean it's the only envelope shape possible.

Generic "time" controls: Some percussion-oriented synths lack specific ADSR envelope controls. Instead, they include a single parameter like "time" or "decay" that impacts the overall envelope shape or one aspect of the envelope.

Rates versus times: SoundSchool measures envelope settings as time amounts, but some envelopes use rate, a measurement of the slope of each envelope segment. The distinction is mainly semantic.

More segments: By adding breakpoints, you can create an envelope that gives you additional segments with which you can control the sound, or even delay the start of an envelope (a DADSR envelope, for instance, adds a delay segment at the beginning of the envelope). You can see an example of a more flexible envelope in **Figure 9.29**. The envelopes in Native Instruments' Absynth, for instance, are virtually unlimited, allowing fine-tuned control of sound even in surround-sound setups—a far cry from the simple ADSR envelope.

Looping envelopes: You can use looped envelopes to produce rhythmic effects by creating percussive amplitude patterns that repeat over time. Hold down a key and the envelopes do the rest, creating even one-note drum machines and groove boxes. Some, like the looped envelopes in Ableton Operator (included with the demo on the disc), can be synced with host tempo so the groove produced by the envelope runs at the same tempo as your song.

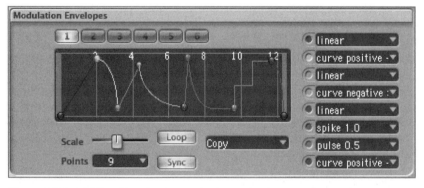

Figure 9.29 Additional breakpoints and other controls can make envelopes more flexible, as shown here in the free Mac/Windows virtual instrument Crystal (included on the disc).

Mixing Oscillators

So far, we've been using only one oscillator at a time, limiting us to basic waveform choices—square, triangle, sawtooth, sine, and noise. That's fine for some sound designs, but fairly vanilla.

By mixing oscillators, you can create richer sounds. SoundSchool provides two oscillators that can be mixed together in the Mix section (**Figure 9.30**).

Many synths have four oscillators or even more, but the two included in SoundSchool allow for most basic techniques.

The simplest way to use two oscillators is by detuning one from the other. When two identical or similar waveforms are not perfectly in tune with one another, natural phasing produces a more complex waveform. Let's watch and hear it.

Figure 9.30
Adjust the balance of Sound-School's two oscillators in the Mix section.

 ## Hands-on: Mixing and detuning

Load preset 28—Basic Sine. Look at the Mix section: by default on this preset, you hear only SoundSchool's second oscillator. The Osc 2 volume is turned all the way up (1), but Osc 1 is set to silent (0). While holding down a note, turn up the volume for Osc 2. Since both are sine waves and are set to the same frequency, the two waveforms will overlap exactly, so you'll get the same sound but twice as loud. (If that doesn't happen, the two oscillators are out of sync: check the Sync Osc 1 > 2 check box and then uncheck it again to place them back in phase.)

With the two oscillators in phase, one waveform is added to the other, as shown in **Figure 9.31**. (Watch the amplitude of the wave on the Scope.) If they're detuned, the waveforms will move in and out of phase. Adjust the detune knob on Oscillator 2 and listen while watching the Scope. As the waveform shifts out of phase, it produces a pulsing sound as it cancels out the sound from Oscillator 1.

With sine waves, this effect isn't very interesting or useful. Load preset 26—Basic Square. (Both oscillators are set to square waves in this patch.) Increase the level of Mix > Osc 2 to 1 (turning it all the way up). Now hold down a note and gradually turn the detune knob down for Oscillator 2, just slightly below 0 in the 0–0.03 range. Huge difference, right? We've gone from a boring electronic sound to a lead sound reminiscent of a distorted electric guitar. Let's take a look at what's going on: decrease the amplitude knob on the Scope so you can see the whole dynamic range of the waveform. As the two waves superimpose, they move in and out of phase with one another, alternately adding and cancelling one another out, creating a dynamically shifting range of overtones in the sound. With the Osc 2 mix set to 100%, the effect is similar to pulse width modulation, because the "stair-steps" appear above and below zero amplitude and shift in width. (For true pulse width modulation, you can assign the filter envelope or LFO to the symmetry of a pulse wave.) To adjust the resulting timbre, adjust the Puls-Sym knob of Oscillator 2, and try replacing the waveforms with Pulse and Saw, Tri/Saw and Saw, and so on.

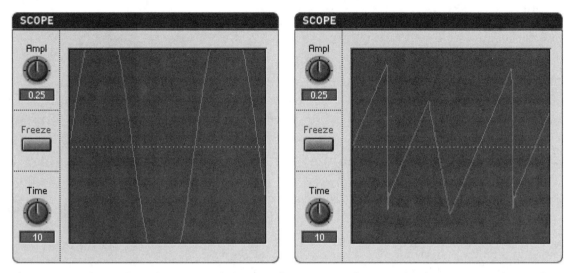

Figure 9.31 With two identical sine waves in phase, combining two oscillators just produces a wave with twice the original amplitude (left). When one wave is detuned from another, the result is a new waveform that changes over time. Try combining two sawtooth waves and adjusting the detune and Symm/Puls-Sym knobs to create a richer sound (right).

Ring modulation

Other means of combining oscillators can result in some pretty far-out effects. By using the Osc 1 and Osc 2 controls under Mix, you're adding the waveforms. To hear what happens when you multiply waveforms, turn up the Mix > RingMod knob. RingMod, or *ring modulation,* is sometimes called *multiplicative synthesis* because it multiplies one signal by another. The net result of multiplying two signals is both the sums and differences of all of the overtones present in the two sources. (For more on ring modulation used as an audio effect—with any signal source, not just these common synthesized waveforms—see Chapter 7.)

Theory aside, ring modulation is useful for clanging, sonorous timbres and special effects. Let's try one extreme example. You'll need two waveforms, since ring modulation requires two inputs. Select preset 26—Basic Square, and turn up the RingMod knob all the way to 1. Note that you don't have to turn up the Osc 2 knob, because RingMod by definition uses both oscillators. In fact, turn down Mix > Osc1 so you hear only the ring-modulated output (**Figure 9.32**).

The two signals are the same at the moment, so change the pitch of one. Turn up the Interval knob on Oscillator 2 to 30. Now try hitting a note: you'll hear a variety of partials, the sum and difference pitches. Sounds horrible, right?

You can make the ring modulation more active by having one of the two signals sweep in pitch. Unlike the amplitude envelope, the filter envelope in SoundSchool can be routed to other parameters. Let's first set up the envelope shape: set the filter envelope's attack to 0, decay to 60, sustain to 0, and release to 30 for a gradual sweep from high to low. Under Filter Env → Oscillator, select the Pitch and Sym check boxes next to Osc 2 (**Figure 9.33**). By selecting these boxes, you're routing the envelope generator to those parameters. So instead of the pitch and symmetry of the second oscillator staying where you put the knobs, they'll shift along the contour of the envelope as you hold down a note. Next, choose the amount of the modulation by increasing Filter Env → Oscillator > Amount to 1. (For a sweep in the reverse direction, from low to high, you'd choose –1.)

Now hold down a note for a wild, sweeping, ring mod pulse wave. You wouldn't want to use this for anything other than a brief special effect, but keeping in mind how simple the ingredients were (two pulse waves and a single envelope), you'll likely agree that the result is more dramatic. (Fans of the British sci-fi hit *Doctor Who* will immediately recognize this sound as the screaming sound that opened the theme music during the '70s and '80s.)

Figure 9.32 For a pure ring-modulated sound, turn up RingMod while turning down the level of the oscillators.

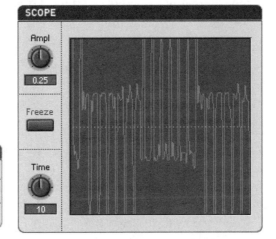

Figure 9.33 You've used envelopes to modulate amplitude; here you modulate the oscillator with the filter envelope using SoundSchool's Filter Env → Oscillator check boxes (left). The ring-modulated result multiplies the two signals, producing the waveform shown at right, while the envelope sweeps oscillator pitch and symmetry downward.

You can also use subtler ring modulation to add timbral color to a patch. For example, load preset 85—Clav. Try playing it with the RingMod knob at 0, then return the knob to the preset's value of 0.2. In this case, ring modulation is simply icing on the cake, turning a somewhat lifeless sound into a more biting one.

Oscillator sync and timbre

Oscillator sync synchronizes the period of two oscillators' waveforms, forcing the "slave" oscillator to have the same fundamental frequency as the "master" oscillator. Unlike what happens when beats are synchronized, you'll hear a timbral, not a rhythmic effect, since you don't hear individual periods of waves. So why would you want to synchronize waveforms? Oscillator sync produces some unique sound design twists that make it useful.

In SoundSchool, with oscillator sync turned on, Oscillator 1 is the master and Oscillator 2 is the slave. If you open a preset like 28—Basic Sine, Oscillator 2 will sound by default. Turn sync on, and nothing audible happens. A sine wave operating at a regular frequency can be synced to another sine wave operating at the same frequency. It's the same effect as tuning two oscillators to the same pitch; nothing interesting happens. However, if you raise the frequency of the master oscillator, Oscillator 1, using its Interval knob, the slave oscillator, Oscillator 2, has to change its waveform to maintain the same frequency as the master. It gets only part way through its period before it must start over again (**Figure 9.34**). The waveform produced will have a unique timbre as a result.

Why is this useful, other than for creating oddly shaped waveforms? If the pitch of your second oscillator is being modulated, synchronizing it to the first oscillator will maintain a prominent fundamental frequency while other overtones change.

The whole point of oscillator sync is to open up new timbral effects, so let's give it a listen. Load preset 40—Basic Sync and play a note. The Filter Envelope controls the pitch of Oscillator 2, but the pitch is not just sweeping down from high to low as you'd expect. You hear the sweep, but you also hear a prominent fundamental tone below it. Looking at the Scope, you can see why this is happening: the waveform of Oscillator 2 is locked to the pitch of the pulse wave in Oscillator 1, and the fundamental pitch is preserved. You can change this fundamental pitch by adjusting the Interval knob on Oscillator 1.

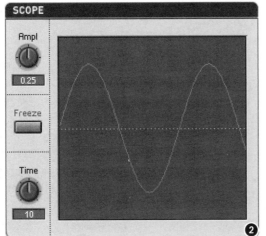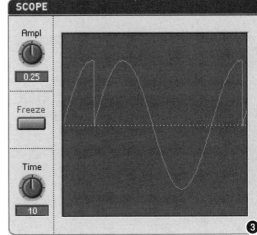

Figure 9.34 Oscillator sync adds another timbral option to your synth. With oscillator sync turned on (1), one waveform will be a slave to the wavelength of another. So a standard sine wave (2), for instance, will have to restart its waveform before it completes a full period (3).

By contrast, if you turn off Sync Osc 1 > 2, all you'll hear is the sweep with no fundamental. Watching the Scope, you'll see the width of the fundamental waveform shifting (which indicates why you're perceiving the fundamental pitch changing).

Frequency modulation (FM)

FM synthesis is often described as sounding metallic or bell-like. The reason is that the process has the perceived effect of adding harmonics. As the name implies, FM modulates the frequency of one oscillator with a signal from another oscillator. The reason FM synthesis differs from other forms of FM, such as vibrato, is that the modulating oscillator is in the audio range, the frequency range above 20 Hz. You need at least two oscillators to do FM, although some synths will give you four or more.

Like many virtual analog synths, SoundSchool focuses on subtractive synthesis but adds some basic FM. FM is hard-wired to the most common case: Oscillator 1 modulates Oscillator 2 via the FM knob (**Figure 9.35**). In basic two-oscillator FM, the wave you hear as the output is called the *carrier,* whereas the wave modulating the carrier is called (oddly enough) the *modulator.* In SoundSchool, that makes Oscillator 2 the carrier and Oscillator 1, the oscillator with the FM knob, the modulator.

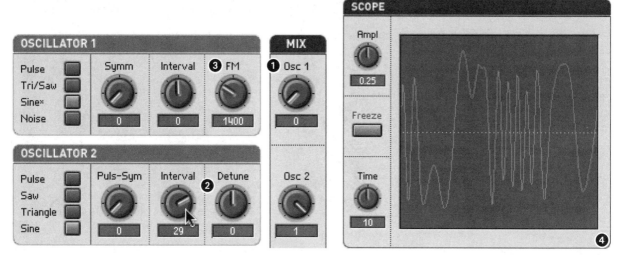

Figure 9.35 The one lowly FM knob in SoundSchool is the key to some timbres that are very different from other subtractive sounds discussed in this chapter. Oscillator 1 is the FM modulator, so you can turn down the Osc 1 level in the mixer (1). Adjust the harmonic relationship of the two oscillators with Oscillator 2's Interval and Detune knobs (2), and choose how much of an effect you want to have on the waveform of the carrier (that is, on the harmonic spectrum) with the FM knob (3). Watch the Scope (4) to see why you hear additional harmonics in the sound.

Load preset 39—Basic FM for a typical FM patch that uses two sine waves. Notice that the designer opted for a bell-like amplitude envelope, and via a similar filter envelope routed to Oscillator 1, diminishes the FM effect as the pitch sounds. This mimics the decay of overtones in a bell or other resonant metal. (To hear the pure tone throughout, uncheck Filter Env → Oscillator > Ampl.)

Using this preset as a template, you can experiment with some basic properties of FM:

- Try changing the Oscillator 2 Interval parameter one increment at a time. As the ratio of the frequencies changes, there's a significant change in timbre.

- For more complex timbres, adjust the Oscillator 2 detune parameter in conjunction with Interval. With detune set to 0, the two oscillators have a whole-number frequency relationship. Detuning sets up an inharmonic relationship that changes the timbre.

- The FM knob increases the amount of effect the modulator (Oscillator 1) has on the carrier (Oscillator 2). Using this knob, you can try more radical changes: a higher value will generally sound more metallic and biting, while a lower value will sound more muted and bell-like. (To hear the difference clearly, adjust the control while the pitch is sounding.)

- Different waveforms will give you different results. Substitute, for instance, two pulse waves for the sine waves.

- Try additional filter and amplitude modulation as employed in this patch to further shape the tone.

Filters and Subtractive Synthesis

Sculptors work in two fundamental ways: they either start with a big block of stone and chip away, subtracting material until they have the shape they want, or they start with a material like clay, adding material to produce a finished form. Likewise, synth designers can start with a basic sound and add harmonic content or start with a harmonically rich sound and remove harmonics for the desired timbre. To put it more accurately, they can use frequency modulation and additive synthesis to strengthen the energy of certain partials, or they can use subtractive synthesis to weaken the energy of the partials within an existing sound.

To do the latter, subtractive synthesis uses filters, just as we used in Chapter 7. In SoundSchool Analog, you'll see familiar filter shapes: notch, lowpass, bandpass, and highpass. By feeding a sound source rich in harmonic content through this filter, you can adjust the timbre of the sound by weakening partials, most commonly with a lowpass filter.

But if the goal is to produce "richer" sounds, why would we want to weaken the harmonics? Isn't it "the more harmonics, the merrier?" Not necessarily: you might want to use filters for several reasons. First, you can use them to achieve specific timbral effects. You might want to weaken certain harmonics to create a more focused timbre. In addition, by adding resonance to the filter, you can accentuate certain partials while weakening others. Second, by using a filter in conjunction with a filter envelope, you can sweep through different harmonics, shaping sounds over time.

Let's take a look at how classic analog filtering works; then, see how that translates into music making.

More FM and subtractive synthesis: For more sound design tips that combine extensive FM synthesis with subtractive synthesis, open the demo tutorials for Ableton Operator, included with the Live demo on the disc. Work through the tutorials to see how classic FM and subtractive techniques can be used to build common sounds. Operator is a four-oscillator synthesizer in which the oscillators can be routed as FM oscillators, virtual analog oscillators, or both.

Anatomy of a filter

As opposed to some of the more elaborate filters you learned about in Chapter 7, most filters used in synthesis are fairly simple. You'll use the cutoff frequency knob to zoom in on the part of the spectrum you want to attenuate, and then add resonance where you want to emphasize specific frequencies near the cutoff.

SoundSchool Analog offers a typical filter bank with a choice of fixed filter types (which SoundSchool calls "Modes"), Cutoff, and resonance ("Reson"). Separate controls adjust how much effect the envelope has on the filter over time (Env) and how much the cutoff frequency changes depending on where you play your keyboard (K-Track) (**Figure 9.36**).

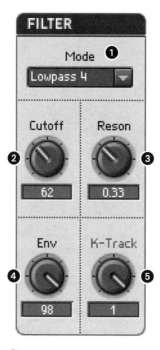

Figure 9.36 SoundSchool's filter controls.

❶ Mode: Selects a specific fixed filter type (lowpass, bandpass, etc.) and slope.

❷ Cutoff: Determines the cutoff frequency for the filter; measure in semitones (60 is middle C).

❸ Reson: Sets the amount of resonance, from no resonance to self-oscillation (1.0).

❹ Env: Determines the extent to which the filter envelope changes the cutoff frequency, in positive or negative semitones.

❺ K-Track: Short for Keyboard Tracking, determines the extent to which the filter cutoff is affected by what note is played.

Mode

Some synths have just one fixed-slope lowpass filter, in which case all you'll see are cutoff and possibly a resonance control. Most will offer you a choice by letting you adjust the filter type (lowpass, bandpass, highpass, and notch), slope (in db/Octave), or both.

In SoundSchool Analog, there is a number after each filter type in the Mode menu. These numbers refer to filters of different slopes: lowpass 1 is 6 dB per octave, lowpass 2 is 12 dB per octave, and so on. (See the explanation of *slope* in Chapter 7.) To find out which is which, turn on hints (View > Show Hints) and mouse over the Mode menu for a full description.

Cutoff frequency

The cutoff frequency setting is the most important to consider first. In fact, with some synths, if you have a lowpass filter with a cutoff of zero or a highpass filter with a maximum cutoff, you may not hear any sound at all. (SoundSchool's cutoff range is intentionally limited so that doesn't happen.) If you choose a lowpass filter with the cutoff set at the maximum value, for instance, you won't hear much or any filtering until you turn down the knob.

Hands-on: Resonance and self-oscillation

Once you've adjusted the cutoff frequency, you can add a resonant peak just below the cutoff frequency by increasing the resonance parameter. Resonance is the amount of emphasis added around the cutoff frequency and ranges from no resonance (Reson=0, a standard, nonresonant cutoff filter) to maximum resonance (1.0). At maximum resonance, a phenomenon called *self-oscillation* occurs in some filters. As the filter approaches its highest resonance value or Q, instead of simply emphasizing frequencies around the cutoff, the filter oscillates at the cutoff frequency. Think back to the discussion of Q in Chapter 7: as the resonance filter increases, you're effectively adding a peaking filter around the cutoff frequency.

It's easier to understand resonance and self-oscillation by trying them out. (Warning: turn your speakers down first, since the result can be dangerously loud!)

1. **Load preset 29—Basic Tri.** By default, this patch includes a lowpass filter, but the cutoff frequency is set to the maximum value of 140, so you can't hear it.

2. **Reduce the cutoff frequency,** and you'll gradually attenuate the harmonic content. Notice what happens: your triangle wave gradually turns into a sine wave as you reduce its upper harmonics.

3. **Set Reson to 0.75** and move the cutoff knob around. You'll be able to hear an emphasis at the cutoff frequency. It sounds somewhat like an additional note sounding at that pitch. If you watch the Scope closely with Cutoff set just above its center position, you'll be able to see this frequency. Incidentally, if you've ever heard overtone chanting as practiced by singers of cultures like Tibet and Tuva, the sound is similar. These singers are able to use their mouths or throats as resonant filters.

4. **Now try self-oscillation.** (Don't forget to turn your speakers down first.) Increase Reson to 1.0 and again move the cutoff knob. The tone at the cutoff frequency is so distorted that the filter literally self-oscillates. If this effect is reminiscent of someone tuning a shortwave radio in an old movie, it's because that tuning circuitry had a tendency to self-oscillate.

Tracking filters to time and pitch

Filter type, cutoff, and resonance are all settings that remain stable in performance, affecting sound equally no matter what notes you play or how short or long the notes may be. To shape the way the filter behaves as a function of time (the length of time a given note has been sounding) or the note played on the keyboard, you'll need to use envelopes and keyboard tracking.

By using an envelope to modulate filter cutoff, you can sweep the cutoff frequency of the filter as the note sounds, making the sound's frequency spectrum morph as it plays for subtle or dramatic effects. In SoundSchool, you can adjust the amount of filter envelope that will be applied to the cutoff by setting the Env knob to either a positive or negative value. Set to positive, the Env setting increases the cutoff frequency as the envelope rises. When the Env control is set to negative, a rising envelope lowers the cutoff frequency. When this knob is set to zero, the envelope has no impact.

Keyboard tracking is significant, too. Normally, the filter cutoff remains at a fixed point regardless of what note you play. (If you're not using key tracking, double-check what the filter sounds like in different registers by playing different notes as you adjust the filter settings.) By adjusting the K-Track knob in SoundSchool, you can determine how closely the cutoff frequency follows the notes you're playing. With the K-Track knob set to 1, the cutoff frequency increases as you play higher notes and decreases when you play lower notes. With K-Track set at zero, the cutoff remains wherever you set it regardless of the note you play. Tracking is sometimes called "following," because with tracking enabled the cutoff frequency "follows" whatever note you've played.

 ## Hands-on: Fine-tune a "brass" timbre with a filter

Analog synthesis has traditionally involved starting with a basic waveform, then fine-tuning it with a filter. You can try this out by creating a textbook brass patch. Okay, so it won't sound much like real brass so much as a retro electronic sound. Most likely you'll use this technique to create distinctive, fat analog electronic sounds or apply similar filtering techniques to digital sounds. If you listen closely, there are some key similarities to real brass that give it that association.

Sawtooth waves are often said to be "brasslike" because they share a similar harmonic profile, so let's start there. Load preset 27—Basic Saw, which sets Oscillator 1 to a sawtooth wave (a triangle wave with a Symm value of 1).

Try playing a note in the middle of the keyboard. It sounds vaguely brassy, but it's a little overly electronic and buzzy. It actually has too much energy in the upper part of the frequency spectrum. You can correct this with a slight filtering of that part of the spectrum. Try reducing the filter cutoff to 110. The result is not as buzzy, but now the patch sounds dead and muted. (Notice on the Scope that what you've done is round off the waveform, making it more like a sine wave.) Give it back some buzz by increasing the Filter Reson to 0.3.

Now you have a slightly richer sound, but it's still missing something. You can make this sound like a brass section by creating some artificial chorusing, slightly detuning a second oscillator to throw it out of phase with the first. Set Oscillator 2 to saw (that is, the same waveform as Oscillator 1) and increase its Mix value to 1. Then set detune to 0.15. Now you have a basic brass patch.

 Still not satisfied? For a slightly different effect, adjust detune, cutoff, and resonance to taste. For fit and finish, tweak the Amp Envelope. (Try a release value of 30.)

Hands-on: Create a filter sweep

 More hands-on filters: Instrument designs often combine amplitude and filter envelopes for useful musical shapes. Try preset 47—Bassh for an example. You can create a more pronounced effect by increasing filter envelope decay and filter envelope amount settings.

You can use filters to modulate sounds over time, thanks to filter envelopes. Let's start with a sound that's rich harmonically: two detuned sawtooth waves. Load preset 27—Basic Saw. Set Oscillator 2 to a saw wave. Set its detune to 0.2 and its mix to 1. Now, let's give it a basic sweep from high to low. On the filter envelope, set attack, sustain, and release to 0, but set decay to 70. With just a decay value, the filter envelope becomes a straight line, dropping from top to bottom. Set the filter cutoff to 50 and the resonance to 80. Hold down a note and listen as the filter sweeps through the harmonic spectrum. (The resonance value makes that sweep more noticeable, and once the filter is at its lowest, you hear two phasing sine waves.)

You can use this technique for other filter envelope shapes as well. Instead of sweeping high to low, try sweeping low to high by setting the Filter > Env control to a negative value. Or, for a filter that opens up and closes again, try setting a larger value for the filter envelope attack parameter, creating a triangular or "mountain-shaped" envelope. Preset 80—OpeningReso makes excellent use of this idea, by modulating the filter with a peak-shaped envelope with a high resonance value. Try different cutoff values to hear what the filter sweep sounds like at different frequencies.

 More Quick and Dirty Analog Subtractive Tips

- Mix together two sawtooth oscillators with one slightly detuned for a thick, analog bass sound. Make it even richer by adding ring modulation. (In Sound-School, access the saw for Oscillator 1 by setting Symm to 1.)

- Turn a static sound into one that moves: shape your sound by adding a filter with an envelope. Set the Sustain value to 0, then adjust cutoff and resonance. Pitch doesn't have to be static, either: try routing an envelope to pitch for a slight change in pitch on each attack. (In SoundSchool, under Filter Env → Oscillator, route the filter envelope to pitch and slightly increase the Amount.)

- Create a quick Clavinet-type sound by slightly detuning two pulse waves, each with a thin pulse width (increase the Symm and Puls-Sym knobs in Sound-School), and creating fast decays (attack at 0, sustain near 0, and a decay lower than 50).

MODULATION AND EFFECTS

What Is Modulation?

In Chapter 8, we talked about modulation as it's understood in the world of MIDI. Modulation is a form of MIDI message. It's used to control an aspect of the sound. For instance, MIDI Control Change 1 (modulation wheel) messages are often used to add vibrato.

Modulation in synthesis can have much the same musical effect, but in this case the modulation signal is created within the synthesizer itself rather than being received via MIDI. Whether the source of the modulation signal is internal or external, modulation is the use of a control signal to change a sound over time. You learned about many of the basic types of modulation in Chapter 7, in the discusion of effects. There we discussed how modulation sources like LFOs (low-frequency oscillators) work. In synthesis, control signals from LFOs and other modulation sources are used in some additional ways.

Modulation Routing

Just as you can route effects, you can also route modulation—either using the fixed, preset routings that came with your gear, or else designing your own.

A few routings are the most common musically, and these are the routings that tend to be built into virtual analog synths like SoundSchool. Let's take a look at the modulation routing within SoundSchool. Normally, this is hidden, but if you click the B icon in the upper-right corner of SoundSchool's interface, you're presented with a diagram of how the different modules of SoundSchool are routed to one another (**Figure 9.37**). If you think of the A button as the "front panel" interface, this is the "back panel" that represents what's going on behind the scenes.

Let's look at Figure 9.37 to see how SoundSchool works. Following the flow of signal from left to right:

1. Two oscillators are at the heart of the sound (labeled in gold, as on the front panel). These aren't all the way to the left in the signal diagram, because two oscillator parameters—pitch (frequency) and symmetry— can be controlled externally.

2. These two parameters can be controlled by either a filter envelope or an LFO (or both), so those are shown just to the left of the oscillators.

Figure 9.37 Click the B button (1) to see how Sound-School's modules are routed. You can follow signal flow visually from left to right and by following the arrows. This is a textbook modular design, so you'll find countless other synths, hardware and software, virtual analog and otherwise, that would match this basic graphic.

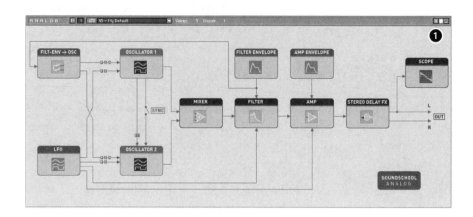

3. The two oscillators are connected to each other, because the first oscillator can modulate the second (frequency modulation), and they can optionally be synchronized.

4. Output from the two oscillators is mixed together.

5. The mixed output is fed into a filter and amplifier, each of which is controlled by an ADSR envelope. The LFO can modulate each of these as well, so there are additional arrows from the LFO to these stages.

6. The final stage is the stereo delay effects.

7. The output of all the above stages is fed to the Scope for viewing and to your stereo output (your speakers).

This isn't just a routing scheme for SoundSchool: it's the classic, textbook routing scheme for almost any traditional synth, even many that use sampled sound. You produce a basic sound via one or more oscillator signal sources, mix those sources together, filter them, apply an amplitude envelope, add effects, and output the result. With that basic routing in mind, you'll be able to figure out most prebuilt soft synths, or construct your own by patching together modules in software like Reaktor (as the designers of SoundSchool did), Max/MSP, Pd, SynthEdit, and so on, or connect modules in the traditional analog style with software like Arturia's Moog Modular.

LFOs

In Chapter 7, you learned how LFOs can create slow sweeping and fast warbling effects like vibrato (when modulating pitch), tremolo (when modulating amplitude), chorus and flanging (when modulating the delay time in a delay), and phasing (when modulating a comb filter). LFOs typically use a simple waveshape as a signal source.

Now that you're a little better acquainted with each of those basic waveforms as they're used as oscillators, let's see what the different waveshapes can do when used in an LFO to perform modulation. Like the filter envelope, the LFO section in SoundSchool has an amount knob and various check boxes that determine which parameters it's modulating (**Figure 9.38**).

Figure 9.38 To modulate your sound using an LFO, choose a rate and waveshape (1), select an amount by which you want the LFO to modulate the destination parameters (2), then check the boxes of the settings you want to modulate (3).

Sine

Sine waves create gradual sweeping effects at low frequencies. Think about the shape of a sine wave: it travels up and down again in smooth sweeps. When you listen to a sine wave at audible frequencies, you can't hear those individual sweeps, because the ear perceives the oscillations as a continuous pitch. At low frequencies, however, when the sine wave is used to modulate something else, you'll hear the individual rising and falling cycles distinctly.

Load Preset 26—Basic Square. By default, its LFO is set to a sine wave and routed to pitch, but the Amount is set to 0. Increase the LFO > Amount to 0.6 and decrease the LFO > Rate to 0.5. Hold down a note, and you'll be able to easily hear and see your square wave oscillator sweep up and down in pitch. (You might want to let go of the note before you get seasick.) Increase the LFO > Rate to 10 and, instead of distinct sweeps of pitch, you'll hear a fast warbling vibrato.

Triangle and sawtooth (ramp up/down)

Like sine waves, the shape of triangle waves travels up and down. But a sine wave spends a disproportionate amount of time at the top and bottom (a bit like a particularly nasty roller coaster), whereas a triangle wave moves at a regular speed from high to low and back again. The difference is subtle, but sometimes audible. With the LFO > Rate still at 10 from the previous experiment, switch the LFO to a triangle wave. You'll hear a change in the resulting pitch, but otherwise the effect is similar to the sine wave. As you decrease the rate again to 0.5, you may notice that although the LFO is still sweeping up and down, the effect is more mechanical than the roller coaster-style sweeps of the sine wave. (Try switching back and forth between sine and triangle waves with the rate at 0.5; pay particular attention to the movement of the square wave on the Scope.)

The triangle wave will start to differentiate itself from the sine wave if you adjust the symmetry of the wave, making it more like a sawtooth wave. Holding a note down, increase the Symm knob gradually. The pitch will begin to sweep up faster than it sweeps down. Increase the Symm knob all the way to 1, and instead of a triangle wave, the LFO becomes a sawtooth wave. When it's used in modulation like this, sawtooth waves are often called *ramp up* or *ramp down* waves because that's the effect they have on whatever parameter they're modulating. For the ramp down effect, reduce the Symm knob to −1.

Pulse

When used for modulation, the pulse wave simply switches between the high and low values, like a quick on/off switch. Return the Symm knob to 0 for a perfect square wave. Decrease the LFO > Rate to 6 and hold down a note. This is an extreme example of pulse modulation, but having the modulated frequency jump back and forth quickly so dramatically isn't musically useful. Decrease the LFO > Amount to 0.02, and decrease the rate to 0.55. Hold down a note again: you've created a simple, automatic trill. (You can edit the Amount and Rate to your liking.)

Random

The last of SoundSchool's LFO modulation sources is a random source, which, as its name implies, outputs a random series of values. To give it a try, continue with the previous example. Switch to the LFO > Random source and increase the Amount. Try routing it to the other parameters as well (Sym, Filter, and Amp) in different combinations. In large doses, the random waveform can be used for special effects. Set to a very small value (0.01 or less), it can simulate an oscillator with tuning drift or make an oscillator sound a little more organic. It's not quite the same effect you'd get with a poorly maintained or dirty oscillator on a piece of vintage gear, but it can provide a twist to a patch design.

Many synths refer to this source as noise instead of random, because random values are typically used to create white noise oscillators.

To review how you can apply all of these settings in patches, see an overview of basic LFO modulations in **Table 9.2**. (Again, these apply to many synths, not just SoundSchool.)

Table 9.2 Using LFOs in Patches

Functions of the waveshapes	
Sine	Sweeps (more time spent at top and bottom)
Triangle	Sweeps (equal amount of time spent throughout value range)
Sawtooth	Ramps up or down
Pulse	Switches between high and low
Random	Random values; noise

Effect of the different modulations	
Pitch	Vibrato
Sym	Pulse Width Modulation
Filter	Wah-wah
Amplitude	Tremolo

For more on these audio effects, see the extended discussion in Chapter 7.

Effects

Many of the effects discussed in Chapter 7 are used not only in mixing and audio production but in synthesis, too. We've already looked at filtering and ring modulation in this chapter. In no particular order, here are some of the other effects typically found in synthesizers and used for synth sound design:

- Delay
- Reverb
- Chorus/Flanger/Phaser
- Overdrive/Waveshaper Distortion
- Multiband EQ
- Dynamics Processors

Hands-on: Warped Delay Effects with an LFO

You've already learned how to create traditional stereo delay effects in Chapter 7. Looking at the effects stage in Sound-School, you should see some familiar controls (**Figure 9.39**): Delay time in ms, Del L-R amount and other stereo phasing controls to manipulate the stereo image, a Feedback knob, and a Dry/Wet control. Using those controls, you can create basic stereo delays.

For a little more fun, you can vary the LFO Rate and Amount knobs, which modulate the delayed signal with an LFO. In addition, although this is undocumented in SoundSchool's signal flow, the LFO waveform is synced to the synth's main LFO in the bottom-left corner of the screen. That means you can get creative, combining LFO modulation of the delay with modulation of other parameters.

STEREO DELAY FX

Delay	Del L-R	LFO Rate	Amount	Feedback	Lowpass	Dry/Wet
63	5	6.85	0.405	-12.5	110	0.33

| Inv L | Inv R | | 180? | Cross FB | | Bypass |

Figure 9.39 SoundSchool's effects section looks like a generic stereo delay at first, but like many analog-style synths, it also has LFO modulation. The LFO Rate and Amount knobs will make this echo more fun.

Load preset 43—Basic Modular Echo. Hit a few notes, and you'll hear a simple stereo delay. Note the routing of the main LFO on the bottom left: since it's modulating amplitude, the sound pulses in and out in sync with the delay. (For an illustration, turn off the LFO > Amp check box and listen to what the same sound is like without amplitude modulation. Switch it on again when you're finished.)

Let's add more LFO spice to this sound. Turn up the Stereo Delay FX > LFO Rate and Amount knobs. (Try some different values above the 9:00 position on each knob.) You should hear a wild, rubbery-sounding echo.

For a variation, combine this effect with an additional LFO effect. Check LFO > Sym and LFO > Filter for a biting, squelchy modulation.

Now let's see what happens when you change the LFO's waveform. Select LFO > Random. The random LFO modulates symmetry, filter cutoff, and the delay. Because it's all synchronized, this gives a rhythmically sequenced sound to the patch, even though all you're really hearing is the impact of a single LFO.

You'll see more exotic processors like vocoders as well, and in the case of some synths, wild morphing and convolution effects. Aside from the possible exception of reverb, you'll usually want control of each of these effects on your individual synth sounds. You'll often combine two or more at a time, for instance, adding both phaser and a delay to a sound, or both chorus and reverb, or distortion and compression.

In the world of soft synths, built-in effects aren't strictly necessary. Since many soft synths are used as plug-ins or (as in software like Reason) are connected to a host via ReWire, it's a small matter to add standard audio effects to the signal chain. Even when using hardware synths, it's not uncommon to plug the outputs of a keyboard into an effects pedal or two.

So why bother with built-in synth effects? They're a convenience. First, there's the content of the effects. Many synths include effects designed specifically for use with the instrument at hand. They might be distinctive effects unique to the instrument or simply bread-and-butter effects you're likely to want (like a chorus or delay). Second, there's the issue of syncing modulation and easy signal routing: if a synth's LFO, for instance, can't be synced to the tempo of the host, you'll need a built-in effect to sync the effect to the synth LFO. (If everything can be synced to host, this is less of an issue.) Third, and probably most important, when effects are built into a synth, your effects settings stay within your synth. If you switch patches, effects settings switch with it.

 Hold the mayo: Soft synth designers sometimes get carried away with built-in effects. Some, for instance, include lavish reverb settings in all their presets, eating up CPU cycles and muddying your sound. Watch for "effects creep" in synth design. It's not a bad idea to turn off all the effects, design a sound, and then turn them back on as desired.

Next Steps

Synthesizer sound design is very much an art, but understanding the basic ingredients is half the battle. Now that you understand what each knob and check box in SoundSchool does and how they impact the sound, you'll find that a lot of faders in other synths look familiar. In addition, because you know some of the basic tools, you can build your own modular instruments in an environment like Reaktor (**Figure 9.40**) or Max/MSP.

Figure 9.40 Behind Sound-School's front panel (top) is a set of interconnected software modules that actually produce the sound ("Structure," bottom). You can view and edit this layer in Native Instruments Reaktor 5. (Photo courtesy Native Instruments, Inc.)

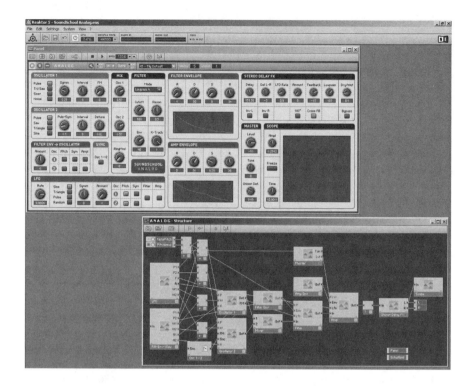

For more advanced discussions of the underlying technologies behind each of these synthesis techniques, check out some of the following books. Of these, Jim Aikin's book is the best place to start for practical programming tips. The others are more academic in tone and challenging for beginners, but even a quick skim can reveal some insights into the nuts and bolts that drive sound design. (The Roads and Dodge & Jerse books are both seminal works.)

- *Power Tools for Synthesizer Programming* by Jim Aikin (Backbeat Books, 2004)

- *Computer Music: Synthesis, Composition, and Performance* by Charles Dodge and Thomas A. Jerse (Wadsworth Publishing, 1997)

- *The Computer Music Tutorial*, edited by Curtis Roads (MIT Press, 1996)

- *Computer Sound Design: Synthesis Techniques and Programming* by Eduardo Miranda (Focal Press, 2002)

CHAPTER 10

Put It Together:
Arrange, Mix, and Master

Now that you've learned about all the components of a project, from MIDI tracks and synthesis to recorded audio and effects, it's time to bring it all together. You'll use arranging features to assemble your finished composition, mixing to ensure that your elements sound balanced and polished, and mastering to prepare your work for distribution.

 Essentials

Put It Together

We'll follow the process of finishing a piece of music, from arranging to mixing to mastering, export, and sharing. Topics include:

- File management, nondestructive editing, and the arrangement view
- Editing, arranging, and beat slicing
- Balancing the elements of your mix
- Surround mixing and delivery
- Mix automation and envelopes
- Mastering and polishing your finished mix
- Sharing your work via different media

Essential Terms

- Beat detection/analysis, beat matching, beat slicing, audio quantization
- Regions; strip silence
- Markers/locators; tempo track; subsequences
- Mixing; mixdown
- Gain; unity gain; metering; over
- Spatialization; stereo; panning and pan pots; surround (quad, 5.1, 7.1, LFE)
- Automation; envelopes and breakpoints
- Mastering; reference mix; bouncing
- Dithering; noise shaping

Where to Start

Learn the basics of your program's arrangement view to arrange the structure of your music. Then focus on listening to the impact of gain and effects in the overall mix for effective balancing of mixed elements.

ARRANGING

With all the raw materials of a song, composition, or other digital audio project in place, the next step is to assemble those materials into a finished form. Part of the appeal of digital audio software is the flexibility with which you can creatively manipulate a project's structure. Traditional composers like Beethoven littered their studios with sketches and scraps of notation on paper. Even a couple of decades ago, arranging with analog reel-to-reel tape involved cutting the tape apart with a razor blade. Digital audio software, in contrast, offers nearly endless "what-if" scenarios. Far from being limited to the structure you created when you recorded your tracks, you have a great deal of compositional control in rearranging materials, from making minor adjustments to radically recomposing your music.

Arranging music can mean adjusting a wide range of different elements, including bass lines and harmonies, chord voicings, and instrumentations. All of these are vital to music, but they're well beyond the scope of this book. What we'll examine here is how you'll assemble audio and MIDI elements into your finished music, arranging them on the timeline of a project in your digital audio software.

Mix Project Files

Audio Files

Project File

A digital audio mix project is a collection of audio files and/or MIDI data. These chunks of sound and notes could include a range of different kinds of content, like looped MIDI patterns and looped audio (as in Chapter 5), recorded vocals, spoken word, instruments, and field recordings (Chapter 6), or MIDI-recorded phrases and soft synth lines (Chapters 8 and 9). The mix project file, or simply "the project," brings all of these pieces together and organizes them into a finished piece of music.

When you make a new multitrack file in your DAW, whether you're starting a new "session" in Pro Tools or creating a new "set" file in Live, you're creating a project file. It's the file that will hold (or refer to) audio files and note data, your arrangement, mix information, and other edits. You'll notice that the size of this file is relatively small, often less than a megabyte. That's because recorded audio data, whether you recorded it directly into your project or imported it from another source, is stored in separate files. (MIDI data is stored in the project file, but, as we've seen, it's very compact.)

Nondestructive editing

Audio files you record or import into the mix project are stored in files on your hard drive, independent from the project file. That way, when you move the audio as represented graphically on the screen or process the track's output with effects plug-ins, you don't directly impact the original audio files. The rectangular blocks you see on the screen in an arrangement view, which act as pointers to the underlying audio files, are called *regions* (**Figure 10.1**).

Nondestructive regions   Underlying audio files
❶   **❷**

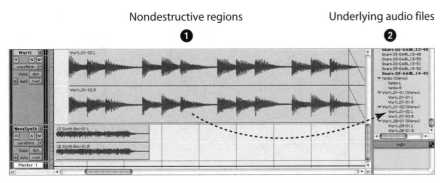

Figure 10.1 The rectangular blocks (regions) you see onscreen in your DAW (1) act as placeholders for audio files (2) stored on your hard drive, as seen here in Pro Tools. You can slice up, alter, and move the regions without damaging the associated file. Your DAW then plays back the mix by streaming the audio from the files on the hard drive or by preloading them into RAM prior to playback.

When separate copies of audio are kept on the hard drive, independent of and unaffected by any edits you make, your manipulations of the audio are called *nondestructive editing*. Editing the audio in the project files has no impact on the original audio files. Your software reads the audio files from your hard drive, so that you hear the audio edits in the mix project. But if you need to go back to the original audio for any reason, you'll find that the files are unchanged.

Certain edits do require modifications to the file. For these, most DAWs automatically make duplicate copies of the file. Automatic duplication can sometimes create redundant files you don't need, so you might routinely take a look at the file window in your audio editor to see if there are files you can delete (see "File management," next page).

Tip: When you save your work, most programs empty the undo buffer, so you won't be able to undo an edit that was made before you saved.

Not all audio tools are nondestructive. Typically, waveform editors like BIAS Peak and Sony Sound Forge edit destructively. That doesn't mean you can't undo changes: most of these programs have multiple levels of undo, so you can use a keyboard shortcut like Ctrl-Z or Cmd-Z on the Mac and reverse changes you've made one by one. Multiple undo and nondestructive editing aren't quite the same thing, though: multiple undo retains a list of actions performed so you can reverse actions later if you change your mind. A program that does nondestructive editing always retains separate copies of original files.

DAWs use nondestructive edits to audio only in certain views. Many DAWs include integrated waveform editors in a "waveform view" or "audio file view." These editors allow you to make edits to individual audio files. Perform a fade-in or trim the end of a file, for instance, and the editor destructively makes that change to the audio file. You'll still be able to undo the change via the undo command until you save your project. You can make a duplicate of the file first if you want to retain an unmodified copy. (Some waveform editor views will even make the duplicate copy for you automatically.)

File management

In a multitrack audio project, you'll probably have many audio files that need to retain their associations with the project file. You might have files you imported from an external source, such as field recordings transferred from a portable recorder. You might also have files you recorded while creating the project, such as vocal or instrumental tracks you recorded onto your computer. You might even have additional audio that was recorded internally from the output of soft synths, if you recorded this audio to a track, or audio imported from a third-party CD-ROM or DVD.

Since the project file only points at these external files rather than including the audio content from them directly, it's important to keep all of the files organized. Most often, when you create a new project, your DAW will create a folder called something like "Audio Files" or "Clips" in which to store these files. Any new audio created in the project will be stored in this folder. You can also automatically copy imported files to the folder, although this feature is often turned off by default (check your DAW's preferences). When importing an audio file into a project, you may see a dialog box that asks if you want to copy it to the folder for the project.

If your audio application can't find associated audio files, it will display an error message and disable that audio content in your mix. (The error message usually reads "disconnected media," "can't find file," or some similar text.) To avoid such errors, make sure all the media in the project is located in the project's audio file folder, and that you move that folder when you move the project. Some applications automatically search for missing files, but of course it's better to keep them organized to avoid this extra step in the first place.

Although keeping track of audio files that are used in your project is important, you may want to unload audio files that aren't used. You might record or import audio that doesn't wind up in your mix, or your audio application might produce redundant copies of an audio file while editing. Most DAWs include file management tools that identify unused audio. Usually, you'll employ these tools when a project is nearly done, so you can delete those files to save hard drive space.

Arrangement View and the Timeline

Audio files and MIDI data form the component parts of a mix. In an arranged song, these are assembled into a whole musical structure. For instance, you might have recorded audio files for a violin part and a piano part and a multitrack mix combining the two. Waveform audio views and MIDI edit views, as discussed in previous chapters, let you work with the components. An *arrangement view* displays a multitrack overview of your mix project, showing how all of the parts fit together over time (**Figure 10.2**).

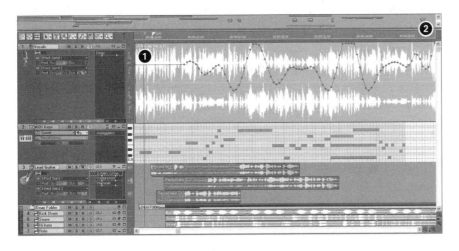

Figure 10.2 An arrangement view (1) displays an overview of different tracks, with MIDI and audio data, as shown here in Cakewalk SONAR. The timeline (2) at the top indicates metrical and/or clock time in the project. (Image courtesy Twelve Tone Systems, Inc.)

Different software, as usual, uses different names for this view. Apple Logic Pro calls it the Arrange window, whereas Pro Tools calls a similar view the Edit window. The features of these windows vary as well. Some applications allow in-line editing of individual MIDI notes, for instance, while others do not. There are more similarities than differences, however. Generally speaking, any window that displays audio and MIDI side-by-side in tracks that run horizontally across the screen and allows basic editing, arranging, and mixing can be considered an arrangement view. Since you can see an overview of your mix, you'll do most of your large-scale arranging in this window, even if you occasionally switch to a more detailed editing window to fine-tune changes.

The *timeline* is the reference to metrical and/or clock time displayed at the top of the arrangement window. It gives a linear structure to your song or other composition. This timeline also shows changes in meter that occur during your song. Changes in tempo are also displayed in the timeline in some programs.

Most digital audio software lets you view and edit your music in familiar, musically meaningful units like beats, bars, and larger sections with names you supply yourself, such as "intro," "verse," and "chorus." You can edit these larger sections to change the overall structure of your music or work at a microscopic level, like individual beats, for finer editing. In this chapter we'll start small and work up to the level of bigger "chunks" of the musical structure.

Slices and Beats in Audio

Let's start by considering audio slices and beats. There are various reasons you might want to work at the level of beats, even when you're arranging your music. You might want to work with beats to match loops for DJ-style beat juggling, remixing, mash-ups, and groove creation. You might want to tighten up an existing performance, for example, to change the rhythmic feel of a bassline or repair slightly inaccurate rhythms in a recorded performance. You might want to reorder the rhythms in a drum part for a creative effect or slice up spoken word vocals. You might want to chop up and reconceive an instrumental part one beat at a time.

Regardless of the aim, working with beats in audio has some special requirements. It's easy to work with beats and bars when you've recorded MIDI to a metronome or when you're working with preformatted loops that contain beat information. (See Chapter 5 for a discussion of loop formats like Apple

Loops, REX, and ACIDized WAV, and how they can be used in music.) But even if it has been recorded to a metronome, audio in a DAW is usually displayed as whole waveforms, so slicing individual beats requires manual work. And on occasion the organic rhythms contained in imported audio or other recorded audio will lack a clear reference to a metronome.

Automatic beat detection features

Audio data isn't inherently organized into specific note or beat events, so the only way to match the flexibility with which MIDI data can be edited is to slice up audio into rhythmic subdivisions and then work with those. To accomplish this, many audio applications can recognize and manipulate beats inside audio using several related features:

- **Beat detection/analysis:** The software detects transients (as would be generated by a drum hit or the attack of a bass note) or other features that indicate likely beat locations. Based on the locations of the transients and other types of analysis, the software "guesses" where beats are located in a segment of audio (**Figure 10.3**).

- **Beat matching:** By aligning beats within the audio to a grid, moving individual beats forward and backward to conform them to tempo, you can match different pieces of audio to a single tempo, irrespective of their original tempo. This feature is commonly used with loops, particularly for DJ-style beat matching, but can be used with nonlooped audio as well.

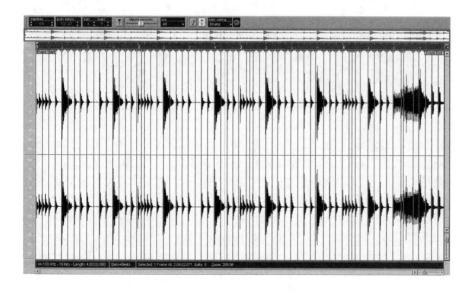

Figure 10.3 Beat analysis, as shown here in Cubase SX, identifies beat locations by applying a detection algorithm to audio. You can then fine-tune the results if needed. Once the beats are identified, you can manipulate audio with as much rhythmic flexibility as MIDI notes.

- **Beat slicing:** Once these beats are identified, they can be (optionally) sliced apart so as to be independently manipulated and/or moved (**Figure 10.4**).

- **Audio quantization:** Some programs can apply rhythmic quantization to the sliced beats from a MIDI track or another audio track, or create a groove quantization template from the unique rhythmic feel of an audio track that can then be applied to other regions. (See Chapter 8 for more on groove quantization.)

Figure 10.4 Slicing audio based on automatic beat detection can save time editing. In Digital Performer, for instance, the Create Soundbites From Beats command converts each identified beat into a separately editable slice, a technique as useful for audio like spoken word recordings as it is for percussion.

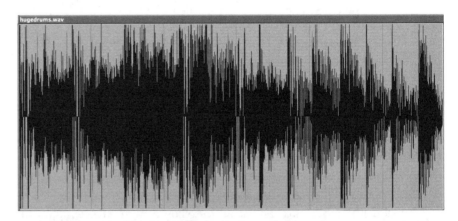

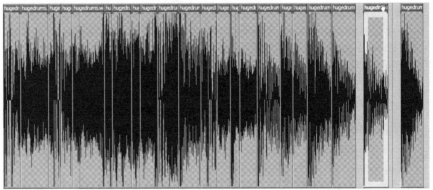

As beat detection, matching, slicing, and audio quantization have grown in popularity, they have become meshed with the audio features in various DAWs. These features tend to be named differently in different software applications: in Digidesign Pro Tools they're located in a separate window called the Beat Detective, in Steinberg Cubase they're collectively called Audio Warp, in Cakewalk SONAR they're grouped into a Loop Construction View, and in MOTU Digital Performer they're called the Beat Detection Engine and located on the Audio menu and in the Soundbite window.

Ableton Live has a unique take on the concept via what is termed Warp Markers and (for automatic analysis) Auto Warp, which are both displayed at the level of clips, although Live lacks audio-to-MIDI and MIDI-to-audio quantization.

Integrated beat detection is growing in popularity, but some stand-alone tools are powerful, too. One of the most popular tools for detecting beats and slicing audio is Propellerhead's ReCycle application (www.propeller-heads.se). ReCycle lets you prep audio in advance for use in another application via the REX file format (as discussed in Chapter 5). Many DAWs can load and play REX files. What makes REX files unique is that each individual slice is associated with a MIDI note, so you can play the slices like a drum kit or reorder and arrange them using MIDI pitches. This affords some unique possibilities, like transposing a MIDI pattern in order to generate a completely different drum pattern. Rather than use ReCycle on a Mac or Windows to create your own prepped audio, you can purchase vast libraries of REX soundware content. ReCycle was the first app to popularize the idea of beat detection and slicing, and some of the tricks that can be done with REX files are not easy to duplicate with any other technology.

How "warping" works

One major advantage of beat detection and slicing is that it enables easier and more accurate "warping" of audio to tempo. Warping is also called "time-stretching."

Changing the tempo of MIDI data is easy: all your audio software has to do is transmit the individual MIDI messages more slowly or more quickly. A MIDI note, for instance, consists of two messages—a note-on followed by a note-off. If the note-on and note-off are ¼ second apart at 120 bpm, at 60 bpm they'll be separated by ½ second. Changing the tempo of audio is much more difficult, however. As discussed in Chapter 5, it's possible to stretch out the audio digitally without changing pitch (unlike tape players and turntables, for which speed and pitch are interdependent). One problem is that you'll stretch out the whole sound, so the hits on a drum pattern will become stretched out and will lose their distinctive, sharp attack. Another problem is that stretching a whole audio wave file at once doesn't discriminate between its individual, internal beats, so those beats may not line up with the tempo of the project. (The beginning and ending of the audio file may be in the right places, but the internal beats may be out of time.)

Warping algorithms slice up the audio, maintaining the transient hits of percussive notes and more accurately time-stretching individual beats. This also means that you can control the lengths of individual beats: by marking the location of each beat, you can move internal beats around or stretch them independently, and the software can accurately match them with the tempo of the music.

Using warping with music

Although the audio warping features of various programs work in slightly different ways, they do share some commonalities:

1. **Set meter, length:** It's easy for human musicians to listen to music and recognize meter and phrase length, but not for software. Generally, you'll have to specify that a given audio sample is four beats long and contains musical content in 4/4 time.

2. **Recognize beats:** The next step is to automatically detect the beats; the software will detect percussive transients and add a marker to each beat (**Figure 10.5**).

Figure 10.5 Automatic beat detection and audio warping features can sometimes make guesses about tempo, but additional controls let you produce more reliable results or correct the application's guesses. Pro Tools' Beat Detective, for instance, provides options for method, for sensitivity, and for specifying information about the content of the audio being analyzed.

3. **Adjust for accuracy:** Some applications let you adjust the sensitivity of this operation to fine-tune its accuracy. Nearly all will let you manually move markers around, relocating marker positions to make sure they accurately fall on beats.

4. **Work with beats:** Once the analysis is done, the fun can begin. You can shift beats forward and backward in time, "beat-match" loops originally in different tempi to a single tempo, or (in some programs) quantize MIDI to audio and vice versa. Since the audio already has the

Slices—not just for drum loops: Despite the beat-oriented names, audio slicing features work well for other instrumental parts, too. You can also try applying your loop construction/beat marker tool to spoken word or vocals for dividing words into slices or (using the Strip Silence function illustrated in Figure 10.7) regions. Once the slicing is done, you can easily reorder, regroove, edit, and arrange.

Hands on with audio warping in Ableton Live: Try out audio warping on the disc, using a sample drum loop for manipulation. See the Live Drum Lesson in the Extras folder.

beats marked, these operations can be performed fairly seamlessly. For instance, you can apply a quantization command to audio as if it were MIDI data, or increase the tempo of the project and automatically speed up warped loops to match.

There are a number of creative applications of this technique:

- **Tighten up performances:** Is the drum take nearly perfect, with just a couple of hits that are a little early or a little late? By slicing up the audio segment in which the hits occur and adjusting them, you can perform delicate surgery on a recording.

- **Change a rhythmic feel:** With an application that supports groove quantization based on audio, you can apply the feel of an audio sample to any other audio or MIDI materials. In the reverse direction, you can apply a groove quantization to audio in the same way you would to MIDI notes.

- **Match loops and other audio materials:** For remixes, resampling, live sampling, or a variety of other applications, warping beats to conform to a synchronized tempo lets you combine audio materials that otherwise would clash rhythmically. Audio files that originally had different tempi, or even audio files that have the same tempo but different grooves or rhythmic feels, can be matched. (See Chapter 13 for more on how you can use these techniques in live performance.)

- **Create regions and markers for arranging:** There are other reasons you might want to slice up audio that have nothing to do with mapping to meter and beat. For instance, you might need to separate the words of a dialogue track. Once the words are defined as regions, you can easily manipulate them individually, applying effects, making certain words louder or softer, or performing whatever other edits you want to make.

Regions

Regions are blocks of data (audio, MIDI, or both) within your larger project. For instance, your project might have several recordings of a horn section, different drum licks, a couple of piano solos, and so on; each of these is a region within the larger project.

If you've worked with looping software, you've already worked with regions. The loops and patterns discussed in Chapter 5 are simply phrases of audio or MIDI notes that are automatically repeated. Apple's GarageBand even calls these blocks of sound or notes "regions," not loops, indicating that they don't necessarily have to be looped. Mackie Tracktion and Ableton Live call these units "clips"; Cubase calls them "parts." Other programs call them sequences or patterns. Here, we'll use the generic term *regions*.

If you're working with audio, each region will usually contain, initially, a single audio file. Each time you record a take or drag an imported audio file into your arrangement, you'll see a rectangular graphic on the screen representing the data, as shown in **Figure 10.6**. To rearrange the audio files, you can drag the edges of the rectangle to stretch, compress, or loop the audio, drag the center of the rectangle to move it forward or backward in time, or drag it up or down to a different track. The exact methods you'll use for these operations will depend on the software you're using.

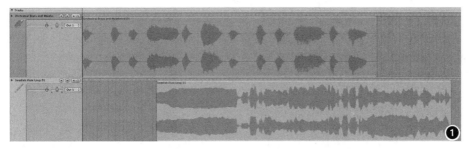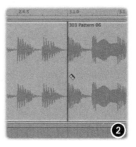

Figure 10.6 A typical display showing two audio regions in Apple Soundtrack Pro (1). This type of interface is now so commonplace it's easily taken for granted. By moving regions forward or backward on the screen, and cutting, copying, and pasting regions, you can more fully control your arrangement—especially with the addition of a razor blade tool to cut regions into smaller segments when needed (2).

Most applications have a razor blade tool or some equivalent for dividing regions into smaller pieces. (Even though few people today have edited analog tape, slicing it with a razor blade, the old analog image remains.) The razor blade tool "slices" the region into two independent sections that can be moved separately.

Nondestructive editing: Nondestructive editing stores audio files separately from the project arrangement; regions in the arrangement define where these files are played.

With audio, razor blade "cuts" are nondestructive. Thus, you could take a recording of someone singing the words "Since my baby left me," divide the audio into the individual words, and create a stuttered track that sounds like "since since since since my my my my . . . ." and so on. Each region would use the data stored in the original audio file of the vocalist singing, and the file would not be changed by your edits, even though you'd see a series of audio regions in the timeline.

Another way to define audio regions is to use a *Strip Silence* command, which defines portions of an audio source as "gaps" by establishing a minimum dynamic threshold and length for a pause in the material (**Figure 10.7**). For instance, you might use a strip silence command to find pauses in a spoken word recording, and then tighten up the gaps between them. Stripping silences can not only close the gap between portions of recordings like vocals, but can also create new regions based on the material between gaps for further editing.

For MIDI data, you can either set rigid metrical points to define regions in terms of beats and bars, or flexibly adjust where regions begin and end. (Some applications, like MOTU Digital Performer, will even let you adjust an automatic sensitivity fader to guess where phrases begin and end so you can make selections more easily.) Once you've defined a region's start and end points, MIDI regions function similarly to audio regions in most programs. You can slice them, move them, copy them, and reshape them at will. The one critical difference is that edits to MIDI regions are usually destructive. If you slice them up or move notes around, you're editing the actual MIDI data, so you may want to copy a MIDI recording to a muted track to serve as a backup before undertaking major edits if you're concerned you might change your mind about the edits later.

 Don't get disconnected: Because arrangements simply point to files somewhere on the hard drive, it's essential that your arrangement not get disconnected from its files. Make sure your application is set to automatically copy files to an audio folder in your project folder, and don't move them once they're there. (This is even more important when you move files around; see "Sharing full projects and collaboration" later in the chapter.)

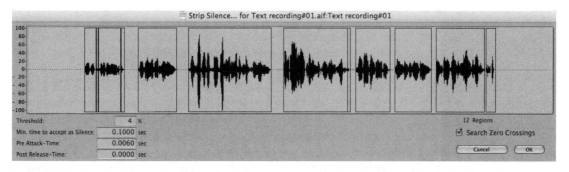

Figure 10.7 The Strip Silence function in Logic Pro creates new regions from an audio file by identifying areas below a threshold as silences.

Markers and Grids

There are likely to be blocks of time in your project that are significant, like a verse or chorus in a song, an instrumental break, a movement in a string quartet, or a cue in a film score. Other blocks of time will be more relative, like those two bars that you want to fix where your drummer got behind the beat. As your project develops, you'll often be working within these specific blocks of time. To work with shorter sections within your overall project timeline, several basic techniques are at your disposal:

- **In/out/cycle:** Using the in and out or "punch" settings on the transport control, you can not only record materials into a specific location, but also edit events within that area. Most applications also let you loop (cycle) the playback of certain time regions, marking them to be repeated temporarily while you make edits and recordings. (The beginning and ending of the looped region are sometimes called in and out points, sometimes left and right locators, as shown in **Figure 10.8**.)

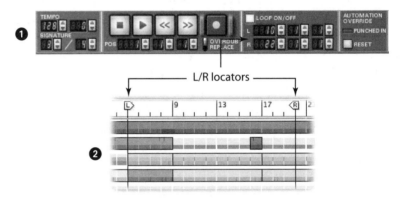

Figure 10.8 Punch in/out controls aren't just for recording: in many programs, they double as a means of defining editing areas. The Left and Right locators on Reason's transport controls (1) can be used for punch recording or for defining an edit selection area in the timeline (2).

- **Snap to grid:** Using your cursor, you can select specific blocks of time by bars, beats, rhythmic values (like eighth-notes), seconds, frames, or other divisions using the *snap to grid* function of your arrangement view or editor. (Depending on the application you're using, this may or may not be available in certain views.) With snap turned on, dragging your cursor to create a selection will increase or decrease a selection by the unit selected, and selected events will snap to the nearest grid location when dragged left or right along the timeline. With snap turned off, selecting is usually accurate to the onscreen pixel, which may be a larger or smaller amount of time depending on how far the view is zoomed in or out. (Some programs display a numerical value as you drag or let you enter numerical values for a selection. Entering values by typing numbers can be slower, but in some situations the additional accuracy makes it worth the effort.)

- **Cursor position:** Another way to get an accurate selection is to set your cursor position to a specific location (usually by clicking your playback cursor), then either drag or use keyboard shortcuts to create a selection relative to that point. For instance, you might set your playback cursor to bar 4, beat 1, and then add the beats after that point to a selection. Most programs also have a nudge command or other incremental selection that lets you move a selection or expand/contract it by a small increment, such as a metronome tick or a video frame.

- **Markers:** Rather than manually entering certain cursor positions over and over again, you can use *markers* to define critical moments in your project and quickly move the editing/playback cursor to them. Markers are often called *locators*, and moving the cursor to a marker is often referred to as "locating" to the marker. Some programs let you snap editing movements to markers, so you can drag chunks of audio and MIDI data so they start at the markers even if the markers aren't on standard rhythmic subdivisions. You can also define selections by using markers (**Figure 10.9**).

Markers also serve a key role when combining sound and video. Since video time uses minutes, seconds, and frames rather than metrical divisions like bars and beats, you'll need to mark moments in the video as landmarks to figure out where critical juxtapositions of sound and image occur. For details of these techniques, see Chapter 12.

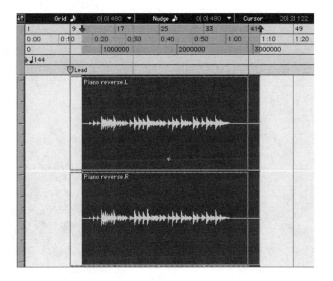

Figure 10.9 With snap-to-marker turned on in your DAW, you can drag regions so their start points line up with a marker, saving some manual labor. (Notice the various time references on the timeline at the top of the Pro Tools Edit window.)

Tempo Track

If your songs never change meter, speed up, or slow down, you won't need a tempo track. You can set a tempo (like 120 bpm) and a meter (like 3/4 time) when creating a song and never worry about either again. But lots of music speeds up or slows down, or changes meter for variety. This is less common in pop songs and dance music than in filmscores, but it happens more often than you may think. A *tempo track* is a track containing only tempo and meter changes. These changes apply globally to all tracks in a song. (If tempo changes were specific to individual tracks, you'd wind up with different racks running at different tempos or different meters—possible in the occasional avant-garde piece, but unlikely in the vast majority of music.)

Tempo tracks are often called "conductor tracks" because they perform a similar role to that of a conductor. A conductor leading a group indicates when to speed up and slow down, and indicates the meter with baton patterns, just as the tempo track affects these parameters for all tracks in a song. Tempo tracks are also sometimes called "global tracks" or "master tracks"; in this case they might also contain other global settings like master volume.

To add tempo and meter changes to a tempo track, you can either manually insert events, or, in many programs, create them graphically with the mouse using envelopes (a technique described in "Mix Automation and Envelopes," later in this chapter). Abrupt changes will appear visually as vertical lines. To create a gradual change in tempo (for an *accelerando* or *ritardando*), you can create a ramp (**Figure 10.10**).

Figure 10.10 In Pro Tools, the tempo track is normally hidden, but click its disclosure triangle (1) and you can edit tempo changes for your project. You can create abrupt changes or draw gradual ramps (2). The conductor icon (3) determines whether the project follows the tempo track or ignores it and lets you set tempo manually.

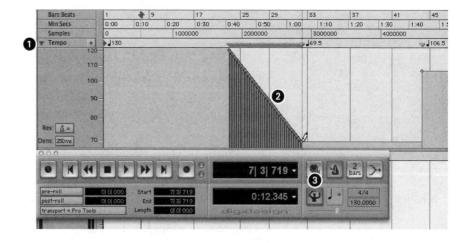

Tempo tracks take on a special significance when they're used to align sound and musical material to the timing of video, as explained in Chapter 12.

Arrangement Markers and Reordering

Many applications have means of organizing the overall order and arrangement of a piece of music. Steinberg Cubase SX, for instance, has a Play Order track, which lets you draw different orderings into a dedicated track to create an arrangement (**Figure 10.11**). When you decide on the best ordering of sections, you can "freeze" the play order, making it permanent.

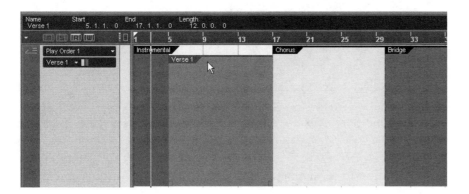

Figure 10.11 Cubase's Play Order track lets you experiment with song arrangements by drawing and dragging different sections. Like the tempo track, it's a separate track that controls the playback of the arrangement.

Other applications may use some kind of arrangement marker or consider different sections *subsequences*, self-contained mini-sequences that are combined to form the overall mix or arrangement. Just as with Cubase's Play Order track, you'll define these larger sections based on the structure of your project, so the chunks might be a "verse" and "chorus" or some other meaningful subdivisions. Like regions, these sections define chunks of data, but unlike regions, they apply to all tracks at once, and represent bigger pieces of the structure. (Some programs even let you use subsequences as a means of organizing multisong sets.)

Ableton Live takes a slightly different approach to this feature using Arrangement Locators. You can add locators to the mix's arrangement in strategic positions (like the beginning of a verse or chorus), then trigger those at any time. This will change the order in which sections of the piece are played, but only during real-time playback; it's not an editing tool. Alternatively, you can form scenes in the Session View comprising different clips and trigger the scenes to create your arrangement. In an onstage situation, this could let you flexibly move through arrangements, improvising as you play. See Chapter 13 for more on creating live arrangements for performance.

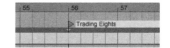

 Jump sections with Arrangement Locators: By mapping Live's Arrangement Locators to MIDI or keyboard keys, you can easily jump to specific sections for editing, or jump through the song structure during playback (from a verse to a chorus, for instance).

MIXING

Mixing is the process of combining all of the sonic ingredients of an arrangement or song, including recorded audio tracks and the playback of software and hardware synths. The resulting sound is the *mix*, the combination of all those elements. In the strictest sense, the mix is defined simply by the relative volume levels of the various audio channels and their spatial placement (either in a stereo field or in a surround monitoring system). But because signal processing has a profound effect on the way you'll hear the mix, you can think of any effects that have been added as part of the mix, too.

Before the advent of computers fast enough to handle digital audio in real time, mixing was handled by a single piece of hardware—the mixer, also called the console or mixing desk. Although hardware mixers remain popular, now that software can perform all the functions of a mixer, there may not be a mixer involved at all. The entire mix may be created in the computer. But the basic concept remains the same. Mixing includes three basic elements:

- **Volume:** The level of each track throughout the arrangement

- **Spatialization:** Panning, the positioning of each track in speaker space (in stereo or surround)

- **Effects:** Levels and settings of effects that impact the sound (particularly EQ settings, since they impact the relative volume of certain frequencies, as detailed in Chapter 7)

The Mixer Fader and Channel Strip

At the heart of the mixer is the channel strip. We looked at the channel strip in Chapter 7 in the context of adding effects, but now let's consider how it functions in the final mix. As discussed earlier, the channel strip is a visual representation of signal flow through each element necessary to mixing: effects (inserts and sends), positioning in stereo or surround space (pan pot), and volume and balancing (the mixer fader). Most channel strips also have their own equalizers, but if an EQ isn't built into the channel strip, you can add it as an insert.

Accurate Monitoring: What You Need, How to Use It

It's a fact of life: eventually your mix is likely to be heard on awful speakers, whether it's someone's computer speakers or car speakers or a live club with a terrible P.A. system. That means you shouldn't mix on high-end studio monitors, since they'll make your mix sound too good, right?

Wrong: you'll want to mix on real studio monitors so that you can hear your whole mix accurately. Good monitors and headphones are designed to be as neutral as possible. Far from sounding "too good," they should faithfully reproduce what's really in your mix.

Consumer-grade speakers tend to sweeten the sound by accentuating certain frequencies. That's the opposite of what you want, because it means you won't have a "clean" reference from which to set levels, effects, and equalization. Worse, inexpensive speakers and headphones lack bass response, which means rumble introduced by leakage or other sources can go unnoticed in the mixing process. (That's an especially big deal when you're making a surround mix, because the low-frequency channel routing on some playback systems can turn a small floor rumble you missed in mixing into a giant, Godzilla-sized boom.)

The ideal monitoring system includes:

- **Good studio monitors:** These should have a decent bass response so you know what's happening at the low end of your mix, and should be neutral in their playback so they don't unfairly sweeten certain registers. If you have both smaller near-field monitors and larger monitors, try switching between the two. This will help deal with ear fatigue and will provide an additional reference as to how your mix sounds.

- **Proper stereo placement:** As discussed in Chapter 3, placing your monitors in an equilateral triangle with your head will help you accurately hear stereo panning. (Surround placement is a bit more complex, but proper placement again is an issue; see a basic description later in this section.)

- **A good pair of headphones:** Occasionally try switching to a pair of studio headphones to get an additional perspective on your mix. Stereo panning, in particular, sounds different through headphones than it does through speakers. Headphones will also give you an additional reference to double-check your mix. You may notice "rough edges" or tiny audio glitches that are not as audible when the music is played through speakers.

You can always test on low-end systems once your mixing is done (see "Mixdown, Mastering, Sharing" later in this chapter), but monitoring on good studio speakers and headphones will ensure that you get the best results from your mix.

Figure 10.12 A fader strip and meter in Cakewalk SONAR. Because the fader controls gain, it's labeled in decibels relative to the input signal (1). The resulting level in power is displayed on the meter at right (2).

 "I can't get rid of the red light!" If a signal is clipping and you still want it to sound louder, you have several options. Compression allows you to reduce the level of the loudest sections, thus boosting the level of the overall signal. Downward expansion won't make the material louder, but it can have the perception of a louder sound by increasing contrast between soft and loud. Also, equalization can impact the perception of a sound. These effects are discussed in Chapter 7.

Adjusting gain

Most people take the mixer fader for granted: that just controls volume, right? Upon closer inspection, you'll see immediately that it's a little more complex: for starters, "0" is in the upper third of the fader, the top is (usually) at +6, and the bottom at negative infinity (–∞) (**Figure 10.12**). That might seem counterintuitive, but it makes sense if you understand what it is that a mixer fader represents.

The numbers printed next to the mixer fader don't actually show how loud the output will be, because the output level is also dependent on what you feed into the channel. The loudness will vary over time as your source sound gets louder and softer. Instead, the fader measures the gain of a signal. *Gain* is a measure of how strong the output signal is relative to the input. When the fader is set to 0 dB, or what is called *unity gain*, the output should theoretically be the same as the input, assuming your equipment is properly calibrated and assuming no insert effects (including EQ) have altered the level before the signal reached the fader. That's why 0 dB is toward the top of your mixer fader instead of at the bottom: 0 dB doesn't represent silence; it represents "zero change" from the level of the input. To achieve silence from any signal, you have to set the output to be infinitely less than the input, which is why the bottom of the mixer fader is labeled –∞.

Theoretically, you should adjust all levels to the 0 dB level as the maximum, and reduce volume (to reduce or fade out a track) by moving the fader downward toward –∞. But all audio systems—digital systems included—have some additional headroom beyond unity gain in which you can increase level without introducing distortion and clipping. (See "Headroom" on p. 187 for a general explanation of the topic.) Usually, 6 dB of headroom is available on each channel strip—not a huge increase over 0 dB but a noticeable one. (Some pro systems offer the option of setting the increase in gain above 0 dB to +12 dB, as you'll find in Pro Tools HD systems.)

All of these numbers are relative until you mix all your channels together. The relationship of the level on individual channels to the mixed level is dependent on the design of your hardware or software mixer. To increase the headroom of the mixed signal, many mixers (digital and analog alike) reduce the gain prior to the final mix to compensate for the fact that the mixed signal will naturally have a greater amplitude when combined than the level of any of the original channels.

You'll need to employ two tools to set the proper level: your eyes and your ears. Using your eyes, watch the level displayed on your individual and master channels. Since these displays are called meters, observing levels is called *metering*. You'll want to watch carefully for an *over*, the moment at which the level exceeds the available signal level. Usually, this is shown by a red light that stays on until you turn it off, to make sure you don't miss the over. As mentioned in Chapter 6, an over in a digital system causes clipping and unpleasant distortion. Metering alone isn't enough, though; you should also listen to the track for distortion and balance.

Grouping faders and tracks

There are times when you won't want individual control over every fader. Grouping faders together lets you manipulate the level of multiple faders at once. For instance, if you're close miking a drum kit, you'll typically have as many as five or more microphones, all associated with the drums. It'd be pretty tedious to have to adjust the level of the kick, snare, hats, and so on individually. Instead, you can adjust the level for all of them using a *fader group* (**Figure 10.13**).

 Pre/post metering: Just as you can insert effects pre-fader or post-fader, you can monitor the level as it reaches the fader (pre-fader metering) or after the fader has adjusted its level (post-fader metering). Pre-fader metering lets you see the input level of the signal, for adjusting input gain, while post-fader metering indicates how hot the signal is in the mix.

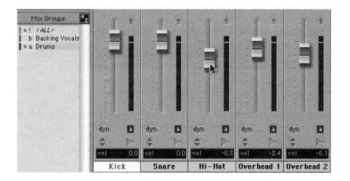

Figure 10.13 A Pro Tools fader group representing the multiple mics for a drum kit. Ordinarily, moving one fader would affect just that fader. When the faders are linked in a group, the entire group will move, and the facers in the group will maintain their relative positions.

Call a group "drums," for instance, and you can control your whole kit at once. (You can always drill down below the group level later, so you could, for instance, tweak the snare level a little while maintaining the overall level of the kit.) Drums are just one example: grouping can help you structure other elements in a mix, letting you manage vocals and other layered sounds. The more complex your mix becomes, the more significant this feature is for keeping your mix manageable. It's especially useful with surround mixing, for example.

Subs and traditional consoles: On a traditional hardware mixer console, you'll often see a set of eight faders called subfaders or subs. Having eight subs naturally facilitates sending channels in useful configurations to 8-track recorders, either in the form of analog reel-to-reel decks or (later) digital recorders like the ubiquitous Tascam DA-88. Now it's not as necessary to set up channels in this way, although it can still be useful to create eight output buses for use with computer audio interfaces that have eight analog outputs.

In addition to grouping channels via fader groups, some programs let you group recorded tracks as well. This gives you control over fades, as with grouped faders, but also gives you mute/play controls for tracks and group control over audio and MIDI edits to multiple tracks at once. You'll find *track folders* (or *folder tracks*) in tools like Steinberg's Cubase and Nuendo, Cakewalk's SONAR (**Figure 10.14**), and Digidesign's Pro Tools (where they're called *track groups*).

Figure 10.14 Track folders for a drum kit in SONAR. Just as fader groups let you link channels, grouping tracks lets you link recorded audio.

Mixing Strategies

Just as the individual flavors of the ingredients in a recipe taste different when they're combined in a pot, individual sounds are heard differently when they're mixed together in the same speaker space. The total is different from the sum of its parts.

Recall that when audio waveforms combine, they cancel and reinforce one another. The audio output can literally change when you add different elements together. Beyond that, your perception of individual elements will change, both in terms of the way your ear perceives volume and frequency content, and in terms of what the combination sounds like artistically (whether the mix is too "busy" or too "sparse").

Fortunately, you don't have to be a trained acoustician to get the sound you want. You're ultimately mixing to satisfy your ears. Some basic strategies will help you achieve the mix you want.

Balancing

Balancing is the art of making all the components sound correct in proportion to one another. The desired proportions depend entirely on your taste, of course: what you want in the "foreground" or "background" of your mix may be quite different from what someone else would do with the same mix. Balancing is simply a means of achieving the desired effect. You'll want to be able to hear each element, but it's also desirable to create the impression that those elements belong together, so the mix sounds like a coherent whole to your ears.

The challenge, whether you're dealing with pan, volume, or effects, is that you can't listen to any individual track out of context and get an accurate aural picture of the results. Ideally, you need to make the most of your adjustments while listening to the entire mix at once. That's part of the reason that you should try to think of the recording/creation and mixing stages as separate tasks, even if you're working in an improvisatory way and making lots of changes to the mix while composing. The temptation when faced with lots of virtual toys, from advanced effects to powerful mixer automation, is to begin adding effects and mixing as you work. It's tempting even for those with a fair amount of experience in studios.

It's better to plan on the early recording, playing, and improvisation phase as being a "roughed-out" version of what will become the final mix. Otherwise, you'll likely wind up with a mix that's overcluttered and has balancing problems created by effects and mixer settings that were adjusted before you knew what the overall combination of elements would be. The compressor setting that sounded great on the vocals alone might destroy the effectiveness of the vocals when they're mixed with everything else.

Relative volume alone, of course, can make a huge difference. Let's start with a simple example: imagine a mix that has no effects whatsoever and is being output in mono to a single speaker. The relative volumes of the tracks determine how the overall balance of components sounds. Ideally, you've already made some adjustments to dynamic level and range. As discussed in Chapters 6 and 7, you probably made these adjustments when inputting and recording the tracks, but you might rough out individual components further with dynamic processing or by changing the overall gain of each.

To change the volumes of the various channels in proportion to one another, there are a few strategies you might use. Some engineers take the extreme first step of setting all the levels to 0 dB and making relative adjustments from there. You won't want to leave everything at the same level, of course, so you'd begin by reducing the parts you want to recede into the background; for instance, maybe the cowbell is a bit too loud initially. Starting with all channels at 0 dB can help "clear the board," but most of us start with the basic levels we set while tracking, which has likely already established roughed-out levels for different channels. Making minute changes to each channel while listening to the full mix, you'll make gradual adjustments until the proportions are perfect. At this point, it's not a good idea to make level adjustments that change during the course of the arrangement. You want to find some level that works reasonably well for the entire mix. From there, you can add up and down adjustments to faders where needed (see "Mix Automation and Envelopes," p. 429).

Listening to a whole mix can sometimes be difficult, especially if you're not an experienced engineer or producer. Using the solo and/or mute buttons, you may want to isolate groups of tracks to identify balance problems. For instance, you might solo the guitar and drums to evaluate the balance between just those two tracks without the distraction of the other tracks, setting rough levels for them. Then, by unsoloing the tracks to hear all the tracks in the mix, you could fine-tune the overall mix again. It's not worth making fine adjustments to individual tracks, though, without listening to the whole mix, because you're likely to wind up making further changes once you hear the whole mix again.

Space and signal processing

What makes various elements fit together is what audio engineers describe as "space." As you listen to a finished track on an album, you're probably aware of the space in the track: the frequency space, the dynamic space, and the localization of sounds in stereo or surround. Within that three-dimensional space, various elements must coexist.

Making use of the available space by mixing elements is not necessarily just a matter of cramming in as much sound as possible: in fact, it's quite the opposite. You'll hear more contrast when elements are differentiated. Even if you want a "full" sound in which the dynamic and frequency range of the mix are both relatively saturated, contrast between loud and soft and between different frequencies will maintain the clarity of each element.

Although you've probably set levels for dynamics processors prior to balancing the mix, you may want to make further adjustments when you're listening to the whole mix at once. Try hitting the bypass button on your effect to hear what the same mix sounds like without processing. In the case of equalization, it's usually best to wait until the mixing stage before adding any EQ at all. If for some reason you did try EQ on individual channels, you may want to try making further adjustments while balancing the mix or even try bypassing EQ to hear how the mix sounds without it.

Dynamics processors and balance

You've seen how dynamics processing can impact the sound of an individual channel, but there's a resulting impact on overall perception of dynamic space:

- **Compressors:** Since compressors reduce the contrast between loud and soft, they make the sound "fuller" at the expense of the sense of space. You may actually want to reduce compression on some tracks to make more room in a mix. Compression isn't always bad, but you should consider how you're using it. This is another reason why it makes sense to initially mix without dynamics processing, EQ, and reverb, and then add dynamics processing and other effects in small amounts while listening to the effect on the mix.

- **Expanders:** By increasing overall dynamic range, an expander can increase the sense of space in a track while maintaining loudness for peak volumes (which is often why people mistakenly add compression in places where it hurts, not helps).

"Squashing" all your dynamics together to achieve greater loudness can quickly overcrowd a mix. You'll want to balance your use of compression with overall dynamic contrast.

Equalization and balance

It's unwise to consider dynamic balance without also considering *tonal balance*, the balance of different sounds in the frequency domain. Too much sound "traffic" in any frequency range can reduce the impact of space. If instruments are "stepping on one another" within a given frequency range, the mix will sound cluttered or confused. You have two basic tools at your disposal with which to resolve this issue: you can use equalization to reduce the sonic energy in certain frequency ranges of certain tracks, or dynamic equalization (dynamics processors with frequency-specific controls) to apply dynamics processing in targeted frequency ranges.

When it comes to balancing a mix, the trick with equalization is to focus more on cutting frequency content than on adding it. The so-called "presence" range, the higher-frequency range around 5 kHz (depending on the instrument), will in fact add audible "sparkle" to a sound. In very small doses, this can brighten a dull-sounding mix. But it's very easy to overdo it and distort the sound of the instruments you're trying to mix, reduce the

You deserve a break today: One of the biggest enemies of good mixing and proper equalization is, believe it or not, working too hard. The problem is, when you listen too long to a mix, your ears fatigue and it becomes harder to objectively judge your work (especially when you're a beginner and balancing and EQ don't come easily). Take a break, and then come back and listen to the same mix a few minutes later. You may be surprised by what you hear. Try turning off your EQ settings to go back to "flat," as well, so you don't lose track of the original source.

sense of "warmth" in a mix (by reducing the perception of the midrange), and create an overcrowded sound. Novices often try to add sparkle to everything by boosting those tempting high-frequency EQs; the result is ear fatigue and a thin, unpleasant, harsh mix.

It's often a sound's overtone content that can cause balance problems. These overtones overlap as you blend multiple sounds together in a mix, causing a lot of competition between sounds. By reducing the amount of competition with precise EQ filtering, you can help different channels coexist more effectively, giving you the full, dynamic sound you're likely trying to achieve.

Rather than warming up a track that sounds too cold by increasing the midrange, for instance, try reducing its presence range. Since our ears aren't as sensitive to the low end, try reducing the very low bass "rumble" area by filtering frequencies below about 40 Hz to make more room for high and mid frequencies in a cluttered track. This is especially useful, in combination with compression, for keeping a bass track from overwhelming the rest of the mix. It doesn't have to mean sacrificing a powerful bass sound: paradoxically, the bass will often "sit" better in the mix with some added compression and a low-end cut than it will without.

The reason this approach works is that, in equalization, each action has an equal and opposite reaction. Cut the harsh high-frequency range (15–20k) and you'll perceive a fuller, warmer sound in the mids. Cut the bass rumble below 40 Hz and you'll hear a clearer bass sound above 40 Hz. Cut the midrange of a dull sound and you'll perceive additional presence in the higher frequencies. Assuming you're starting with a full-spectrum recording provided by good mics, proper levels, and proper placement, you'll be able to accentuate the frequencies you want to hear by reducing other frequency content that's masking that range. The only way to really get good at this is to practice, but by listening to the mix as a whole and making small changes, you'll gradually get closer to the sound you want.

(For more on this topic, see Chapter 1 for details on how we hear, and Chapter 7 for how to use equalization and how different frequency ranges sound.)

Spatialization

So far, we've covered dynamics and frequency range in balancing, but only in one "dimension," as if everything were coming out of just one speaker. That's ignoring the ability to use positioning in a mix. With only two ears, we're able to perceive very clearly where a real-world sound source is located in the 360-degree space around our head. Because our ears are so sensitive, precise positioning of sound in a stereo or surround mix can be a powerful tool.

The local positioning of sound in a mix is called *spatialization*. It's a way of creatively adopting the mix to our perception of direction. Most projects, of course, will at least mix to stereo, giving you left/right positioning possibilities, and increasingly you may be mixing to some form of surround, giving you even more positioning options. Panning in stereo and panning in surround require different techniques, so let's look at them one at a time.

Stereo sound

Stereo uses two channels (left and right) to create the illusion of sound coming from different directions in aural space. As discussed in Chapter 6 (see Table 6.2, p. 172), you can capture stereo information when you record. This works via one of two basic methods. Two mics located at the same position but pointed in different directions can capture different sound pressure levels. Two mics pointed in the same direction but located some distance apart capture the different times and levels at which sound arrives at each mic. These methods can capture a sense of the relationship between the sound source and the listener because your ear can translate subtle information about delay and loudness into the perception of space.

Stereo recording depends on recording natural phenomena into two channels. Stereo mixing goes in the opposite direction: starting with any number of channels, you can mix down to just two channels, controlling the relative amount of each signal that is sent to each channel using the pan pot on the channel strip. Whereas with stereo recording you're dependent on the location of your sound source, with stereo mixing you can determine where you want your listener to perceive the source's location.

Adjusting the perceived position of a sound in stereo space is called *panning*. The word originally comes from film production and the word *panorama*, which is a good image for stereo mixing. The idea is to position sounds into a broad panorama in aural space, so that the space from left to right sounds full, and each sound is distinctly positioned in that space.

To pan the level of a sound on a traditional hardware mixer, you turn a knob left or right; this adjusts a simple circuit called a *potentiometer*, so the pan knob is called a pan potentiometer or, more commonly, a pan pot. Turning a knob left or right is an intuitive way of controlling the left/right position of the sound, so this approach has been adopted in audio software, too. When a channel is panned center, the same amount of signal travels to the left and right mix channels. As you turn the knob left, you maintain the level on the left channel while decreasing the level on the right. As you turn the knob right, you maintain the right level while decreasing the left level (**Figure 10.15**).

Figure 10.15 When you adjust a pan pot, you're really adjusting the relative balance of signal feeding the left and right mix channels. Most often, the pan pot is in the form of a circular knob, as in Logic Pro (1). Pro Tools uses left/right sliders as well as knobs, and shows separate left and right controls for stereo signals (2).

Because of a combination of how we hear and how signals are routed, a steady change in pan position from left to right won't sound entirely even, particularly once it's placed in the mix. The "quarter-turn left" position of the pan pot probably won't sound exactly like halfway between center and panned hard left. Different numerical models determine how much one channel is turned up as the other channel is turned down, so the key is to use your ears. Listen to how the sound changes as you adjust the pan setting. The visual position of the knobs is only a rough indication of how each channel will sound. (Some engineers don't even look at the knobs.)

As with other elements of the mix, there are no definite rules to panning; practices have evolved over time. If you listen to early stereo recordings from the '60s, you'll notice more dramatic use of sounds panned hard left or hard right; to our modern ears, the panning may even sound a bit silly, especially when a track starts out panned entirely to one direction or a sound flips back and forth. This was done, in many cases, because the original master recordings were made with four or eight-track recorders. There weren't a lot of sonic elements to spread around, so positioning (for instance) the drum track to the right in the stereo field gave the mix some semblance of space, which would have been entirely lacking if the drums (recorded in mono) were panned to the center.

In rock and pop, vocals and bass are usually panned toward the center, anchoring the sound. Because drums are usually close miked with multiple mics, it's easy to spread the sound of the drum set through stereo space to accentuate the percussive quality of a track. Guitars can likewise be spread to the left or right if desired.

One conservative approach is to simply pan to re-create the onstage setup of a live band, although few producers stick slavishly to this. Our ears are used to hearing recorded music with artificially adjusted panning. At the opposite extreme, it is possible to overdo the possibilities of stereo. Although it can be desirable to have a source move through stereo space for special effects, particularly in electronic music, it can sound a little strange if a musician seems to float across the stage.

Because our ears are so sensitive, a lot can be achieved with very small increments of panning. Some engineers never leave anything panned exactly center: even positioning a sound just a few degrees off center will make it seem to "pop" in stereo space. With a subtle adjustment, it will still sound relatively center, but more clarified, particularly when listeners hear the whole mix at once.

It's also possible to create the illusion of depth by using level and reverb. In real-world sounds, a source that is more distant will have a lower level, a greater reverb (since you'll hear more reflected sound than direct sound), and weaker high-frequency content. Simply adding reverb to a sound, even without adjustments in level and EQ, will make it seem to recede into the background of a mix. It's yet another reason you don't want to add reverb to absolutely everything. You'll wind up with a muddy mix in which everything gets lost in the background.

Sounds you want in the foreground should be left as dry as possible. But sounds you'd like to place in the background intentionally can be made to seem further away from the listener. In addition to lowering the level slightly (which you'd probably do anyway), add a small amount of reverb with some predelay and (if your reverb's built-in filtering isn't sufficient) roll off the highs a bit. You'll not only achieve the effect with this sound, but you may help create the perception of increased space in the mix, drawing attention to your foreground sounds.

Whatever you decide to do, it's important to use the available stereo space. With your entire mix panned center, you'll have what amounts to a mono recording, because your listener won't be able to perceive much of a difference in space. Start out with your mixed panned center and gradually

Bass and panning:
Our ears are sensitive to direction, but not equally sensitive across the frequency spectrum. We can't hear direction in very low sounds, so it's sometimes hard to tell exactly where a booming bass sound is coming from. For this reason, bass sounds are usually positioned at or near center.

Reverb and depth:
Just as you can adjust balance with faders while mixing, try adjusting balance with your reverb level. Insert a favorite reverb effect on one bus (or two or more buses, if you want quick access to different reverbs). Turn down all the send levels to make everything dry. Then, try gradually adding small amounts of reverb to position sounds "in the background," creating the illusion of front-to-back panning.

position different elements, just as you did with balancing. You may find you need to make subtle adjustments again to level to complete the aural "picture" of what you want to achieve.

Surround sound

Two-channel stereo sound is good at replicating left/right positioning of sounds, but our ears can localize sound from many more directions than left/right stereo can reproduce. *Surround sound* is any sound format that mimics the larger, 360-degree field of sound placement. It's possible to create the illusion of surround imagery using two speakers and various technologies that introduce subtle aural cues, but usually surround systems add additional channels (and speakers). With discrete channels, it's much easier to control the exact positioning of sound and replicate that positioning reliably. For one thing, the sounds will still have spatial separation even if your listeners should turn their heads.

Early surround techniques used four channels in what was called quadraphonic sound. The four speakers were positioned at the corners of a rectangle with the listener in the center. "Quad" never caught on as a consumer music format, however; most setups now use six or more speakers.

The word "surround" has today become synonymous with the various digital surround sound formats used in movie theaters and home entertainment equipment. In home equipment, surround is often configured as a "5.1" speaker setup, consisting of six speakers. (It's really 5 + 1, not 5.1—that's six speakers, not five and one tenth speakers!)

The five speakers are left and right, as in stereo, plus a center speaker, additional left and right speakers at the center or rear, and a subwoofer (**Figure 10.16**):

- **Front left, right, center:** Like stereo sound, surround has a left and right speaker in the front, but it adds a third, center speaker. The center speaker fills in the forward space and provides more detailed positioning of the front sound. In a movie theater, center speakers are positioned behind the movie screen, and much of the content of the dialog (although, ideally not all) is panned center. Mixed properly, the left/center/right balance should be relatively seamless.

- **Side/rear left, right ("surround" left/right):** In addition to the front left and right speakers, surround adds another left and right that can be positioned to either the side or to the rear (or somewhere in between).

The rear speakers give you that "helicopter flying over your head" effect in movie theaters. (Some home theater buffs will zealously overdo this effect by turning the rear speakers up as high as they can, but the idea is for the rear to be a fairly subtle effect.)

- **Plus one:** The "point-one" speaker is technically a subwoofer channel, or *low frequency effects* (LFE) channel. In home theater setups, the actual routing to your subwoofer is a bit more complex, but it's still basically accurate to think of this as the "large explosion" channel. It's the one that handles the low-end frequency range.

Reference listening position

Figure 10.16 A standard 5.1 surround setup (1) includes five speakers plus a subwoofer. Configured for music as shown, the rear channels ("left surround" and "right surround") are angled about 110° from center, with the left and right speakers angled 30° from center. Placement of the subwoofer isn't critical because your ears are less sensitive to the direction of very low frequencies. You can configure a surround panner in your software, like the panner included with Native Instruments' Kontakt sampler (2), to match the setup of your speakers.

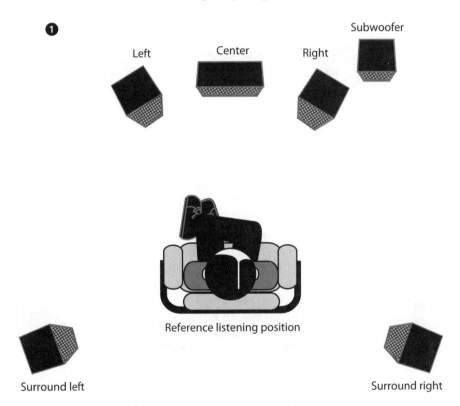

In addition to 5.1 surround, home setups (particularly for gaming) and movie theaters now also use 7.1 or 8.1-channel surround (**Figure 10.17**). You can continue adding channels and speakers along the same lines. Popular current digital specifications allow for up to 14 discrete channels, and technologies have been demonstrated that use dozens of speakers. Of course, with added channels and speakers, the technical requirements become greater, and since you can pan level noticeably with far fewer speakers, the added artistic utility is marginal at best.

Figure 10.17 A typical surround speaker placement for 7.1 surround, as you might find in a home theater setup. While less common than 5.1, 7.1 is growing in popularity even in consumer home setups.

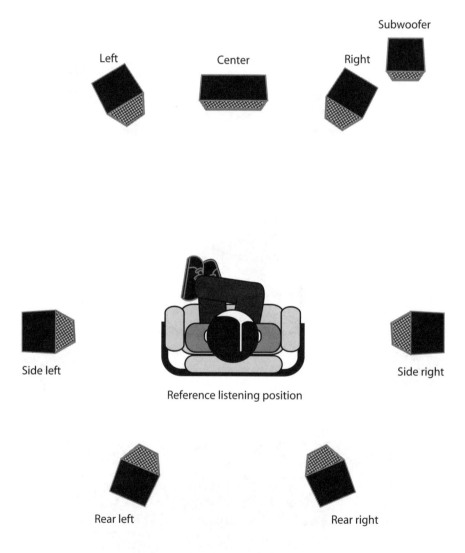

The most common home entertainment setup for TV, movies, and gaming, 5.1 surround has also become the most popular for distributing music in surround. In home setups, 5.1 uses a digital decoder that translates encoded audio stored on formats like DVDs to the different speaker channels. For playing your own digital audio projects on your computer, your audio won't be encoded. You'll simply use your existing multitrack project fed to multiple speakers via a multichannel audio interface. The combination of an encoder and decoder is required only to make surround sound more portable, delivering it via encoded formats such as those found on DVDs. Assuming your audio interface has at least six free outputs, for instance, you'll be able to connect those outputs to the surround speakers. With your software configured for surround sound, you'll use the surround panner in a surround-enabled DAW to pan sound through the surround speakers.

Even the basic 5.1 channels of surround can be a lot to manage in a mix. Stereo mixing is fairly easy to grasp, but surround sound mixing is an art in itself. For music, that art is still evolving, since only a tiny number of tracks have been mixed in surround in comparison to the decades of music history mixed to stereo. If you're having difficulty understanding why musicians should care about surround mixing, pay attention the next time you're listening to music in a concert hall, rock club, cathedral, or other venue. You may be surprised at the amount of sound that can be heard around the space, not just in a frontal, left/right field.

Delivering surround sound

Encoding formats are used to deliver surround sound on formats like DVDs, video games, and movies. To use these formats for your own multichannel content, you need an encoder. The playback device (whether it's in your living room or in the local Cineplex) uses a decoder to separate the audio back into discrete channels and route it to speakers. The major competing formats for surround encoding are Dolby Digital (www.dolby.com), DTS (www.dtsonline.com), and Sony Dynamic Digital Sound or SDDS (www.sdds.com). These brand names apply to slightly different formats used in home entertainment and professionally in movie theaters and other venues. (Lucasfilm's THX, contrary to popular belief, is not a format; in addition to various THX-branded technologies, the THX label is a certification for systems as an assurance of quality.)

The two basic components to surround mixing are panning configuration and encoding. Panning configuration simply requires that you set up your panning environment in a surround-enabled DAW, and then pan your tracks accordingly (**Figure 10.18**).

Figure 10.18 Surround panning requires a specialized panner that can represent 360° space (1), as shown here in Cakewalk SONAR. (Notice the extra columns on the LED meter that are needed to represent all six channels.) SONAR's surround-capable effects include the Sonitus:surround panner (2), which lets you choreograph the motion of sound through surround space.

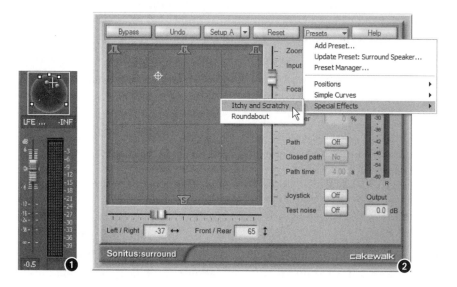

Most surround-capable DAWs provide options for the common configurations, like 5.1, 7.1, and 8.1. To take full advantage of the surround environment, you'll also want surround-sound plug-ins, such as those bundled with applications like Cakewalk SONAR, MOTU Digital Performer, Digidesign Pro Tools TDM, and other DAWs. (You'll even find some instruments capable of surround, like Native Instruments' Kontakt sampler.)

If your mix will be played exclusively on a computer with a multichannel interface, you're done. More likely, you'll want to give someone the mix on a video or audio DVD, or some other format that requires that it be encoded. This means you need encoding software to translate the audio into a format for the targeted delivery medium. Encoders are rarely included with DAWs, although you will find them bundled with video applications like Sony Vegas (the bundled AC-3 encoder) and Apple Final Cut Pro (the bundled Compressor encoder; **Figure 10.19**).

You don't have to be working on a big-budget video production to want to encode to Hollywood-style digital audio formats; you might just want to give your surround mix to friends to play on their home DVD player. Dolby Digital encoders are now bundled with $100 CD/DVD burning software like Roxio's Toast Titanium (Mac) and DigitalMedia Studio (Windows). These burn Dolby Digital-encoded surround mixes (or simply high-definition stereo mixes) on audio DVDs that you can play on any home DVD player. You'll still need a receiver capable of decoding the digital surround sound, but the vast majority of consumer receivers now include surround features as standards, so if your friend can watch *Titanic* in digital surround, your audio DVD should work, too.

 Joysticks and surround: Some surround plug-ins support standard joystick inputs—as in the same joysticks used for gaming. The joystick is designed for 360° control, ideal for surround panning.

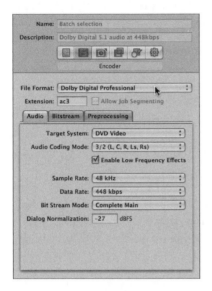

Figure 10.19 Expensive hardware used to be required to encode Dolby Digital sound, but now your PC or Mac can do the job. Apple's Compressor includes Dolby encoding for stereo and surround; presets will guide you to the settings you need for your target medium.

Mix Automation and Envelopes

Now you've seen how you can mix in software exactly as you would on an analog console, by manually adjusting individual faders and knobs (either with your fingers, using a control surface, or with a mouse). So far, all of those changes have been "set-it-and-forget-it": they've applied to a whole song with no changes. But what if you want to make changes in relative levels over the course of the song? For example, you might want the guitar track to be relatively quiet during the vocals, but much more prominent during an instrumental solo. Mixing changes of this sort can, again, be handled manually while the song plays. But performing complex mixes with a mouse is likely to be difficult or impossible. Making manual adjustments of the sliders in a control surface is prone to error, and control surfaces are expensive.

Fortunately, computers offer a far more convenient alternative. Automation and envelopes let you make adjustments in the mix and have them performed automatically. There are two basic ways of doing this—by recording moves manually, and by editing envelopes. Some programs provide one or the other, and some provide both. You may be able to record fader moves one at a time manually with the mouse and then have them played back automatically, or you may be able to create a graphic envelope that will control mixing changes. Such an envelope will typically be displayed on top of or immediately below each audio track.

An automation system typically records not only fader volume level, but other parameters as well, including:

- Pan

- Solo/mute

- Effects send levels, wet/dry level, effect enable/disable

- Plug-in settings, including individual parameters for soft synths and effects

By recording these parameters as automation data, you can create complex mixes and make further changes in your arrangement.

Recording automation

If you're comfortable with the physical gestures of moving faders and knobs directly, you can record mix automation data by recording these physical movements directly into your project file. Because the recorded data "automates" these physical gestures, the process is called mix *automation*. Recording automation is a bit awkward if you're dragging faders with a mouse, but it's an ideal method if you have a control surface for making adjustments to hardware controls. For instance, using a motorized control surface like the Mackie Control, Digidesign Command|8, or even an inexpensive surface like the Behringer BCF2000, you would record each fader slide and knob twist, then play it back with your sequence (**Figure 10.20**). Motorized controls will move unaided automatically and snap to the right position if you move the playback locator to any point in the mix. (You can mix using a mouse, but you'll probably have to go back and edit the data later. You can also use a nonmotorized control surface like the faders on a music keyboard, although you won't have the convenience of the faders automatically following the mix data you've already recorded.)

Figure 10.20 Mackie's Control Universal is a popular choice for controlling software mixes because of its broad out-of-the-box compatibility (1). Simply select it in the settings for programs like Ableton Live (2), and you'll have instant, motorized control over mixing settings in your software without touching your mouse (3).

The basic process for recording automation in many DAWs is

1. Enable automation for each track you want to record. (You may also need to specify what type of data you want to record, like volume, pan, plug-in parameters, etc.)

2. Set the automation settings to make sure you don't overwrite important data. For example, your program may let you set punch-in and -out points so as to record new automation data only within a specific area of the arrangement. Other automation recording options let you control when automation is recorded, so that existing settings are preserved until you adjust a fader or knob to make a change.

3. Press play to begin recording automation. In many programs, you won't click the Record button in the transport controls; that button is intended for recording MIDI and audio. If you only need to record automation data, you will play back the mix using the Play button on the transport. As long as automation recording is enabled on each channel, your adjustments will be recorded.

4. To gradually layer automation, leave playback on loop. (This is especially helpful if you find yourself running out of hands during playback!)

5. Play back your project with automation playback enabled, and all your automated changes will be reproduced with the mix. (Automation playback settings are usually available on a menu separate from the automation recording enable/disable switch, although they may be automatically turned on by default when you enable recording.)

Figure 10.21 Mix automation settings in Digital Performer. To use automation, you'll need to turn on playback/recording of automation data and select an automation recording mode.

When you enable automation, you may be given a choice for how the data will be recorded, and when and how it will overwrite default levels and existing automation, as illustrated in **Figure 10.21**. The names for the different recording modes aren't immediately intuitive, but fortunately most major DAWs use similar basic terminology:

- **Overwrite/write:** Overwrite mode (or auto-write or simply "write" mode) is the simplest form of automation recording. From the moment you hit Play to the moment you hit Stop, you'll be deleting any existing automation data in any track for which automation recording is enabled and replacing it with whatever fader moves and knob tweaks you make. (If you leave a fader in place, it will simply replace any existing level with the position of the fader.) *Overwrite example: You want to create or redo the fade-in and level changes on a track; you click Play, and create new levels from scratch.*

- **Touch:** Unlike overwrite, a touch record mode only records automation as you make an adjustment. When you release an automated control, it snaps back to its previous value. (You may be able to adjust the rate at which it snaps back.) *Touch example: You want to adjust the volume of a keyboard solo down a little bit, but adding compression would be overkill, so you click Play just before the solo, pull down the fader during the solo, and release it once the solo is done.*

- **Latch/autolatch/x-over:** Like touch, latch mode starts recording when you first touch a control, but it doesn't snap back to the original level when you let go. It continues to overwrite any existing data until you stop playback. (The useful X-Over variation in Cubase SX works the same way, but automatically stops recording any time you cross existing automation data to preserve the original automation.) ***Latch example:*** *You decide to fade out a guitar track, so you wait until you want the fade to begin, push the fader down (triggering latch mode recording) and then leave it down once the fade is done, releasing the fader. You'll also generally want to use latch mode on controls like pan, where it would be unusual for you to want the control to revert to its original position when you let go.*

- **Trim:** Some programs (including Cubase SX, Digital Performer, and Pro Tools HD) add a fourth major mode designed to make adjustments to existing volume automation data. (It doesn't make sense for other data types, so it's limited to volume only.) Instead of writing data directly, the trim control centers the volume fader, so any move upward increases the existing data, and any move downward decreases the existing data. (In Pro Tools HD and Digital Performer, trim can operate in touch, latch, and write modes, just like other automation.) ***Trim example:*** *A fader automation move sounds a little too quiet, but you like the curve of the fades, so you enable trim touch and push up the level to add more volume.*

These modes are found in programs like Pro Tools, Digital Performer, Logic, Cubase, Nuendo, and SONAR, but not all applications have this many automation options. Reason, for instance, simply has an automation record enable with an additional override control that you can punch in/out manually. (In other words, Reason uses overwrite mode by default.) Ableton Live takes a still more simplified approach: in place of a separate automation control, controller motions are recorded whenever the main record toggle on the transport is active. Automation only becomes active when you record. (Although Live doesn't call this mode "latch," that's effectively what it is.)

Drawing envelopes

In the world of digital audio software, you're not limited to the position of physical faders and knobs. Most applications also provide the ability to draw automation changes graphically, using what are usually called *automation envelopes*. Like envelopes in synthesis, automation envelopes cause a change in a parameter over time. Unlike the simple envelope shapes in synthesis, automation envelopes can contain dozens or even hundreds of segments and are created using specialized drawing tools.

Various programs provide various tools for drawing automation envelopes. The simplest way of drawing envelopes is to click or double-click to create breakpoints (**Figure 10.22**). The *breakpoint* represents a significant value, like the bottom or top volume level of a fade. The program interpolates intermediate values between breakpoints, either as a straight line or as a curve. (If you've worked with visual software like video and motion graphics software, you'll know that "keyframes" work the same way.) Breakpoint editing is sometimes called "rubber-banding" because in many applications you can drag the line between the breakpoints to reshape it into a curve, just as if it were a rubber band. Some tools also let you freehand curves or draw in specialized shapes like random, wave shapes (triangle, square, sine), and other curves.

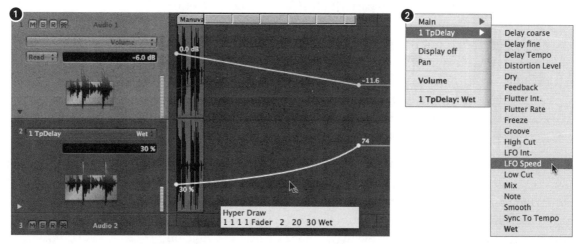

Figure 10.22 Mix automation envelopes in Logic Pro. Breakpoints define begin and end levels; the ramp in between can be left as a straight line or bent into a curve (1). You can control almost any parameter, including individual settings in an effect like the Tape Delay (2).

To create a simple volume fade-in, for instance, you'll create an initial breakpoint at the bottom level (−∞ dB), and then add a breakpoint a few seconds later in the timeline at the level to which you want to fade (e.g., 0 dB). Using those two points, the DAW will automatically ramp the volume from the bottom value to the top value.

Breakpoint editing is important even if you prefer to record automation manually first. By editing breakpoints you can fine-tune automation onscreen after it's recorded. You can view existing automation data in most tools as breakpoint envelopes, so you can easily adjust points up and down (in level), left and right (in time), and create or remove points to add or reduce automation details.

Envelopes aren't limited to volume mix automation. You can record envelopes into tracks for other settings, like plug-in parameters. Some programs also give you additional control of envelopes at the level of regions or clips. These region/clip envelopes are especially fun to use when they're beat-synced. You could, for instance, beat-sync a change in an effect level, or have a sound pan left and right in time with tempo, or make subtle changes to the timbre of a soft synth. You'll find tempo-synced clip/region envelopes in tools like Ableton Live, MOTU Digital Performer, and Cakewalk's SONAR and Project5.

These techniques can also apply to MIDI data and overlap with MIDI production techniques. (For an example of MIDI envelopes in Ableton Live, see "Hands-on: Recording and editing MIDI clips" in Chapter 8.)

MIXDOWN, MASTERING, AND SHARING

Once you have your mix in place, your project should sound exactly the way you want it to. But for others to hear what you've done, they'll need your multichannel setup and exact speaker configuration. Since that isn't likely to be practical, a few additional steps will be needed.

Mixdown is the process of taking all the tracks in your project, whether there are 14, 29, or 128, and combining them into a single digital audio file that contains the same number of tracks as your listener has speakers. Mixdown creates a digital audio file that replicates what you hear as the output of your master faders. If you're recording to stereo, which has two channels (left and right), you'll mix to two tracks. The left and right master channels, fed to your left and right speakers, are recorded as the left and right channels of a stereo audio file. If you're recording for surround sound, you'll mix to four tracks (for quad), six tracks (for 5.1 surround), eight tracks (for 7.1 sound), or however many tracks you need for each speaker of the surround configuration.

In addition to having the right number of channels for the number of speakers, you'll want to think about what those speakers might be. You could just mix down your tracks to a new file and be done, but you'd be taking a big risk. All the mixing you've done has probably been on a single pair of speakers, plus a pair of headphones. But that setup doesn't take all your listeners into consideration: will your audience be listening through computer speakers while on the Web? An audiophile speaker system? A cheap boom box? A TV? A portable player through earbuds?

Mastering is the process of fine-tuning the finished output tracks for their target medium. It's the "icing" on a finished mix, the adjustments that make your track sound as satisfying to people who listen to your audio in other environments as it does to you in your studio. You can perform mastering in a DAW by mixing down to some number of channels and adding effects before export, or after export in another program.

In some cases, you actually shouldn't do any mastering. Mastering for professional CD distribution generally needs to be done by a *bona fide* mastering engineer if you can afford it. In this case, you should leave your tracks as unaltered as possible, reducing mastering and EQ effects to a bare minimum. Of course, in the nondestructive world of digital recording, this isn't such a big deal: if you need to produce a quick one-off demo and want to add some sweetening to the sound, all you have to do is duplicate your project file and add whatever effects you want. You can still give an unmastered version to a mastering engineer later on. But since many people can't afford to hire a studio and engineer for other projects (like a band demo or quick song), you can try some light mastering on your own.

Don't try this at home: If you're planning to have a CD pressed commercially or are producing tracks for other commercial distribution, don't do any mastering. Leave that to the trained professionals.

Reference Mix: Beta Testing for Audio

By the time you're nearing completion of your project, you've probably listened many, many times to your mix. Ideally, you've tried alternating between headphones and monitors, and, if you have multiple speakers, between different sets of speakers. But it will still be difficult to hear your mix in a fresh way or to know what it will sound like outside the controlled environment of your studio.

The single most important step you can take is to try out rough mixes on different playback devices to see how your mix really sounds. This rough "beta test" mix is called a *reference mix*. Listen through the door from the next room. Put your mix on your iPod or MP3 player and listen on the bus. Pull that old cassette Walkman out of storage and listen on that. Play it back on your awful internal laptop speakers. Listen in your car with the windows rolled down. Try playing through the internal speakers on a TV if you're outputting to video. If your studio is equipped with a subwoofer, turn it off, or listen on a small stereo with bookshelf speakers.

"Mastering" for Live Performance?

Traditionally, mastering is the process of preparing sounds for a permanent medium, like a CD album or broadcast (as on FM radio.) Now that you can take your whole studio onstage and perform with it, the equation has changed.

Many of the fundamental techniques described in this chapter can be used if you're performing with your laptop live: you may want to add basic dynamics processing to your master track, for instance, to make it sound better on a particular house P.A. system. The fundamental concept of mastering—adjusting the overall output sound for the delivery medium—remains the same. Best of all, by using audio effects in software, you can rely on your computer alone without having to carry expensive, weighty hardware effects.

If you're running soft synths through a host, you can sweeten the overall sound by bussing to effects. You might try adding a Compressor II device to your Master track in Ableton Live, for instance, or taking advantage of the MClass Mastering Suite in Propellerhead Reason (**Figure 10.23**). Part of the advantage of playing live with a laptop is that when you get to a venue and discover your mix sounds awful on the P.A. system, you can make a quick adjustment during sound check and save the show. (For more tips on live performance, see Chapter 13.)

Figure 10.23 The MClass Mastering Suite in Propellerhead Reason, shown with a typical gentle mastering setting. The Mastering Suite has "mastering" in the title and includes typical mastering effects like EQ, compressor, dynamic maximizer, and stereo imaging, but that doesn't mean you can't use the same effects live onstage.

After hours or weeks of listening under what we'll hope are the optimal conditions in your studio, the goal is to hear the mix as it would sound under poor or simply different conditions. A well-conceived mix should hold up under both circumstances. If your listening tests reveal deficiencies, you'll want to make adjustments. For instance, if the bass is overwhelming on other systems, it may be because your physical studio or your speakers are swallowing the bass, causing you to crank it up in your mix to compensate. Mids are often naturally emphasized on inexpensive speakers, meaning you may want to add additional space in the midrange. Overwhelming highs are usually the result of overly aggressive EQ or a studio monitoring situation that underrepresents the high frequencies. If you've made your mix sound good in a variety of listening situations, you've probably resolved any outstanding problems.

Effects for Mastering

It's common to use certain kinds of effects to make adjustments to the overall balance and character of the mix. Just as you wouldn't want to make dramatic changes to the color of a feature-length movie at the end of production, these effects are generally very subtle. If you've read Chapter 7, you're already familiar with most of the effects used in mastering. You'll just employ them a little differently when they're impacting a whole mix instead of individual channels. The ideal mix wouldn't need mastering; the mix itself would be perfect. In the real world, that seldom happens, but applying effects at the mastering stage, since it applies to all channels, is more like painting with a broad brush. That's why you don't want to overdo it.

Routing mastering effects

When manufacturers refer to a "mastering effect," they usually mean one that's designed to be applied during the last stage of the mixing process. But an effect doesn't have to be a "mastering effect" *per se* for it to be useful for mastering. Any effect can be used for mastering, as long as it's applied to the whole mix at once. You can do this in several ways:

- **In your main mixing project:** If you want to add effects as part of your existing multitrack project, add the effects to the master bus, the main left/right bus that you're recording as the finished mix. When you export the finished audio, the effects will be included. You can also create a separate bus expressly for the purpose of trying out mastering effects, so that you can A/B between the dry mix and the "mastered" mix.

- **In a separate project for mastering:** To create a new project file specifically for the purpose of mastering, create one stereo track (or surround track, if it's a surround project) containing the final mixdown audio, and then add effects to that. Export a bounced mix from your original project, mixing down to either stereo or surround. Then import that mix into a new project and add whatever effects you like. (Most DAWs provide a special "mastering template" for this purpose.) Export the finished recording again to create your mastered version. This method works especially well if you want to apply the same limiter to several tracks at once, but don't want to leave your DAW and its built-in effects.

- **In an audio editor or mastering/authoring application:** If you'd rather add mastering effects to audio tracks outside your DAW after they've been exported, import the unmastered mix into your program of choice and use its internal effects (**Figure 10.24**).

 What makes mastering effects special: Effect designers may add special characteristics to effects intended for mastering by reducing distortion, producing higher-quality (and therefore more processor-intensive) results, and providing additional controls for fine-tuning and tweaking. Other than that, the term "mastering effects" refers more to how you apply effects like dynamics and EQ than to which effects you apply. Careful use of parameters often means more than choosing some sort of magic, "silver bullet" mastering processor.

Figure 10.24 As an alternative to adding effects as inserts on your master faders in your DAW, you can add them after the fact in a CD authoring and mastering application like Apple's WaveBurner (part of Logic Pro).

Generally speaking, you won't apply different effects amounts to the left and right channels, although there are occasions when this is necessary, if the balance of one side or the other needs adjustment. In that case, create separate effect buses for left and right.

Equalizers

Equalization to the master left/right channels can improve the tonal balance of the mix, if used very sparingly. Assuming you've made the proper changes in the mix, and to specific channels, you'll only need to make minor changes to the sound overall. Make small adjustments and listen to your settings for a minute or two to see how they impact different portions of your source material before making a decision. Your ears will react differently to a setting after about 10–30 seconds than when you initially heard the mix.

For a basic sense of what an overall tonal balance should sound like, many people refer to the symphonic sound—the full musical range of a symphony orchestra. It's a frequency range that's large, balanced, and generally pleasing to the ear. The original *Star Wars* movies used the sound of this frequency range as a kind of special effect. Alfred Newman's old mono-only 20th Century Fox theme is immediately followed by a full-range stereo recording of a tutti orchestral chord (with added percussion sparkles for a little extra high-frequency content). This symphonic range isn't just an effective reference for classical music. It's balanced across the "musical" range of acoustic instruments and works quite well for a wide variety of musical genres that have nothing to do with orchestras or classical music (or even acoustic instruments for that matter). Even rock, pop, and jazz engineers, working with a very different instrumentation, often refer to the "symphonic reference."

Balanced properly, a good recording should have an orchestral effect. That's why it's important not to boost any one frequency range too much: adding to a certain range will diminish the perception of the strength of a contrasting range. Conversely, you can often boost the perception of one frequency range by diminishing another. For mastering, a gentle change like the one shown in Figure 10.23 can warm up or increase the presence of a recording. (See Chapter 7 for more details on the effects of EQ on different ranges.)

Certain musical genres (like dance music, reggae, hip-hop, and others) emphasize certain ends of the frequency range more than others. Once you've learned how to get a basic balance, listen closely to recordings you like, and pay attention to biases within the frequencies used. A Schubert piano trio, death metal album, vintage Motown recording, and techno track are (not surprisingly) going to have very different characteristics. You can either match the sound by ear or take advantage of software features like "EQ matching" that can analyze the spectrum of a recording and set an equalizer to match it.

When listening to your reference of choice, keep in mind that microphone choice and placement impacted the sound, not just a blanket EQ setting after the fact. To fully re-create the sound you're hearing, you'll have to reproduce these decisions as well as you can in addition to choosing the right equalizer settings.

Dynamic range

As with equalization, most dynamic manipulations are applied to individual channels, not to the mix. That means it's most important when mastering with these processors to make smaller changes, so that the impact on the mix is not too great. The purpose of compressors, limiters, and expanders for mastering is to balance out the dynamic range for the target medium and to impact the perceived loudness of the resulting mix.

There are several widely held misconceptions about compressors and mastering:

* You should always use a compressor when mastering.

* Compressors are the best way to make a mix sound louder.

* Compression is necessary to make a mix sound good on cheap speakers.

* You need to add compression to make a mix "safe" for playback.

All four assumptions are incorrect. First, although some kind of dynamic manipulation is common in mastering, it doesn't necessarily have to be a compressor; limiters and upward expanders are options, too. Second, although compression does increase the perceived loudness of a mix, it does so by reducing the dynamic range, which can make a mix sound artificially "squashed" if too much compression is used. Third, "safe" playback has nothing to do with compression: digital audio has a fixed maximum peak, and if you're trying to prevent a spike from damaging audio equipment, you'll want a limiter, not a compressor. (Also, you'll want it on the playback equipment, not the mastering software.)

Heavy compression—called *brick-wall limiting* because it produces a dynamic range that resembles a brick wall—is used in commercial broadcast media. The increase of this kind of limiting is very controversial among engineers, because the resulting sound loses the contrast in dynamics that makes music and audio sound exciting to our ears. (You've heard the results in the squashed, unnatural sound of FM radio and TV advertisements.) The trend over the last 20 years has been to apply more compression to popular commercially released CDs—to the disappointment of many audiophiles and engineers.

There's no reason to apply lots of compression while mastering under the misguided belief that it's necessary or that a track will sound "unprofessional" without it. Only use it if you actually like what you're hearing.

What's a "maximizer"?
Although the name sounds like some sort of unusual aerobics exercise equipment, maximizers (also known as "dynamics maximizers") are simply specialized limiters. They make an input sound louder by increasing the level with make-up gain.

Most people simply want to create a mix that will sound loud and exciting, and can sound good on speakers other than studio monitors. Maintaining a broad dynamic range on lesser speakers, for instance, often requires less compression, not more. Your mix will naturally sound more compressed when you play it on a car stereo or boom box than on your monitors, because those speakers are less capable of producing a wide dynamic range.

Your best bet is to apply extremely light compression, or more likely limiting, to reduce only the loudest peaks of the mix. The make-up gain of the processor will then be able to increase the overall gain of your source, making it sound louder or "punchier." This is a delicate process, because you're losing some audio fidelity by reducing dynamic range, but light compression or limiting can often work well. As always, try testing each version of the mix and listen carefully to the change that results.

In some cases, when we say we want something "louder" what we may really want is more dynamic contrast, so expanders are sometimes the right tool for sculpting the dynamic range during mastering.

Stereo imaging, exciter/enhancers, and other "icing"

Although equalization and dynamics processing are the most common two forms of processing for mastering, some additional effects can be added for more "icing" on the finished mix:

- **Stereo imaging:** Stereo imaging processors are specialized processors that widen the perceived sound of a source in stereo space. Unlike a pan pot, the source is always a stereo signal (hence, these are considered mastering effects). Generally speaking, particularly if you're a novice at mixing, you should focus first on broadening the stereo field through the careful use of panning on different channels rather than looking to a stereo effect to magically correct problems in the original mix.

- **Exciters/enhancers:** Exciters and enhancers add small amounts of distortion that give additional "sizzle" or "sparkle" to a sound. (The term "exciter" is trademarked by Aphex Systems [www.aphex.com], but the effect has become so well known that many people refer generically to exciters rather than using the nontrademarked term "enhancers.") Theoretically, these processors are intended to restore harmonic content that's damaged or lost in the recording process, originally due to the limitations of analog recording media. They "restore" this content by adding harmonically related distortion. They should be used sparingly in mastering, since they work better on individual channels, but some engineers will swear by an especially high-quality exciter.

- **Bass boost:** The best way to increase the sound of your bass is to manipulate compression and EQ for an individual track, but there are effects designed to increase bass on the full mix. For most types of music, a bass boost is not necessary, but for dance music production and other genres that exaggerate emphasis to the bass spectrum, you will probably want to give it a try. You'll also find that some high-end bass boost effects are able to perform fixes to the low end of a track without introducing much distortion. If you use a bass boost, make sure you're monitoring with a setup that has a powerful subwoofer; emphasizing the bass can bring out problems like rumble and leakage that would otherwise be inaudible.

Further reading:
Mastering Audio: The Art and the Science (Focal Press, 2002) is an extensive, practical reference on the techniques of mastering from seasoned pro Bob Katz. It's fairly technical and geared for engineers, but it goes into greater detail on how mastering works, scientifically and musically.

Bouncing and Exporting

Once you have your mix sounding the way you want, you'll need to export the mix as a file (or split files) containing 2-channel stereo or multichannel surround. *Bouncing* in digital audio software means mixing together the outputs of all active channels in a selected region and saving that output as a new audio file (**Figure 10.25**). This feature is usually called "bounce," "bounce to disk," or in some cases simply "render to disk" or "export." It really involves two major steps: mixing together outputs, including any effects, and writing the result to a file format of your choosing.

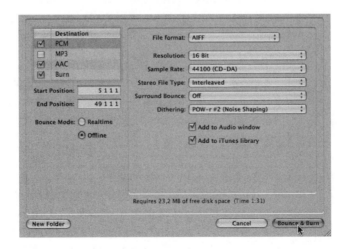

Figure 10.25 A typical bounce dialog lets you export audio to a range of formats. Logic Pro's bounce feature lets you bounce to several formats and burn to CD using one command, and includes high-quality dithering and noise shaping as well.

Here are some of the major options you'll usually be given in the bounce dialog:

- **Region:** If you don't want to capture the entire project length (or if you have a lot of empty bars at the end), set the beginning and end of the material you want to bounce. You'll define the region either by using an active selection (a selected area of the project on the screen chosen by dragging your mouse to highlight it) or by setting start/end points in the bounce dialog, depending on how your DAW works.

- **Source channels:** Some applications let you manually route the channels you want bounced by selecting specific outputs as the bounce target. (You can use this option to easily "print" individual submixes or groups to create an *a cappella* track with no vocals for backing or practice, for instance.)

- **Destination channels:** This option lets you select whether you want to bounce to mono, stereo, or some surround format.

- **Bit depth and sample rate; dithering:** You'll need to choose a bit depth and sample rate that's appropriate for your target medium. For instance, if your project was created in 24-bit/192 kHz sound but you're mastering a CD, you'll need to bounce to 16-bit/44.1 kHz. Dithering can help maintain the fidelity of the original recording when reducing bit depth; more on that in a moment.

- **File format and type:** Here you can choose the output file format, such as AIFF/PCM, WAV, MP3, WMA, AAC, and so on. Many DAWs now let you bounce to multiple formats at once, so if you want to export to your iPod and burn a CD simultaneously, you can save some time.

- **Real time vs. offline:** You may be able to choose whether you want to bounce in real time, playing the output of your bounce, or let your computer render the file as quickly as it can offline with no playback. The advantage of offline rendering is that it's faster. With a fast CPU and light processing, you might render a 15-minute, multichannel mix in just a few minutes. Why would you want to force the playback to go slower? By bouncing in real time, you can listen to your mix to double-check one last time for errors. You can also hook up a real-time recorder like a CD recorder to make a backup or additional copy of the mix. Neither of these tasks is essential, but if you want that one last listen while you bounce, doing it in real time can be helpful.

- **Batch and additional options:** Whereas bouncing was once limited to creating one file at a time, other options are now available in many DAWs, like bouncing multiple files at once, simple batch processing tasks, and even automatically burning a track to a CD or adding files to your iTunes library. These features are unlikely to replace dedicated tools for batch processing and CD mastering, but they may suffice for simple chores.

Dithering and Export Quality

Digital systems have to round off sampled values to discrete numbers. The greater the bit depth, the more values are available to which the samples can be rounded. (See "Quality in the Digital Domain" in Chapter 1.) But what happens if you go from a greater bit depth (with more "grid lines" for dynamic levels) to a lower bit depth (with fewer grid lines)? The digital audio system will have to round off the numbers to different values, reducing the dynamic range. As discussed in Chapter 1, that introduces rounding errors at the bottom end of the dynamic range. These errors are heard as audible harmonic distortion. In other words, areas of a recording that are quieter (lower-level dynamics) will sound noisier when the bit depth is reduced. (See "Digital distortion" in Chapter 7 for examples of employing this creatively, as with Ableton Live's Redux effect.)

The easy solution would be to never decrease bit depth, but that's not practical. Audio CDs require 16-bit depth, for instance. One alternative is to always set your project depth at 16-bit, but that doesn't work well, either. There are many benefits to adding effects and processing at higher bit depths even if the final output medium has a lower bit depth. Some 16-bit projects use 24-bit audio internally (either for internal processing or the audio interface), as on Pro Tools LE and HD systems, for instance.

You need a way to decrease bit depth without adding distortion. You can't eliminate the errors, but you can cover up the audible distortion by using *dithering*. Dithering reduces the perceptibility of the distortion introduced by reducing bit depth by adding random, low-level noise to the downsampled signal. The result is that we perceive less noise during quieter passages because the errors are randomized rather than being harmonically related to the signal. The resulting recording sounds better.

Noise shaping is a related technique. Technically it's not dithering, but shares the aim of reducing audible noise. Noise shaping shifts the frequency range

Dither only once:
Multiple dithering will add distortion rather than reduce it. So dither only once as you're reducing bit depth, since the bit depth algorithm will add dithering prior to bit depth reduction.

CD medium:
Red Book-compatible Audio CD

CD target format:
Stereo, 16-bit, 44.1 kHz

CD tools:
Built-in tools on Windows and Mac, as well as specialized CD authoring and burning software. On the Mac, examples include Roxio Toast with Jam (www.roxio.com), Apple WaveBurner (included with Logic Pro), and BIAS Peak (www.bias-inc.com). On Windows, examples include Sony Sound Forge 8 (www.sonymedi-asoftware.com), Nero (www.nero.com), and Cakewalk Pyro (www.cakewalk.com).

of the noise created by rounding errors into a range in which our ears are less sensitive, so we're less likely to hear the noise. (You'll often see noise shaping grouped together with dithering in audio software.)

Many DAWs will give you the option of dithering and/or noise shaping when you export to a lower bit depth such as 16-bit. The most popular algorithm for both high-quality dithering and noise shaping is a proprietary algorithm called POW-r, or Psychoacoustically Optimized Wordlength Reduction. You'll find POW-r bit reduction algorithms built into programs like Pro Tools, Logic Pro, and SONAR.

You should turn on dithering any time you're reducing your recording from a higher bit depth to a lower bit depth in order to produce a final output file. (Dithering more than once can add distortion, so if for some reason you need to downsample more than once, wait until the last time to add dithering.) Dithering filters sometimes offer additional options (like noise shaping or straight dithering), but because these will have different impacts based on source material, the best way to work with these choices is by trial-and-error, so you can find out which option you like best. If your application doesn't support dithering, you can export as 24-bit, for instance, and then add dithering and reduce bit depth using another program. (Many audio editors, such as BIAS Peak and Sony Sound Forge, as well as CD recording tools like Roxio Jam, include dithering algorithms.)

But keep in mind that you can't reduce bit depth first and then add dithering or noise shaping: dithering is performed by the audio program prior to bit reduction.

Sharing Your Work

Once you've successfully bounced a mixdown of your work and mastered it, you're ready to deliver it in your medium (or media) of choice. Each has different associated technical and format requirements, and specialized tools for creation.

CDs

The standard format for audio CDs is called Red Book or Compact Disc Digital Audio (CDDA). (For more information, see the official CDDA site at www.licensing.philips.com.)

Contrary to popular belief, if you author a CD and burn it in a computer CD drive or CD recorder, you're not creating a Red Book CD. Technically speaking, you're creating an Orange Book CD. This is the standard format for recordable CDs, but it's designed to be compatible with standard CD players for audio playback. That's not terribly important to know; if you decide to produce a commercial CD, you'll need to work with a commercial production house that will specify their own requirements for how you provide audio. (You can be fairly sure they won't be printing your CDs on an internal CD-R drive!)

Your CD burning software will offer you a choice between a data CD format (a CD-R that can be read only by a computer), an audio CD format (the type that is compatible with audio players), or a hybrid format that contains data for computers and audio for CD players (**Figure 10.26**). For simple audio playback, choose the audio CD format.

What's PCM? PCM, which stands for Pulse-Code Modulation, is a means of encoding digital signal that underlies many digital audio formats (including both AIFF and WAV) and most storage formats like audio CD and DVD (although not Super Audio CD).

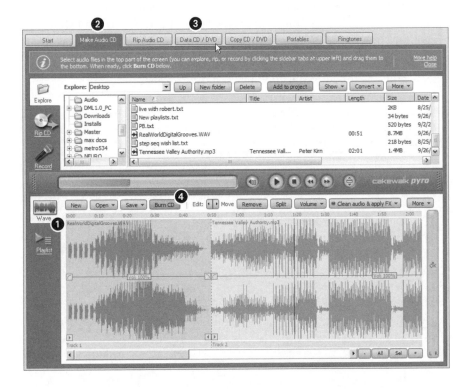

Figure 10.26 Hybrid CDs let you store both audio content readable by an audio CD player and additional files readable by a computer. In Cakewalk's Pyro, for instance, place audio tracks (1) in the Make Audio tab (2), just as you normally would, and then add other files in the Data CD/DVD tab (3). When you select Burn CD (4), Pyro records a disc containing the audio and the files.

The hybrid format (sometimes called CD-Extra, CD-Plus, or Enhanced CD) allows you to add data files to an audio CD. Those files could include music videos for your band, PDF "liner notes," Flash animations, or any other file that's readable by a computer. This data will be invisible to standard CD players but will appear on Mac and PC computers. (Macs are compatible with PC volumes, and Linux is read-compatible, so your best

Mind the gap: Putting space between tracks is important for determining the flow of the album. It's one reason it's worth using a specialized CD authoring tool (many other programs simply default to a value, usually two or three seconds). Try different gaps for different songs based on the feel of the music. Then burn the whole CD and listen to it all at once to see if the gaps you chose work well.

bet is to format the data volume for the PC to ensure cross-platform operation.) Creating a hybrid CD is usually as simple as dragging file content to a folder that will be used for data, and separately dragging audio tracks for the audio CD portion. Virtually all Macs and PCs now properly display the data, and virtually all CD players will correctly ignore the data and play the audio.

You'll find CD burning facilities built into Windows and the Mac OS, and even in many DAWs, but there are advantages to taking the time to author a CD separately. Dedicated tools will give you additional control over crossfades (for continuous blends between tracks, if desired); the lengths of pauses between tracks; and meta-information added to the CD like index numbers (for references within a track) and CD text (displayed on the LCD of a CD player) (**Figure 10.27**). Applications like Sound Forge, Peak, and WaveBurner double as editing and mastering tools, so you can polish the rough mix from your DAW and author your CD in a single program. (Each of these programs also includes built-in effects and supports third-party effects plug-ins for additions to your mastering arsenal.)

Figure 10.27 Full-blown CD authoring tools like Apple WaveBurner let you arrange all your materials on your disc, set pauses and crossfades between tracks, and add CD text to be displayed, among other options.

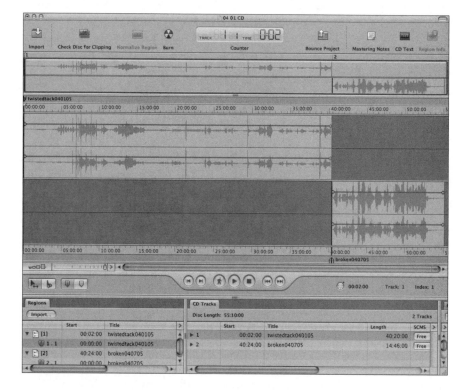

Countdown to zero: CDs can have zero gaps between tracks (for continuous playback between tracks) or some other small amount. You can also define a negative countdown prior to the beginning of a track, but the gap must be at least two seconds.

Many CD burning tools also include basic DVD facilities. They typically lack tools for sophisticated DVD video menus and advanced audio/video encoding, but if your needs are simple, they may suffice.

DVDs

CD authoring is a simple process: there's just one audio format (PCM, 16-bit/44.1 kHz) and the "authoring" required is basically adding a few audio tracks and burning. Not so with DVDs, which support a variety of formats, require specialized tools for certain kinds of encoding, and involve menu design for videos that can rival Web design in complexity.

Focusing on the audio side, though, there are some constants. You first need to distinguish between DVD-Video, the format that's playable by all consumer DVD players, and DVD-Audio, a specialized format that requires a specific player. Unless you're authoring DVD-Audio for a DVD-Audio player, odds are what you're recording is really DVD-Video, even if it's called an "audio DVD" (**Figure 10.28**). The latter usually just means a disc intended for DVD players that contains audio content only.

Figure 10.28 Roxio Toast can record audio to DVDs as well as CDs. Technically, the discs it burns are DVD-Video discs, even though they're audio only—not to be confused with DVD-Audio, which is a specialized format. Technical details aside, the advantages of the music DVD it burns are higher-quality audio, greater length, and compatibility with standard DVD players.

 DVD media:
DVD-Video (most common), DVD-Audio (rarer)

DVD target format:
Uncompressed AIFF or encoded/compressed file (usually MPEG2-compressed or Dolby-encoded); typically 16-bit/48 kHz or 24-bit/96 kHz (192 kHz for DVD Audio)

DVD tools:
Specialized DVD authoring and burning software, including the DVD burning facilities in many consumer CD/DVD creation products. On the Mac, examples include Apple DVD Studio Pro and Roxio Toast Titanium. On the PC, examples include the Sonic Solutions product line, which ranges from under $100 consumer DVD burning to pro authoring, costing tens of thousands of dollars (www. sonicsolutions.com), Roxio Easy Media Creator (www.roxio.com), Pinnacle Studio (www.pinnaclesys.com), and various products from Ulead (www.ulead.com).

DVD-Video supports a variety of audio formats, but the most common are PCM and Dolby Digital (AC-3). PCM is the same format employed by audio CDs. For DVDs you simply use a different bit depth and sampling frequency, usually either 16-bit/48 kHz (instead of 44.1 kHz as on CDs) or 24-bit/96 kHz. *Dolby Digital AC-3* is a special compressed format that can handle both stereo and surround channels (typically 5.1).

So if DVDs are bigger than CDs, why do DVDs use a lossy compressed format? The reason is that video is a file hog; add to that the need for additional channels for surround and the audio gets squeezed. Dolby AC-3 is specially optimized to compress audio for this application without a significant loss in fidelity. Unlike PCM, Dolby Digital sound has to be encoded with a specialized application; this is built into some DVD tools or bundled in the form of Dolby's own A.Pack software.

You can see why DVDs have more appeal than CDs, even for audio-only content. DVD players are now ubiquitous, as are cheap consumer audio setups with digital stereo and surround. Using PCM audio on a DVD, you can either burn a much longer stereo audio recording at 16-bit than you could with a standard audio CD or burn a higher-quality recording (up to 24-bit/96 kHz). Using Dolby Digital, you can encode surround sound, provided you have Dolby Digital encoding software. (That saves you the much more significant cost of hardware; on the Mac, for instance, you could use the $100 Roxio Toast Titanium instead of hardware costing thousands of dollars.)

Other formats are competing for the next generation of content. These include the rival formats for high-resolution audio, SuperAudio CD or SACD (www.superaudio-cd.com) and DVD-Audio. Support for the new formats may be found in high-end audiophile equipment as well as built into game systems like Microsoft's Xbox 360 and Sony's PlayStation 3. Higher-resolution video also has rival formats, Blu-ray (www.bluraydisc.com) and HD-DVD (www.dvdforum.org).

Despite the confusion over formats, audio for the new formats is much the same. With the exception of SACD, which uses a technology called Direct Stream Digital (DSD) in place of PCM, you'll use many of the same encoding formats for the new media. Additional space means that you can also use Dolby Lossless for higher-quality surround on Blu-ray, but PCM and AC-3 will work, too. As these formats gain popularity, consumer-grade audio burning software will become available as well—sometimes in advance of the hardware burning tools. (Apple released HD-DVD support in DVD Studio Pro before a drive was available to burn the disc.)

Online distribution

Uncompressed files are far too large to easily transmit and distribute online, so you'll need one of two solutions: either a compressed format that can be downloaded quickly, like MP3 or WMA, or a streaming server that sends audio to a computer in tiny pieces rather than all at once.

Online media:
Files for download or a streaming media server

Online target format:
Windows Media, Apple AAC/QuickTime, OGG Vorbis, Real, MP3

Online tools:
Most audio programs include basic conversion tools. Mac/Windows tools designed especially for each of the major online formats include Apple QuickTime Player (www.apple.com/quicktime), Apple iTunes (www.apple.com/itunes), Microsoft Windows Media Player and Windows Media Encoder (www.microsoft.com/windows/windowsmedia), Real Networks RealProducer (www.realnetworks.com), and various open-source/free tools for Ogg Vorbis (www.vorbis.com).

Downloadable formats are the easier of these two methods to use: all you need is a tool to convert from the uncompressed file (most likely a bounced AIFF or WAV file) to a compressed version (such as MP3, Ogg Vorbis, Microsoft WMA, or Apple AAC). Most DAWs include at least one of these formats, and many of the programs available from Apple, Microsoft, Real, and others are free to download, at least in a limited basic version. It's not always as easy to use the free program as the more advanced pro applications with batch processing, but the price is right.

Using iTunes on Mac or Windows, for instance, you can convert an AIFF or WAV audio file (or CD audio) to MP3, AAC, or Apple Lossless files (**Figure 10.29**). Set the format you want in Preferences > Advanced > Importing, drag your file into the Library, and once it's imported, drag it out to a destination folder. This task will become tedious if you're converting a lot of files, but for an occasional conversion job, it's fine, and the formats will play back using the QuickTime Player or most Web browsers.

 Batch processing: Performing one or more functions on a whole group of files at once (a batch of files) rather than manually processing them one at a time is called batch processing. Audio editors often include batch processing for converting and adding effects to files. On Windows, for instance, Sony's Sound Forge can script file conversion and effects processing tasks as a batch process. On the Mac, Apple's Soundtrack Pro can automate conversion, edits, and effects via Automator and AppleScript.

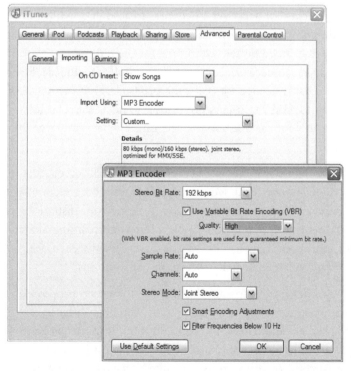

Figure 10.29 iTunes offers an easy way to encode compressed files for free on both Windows and Mac. The options in its built-in importing facility are typical of most MP3 encoders. Bit rate determines the bandwidth of the compression engine, although you'll get different results with different compression formats.

Downloadable, compressed files offer several advantages:

- **Easy creation:** Basic encoding is included in most DAWs; specialized tools are often inexpensive or free. Saving as a file is a simple conversion process.

- **Easy playback:** Using their existing Web browser or digital music player, virtually anyone can play back the music after downloading it without having to worry about varying network performance and other issues.

- **E-commerce:** It's now possible to sell downloadable music in place of CDs.

The major disadvantage is that your listener must wait to hear the track until the file has downloaded completely. (The one exception is an audio file embedded in a Web page. Formats like Flash, QuickTime, Windows Media, and Real can all be used with automatic "instant-on" features so they begin playback while the file is downloading.) For instant delivery advantages, as you'd have with radio broadcasts, the other alternative is streaming. *Streaming* sends sound in tiny packets of data over a network. Instead of downloading an entire file, waiting until it's finished, and then playing it, the client computer loads these packets into a buffer just in time for the music to be played. To account for variations in network bandwidth, this buffer includes a few seconds more than what is needed for real-time playback. So if the network slows down, the sound won't immediately stutter. (This is more or less what the CD player in your car does, so that the music won't stutter when the car hits a bump.)

The major challenge with streaming is that it requires special server software called the *streaming server*. Real, Microsoft, and Apple all have competing commercial servers. If you're comfortable with server administration, various servers are open source and free: Apple's Darwin Streaming Server (http://developer.apple.com/darwin), the Icecast server (www.icecast.org), and VideoLAN (www.videolan.org) are three popular solutions.

More likely, you'd rather have someone else manage the messy proposition of server administration for you. Fortunately, most Web hosts offer inexpensive streaming servers and handle the configuration. If money is tight, you can upload your music to a free, shared solution like Nullsoft's Shoutcast (www.shoutcast.com) or community sites like Yamaha's Player's Paradise (www.playersparadise.net) and electronic music community EM411 (www.em411.com).

Both streaming and downloading employ compression schemes for removing data from sound files to save space. Most of the time you'll be using lossy compression methods, so you'll need to make decisions to balance audio quality with file size or stream bandwidth.

Bit rate, measured in kilobits per second (abbreviated kbps or kbit/s), is the most important relative measure within any given compression format. Bit rate is a measure of the overall bandwidth of the compression algorithm: it's a determination of how much data is contained in a file or flowing through a stream each second. The higher the bit rate, the higher the quality, and the larger the file or stream.

The problem with bit rate as a measure is that not all compression formats are created equal. Apple's AAC format, for instance, is a licensed application of the technology used in the Dolby Digital audio on DVDs; it's more highly optimized than the older MP3 format. As a result, an encoded AAC file at 128 kbit/s should sound as good as or better than an MP3 file encoded at 160 kbit/s, all other factors being equal. For this reason, your best bet for audio fidelity is to use the more recent formats, like the free Ogg Vorbis, or the latest compression schemes from Apple, Real, and Microsoft. Since the newer formats sometimes aren't as broad in the players and browsers they support, you may still want to offer MP3 as an option for maximum compatibility.

Once you have selected a format, bit rate is an excellent relative measure of quality: although it's hard to compare a 128-kbit/s AAC to a 128-kbit/s MP3, you can safely say a 192-kbit/s AAC will sound better than a 128-kbit/s AAC. Which settings you use will depend on your source material, the available space on the hard drive where the files will be stored, and your taste, so you'll want to estimate how much space you can spare and listen to some different settings to find the one that sounds right to you.

Certain parts of a file require more bandwidth for high audio fidelity than others, so one way to make a compression algorithm more efficient is to employ Variable Bit Rate (VBR) encoding. As the name implies, VBR changes the available bandwidth depending on the source instead of using one constant bit rate throughout. It must analyze the audio to do this, so you'll sometimes see 1-pass or 2-pass VBR. Two passes allow the algorithm to more accurately account for variations in the source. In addition to VBR, some encoding tools (including even the lowly iTunes) include other options for increasing fidelity, like filtering out low frequencies that can exhibit noise.

 Going lossless:
Choosing audio formats seems like a choice between extremes: either reduced audio fidelity and smaller files, or full audio fidelity and larger files. Lossless compressed formats offer a middle ground, reducing file size without reducing sound quality. Popular formats include Windows Media Lossless, Real Audio Lossless, Apple Lossless Audio Codec (ALAC), and Ogg Free Lossless Audio Codec (FLAC). For an extensive comparison, see Hydrogen Audio's Lossless Wiki (http://wiki.hydrogenaudio.org/index.php?title=Lossless_comparison).

Promoting and Selling Your Music Online

One major advantage of online distribution is that it offers an alternative to CD sales, and it can make money without physical shipments. If you've already signed with a label, it's up to your label to get you on an online store like iTunes, MSN Music, or Rhapsody. But if you're self-published, you can sell your own music.

Turnkey solutions for Web-based musical promotion are proliferating. In addition to online sales brokers like CD Baby (www.cdbaby.net) and hosting services like GarageBand.com (not affiliated with Apple), there are new tools evolving if you'd prefer to use your own site. Jamroom (www.jamroom.net) lets you build your own Web site for sharing your music; it's as cheap as $19 for individual users and even includes support for streaming files. If you want to make money from downloads, you can pair a site like Jamroom with EasyBe (www.easybe.com) to create your own online music store or the Weed revenue-based file-sharing service (www.weedshare.com). EasyBe even creates an online store in your existing site.

MP3 remains the *lingua franca* of online distribution, and services like EasyBe allow sales of MP3s without copy protection, ensuring maximum compatibility with different platforms and portable devices.

Sharing full projects and collaboration

To exchange files in progress for collaboration, you'll want more than just an "end-result" mixdown of your sound. You'll need raw tracks, so you can easily make changes to individual parts.

If your collaborator uses the same software, you're in luck. To maintain maximum compatibility, you'll want to reduce or eliminate the use of third-party plug-ins (unless you have some agreed upon or freely available selections). A program like Propellerhead Reason, for instance, becomes very useful if both you and your collaborator have copies, because you'll have an arsenal of effects and instruments in common. (Otherwise, you'll have to bounce the audio output of effects and instruments that are exclusive to your setup, which will leave your collaborator unable to edit the original MIDI and audio.)

You'll also want to make sure you include any recorded audio files as you send the project back and forth. (See "File management," earlier in this chapter.) In Ableton Live, you can "Save Set as Self-Contained" so that all of the audio files being used in the project are located in a single folder. If your program doesn't give you this option, double-check file locations so your collaborator isn't treated to a barrage of "file not found" or "media disconnected" errors when opening your work.

Sending big files back and forth tends not to work well over email, so investigate Web-based file services or try setting up an FTP account. (If you don't have your own Web site, you'll find that many Internet providers include Web/FTP space with their service, so this is worth looking into.) You may also want to compress audio tracks to a format like MP3, and then

---

 Interchange Formats

For exchange of file information between applications from different manufacturers, you'll need a format that ensures critical information like fades and timing can be imported and exported. This is an issue in particular when working with video and audio, because audio production and video production specialists have to collaborate, each using a different program. (The audio person might work with Pro Tools or Logic Pro, for instance, whereas the video person might work with Avid or Final Cut.)

You'll need to check the specifications of each program you're using to find the format you need. The most widely supported format is called OMF, but you may encounter a number of other competing formats, each (strangely enough) with its own archaic three-letter acronym:

- **OMF (Open Media Framework):** Developed by Avid (www.avid.com) in 1991, the OMF format is especially popular for use with Avid video and Digidesign Pro Tools audio systems. Because interchanges between those systems are common, the format is supported by a variety of DAWs.

- **AAF (Advanced Authoring Format):** AAF is a cross-platform format maintained by the AAF Association (www.aafassociation.org), an industry group intended to promote and develop the format. Because its SDK is open source and free, AAF also has wide support; much of the code for the format was contributed by Avid, and Avid video systems and Pro Tools aggressively support this format.

- **MFX (Material eXchange Format):** MFX is similar to AAF, with efforts to make it an industry-standard format. It's actually closely related to AAF, developed in part by the AAF Association with the Pro-MPEG Forum, providing AAF-like functionality with smaller files.

- **XML (Final Cut Pro):** Because AAF and MFX contain XML-formatted information, it's possible to add proprietary data to the file formats, as employed by applications like Final Cut Pro. You can exchange XML project files between Logic Pro and Final Cut Pro, for instance.

decompress them when they reach the other side. As long as you maintain uncompressed versions on your local hard drive, you can always go back to the uncompressed audio when you finalize the project.

If you aren't using the same recording software, your choices are more limited. If both programs support a file interchange format, you should opt for that so you don't lose information about plug-ins, mix automation, and so on. (See the sidebar "Interchange Formats"). Barring that, your only common ground formats are raw audio files in WAV, AIFF, or a compressed format, and Standard MIDI Files for MIDI data. (See "Standard MIDI Files" in Chapter 8.) But Standard MIDI Files will work only if you and your collaborator have exactly the same MIDI instruments (or something comparable, like a similar acoustic piano sound you could substitute for your collaborator's piano plug-in).

Plug-in based online collaboration tools can ease all these tasks even if you're working in different applications. Some promising new services have appeared, including Digital Musician Net (www.digitalmusician.net), which allows real-time MIDI and audio collaboration via a cross-platform VST plug-in, plus community features, file exchange services, and video chat.

CHAPTER 11

Producing Printed Scores

Whether you're just creating a simple lead sheet with lyrics and chords or a full-blown orchestral composition, scores are an essential tool for communicating musical ideas to live players. Notation software is designed for creating and editing scores and printing them on paper.

 Essentials

Producing Printed Scores

Following the sequential process of producing a score and understanding some basic notation strategies can help you create the score you want. We'll look at the available tools and how to best use them:

- What notation software does, and how to choose the right tool for the job
- Starting a score with templates and quick-start features
- Methods for entering notes with a QWERTY keyboard, MIDI, scanning, or audio
- Assembling a score, laying out the page, and extracting parts
- Playing back your music
- Sharing files with other applications and users

Where to Start

Essential Terms

- Lead sheet
- Split/split point
- Input quantization vs. display quantization
- Tablature; guitar frames
- Parts; part extraction
- Cues; multi-bar rests
- SoundFonts/DLS
- MusicXML

Try entering and editing a basic score, like a lead sheet, using a dedicated notation product. If you don't have notation software, try the free notation tool Mac/Windows Finale Notepad (www.finalenotepad.com); it's limited, but provides a good introduction to notation tools.

WHAT NOTATION SOFTWARE DOES

You don't have to be an aspiring Beethoven to need software that lets you create music notation. At one time or another, you might need to print melodies with lyrics to keep a written record of your original songs, or lead sheets and parts for your band, or worksheets for your music class, or, at the opposite extreme, something as complex as a full orchestral score. If your work fits into any of these categories, and if you have some basic music-reading skills, you'll find it useful to be able to print notation. In this book we've looked at a variety of tools whose principle goal is to output sound; scoring tools focus instead on creating printed notation on paper.

"Printing notation" may sound at first like a simple task, but because of the complexity and variability of music notation, it involves a lot of components. Whether you're using the notation feature in your DAW or dedicated software, even a simple *lead sheet* (a song score with melody, lyrics, and chord changes) requires that your software handle a number of tasks:

- **Note entry and editing:** You'll need a way of entering and editing the pitches. If you're using a MIDI keyboard for input, the software needs to know how notes are spelled (whether a G♯ or A♭, for instance). You'll also need to be able to handle rhythms like triplets (three notes in the space of two), rests, and other complexities (**Figure 11.1**).

Figure 11.1 The first step in notation is entering notes; you can input notes using a mouse, QWERTY keyboard, or live or step MIDI input. (Shown: Sibelius)

- **Symbols:** Music notation uses a range of specialized symbols (**Figure 11.2**), from staccato indications (dots above the notehead) to guitar tablature and guitar frames (graphics that represent how to place your fingers on frets).

- **Spacing:** Using a complex "engraving" algorithm, the software will keep elements on the page appropriately spaced so they don't collide with one another and remain easy to read. Because the program may not always produce the spacing you want, it also needs tools for editing the spacing.

- **Lines and curves:** Shapes like slurs, hairpins (crescendo and decrescendo marks), and pedal indications can't easily be drawn free hand as with a drawing program. These shapes require very specific appearances (the thickness of a slur, for instance) and must be precisely aligned with other elements on the page (**Figure 11.3**). If the page layout changes, slurs need to be extended or shortened automatically.

- **Text:** Your music's title, dynamic markings, performance indications, and other text (**Figure 11.4**) all have specific placement and spacing requirements of their own. In the case of the lead sheet, lyrics have to be lined up with individual notes, and chord changes with each measure or beat.

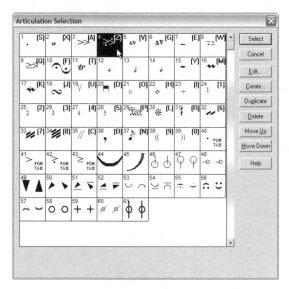

Figure 11.2 Specialized symbols for music notation include articulations like staccato, bowing for strings, and guitar notations; notation software has tools for adding them to individual notes or groups of notes. (Shown: Finale)

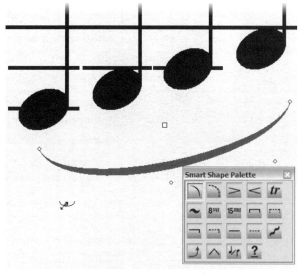

Figure 11.3 Notation software must double as graphics software for precise editing of curves and lines like slur markings. These objects have built-in behaviors for ensuring that they look correct and remain attached to certain notes. (Shown: Finale)

Figure 11.4 Text includes lyrics, dynamics, expressive and technical indications, and more general words added to the score: titles, composer name, copyright notice, headers and footers, and page and measure numbers. (Shown: Sibelius)

- **Layout:** In addition to the spacing of all the individual elements, the notation software must lay out the space between systems on the page to fill the page area and make the overall appearance friendly and readable.

- **Printing:** Once all this is done, you'll need to be able to print the results.

In order to handle these challenges, notation software must be much more sophisticated than a word processor, even though we'd ultimately like it to be just as easy to use. The list above is just the beginning, too. More advanced scores need additional features, such as:

- **Handling multiple instruments:** Instruments have specific ranges of notes they can play and sometimes a different appearance in the score, and, in cases like the clarinet or French Horn, they require transposition (**Figure 11.5**). Transposing instruments play a note that sounds at a different pitch from the one written on the score.

- **Alternative staff and notehead types:** Percussion and other instruments may play on a one-line staff or other variations on the five-line staff. Percussion and special techniques on other instruments require different noteheads for certain notations (**Figure 11.6**).

- **Part extraction:** In chamber ensembles, bands, and orchestras, players read from individual parts that show only the music they're playing rather than a full score.

- **High-quality playback:** If you need to create an audio demo of your piece or just listen to the score to check for errors (which are often easier to hear than to see), you'll need features for controlling how the notation software renders the music with virtual instruments.

- **Exporting and sharing:** For working with other applications, distance learning, collaboration, online demos and sales, or just sending scores faster than the mail, export and online sharing features become essential.

Now with a basic sense of what you may need from notation software, we can look at how to find tools that will fulfill these needs and find out how to use them.

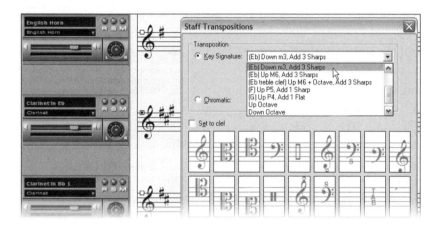

Figure 11.5 Many instruments require transposition; their key signature and notes are notated in a different key from "concert pitch" instruments like the piano and flute. Using Finale or Sibelius, you can easily switch between transposed and nontransposed display. (Shown: Finale)

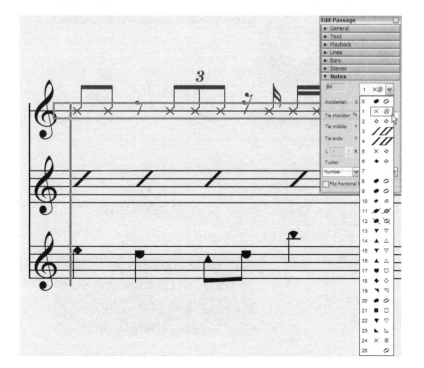

Figure 11.6 From run-of-the-mill, everyday notations (like percussion) to more obscure and archaic possibilities (like "shape note" notation), different scores need different staff types and noteheads. By changing the attributes of the notes and staves, you can accommodate many of these notations throughout a score, saving you the work of manually entering lots of custom symbols. (Shown: Sibelius)

DAWs vs. Dedicated Notation

Your first step is to decide which tool to use. If your primary goal is to print out basic scores from MIDI tracks you've recorded in your DAW, the built-in notation features of that program could be a good solution (**Figure 11.7**).

There are several advantages to working inside your DAW. First, you'll probably have already recorded, edited, and tweaked your MIDI tracks within the interface you're used to using. Simply click the MIDI track or tracks you want to edit as a score and open the score or notation view to begin working. Second, since notation is simply a "view" of the same data, you can generally make edits to either the score or the sequence: the two are effectively one and the same. (You will still need to edit parts separately, and you may need to make a second copy of tracks that require trickier notation, like percussion parts.) In contrast, maintaining separate copies of a project as a sequence in a DAW and a project file in notation software will require updating each independently. Third, working within a DAW provides more flexibility for rendering the score's playback using soft synths. Many notation programs provide access to built-in sound libraries, and Finale 2006 and later supports VST/AU plug-ins from Native Instruments. But a DAW is more likely to let you work with all of your existing soft synths.

Figure 11.7 Some DAWs, like Apple's Logic Pro, let you view, edit, and print notation via an integrated score view. The major advantage of working this way is that switching between editing the score and editing your MIDI project is relatively seamless.

Not all DAWs can print scores, however. Apple Logic Pro and Logic Express, Steinberg Cubase SX, and MOTU Digital Performer all have fairly mature notation features; Cakewalk SONAR has a more basic but usable scoring and printing facility. Most other digital audio software lacks notation capabilities. DAWs like Digidesign Pro Tools, Ableton Live, Sony ACID, and Mackie Tracktion lack notation entirely. Apple GarageBand has a notation view, but it can't print your scores. You'll need to export MIDI tracks from these programs to open them in a dedicated notation application (or, in the case of GarageBand, open your project in Logic).

For more complex tasks and better-looking scores, you'll be better off using a dedicated notation program. Many scores can't be produced any other way: even entry-level notation products have more advanced scoring features than the integrated notation functions of DAWs. Even if you're a beginner, having access to so-called "pro" features can be essential: the major notation applications have built-in time-savers for working more quickly. Even if your scoring needs are modest, you may find that features like Web sharing, pro page layout, and others are essential.

In this chapter, because of the popularity and power of Sibelius and Finale, we'll look at examples in those two programs. They tend to engage each other in an ongoing feature war. Each also comes in various dedicated versions. Sibelius has a Student Edition, an Educational Suite, and G7 software for guitarists; MakeMusic! produces a large variety of versions of Finale, from the flagship version to the free Finale NotePad and SmartMusic educational software (www.smartmusic.com). Many of the principles we'll discuss using Sibelius and Finale as examples will apply to other notation software, as well, including the notation features in your DAW.

GETTING STARTED WITH A SCORE

When you're ready to start your score, you'll need to set up the kind of score you need and begin entering notes and other elements. Thanks to templates and quick-start features or "wizards," you can avoid some of the grunt work of setting up instruments, title and composer text, time and key signatures, and the other elements you'd add at the beginning. When it comes to note entry, you have a variety of options: choose the one that's fastest and easiest for you. QWERTY and mouse entry work well if you don't have a MIDI keyboard handy, whereas step entry and real-time entry can save additional time.

 DAWs with notation:
MOTU Digital Performer (Mac; www.motu.com)

Apple Logic Pro (Mac; www.apple.com)

Steinberg Cubase SX (Mac/Windows; www.steinberg.net)

Popular dedicated notation applications:
Sibelius (Mac/Windows product line; www.sibelius.com)

MakeMusic! Finale (Mac/Windows product line; www. finalemusic.com)

 Notating audio (not): Your audio tracks are basically useless to notation software; since they contain recorded sound, not note values, they can't be converted to notation. To notate them, you'll need to transcribe them by hand. Technologies for automatically transcribing audio are still developing.

Templates and Quick-Start Features

If you're creating a score from scratch, it's best to add all of the instruments, key signatures, time signatures, and other text at the outset. You'll avoid creating more work for yourself later—or winding up with a score with missing information. Instead of skipping the launch dialog in Sibelius or Finale, you can use it to add these elements to the score (**Figure 11.8**). Both programs let you start with a basic template (either a blank page or a preformatted design) and add these elements by using a wizard so you don't forget any steps. (Yes, even pro composers sometimes accidentally leave out the time signature.)

If you start with a preformatted design, you'll have a document set up for an ensemble, meaning you only need to add a title, key signature, time signature, tempo, and so on. These templates are the digital equivalent of the manuscript paper you can buy in a music store, with blank staves laid out

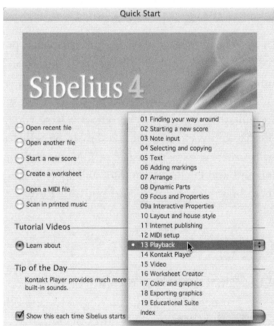
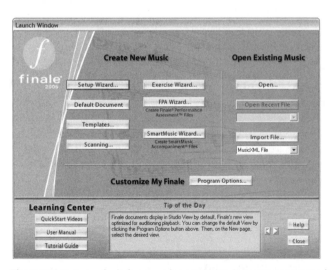

Figure 11.8 Launch dialogs can be annoying in some programs, but in notation software they can actually save you time. The "Launch Window" in Finale (left) and "Quick Start" in Sibelius (right) provide quick access to tutorials, templates, and other features.

for orchestra, choir, string quartet, band, or other typical scenarios. If none of the templates fits your purpose, choose a blank document and add instruments (**Figure 11.9**). Keep in mind that different score types place staves in different orders. Sibelius defaults to normal orchestral order, which works for most cases, while Finale has options for different ensembles. You can reorder staves after you create them; it's not uncommon in smaller groups to change the order for convenience.

Most of us tend to create similar score layouts over and over again, so once you have your score set up, before you begin adding notes, consider saving it as a template. That way, the next time you want to quickly create a score for your harmonium, saxophone, and didgeridoo trio, you'll be able to load your template with staves, fonts, and other options set up the way you like them.

Figure 11.9 To create a score from scratch, select a blank template and add the instruments you need, as shown here in Sibelius. (You'll find an almost identical dialog in Finale.) In the future, you can save yourself this step by creating templates for scores you create regularly.

Entering Notes

Your next step is to get notes into your score. If you're working with integrated notation in a DAW, you may already have the parts you want to notate entered as MIDI tracks; see the sidebar "Display Quantization and Maintaining Your Performance" for an explanation of how displayed notation derives rhythmic values from your sequenced track. If you're starting from scratch, however, you have several means by which you can input notes:

• Using a mouse for point-and-click note entry

• Using a QWERTY computer keyboard for "touch-typing" a score

• Using MIDI input for either step entry (one note or chord at a time) or real-time recording (most often while playing to a metronome)

- Importing presequenced MIDI tracks as a Standard MIDI File

- Turning printed notation into computer notation by scanning it

- Transcribing one line at a time using an audio input to enter notes with an acoustic instrument (like a trumpet)

Figure 11.10 Finale's interface centers around using different tools for different jobs, including different data entry methods, such as Simple Entry, Speedy Entry, and HyperScribe. To select a specific entry method and its associated settings, you must first select a tool.

We'll look at each of these in turn, but you'll most often use QWERTY keyboard touch-typing or MIDI input (or a combination of the two), because they tend to be the fastest and most reliable methods. Scanning and audio transcription are the newest technologies, and although they're often the most exciting to those who want to save time with computer notation, they don't yet work as well as many of us would like. (Another emerging technology, tablet input, holds promise as well; see the sidebar, "Tablet Input: The Future of Computer Notation?")

Most notation software supports at least mouse, QWERTY, and MIDI input methods. In Finale, for instance, these are given different names because they're associated with different tools (Simple Entry, Speedy Entry, and HyperScribe) (**Figure 11.10**). In Sibelius, all these methods are available, although you don't need to select a tool to use them.

Point-and-click entry

Most people new to notation enter scores by pointing and clicking with a mouse. Virtually all notation software has clickable palettes of common rhythmic values and musical symbols, so the most obvious way to add these elements to the score is to click on the object, then click on the score. Although this will work and is necessary for some scoring tasks, it's also unnecessarily slow.

QWERTY keyboard entry

"Touch-typing" music with the QWERTY computer keyboard is a much faster way of entering music than the point-and-click method. All major notation programs and most notation facilities in DAWs have a wide range of keyboard shortcuts for entering notes without using a mouse. Early versions of the manual for Sibelius even suggested users hide their mouse under the desk to force them to use keyboard shortcuts. That's a little extreme, but you can enter music more quickly by becoming comfortable with QWERTY note entry.

Tablet Input: The Future of Computer Notation?

As much as composers and musicians have embraced computer technology for notation, many will tell you they miss the intuitive feel of a pencil and the ability to place paper on a music stand or a piano's desk. Computers built on Microsoft's Tablet PC platform offer a user experience that's closer to paper than a laptop, and they can be placed on sturdy music stands.

For input, Microsoft partnered with a research group at Brown University to build a tool that would let tablet users input music. Microsoft released the result as a PowerToy called the Tablet PC Music Composition Tool, which the Brown team has distributed under a BSD open source license as Music Notepad (**Figure 11.11**).

Instead of tapping keys or moving a mouse, the Music Notepad lets you draw in notes and text by hand and automatically converts them to computer notation for playback and saving. You can't use your normal handwriting unaltered; as with the handwriting recognition on many PDAs, you have to make minor adjustments so the software can recognize your writing correctly. The gestural interface is not diffi-cult to learn, though, and the ability to draw in notation is addictive. You can save the result as a MIDI file for use in a full-featured notation program. The one caveat is that you'll need a Tablet PC to use the program; the installer won't work on any other Windows computer. With the code released as open source, however, this could be a glimpse of notation technologies to come. The UI is primitive, but the quality of the recognition is promising.

 More information:

Microsoft Tablet PC platform (www.microsoft.com/ windowsxp/tabletpc/)

Microsoft Tablet PC PowerToys (www.microsoft.com/ windowsxp/downloads/ powertoys/tabletpc.mspx)

Music Notepad research project, Brown University (http://graphics.cs. brown.edu/research/ music/tpc.html)

Guide to using Tablet PCs in nota-tion and education (http://kellysmusic.mb.ca /articles/anmviewer.asp? a=335)

Figure 11.11 Using Music Notepad, you can draw in note shapes on a Microsoft Windows Tablet PC almost as if you were writing on paper. The software automatically converts your writing into editable computer notation for playback or export. (Image cour-tesy Brown University Computer Graphic Group Research)

Figure 11.12 Learning keyboard shortcuts can dramatically reduce the amount of time required to enter scores. To encourage you to do so, Sibelius maps many of its shortcuts to an onscreen display of the numeric keyboard.

In most applications, you can type to input notes, and use the left and right arrow keys to navigate forward and backward along the staff, just as you would in a word processor. In Sibelius and in Finale's Simple Entry mode, you can select rhythmic values (sixteenth-note, quarter-note, and so on) using the numeric keypad—the numbered keys on the right of a computer keyboard that look like a calculator (**Figure 11.12**). For pitches, you can select note names by using their associated letter (A–G). (Some applications, including Finale's Speedy Entry mode, map pitches to rows of the QWERTY keyboard, so that the notes C D E F will be Q W E R or A S D F instead of the keys C D E F.) With some practice, you can enter notes almost as quickly as you could type an email. (Sibelius even sells a color-coded computer keyboard.)

Once you learn keyboard shortcuts for other objects, like slurs, tuplets, and text, you can often enter pages of music without ever touching the mouse. If you add up all the time it takes to move the mouse around to select menu commands, that can make a big difference.

Scores to Go: Entering Music on Laptops

QWERTY input is perfect for creating scores using a laptop in situations when you don't have access to a MIDI keyboard. Unfortunately, most laptops lack numeric keypads, onto which many programs map rhythmic values. There are a few ways around this problem, however:

- **Use the Function modifier:** Most PC laptops and all Mac laptops hide a numeric keypad on the right side of the QWERTY keyboard (look at 7 U J M and the keys to their right). To turn those keys into a numeric keypad, hold down the Function (Fn) modifier.

- **Plug in an external keypad:** Targus and several other manufacturers make USB numeric keypads for use with laptops.

- **Use specialized keyboard shortcuts:** Most notation programs let you remap keyboard shortcuts, so you can use keys that are more convenient on your laptop. If you're using Sibelius 4 or later, you can switch to a special prebuilt laptop mapping on Windows or alternate shortcuts on the Mac.

If you can spare the room to carry an ultraportable MIDI keyboard like the Edirol PCR-M1 (www.edirol.com), you can also use MIDI to input notes on your laptop.

MIDI step entry

QWERTY input is reasonably fast. But for chords or lines that jump octaves frequently, entering pitches from a MIDI keyboard is faster and easier. Instead of selecting pitches on the QWERTY keyboard, you can select pitches as you go with a MIDI keyboard or other MIDI input. (You'll still select rhythmic values, articulations, and other elements via the QWERTY keyboard or mouse.) As with MIDI step entry in a sequencer, you'll enter notes or chords one at a time, manually selecting how long each step is rhythmically instead of playing in real time. Unlike a sequencer, most notation software doesn't have a dedicated "step entry mode": most of the time, you can simply press keys on your MIDI keyboard in place of your QWERTY keyboard.

Real-time recording

If you prefer to play musical lines live, you'll want to use real-time MIDI entry. Most often, this will require that you play to a metronome so that your notation software can align the notes you're playing with your score's meter and beats.

Real-time input in notation software is basically identical to recording MIDI in a sequencer. Select the part onto which you want to record; set up the tempo, count-off, and metronome playback; and then hit Record and begin playing. As with a MIDI sequencer, you may want to slow down the tempo so you can play more accurately.

You'll usually input on only one staff at a time unless you're recording piano music. Since piano music usually involves two staves—treble and bass, for left and right hands—notation software uses a *split* to determine which input note goes on which staff. The simplest way of doing this is to define a fixed *split point*: if a note falls below the split point's pitch, such as middle C, it will fall on the lower staff; otherwise, it will fall on the upper staff. Some programs have additional, more advanced options. Sibelius has an automatic split point option, which attempts to intelligently guess where the split should be based on the musical context. Finale lets you set customizable moving split points and splits based on a fixed interval between hands.

Split points are most often used for piano input, but they work for inputting any two instruments simultaneously. Instead of the left and right hand of a piano, for instance, you could split input between a violin and a flute. (In Finale, you can record multiple tracks at once using multitrack record mode instead of split points to route different MIDI channels to different staves.)

Quantization is especially vital when inputting notation. MIDI can record rhythmic values of a tiny fraction of a second, but musical scores rarely use values smaller than a 32nd-note. Notation software must quantize the notes you play to the grid of the notation used (**Figure 11.13**). (Some software will let you preserve your original performance, independent of the notation displayed; see the sidebar, "Display Quantization and Maintaining Your Performance.") Set the quantization grid close to the rhythmic values you'll be playing. Consider the smallest rhythmic value of the music you're entering: if you're not going to play a note shorter than a sixteenth-note triplet, select that rhythmic duration in the quantization options for recording. Otherwise, notes that you play just slightly off the beat may appear as strange, complex rhythms rather than what you intended. (Keep in mind that, for instance, a sixteenth-note triplet is shorter than a sixteenth-note duplet, but longer than a 32nd-note.) Another common problem is that staccato notes can be mistaken for shorter notes followed by a rest. Sibelius can automatically guess which notes are staccato, and Finale has various options for "smoothing out" or ignoring these and other short notes.

Figure 11.13 Are strange, complex rhythms showing up in your notation software's transcription? You probably need to adjust the quantization setting: the minimum value should be no smaller than the shortest rhythm you'll play, and triplets should be adjusted to the material you're recording, as shown here in Finale's Quantization Settings.

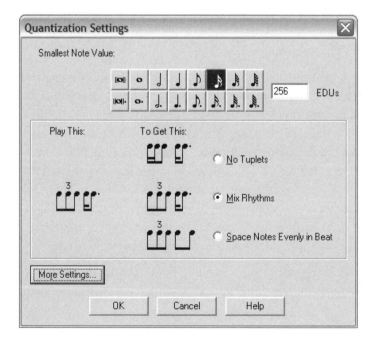

Display Quantization and Maintaining Your Performance

You'll encounter two forms of quantization when working with computer notation. *Input quantization* alters the rhythmic values of notes as you input them; that is, it actually alters your performance as it records it. *Display quantization* leaves your performance untouched, and simply changes what is displayed in notation. The latter is useful if you want to hear your original performance but see readable notation.

Display quantization is supported in some notation software, and it's the form of quantization most often used in a DAW or sequencer. The DAW's MIDI track can be destructively quantized, but it must use display quantization so that, for instance, you aren't looking at 128th-notes—or worse!

In addition to rhythms, via MIDI, you're recording other elements of your performance, like velocity. As you'll see in the "Playback and Rendering" section later in this chapter, most dedicated notation software will make an attempt to replicate the score as written when playing it back. A forte or piano indication in the score, for instance, should affect the loudness of the playback. If you want to instead use your original performance for playback, some notation software will let you switch between your performance and the application's rendering of the score. In Sibelius, the Live Playback toggle on the toolbar switches between the standard software interpretation of the score as shown and an editable record of the MIDI data as you recorded it. In Finale, you can hear your original performance data in Playback Controls > Human Playback Style (**Figure 11.14**).

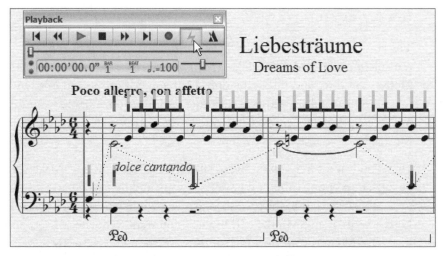

Figure 11.14 Switching on Sibelius's Live Playback toggle restores your original performance and lets you modify MIDI velocity data for notes you played.

You'll find that careful attention to these and other recording settings can improve accuracy. In Sibelius, choose Notes > FlexiTime Options for recording settings; in Finale, select HyperScribe > HyperScribe Options > Quant Settings. Although all these settings will help, you may also want to alter your playing style if you're getting stuck on certain errors. Remember, you're really "performing" for the computer, so it often helps to make your playing as obvious and mechanical as possible.

If you don't like playing to a metronome, you'll be happy to learn that both Sibelius and Finale have alternative options. Sibelius has a flexible metronome called FlexiTime that can adapt to your playing, so that the metronome speeds up and slows down as you do. (Getting it to work right often takes some adjustment, so just as with quantization, you'll want to experiment with different options and tailor recording settings to what you're playing.) Finale and some sequencers let you tap tempo for a freely definable beat, independent of a metronome. Instead of playing to a regular metronome click, using Finale's TempoTap you would tap a foot pedal or other input to define beats, either during or after recording.

Importing from an SMF

The common file format for exchanging music data between applications remains the Standard MIDI File (SMF), as described in Chapter 8, "MIDI: Notes, Rhythms, and Physical Control." If you want to record in a DAW first via MIDI and then import that note data into your notation software to produce a printed score, exporting the DAW's MIDI tracks in SMF format is usually the easiest way.

First, you'll want to clean up the tracks in your MIDI project. Make sure quantization options are set the way you want and that each part you want to be a separate staff in the final score has its own independent, labeled track. Next, export as an SMF the MIDI tracks you want to notate. Then import that SMF file into your notation software. (Although technically this is an import function, you'll often need to use the File > Open command with .MID as the file type. Neither Finale nor Sibelius uses an Import command for SMF files.) Your notation software will give you quantization options much like those for recording, and further options for how the SMF is to be interpreted in the score (**Figure 11.15**). Because SMFs contain less information than most scores do, you'll need to add markings like slurs to create a good-looking score. You may also need to perform other chores, such as replacing accidentals with their enharmonic equivalents (for instance, replacing the note E♭ with D♯).

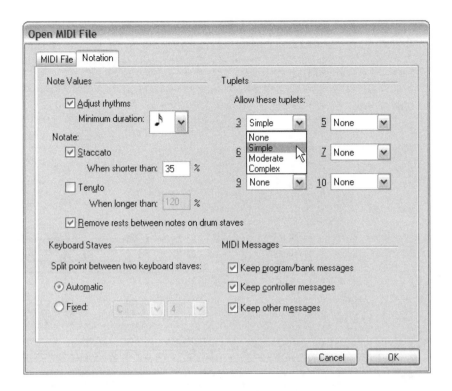

Figure 11.15 Standard MIDI Files contain more detail than you'd want for your score, so you'll find quantization, among other features, useful. Sibelius's SMF import looks just like its recording options: you can quantize rhythms and use split points. Additionally, there's a filter for choosing which MIDI messages are imported.

Going in the opposite direction, from notation software to a sequencer, allows you to tweak playback of a score in your DAW, with full access to your software or hardware synths and effects. Exporting SMFs is usually much easier than importing them. You won't have to worry about quantization, and many notation applications are smart enough to export scores complete with MIDI interpretations of expression text and dynamics rather than just raw notes.

Scanning notation

Ever wish you could just scribble notation in pencil, as sloppily as you wanted, and then scan it into a computer and have it magically converted into notation? Too bad: that's not yet possible. What is possible is to scan printed notation and convert that into a file that can be edited in your notation software. Scanning software such as SmartScore is the musical equivalent of *optical character recognition* software. Instead of converting scanned images into editable text, it converts images into editable musical scores (**Figure 11.16**). This can be a godsend if you've ever needed to edit or transpose a printed score. Once the process is done, you have a notation file you can edit just like any other.

 Don't lose the groove: Your best bet is to quantize MIDI tracks in the DAW, then set your notation software to exactly the same minimum quantization settings before importing the SMF. That way, you can check that the quantization is correct in your DAW rather than having to do lots of cleanup in the notation software. (Additional, detailed quantization and editing will probably still be necessary in some places.)

Figure 11.16 Music scanning software like SmartScore Pro, shown here, converts ordinary printed music (1) into editable notation files (2). By mousing over the notation at the top, you can compare the computer-recognized score to the original image to correct any mistakes made by the recognition algorithm. A zoomed-in image (3) of the original score shows the scanned location, close-up. You can edit directly in the scanning program or bring the file into your notation software for further editing or transposition.

The accuracy of scanned notation depends primarily on two factors: the image settings of the scanning software and the quality of the source. For the former, you'll need to check the documentation for your scanning software, because different software works better with different settings. (Typical settings to adjust for better accuracy include color depth and resolution.)

The quality of your source is often the most critical issue, especially since one of the most important uses of notation scanning software is recovering old, long-out-of-print scores that may be in poor condition. Recent computer-engraved published scores tend to work best, but they'll probably still be protected by copyright law, which means that scanning them (other than for personal use, such as transposing a song to an easier key) would be strictly illegal. Older engraved scores, often using slightly different-looking symbols and suffering from deterioration over the years, tend to require more hand corrections, although that may still save time versus hand entry. Music scanning software will let you compare the scanned image to the converted notation so you can correct the recognition algorithm's mistakes. You'll probably find that you're better at reading notation than the computer is, but notation scanning can still save a lot of time.

Both Finale and Sibelius include a "lite" version of integrated scanning software. These are too crippled for regular use, typically lacking support for text, tuplets, slurs, and other features that hardly qualify as "pro." They should work enough for you to see if you like the process, however; if you get hooked, you can update to the full version. The full version supports more recognition and editing features. Using a program like SmartScore for editing and playback, you might not even need a dedicated notation application.

Keep in mind that many musical scores are protected by copyright law, even if the music is old. Beethoven's symphonies aren't copyrighted, for instance, but your edition may be. Again, scanning for personal use is not going to get you in trouble, but before distributing a scanned score publicly, you should check with an attorney who is familiar with copyright law.

Audio transcription

The last frontier for notation input is audio transcription. Again, the ideal scenario—being able to convert recordings of whole ensembles into notation—isn't yet possible. More basic audio transcription is within reach, however, with some caveats. Finale integrates a feature called MicNotator that allows you to use an audio input alongside other input methods. Your instrument needs to be monophonic, playing only a single note at a time, and MicNotator only claims to work with winds and brass, not voice. If you're a flute or trumpet player and lousy on the keyboard, mic input via Finale's MicNotator or a similar function could be terrific for you. For other tasks, QWERTY and MIDI input remain the preferred methods, at least until the technology develops further.

Assembling Your Score

Computer notation was once a laborious process. Users had to lay out scores manually, carefully adjusting the number of measures on a line and lines on a page by hand. Now, these aspects of layout are fairly automatic. Notation software automatically places symbols and notes, lays out measures, respaces and reflows measures to fit everything while keeping your music legible, and generally does much of the work engravers once did by hand.

Notation scanning software:

Musitek SmartScore (www.musitek.com): Export to Finale 2003 or later, audio CD, PDF, MIDI

Neuratron PhotoScore (www.neuratron.com/ photoscore.htm): Export to Sibelius, MusicXML, NIFF, MIDI

Notation for Guitar

Music for fretted instruments like the guitar has some unique notation requirements. Although fretted instrument players sometimes read from conventional staff notation, they often use types of notation specialized for their instruments. These types of notation show you where to place your fingers on the instrument instead of showing the resulting pitch as 5-line staff notation does. A nonguitarist wouldn't even know what pitch this would create, because it's specific to the instrument, and the sounding pitch isn't shown in the notation.

There are two main forms of guitar notation (see **Figure 11.17**):

- **Tablature:** A 6-line staff represents a guitar's fingerboard. The top line is the first string (high E), and the bottom line is the bottom string (low E). Numbers placed on each line indicate where to finger a note or chord. Stems to show rhythm are sometimes included. Tablature generally replaces 5-line staff notation.

- **Guitar frame:** Also known as a chord diagram, the guitar frame is placed above the staff with indications for chords. Guitar frames generally replace or supplement a written chord symbol like Gm7. If you didn't know how to finger the chord Gm7, you could look at the guitar frame to find out.

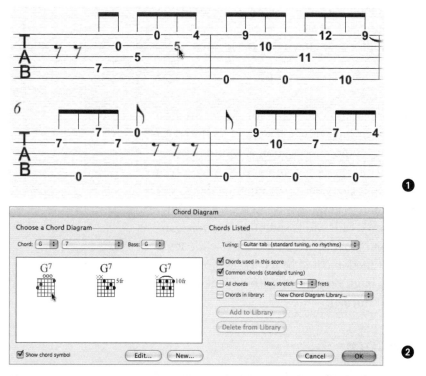

Figure 11.17 Guitar parts can be notated with standard staff notation, but they also use two other major means of notating. Tablature (1) substitutes a specialized staff for the 5-line staff used by other instruments; instead of showing resulting pitch, it shows where to place your fingers on the strings. Each line represents a separate string. Guitar frames (2), also called chord diagrams, show how to finger specific chords.

Both convey fingerings on the strings, but each conveys a different kind of musical information. Tablature can include rhythms and melodies, but guitar frames show individual chords only, akin to chord symbols.

Since tablature is a staff type, you'll select it in notation software as a staff type. Using dedicated notation software like Finale or specialized guitar products like Sibelius G7, you can copy and paste between 5-line staff notation and tablature and the software will convert to the correct numbers.

Guitar frames appear above the staff as chord symbols do and can also be generated automatically, although for tricky chords you may want to substitute your own fingering details.

Hundreds of thousands of *ASCII tablature* files are available online; they encode basic guitar or bass tablature as raw text and symbols (**Figure 11.18**). The level of detail included can vary, but even if the tab files lack rhythms, they'll include basic fret positions, meaning this format can represent simple song structures. (Copyrighted music cannot legally be distributed as tablature without permission of the copyright owner. For this reason, *Real World Digital Audio* won't recommend specific sites from which you can download tab music, but they're not hard to find using a search engine.)

Many notation programs, including Sibelius, Sibelius G7, and Finale Guitar, can import and/or export guitar tablature. Tablature notation has been used for drums as well. (You may need to substitute a file extension; Sibelius, for instance, can only recognize ASCII tab if you add the .tab file extension to the text file.)

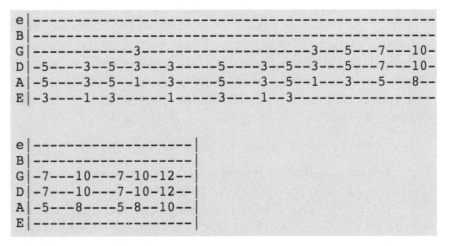

Figure 11.18 Hundreds of thousands of songs are available for free download online as ASCII tablature, a format that uses a standardized, all-text means of recording chords, rhythms, and other information.

The reason this is possible is that long before computers, engravers codified complex rules by which scores were laid out. Computer notation incorporates these principles into algorithms that make reasonable decisions on spacing for you. It's not perfect: many engraving decisions were subjective, so you'll often need to manually adjust elements to make them look better or improve readability. Sometimes, the automatic layout just doesn't work right: the computer algorithms sometimes make decisions that are obviously wrong, or simply not what you want. But rather than adjust 100% of your score manually, you can make minor adjustments later, after the automatic algorithm has taken its best shot.

You can use these principles to save yourself time adjusting a score. While you're entering notes and other elements, don't worry about how many bars are on a line. Let the computer algorithm adjust them, and then go back and make changes later once you've finished entering the music. Some notation users prefer to enter all notes, then slurs and articulations, then dynamics and other text, or otherwise segregate various tasks. This can be useful if you're copying music from paper, because it reduces the chance that you'll forget a slur somewhere. Thanks to more streamlined, automatic text and musical symbol features in newer notation products, though, you can often mix notes and other elements as you input music. Just remember to enter music first, then adjust layout—it almost always saves some duplication of work.

Here are some other strategies that could save you time:

- **Freehand as little as possible:** Most notation software, Sibelius and Finale included, has options that let you choose between automatic placement of shapes like slurs and manual, freehand placement. Always try the automatic placement option first. Manually drawing in slurs not only tests your mouse-eye coordination skills and takes more time, but also increases the number of readjustments you'll have to make later.

- **Select multiple items:** Don't let repetitive work slow you down. You've probably already figured out how you can use copy and paste to reduce the amount of entry you have to do. Using multiple selections can reduce work, too. For instance, if you needed to add staccato marks to a whole range of notes, don't add them one at a time. Use a multiple-select tool to select the notes you need, then apply the change to all of them at once. In Finale, use the Mass Edit tool; in Sibelius, try the Edit > Filter menu options.

- **Take advantage of the incredible disappearing score:** Despite outward appearances, notation software is very different from page layout software. Notation software usually assumes that every object and text element has some relative position to a staff. That usually saves you time, because most notation objects are naturally tied to staves: move a staff around, change the layout, extract parts, and everything should "snap" to its proper place. There are cases, however, where you want a more free-form layout, for tasks like adding large blocks of text to a score, creating specialized notations, or building a quiz for a classroom. The secret for such layout tricks is to hide staves, notes, or other elements. This is especially easy in Sibelius: you can use the Properties window or staff type to hide anything on the score. In Finale, you'll have to use the associated tool for whatever you want to hide; for staves, for instance, select the Staff Tool and use Staff Attributes for hiding. You can use hidden staves and bars to line up notes: elements will stay in place, even though they look on the page as if they're free-form.

PRINT, PLAY, AND SHARE YOUR SCORE

Getting your score from your computer screen to musicians, collaborators, customers, and everyone else has its own considerations. If the final stage will be paper, you'll need to think about the needs of your players as you refine the layout of the page and (if needed) extract individual parts. Part of the advantage of digital notation is that you don't have to stop with paper: you can create high-quality audio renderings of your work, exchange editable files with other applications and users, and share or sell your scores online.

Page Layout

Once you've added the basic elements of your score—notes, slurs and articulations, dynamics and text, lyrics, and other elements—you can think about how best to lay it out on the page. The single most significant setting to adjust is the default staff size. Since the layout algorithms of notation applications adjust all elements relative to one another, it's this basic size value that will have the most impact on the overall layout. If notation is too hard to see, you'll probably want to increase the staff size. If it's too spread out, requiring too many page turns, you'll want to decrease it. In Sibelius, the global staff size is included in the Layout > Document Setup dialog, making it easy to see how this setting interacts with the page layout (**Figure 11.19**). In Finale, you can use the Resize Tool from page layout view by clicking on a staff.

Figure 11.19 Making a change to the overall default staff size, as shown in Sibelius, can dramatically affect how your score fits on the page.

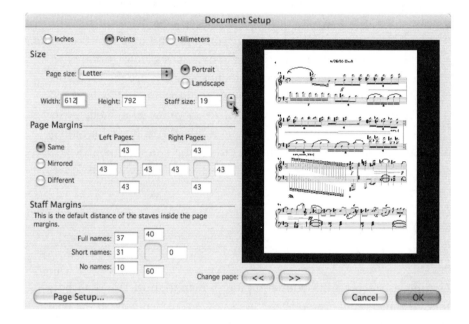

After you've established a staff size that fits the music efficiently, the next parameter to consider is the distance between staves. You'll sometimes need to adjust this manually on individual pages, as when one part extends to lower or higher ledger lines, requiring more vertical space.

Finally, look at the spacing of individual measures. Although the default spacing algorithms should work most of the time, there are cases in which you'll want to override the defaults. You might want to avoid nasty page turns in the middle of dense passages: try using a page break to force the music to break where you want it. In other cases, you might have a measure with a lot of fast notes that looks especially crowded: try reducing the number of measures on that line by using a system break, or enlarging or reducing the proportional space of the bar itself.

Although these techniques will work in most cases, specialized notational tasks can require specialized tools:

- **Locked formatting:** In cases where you need a fixed number of measures per line, such as for a worksheet for a classroom or a basic lead sheet, chord chart, or other simple music, most programs will let you fix the number of measures per system or systems per page. Sibelius and Finale will let you lock formatting for specific measures as well.

- **Automatic fit:** Both Sibelius and Finale offer automatic layout tools for when you need to fit a certain amount of music to a page.

Scores and Parts

As any orchestral player will tell you, it's almost always more convenient to read from a *part*, printed notation that includes only the instrument you're playing, than from a full score. As a composer or arranger, you'll need to produce separate parts from your full score for orchestral music, chamber music, and any other music in which the full score is too cumbersome for individual players to read.

The most common method is to *extract parts* from the full score: that is, the notation software will generate new files for each part or parts. Extracting parts will create a whole set of files, usually organized into a folder, each file containing a separate part. (In some cases, it's customary to include more than one instrument on a part: a first and second flute might read from a single part, for instance. Extraction features usually provide this ability.)

The problem with extracting parts from a full score into separate files is that any later changes made to the full score must be manually added to each affected part, and vice versa. You can re-extract parts each time you make changes, but that can still mean a lot of additional editing. In theory, automatic part extraction should create perfect parts with no need for editing, but in reality you'll often have to adjust parts for aesthetics, page turns, and the like. Usually, the only way to avoid additional work is to extract parts as a final task, and then hope you don't need to make any more changes.

The solution employed by some notation software, including Sibelius 4 and later, is to link parts and full score (**Figure 11.20**). With parts and score connected as two "views" of the same music, you can view or print individual parts and change their appearance individually or globally, but edits in either the score or the part will be reflected in both.

Figure 11.20 Parts require that the same musical information for an instrument appear in the individual part that appears in the full score. Using Sibelius's scores and parts feature, you can edit both simultaneously, and switch between views of each without extracting separate files.

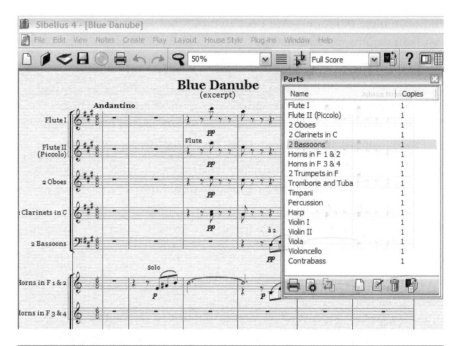

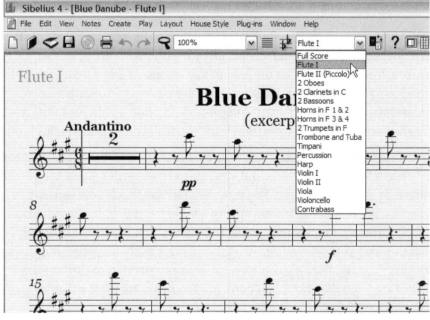

Parts need to include all the information from the full score relevant to that instrument, but they also need elements specific to the part. That includes instrument-specific information like fingering, or anything else that would be distracting to the conductor but essential to the player. In Finale and other applications that extract parts, you'll add these to the part file; there's no need to add them to the score since they're not needed there. In Sibelius, since part and score are linked, you can specify which elements are shown in each.

Since players reading from parts can't see the rest of the score and often have long periods of time during which they're not playing, it's helpful to include *cues*, phrases from other instruments that help them see where they begin playing after multimeasure rests. If a violinist drops out for a measure, cues are overkill, but after a half dozen or more bars, you should consider whether a cue may help a player feel more comfortable about an entrance. Cues are displayed using smaller notation so a player can tell they're cues. Finale generates cues using the Smart Cue Notes feature, based on rules you select. It's not entirely automatic, because you'll need to do a fair amount of shepherding of the feature, but it can save time. Using programs like Sibelius, you can manually add cues; copy-and-paste is usually the fastest way.

Because players have time during which they're not playing, parts also have a specific notation called *multi-bar rests* (**Figure 11.21**). These are markings that appear as one bar in length in the parts. They indicate the number of measures of rest during which the player isn't playing, whether for an interval of two bars or two dozen.

Multi-bar rests are added automatically to parts by the notation software, but the spacing of parts sometimes needs to be changed to put a long rest at the end of a page, thus giving the player time to turn the page.

Figure 11.21 Multi-bar rests are used to indicate periods of time during which the player or players of a part aren't playing. Here, the number three above a measure indicates three bars of rest. The dotted-line page icon is a forced page break, added to make page turns easier.

Playback and Rendering

Musicians reading a score read more than just the notes: they interpret dynamics and tempo, follow expressive and technical indications, and phrase rhythms and gestures in musical ways. If you're using a DAW for notation, you'll add expression to the performance the way you would with any other MIDI sequence, by adding MIDI data to shape playback. Using dedicated notation software, however, you can use built-in features designed to interpret a score automatically.

You'll find global settings for options like groove/swing (in Sibelius, use Play > Performance; in Finale, select Playback Settings > HP Preferences to access Human Playback). These options let you tailor playback to the kind of music in your score, "pulling out all the stops" by interpreting all indications and swinging rhythms, or turning off playback interpretation to play the score "dry" (**Figure 11.22**). In Sibelius, you can set interpretation individually for each text indication and symbol using the Playback Dictionary, although generally you'll probably keep the defaults.

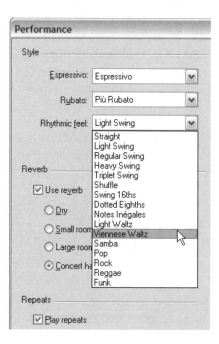

Figure 11.22 Dedicated notation software can automatically interpret what it sees in your score. By adjusting the rhythmic feel and other settings, you can give the computer playback some indications of what you want your music to sound like, as shown here in Sibelius's Performance settings.

Using automatic playback interpretation has several advantages. Aside from the obvious advantage that you'll be able to hear your music in a less robotic, mechanical form, you can use playback to check your score for errors. You can also include these interpretations when exporting to MIDI or audio, or when sharing your music online. To add expressive detail, however, Finale and Sibelius have features for editing underlying MIDI data or using the original performance; see the sidebar earlier in the chapter, "Display Quantization and Maintaining Your Performance."

While MIDI editing, playback, and soft synth options are almost always more advanced in a DAW, dedicated notation software has some of the same basic functionality—possibly enough that you'll never have to leave your notation software to tweak playback. Typically, sounds will default to General MIDI patch numbers, so a violin line should automatically sound like a violin if you're using a synth in GM mode. (For more on General MIDI, see Chapter 8.) You'll even find sequencer-like mixer controls for instruments and playback, as in Finale's Studio View (**Figure 11.23**).

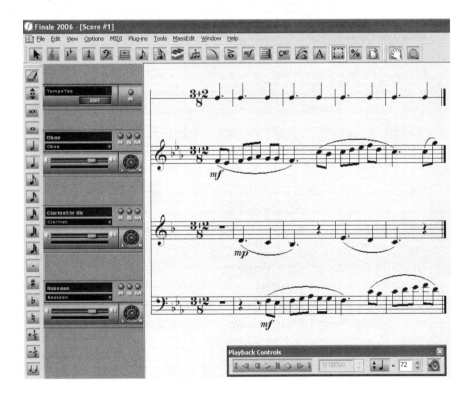

Figure 11.23 Basic sequencing, MIDI, and playback controls in notation software can save you an extra trip to your DAW. Using Studio View in Finale 2006 or later, you can display instruments horizontally, with controls at the left for playback settings. (Photo courtesy MakeMusic!)

You can play back your music in notation software using any of several methods:

- **Built-in computer soft synths:** All Macs and most PCs can access a very simple General MIDI soft synth for playback, like the Microsoft GS Wavetable SW Synth on Windows or the QuickTime Musical Instruments included with QuickTime for Windows and Mac. The quality of these soft synths is extremely limited, but they serve as good common-denominator sound sets, especially for sharing your music online.

- **External MIDI synths:** If you have MIDI hardware hooked up to your computer, you can use that for playback; just be prepared to manually set program change numbers if your synth doesn't have a General MIDI mode.

- **SoundFonts:** On all Macs and many Windows setups, you can use inexpensive or freeware SoundFonts, which are simple sets of sounds that are loaded by the OS (see the sidebar, "SoundFonts").

- **Bundled soft synths:** Recent versions of Finale and Sibelius each include a high-quality orchestral sound library based on the Kontakt Player sample playback engine from Native Instruments. You can upgrade these included libraries to more extensive ones if you're doing a lot of playback. Finale, in particular, has included features for optimizing playback via the Garritan Personal Orchestra orchestral library. (See Chapter 9, "Synthesis and Software Instruments," for more on how orchestral sample libraries can be used expressively.)

- **Your own soft synths:** If your soft synth of choice has a stand-alone mode, you can route MIDI to it from your notation software just like a hardware synth. (On Windows, you may need to use MIDI Yoke to route MIDI; see Chapter 4, "Preparing Your Computer for Audio," for more details.) Integrated soft synths may be the wave of the future: Finale 2006 and later supports the use of all Native Instruments soft synths and sample libraries based on the Kontakt/Intakt sample playback engines. As soft synths continue to grow in popularity, you can expect more features like this to emerge.

SoundFonts

SoundFonts are a standard format for distributing simple sample libraries, developed by Creative Labs and its music subsidiary E-MU. For links to sounds and tutorials, check out Creative Labs' own SoundFont site or the many online community resources like SynthZone. SoundFont files appear with the .SF2 extension. The similar DLS (DownLoadable Sounds) format is an open format developed by the MIDI Manufacturers' Association; DLS files appear with the .DLS file extension.

SoundFonts are especially useful for notation playback because a wide range of General MIDI-compliant sound banks are available, and they can be used in notation applications without the need for additional soft synths.

If you're a PC user, you can use SoundFonts with Creative's AWE, Live!, and Audigy sound cards, or with software that supports the SoundFont format, including the built-in sound engine in Finale. In Finale, you can select a SoundFont by selecting MIDI > MIDI Setup > SoftSynth Settings > Current Sound Font. DLS is also supported via Microsoft's DirectX architecture.

Mac OS X natively supports SoundFont and DLS files. You can change the QuickTime Instruments synth to a font from System Preferences > QuickTime > Default Synthesizer, or select the DLS Instrument in your DAW or notation software, which despite the name, supports both DLS and SoundFont files. (For these instruments to see sound banks, you'll need to install them in your ~/Library/Audio/Sounds/Banks folder.)

 Resources

SoundFont
www.soundblaster.com/
soundfont

SynthZone
www.synthzone.com/
soundfont.htm

**MIDI Manufacturers'
Association**
www.midi.org

Sharing Files

Once your score is ready, digital notation offers a wide range of sharing options beyond just printing. You can distribute your music using various standard formats, so with their existing software or additional free software, anyone can view, hear, edit, print, or even purchase your music.

PDF

PDF remains the most foolproof means of distributing scores. It lacks bells and whistles like security and playback, but it's also easy and free for musicians to print your files. In addition to integrated PDF printing capabilities in Mac OS X, many notation applications natively produce PDF on Windows. If your notation software won't produce PDFs, you can consider free

PDF tools like Cute PDF Writer or PDF4Free, each of which can be upgraded for a fee for additional capabilities. Adobe has a free viewer, pro-level products, and even an online subscription service for creating PDFs.

MIDI

SMF export is a good format for moving notation to a sequencer, but it also works well for distributing files. QuickTime Player can play MIDI files using General MIDI patches on both Mac and Windows, as can many other applications. QuickTime Pro can convert GM playback of MIDI to audio files, for saving as an MP3 or burning to a CD.

Audio

Many notation applications, including Sibelius and Finale, can export audio files. Export as audio, and the application will render playback as you hear it on your software's included soft synths. (If that doesn't work, see other options for routing and recording audio in Chapter 4.) Once you have the audio file, you can open it in free applications like Windows Media Player and Apple's iTunes to convert it to a compressed file or burn it to a CD.

Web publishing and e-commerce

Both Sibelius and MakeMusic maintain tools and Web sites for distributing your music online; each has its own strengths and weaknesses. MakeMusic's emphasis is generally on distributing full, editable files; Sibelius's emphasis is on e-commerce and Web browsing.

Because Finale has a free application for opening and editing notation files, Finale Notepad, it's easier to distribute an editable Finale file on your own site or the Finale Showcase. As long as people are using one of the recent versions of Finale, or can download the free application for Windows or Mac, they'll be able to work directly with your score. This makes it perfect for distributing scores you want people to be able to edit, whether it's a score on which you're collaborating or an exercise for a class. (Since Sibelius lacks a free version, your collaborators would have to buy Sibelius to have the same flexibility.) On the downside, you won't be able to control how people use your Finale score, because you can't prevent them from changing or printing it, so this method won't work for online sales.

Sibelius uses a browser plug-in called Scorch for in-browser transposition, playback, viewing, and printing (**Figure 11.24**). The plug-in works on a variety of browsers on Mac and Windows, including Microsoft Internet Explorer, Firefox, Netscape, and Safari. Because Scorch is built for e-commerce, you can control whether people can save or print the scores, and whether they can play and view an entire score or just an excerpt. Sibelius also maintains an extensive Web site for hosting and (optionally) selling your music for profit at www.sibeliusmusic.com. (If you'd rather your music be distributed free of charge, SibeliusMusic has that option as well.) If your purposes are educational rather than commercial, you may prefer to use the educational Web site at www.sibeliuseducation.com. Pro publishers might evaluate the Sibelius Internet Edition, as well, for more advanced e-commerce.

Whether you want to use one of the Sibelius sites or publish to your own Web page, there are simple export commands within Sibelius that do the work for you; you don't need to do any HTML coding if you don't want to. On the upside, you'll be able to sell your scores and promote yourself with a SibeliusMusic Web site with contact information and bio; on the downside, if anyone needs to edit your score, they'll have to buy Sibelius.

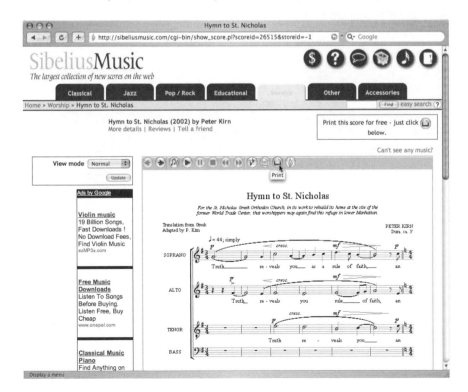

Figure 11.24 One advantage of going digital with notation is the ability to share or sell your work on the Web. By downloading the Mac/Windows Scorch plug-in for your Web browser, you can browse, play, and print tens of thousands of works of music available at SibeliusMusic.com, either for free or for purchase. Music publishers are beginning to distribute online as well.

MusicXML

None of the aforementioned formats is a substitute for being able to exchange entire, editable scores with users of other applications. Various formats have attempted to standardize the many complex variations that are possible in notation, and applications have added individual, app-specific import/export filters for programs like Encore and SCORE. These solutions tend to work under certain circumstances for certain users, depending on the content of their score and the application they're trying to use.

Fortunately, there is finally an interchange format that actually works, and it's gaining acceptance: MusicXML, developed by Recordare (www.recordare.com). MusicXML import/export is built into Finale 2003 and later, and import is allowed into Sibelius 4 and later, among other applications. Even if your application doesn't natively support MusicXML, you may be able to use a Recordare plug-in for import and export. (Finale and Sibelius, although they each include basic MusicXML support, can be upgraded to more extensive import/export functionality.)

Aside from MusicXML, you'll occasionally see other interchange formats. The NIFF (Notation Interchange File Format) has mostly fallen out of use and has been supplanted by MusicXML.

CHAPTER 12

Music and Sound for Video

Producing audio for video requires specialized techniques for synchronizing sound and picture. Whether your end result is an edited audio soundtrack, recorded dialog, sound effects, or a musical score, you'll need to understand how timing and synchronization function in video, and how to match your sound to image.

Essentials

Music and Sound for Video

We'll look at the technology for adding audio to video, including tools and formats:

- Synchronization, spotting hit points, and adjusting cues to fit music to picture
- Workflow, integrated software suites, and file exchange
- SMPTE timecode and measuring time in seconds and frames
- Recording sound so it can easily be synchronized
- Synchronizing sound and video when they've been recorded separately; recording dialog

Essential Terms

- Cues/hit points; spotting
- Postproduction
- Codecs
- Frame rate; SMPTE timecode
- Click track
- Slate/clapperboard
- Free run/record run/jam-sync synchronization
- File formats: MPEG, BWF
- ADR

Where to Start

If your goal is creating music for film, you'll want to learn to identify hit points and match musical tempos to cues. If your goal is sound editing and video postproduction, take a look at slates and synchronization based on in/out points for use in a video editing program like Final Cut Pro or Vegas.

SYNCHRONIZATION, TOOLS, AND FORMATS

Building on what you have already learned about producing digital audio, you'll be able to utilize a variety of tasks specific to producing sound for video:

- **Composing digital music:** Creating musical soundtracks using recorded sound and/or soft synths

- **Composing printed scores:** Producing printed scores for musicians to perform live in order to record soundtracks

- **Postproduction:** Editing existing sound from a video soundtrack, matching separately recorded sound to video, and adding new sound to a video (sound effects, spoken dialog, narration, and other audio)

All of these tasks involve processes we've looked at, from recording, editing, and mixing to scoring notation and using virtual instruments. In addition, soundtrack work requires coming to terms with a new issue: synchronization.

Matching Sound and Image

Synchronization in video extends both to literal sync of image and sounds and to the looser synchronization of image and music. You'll obviously need dialog, sound effects, and other sounds to synchronize exactly with what's onscreen so the sound matches the action. Music is more loosely synchronized based on where you want it aesthetically.

Music doesn't always need to line up exactly with picture, but it may need to start or end at certain times (like the beginning of the opening credits or a change of scene) and to line up with specific events onscreen for maximum impact (like a swell of music when the villain in a horror flick appears). These specific events are called *cues* or *hit points*.

Because you're matching up two different elements, audio and visual, it helps to have a reference as you're working. Usually, this is in the form of a video file, which gives you both a reference to the timing of the video you're scoring and the literal visual content of the movie itself. The video will usually run in a small window in your DAW or audio editing software. It will automatically play back in synchrony with the audio. In addition, you may see a visual indication of the video time in the form of a *burn-in*, in which video timecode is overlaid on one corner of the picture. It's also possible to view the video in a VCR (if you still have one) while scoring the music, but this requires expensive synchronization hardware and entails other headaches, so almost all composers who work with film and video have moved to computer-based video playback.

You're already accustomed to working with two kinds of time in digital audio: clock time (3 minutes, 47 seconds) and musical time (4/4 time, 90 bpm, bar 17, beat 3). With audio alone, you rarely have to convert between the two: if two tracks are lined up at 120 bpm, it doesn't really matter when events occur in seconds. Working with video and music, though, you'll need to be able to make those conversions. You'll also need to resynchronize media that were recorded separately, such as audio that was recorded on a separate recorder from the video.

Video Capabilities in Audio Software

Working with video makes new demands on your audio software. Here are some of the features you'll want to look for when using music software during the process of producing sound for video:

- Video import capability, so you can associate your audio project with the video file you're scoring.

- A preview display for watching the video while you're working; this is usually in the form of a video window, but some programs provide a still-by-still track preview, displayed horizontally (**Figure 12.1**).

- Markers, for indicating cues where sound and picture need to be associated (**Figure 12.2**).

- Some means of changing the music's tempo so that cues line up with key moments ("hit points") in the video.

- Video export capability, so you can embed your finished audio in the video (not always necessary, but often useful).

Most often, the tool that fulfills these requirements is a DAW. Pro Tools, SONAR, Cubase, Logic, Digital Performer, Sony Acid, and Mackie Traction all have integrated video features, as do tools specializing in video scoring like Apple Soundtrack Pro and Adobe Audition. Using these tools, you can record dialog and sound effects, and edit and clean up an existing soundtrack from the video.

Figure 12.1 You can import video files into your audio software (1) so that they will serve as a reference while you're creating the music. In software like Cakewalk SONAR Producer Edition, you can watch a synced video in a window (2) or in a horizontal, timeline display of frames (3).

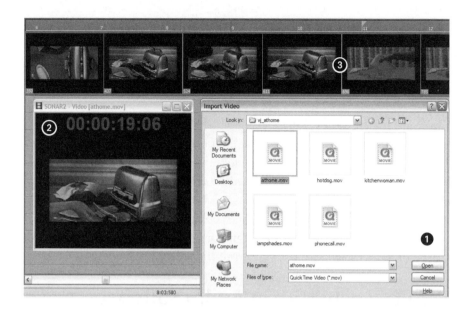

Figure 12.2 Markers, as shown here in SONAR, are essential for keeping track of cues and other important moments in the video.

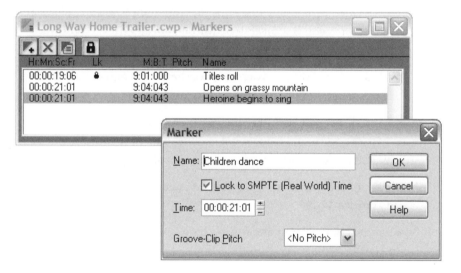

If you're creating your own original music soundtrack for video, you have several choices:

- **"Temp" tracks:** If the end result is a temporary music recording to give a director an illustration of what a finished track might sound like, your quickest solution will be to assemble prebuilt loops in a program like Apple Soundtrack Pro or Sony ACID.

- **Soft synth soundtracks:** If you're producing music for the video entirely with soft synths, a DAW will be the best way to go, since it incorporates both necessary video features and extensive MIDI and soft synth hosting features. (The latter are missing from programs like Soundtrack Pro and Audition.)

- **Live musical scores:** If you need to print out scores for musicians to play, complete with cues and timing information where needed, you'll want to use either the notation capability of a DAW like SONAR or Logic, or a dedicated notation application like Sibelius. (See Chapter 11, "Producing Printed Scores," for more information on deciding between a DAW and a dedicated notation tool for creating scores.)

Managing Video Files

There are two reasons you might need to work with video files when doing sound scoring. The first, obvious reason is that you'll need to look at the video for reference. The second is that you might need to embed your own audio in the video, either to ensure that timing is synced in a final project or to provide a mock-up for a director or collaborator of how video and sound will mesh.

Workflows

When it comes to working on video, workflow, which is a fancy word for the order in which you complete a series of tasks on a project, becomes a vital consideration. You might edit all your audio first, then bring it into a video editor. You might take a preedited video and create music that fits it, or (as would be the case in a music video), you might create the music first and bring that into a video editing application, making the music the reference while you assemble a video.

Your workflow becomes more significant if you're collaborating with other people in the phase video producers call *postproduction*, or simply "post." (Postproduction is, literally, everything that happens after the video has been shot.) A standard video production workflow is to shoot first, then edit the video, then edit sound. In this case, a video editor will cut the picture, then send all the audio at once for editing by a sound editor, who will return the edited sound to the video editor for the last stage in the video mastering process, which is referred to as the final cut. Even in professional work, this process isn't totally fixed: film composers, for instance, often work from rough cuts of the film and wind up making revisions to the music as the film changes. If the video editor trims two and a half seconds from a scene, the composer is expected to edit the existing music so that it still fits the shorter scene.

Even if you're just one person, you'll probably need a way of moving video and audio content between your audio editing application and your video editing application. If you're working with other people, you'll need a way of sending projects back and forth. This could be as simple as receiving a low-res copy of the video to use as reference, or as complex as sending full multitrack audio for each scene as it's edited.

File formats and encoding

Digital workflows:
Read an interview with D.A. Young at www.real-worlddigitalaudio.com for a glimpse of how rapid postproduction for TV can be. Don't expect anything exotic as far as file transmission: the sound you hear in a South Park episode is an emailed MP3.

Digital video files are necessary both for exchanging video files with other collaborators and for keeping a reference for video scores and soundtracks. You'll find a variety of typical formats, including Apple QuickTime (.MOV) files, Microsoft Windows Media files (usually labeled .AVI), and MPEG files (.MPG or another .MPx extension). Just because a file appears to have a supported file extension doesn't necessarily mean your music software will be able to read it. MPEG files are available in different flavors like MPEG-4 and MPEG-2, and QuickTime and Windows Media files may require the current version of the player software (usually a free download). Furthermore, QuickTime and Windows Media formats are often compressed using different *codecs* (short for coder-decoder). Fortunately, downloading the latest QuickTime or Windows Media software will let you handle many of these formats.

The preferred file format for audio production for video remains Apple's QuickTime, which supports a variety of video compression codecs and content types. Despite the Apple brand name, QuickTime is often preferred even by PC users, because so many video and audio applications on Windows and Mac alike are able to open and save QuickTime .MOV files. As a result, this format is popular for sharing videos.

To work with QuickTime files, you'll probably want to invest the $29.95 needed to upgrade to QuickTime Pro, which unlocks a slew of conversion options for audio and video on both Windows and Mac (**Figure 12.3**). QuickTime Pro is adept at handling both Apple formats like .MOV and

AAC and standard formats like MPEG-4. Using QuickTime Pro, you can also capture video and audio and create surround sound. If you're on a Mac, you can automate video conversion tasks using Mac OS X's Automator and AppleScript. If you're a Final Cut Pro user, you'll have additional encoding options using the Compressor application included with Soundtrack Pro, Final Cut Pro, and Final Cut Studio.

Figure 12.3 Apple's Quick-Time Pro serves as an inexpensive Swiss Army knife for handling video on both Windows and Mac, with extensive import/export options and basic editing.

Windows Media videos (.AVI files) are also typical in video and audio work. (Windows Media files can be opened easily on the Mac using Windows Media Player for Mac, but not all audio and video applications support it.) Unlike Apple's tools, most of Microsoft's tools are free. You can handle many conversion tasks in the Windows Media Player application and, for heavy-duty batch conversion and encoding, can download the free Encoder tools. The Mac encoding tools for Windows Media are more limited than the Windows tools, as you might expect, but can still be worth a download.

If you're using video only for reference, you won't need to use a full-resolution file. Reducing the quality of the file can conserve hard disk space and CPU bandwidth, so that you can devote more resources to your audio work instead. You'll want to maintain the original *frame rate* (the number of frames displayed per second), but you can use a lower display resolution (like 320x240 instead of 640x480 or HD) and compress the video.

 Web resources:

Apple and Microsoft each maintain pages that contain necessary software downloads, free tools, and tutorials. If you're working with video files, each is a must-visit; skip the glitzier pages advertising movie trailers and head straight to these resources:

QuickTime Pro (www.apple.com/quick-time/pro)

Windows Media (www.microsoft.com/windows/windowsmedia)

Cheap/free video editors:

For simple video editing (like trimming down a video file or converting it), use QuickTime Pro for Windows or Mac. If your needs are slightly more advanced but you're on a budget, try one of these tools:

Windows Movie Maker, free with Microsoft Windows XP Service Pack 2 and later; find tips, tutorials, and forums at the community site Windows Movie Makers (www.windows-moviemakers.net)

Apple iMovie HD, part of Apple's $79 iLife suite and free on new Macs; integrated with GarageBand (www.apple.com/ilife/imovie/)

Integrated tools

If all you need to do is import video footage, edit the soundtrack or add a score, and give it to your video editor, opening a small QuickTime file or sending it to a collaborator may be all you need to do. But what if you need to edit audio tracks while working on a video project? A major selling point of the leading video and audio suites is their ability to select audio in a project, switch over to an audio application to edit it, and modify the original video project without manually exporting and importing. Since a single manufacturer (like Apple) sells a suite of products (including Final Cut Studio), it's in the manufacturer's best interest to make it easy to integrate the included applications.

For instance, using Final Cut Studio, you can select audio in Final Cut Pro, DVD Studio Pro, or Motion, and by right-clicking on audio (Ctrl-clicking on a one-button Mac mouse), send it to Soundtrack Pro for either destructive or nondestructive editing (**Figure 12.4**). You'll see the associated video in Soundtrack Pro while editing, and when you save, the audio will automatically update in the original project. Similarly, in Sony's Vegas Pro for Windows, you can use ACID files and loops directly from the interface, and by right-clicking on audio in the timeline, can choose Edit Source Project to make changes in your original ACID audio project.

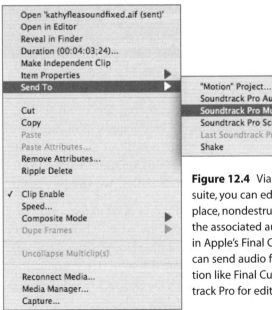

Figure 12.4 Via an integrated suite, you can edit audio in place, nondestructively, with the associated audio tool. Here in Apple's Final Cut Studio, you can send audio from an application like Final Cut Pro to Soundtrack Pro for editing.

These features are especially useful if your video project and audio project are both on the same machine, since they facilitate switching between video and audio applications. However, by exporting and importing video and audio files, you can use these features to exchange files remotely as well, in case your video editor is in Melbourne, Australia, and you're editing audio in Madrid. The projects may include not only basic audio and video information, but also editable multitrack sound complete with plug-ins, edits, and automation.

Interchange formats

Working with integrated software suites works well for many purposes, but that doesn't mean you have to limit yourself to working with applications that share a brand name. File exchange formats like OMF, AAF, MFX, and Final Cut Pro/XML all allow easy import/export of multichannel audio projects. At the very least, these formats include multichannel audio information as separate, editable channels; also, some formats (AAF, MFX, XML) include additional information like track automation. (See Chapter 10, "Put It Together: Arrange, Mix, and Master," for more details on these file formats.)

Support for formats like AAF is growing not only in DAWs but in other media programs like Adobe After Effects and Premiere. OMF is popular in postproduction because the format, developed by Avid, is compatible with Avid video systems, Pro Tools audio systems, and many DAWs and video programs. A typical workflow might include exporting multitrack sound from Pro Tools as an OMF and opening it on an Avid or other video system, or vice versa. Other formats include application-specific information. Apple's Final Cut Pro/XML format, for instance, lets you move audio between Logic Pro and Final Cut Pro. You could assemble a multitrack audio soundtrack in Logic, and then export it to Final Cut with mixing settings intact and editable.

Time, Frames, and SMPTE

In order to properly measure time in video, for synchronization and cueing, you need a standard way of calculating locations in time. It'd be pretty useless to figure out that you wanted an orchestral hit to be heard at a certain point in the action if you couldn't describe exactly where that point was, and you can't synchronize two media files if you don't know where the correct starting point is.

 Get self-contained before you move: If you're moving files between machines, make sure you save your audio and video project files as self-contained files, not reference files. Reference files include pointers to the actual audio and/or video data, which is stored in another location. If the reference file can't find that data (which will happen if the reference file is moved to another machine), the file will appear "offline"; you won't be able to use it. A self-contained project file is larger, because it includes all the associated video and audio data, but it's portable.

The standard means of expressing time in film and video is *SMPTE time-code*, a set of industry standards for designating each frame of the video. SMPTE timecode (usually pronounced "simp-tee") is used both to synchronize equipment, by providing a standard frame of time reference, and to measure relative location in video and film. Technically, it's called SMPTE/EBU, named for the Society of Motion Picture and Television Engineers (www.smpte.org) and European Broadcasting Union (EBU/UER, www.ebu.ch), the standards organizations that developed it.

Unless you're connecting multiple pieces of pro video gear, one thing you won't have to worry about is how SMPTE is used for synchronization. Instead, you'll probably first see SMPTE timecode as a simple series of numbers in this format:

Hours : Minutes : Seconds : Frames (xx : xx : xx : xx)

For example, 2 hours, 7 minutes, 23 seconds, 14 frames would be written 02:07:23:14. The nuts and bolts of how this works when it's encoded in media like film and digital video (DV) tape are a great deal more complicated, but for most tasks you only need to understand how to read the timecode as it's displayed in your DAW or video tool (**Figure 12.5**). (Technically, your DV tape or QuickTime file uses its own means of encoding timecode digitally, not literal SMPTE timecode signal as is used on analog tape and film. But the formatting of minutes, seconds, and frames is displayed to the end user the same way.)

Figure 12.5 Transport controls of programs like Cubase SX can display timecode in various frame rates, alongside musical measurements of time.

There's one twist: what a frame means depends on the *frame rate*. TV, digital video, and film all provide the illusion of motion by displaying a series of successive still images called frames. They do so at a constant rate, but what that rate is depends on the medium and even the country you're in. **Table 12.1** contains a comparison of commonly found frame rates.

Table 12.1 Common Frame Rates (frames per second, fps)

Frame Rate	Format	Where It's Used
24 fps	Film	Worldwide
25 fps	PAL, SECAM-encoded TV and video	Europe, Africa, Australia, much of Asia and Latin America
29.97 fps/30 drop fps	NTSC-encoded TV and video	North America, much of South America, Japan and parts of Asia and the Pacific
24, 25, 30, 60 fps	HD (High-Definition) video	Worldwide; frame rate typically mirrors historic analog encoding and broadcast

You'll need to make sure your audio software is set to display timecode at the correct frame rate so you can properly locate each frame. These frame rates are mostly straightforward, except for the 29.97 fps rate used by default for NTSC in certain parts of the world. Because of a quirk of engineering, when American broadcasters tried to create a new color broadcast format that was compatible with black-and-white receivers, they had to use the oddly numbered frame rate (29.97 is an approximation; the rate is actually an even stranger $30 \times 1000/1001$ fps, or 29.97003 fps). The 30 drop frame rate is the same as 30 fps, but "drops" frames at regular intervals so that it doesn't fall out of sync with the 29.97003 fps rate. (If you're in Europe or most of the rest of the world except the United States or Japan, you don't have to worry about drop-frame, because it's not used by the popular PAL format.)

Bizarre frame rates and regional differences aside, what's important is that all your audio and video be set to the same frame rate. You can synchronize media that uses different frame rates, but it can cause a range of problems. If you're involved with a project in which you're mixing film and video, for instance, you may want to communicate with the postproduction house or processing facility that you're dealing with. At the very least, make sure you know in advance what your target medium is, and ensure that all your recordings match up.

MUSIC FOR VIDEO

Before we look at the thornier issues of exact synchronization as it's used in dialog and sound effects, let's start with the rougher sync that's used in creating music for film and video. While dialog that's even a frame or two out of sync is immediately noticeable, music often benefits from having different internal timing than what's happening onscreen. Just ask anyone who's played Pink Floyd's *Dark Side of the Moon* to the movie *The Wizard of Oz*: sometimes accidental synchronicity is more interesting than intentional synchronicity. Making music work in terms of timing involves balancing intentional synchronization (usually within a few frames), and more flexible, unintentional synchronization. For those moments when you do want control over how music is fitting to picture, digital video and audio software provides a number of tools for aligning the two.

Spotting and Hit Points

The music swells as the heroine leans in for a kiss. A metallic scrape of piano strings screeches as the murderer's hand slides across the knife. *Duh-duh*: A string motive tells you that Jaws is lurking underwater. As comedians say, "it's all in the timing." Although there are many expressive elements to film scoring other than just lining up cues, timing is an essential ingredient.

A *hit point* is an event in the video, a cue, at which you want some musical event to coincide with what's on screen. Even before any sound is added, just deciding what will be a hit point is an art in itself. Choose too few hits, and music will just sit over top of the film as background, lifeless and failing to interact with the image. Choose too many, and the music becomes distracting.

Spotting is the act of watching a video, usually many times over, and finding points that make effective hit points. A master film composer can slip in subtle hit points so they trigger an emotional reaction without you even noticing the coincidence. That's why a lot of energy and finesse goes into the spotting process.

Before computers, film composers like Bernard Herrmann and Alfred Newman would spot using pencil and paper. Now, you can use markers to keep track of hit point locations (**Figure 12.6**). Most DAWs have a marker function, so while watching a digital video of the material you want to score, you can add a marker each time you come across a desired hit point. (It's a good idea to memorize the keyboard shortcut for adding a marker.)

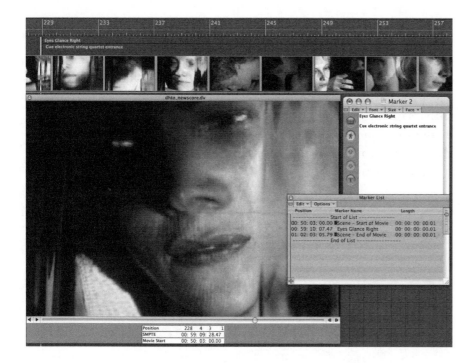

Figure 12.6 Spotting with markers involves selecting points at which you'd like something to occur in the music in a DAW like Logic Pro. With the crucial points marked in real time (SMPTE time), you can refer to these landmarks later to adjust sound and music to fit.

Adjusting Tempo

Once you've marked the hit points, your second challenge is to find a way to make music fit them. Music is usually measured in beats and bars, not seconds and frames, so if you're creating regularly metered music, some thought needs to go into tempo and meter. Usually, you'll assemble most or all of your hit points first, marking their timecode locations, and then adjust meter and tempo to see how the music's beats and bars correspond to the video's seconds and frames. (You may need to use a "lock markers" feature to make sure you can remap tempi while leaving your time markers in place, since it's the music that's changing, not the video.)

Finding a musical flow that fits the video depends on what's happening onscreen, and on how the video is edited. Expert video editors often build a musical rhythm into their edits, either intentionally (by watching timecode) or intuitively. Choosing certain tempi can help images onscreen fall naturally into the musical rhythm. Multiples of 60 work especially well. For instance, at 120 bpm (beats per minute), two beats will fall every second; that's every 12 frames at 24 fps, or every 15 frames at 30 fps.

For a simple score, you might opt for a 4/4 meter at 60 or 120 bpm and then leave everything else to the music. You won't want regular meters and static tempi all the time, though. Some applications, like MOTU Digital Performer and Steinberg Cubase SX, include tools for automatically calculating initial tempo and subsequent tempo changes so that even gradual changes can be shaped to fit hit points (**Figure 12.7**). If your DAW can't do this, you can try adjusting tempo envelopes/automation, or simply make changes and compare the timecode values in your Markers window to the resulting musical values.

Figure 12.7 MOTU Digital Performer can automatically calculate different tempi, displaying how they'll fit with the markers you've selected. At some tempi, beats will come close to certain hit points, whereas others are farther off; they're displayed in descending order of accuracy.

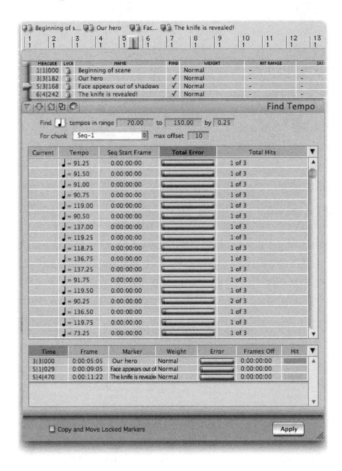

You won't necessarily spot on every project. The phrase "cut picture to music" refers to editors who cut the film to the music's rhythmic events rather than the other way around. Some directors will even find existing music that naturally fits the rhythm of editing, without substantial modification to either. Digital audio technology makes these techniques easier than ever: you can quickly try a what-if scenario and see and hear what happens. You can also cut segments of recorded audio without micromanaging tempi and meters, for a relaxed relationship between sound and picture.

Timing and Notation

Traditionally, working with notation software has meant spotting first, then moving to the notation software to do the actual scoring. A composer would set up markers in a DAW like Digital Performer, then either manually copy them into a program like Finale or export tempo and meter changes as an SMF file. Some composers still spot on pencil and paper, watching the video on a computer or TV display.

Once video is integrated with notation software, however, it's possible to spot timecodes within the notation application, which is much more flexible (**Figure 12.8**). Using Sibelius 4 (www.sibelius.com), you can import video, play back video in sync with the score, mark hit points, and export an audio rendering of your score with the video file. The quality of such a rendering is limited, but it's very convenient for running the music past a director before you hire musicians to play an expensive session.

Whichever way you choose to work, you'll want to print timecode indications above the score, as shown in Figure 12.8, with annotated markers for significant hit points. That way, you'll know which points you most urgently need to hit, and you'll have a reference for lining up the score with the video when you record a performance with live musicians.

 See spot hit: Digital video is now so precise that some composers and editors find spotting has gotten too accurate. Instead of carefully spotting to the exact frame where a hit occurs, they play the video at normal speed and intuitively hit the add marker keystroke where they feel the hit should go. Being slightly off can make the hits seem more organic.

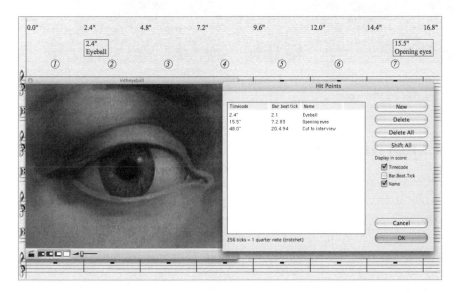

Figure 12.8 Sibelius's Hit Points display lets you spot video from within the scoring application. Timecode and bar/beat/tick are displayed side by side, so you can see how each cue will line up in musical time.

Performing with Live Musicians

Working entirely in the hermetically sealed realm of digital audio and video, resolving timing issues is reasonably easy. Working with live musicians, though, means mixing accurate digital technology with decidedly organic technology (namely, human beings). That doesn't make computers any less handy. You can either designate a conductor to keep players in time with the music, have ensemble members watch a display, or give players headphones and play a *click track* as they record their parts. (A click track is a generated metronome that corresponds to the tempo of the score, including any meter or tempo changes that might occur.)

Many DAWs include oversized or scalable timecode displays (**Figure 12.9**). Even in high-end professional settings, many conductors simply project these displays so that they can watch the timecode and the score at the same time. Alternatively, with real-time display of scores improving and simultaneous video playback possible in DAWs and programs like Sibelius, they can simply open a video window, open a timecode display, and hit Play, watching the score from a screen. To replicate this Hollywood setup on a budget, you'll want a projector or a large television or computer display so you can see what you're doing while you record.

Figure 12.9 An oversized timecode display like Logic Pro's is useful for dragging to a second monitor or projector so you can watch the counter while live musicians play the score.

Exporting Audio for Video

Once you have your mix, you'll want to export your audio in a form that makes it easy to drop it into a video editing application. We'll look at synchronization issues in the second half of this chapter, but suffice it to say, whether you're doing the video editing and postproduction or someone else is, exporting the audio in a suitable file format is essential.

Most of the time, you'll want to export as follows:

1. AIFF or WAV file

2. 48 kHz, 16-bit audio

3. The file should contain a "2-beep," a short beep two seconds before the beginning of the actual audio; see the sidebar, "The 2-beep," p. 511.

Recording for Video

Most of what has been discussed in this book about audio recording applies to music created for video; see, in particular, Chapter 3 for information on how to connect devices and Chapter 6 for information about microphones and recording, as well as Chapter 10 for general mixing strategies. There are some techniques that are specific to sound production for video, however. The single thorniest issue to deal with is synchronization.

Separately Recorded Film/Video and Audio

If audio and video are recorded on the same storage medium at the same time on the same device, you shouldn't have to worry about synchronization. For instance, if you recorded sound to your DV camera by connecting a microphone to its audio input while shooting video, that recorded sound should be synced to picture. (If it falls out of sync, you probably need to get a better camera.)

There are many cases when you'll need or want more than one recorder. You can't record sound onto film formats like 16mm and 35mm, so if you're using one of those formats you'll have to carry a second deck for audio. Video formats like DV and HDV can contain audio as well as video, but a dedicated audio recorder can provide higher-quality sound. Many video cameras are geared for video footage, not for pro audio inputs, and lack good quality XLR mic inputs. By bringing along a separate audio recorder, you can avoid the video camera's low-fidelity audio capture.

The use of separate recorders for picture and sound is called *dual system recording*. It requires that you put the two media files together again in the postproduction phase. Pro video editing software is capable of merging the two recordings so that they're synchronized, using time information recorded on the storage medium (timecode), or some other reference point.

There are three basic elements to the process of preparing synced video and audio via the dual system recording method:

1. **Recording:** The audio and video captured during production should ideally have some form of timecode stream or other common time reference, which is included in each of the recordings when they are made.

2. **Capture:** Transferring your audio and video content onto your hard drive system and into your editing program (Final Cut Pro, Avid, etc.) should preserve timecode information for editing purposes.

3. **Synchronization:** Once you've brought in video and audio using either timecode or another reference, you'll use your software to merge your clips based on that time reference so that they're perfected synced.

The first step is to make sure there's some kind of reference in the recordings that you can use to synchronize them.

Recordings and Time Reference

 Get all your devices on the same page: The most important task when recording is to set timecode to the same frame rate in all your devices and software. Otherwise, you'll have to deal with *pulldown:* the conversion between timecodes with different frame rates. Considering pulldown could be conversion between 29.97 fps and 25 fps, it can obviously cause some major problems, so it's best to avoid the issue entirely by matching all your media's frame rates when possible.

Technical details aside, it's pretty easy to understand the need for recording a time reference by which you can sync. Imagine you're at a track-and-field race between two runners. Instead of shouting "3, 2, 1, go!" or firing a starting pistol, each runner just runs the 100 yards at a different time, and no one has a stop watch.

Who was faster? There's no way to tell, because there's no common time reference. The start point (the moment they started running) and the end point (the moment they crossed the finish line) happened at different times, and there was no common measurement of time (no stopwatch). Any one of these three elements would solve this problem: if they crossed the finish line at the same time, whoever started running first lost. If they started at the same time, whoever crossed the finish line first won. If someone was watching a stopwatch, he or she would be able to easily measure the length of each run, even if the runners started and finished at different times. Notice that you don't necessarily need the stopwatch: you just need some common reference for a starting or ending point.

The same is true for video production. To synchronize your recordings, you need at least one of three elements: an in point (the starting line from the example), an out point (the finish line), or a common stream of timecode (the stopwatch).

Slates and clapperboards

Professional film and video crews begin shooting by adding a *slate*, a visual and auditory marker that designates the start of each take. Even if you've never seen a professional production, you probably know what this looks like: someone shouts, "Take 4!", holds a flat board in front of the camera, and then "claps" the hinged top of the board.

You can buy a slate, also called a clapboard, clapperboard, or "clapper," at a video supply store (**Figure 12.10**). Simple models run as little as $10, so there's not much excuse for not using one. The old-style models were made of wood and had chalkboard fronts for labeling which scene was which. Modern models are fancier, with dry-erase whiteboards, and even digital timecode readouts on high-end slates. The design is significant because it actually creates two reference points at once: you can align the sound of the transient, the "clap sound," with the visual reference of the top of the hinged clapper coming in contact with the base. (With a digital LED readout, there's a third, numeric timecode reference; you can literally see the numbers of the timecode as the stream is received electronically by the slate.)

Figure 12.10 Slates range from simple to sophisticated, but they have one thing in common: "clapping" the hinged top provides both a visual and auditory cue for synchronizing sound and picture. Advanced "smart slates" like the Denecke Time Code slates can also generate, read, and display timecode. (Photo courtesy Pawel Wdowczak)

Slate and timecode equipment makers:

Ambient Recording
(www.ambientaudio.com)

Denecke, Inc.
(www.denecke.com)

Even if you don't have a pro clapper, any sharp transient sound with a clear accompanying visual will do. You can even clap your hands in front of the camera. (Banging the actor on the head is not generally suggested, although in the underwater shooting of James Cameron's *The Abyss*, the crew banged the helmets of their actors to get a good sound.)

Using a slate at the beginning of a take gives you your in point, but to be safe, you should also add a slate to the end of your take; in other words, clap your clapboard at the beginning and ending of everything you shoot. This serves two functions. First, if something goes wrong with your start slate, you have a backup slate from which you can sync video and audio. Second, if a problem with one of your recording devices is causing timing to drift, you'll be able to identify and more easily fix the problem.

Even if you're generating timecode for automatic synchronization, adding slates to the beginning and end of a take is a good idea. The additional reference points can be used if your timecode fails, and can help trouble-shoot timecode issues. To save yourself headaches, then, even if you're not involved in shooting, make sure whoever is in charge at least adds slates, even if they're doing nothing fancier than clapping their hands.

Slates are also typically added in video and audio editing; in this case the "slate" is a screen added to the front end of the footage, not the physical object shown in Figure 12.10. This screen also includes the auditory cue of the 2-beep, which is the editing equivalent of the "clap" sound added to footage by the physical slate.

Timecode signal

With pro recording equipment that can synchronize to and record an external timecode signal, you can perform more sophisticated, automatic synchronization. When you record a common timecode signal onto multiple devices, everything you record should be coded with the same time information regardless of which device recorded it. That way, your editing software will be able to automatically merge footage from any device. For instance, 3 minutes, 2 seconds, 4 frames will mean the same thing on your two DV cameras and your audio recorder, because each recorded not only audio and/or video but also a signal printed to the tape at that moment identifying time at which the recording took place.

The 2-beep

Despite the name, the "2-beep" doesn't sound like the Road Runner. The "two" stands for two seconds, not two beeps. The 2-beep is a single beep used to assist synchronization:

- The beep is a sine wave with a frequency of 1 kHz.
- It is always added two seconds before the start of picture. (This is most often at –00:00:02:00, but can also be two seconds before the beginning of a video take, or two seconds before the beginning of an audio mix, such as a specific audio or music cue.)
- Its duration is just one frame.

Assuming you haven't already been handed footage with a 2-beep and are providing your own, you'll add it manually in your DAW or other audio software (**Figure 12.11**).

Pro Tools and other applications have simple sine wave generation facilities that let you determine the duration of the synthesized sound in frames. First, set your audio editor's playback head to two seconds before the beginning of your mix. (You may need to insert empty bars or audio time at the beginning of your project.) Then use your audio editor's tone generator command to create the beep, setting the frequency and setting length to 1 frame. (If your tone generator doesn't give you a length option, set the ruler of your audio editor or DAW to frames and select 1 frame of audio, starting at 2 seconds before 0:00.) That's all there is to it: export your mix to AIFF/WAV, and you're done.

If you're exporting an audio mix to give to a video editor or postproduction house, they'll use your 2-beep to sync your file to their video. You can also do it yourself if you need to; the only specialized equipment you need is your ears. If both clips have a 2-beep on them and are played simultaneously, you'll be able to immediately hear whether they're in sync. If they are, the two sine waves will combine, and you'll hear a single, louder beep of the same duration. If the sync is off by even part of a frame, you'll hear either a longer beep or multiple beeps.

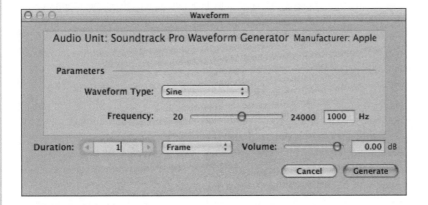

Figure 12.11 To generate a 2-beep, you need a basic waveform generator in an audio editing application or DAW that can select length in frames. For instance, in Soundtrack Pro, choose Process > Insert > Waveform. Set the frequency to 1 kHz (1000 Hz), amplitude to 0 dB, and the length to 1 frame.

Most recording devices write some kind of timecode as they record: if you look at the display of a DAT or DV recorder, for instance, you'll see time-code displayed on the counter. Not all counters show timecode; the way you can tell this display represents the timecode written to the tape is by moving the tape to another machine and viewing its counter.

The trick for synchronization is that this can't just be any timecode; you need to make sure every device that's recording has exactly the same timecode. This timecode source is usually provided as a SMPTE timecode signal.

You won't normally hear the SMPTE signal, but a device capable of reading the timecode will be able to extract it from an otherwise inaudible track, so that everything recorded on that device contains the timecode reference. (On tape, this is an extra physical track; in digital video and audio files, it's encoded digitally into the file.) When you capture the clip to a pro video application, the timecode is included in your video project, so the software can automatically synchronize clips. (Most often, but not always, this source is encoded as SMPTE timecode; see the sidebar, "SMPTE and Other Timecode Formats.")

 SMPTE and Other Timecode Formats

SMPTE Timecode signal is an analog signal containing encoded time information. (It's a modulated pulse wave, to be specific.) Recorders that store SMPTE information "stripe" this signal onto the tape, usually by recording it onto an unused portion of the tape. (Older analog decks interlaced the SMPTE data with the frames of the video signal.)

"Timecode" and "SMPTE" are, contrary to popular belief, not synonymous terms. SMPTE is just one kind of timecode. SMPTE was originally developed for film and was later adapted to tape and other formats. Your hardware and software may support or require other formats, and even many SMPTE-compatible devices convert the actual information into other encodings. (Different digital video tape formats, like MiniDV, DVCAM, DVCPro HD, and HDV, can use different formats.)

The good news is, most of the time you won't have to worry about these details. Most of the conversion between the different formats occurs behind-the-scenes, by the recorder hardware capable of receiving timecode and your digital video software during capture. An important first step is to check to see if your devices and software support timecode capture and encoding. You may need to check your product specs and documentation for details.

To generate timecode during the recording process, you need a timecode source or generator. This can be a computer with peripheral hardware capable of generating timecode signal, or a recording device—anything with a timecode out. (To use a computer, you'll need either an audio interface that includes SMPTE timecode inputs and output jacks, like the MOTU 828 mkII and Traveler, or a dedicated synchronizer hardware unit; see the sidebar, "Digital Recorders and Formats.") Second, you need a way of receiving and recording the signal; each device needs to be compatible with the timecode signal. These devices usually receive this signal via a timecode-in jack, a dedicated audio connection. You'll need to check your audio recorder's specs to see if it can send and/or receive timecode information; many cannot, particularly if you're using inexpensive semi-pro equipment. (In that case, you'll need to sync via a clapperboard or other reference instead.)

Once you have both a generator and a device or devices to receive timecode, you'll have several options for what kind of timecode to use, but you'll most frequently encounter one of three popular types:

- **Free run:** Like two spies in a James Bond movie synchronizing watches before a mission, equipment using free run sync sets a synchronized point and then starts running, disregarding any incoming timecode. The camera, the audio recorder, the computer, and all other devices simply start their clocks and run as long as they're on. The timecode can be encoded as either time of day or an arbitrary specified start point.

- **Record run:** Instead of running continuously, record run devices record timecode only when they're on. The problem is that stopping recording or switching off a device will throw timecode out of sync.

- **Jam-sync:** Jam-sync synchronizes your device (such as a camera) to an external synchronization source. For instance, cameras set to jam-sync might receive a SMPTE timecode signal from a computer or audio recorder, overriding their internal timecode with that external signal, as recorded to their audio track.

The advantage of free run and jam-sync over record run is that they'll work even if devices are stopped or started at different times, or even powered down, because they're all using the same timecode.

 Leaving a sufficient lead-in and lead-out: Even digital equipment needs a margin of error for accurate timecode. Any mechanical glitch on a DV tape or other delay can cause a tiny timeout dropout. So to get a fully synchronized tape, leave a few seconds before the critical part of your recording to ensure complete timecode recording (10 counts is a safe reference typically used by pros). Don't hit Stop once you're done recording; leave a sufficient lead-out. If you're using tape, you'll also want to rewind slightly over the lead-out prior to restarting recording so there isn't a timecode break between subsequent takes.

 Shooting on HD: New HD (High Definition) video formats pose new challenges for synchronization; slate manufacturer Denecke has a good overview of these issues entitled "24P Info: Time Code and the High Definition Camera" (http://denecke.com/24pinfo.htm).

Recording Formats

Popular pro audio recorder vendors:

Fostex (www.fostexinternational.com)

Marantz (www.d-mpro.com)

Nagra (www.nagraaudio.com)

Sony (http://bssc.sel.sony.com/Broadcastand-Business)

Zaxcom (www.zaxcom.com)

Recording formats can be complex, so here's some general advice: when in doubt, opt for 48 kHz, 16-bit audio, and make sure there's some kind of time reference embedded in the recording: an in point, an out point, a timecode stream, or some combination of the three.

Generally speaking, digital video footage is shot at its highest-quality setting at 48 kHz, 16-bit. (DV cameras can be set to other settings, but the highest-quality setting is preferable.) Stereo sound for DV will usually be delivered at this quality.

Surround (theatre-style, multichannel mixing) and other audiovisual formats open up other possibilities, but are dependent on delivery method; see Chapter 10 for an extended discussion of surround mixing. Here again, recording at 48 kHz is preferred, because DTS surround sound (Digital Theater Systems) and Linear PCM (LPCM) both encode each audio channel at 48 kHz. (See the sidebar, "Digital Recorders and Formats.")

High-end recorders geared for video work often encode audio in the Broadcast Wave Format (BWF). BWF is a format based on the Microsoft WAV file format that adds additional timecode information to the file, making it easier to sync with video. The format was approved by the European Broadcast Union and is used as a standard internationally. BWFs can be read by most DAWs and high-end video editors on both Windows and Mac, so all you have to do is drag them off your hard drive recorder onto your computer, usually via USB. (Note that if you have a semipro digital audio recorder that uses plain-vanilla WAV or AIFF, you'll lack this timecode information and will need to sync it manually.)

 Digital Recorders and Formats

Back when analog was the norm, film crews would travel with portable cassette decks made by companies like Nagra and Marantz. Later, even VHS decks were used as audio-only recorders. Digital recording has actually broadened the number of recording options rather than simplifying them. Knowing where your content has come from will help you prepare for editing—especially if you're relying on sound given to you by a video production crew, who may not have thought much about the audio they were recording.

Note that many of these recorders—semipro recorders, solid-state recorders, and even many DV cameras—are unable to sync to timecode. With these devices, you'll absolutely want to record slate information, including both a 2-beep before the recording and a clap at the beginning and end, if possible.

Common recorders include:

- **DV recorders/cameras:** The most common place to find sound is on the DV tape. DV always includes timecode, although you'll need some additional time reference if you're using sources from more than one DV recorder, as in a multicamera setup.

- **Computer:** Although a laptop is a bit unwieldy on-location compared to a recording deck, you can record directly into your digital audio software. Interfaces like MOTU's Traveler include SMPTE timecode features that allow you to sync without additional hardware, using software to generate timecode (**Figure 12.12**).

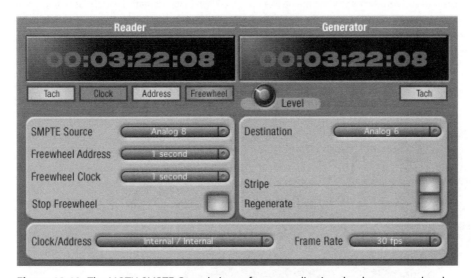

Figure 12.12 The MOTU SMPTE Console is a software application that lets you read and generate SMPTE timecode via your computer, using interfaces like the FireWire-based MOTU Traveler and 828 mk II. In addition to enabling sync in the studio, this lets you sync with recorders on the road, using your computer as a recording device, synchronization source, or both. (Image courtesy MOTU, Inc.)

- **DAT recorder:** DAT recorders have the disadvantage of using linear media (that is, tape), so transfers are slower. A variety of reliable, high-quality recorders are available from companies like Sony and Tascam, and DAT remains a popular format for video production.

- **Nagra:** The Nagra open-reel tape recorders have been so wildly popular among filmmakers for decades that if you hear someone generically refer to "a Nagra," they probably mean the classic reel-to-reel analog version. Nagra Audio still makes high-end tape recorders, although they now make digital recorders as well.

- **Pro Hard Disk recorders:** Since linear tape isn't as convenient as a nonlinear hard drive, broadcast audio recorders now often use hard drives to store sound, outputting to DVD or connecting to a computer via USB. These recorders have important pro features like timecode input jacks, high sample rates, and reliable timing encoding and recording geared for on-location and production work. They usually use the Broadcast Wave Format (BWF). You might also consider a digital recording workstation from a company like Roland, Yamaha, or Korg as a more portable replacement for a laptop.

continues

Digital Recorders and Formats (*continued*)

- **MiniDisc recorders:** MiniDisc should generally be avoided for serious audio work, because the standard MD format uses lossy compressed audio and can cause timing and sync issues. You'll also need to manually sync MD audio, since consumer MD recorders lack timecode input. (Sony's Hi-MD format records directly to uncompressed Linear PCM audio, which is the basis of both Broadcast Wave and Microsoft WAV formats; it's slightly more usable, although you may need to manually resample audio at 48 kHz.)

- **Semipro recorders and solid-state:** As storage media like CompactFlash have dramatically decreased in price, solid-state recorders are becoming more popular. Make sure yours supports 48 kHz uncompressed audio, and be prepared to manually insert some kind of timing reference, because few of these recorders have timecode inputs. (Exceptions include the Fostex FR-2 CompactFlash recorder, shown in **Figure 12.13**, and the Tascam HD-P2.)

Figure 12.13 In years past, tape (analog or digital) was the only way to do field recording, but now solid-state recorders are gaining popularity. The Fostex FR-2 records high-resolution audio (up to 192 kHz) onto CompactFlash cards using the BWF file format, and with an optional sync card can read and generate SMPTE. Simpler, cheaper consumer devices lack sync but also record onto affordable, tiny CF cards. (Photo courtesy Fostex Corporation)

Postproduction: Capture and Synchronization

Once all your audio and video has been recorded, the final step is to bring it into the editing environment for postproduction. Even working with digital media, some additional steps are necessary to bring your media together. You'll need to make sure your media is captured properly to the computer so that you retain timecode information. The best way to do this is by importing it into a video editing project using your video editing software's capture utility. (If you're not doing the video editing, you can have an editor do the capture for you and send you a file with the video for timing reference.)

Capturing video and audio

So you have your DV video on tape, you have your computer, and you have your video editing software: everything's digital, so you're done, right? Not exactly: since DV (and HD digital video cameras) all shoot to tape, you'll have to capture your media to your hard drive in real time. The tape will play back at normal speed, and the computer will record video signal, most often through a FireWire connection to a camera or tape deck. You need to make sure the capture software is capable of recording timecode information along with the video and/or audio content, so that when the software records that information to your hard drive, the timecode is maintained.

There are three elements to this capture process: a device playing your source content, a computer, and video editing software. The source is called a Video Tape Recorder (VTR); it's typically either a DV camera or a dedicated DV playback deck. With DV, the computer is connected to the VTR via a simple FireWire cable. You click Record in your video software, and the software records whatever is on your tape to a file on the hard drive.

Device Control is a protocol that's used to remotely control the deck or camera (for start, stop, and other transport operations), enabling you to capture video and audio from a device and write edited video and audio back to the device. Device Control is essential for synchronization, because it also transfers timecode from your recording device to your computer. Using a DV camera or deck, Device Control is usually plug-and-play, even with cheap consumer-grade cameras. Connect the camera via FireWire, and when you click Record in your video editing application, the camera will start playing and will transmit timecode information to your software. (If you're working with a professional audio recorder, you might also use a serial RS-232 or RS-422 connector, which can be connected to the computer via an adapter or a pro-level video/audio capture card.)

To keep everything in sync, you need a tool that's up to the job. Entry-level tools like Apple iMovie, Adobe Premiere LE, and Microsoft Windows Movie Maker can all record video from a DV camera and other sources, but they generally don't support timecode capture and synchronization. Even the full version of Adobe Premiere requires a third-party plug-in for Device Control support. Fortunately, Sony Vegas, Apple Final Cut Express and Final Cut Pro, and Avid's product line all support Device Control and synchronization. You can also use specialized capture, logging, and batch processing tools like Squarebox's CatDV (www.squarebox.co.uk).

Using the capture feature in one of these applications, you'll record video and audio to a hard drive file and import it (along with any meta-information) into your video project. Capture tools perform other useful tasks in addition to retaining timecode information. They *log* recorded information, so you can keep track of what footage came from which camera or recorder on which date and what it contains—not much of a consideration for your home movie, perhaps, but a big deal for industrial-strength, full-length projects. (Specifically, logging records a *reel number*, among other information like comments. Although the word "reel" used to designate a physical spool of film, it now identifies clips of video that came from the same video tape.) Digital video editing software can also organize content based on related media (like audio and video from a multicamera, multirecorder shoot), subject matter, or any other system you want to use.

Importing audio is usually even easier. To add audio with embedded timecode in Broadcast Wave files, you might connect your BWF digital recorder via USB, drag the files to your hard drive, and then import them to a DAW or audio editor with BWF compatibility, or directly into your video software.

With other formats like ordinary WAV files, you can also drag-and-drop, although you won't retain timecode information since it's not included in the file; the file always begins at 0:00:00. Audio and video captured without timecode can either be imported as is or dubbed onto a DV deck to add timecode information. Either way, you'll need to sync it manually.

Synchronization

If you've shot video and audio in a dual system recording setup (via separate decks), your final step will be to synchronize the two media. To reconnect the video with its associated audio, you'll use the "merge" function in your video editing software (**Figure 12.14**). If all your clips have the same time-code, you'll be able to merge them automatically. If not, here are the methods by which you can manually sync them:

- **Match a slate:** If your footage has a slate at its beginning or end, you can sync with that. If the slate is at the beginning, you'll mark the in points; if it's at the end, you'll mark the out points. Let's use the in point as an example. To find the slate in the sound, scrub over the audio until the playback cursor is right over top of the "clap" sound, and mark that spot as an in point. To find it in the video, move in slow motion to the exact frame where the top hinge of the slate makes contact with the bottom of the slate. Mark that spot as the video's in point. Then merge the clips using the in points. (This method will also work if you use a person clapping his or her hands as a "poor man's slate.")

- **Synchronize a 2-beep:** Using the 2-beep, you can either visually overlay the clips by looking at the waveforms or scrub over the audio to the right location and place a marker on each. Then set your audio editing software so that segments will snap to markers when dragged.

- **Synchronize identical timecode:** Your video application should be able to select a timecode source from a group of clips to merge them according to identical timecode. You should still check the 2-beep and/or in and out slates to double-check that they've synced successfully.

- **If there's no reference at all, synchronize manually:** This is the trickiest case. In this situation, you'll need to manually overlay audio and video using your video editor's nudge feature. First, get the two elements in the same ballpark: look for any reference at all, like a clear transient, start, or end part that you can identify visually or aurally, checking the waveform display in the timeline view or any other landmark contained in both audio and video. Next, align that element as well as you can so you're at least in nudge range. Then nudge by seconds, then by frames, for a frame-accurate sync. (Many applications even let you edit at the subframe level, if needed.)

 Do you really need timecode sync? The short answer is no. The reality is, many shoots—not just independent films, but commercial ones as well—record video and audio without true timecode sync. The reason is that many recorders lack this feature, and, on a nontechnical note, audio and video people often don't pay much attention to each other on a shoot. Using a slate (even if it's someone clapping their hands at the beginning and end of a take mimicking a slate) is the next best thing. In the absence of a clap, you can use the manual method of nudging your audio until it lines up with video. It's more work, but once you've aligned the two, assuming neither recording drifted in timing over the take, you're done.

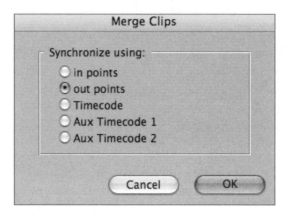

Figure 12.14 Merge clips using one of your time references to align video and audio. In Final Cut Pro, for instance, select audio and video clips and choose Modify > Merge Clips.

Dialog

Matching music to video involves marrying the dual sciences of video and music. Matching spoken word to video usually just comes down to a lot of takes and raw human skill. It's often impossible to get clean dialog recordings on location because of ambient noise or technical problems. Adding dialog to video after it's been shot is called Automated Dialog Replacement (ADR). (Alternatively, ADR is sometimes said to be an acronym for Additional Dialog Recording, which would be more accurate, since there's nothing particularly automated about it.) The challenge of ADR, like dubbing, is to make the words line up with the pacing of the footage, especially if there are onscreen lips the viewer will be able to see. If the timing of the dialog is off, your video will look like a cheap English dub of a Hong Kong action flick.

You can perform ADR very easily with any audio software that supports video playback during looped audio recording with multiple takes (**Figure 12.15**). The computer software duplicates what filmmakers have done for decades: you'll keep looping the video while your actor or actors perform the lines. Once you're satisfied that you have enough takes, you can choose whichever take works best with the picture. The advantages of looping are twofold: first, your actors have plenty of shots at getting it right, and second, after a few loops they'll start to memorize the pacing.

Since you'll typically be recording directly to a precaptured digital video file, you can then export the video clip with the new dialog audio mixed in, and the two will be synchronized.

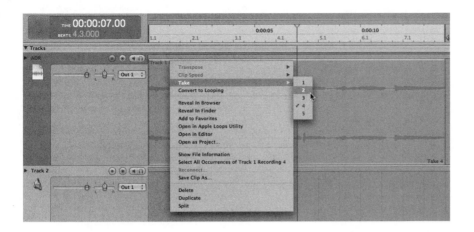

Figure 12.15 Having trouble getting your narration or dialog right the first time? Try looping recording so you can do multiple takes, rapid-fire, until you get it right. Soundtrack Pro, for example, will record multiple takes automatically with cycling turned on and will keep rolling the video file as you record.

Further Reading

Sound for video and film is a discipline all its own. Here are just a few of the many resources dedicated to the topic or to video/film production in general:

Real World Digital Video, second edition (Peachpit Press, 2004): General reference on video production with extensive coverage of audio production topics.

Sound for Film and Television; Sound for Digital Video (Focal Press, 2001): Seminal works on creating sound for motion pictures, both by Tomlinson Holman, the creator of THX sound and a veteran of films like *Star Wars* and *Indiana Jones*.

The Reel World: Scoring for Pictures (Backbeat Books, 2000): The TV composer behind *Chicago Hope* and *Homicide* talks about the ins and outs of composing for film, video, and TV; additional useful links can be found at the Jeff Rona Web site (www.jeffrona.com).

From Score to Screen: Sequencers, Scores, and Second Thoughts: The New Film Scoring Process (Schirmer Books, 2004): Sonny Kompanek, composer and NYU teacher, updates traditional scoring and composing techniques for new digital technologies.

You can also find a wealth of references on the Web: a couple of good sources for technical expertise include the HD for Indies weblog (www.hdforindies.com), which covers the fast-changing world of HD production while remaining mindful of budget, and the articles at DV Info (www.dvinfo.net).

CHAPTER 13

Playing Live

Computers open up new performance techniques that were never possible before. But creating a dynamic, spontaneous performance paradoxically requires lots of preplanning, and what makes a good performance rig depends on your musical vision. With approaches ranging from DJing to playing live instruments with computerized backing tracks, making your digital music road-ready is a many-faceted challenge.

 Essentials

Playing Live

We'll look at the range of possibilities:

- How to play soft synths onstage, including switching between sounds, playing multiple instruments at once, and playing patterns

- Using live audio inputs and effects with real-time control

- Synchronizing multiple pieces of software, computers, and outboard equipment

- Triggering live arrangements, from simple backing tracks to elaborate combinations of audio loops, samples, and MIDI clips

- Live sampling

Where to Start

- DJing with a computer; cueing with headphones

- Using a vinyl turntable for scratching and control

- Creating custom software using modular software environments

Essential Terms

- Clips and one-shots

- Cross-faders and segues

- Cueing and beat matching

- Distributed computing

- Patcher interfaces

Try some basic synth hosting and playing, setting up software so you can quickly access sounds and controls. Experiment with Ableton Live on the disc for interactive arrangements and DJing. When you're ready, dive into more advanced custom projects in Max, Pd, and Reaktor.

Digital Audio Onstage

The more widespread computers have become in performance, the more wide open their uses. Some computer performances expand upon conventional techniques. There are keyboardists playing soft synths, guitarists using computers for effects, turntablists using real vinyl to scratch digital files, and drummers hitting pads to trigger cues in a flexible backing track. Other possibilities include:

- Sampling an instrument or voice and manipulating layers of loops

- Creating improvised, mashed-up soundscapes by remixing samples

- Assembling a custom piece of software for creating sounds, mixing beats, and generating musical patterns

- Running theatrical cues (sound, music, and even video and lighting)

- Manipulating visuals in time with music (VJing)

- Using sensors and home-built physical controllers to generate interactive music

Despite such a wide range, you may be surprised at how much computer performers—from the rock guitarist to the DJ to the experimental sound composer—have in common.

The main challenge all computer performers face is to adapt software and hardware tools, most of which are intended primarily for a studio environment, to playing live in front of an audience. This requires that you set up easy-to-see onscreen setups and easy-to-play hardware controls, so that you have access to what you need at the touch of your hands or feet.

Certain tools work well for many kinds of live performances. Software like Ableton Live is popular with musicians in divergent genres because it can perform tasks normally associated with DAWs and samplers in real time onstage, and has an interface that's easy to see and control while performing. For those willing to invest time in making their own custom performance tools, modular environments like Cycling '74 Max/MSP (www.cycling74.com), Pure Data (www.puredata.info), and Native Instruments Reaktor (www.native-instruments.com) can help tailor the computer to fulfill almost any set of needs without the necessity of writing a line of actual programming code. Many performers have musical techniques in common, too. DJs were among the first to manipulate audio in performance, and some of the methods they have developed are reflected in a broad cross-section of musical genres.

Underneath all of these techniques are specific applications of technologies we've already looked at. MIDI is still the most readily available way to translate physical gestures into musical control. The ability to control the virtual world of the computer with physical movement is essential to making a computer a performance instrument, even if the movements are as simple as playing a QWERTY keyboard in a dramatic, virtuosic way. And the basic techniques of synchronization, used by many performers, are key to making events onstage match musical time.

 Hooking Up to the House: What to Bring

Anyone who's ever been on the road knows the variability of house P.A. systems, but there are a few measures you can take to prepare:

Bring lots of cables: A set of cables and adapters will ensure that you're ready to plug into whatever you find.

Bring a power strip: A good quality power strip can guarantee that you won't generate your own ground loop and will help protect your equipment from unreliable wiring.

Stay balanced: Use an audio interface with balanced outputs if you can. You can also plug audio outputs into a DI (direct injection) box to balance the audio output.

Multiple outs: A multichannel audio interface can help you feed "front of house" speakers, onstage amps (for guitars, bass, and keyboards), and additional speakers that might be available, and help you control the mix yourself.

Consider a portable mixer: Having a mixer along can help with routing; aside from stand-alone mixers, there are various inexpensive portable mixers from makers like Alesis and Mackie/Tapco with self-contained audio interfaces. Audio interfaces like the 8-channel MOTU Traveler and 4-channel Lexicon Omega double as self-contained mixers, too.

If you want to record your set, you might consider bringing a portable recorder. In addition to lossless HD MiniDisc recorders, consider portable CompactFlash-based recorders like the Edirol R-1 or M-Audio MicroTrack. These players have decent mic inputs, line inputs, and (in the case of the MicroTrack) digital inputs, and record to increasingly affordable removable media. If you just need a line output from the board, the Gemini iKey (www.geminidj.com) lets you attach a USB 2 flash drive, portable hard drive, or hard drive-enabled music player to record a line input, with full start/stop and level trim controls. (Many DJ mixer/audio interface combinations also support bidirectional recording, so you can capture your performance or DJ set.)

Sadly, most digital audio players like the Apple iPod lack high-quality line-in recording capability. The iPod can be hacked to support better recording via a minijack by installing iPodLinux (www.ipodlinux.org). If you can settle for MP3- or WMA-encoded files (which are fine if you just want to post your set on your Web site the next day), you'll also find line-in recording on select players from makers like iRiver (www.iriver.com), Creative Labs (www.creative.com), and Cowon (www.iaudio.com).

If you're using software like Ableton Live or Propellerhead Reason that lets you easily record MIDI and arrangement actions, don't forget to hit Record while performing your set. Since in most cases you won't be recording audio, you can preserve some of your performance without having to use up significant hard-drive space or system resources.

The process of preparing for a performance begins with some basic questions. What do you want to be able to control directly, and what do you want the computer do for you (for those tasks for which you don't have enough hands and feet)? For the elements you want to control, what's the best interface for making your performance expressive and fun?

Live Instruments

A big draw of having a laptop onstage is being able to play your collection of software synths live. A keyboard or other MIDI instrument and a computer are a viable choice for replacing or supplementing outboard hardware synths and instruments. With a little preplanning, they can make it easy to call up, play, and manipulate a broad arsenal of sounds. All you need is a low-latency audio interface for the computer and a MIDI input to the computer (possibly in the form of a USB output from the keyboard), and you're ready to go.

Switching sounds

Your primary need onstage is probably being able to easily play different sounds. Using a single soft synth, that means being able to switch patches. If your soft synth lets you create different folders of patches, it's a good idea to copy the patches you intend to use (or a selection of favorites) into a separate folder to make them more manageable. To avoid having to click the mouse, assign the "next patch" or "next program" control to a MIDI parameter. In Propellerhead Reason, for instance, the "next" and "previous" patch controls are MIDI-assignable, so you can scroll between them with MIDI buttons (**Figure 13.1**). In Reason 3 or later, you should assign these buttons to a folder of Combinator patches, since that module can contain any combination of Reason's devices.

When using multiple instruments, it's often easiest to set up each instrument on its own MIDI channel. Most hosts will use processor resources only if a signal is being generated by the plug-in, so you can switch which instrument you're playing by switching which channel is enabled for MIDI input, or change the MIDI transmit channel on your master keyboard. For instance, you might put a piano sound on the first channel and an organ sound on the second channel. In Ableton Live, you can switch between sounds by assigning the record-enable for each track to a different button on your keyboard or foot pedal. If you're using Steinberg Cubase as a host, you can use the computer keyboard's up and down arrow keys for switching. Other programs may require a little mouse work.

Figure 13.1 Assign the program change control to a MIDI controller, and it'll be easy to change patches on your soft synth without using your mouse or computer keyboard. In Reason, the next and previous program controls are configured by default for keyboards that support Reason's Remote communications protocol, but you can create your own assignments, which you can access via Options > Remote Override Edit Mode. If you're using Reason 3 or later, set up all your patches with the Combinator so you can easily control splits, layers, and MIDI assignments for any of Reason's built-in synths.

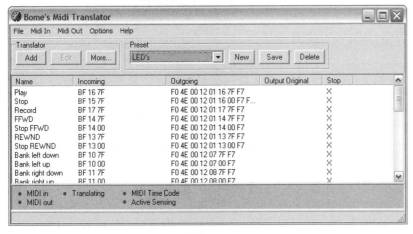

Figure 13.2 Bome's MIDI Translator for Windows can remap incoming MIDI to other MIDI or to keystrokes. It's useful for bridging the divide between hardware and software that aren't designed to work with each other.

 Mapping MIDI to QWERTY: Do you have a software control you want to use during performance, but it includes only QWERTY keyboard shortcuts and doesn't allow MIDI messages to be mapped to commands? On the Mac, you can use MIDI to trigger keyboard shortcuts (and even AppleScripts) with MidiPipe (http://homepage.mac.com/nicowald/SubtleSoft). On the PC, you can create extensive mappings of incoming MIDI messages to QWERTY keystrokes, assignable to different programs, using the "postcardware"/EUR20 Bome MIDI Translator, shown in **Figure 13.2** (www.bome.com).

If your keyboard is doing double-duty, both generating its own internal sounds and controlling sounds on your computer's soft synth, you can switch between them using a hardware mixer, or, if your hardware synth is routed into software, the mixer in your DAW. That way, to switch from one to the other, you can grab a mixer fader instead of having to work with the menus on your synth. (Note that you may experience in-to-out latency issues routing analog inputs from a hardware synth when mixing with software. This is avoided with synths that include low-latency drivers for audio input like the Novation X-Station and Access Virus TI.)

Most of the time, you'll probably use your hardware synth's built-in program change controls to switch its sounds. But if you want automatic software control for quicker changes or automatic changes during the course of a song, you can store program changes in software and transmit them from the computer to the keyboard while the music plays. In Ableton Live, for instance, you can give each MIDI clip an associated program change: double-click a MIDI clip, and then select bank, sub-bank, and program numbers for that clip in the Note Box. (For more on bank select messages, see "Programs and Banks" in Chapter 8. Ableton's bank values correspond to the bank select MSB, and their sub-banks are the bank select LSB.) You can quickly fire off different patterns, each of which will transmit a different program number to your external synth. In Cakewalk's Project5, you can do the same by clicking on any MIDI track. (You'll need a different MIDI track for each program change.)

Playing multiple sounds

Program changes let you switch between sounds quickly and easily. But what if you want to play more than one sound at once?

One option is to use multiple input devices, each assigned to a different synth. For instance, you might place two or three keyboards on a multitier rack or use a keyboard and drum pad. Place different plug-ins on different tracks in your host (or different instances of the same plug-in with different patches loaded) and set the input of each to a different keyboard. (If the keyboards are plugged into different MIDI ports or use USB, you can select them by port. If they're chained together via MIDI, set them to different MIDI channels and set each track to the corresponding channel.)

To play more than one sound simultaneously from a single keyboard, you can use splits and layers. Splits assign different sounds to different areas of the keyboard, and layers assign multiple sounds to each note. (For more information on what splits and layers are and how to configure them, see Chapter 8.) There are several ways to set up splits and layers (**Figure 13.3**):

- **Using your keyboard:** You may be able to set up splits and other routing options on your keyboard. Most MIDI keyboards, other than the most bare-bones, entry-level models, can be configured to assign different key zones to different MIDI channels. This is usually the best approach if you want to play external hardware synths and soft synths at the same time.

- **Internally, in a soft synth:** If your soft synth supports combination patches involving more than one sound, you can set up splits or layers within the synth. (SampleTank FREE, included on the DVD, supports combi patches, which are demonstrated in some of the included tutorials.)

- **Using your host:** Many hosts have their own split and layer functions that work independently of the plug-ins. This can allow you to assign more than one plug-in at a time to a keyboard. (This technique works particularly well with hosts designed for hosting plug-ins for performance, such as V-STACK and Rax. Logic Pro's Environment, Cakewalk Project5, and Reason 3's Combinator all have extensive options for configuring layers, splits, and other MIDI options.)

- **Using an extra tool:** If you can't accomplish what you want in your host of choice, you may want to combine it with another tool. Using MIDI-OX on Windows or MIDI Pipe on the Mac, you can perform splits, layers, and various routing tasks.

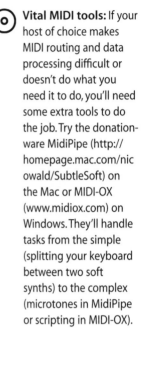

Vital MIDI tools: If your host of choice makes MIDI routing and data processing difficult or doesn't do what you need it to do, you'll need some extra tools to do the job. Try the donationware MidiPipe (http://homepage.mac.com/nicowald/SubtleSoft) on the Mac or MIDI-OX (www.midiox.com) on Windows. They'll handle tasks from the simple (splitting your keyboard between two soft synths) to the complex (microtones in MidiPipe or scripting in MIDI-OX).

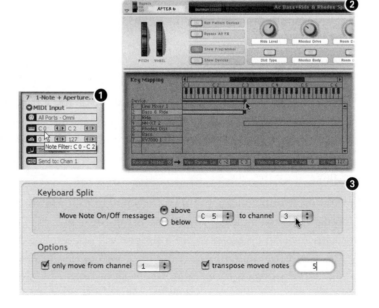

Figure 13.3 Mapping inputs can help you play more than one instrument at a time. Cakewalk's Project5 lets you configure which ports, note ranges, and even velocities go where just by clicking on an instrument. This makes Project5 an ideal host for playing live on Windows (1). Reason's Combinator lets you combine splits into a single instrument (2). If you need additional settings beyond what your software and keyboards provide, turn to a tool like MidiPipe on the Mac (3) or MIDI-OX in Windows.

Tools for hosting soft synths

If you're opting for plug-in instruments (rather than software with built-in instruments), you'll need a host environment. That can be your DAW or workstation software, which often has the advantage of providing its own built-in instruments and effects, plus arrangement and backing track features.

Alternatively, if you just want a simple way to host a couple of plug-ins, you can opt for a more basic plug-in host. There are several potential advantages to using a host: this type of software can be simpler to configure, less expensive, and more lightweight in terms of system resources. A host can also provide additional features. Some of the more useful possibilities include:

- **AU Lab** (Mac OS X 10.4 and later; free): Apple's free testing tool for developers doubles as a surprisingly feature-rich Audio Unit host, with extras like side-chaining, custom channel strips and groups, MIDI splits, tempo controls, and network routing. Install the Xcode Tools option from your OS install disc; it can be found in Developer > Applications > Audio > AU Lab.

- **Rax** (Mac; $30; www.plasq.com): Rax is a simple, reliable Audio Unit instrument and effect host and mixer. It's especially good at easy, powerful MIDI assignments, including layers, keyboard and velocity splits, and MIDI learn. You can even assign MIDI to those pesky plug-ins that don't support it natively. Rax supports audio input and has a built-in reverb as well.

- **Steinberg V-STACK** (Mac/Windows; $50; www.steinberg.de): Using Steinberg's VST and ReWire host is a bit like having Cubase's channel strip and instrument routing, without the sequencer (**Figure 13.4**). It has some handy effects send capabilities, preset management and keyboard splits, and network features via System Link. (Despite its name, it also supports DirectX instruments and effects on Windows, although not AU on the Mac.)

Several more sophisticated tools can also be used for hosting, adding in modular tools for building your own custom instruments. These tools are probably overkill if you just want a simple way of hosting a couple of soft synths or effects, but if you want to tinker with more advanced, "under-the-hood" MIDI and audio operations, they can be invaluable. In addition to options like Max/MSP, Reaktor, and Pd, other tools especially well-suited to the task include:

- **Buzz** (Windows; free; www.buzzmachines.com): Buzz is popular as a performance tool because it's free, has a broad user community with lots of sample content, and doubles as a modular MIDI and audio environment, and synth in its own right. It can be complex to learn, but the payoff is some sophisticated custom patch design capabilities normally found only in environments like Max/MSP, Pd, and Reaktor.

- **Plogue Bidule** (Windows/Mac; $75; www.plogue.com): Like Buzz, Bidule is a modular audio environment as much as it is a host. But because it supports cross-platform VST and Mac AU, as well as both ReWire slave and master mode and Open Sound Control (OSC), it's also popular as a performance host. It has some sophisticated audio and MIDI routing that make it useful as a Swiss Army knife tool. You may not need to perform spectral manipulations to the audio signal from your piano plug-in, but if you do, Plogue Bidule can handle that as well.

- **Energy XT** (Windows; $50; www.xt-hq.com): Energy XT offers a little bit of everything. Its modular design lets you create splits, layers, and chains of instruments, but it also has a sequencer, an automatic chord generator, a piano roll editor, and envelopes. Some musicians use it simply as a host or a way of extending their existing tools; others use it as a more extensive environment, although it lacks some of the more advanced features of Plogue Bidule. Like the other programs listed on this page, it has a passionate user community.

Figure 13.4 Steinberg's V-STACK serves as a mixer and a host for effects and instruments (DirectX on PC and VST on PC and Mac). Used alone, it acts as a "mini-DAW" for live mixing and hosting. Steinberg's System Link lets you synchronize multiple machines and transmit audio and MIDI data, which is useful for multicomputer performances.

Arpeggiators and Patterns

Using pattern-based software and arpeggiators, it's possible to "perform" complex rhythmic phrases that would be difficult or impossible to play yourself. You can use these for rhythmic pitched effects or to control effects and other parameters in sequence.

Arpeggiators

An *arpeggiator* is a special MIDI effect that automatically plays a sequenced pattern based on an input note or notes. In musical terms, an *arpeggio* is the notes of a chord played in a series from bottom to top or top to bottom rather than all at once. (It's also called a "broken chord"; the sound of a harp or guitar strum is a fast arpeggio.) In its simplest form, an arpeggiator plays the notes of a chord you're holding down in sequence.

You can use an arpeggiator for more dramatic rhythmic effects, however, depending on the parameters it provides. Different arpeggiator shapes or "styles" can be used for different effects, like playing up and down the chord in series. Some can play prerecorded, polyphonic patterns. By adjusting the rhythmic interval of the pattern or using an arpeggiator that's synchronized to tempo, you can create unique, rhythmic special effects.

Some arpeggiators can automatically generate chords as well as sequential patterns. It's the opposite of an arpeggio, really, but the term has come to mean any software effect that adds notes based on the ones you're playing. Some arpeggiators might best be considered "interactive pattern generators," because they're capable of generating various patterns based on input pitch. Up and down scales can get fairly boring, but with a full-featured arpeggiator or pattern sequencer, you can use arpeggiators to produce otherwise unplayable patterns.

Although an arpeggiator is most often used with a pitched soft synth, you can route an arpeggiator's MIDI output to any instrument or effect parameter with a MIDI input. For instance, applying an arpeggiator to a drum track can "mix up" a drum pattern or create doubling effects. You can even use an arpeggiator with a keyboard input to automatically control a MIDI-assigned effect, such as a filter, in an interactive way.

You can even use arpeggiator parameters as performance tools. The effect is somewhat less than subtle, but you can accentuate the pattern of the arpeggiator by assigning knobs or faders to parameters like the step length (the length of each arpeggiator note) or speed, and then adjust that knob during a performance.

Custom pattern generators

What if you're not happy with preset arpeggiator patterns or static pattern clips that aren't based on input pitch? You're a candidate for building your own custom interactive patterns.

Modular environments like Pure Data, Max, and Plogue Bidule are all designed for the job. In fact, creating MIDI processing patches is often the best way to begin learning one of these environments, because such patches tend to be the simplest. For instance, you can create chords automatically using basic arithmetic: for each note-on event, use an "add" module to output an additional note event some number of scale steps higher. For a triad, use two add objects, each connected to an output object (**Figure 13.5**).

 Building a pattern generator: Try out a custom Mac/Windows interactive pattern generator/step sequencer built in Max/MSP (included on the DVD) and learn how it was built.

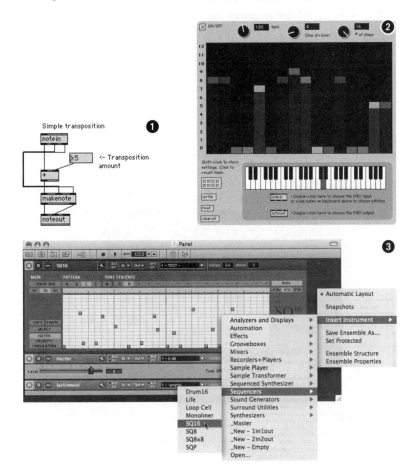

Figure 13.5 Three approaches for controlling MIDI data live using custom software patches. Using basic arithmetic, you can patch together objects in software like Max/MSP to change notes (1). By building up various objects in this manner, you can create a custom pattern sequencer, for example, based on your own needs (2). Using prebuilt "macros" (components of a larger patch) or "ensembles" (prebuilt instruments), you can jump-start custom performance software creation in Reaktor using objects like this step sequencer (3).

Double duty: Switching between guitar or bass and keyboard parts? Since guitar effects like Guitar Rig, AmpliTube, and Line6's GearBox software run as plug-ins, try feeding your keyboard parts through them for some grungy effects. These effects can also create unusual timbres with string instruments like violin, cello, and sitar, and can create unique distortion effects with drums.

More sophisticated users may create elaborate random note generation algorithms. Taking the concept to the extreme, you can reduce your "performance" to pressing a single key. When designing your own pattern generator, keep in mind that you can use patterns to control any number of parameters, not just pitch.

If the prospect of digging into a modular software environment is frightening, you can simply chain MIDI effect devices in Ableton Live. The Random effect, since it has a variable amount of randomness, is particularly useful for creating complex effects. You can also design rule-based pattern generators using MIDI-OX or MidiPipe.

Live Effects

By using software-based effects live, you can apply your full arsenal of sonic tools to both live audio input and recorded sources (**Figure 13.6**). When effects parameters are manipulated onstage, effects become part of the performance. If you're just adding effects to existing elements, like loops, prerecorded audio materials, and soft synths, the process is fairly simple. You'll route effects just as you would for studio recording. (For more on using effects, see Chapter 7.)

Live performance can pose two special challenges: how to minimize or manage the latency of live audio being sent to the computer, and how to easily turn effects on and off and control their settings in real time. (Note

Figure 13.6 A multi-effects package like the Line6 TonePort can help you emulate studio equipment when you're onstage. These packages are favored by electric guitar and bass players, but mic preamp models are ideal for vocals, and you can use the distortion, amps, and effects with other instruments, too. (Photo courtesy Line6, Inc.)

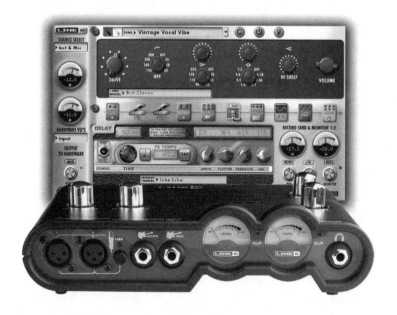

that you should be especially careful managing CPU load with Ableton Live, because, unless you've frozen tracks, it's also performing time-stretching in real time.)

Live audio input and latency

With live input, signal must pass through the audio interface, through whatever software you're using, and back out through the interface again. As a result, the time lag (latency) becomes particularly significant. (If you're using your software for mixing, you'll face the same issue.)

Above about 10–11 ms, latency becomes great enough that instrumentalists who are playing live will notice it. Generally, 3 ms is the minimum practical latency that can be achieved on computers; it's nearly undetectable. (The range in between is usually tolerable.)

You should double-check two basic elements for low-latency operation:

- **Low-latency drivers:** On Windows, ASIO 2.0 drivers are your best bet for lowest latency. (Windows Vista will incorporate lower-latency drivers into the Windows Driver Model.) On Mac, drivers are essentially a non-issue; all Core Audio drivers are low latency. (That's assuming the drivers work, of course, but if functioning properly they should be low-latency.)

- **Low-latency settings:** Some programs let you adjust the latency of the audio driver; obviously, for live audio applications, you'll want to err on the side of less latency. (See Chapter 4 for more on configuring your audio interface.)

Some effects plug-ins introduce more latency than others, so try auditioning different effects if one seems to be causing too much latency. Also, latency is dependent on the speed of your computer's CPU. A slower computer will run out of processing headroom more quickly when set to a low latency. This means that you may have to make a trade-off between low latency and running all of the effects or soft synths you'd like to. Native Instruments, for instance, recommends a relatively high-powered processor for live operation of its Guitar Rig live effects software (minimum 1.25 GHz Mac or 1.4 GHz PC).

Note that "latency compensation" or *delay compensation* features have no bearing on live audio input. They work with plug-ins only during track playback. See "Delay Compensation" in Chapter 7.

Hardware first? If your computer is overburdened with live processing tasks, you can plug a live input into a hardware effects processor prior to connecting it to your computer or use an effects processor that's built into an audio interface. Examples include the inexpensive, MIDI-controlled Lexicon MPX 110 processor with a digital out (www.lexiconpro.com) and audio interface/processor combinations like the MindPrint Trio USB (www.mindprint.com) and M-Audio Black Box guitar processor (www.m-audio.com).

Adding horsepower: A DSP hardware-based effect doesn't rely on your CPU, making it highly desirable in performance situations where your computer is handling a lot of tasks at once. Various effects, including live vocal and guitar processing, are available for the portable, FireWire-based PowerCore Compact system (www.tcelectronic.com), for instance. If you're using Windows, you might also consider the E-MU 1616M (www.emu.com), which includes a suite of DSP-based effects.

Turning effects on and off

 All about sends: You'll want to be even more mindful of using sends in live performance than when mixing prerecorded tracks. Using CPU-hungry effects like reverb on a send instead of multiple inserts will save computer resources, and it's often easier to assign a send level to an external MIDI control than it is a wet/dry level in an effect.

Running effects constantly can quickly get unwieldy, both musically and in terms of CPU resources. If you're using insert effects in Ableton Live or plug-ins that support MIDI mapping, make sure you assign the bypass switch on your effect (or the enable/disable switch) to an easily accessible MIDI control. You can also assign sends to a fader for easy adjustment of level feeding the effect.

Using software effects doesn't mean giving up the easy footswitch method of enabling and disabling effects to which guitarists and bass players are accustomed. A MIDI pedalboard or foot controller can provide control. They're useful for laptop-based musicians who need their hands to play their instruments (like horn players, string players, and keyboardists), not just guitarists (**Figure 13.7**).

Native Instruments' Guitar Rig includes its own pedalboard called the Rig Kontrol 2; IK Multimedia's AmpliTube is available with an optional StompIO controller. You can also use MIDI pedalboards to control these and other sets of effects.

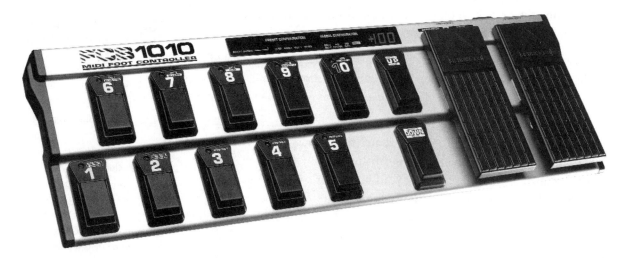

Figure 13.7 A MIDI-only footswitch like the Behringer FCB1010 lets you add pedal control to any software that can be mapped to MIDI notes or control changes. The large pedals send continuous expression data (useful for controlling the level of an effect). (Photo courtesy Behringer Spezielle Studiotechnik GmbH)

Real-Time Control

With just two hands, two feet, and a performance to focus on, assigning live control of parameters to easily accessible knobs, faders, buttons, and foot pedals is essential. (See "Using Control Surfaces" in Chapter 8 for more information on choosing and configuring control surfaces.)

- **Combine controls:** You can make a knob or fader do multiple duty by routing its control change output to multiple destinations. (This sometimes requires a third-party tool for remapping, since many programs let you map a controller to only one parameter at a time.)

- **Combine instruments:** Many DAWs let you combine effects parameters, instrument settings, and so on into single settings for easier switching. Try features like Logic Pro's channel strip preset save and recall, Project5's device chains, Live's Device Groups and Live Clips format, and Reason's Combinator patches.

- **Combine changes:** When changing from song to song, you may have a whole set of device changes that need to happen: fader changes, program changes for effects and synths, effects chains, and so on. You can combine these by loading a new song into your DAW or by inserting these events at a marker/locator position and triggering them that way. (In Ableton Live, you can use the "Macro Track" trick discussed later in the chapter.) If these methods don't work well, you can store changes in a custom patch in a program like Max, Pd, or Reaktor and launch them from there. It's not as elegant as having a prebuilt solution, but unlike the frequent frustration of having to rely on developers, you're guaranteed it'll work the way you want since you built it yourself.

It's useful to have a "tool belt" for handling MIDI routing and assignment chores. Some routing tools may be included in the program you're using. Logic Pro's Environment, although initially daunting, can be used for sophisticated MIDI routing and automation tasks. For instance, you can combine a number of changes to instruments and effects into a selector patch, as shown in **Figure 13.8**. Hosts like Plogue Bidule and EnergyXT also have modular MIDI routing and assignment tools.

Controlling FL Studio: FL Studio provides some powerful hooks for external control. You can use a Logitech gamepad (www.logitech.com) like the Cordless Rumbleman 2 with FL Studio's X-Y Controller (**Figure 13.10**). With two analog joysticks, you can control two Fruity X-Y Controllers at once for control over four parameters. Also try the unique Peak Controller to have peaks in a mixer automatically control some other parameter (like a synth or plug-in).

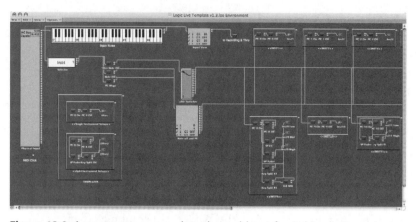

Figure 13.8 A power-user approach to the problem of switching between instrument and effect settings is to create a virtual patch bay to route notes and change parameters, as in this custom Environment for Apple's Logic Pro. (File courtesy of Christopher Scheidel, www.heavyliftmusic.com)

 Game on: For game controllers in other applications, try the hi object for Max/MSP or junXion for Mac OS X (www.steim.org/steim/junxion.html).

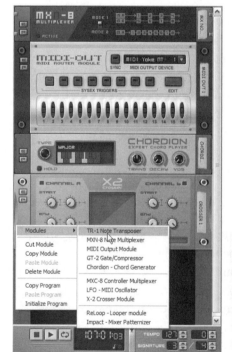

Figure 13.9 LiveSet (left) is a Windows-based ReWire host that fills in a lot of the performance MIDI features other applications lack. It includes a collection of devices that can combine MIDI control, facilitate custom routing to soft synths, create chords, patterns, and loops, and handle other tasks. Just as in Reason, press the Tab key and you can create custom signal routings (right), which are vital for getting your MIDI data to go where you want.

The other option is to use a tool to intercept MIDI data between your input device and your software of choice. MIDI-OX on Windows and MidiPipe on Mac both work well for basic MIDI routing and assignment. If that's too limiting, you can also build your own custom tool in a program like Max/MSP or Pd.

One especially useful tool on Windows is PeterTools LiveSet (www.peter-tools.com), a Reason-like rack of MIDI tools. It includes multiplexers for manually creating layers of synth and effect controllers, transposers, chord players, and a MIDI routing module, among other elements (**Figure 13.9**). LiveSet is clearly designed to work with Reason, but it works equally well with other software that benefits from these features; it's compatible with any Windows ReWire client.

 Need a spare screen?
If the Lemur multi-touch interface exceeds your budget (see p. 325), you still have other options. You can find affordable single-touch touch-screens for quickly navigating parameters from vendors like ELO Touch-Systems (www.elotouch.com) for as little as $300. If visual feedback is all you need, so you can tell what you're doing with your MIDI controller, Lil-liput Electronic (www.lil-liput.com) makes tiny LCD screens designed for use in automobiles that you can place discreetly on your rig.

The Joy of X and Y

X/Y controllers can be especially powerful because they let you control two effects parameters at once, like cutoff and resonance of a filter, or delay time and wet/dry level of a delay or reverb. You'll find X/Y touchpads on hardware like the Novation X-Station and ReMote, Korg Kaoss Pad, and joysticks on many keyboards. To manually assign these to two parameters, turn on MIDI learn and assign each axis separately by moving or touching the controller carefully in a single direction. Software tools like the Fruity X-Y Controller in FL Studio (Figure 13.10) and the X-2 Cross-fader in PeterTools LiveSet provide additional options.

If you lack an X/Y controller, the Mercurial Innovations STC-1000 is worth a look. It's a specialized MIDI touch controller that can work in an X/Y mode or double as a 16-zone percussion-style trigger (www.thinkmig.com).

 **Figure 13.10** X/Y controllers give you simultaneous control of two parameters. You can use FL Studio's X-Y Controller with a mouse, but it's more fun with joystick input.

Synchronization

Once you start playing with multiple software applications, multiple pieces of music gear, or multiple computers, you'll probably want to sync everything to a single tempo to keep all your gear and software in time. By using synchronization, you can:

- Sync two pieces of software on the same computer. (Example: one piece of software running a soft synth arpeggiator is synced to another piece of software running drum loops.)

- Sync your computer to external hardware. (Example: an external drum machine or loop sampler with a tap tempo button controls the tempo of a computer running loops, patterns, or backing tracks.)

- Sync your external hardware to your computer. (Example: VJ hardware running live video clips is synced to the tempo of a music program.)

- Sync two computers to each other. (Example: you and a friend play a computer duet with tempo-dependent effects that are synced.)

Tempo master and slave

Common to all these techniques is the need to have what is usually called a single "master" and one or more "slaves" for tempo. You need a single piece of hardware or software to act as the master, setting the tempo for all of the other pieces of hardware and software and transmitting the necessary clock information to the slaves on a continual basis. There can be only one master. If you had more than one, it'd be like having more than one conductor running a symphony orchestra. You can have any number of pieces of hardware and software following the tempo, but only one can set the tempo.

ReWire

Plug-ins are able to route MIDI and audio to a host, and some are able to synchronize timing to the host tempo (for tempo-synced delays, for example). If you want to use different stand-alone applications for this task, however, you need *ReWire*. ReWire is a technology developed by Propellerhead that has become an industry standard for interconnecting different pieces of software on the same machine. ReWire transmits the following data:

- **Synchronization:** Tempo, meter, start/stop, position within an arrangement, looping on/off, and loop start and end points.

- **Audio:** Multichannel audio (both independent audio channels and a left/right master mix).

- **MIDI:** Multiple simultaneous channels of MIDI performance and/or control data.

- **Device labels:** Instead of channel numbers, connected slaves will show the names of soft synths, drum machines, and the like. (This feature is found in ReWire 2 and later.)

In other words, you have full audio and MIDI routing, and complete control over the transport. Synchronization is sample-accurate (a far cry from MIDI clock, as you'll see in a moment), and once a ReWire client is loaded into the host application, the management of resources is handled by the host. A client ReWired into a host takes up fewer system resources than the two would on their own, and they're able to share a sound card and external sync settings (controlled by the master).

Unlike other synchronization methods, ReWire accomplishes all this transparently without your intervention. The process sometimes confuses beginners because you don't have to do anything with most applications to make ReWire work. The process is simple (**Figure 13.11**):

1. Launch the host application first.

2. Launch the client application second. (The order is crucial; otherwise, ReWire won't work.)

3. Route audio and MIDI. (You may need to switch on ReWire audio reception or record-enable an audio track in the host in order to monitor the signal coming from the ReWire client; otherwise, audio may be properly routed but you won't hear anything.)

A common usage of ReWire is to set up the host application as "mixer," controlling tempo and backing track arrangements, and a client application as the "instrument" for adding a synthesizer, virtual instrument, drum machine, sampler, arpeggiator, or other instrument that isn't available in the host application. (You'll sometimes even see the terms "mixer" and "instrument" in place of master and slave or host and client, although the latter is more common.)

For audio and MIDI routing, depending on your host's ReWire implementation, you should have several options. If you just want to play a client as a synth, you may just route the left/right audio mix into your host. If you want multichannel control of each separate output, you can route channels independently into your host. If you want to play MIDI patterns from a program like Live or Project5 back into the ReWire client, set a MIDI track output from your host to the input of your client.

Figure 13.11 ReWire can extend your available software instruments without taxing system resources. Reason, for instance, can be loaded into Live so you can play synths from Reason together with synths, audio loops, and MIDI patterns in Live. In this example, to access just one synth we've routed the left/right audio output mix from Reason into a Live track while routing a MIDI track back to the Reason synth so it can be played by Live's MIDI patterns.

One particularly popular combination is the use of Propellerhead Reason with Ableton Live. Live provides the audio input, more extensive loop, pattern, and arrangement triggering, arpeggiator, and MIDI tools that Reason lacks, while Reason fills out Live's built-in instruments with a healthy collection of samplers, drum machines, and synths. That's just one example, though; the appeal of ReWire is being able to mix and match any applications you like. Some examples of applications with ReWire support include:

- **Host ("mixer"):** Digidesign Pro Tools, Apple Logic Pro, Apple GarageBand, MOTU Digital Performer, Steinberg Cubase and Nuendo, Cakewalk SONAR, Adobe Audition, Steinberg V-STACK

- **Client ("synth"):** Propellerhead Reason, Cakewalk Kinetic, ArKaos VJ

- **Both host and client:** Ableton Live, Cakewalk Project5, Cycling '74 Max/MSP, Plogue Bidule, Arturia Storm, FL Studio, Sony ACID (Pro version 5 or later)

If an application can run as either a host or a client, its role will depend on the order in which it is loaded. For instance, if you load Live and then load Max/MSP, Live will be the host and Max the client. If you load Max and then load Live, Max will be the host and Live the client. Usually, you'll use only one client at a time, although some hosts can support more than one client at once. As with other sync methods, there can be only one master clock source, so two hosts can't operate together.

ReWire gives you significantly more control than other synchronization methods. It does require that all the software be running on the same machine. For information on how to synchronize between computers, see the upcoming sections, "MIDI clock synchronization" and "Networking computers and distributed computing."

If you want to use stand-alone applications that don't support ReWire, you can use MIDI data routed between the applications; see "MIDI clock synchronization." Some applications that don't support ReWire, such as Native Instruments Reaktor, can instead be loaded as plug-ins. Plug-ins share many of the advantages of ReWire, including clock sync. For more information comparing ReWire to using plug-ins or stand-alone applications, see "Combine software for a custom studio" in Chapter 2.

MIDI clock synchronization

The easiest and most reliable way of providing synchronization between devices is with MIDI clock. Most often, MIDI clock is used to synchronize hardware to hardware or hardware to software rather than software to software. You'll need devices capable of sending and/or receiving MIDI clock data, and they'll need to be connected using MIDI cables (or via MIDI over USB or FireWire).

You can synchronize different software applications using MIDI clock. On the Mac, use the Inter-Application Communications driver or a virtual MIDI driver. On Windows, use MIDI Yoke. (For more information on utilities to use with Windows and Mac for MIDI, see "Essential MIDI Tool Belt" in Chapter 8.)

For a full explanation of how MIDI clock works, see "MIDI Time Code and MIDI clock" in Chapter 8. With that in mind, let's look at the specifics of how MIDI clock is relevant to performance.

It's important to understand what data a MIDI clock connection transmits:

- Start and stop

- Position and "continue" (to start playback from a position)

- Tempo

Testing ReWire: If you don't hear anything, make sure you've set up an audio track to receive audio from the ReWire slave and have record-enabled that track and/or turned on monitoring. (A good source to try for testing is the master L/R input from the ReWire slave, because it mixes all the audio channels from the slave together; you don't have to worry about selecting the right channel.)

Pure Data and Jack: The free interactive application Pure Data (Pd) doesn't support ReWire, but it does work with interapplication MIDI drivers like the IAC driver on Mac and MIDI-Yoke on Windows. On Mac and Linux, Pd also supports Jack, which allows synchronous interapplication audio (jackit.sourceforge.net).

Tempo isn't transmitted explicitly: the master doesn't transmit "120 bpm" to receiving devices. Instead, the MIDI clock signal consists of a regular "pulse" of messages at a resolution of 24 pulses per quarter-note. The receiving device has to count those 24 messages, or at least measure the time gap between two of them, before it knows what the tempo is. It's a bit like watching a conductor: the conductor doesn't say, "okay, we'll do this at 133.34 bpm." Instead, musicians simply watch the steady pulse provided by the movements of the conductor's hand.

A resolution of 24 messages per quarter-note (24 PPQN) is significantly less than the MIDI editing resolution of most audio software, but it's enough for performance synchronization. You'll encounter sync issues only if you make tempo changes that are too sudden. You might not want to go from 40 bpm to 240 bpm instantaneously, for instance. Gradual tempo changes, or small intervals, will usually work fine.

MIDI clock, not MIDI Time Code: Make sure you're syncing with MIDI clock, not MIDI Time Code (MTC). Many software applications will let you use either type of synchronization. MTC is intended for transmitting time data in seconds and frames. That's useful for syncing with video devices, but useless for musical performances (or even performing with musically synced video, as VJs do). If two tempo-based devices are synced using MTC, each will have its own tempo control and can speed up or slow down independent of the other. MIDI clock gives you musical tempos and pointers to song position.

You can use the combination of tempo data and start and stop messages to quickly sync software, computers, and hardware. Here's the basic process:

1. **Choose a MIDI clock master.** Designate a piece of hardware or software for transmitting MIDI clock. Not all devices and applications have both send and receive capability; some have only receive capability. (Propellerhead Reason can only receive, for instance, although you can load it as a ReWire slave and use your ReWire host for MIDI clock transmission.)

2. **Connect your gear.** Connect all of the gear you need to receive MIDI from the master. Multiport MIDI interfaces can be handy if you have a complex hardware setup, but for most setups you'll just need the usual MIDI cables and/or USB/FireWire connections.

3. **Configure the sending device.** Most software (including Ableton Live and DAWs like Cakewalk SONAR) will let you choose the ports to which you want to transmit synchronization data.

4. **Configure the receiving devices.** You'll need to set sync to "external" for each receiving device to receive MIDI clock. Once you've done this, depending on the device, certain features (such as an arpeggiator) may operate only when MIDI clock messages are actually being received. When the master clock source is stopped, the synchronized device may produce unexpected sounds, or even no sound at all.

5. **Start me up.** Once you're ready to go, hit play. If you want to adjust the tempo during a performance, you can do so with a tempo control or by tapping in a tempo (see "Tap tempo," below); all the receiving devices will stay synced. Hit stop, and all the devices will stop.

If you want to get a little fancier and have software and hardware that support it, you can use MIDI clock to locate to specific points in an arrangement or to select songs using position and song select messages.

Not all devices support position messages (called Song Position Pointer, or SPP), but most recent devices that support MIDI clock do. Position is defined in terms of the number of sixteenth-notes since the start of the music. But you're probably only jumping to a downbeat in a performance anyway, so the fact that you can't locate to a position between sixteenth-notes is unlikely to matter. You can use SPP to jump to certain parts in a arrangement if you have a sequence in a piece of software that's synced to a drum machine pattern, for instance.

Most hardware devices also support a song select message, which lets you jump to a specific song. For example, you can store various patterns on a piece of hardware like a Korg ElecTribe and call them up by transmitting song select messages. (Software is less likely to receive this message, but some sequencers that support subsequences and MIDI remote control do.)

Tap tempo

Depending on the features of your software, you can set a tempo by typing a number directly into a tempo box, turning a knob on a control surface assigned to the software, or using the tempo controls on a piece of hardware that's transmitting MIDI clock. For dynamic control of tempo, however, tap tempo is the way to go. By pressing a tap button on hardware or (better yet) assigning hardware or software tap tempo to a MIDI foot pedal, you can set a tempo for your gear much the way you would do a countoff for your band. (You'll find a handy tap tempo button in Ableton Live.)

Using tap tempo, you can dispense with other synchronization methods altogether. For instance, a VJ or electronic musician might follow a live instrumental performance by an acoustic jazz quartet by tapping along to the tempo manually. (You can either tap continuously through the song or simply tap to set a tempo and leave it there, then begin tapping again when

 Hardware patterns at the ready: MIDI clock can help you integrate hardware and software. Using a device like a Korg ElecTribe, for instance, you can store song patterns and tempo-synced parameter automation in "Pattern Sets" and call them up using the front-panel button devices. In external sync mode, they'll sync to your computer or other clock source. When it's functioning as a MIDI clock master, ElecTribe lets you use the pattern buttons containing different tempi to trigger your computer sequence or other devices.

the tempo needs adjustment.) One advantage of this method is that it allows you to synchronize with live instruments. (An acoustic jazz quartet is made up of human beings without a MIDI out port!) But it can also be used with electronic instruments to keep the tempo feel of a performance loose and improvisatory.

Networking computers and distributed computing

MIDI and audio are ultimately just data, so there's no reason the "pipe" for the data can't be a network. The reason we're not all using Wi-Fi-enabled MIDI and audio for performance is synchronization: keeping data in perfect sync while it's transmitted over a busy network is a challenge. Although there's still no major standard for networked transmission of MIDI and audio, you can accomplish the task with specialized tools.

An additional benefit becomes the ability to implement *distributed computing,* in which the resources of multiple computers are combined to accomplish a single task. At the simplest level, this can be using one computer to run backing tracks and reverb while another runs a synthesizer. This requires that you manually choose which computer does what, although with audio and MIDI flowing between two synchronized computers, you have some flexibility. Dynamically distributed processing systems like Logic Node have the ability to distribute processing load automatically among computers without human intervention.

Several tools, some free, can provide these features, though they're specific to different platforms (note that these tools assume you're using a local network, such as an Ethernet connection between laptops; using the Internet poses other challenges):

- **Steinberg VST System Link; Inter-computer audio and sync** (Windows/Mac): VST System Link transmits sync, transport position, and audio data between computers via standard digital audio cables (ADAT, S/PDIF, AES/EBU, and TDIF). It's a bit like having ReWire between computers: it provides the sample-accurate synchronization MIDI clock lacks plus audio data routing, and it works with as many computers as you can connect via cables. Connect the S/PDIF ins and outs of two laptop audio interfaces, for instance, plus MIDI if you want cross-machine performance of soft synths, and you're ready to go. System Link is a feature, not a separate product; Cubase and Nuendo both support System Link natively on both Mac and Windows. If you're not a Steinberg user, System Link is the most reliable cross-platform means of syncing transports between computers, and since the $50 V-STACK supports ReWire, it can be an easy way of syncing up an application like Reason or Live on two machines.

- **Wormhole; Intercomputer audio plug-in** (Windows/Mac): The easiest way to route audio between applications and computers on Mac/PC is to use Wormhole, a $50 plug-in available as Windows VST and Mac VST and AU (**Figure 13.12**). Wormhole automatically configures itself and negotiates network connections. Beyond simply routing S/PDIF digital audio, Wormhole lets you route audio as part of your insert chain, so you could route audio to another computer as an insert in a single channel strip. That makes it ideal for onstage routing applications or for manually distributing effects between computers and even platforms.

- **Jack; Intercomputer audio** (Mac/Linux): The open-source, interapplication audio app Jack (www.jackit.sourceforge.net) supports audio over a network. Jack on Mac OS X (www.jackosx.com) supports the Mac's distributed devices features and audio-over-network. There's also a UDP module for the Jack audio system called jack.udp (www.alphalink.com.au/~rd/sw/jack.html) Although you could theoretically send UDP packets over the Internet, the module works best over a local network.

- **AUNetSend; Intercomputer audio** (Mac): While it lacks some of the features of tools like Wormhole, Mac OS X (10.4 and later) has the ability to route audio over a network to another Mac with an Apple Audio Unit included with the OS. Insert the AUNetSend object on a track in any AudioUnit host, and you can connect to other Macs via Apple's Bonjour zero-configuration networking technology.

- **Logic Node; Distributed processing** (Mac): Apple's Logic Pro supports distributed audio processing, automatically using additional Macs for processing power via a Gigabit Ethernet connection, even if those Macs don't have a copy of Logic on them. You also don't need a display on those machines, so additional Macs can supplement processing power at a gig. Effectively, you'll have a little render farm of Macs accompanying you onstage. (Apple recommends G5 computers, but many users report success using high-end G4s.)

 Interapplication audio: Jack and Wormhole both support routing audio between applications on a computer, which is useful for applications that don't support ReWire. (Note that Pro Tools doesn't work with either tool.)

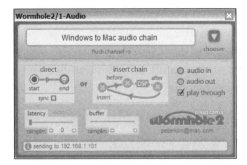

Figure 13.12 Using Plasq's Wormhole plug-in, you can route audio between two applications on your computer or between two different computers over a network. Operation is fairly simple: add Wormhole as an insert effect on each end, make up a name for your virtual audio channel on one end, and select that channel on the other. The rest is automatic.

Live Arranging and Clips

There was a time when you could draw a clear line between live performance and recordings. Live performance was exclusively composed of what was played on instruments onstage. Recordings, whether captured onstage or in a studio, were a fixed, unchanging representation of the music. DJs first began to change that by extending certain sections of a record to make them last longer, keeping people on the dance floor. After that, sampling hardware helped erase what remained of the boundary between recordings and performance. With the ability to trigger sliced and manipulated audio, you can take the output of a studio (a recording) and turn it into a performance.

Prerecorded Arrangements

The simplest way to bridge the studio and stage is to adapt a static recording to a live performance. It's common to wind up with parts recorded in a studio version of a song that can't be played onstage because of overdubs made by a single performer, performers who are not available, or complex arrangements or audio processing that aren't possible live. A computer can play a "backing track" or prerecorded arrangement in the background of a live performance to fill in these parts.

Why not just play back the finished track from a CD or portable digital audio player? Cueing start and stop points is often much easier using a computer, particularly with the help of MIDI controllers. You can adjust levels of individual channels in your DAW project file, which isn't possible with a CD, and you can move instantly to different parts of the arrangement for a flexible song structure.

Internal cues

In the simplest form, you'll just bring your existing multitrack project file with the tracks you need enabled, hit Start and Stop, and play the arrangement as is. You could just leave it at that (and many big-budget pop tours let a tech do the start/stop work), but part of the appeal of taking a computer onstage is giving the performer control over a flexible song structure.

Using a program like MOTU Digital Performer, you can add subsequences to a single project. You'd then call up songs in your set by triggering subsequences and navigate the structure of the song by locating to individual markers. (For more information on arranging the structure of a project, see Chapter 10.) With MIDI remote control, you can assign these events to something easy to control onstage, like a drum pad or foot pedal. Ableton Live also lets you locate to points in a fixed arrangement using MIDI- and key-assignable Arrangement Locators, although since the Arrangement View is linear, you'll have more flexibility in the Session View using Scenes. Either way, you can use an inexpensive two-octave keyboard to line up cues on different notes, using a keyboard like the M-Audio Oxygen8.

Click tracks

The main challenge is making sure your live playing lines up with the tempo of the backing track. If the backing track enters first, you can simply use your ear, though starting a song with a backing track defeats or at least dilutes the audience's sense that they're hearing a live performance.

One solution is to provide a click track for the performer or performers, starting it before the music enters and, if needed, playing it throughout the song to keep everyone in sync. You can create a click track by routing your metronome click to a separate audio output if that option is provided or by creating a click track manually using a snare sidestick sample, for instance.

You'd route the click track as a separate audio feed to in-ear monitors worn by the player. (Specialized earbuds like the Shure E series monitors shown in **Figure 13.13** are made just for this purpose, blocking enough external sound that the click will be audible onstage, with the added benefit of

Figure 13.13
Sound-isolating earbuds like Shure's E4 earphones block outside noise for use onstage as personal monitors or for listening to a click track. (Photo courtesy Shure Incorporated)

Do you need a backup? Pro tours running backing tracks usually have one or more backup computers synchronized to the tempo of the main playback computer. If the main computer crashes, the other one can immediately take over. That's overkill for most people. If you can't spare an extra computer, focus on testing the system you have or consider a worst-case-scenario backup like a prerecorded audio CD.

providing some ear protection.) If your band has a drummer, you may need a click feed only for him or her. In other music, multiple musicians may want to monitor the click track. Even performers of new concert music are now likely to be accustomed to working with click tracks.

The alternative to a click track is to use a tap tempo or other tracking method to set your backing track tempo, so that you can set the tempo yourself instead of relying on your backing track to set it. (See "Tap tempo," earlier in the chapter.)

Arrangements on the Fly: Live Audio and MIDI Clips

Onstage digital arrangements are no longer limited to static backing tracks. You can perform with audio samples and audio and MIDI *clips*—blocks of data that can be looped, triggered, edited, and manipulated at will. You can use these clips to augment an instrumental/vocal performance or make a collection of clips the entire basis of a live performance.

You can use several different kinds of clips in performance (**Figure 13.14**):

- **MIDI clips** need to be assigned to a MIDI instrument to make any sound. They're useful for triggering synths (software or hardware), particularly if you want real-time control over parameters. A MIDI clip can even contain control data but no notes.

- **Audio clips** can be loops that play repeatedly or "one-off" audio files that play once, then stop.

- **Automation** can be embedded in a clip for real-time control of MIDI or audio, or as an automated means of controlling effects.

Unfortunately, although most DAWs are good at manipulating segments of audio and MIDI in the studio, they're more limited when it comes to triggering these in real time, without any audio dropouts, onstage. DAWs can work well for playing backing tracks, but for more interactive musical control, you'll be better off with a specialized tool. These tools can include:

- MIDI pattern sequencers (hardware and software)

- Samplers and drum samplers

- Software geared for performance and interactive arrangement; most commonly, Ableton Live

Using pattern-sequencing hardware like a Korg ElecTribe, you can trigger MIDI clips externally. You can use audio clips with any software or drum sampler, some of which include basic MIDI step sequencers. You can also trigger looped sounds and MIDI patterns in a program like FL Studio or Propellerhead Reason, assigning different layers to MIDI notes so you can turn them on and off.

Samplers (particularly drum samplers) are often the best bet for playing audio clips as a musical instrument. They let you load samples into virtual drum kits and play more expressively by assigning key elements like note velocity to playback parameters.

For interactive arrangements, Ableton Live has its own unique set of capabilities that haven't yet been fully duplicated in any other product, making it a kind of real-time DAW-sampler hybrid. Cakewalk Project5 isn't as focused on clip triggering as Live is, but it does offer the ability to control audio and MIDI clips, and has some other useful performance features (like arpeggiators, extensive MIDI pattern control, and a collection of instruments).

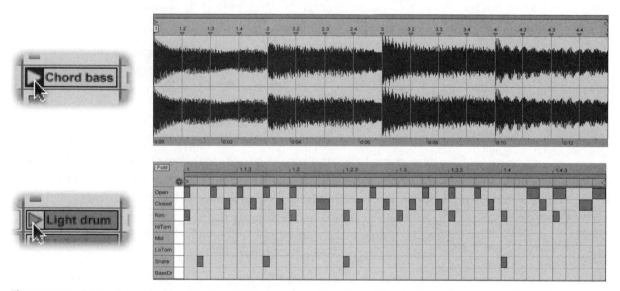

Figure 13.14 Triggering audio clips (top) and MIDI clips routed to soft synths or hardware instruments (bottom) can put a full, interactive arrangement at your disposal, as shown here in Ableton Live.

Triggering MIDI and audio clips with Ableton Live

Ableton Live is unusual enough in its design that the ways of using it onstage deserve special explanation. Several features of Live in particular make it well-suited to clip-based performance:

- It's possible to map most functions of Live to MIDI control (or to QWERTY keyboard shortcuts, which can in turn be mapped to external hardware via specialized utilities).

- Live is designed so that functions rarely cause audio dropouts, including those that normally would (like adding an effect to a channel insert).

- Live's Session View includes various controls for how clips are triggered—individually, in groups, and in sequences—that aren't possible with other hardware or software (**Figure 13.15**).

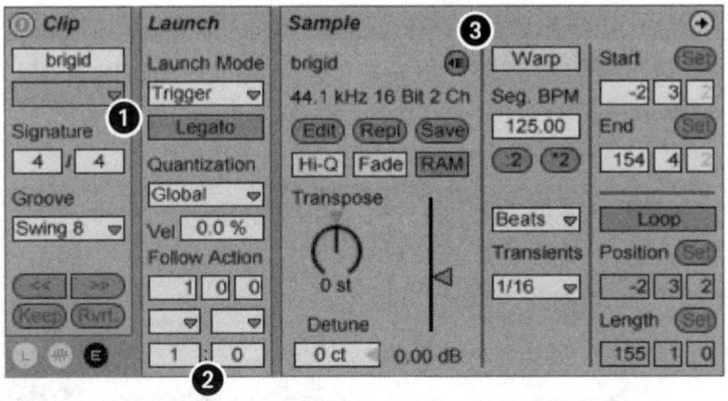

Figure 13.15 The appeal of using Live instead of drum sampler or other sampling instrument software is the ability to control how clips are triggered in an arrangement. You can use different launch modes to perform with clips via MIDI (1), setting quantization levels to sync clips to different rhythmic values or leave them unquantized. You can follow clip launches with other events (2) to create chains of clips. Sample settings determine warping, looping, and the timbral quality of clips (3).

In Live, you can use audio clips and MIDI clips to create a truly interactive musical arrangement. You can load larger phrases (like a verse or multibar phrase) and then trigger backing tracks with more flexibility than is possible with the markers and subsequences found in some other programs. For finer control over musical details, you can load individual drum patterns and breaks as clips. You can then use them to create a spontaneous backing track, or even make your improvisation with clips the basis of an entire performance, in combination with live effects.

There's no reason why all clips need to be perfectly beat-synced and looped. You can turn looping off and launch clips as *one-shot* samples (audio that plays once, then stops, rather than playing as a loop). A bank of clips could easily be a series of audio and musical cues for a dance or theater performance, with either individual clips as cues or cues grouped and triggered together.

Clip triggering settings are prime opportunities for configuring a set to be more expressive. For instance, you can choose whether or not the start of each individual clip is quantized, and to what beat. By setting quantization to a value shorter than a bar, you can create syncopations by triggering certain clips before or after the downbeat. This is especially important if you want to mix meters: if you have a song with bars in both 4/4 and 3/4 time, for instance, you may want to set the global quantization to the quarter-note so that you can easily switch between the two meters at will.

In addition to triggering clips one at a time, you can trigger an entire row of clips at once with just one MIDI input, keystroke, or mouse click (**Figure 13.16**). Triggerable groups are called "scenes" in Live and "grooves" in Project5 (which lines them up in columns instead of rows), but what those terms mean to you will depend on how you want to structure your performance. For instance, you could group together a series of clips that needs to start at a certain point in a song structure, like a verse or chorus. You could use something more arbitrary in which each group is a slightly different texture. In a theatrical performance, a scene could be a multitrack musical cue.

 Optimizing audio clips for performance: Running Live can be processor-intensive, because it's warping sound in real time and (by default) streaming audio from the disk. The "Hi-Q" setting for clips (turned off by default) uses up CPU cycles, so turn it off if your CPU meter is high. If you're getting skips and stutters even when the CPU meter is low, consider using a faster external hard drive or switching playback of some clips to RAM.

Figure 13.16 Triggering clips in groups lets you layer clips and create song structures. In Ableton Live (left), "scenes" trigger rows of clips; in Cakewalk Project5 (right), "grooves" trigger columns. Combining scenes with Follow Actions in Live can keep the groups from sounding rigid or mechanical (especially with the use of the Random setting).

Trying to trigger a number of clips at once is often awkward. Usually, what happens is the player gets overwhelmed and falls back on using a bunch of endlessly repeating loops. One solution is to employ Live's scene triggering and remove the stop buttons from selected columns. Another solution is to employ Live's Follow Actions, which let you determine what happens *after* a clip plays. You'll find two customizable Follow Actions, which can either automatically shut off a loop or play one of the other clips in the same track.

Clips and rhythm: Launch quantization is a useful way to control the rhythms of your clips as you play. With quantization set to a bar or beat, you can make sure everything stays synchronized. (If you're mixing meters at will, set quantization to a beat instead, such as a quarter- or eighth-note.) With quantization at a smaller level or even off, you can create syncopations, swing sounds, or non-metrical "ambient" textures, especially if you mix clips of different lengths.

Clip launching isn't necessarily exclusive to Live, although some specific techniques are, at least if you're using off-the-shelf tools. It's possible to build your own clip-launching tools using software like Reaktor or Max/MSP, though this requires significantly more work. (See "Custom Performance Software," later in the chapter.) Custom software does provide additional flexibility, and some performers combine custom software with a program like Live.

 Hands-on: Hacking a "Macro" Track in Ableton Live

Ableton Live's scenes are useful for performance, but they can only be used to launch clips, not for other kinds of control. Thanks to Live's support for MIDI content in clips, though, you can store MIDI data in clips for additional control. The only problem is that you can't use that MIDI data to control Live, only external hardware or other software. Fortunately, there is a workaround.

You first need a way of routing MIDI "between" applications. (For this trick, you'll be routing MIDI back to Live, but you'll use the same tools.) On the Mac, you'll use the Inter-Application Communications bus (IAC). On Windows, you'll need a third-party virtual MIDI driver like MIDI Yoke, included on the DVD.

1. With IAC or MIDI Yoke activated, launch Live.

2. Create a new MIDI track and name it the "Macro track."

3. Assign the MIDI output of the Macro track to IAC or MIDI Yoke.

4. In Preferences > MIDI/Sync > Active Devices, turn Remote on for IAC or MIDI Yoke to establish it as the remote control input. You've now routed MIDI from your "Macro" track in Live back to Live as a remote control source.

Now a single MIDI clip in the Macro track can have an arbitrary number of note messages and/or controller contours, each of which can perform a different function in Live. By triggering a single macro clip, you can turn five or six devices on or off, start and stop clips in various tracks, and so on. To record a macro, you can either manually draw in data in the Clip View or hit record on the Macro clip to record controller actions manually. (Record over the clip multiple times, and you can layer events into the Macro.)

Using a Macro track is much more convenient and flexible than using scenes because instead of just starting clips, you can control anything in Live that can be mapped to MIDI. You could create a cross-fade macro that also alters the wet/dry level or delay time of an effect during the cross-fade. You could trigger multiple clips, then gradually shift multiple effects parameters for those clips. The possibilities are limited only by what can be controlled by MIDI in Live. (And, of course, you can continue triggering scenes and clips, using live inputs, and playing soft synths while the macro plays.)

Triggering audio clips with drum samplers

Although Ableton Live has extensive arrangement and clip-triggering features, it tends to lack some of the performance features associated with
drum samplers. A true drum sampler has some advantages for live performance. Most important, drum samplers let you modulate specific features
with MIDI key velocity, so that how hard you hit a MIDI note or drum pad
can translate into how loud a clip plays, the cutoff frequency of a filter, or
even the point in a clip at which playback begins. You can use these features
to create more realistic-sounding drums, but even if you're using samples
other than drums, they can be useful for more expressive performance of
samples (**Figure 13.17**).

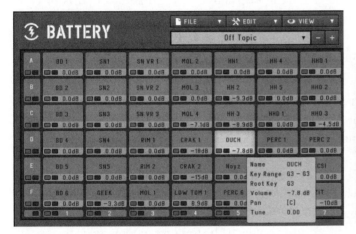 

Figure 13.17 A drum sampler is useful not only for sampled drum sounds but for other kinds of samples as well.
Native Instruments' Battery can load audio clips into banks and slots that you can trigger via MIDI (left). Although
the start of sample playback in Battery isn't synced to the bar or beat of an arrangement as it would be in Live, Battery's
slots are velocity-sensitive and include various performance controls. Battery provides extensive modulation control
(right) that can let you further control the clips while playing them live.

Even though it isn't quite as full-featured in terms of drum sample editing,
FXpansion's GURU groove machine-style instrument can group sets of
sliced audio into scenes for triggering. Like Live, it also incorporates MIDI
patterns, so you can create step-sequenced grooves and trigger them as well.

How do you decide which tool to use? Drum samplers can be more expressive to play if you're using them as your primary instrument rather than
just for backing grooves, sound effects, or static cues. On the other hand,

drum samplers don't offer the arrangement features and beat-synchronized triggering of a program like Live. Fortunately, the decision doesn't necessarily have to be either/or: you can load a drum sampler plug-in like Native Instruments Battery into Live. Having done so, you can trigger beat-synced backing loops in Live with a keyboard or foot controller while performing samples and drum kits live on a velocity-sensitive drum trigger pad or MIDI-enabled drums.

Mapping clips to hardware control

Clips at your feet:
If you can't spare a finger even for a moment to start clips, you'll want to consider a foot pedal. Look for a pedal board that has "scene pedals" so you can switch between different groups of pedals. (Otherwise, you'll be limited to seven or eight clips for your whole session.)

You can trigger clips in many sample-playback-oriented programs with a mouse, but it's not much fun. Instead, you'll probably want to play them using MIDI hardware. You can map clips to a MIDI keyboard, making each clip a different note. This can work well with a compact, two-octave keyboard, and you may want to use a spare so you can use your main keyboard to play soft synths.

Keeping track of where clips are located on a keyboard can be a little disorienting, so for many people the preferred hardware performance interface is a drum pad. The 4x4 drum pad on the Korg Kontrol49 has the advantage of being conveniently located above a keyboard, although it's not as useful if you want expressive velocity-sensitive control (for example, of a jazz ride cymbal sound), because its velocity response is rather coarse. Dedicated drum triggers like the Akai MPD-16 (www.akai.com) and M-Audio Trigger Finger work especially well if you're using velocity response to change the sound of clips, as in a drum sampler. (Ableton Live ignores velocity data when triggering clips.) You can play drum pads with your fingers or sticks and balance them on a keyboard or music stand so you can keep playing your primary instrument.

Using two drum pad modules, you can access additional triggers simultaneously or use one for clips and one for moving between clip groups (in the form of "scenes" or "songs," depending on what you're controlling). With the knobs and faders on the M-Audio Trigger Finger (**Figure 13.18**), you can simultaneously control effects levels in some percussion-oriented programs, including Battery.

Figure 13.18 Map clips, samples, loops, or drum kits to the pads of a control surface like the M-Audio Trigger Finger to play them with your fingers. The Trigger Finger has velocity-sensitive pads for more expressive playing. (Photo courtesy Avid Technology, Inc.)

Live Sampling

You can make a lot of music using prerecorded samples, but many vocalists, guitarists, beatboxers, and players of acoustic instruments want to sample their own sounds onstage.

Many popular pieces of hardware are available for the task. The Boss Loop Station RC-20 "phrase recorder" pedal is inexpensive and ubiquitous, but doesn't support MIDI. Most hardware samplers or "phrase samplers" do have MIDI connections and support MIDI clock synchronization, so if you prefer to use hardware, you can sync them to your computer as a master or slave.

Using software, however, you have the advantage of being able to easily use your software effects and integrate recorded audio in your existing arrangement. The one thing you can't do with some software that you can do with hardware like the Loop Station is create a "first-record" loop, where the loop length you record (how long you hold down a record pedal, for instance) defines the tempo. You'll find that sampling software provides various capabilities that aren't available in hardware, not the least of which is that your audio is recorded to your computer's hard drive and thus can be saved for later reuse.

Using Ableton Live, it's possible to record directly into Live's clips interface, so you can use the program as a flexible live looper and, if desired, integrate your own recordings with other audio and MIDI clips live onstage. One of the most full-featured looping effects is built into Native Instruments Guitar Rig 2; the Loop Machine supports extended layering, undo for deleting mistakes, first-record loops of any duration, and export of audio.

Try Musolomo on the DVD: Loop live with a free copy of Musolomo, included on the disc.

On the Mac, the free Musolomo "sampling instrument" from Plasq (www.plasq.com) provides easy MIDI assignments and enhanced real-time loop slicing (**Figure 13.19**). Some Live-based musicians even use Musolomo in conjunction with Live's built-in features, although it's available as a Mac Audio Unit plug-in and will work in other hosts, like Logic. As with recording into Live, everything you record into Musolomo is tempo-synced and time-stretched. Musolomo also scratches audio, emulates tape speed and pitch-shifting, can automatically jump through beats in the loop, and is designed to be used without having to glue your eyes to the screen. (You can see the interface from the corner of your eye thanks to a flashing color border for feedback, and MIDI assignments can be made on the fly using MIDI shortcuts instead of in advance.)

Figure 13.19 Using the free Plasq Musolomo plug-in for Mac, included on the DVD, you can record, play back, and layer loops with full control over speed, pitch, chopping, and scratching. The interface is attractive, but the idea is not to look at it; everything can be controlled with MIDI. (For visual feedback you don't have to look directly at the screen; the border flashes in color.)

Hands-on: Live Looping in Live

Using Ableton Live, you can record audio into clip slots and loop them there (**Figure 13.20**):

1. Create a set with multiple audio tracks, all set to your mic or instrument input, and record-enable all of them. (Cmd-click on Mac or Ctrl-click on PC on the record-enable button on multiple tracks to enable all of them at once.) All clip slots should be left to the default launch mode, Trigger.

2. If you want to sync your samples to the tempo of the project, you'll need some reference to the tempo. You can load a click track to your cue output, play an existing loop to give you a reference, or tap a tempo.

3. Set a global quantization value. Set the value to a bar (or other larger value) if you just want to quickly record bar-length loops. For more control, choose a smaller value (like a quarter-note); that way you can easily adjust start/end, length, position, and "nudge" values to play different parts of the loop.

4. When you're ready, hit the record button on an empty clip slot to begin recording. (For mouse-free operation, you'll probably want to set up MIDI assignments to clip slots first or use a precon-figured MIDI template.)

5. To stop recording and immediately begin looping what you've just recorded, trigger the *same* clip slot again. Your audio will begin looping at the project tempo. (If you don't want to hear your loop right away, just trigger an empty slot to stop.)

Figure 13.20 Using Live's clip recording abilities, you can layer loops from a mic, instrument, or other source and, if you desire, mix them with an existing Live arrangement.

If you want to layer looped samples, repeat steps 3 and 4 for additional tracks. Alternatively, you can trigger an empty slot instead of retriggering in step 3, then drag the clip with the mouse to Live's Simpler sampler to play the same sound (repitched) across a MIDI keyboard, or to a free slot in an Impulse drum machine. (Unfortunately, there's no way to perform this step without the mouse.)

For more advanced control, you can control loop playback position using the quantization setting in step 3. For instance, you could play just the third and fourth beats from a one-bar phrase. The nudge left/right, start/end, and position controls in Clip View are all MIDI-assignable, so you can trigger all these without grabbing your mouse or even watching the screen.

Other free alternatives include the Windows-only Zone Mobius (www. zonemobius.com), which emulates the Echoplex Digital Pro with Loop IV, and the Mac/Linux SooperLooper (http://essej.net/sooperlooper).

There's lots of crossover between DJing and the techniques used in live sampling and looping. Aside from the actual techniques, looping can also be made easier by using DJ-style hardware control surfaces like those from Behringer and Hercules. See "Alternative scratching hardware," later in the chapter.

DJING AND THE LIVE REMIX

DJing is a far cry from what it once was, playing records on a radio station or at a dance hall in careful, unaltered succession. Now, the word "DJing" can apply to the live creation of original electronic music onstage, sometimes even without the use of prerecorded music. DJing can involve free manipulation of beats, improvisation, and live remixing of sound materials. Although the traditional DJ setup involves two vinyl turntables hooked up to a mixer, some DJs also use samplers, groove boxes, synthesizers, and other equipment. Computer DJing can therefore involve both the emulation of traditional turntable mixing and scratching and other performance techniques that overlap with other genres.

 DJ Mixers and Digital Audio

One of the nicest features for computer users that is starting to appear on DJ mixers is a USB audio connection. USB can facilitate both easier mixing and easier recording. For mixing, it's easier to integrate a computer audio source (or multiple computers) with turntables and effects. For recording, many of the USB mixers provide bidirectional audio, meaning they can route audio from your computer to the mixer while simultaneously recording your finished mix, preserving your set for posterity if you desire.

With or without USB, you may want to look for a digitally oriented DJ mixer with S/PDIF ins and outs for your computer or other gear.

Mixers with USB include the 3-channel Gemini PS-02 USB (www.geminidj.com), various models from Numark (www.numark.com), and the Rane MP4 hardware/software bundle (www.rane.com). Allen & Heath's high-end Xone:3D includes a mixer, control surface, and USB audio interface (www.xone.co.uk). Using the MIDI controller features on the Xone:3D's mixer/audio interface, you can integrate software like Traktor or Live as though it were hardware.

Many of these mixers are rack-mountable and/or portable, so you won't be stuck with lousy house mixers.

DJ Mixers

The key device in DJing, whether you're using a computer or not, is the mixer. You can think of DJ mixers as performance mixers: they have special features, making them better suited to live work. For that reason, many computer musicians have embraced the design, even if there's not a turntable in sight.

At its simplest, a DJ mixer involves only two channels, although some DJ mixers will have four or more channels, allowing them to mix additional decks, vocals, or other sound sources. What makes the mixer work in performance is a *cross-fader*: a horizontal fader that lets you transition easily between the signals on the two channels. (An even fade from one channel to the other is known as a *segue*.)

You'll need a true cross-fader in order to fade effectively between two channels; a traditional mixer requires two hands for a cross-fade (one on each fader), which makes it more difficult to transition smoothly from one channel to another. Dedicated DJ software such as Native Instruments Traktor DJ Studio universally includes a cross-fader. Outside of dedicated DJ software, cross-faders can be harder to find. One exception is Ableton Live, which can assign any track (or multiple tracks) to a global A/B cross-fader. You'll also want a hardware cross-fader control to which you can assign the software cross-fader, like the Evolution X-Session from M-Audio (**Figure 13.21**).

Figure 13.21 If all you need is a cross-fader, M-Audio's Evolution X-Session can provide a cross-fader control surface. It's small enough to fit atop a MIDI keyboard. (Photo courtesy Avid Technology, Inc.)

If your software lacks a cross-fader feature, you can connect a DJ-style hardware mixer to your computer so you can cross-fade between the computer and something else (like a turntable, groove box, or another computer). Hardware mixers may give you additional access to mic/phono preamps, effects (like 3-band EQs and beat-synced delays), and other features. Of course, with a computer, you may want to substitute software effects for those on hardware.

DJ Software

DJ applications are able to emulate in software many of the features you'd have in a hardware DJ setup. They're effectively:

- **Virtual decks:** With full pitch control and "needle drop"-style cueing.

- **A collection of "vinyl":** Digital audio file library management gives you access to a collection of digital albums to spin.

- **A DJ mixer:** Multichannel mixing (with a cross-fader) of two to four decks, audio input (for a mic), and separate outputs for cueing and P.A. provide the capabilities of a mixer. (Traktor DJ 3 and later goes as far as fully emulating the sound, effects, and features of an Allen & Heath Xone:92 hardware mixer.)

- **Effects:** Many applications add DJ-style effects like 3-band EQ (the type found on a mixer) and delays (such as those found in an external effect).

- **A sampler:** Beat jumping and loop setting features give you functionality you wouldn't find on a turntable but might find on digital sampling hardware.

With the ability to customize the interface on the screen and the way in which it's mapped to MIDI and turntable hardware, the DJ application effectively becomes customizable virtual hardware.

Of course, computer DJ software can do things a hardware setup can't. Waveform displays and automatic beat-matching and looping, for instance, can completely change how you would align beats with hardware. To some, that's cheating. To others, it may make possible new sounds and new approaches to performing. DJ software also allows access to digital files and the ability to treat digital samples as though they were vinyl records.

Several software applications can be purchased without hardware:

- **Traktor DJ Studio** by Native Instruments (Windows/Mac, www.native-instruments.com) is the flagship of Native's DJ line, with power features like four-deck mixing and hardware-emulated, tempo-synced effects (**Figure 13.22**).

- **VirtualDJ** by PCDJ (Windows, www.pcdj.com) is also a full-blown "virtual turntablist" application with usability features like a virtual record case and integrated CD ripping.

- **djDecks** (Windows, www.djdecks.be) features an absurdly low price in comparison to its rivals ($30) but manages to include a full complement of features and multiplatform support for hardware control systems.

If your interest is limited to mixing and cueing, you might also consider the Mac-only MegaSeg (www.megaseg.com). It lacks features needed by turntablists, such as scratching support, but it focuses on library and playlist management and can even output to broadcast or Internet radio.

What about an "alternative" DJing application like Ableton Live that doesn't directly emulate hardware? Live is lacking in library management, but Live 5 can search quickly through MP3, AIFF, and WAV files by filename. It also lacks some vinyl emulation features, like true pitch control and scratching capability, as well as the ability to interface with most turntable scratching interfaces.

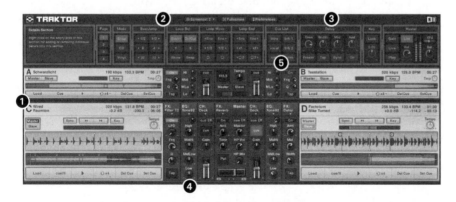

Figure 13.22 The hardware-style interface of Native Instruments Traktor DJ reveals some of the basic features of generalized DJ software. Virtual decks load loops or full songs from a library of music (1). You can then loop individual clips using extensive loop controls (2) and add beat-synced effects (3) with mixer-style EQ (4). Using these features together, you can construct entirely new songs from loops, with cued song structures (5). (Image courtesy Native Instruments, Inc.)

On the other hand, either a program like Live or the custom DJing software that DJs are building in tools like Max/MSP and Native Instruments Reaktor is better understood as a bridge between traditional DJing and electronic music production. Although these software solutions lack some capabilities, they add others. A program like Live can also double as a full DAW, giving you greater arrangement options and access to your library of plug-in effects and instruments. If you're entirely dedicated to scratching and mixing, you may not care that you can throw in a synth pattern on top of a beat loop. For others, that feature could make their performances more flexible and exciting. The kind of application you choose will depend on your musical temperament and working style.

Managing files

Computers shine not only in their ability to time-stretch and otherwise manipulate audio in ways turntables can't, but in their file management capabilities. DJ applications support various file formats, not only the expected AIFF/WAV but compressed formats like WMA, OGG, AAC, and MP3. With cataloging and searching facilities, it's reasonably easy to find the music you want.

Traktor and MegaSeg both integrate with your existing iTunes music library. Unfortunately, because of copy protection restrictions you won't be able to use songs purchased from the iTunes Music Store with most software (or copy-protected Windows Media files on a PC), but you will have easy access to CDs you've ripped yourself. (MegaSeg is the one exception; it actually does support iTunes Music Store-purchased music. Traktor DJ 3 and later integrates purchasing from the DJ-oriented Beatport music store.)

Since DJ applications don't play very many channels of stereo audio simultaneously (typically only two to four), they're not as picky about hard drive performance as some audio applications are. You can use the hard drive feature of your portable music player, for instance, to store music. Some applications (including Traktor and MegaSeg) can read music directly from your iPod.

Cueing and pitch control

DJ mixing starts to get interesting once it's combined with *cueing*, or controlling the point from which a deck plays back audio. By cueing and mixing beats, a DJ is able to slice up the way the records are heard, thereby composing new musical phrases. In computer software, it's possible to cue in ways that aren't normally possible with a turntable, by previewing the waveform of the file and adjusting cue points by small increments or tempo-locked beats.

Virtually all DJ software and audio looping software lets you set start and end points with a mouse; some programs add the ability to use MIDI controllers. (Ableton Live allows only MIDI mapping of in and out points, not direct scratching of the audio file.)

Using cueing, you can synchronize the start point of an audio file. With control over speed, it's possible to *beat match*, or synchronize the tempo of one deck to the tempo of the other. On turntables, there's only one way to do this: change the speed, sometimes called the "pitch control." On a turntable, pitch and speed are linked: slow down the speed at which the turntable is rotating, and the pitch gets lower.

Using computers, it's possible to adjust pitch and tempo independently; for more information see Chapter 5 and "Slices and Beats in Audio" in Chapter 10. But because the sound of beat matching using turntable pitch controls is so distinctive, many DJ programs can be configured to use pitch to change tempo, effectively emulating turntables. With drum machines, samplers, or a program like Ableton Live, set clips to change pitch with tempo instead of using the default pitch-independent warping. (In Ableton Live, double-click an audio clip, then select Re-Pitch from the Warp Mode drop-down menu in the Sample Box.)

Headphone cueing

Listening to sound through headphones before it's sent to the house mix is critical not only for DJing but for any music in which you want to "prelisten" to loops or other beat-synced materials. The ability to cue through headphones is so vital that "cueing" has come to mean any sound cued up while listening through headphones. Unfortunately, only a handful of laptop audio interfaces have separately assignable headphone outputs. Usually, although the headphone jack may have its own volume knob, it simply duplicates whatever signal is emerging from the main left/right mix. Laptop performers who want to control the headphone mix separately should look for an audio interface that does have an assignable headphone bus. If that's not an option, look for an interface that has additional outputs you can route to a headphone amp or mixer, then plug your headphones into that.

Portable interfaces with assignable headphone jacks:

Echo Audio PCMCIA Indigo DJ
(www.echoaudio.com)

E-MU 1616 / 1616M
(www.emu.com)

Focusrite Saffire
(www.focusrite.com)

M-Audio Fast Track Pro and FireWire 1814
(www.m-audio.com)

PreSonus FireBox
(www.presonus.com)

You'll also need to route a signal in your software so that it's sent to the headphone output (**Figure 13.23**). Ableton Live and most DJ applications have separate controls for cueing headphone outputs. (If they can route to two audio interfaces at once, you can even use the internal headphone output on your laptop, meaning you may be able to get away with using an audio interface that lacks an assignable headphone out. Be aware that some Windows drivers for internal audio cards may be higher latency, making them less suitable for cueing.)

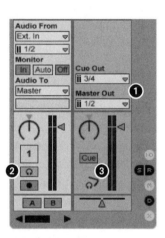

Figure 13.23 Cueing tracks, as shown here in Live, requires two basic elements: a separate cue output on your interface to which you're routing cues (1) and a way of switching outputs to that cue output (2). These are usually established globally in a DJ app, but in Live, since the cue switch on each track doubles as a conventional solo switch, you also need to change the solo mode to cue mode (3).

Scratching with a Computer

Once a computer enters the picture, you have three options:

- **Scratch the old-fashioned way:** You can mix the sound of your existing turntable scratching vinyl with the sounds of your computer either by plugging the turntable into a mixer or by plugging it into your computer via an audio interface.

- **Use your turntable to control your computer:** Using a specialized software interface, you can translate the motions of scratching to your computer software, controlling audio files on the computer instead of playing a record directly.

- **Replace your turntable with a new interface:** Since you're controlling your computer at this point, you're not limited to using a traditional turntable at all. New hardware devices, connected via USB or MIDI, can provide alternative physical interfaces for scratching.

Scratching with Vinyl: What You Need

If you're thinking of using vinyl to scratch, be aware that you need special equipment:

The table: A heavy, direct-drive turntable

The cartridge: A scratch-worthy cartridge

Direct-drive turntables are critical, because manipulating the record on the platter puts pressure on the drive, which can cause skips and unreliable speed, and can damage the turntable over time. A belt drive, of the type found on most consumer turntables and lightweight portable models, won't track reliably enough during scratching. Belt drives are likely to cause the record to skip or, if you apply pressure to the turntable platter, break. (Numark claims that you can scratch on their portable PT01 turntable by way of an included felt slipmat, but you'll find the results are much less effective than on a good direct-drive model on which you can directly handle the platter.)

Any cartridge can theoretically scratch, but certain cartridges are better suited to the task. Hi-fi audiophile cartridges are designed for picking up subtle nuances on the disk; they're exactly the opposite of what you want for scratching. Instead, opt for a good-quality cartridge that's specifically made for scratching, like the Stanton 505 or Shure M44-7. They'll last longer and perform better (scratching reliably and causing fewer skips), and they have high-output signals.

Connecting turntables

Whether you're using a turntable to directly input sound or using specialized software control via vinyl, you'll need to properly connect the turntable's audio out. (All of the computer control schemes use the audio signal from the turntable for control.)

Turntables have unbalanced RCA ("phono") outputs, but you can't just plug them in like other unbalanced audio gear. A standard phono output produces an audio signal voltage that's well below line level, so you need a preamp to amplify the level of the signal. Because of the way records are mastered, the preamps also need to apply a special equalization curve to reproduce the sound of the record accurately.

Fortunately, phono preamps are simple, cheap circuits. When turntables were still popular equipment for consumers, phono inputs were standard issue on all consumer receivers. Today that's not the case, but stand-alone phono preamps are readily available and run $40 or less. Good-quality, popular models include the ARTcessories DeeJayPre and Rolls VP29 (www.artproaudio.com). Make sure the phono input includes a ground screw for connecting the turntable's ground wire; this prevents ground loops and accompanying hum.

Once you have the phono preamp, connect the output of your turntable to the input of the preamp and the output of the preamp to your computer audio interface. You'll need a separate preamp or dedicated phono input for each turntable you want to use. Some preamps are now available with onboard USB, so you can skip the interface altogether. (The ARTcessories USB Phono Plus is an especially good choice because of its front-panel trims and LEDs, switchable inputs, and low cut filter for removing rumble; **Figure 13.24**.) Some DJ-oriented audio interfaces, like the Rane MP4, PreSonus Inspire (www.presonus.com), and E-MU 1616 / 1616M, also include turntable connections.

Figure 13.24 The ARTcessories USB Phono Plus (www.artproaudio.com) provides an easy way of connecting a turntable to your computer, whether you're recording scratching as audio or using a turntable for control. (Photo courtesy Applied Research & Technology)

Even if you're using your turntable exclusively for controlling your computer rather than letting your audiences hear its signal, you'll still need a proper phono preamp. Some turntables now include S/PDIF digital outputs in addition to phono or full line outputs. Effectively, these turntables build the phono preamp, equalization stage, and digital-to-analog conversion circuitry into the turntable, eliminating the need for a dedicated connection on the other end. With these turntables, you simply connect the S/PDIF output to the digital input on your computer's audio interface.

Controlling computers with vinyl

The basic innovation of the turntable-to-computer interface is the control record. It looks like an ordinary vinyl record, but instead of containing music, it contains time information. Place it on an ordinary turntable, and the turntable plays the timecode as audio signal through its audio outputs. You then connect the turntable to your computer, and special software translates the timecode signal into control data. As you cue or scratch the record, the software responds as you'd expect a turntable to respond. Some early systems were unable to recognize when you picked up the needle and dropped it in a different location, but records are now encoded to provide this information. (Incidentally, you should make sure you don't inadvertently feed the audio from the turntable to the mixer out, or you'll broadcast the timecode signal. It won't sound pretty.)

Two major competing systems for computer-based DJs combine hardware with vinyl control records and control CDs. Both are Windows/Mac-compatible:

- **Stanton Final Scratch** (www.stantondj.com) includes a FireWire interface called the ScratchAmp for connecting turntables, audio, mics, and MIDI, plus a limited version of Native Instruments' Traktor DJ Studio software (upgradeable to the full version) (**Figure 13.25**).

- **Serato Scratch LIVE** (www.serato.com), with hardware manufactured and distributed by Rane, includes a USB interface for connecting turntables, audio, and mics (though not MIDI), plus Serato Scratch LIVE software.

Final Scratch and Serato Scratch Live are often abbreviated FS and SSL, respectively.

Figure 13.25 Stanton Final Scratch is a combined hardware/software solution for integrating computers with other gear for sound production and control. The FireWire-based ScratchAmp interface connects not only with mixers, turntables, and CD players, but with MIDI gear and, via a FireWire thru port, FireWire hard drives and iPods. Phono inputs eliminate the need for separate phono amps. (Photo courtesy Stanton Magnetics)

Since both the Rane and Stanton products include two control CDs in addition to two or three control vinyl discs, you can combine them with CD players with scratch interfaces. These products have made big inroads among mainstream DJs; Stanton even maintains a list on its Web site of clubs around the world that have Final Scratch preinstalled.

Various other solutions involve vinyl records sold *a la carte* or bundled with software; you provide your own preamp and audio interface. These solutions can be much less expensive than the Rane or Stanton offerings, particularly if you already have the gear:

- **Ms. Pinky** (www.mspinky.com) makes an integrated Windows/Mac solution called the International Wrecked ("Rekkid") System, or IWS. Instead of straight timecode, Ms. Pinky uses an advanced system called "physical location stamps," which allow it to track extremely accurately, particularly when needle-dropping a record in reverse, which can foul up timecode systems. Ms. Pinky is also designed to interface with Max/MSP/Jitter patches as well as bundled DJ and VJ/video software. Bundles run around $100 for multiple discs and software (**Figure 13.26**).

- **PCDJ** (www.pcdj.com) is based on Ms. Pinky technology but is coded specifically to work exclusively with Windows-only DJ software.

- **MixVibes** (www.mixvibes.com) and **VirtualDJ** (www.pcdj.com) are both vinyl control solutions designed to accompany Windows-only DJ software. Both vendors also make their own special hardware control surfaces. VirtualDJ vinyl is especially cheap ($15 a record).

- **EJ MIDI Turntable** (www.ejenterprises.tv) has one huge advantage, and the name gives it away: it outputs standard MIDI instead of proprietary data. The EJ system operates on an optical cartridge, instead of using an audio signal, to eliminate skipping and tracking issues. Connect that to the included hardware and connect the MIDI connection to your computer. The package includes the ScratchTV VJ application for scratching and beatmatching videos. The advantage comes at a price, though: at $1,000, it's by far the most expensive option.

With the exception of the EJ MIDI Turntable, all of these options require an application that supports the specialized signal generated by the control vinyl. Usually, that means you're limited to the software bundled with the hardware. One exception is the Windows DJ application djDecks (www.djdecks.be), which has plug-ins for Serato Scratch, Final Scratch, Ms. Pinky, and VirtualDJ vinyl.

Ms. Pinky deserves special mention in this regard. Because the package includes a basic Max/MSP object, it's possible to translate control signals into anything you like, making it possible to control custom sound patches and instruments or manipulate video. You can even configure it to work with MIDI-compatible software, although you'll have to manually set up the translation in Max/MSP.

Figure 13.26 Ms. Pinky involves a pink control record (left) you can place on any conventional turntable capable of scratching. You can use the data to control whatever you want; aside from the expected DJ applications, Ms. Pinky has appeared in interactive art installations and has even controlled a vibrating chaise longue (right). (Control record photo courtesy Scott Wardle; chaise longue photo courtesy DJ Daito Manabe, www.daito.ws)

Alternative scratching hardware

Other methods of controlling DJ software don't use a turntable at all. At the low end (under $300), there are two major control surface contenders. The Behringer B-Control DeeJay BCD2000 is a combination analog mixer, control surface, and 4-channel audio interface (**Figure 13.27**). The Hercules DJ Console is a lightweight control surface with MIDI, digital audio, and analog I/O. Neither of these feels like a real turntable, because they lack a full-sized platter and direct-drive mechanism, but they're a big step up from a mouse and QWERTY keyboard.

Figure 13.27 Behringer's BCD2000 is a control surface that doubles as a mixer and audio interface. Its controls output MIDI, making them perfect for mapping to DJ software, live performance software, or even VJ applications. (Photo courtesy Behringer Spezielle Studiotechnik GmbH)

Some users have even gotten by with inexpensive toys like the Mixman DM2 (www.mixman.com), which can often be found for under $50. Combined with the donationware DM2MIDI (www.pdoom.ch/dm2) for Windows and a virtual MIDI driver like MIDI Yoke, the DM2 is a full-featured control surface. The DM2 is supported natively by some pro-level DJ software, including MixVibes. (The included Mixman software, although it's fun to play with, won't satisfy serious DJs; it's aimed at casual users only.) Unfortunately, Mixman doesn't approve of the DM2MIDI tool, which it says is illegal, and doesn't even distribute its USB drivers outside the retail package.

At the higher end, you'll find hardware like the Numark HDX. Instead of providing just a CD player, it has a full 80 GB hard drive. And instead of a lightweight plastic platter, it replicates a full platter with a direct-drive mechanism underneath. Via a USB 2.0 connection, it can plug directly into your computer.

CUSTOM PERFORMANCE SOFTWARE

When off-the-shelf software doesn't provide what you need, you can turn to more customizable systems for developing solutions tailored to your unique performance needs.

Fortunately, although using an environment like Max/MSP can be technically considered object-oriented programming, it won't feel like coding in a programming language. Instead of writing text code to create software, these applications let you connect prebuilt objects onscreen via a *"patcher"* interface (**Figure 13.28**). Like the patch cords on modular synths or the audio cables plugged into a mixer, each cord represents the flow of a signal. (In Max, signals flow from top to bottom and right to left through the objects you have onscreen, although occasionally they will be rerouted by the objects through which they pass.)

Start simple: One of the common misconceptions about customizable software, because of its depth, is that you have to immediately create something complex. In fact, not only is solving simple problems usually the best way to begin to learn about the software and what you can do with it, but simple tools—like a transposition tool that you've designed just the way you want it—are often the most useful.

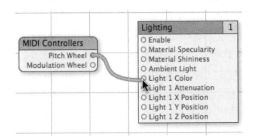

Figure 13.28 The basic idea of a patcher interface is to use virtual cables to represent the flow of data. That allows you to use one device to control another, such as mapping a control change value from MIDI to the color of a live-rendered 3D environment in Apple's Quartz Composer utility, shown here.

Users of software like Max or Reaktor will sometimes say they've "programmed" custom software, but part of the power of these packages is that much of the work is already done for you. The hundreds of objects in Max, Reaktor, and Pd handle many of the basic things you'll need to do. The available objects include items like oscillators, which generate signals for synthesis, audio and MIDI routing objects; control objects like knobs and sliders; and even menu objects. As if playing with a pile of Legos, you can combine these objects into a virtually infinite number of possibilities and not have to create anything from scratch. (Those who do code can use languages like Java and JavaScript in Max/MSP and Pd.)

Choosing the Right Interactive Tool

A broad variety of "interactive" or "modular" environments exist for music. There are hosting tools like Plogue Bidule and Buzz, mentioned earlier in the chapter, as well as custom synth and effects construction tools like the $50 Windows-only AudioMulch (www.audiomulch.com), the free Mac-only sound creation environment SuperCollider (www.audiosynth.com), and tools for building your own effects and synthesizers like the wildly popular $50 Windows shareware for constructive VSTs, SynthEdit (www.synthedit.com). Several tools deserve special mention, however, for their unique depth of capabilities.

The best known of these tools is popularly called Max (**Figure 13.29**), although the version that includes audio is technically called Max/MSP. Max is used for everything from simple MIDI and arrangement tasks to driving musical robots and flaming propane-powered sound organs called pyrophones. Max and Cycling '74's Jitter video, data processing, and 3D add-on can cost as much as $850 (less if you're a student), but the investment is often worth it. Max contains thousands of objects, with many more "externals" contributed by a robust user community. Other environments rival Max for creating custom synthesizers and effects, but Max has unmatched tools for processing data, building custom interfaces, and even adding code in languages like Java and JavaScript.

ElectroTap Jade (www.electrotap.com/jade) is built from the ground up for managing complex live performances with computers. On its own, it's a performance tool for audio and video that makes it especially easy to link events in audio and MIDI to complex series of events and controls (**Figure 13.30**). Combined with Max/MSP/Jitter, Jade makes it easier to create elaborate scripted events and reuse modular components, something that's essential to building extended custom performance environments. It costs $200 or less and doesn't require Max/MSP to operate, making it both affordable and approachable. Unfortunately, unlike Max/MSP, it's not cross-platform; the software is Mac-only.

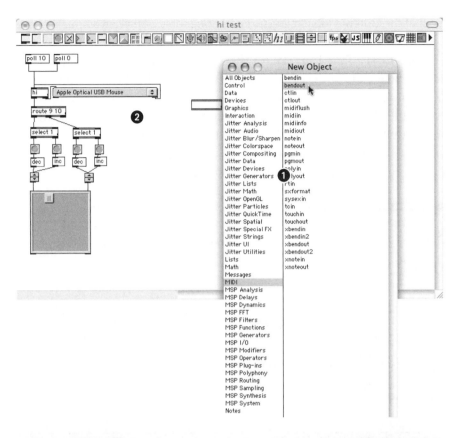

Figure 13.29 Max/MSP is a full-blown visual development environment for MIDI, sound, video, 3D, and other data. Even with a broad library of objects (1) for every kind of function, Max is often useful as simple interactive "glue," like this patch to pull data from a USB input (2). (This patch turns the scroll ball on the Apple Mighty Mouse into an X/Y controller. The "hi" object works well with other controllers, such as USB game controllers.)

Figure 13.30 Custom performance software lets you create a patch that's designed for the specific needs of a piece of music. Composer and developer Tim Place created this patch in Max/MSP/Jitter and Jade for a piece that "watches" a marimba performer. Specialized modules analyze video imagery to track the color of the yarn on the mallets. Different modules are assigned to different tasks, making the patch easier to navigate (and making it easier to reuse those components in other patches). (Image courtesy Tim Place)

Pd on the DVD: Try out the free, interactive, cross-platform environment Pure Data (Pd) on the disc. Also on the disc are three sample Pd patches from Jim Aikin, including the one shown in Figure 13.31.

If all of the aforementioned tools are sounding too expensive, you might want to consider Pure Data (www.puredata.info) for Mac, Windows, and Linux (**Figure 13.31**). Pure Data (Pd for short) is open source and entirely free. It's the brainchild of the original creator of Max, Miller Puckette. It shares a similar patching structure and even some compatibility of objects with Max/MSP. Pd is quite a bit rougher around the edges and is not as easy to use or well-documented as Max, but it has some unique capabilities of its own and its abilities are growing fast thanks to the contributions of the open-source community to add-ons for the program.

Figure 13.31 Like Max/MSP, Pd uses simpler objects that can be patched together to form larger creations of your own design. This chord/delay generator is an example of some of the kinds of creative control over MIDI note processing these environments provide. It's included on the DVD in case you want to try it out, see how it works, and customize it for your own needs.

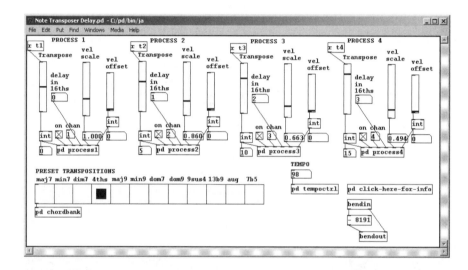

If you are ready to learn how to code, you may want to look into Processing (www.processing.org), a new, object-oriented language designed for musicians, artists, and sculptors instead of computer science majors. On its own, it's not terribly useful for sound, but with the addition of the free Sonia Library (http://sonia.pitaru.com), it's capable of audio features like sample playback and recording, synthesis, and analysis of audio inputs.

Sophisticated interactive capabilities aside, what many people want is simply to build custom tools for sound. Native Instruments Reaktor has perhaps the deepest sound engine of any of these tools, comprising everything from analog synthesis to less familiar techniques like granular synthesis and digital effects. Although it tends to be weaker at processing data in interactive ways and isn't as customizable as Pd or Max, Reaktor's focus on synths and effects can make it a better choice if that's your primary interest.

How to Learn the Tools

Make no mistake about it: it takes a significant investment of time to become adept with any of these customizable tools, and they can be intimidating to a beginner. The good news is that many non-programmer musicians have been able to approach them successfully. Keep in mind that the lessons you learn, as well as the custom patches you build, can be reused many times over.

The one approach that works well for most musicians is to pick a simple problem and attempt to solve it rather than build an over-ambitious, granular physical modeling aleatoric laser-powered composer robot you've been dreaming about. Simple problems like building a time-stretching audio playback module, a custom MIDI split tool, or a simple sequencer are often the best place to start.

Reaktor is probably the easiest of these programs to use right out of the box, because unlike the others, it comes with many powerful example files (**Figure 13.32**). In fact, the included content is so good that many Reaktor users never get around to developing their own custom patches. By looking at the underlying workings of some of the simpler examples, you can learn a lot about how Reaktor works, and you'll have a good starting place from which to build your own patches.

With Pd, the simple answer is to head for the Web. Because of the open-source nature of the software, most of the documentation is online. There's actually very little chance you'll be able to start up the program and have any idea what's going on until you read the documentation. You'll find various links at the Pd Web site; one of the best is an extensive tutorial Wiki or a collaborative online document (http://puredata.info/community/pdwiki?PdTutorialIntro).

With Max/MSP, most of the documentation is included in the software. You'll find two especially handy tools: the "Tutorials and Topics" documentation and accompanying patches, and the online help. Resist the temptation to dive into MSP and audio or Jitter and video, and begin with the basic Max "Tutorials and Topics" document. Fundamental MIDI and data processing is the most significant topic to understand first, in depth.

 Max plays Taps: Add-ons can make Max and Pd more useful in performance. For more advanced construction of modular components in Max/Jitter, Jade's author Tim Place has created a free, open-source module structure called Jamoma (www.jamoma.org). ElectroTap also makes a useful library of extensions for Max called Tap.Tools, which fills some gaps in the built-in library of modules, as well as a sensor interface called the Teabox that works well with all these applications.

Figure 13.32 If you're looking for help dreaming up some crazy, new, improvisatory instrument with which to perform in Reaktor, check out some of the example files, such as Skrewell, for inspiration.

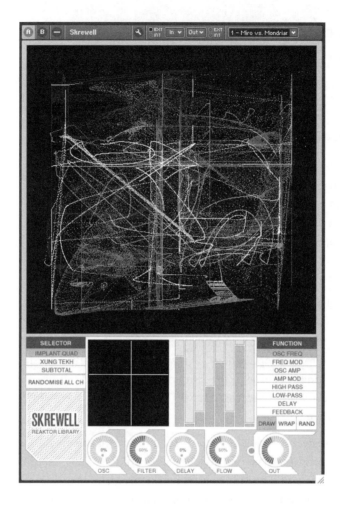

You'll probably spot patches among the tutorials that you want to reuse in your own work, so the best strategy is to participate in the time-honored tradition of beginning programming, which is to copy and paste code ("code" being, in this case, Max patches). The other learning approach is, if you find an object and want to know more about it, Option-click or Alt-click the object to open extensive online help and sample code (**Figure 13.33**). The sample code in the help files can be cut and pasted into your own work: unlock the patch and you'll see and be able to edit the underlying patch structure. Don't save, or you'll overwrite the help file.

For each of these tools, you'll find additional learning resources in workshops and conferences. Harvestworks in New York City (www.harvestworks.org)

is dedicated to teaching advanced music technologies and has a particular specialization in Max/MSP. It welcomes students from around the world. The growing movement behind Pd is staging regular free workshops internationally.

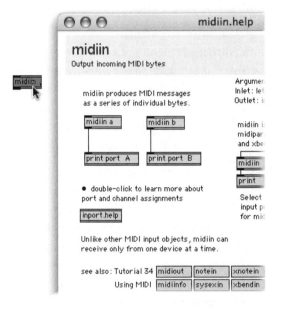

Figure 13.33 Online help is useful in any program, but in Max/MSP it's essential for understanding how an object can be used. You can operate the patch in the help window to understand it better or copy and paste it to incorporate it into your own work.

 What's next: For additional tutorials and resources for Pd, Reaktor, and Max/MSP, as well as examples in action, see the Real World Digital Audio Web site (www.realworlddigital-audio.com).

Futuristic Interactive Music

For many of us, the "future" of computer music may be fairly modest, like coming up with a better MIDI control mapping scheme for our favorite soft synth. But if you are ready to take the plunge into something more experimental, there are plenty of resources for you.

One of the primary areas of interest is finding new input methods. The sonic potential of computers and digital audio technology has exploded over the past decades, but the hardware interface—keyboards, knobs, and faders—harkens back to the early part of the 20th century or, in some cases, the 17th.

With open-ended software, it's easier to build new instruments and tools for performance. The data-processing capabilities of software like Max and Pd in particular make it more practical to interpret data streaming into the computer from hardware.

There are many frontiers to explore:

- **DIY hardware:** Sites like Midibox (www.midibox.org) and vendors like Doepfer (www.doepfer.de) have resources for designing and building your own custom hardware. So if M-Audio doesn't ship exactly the fader box you want, you can create your own.

- **Sensors:** So-called "real-world" interfaces translate data from simple electrical sensors, which measure movement, light, pressure, tilt, "flex" or "bend," and other data. You can purchase the sensors from electrical supply houses like Jameco; the challenge is to translate the data into computer form via MIDI, USB, or Wi-Fi. You'll find several solutions on the Cycling '74 Web site, but the most affordable and flexible MIDI solution is the $149 MidiTron (www.eroktronix.com).

- **Interactive smart tables:** What if, instead of using a mouse and keyboard, you could create music by moving tangible objects like blocks on a smart table, with visual feedback for your actions projected on the surface? That somewhat far-out scenario has been the target of a surprising number of research projects, ranging from academia to automaker Lexus (**Figure 13.34**). A team working on the problem in Spain has made a list of numerous related projects (www.iua.upf.es/mtg/reacTable/MusicTables). If you're ready to try your hand at using free, open-source software tools, you'll want to know about SonicForms, a research project that aims to collect and share methods for building new interfaces (www.sonicforms.org).

- **Cameras:** Tracking motion and converting it into control signals is a challenge, but it continues to entice musicians with the promise of controlling music without hardware, just using your body. If you're using Jitter, you'll find excellent tracking tools in Tap.Tools and the free cv.jit object library (www.iamas.ac.jp/~jovan02/cv). The free Windows-only EyesWeb stand-alone software (www.eyesweb.org) can be interfaced with other software via OSC. If you just want to play with your webcam, check out Cycling '74's prebuilt Hipno, a suite of camera-controlled effects processors.

- **Networked data:** Using OSC, it's possible to send network-friendly control data over the Web. The timing latency increases over great distances, so beat-accurate jamming may be a long way off. But projects like Monolake's Atlantic Waves collaborative music software (www.monolake.de/atlantic.html) are already using the Internet for music creation (**Figure 13.35**). The keys are the OSC and UDP objects for Max/MSP on Windows and Mac, which allow data to be easily routed between Max patches running on different computers (www.cnmat.berkeley.edu/OpenSoundControl/Max). Although routing data halfway around the world can be tricky, the system works quite well for two people in the same room.

Figure 13.34 The Audiopad (www.jamespatten.com/audiopad) by James Patten and Ben Recht is one of a number of experiments in using interactive tables for music production instead of a conventional interface. Antennae track tagged objects on the table and generate visual feedback and interactive music. (Photo courtesy Mariliana Arvelo)

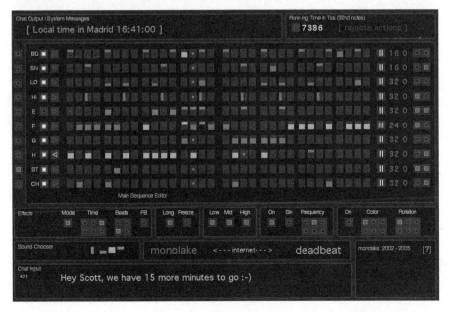

Figure 13.35 Atlantic Waves, a software project developed in Max/MSP by Monolake and Deadbeat, allows collaboration across the Web from remote locations. You can try some similar experiments using Max or other tools that support the use of OSC over a network. (Image courtesy Robert Henke [Monolake])

APPENDIX

What's on the DVD

The DVD included with this book is a cross-platform data DVD compatible with both Mac and Windows computers. We've assembled over two gigabytes of sound content, instruments, and software tools you can use immediately in your music, and to explore topics in the book.

TOOLS AND EXTRAS

The Tools folder includes nearly a gigabyte of software, much of it free for unlimited use. The software is compatible with both Mac and Windows, unless otherwise indicated:

- **Ableton Live** (save-disabled, time-unlimited demo): Live performance, recording, editing, and arranging digital audio workstation

- **Audacity** (full version): Open-source audio editor

- **Cakewalk Kinetic** (30-day demo, Windows only): Groove box/electronic music production software

- **IK Multimedia AmpliTube UNO** (full version): Standalone guitar amp simulation and effects

- **IK Multimedia SampleTank FREE** (full version, limited to included sounds): Sample playback instrument, including nearly 50 MB of instruments

- **Native Instruments SoundSchool Analog** (full version): Standalone virtual analog synthesizer built in Reaktor 5

DVD examples: Look for the DVD icon throughout the book for references to software included on the disc. You'll find specific hands-on examples in the text that you can try with Ableton Live, SampleTank FREE, Kinetic for Windows, Sound-School Analog, and the tools in the Utilities folder.

- **Instruments and Effects** (full versions, some in standalone mode only): A collection of free plug-in and standalone instruments and effects for Mac and Windows, assembled exclusively for this DVD, including the Crystal soft synth and contributions from Audio Damage, Plasq, Ohmforce, and Smartelectronix

- **Utilities** (full versions): Essential utilities for monitoring and managing MIDI data for Mac and Windows

You'll find additional sample files and other content in the Extras folder, as well as tutorials for some of the software in the associated folder on the disc.

SOUNDWARE

The Soundware folder includes approximately one gigabyte of loops, sampled instruments, and other content, free for use with your software of choice. The sounds and software are compatible with both Mac and Windows:

- **East West:** Over 600 MB of sampled instruments from the East West and Zero-G sound libraries, for use in the free, included Native Instruments Kompakt and Intakt players

- **SmartLoops:** Over 200 MB of loops (including percussion and instrumental content), provided in ACID, Apple Loops, and REX formats compatible with a wide variety of audio programs

- **TrackTeam:** Nearly 200 MB of sample content for Ableton Live and Propellerhead Reason

INDEX